# Democracy Challenged

# Democracy Challenged

## The United States Since World War II

JOHN EDWARD WILZ

*Indiana University*

1817

**HARPER & ROW, PUBLISHERS, NEW YORK**
Grand Rapids   Philadelphia   St. Louis   San Francisco
London   Singapore   Sydney   Tokyo

All the photos in the text are from AP/Wide World, except for the following: page 96, NASA; 241, © 1981, Englebert, Photo Researchers; 276, NASA; 307, Sygma; 319, Grunnitus Studios; 335, Tiziod/Sygma; 354, Sygma; 369, Sygma; 428, Philipott/Sygma; 440, Franken/Sygma; 456, Nogues/Sygma; 493, Tannenbaum/Sygma; 505, Sygma; 510, Philipott/Sygma.

**Sponsoring Editor:** Lauren Silverman
**Project Editor:** Paula Cousin
**Art Direction:** Heather A. Ziegler
**Cover Coordinator:** Mary Archondes
**Cover Design:** Lucy Krikorian
**Photo Research:** Mira Schachne
**Production:** William Lane

DEMOCRACY CHALLENGED: The United States Since World War II

**Library of Congress Cataloging-in-Publication Data**

Wilz, John Edward.
    Democracy challenged: the United States since World War II / John Edward Wilz.
      p.    cm.
    Includes bibliographical references.
    ISBN 0-06-047167-0
    1. United States—Politics and government—1945-    I.  Title.
E743.W64 1990
973.9—dc20                                   89-38682
                                                    CIP

89  90  91  92  9 8 7 6 5 4 3 2 1

*For Ellen, John, Mary,*
*Cathy, Jennie, Paul,*
*Stark, and Jim*
*—and in memory of*
*their sister Barbara.*

# Contents

# CHAPTER 2    A Time of Tribulation    37

# CHAPTER 3    Holding the Line    70

# CHAPTER 4    A Pulsating Society    109

# CHAPTER 5    The Torch Is Passed    145

# CHAPTER 8  Anguish and Triumph  264

# CHAPTER 9  Tragedy and Transformation  304

# CHAPTER 12    Conservatism Triumphant    433

# CHAPTER 13    In the Second Term of Reagan    476

# CHAPTER 14    Beginning of the Bush Era    519

# *Preface*

The historian who sets about to survey the experience of any nation and its people across a period of forty or so years in a few hundred pages of text confronts a formidable challenge. History, after all, is the sum of human experience. Every thought that has crossed the minds of the billions of men and women who have trod the earth over uncounted millennia, every word that humans have uttered, every step they have taken, is a fragment of history. Awareness of this truth should suffice to guarantee the humility of the most cerebral and erudite historical scholar. Still, historians from the time of Thucydides have taken up the challenge of describing and interpreting the experiences of nations and peoples. And a dozen or so scholars of history have marshaled their powers of intellect and expression to make intelligible the experience of the United States and its citizenry during the forty-plus years since World War II. Inevitably different in emphasis and perspective, the resultant books are uniformly first rate; some are excellent.

Like the authors of most of the volumes that survey the post-World War II American experience, I have used politics (or public life and power) and the economic life of the republic as the scaffolding (or essential structure) for *Democracy Challenged.* But I have sought to strike a rational balance between politics and the economy on the one hand and social and cultural—also scientific and technological—happenings and developments on the other. Fortunately, my editors at Harper & Row encouraged me to go into more depth with my subject matter than the other volumes which have surveyed the passage of the people of the North American superpower in the post-1945 years. This has enabled me to prepare a more comprehensive and more anecdotal volume than otherwise would have been possible.

*Democracy Challenged* attempts to drive home the point that, day in and day out, most Americans during the decades following World War II gave only passing thought to such cosmic concerns as the Cold War, the crusade for civil equality, and the ups and downs of the stock market. Rather, ordinary citizens tended to be preoccupied by their own personal problems, particularly those relating to family, health, and employment, and an almost frenetic quest for personal satisfaction and fulfillment. Still, the overall theme (i.e., "a recurring, unifying subject or idea") of *Democracy Challenged* is that across the four-plus decades following the global war, the world's longest-surviving democratic republic, one beset by manifest imperfection, sought to meet an array of challenges, most of which, inevitably perhaps, it met with mixed success—in a word, imperfectly.

As set out in the chapters of *Democracy Challenged*, the challenges faced by the United States during the decades after 1945 were nothing if not diverse. One can readily enumerate some of the most pressing and obvious of those challenges (not necessarily in the order of their importance): (1) the challenge of facing up to responsibilities and paying the price accruing to the republic as a consequence of its new status as a global superpower—the challenge, in the main, of standing up to what a preponderance of Americans perceived to be the deadly threat to American institutions and ideals presented by the Soviet behemoth and Marxist-Leninist ideology; (2) the challenge of standing up to the foregoing Soviet-Marxist-Leninist threat while at the same time avoiding "doomsday," to wit, a nuclear holocaust; (3) the challenge presented by the imperative that the self-anointed citadel of liberty and justice and opportunity undertake a renewed effort to honor its hallowed principles and eradicate the infamous racial caste system, not to mention a gender caste system, that had made a mockery of those principles since the founding of the republic in the 1770s; (4) the challenge of taking maximum advantage of an incredible succession of scientific discoveries and technological developments to forward the frontiers of knowledge and improve the conditions of life of all earthlings; (5) the challenge of adjusting to changing economic realities, notably the revival of nations that had suffered devastation in the war of 1939–1945, and the increasing integration of the American economy into a global economy over which the people of the United States and their institutions exercised limited control; (6) challenges resulting from the continued growth of America's cities and the continuing shift in the geographical balance of the national population; (7) the challenge of providing adequate schooling, housing, and health care for all citizens; (8) the challenge presented by the scandal of persistent and widespread poverty in the most affluent society in the history of the world; (9) challenges presented by what appeared to many Americans to be revolutionary changes in the values and modes of behavior of legions of citizens, particularly those who were born after World War II; and (8) the challenge presented by an increasing awareness of the fragility of the natural environment.

However flawed or imperfect their society—and here is another theme of the present volume—a preponderance of Americans clung to their faith in the traditional foundations of their national system, namely, representative democracy and free enterprise. Indeed, despite occasional (or perhaps frequent) misgivings along the way, their faith in those foundations was, arguably, at least as great in 1989 as it had been in 1945. If manifestly more mature in their patriotism by 1989 (that is, painfully conscious of national blemishes and shortcomings to an extent that they transparently had not been in 1945) most Americans nonetheless completed that forty-plus-year period of their voyage across history secure in their conviction that their democratic society, for all of its obvious imperfections, remained the world's best hope for men and women who valued freedom of expression, freedom of initiative, and freedom of movement, not to mention economic security, political institutions that were directly responsible to the popular will, and something approximating equal justice and equal opportunity for all people. In a word, a preponderance of U.S. citizens continued to believe in the early 1990s (as had one generation of Americans after another since the founding of their republic in the closing decades of the eighteenth century) that their nation was the veritable gem of the ocean.

## ACKNOWLEDGMENTS

By way of acknowledgment, I should like to thank Marianne Russell, Lauren Silverman, and Paula Cousin, my editors at Harper & Row, for their encouragement, guidance, and patience during the preparation of *Democracy Challenged*; Anne Lesser, the copy editor; Harvey C. Bunke and Elmus R. Wicker for criticism of sections of *DC* that treat economic developments; Philip C. Bobbitt for providing a copy of his manuscript on the nuclear strategy of the United States; and D. Dean Cofield and Bernard P. Kemker for guidance regarding trends in the field of medicine since World War II.

I also thank the following reviewers for their comments: John Andrew, Franklin & Marshall College; Roger Bilstein, University of Houston, Clearlake; Peter Buzanski, San Jose State; Charles Eagles, University of Mississippi; Mitchell Hall, University of Kentucky; Richard A. Hunt, Nassau Community College; Alton Lee, University of South Dakota; Blanche Linden-Ward, Emerson College; Michael Mayer, University of Montana; Jesse T. Moore, University of Rochester; Keith W. Olson, University of Maryland; William O'Neill, Rutgers University; Leo Rebuffo, George Washington Univ.; Jerry Rodnitzky, University of Texas at Arlington; Carlos Schwantes, University of Idaho; Richard B. Sherman, College of William & Mary; Michael Sherry, Northwestern University; and Sara Lee Silberman, Connecticut College.

I also want to thank Alice F. Wickizer and her splendid staff in the government publications department of the Indiana University library for locating obscure materials and for dredging up answers to uncounted questions regarding the experience of the United States over the past forty years; my daughter, Mary, and son, Jim, for tutoring me in the mysteries of word processing; the former chairman of the Indiana University history department, William B. Cohen, who provided encouragement and support when I was trying to convalesce from a health crisis and pick up the threads of *Democracy Challenged*; and the gifted surgeon, Yousuf Mahomed, and the equally gifted cardiologists, Carter F. Henrick and Lawrence D. Rink, whose medical knowledge and skills enabled me to survive that health crisis and complete the present book. Most of all, I wish to thank my wife Susan, my precious "Kentucky Babe," for her love and unflagging support while I was recuperating and putting together *Democracy Challenged.*

John Edward Wilz

# Chapter
# 1

---

# After Victory

"We will gain the inevitable triumph—so help us God." So promised Pres. Franklin D. Roosevelt on the day following that infamous Sunday in December of 1941 when Japanese bombing planes swooped down on Pearl Harbor and plunged the United States into World War II. No American at the outset of 1945 doubted that the presidential promise would be fulfilled—with or without the help of God. Still, the end of the global war did not appear imminent when dawn broke across the national landscape on New Year's Day, 1945. As matters turned out, of course, the war careened to its termination with unexpected suddenness over the next seven months, and the drama that unfolded during that time of national triumph remains etched in the memory of tens of millions of Americans. Those indeed were momentous times.

Elected to a fourth term the previous autumn, Roosevelt repeated the presidential oath in a quiet ceremony at the White House on January 20, 1945. An obscure politician from Missouri, Harry S. Truman, repeated the vice presidential oath. The following month, Roosevelt traveled to Yalta in the Crimea to discuss political and territorial arrangements in Europe and Northeast Asia with Premier Josef Stalin of the Soviet Union and Prime Minister Winston Churchill of Great Britain. Three months later, delegates representing 50 governments assembled in San Francisco to draft a covenant for a new international organization that would displace the discredited League of Nations. After eight weeks of toil, on June 26, 1945, they put their hands to the charter of the United Nations Organization.

On the global battlefront, meanwhile, the military-naval campaign of the United States and its allies was progressing at full throttle. Armies of the United States, Britain, and Canada, from February to April 1945, hammered those of the tyrant Adolf Hitler in the Low Countries, crossed the Rhine, and drove into Germany's industrial heartland. Stalin's mighty Red Army smashed at German defenses from the east; bombing planes of the Western Allies turned the cities of Hitler's Reich to rubble. In the Far Pacific, U.S. forces drove the Japanese from Manila, expelled them from the tiny volcanic island of Iwo Jima, and undertook what would prove for Americans the most sanguinary action of the entire war—in the waters adjacent to and on Okinawa. From bases in the Marianas Islands, U.S. B-29 bombing planes incinerated one Japanese city after another.

The sudden death of Roosevelt and accession of Truman to the presidency, on April 12, 1945, brought no interruption of the rush of the Allies toward victory. On April 27, American and Soviet troops came together near Torgau, on the Elbe 70 miles south of Berlin. On April 30, as Soviet shells rained down about his bunker in the German capital, Hitler shot himself to death. On May 7, at Rheims in France, German emissaries signed surrender documents. Told of the surrender the next day, "VE (Victory in Europe) Day," the people of the United States gave themselves over to an exuberant celebration.

After completing the conquest of Okinawa, U.S. forces in the Pacific prepared for what promised to be a bloody invasion of Japan's home islands. But unbeknownst to all save a handful of Americans, scientists and engineers on a lonely expanse of desert in New Mexico were about to test an atomic explosive device. If successful, the test appeared certain to rank as one of those epochal events in history, to wit, an event that marks the start of a new period or era in the unfolding of nature or in the affairs of humans.

As dawn broke over the sands of New Mexico's Tularosa Valley on the morning of July 16, a spherical device designated "the Gadget" rested atop a 100-foot steel tower on a remote bombing range of the Alamogordo Air Base of the U.S. Army Air Forces. Four and one-half feet in diameter, the Gadget had a metal casing that was enveloped by detonator wire. The wire, in turn, was connected to a score of electronic detonators that protruded through the casing into tapered circular lenses of high explosive. At the center of the device, less than two feet in diameter, was a subcritical core of plutonium, and at the center of the core was a neutron-laden sphere of less than one inch in diameter—the initiator, or, as it was codenamed, "Urchin." Then, at 5:29, by the action of an electric timing device, a surge of high voltage triggered the electronic detonators, the eruption of the high explosive lenses compressed the plutonium core, and Urchin released its neutrons. In that instant, the core became a seething critical mass.

The result was stupefying. A searing flash that was visible for 250 miles enveloped the desert and nearby mountains in a dazzling glow of orange and violet and gray. A column of smoke and ash jetted skyward, then billowed into a huge mushroomlike cloud. Thirty seconds after the explosion, those who were witnessing the phenomenon (from a distance of 6 miles) felt a blast of hot air, then, in the words of one observer, heard a "strong, sustained, awesome roar which warned of doomsday and made us feel that we puny things were blasphemous to dare tamper with the forces heretofore reserved to the Almighty." Another observer wrote, "It was as though the earth had opened and the skies had split. One felt as though one were present at the moment of creation when God said, 'Let there be light.'" Taking a more mundane view of what had happened, a scientist exclaimed, "It worked, my God, the damned thing worked!" And the corpulent general who had overseen the atomic bomb

August 1945: Japanese women walk along a path cleared through atomic devastation in Hiroshima.

September 2, 1945: Japanese emissaries prepare to sign surrender documents aboard the USS *Missouri*.

project, Leslie R. Groves of the Army, said, "The war's over. One or two of those things, and Japan will be finished." Events proved Groves correct.

Learning of the test of the atomic bomb shortly after arriving at Potsdam (outside devastated Berlin) for a conference with his British and Soviet counterparts, Truman declined to reverse an earlier decision to use atomic bombs when the Tokyo government rejected "the Potsdam Declaration," demanding that Japan surrender unconditionally. Unbeknownst to their enemies, the Japanese were bent on fighting to the death unless permitted to keep their emperor. Thus, on August 6, 1945, an atomic bomb delivered by the B-29 super-fortress *Enola Gay* virtually obliterated the city of Hiroshima from the planet—and brought death to seventy thousand Japanese. Two days later, the Soviet Union declared war on Japan. The next day, August 9, a second atomic bomb devastated Nagasaki and claimed thirty thousand lives. The Japanese thereupon advised the Allied powers that they would quit the war on the condition that they be allowed to retain the imperial throne. When the Allies indicated probable acceptance of that condition, the Japanese agreed to capitulate, and on September 2, 1945, Gen. Douglas MacArthur of the United States presided over an emotion-packed ceremony of surrender aboard the USS *Missouri* as the superdreadnought rode majestically at anchor in Tokyo Bay. World War II, which had claimed the lives of 20 to 35 million people—400,000 of them Americans—belonged to history.

## STATE OF THE UNION

That a U.S. general standing on the deck of a U.S. warship had presided over the ritual of terminating World War II seemed manifestly appropriate. For the United States by any standard of measure—military-naval strength, industrial capacity, agricultural productivity, vitality of citizenry—was the premier power of the world. Because of its inestimable power, and because it had mobilized that power in the recent crusade to crush aggression in Europe and Asia, the United States, almost universally admired as a citadel of liberty and democracy and a land of unbounded opportunity, had achieved a level of influence and prestige across the world that was without precedent.

Most Americans in September 1945 basked in the outer world's admiration of their society and institutions. Never mind the outrageous internment of Japanese Americans during the late war. Never mind the blatant denial of essential democratic rights to racial minorities and the callous and often brutal mistreatment of those minorities in the North American bastion of democracy and justice. Never mind the anomaly of grinding poverty in the land of unparalleled abundance. Seemingly oblivious to the imperfections of their society, exhilarated by their country's magnificent achievements in battle areas and on the home front during the global war, a preponderance of Americans in September 1945 continued to accept uncritically what a preponderance of Americans had accepted uncritically from their republic's birth in the 1770s, to wit, that the United States was a New Israel (or promised land), its citizens a chosen people.

Otherwise, the United States in 1945 was a republic of 140 million people, 124 million of them white, 15 million black, 300,000 Indian, 200,000 Oriental. Eighty million Americans lived in cities and towns, 60 million in the countryside, 14 million in "the Empire State" of New York, a mere 6 million in California. Made up of 48 contiguous states, the United States maintained dominion over a variety of overseas territories: Alaska, American Samoa, Guam, Hawaii, the Philippines, Puerto Rico, part of the Virgin Islands, and an assortment of tiny islands in the Caribbean and Pacific. By a mandate of the United Nations in 1947, it would formally assume administration of the Caroline, Marianas, Marshall, and Palau island groups that reached for more than 2,000 miles across the Western Pacific.

The future looked bright for most of the republic's 140 million citizens in September 1945. Since no bombs had fallen on America's cities and no invading armies had scarred its landscape, Americans faced no problems of rebuilding the physical bases of their civilization in the aftermath of global war. Although the national debt had skyrocketed from $34 billion in 1940 to $258 billion in 1945, the economic boom generated by the war had knocked the Great Depression of the 1930s into the dustbin of history. Happily, that boom appeared fated to continue, as Americans now set about to cash in billions of dollars of government bonds bought during the war when automobiles and refrigerators and other manufactured goods were unobtainable and give themselves over to an orgy of consumption. But might the serpent of war slither anew into America's Garden of Eden? No way—or so reckoned most Americans. The new world organization, the United Nations (UN) would guard the peace and resolve international disputes amicably. Besides, what nation would dare put down a challenge to the United States, the only power whose military arsenal included atomic bombs?

The political center of the United States, of course, was Washington, where the Supreme Court, Congress, and office of the president exercised judicial, legislative, and executive authority that the so-called Founding Fathers in 1787 had accorded the national or federal government. As for the Supreme Court, all save two of its members appointed by Franklin Roosevelt, it was in the parlance of American politics manifestly liberal in orientation in 1945. Across the street from the majestic Supreme Court building stood the equally majestic federal Capitol, the workplace of the U.S. Congress. Although members who claimed membership in the Democratic party, the more liberal of the republic's two principal parties, comprised majorities in both the House of Representatives and Senate, a "conservative coalition" of conservative Democrats of the South and Republicans of the North and West was, as it had been since the latter 1930s, in de facto control of the national legislature. Less than two miles to the west and north of the Capitol, at the opposite end of Pennsylvania Avenue, the national parade thoroughfare, stood the White House, where Harry Truman, a Democrat, presided over the executive branch of the federal government.

Born in the village of Lamar in western Missouri in 1884, Truman had grown up in the town of Independence in middle-income comfort. After graduating from high school, he became a bank clerk, then spent some ten years toiling as a farmer on his family's acreage near the town of Grandview. A member of the Missouri National Guard, he was summoned to active service in the Army a few months after America's entry in the Great War in 1917, and commanded a field artillery battery in the Meuse-Argonne campaign in France during the closing weeks of the war in the autumn of 1918. On returning from the war, he married his childhood sweetheart, and shortly after his marriage he and his former sergeant opened a clothing store in Kansas City, only to see the venture overwhelmed in the economic recession of 1921–1922.

Meanwhile, Truman had become a functionary in the notorious political "machine" of "Boss" Thomas J. Pendergast of Kansas City. He apparently stayed clear of the corruption that pervaded the Pendergast organization, and, supported by Pendergast, won election to county offices, then in 1934 to the U.S. Senate. In the Senate, Truman, a stalwart supporter of the New Deal administration of Franklin Roosevelt, was known as "the senator from Pendergast." When Tom Pendergast in 1938 was convicted of income tax evasion and sent off to prison, Truman's political career appeared to be near its end. But, following a strenuous campaign, he won re-election to the Senate in 1940, and beginning in 1941 gained the respect of colleagues in Congress when he presided over the so-called Truman Committee that moved against greed and self-seeking in the national defense effort. Because he was acceptable to the various factions of the Democratic party, a weary Franklin Roosevelt selected a surprised and somewhat reluctant Truman to be his vice presidential running mate in the electoral contest of 1944. After the Roosevelt-Truman ticket swept to victory on Election Day, Truman in January 1945 repeated the vice presidential oath and, when Roosevelt died of a massive cerebral hemorrhage on April 12, 1945, he became the republic's thirty-third chief executive.

Truman appeared the epitome of the ordinary American. Standing 5 feet, 9 inches, he wore thick glasses and spoke with what was sometimes described as a flat midwestern twang. He had none of the histrionic abilities of the magniloquent Roosevelt. But appearances were deceiving. Notwithstanding the fact that after high school his formal schooling had been limited to a few night classes in Kansas City, Truman had a quick and incisive mind and a capacity for intellectual growth. He had a keen understanding of human nature, a grasp of the mechanism of government, a reverence for history. Most of the time, he was a good judge of ability and character. He was sensitive to the needs and aspirations of ordinary people, had a fine sense of humor, was without guile. After the shock of being catapulted to the presidency had worn off, he never doubted his capacity to meet presidential responsibilities. He was a man who could act decisively. Resting on his desk in the Oval Office, indeed, was a little sign that read "The buck stops here." A Mason and a Baptist who enjoyed a tumbler of bourbon and branch water, he was a combative man, feisty and sometimes profane, one who refused to be intimidated by critics or brood over decisions that had gone awry but were beyond reversal.

## STATE OF THE WORLD

The territory of the republic over which Truman presided in 1945 comprised only 7.1 percent of the earth's land area, the 160 million people under U.S. jurisdiction, only 6.9 percent of the world's population. Still, Americans, as they had since the founding of their republic (notwithstanding an "isolationist" impulse to stay clear of foreign embroilments), took an abiding interest in the state of the outer world.

Like the United States, Canada in September 1945 was experiencing economic prosperity; its citizenry was looking to the future with confidence. Elsewhere in the world, the conditions of life tended to be grim. Inflation, authoritarian and inefficient government, and widespread poverty plagued most of the countries of Latin America. Although nationalist impulses were becoming increasingly evident in Africa, most of the fabled Dark Continent remained under the colonial rule of various governments of Europe. A preponderance of its people could neither read nor write, lived in squalor, and were victims of disease and malnutrition. Not yet the world's center of petroleum production, the Middle East was astir. Iran was striving to rid itself of foreign domination, and Arab states were organizing to resist the demands of Jewish Zionists that Palestine, an Arab domain for more than a thousand years, be opened to large-scale Jewish immigration and much of its territory reconstituted as an independent Jewish nation-state.

To the east, India, inhabited by 400 million people of diverse languages and religions, a land of rampant poverty and illiteracy, was demanding independence from Great Britain. In Vietnam, the followers of the communist patriot Ho Chi Minh were preparing to resist the restoration of the country as a colony of France. Indonesian nationalists led by the flamboyant Achmed Sukarno determined to resist the restoration of Dutch authority in the Netherlands Indies. Far to the north, Japan, 1.3 million of whose people had perished in the late war, was cleaning up its cities and harbors and adjusting to the rule of General MacArthur, the supreme commander of the Allied powers in that battered country. Across the Sea of Japan, Korea, under the yoke of Japan since 1905, was beginning a new chapter in its tragic history as its liberators, the Soviet Union and the United States, set about to address what would prove to be the intractable question of how to redeem their pledge to reestablish Korea as an independent and unified nation-state. Beyond the Yalu and across the Yellow Sea from Korea was China, ravaged by Japan since 1931. The homeland of a half-billion people, weighted down by ignorance and poverty and the ineptitude of an inefficient and corrupt central government, China was bracing for a struggle to the death between the military forces of Generalissimo Chiang Kai-shek and the communist chieftain Mao Zedong.

Beyond China's northern frontier lay the Soviet Union, a Eurasian behemoth of 200 million people representing an array of nationalities and speaking a variety of languages. The recent war had claimed the lives of 10 to 20 million Soviet people and brought devastation to vast reaches of European Russia. Ruling the Soviet Union was the tyrant Stalin, whose impulse to brutality rivaled that of Hitler. Still, the citadel of international communism had emerged triumphant from the war and acquired an assortment of territories, and the country was animated by an élan born of victory.

To the west of the Soviet Union lay the historic heartland of Euro-American civilization. Portugal, Spain, Sweden, and Switzerland had stayed clear of the world war; the rest of the countries of Europe had not. Millions of Europe's people had perished. Particularly in the Low Countries, Germany, parts of France, and Poland, devastation was omnipresent. When not in total ruin, national economies were in disarray. People were confused and dispirited and hungry.

Its citizenry having put aside isolationist impulses of former times, the United States determined to make at least a modest effort to relieve suffering and promote reconstruction in the outer world. Hence it continued in the aftermath of the global conflict to contribute to the UN Relief and Rehabilitation Administration (UNRAA), organized in 1943 to provide relief supplies and assist in the rehabilitation of war-torn countries. By the end of 1945 the United States had contributed $2.5 billion to UNRAA. It also had taken part in the international conference at Bretton Woods, New Hampshire, in 1944, and in the months ahead would implement the so-called Bretton Woods agreement by joining the new International Monetary Fund to achieve stability among the world's currencies and the International Bank for Reconstruction and Development (World Bank) to facilitate long-term investment in countries that had suffered damage during the war, as well as those that were economically underdeveloped.

## WAR CRIMES TRIALS, DEMOBILIZATION, THE UNITED NATIONS

Upon termination of global hostilities, Americans determined to turn their energies to enterprises of peace. But they did not forget a commitment they and their allies had made to bring leaders of the Axis powers, the perpetrators of monstrous "war crimes," to the bar of justice. In addition to ordering unjustifiable and unprovoked attacks against neighboring countries, Axis leaders had ordered the bombing of open cities and enslavement of civilian and military prisoners. Most horrendous, the leaders of Germany had set about with machinelike efficiency to exterminate an entire ethnic-religious population that resided within the Nazi empire. Not only did justice cry out for vengeance against Axis war criminals; Americans and others believed it essential that national leaders be put on notice that they could not escape personal accountability if they ordered wars of aggression and sanctioned brutalities against groups and individuals.

Although some jurists thought the war-crime trials violated widely accepted standards of jurisprudence, the trials of leaders of Germany and Japan, presided over by international tribunals, took place in Nuremberg and Tokyo from 1945 to 1947. Particularly in Nuremberg, where the accused squirmed and grimaced when confronted with photographs of devastated cities and twisted corpses, the trials were often heavy with drama. The outcome? Of the 21 defendants who sat in the dock in Nuremberg, 7 received prison terms, 11 the death sentence. Three were acquitted. The international tribunal in Tokyo found all 27 defendants guilty and sentenced 7 of them to death.

At the same time that Axis war criminals were facing their accusers, the

September 30, 1946: Hermann Goering, Rudolf Hess, and other onetime leaders of Nazi Germany listen as the verdict is read at the war crimes trial in Nuremberg.

United States was dismantling the military-naval mechanism it had assembled during the global war. Training camps were closed. Rifles and artillery pieces, tanks and aircraft, warships and cargo vessels were put in storage or sold as war surplus. Meanwhile, the armed forces discharged millions of servicemen and -women, and by the spring of 1946 their total personnel had dwindled from more than 11 million at the time of Japan's surrender to fewer than 3 million.

If pell-mell demobilization brought scattered protest by people who warned that the United States was apt to find it necessary to flex military-naval muscles in the postwar era, most Americans, confident that the global bloodletting had ushered in a new era of peace and harmony in the world, determined that the federal government press ahead with the task of drastically reducing the military-naval establishment. In any case, the United States would scarcely want for military muscle in the years to come, for it alone had atomic bombs and aircraft capable of unleashing those bombs on any conceivable enemy. Reinforcing the national impulse to demobilization was the popular awareness that the new agency to keep the peace, the UN, had started to function, first in London, then at Flushing Meadows on Long Island in the

United States. (The General Assembly of the world organization would vote in 1946 to locate the UN's permanent headquarters in New York City.)

The United States had declined to join the League of Nations, the dream child of Pres. Woodrow Wilson that had appeared after World War I. A frail instrument, the League proved incapable of preventing a new outbreak of aggression and war in the 1930s, and tens of millions of Americans accepted the argument that the League had failed as a peacekeeping agency because of the absence of the United States from its membership roll. However dubious that argument, most Americans supported the idea of U.S. membership in a new international organization that would take form after World War II—and in July 1945 the Senate in Washington consented to the UN charter by a vote of 89–2.

The charter of the UN stipulated that international disputes were to be settled by peaceful means and that each member was obliged to assist the world organization in any action it might undertake in accord with the charter. Primary responsibility for the maintenance of peace rested with the Security Council, comprised of 11 members, 5 of them permanent (Britain, China, France, the Soviet Union, and the United States), 6 of them elected by the General Assembly for two-year terms. A decision by the Security Council on a "substantive matter" required an affirmative vote by the 5 permanent members, hence any permanent member, by withholding assent, could veto a proposed decision on a matter of substance.

During the UN's pristine months, the General Assembly dealt with problems relating to displaced persons, the shortage of food in the world, and children in war-torn countries. It considered the disposition of territories hitherto administrated under "mandates" of the League of Nations. Meanwhile, the Security Council weighed complaints relating to the presence of Soviet troops in Iran, British troops in Greece and the Netherlands Indies, and British and French troops in Lebanon and Syria—also complaints that Albania, Yugoslavia, and Bulgaria were assisting communist guerrillas who were operating in northern Greece and that the government of Generalissimo Francisco Franco in Spain constituted a threat to peace. Of equal moment, or so it seemed at the time, the General Assembly in January 1946 established the UN's Atomic Energy Commission to prepare proposals to assure that governments would use the awesome energy released when a subcritical core of uranium or plutonium was bombarded by neutrons for peaceful purposes only and to eliminate atomic weapons and other weapons of mass destruction.

## ATOMIC ENERGY

At the time the General Assembly established the UN's Atomic Energy Commission, in early 1946, Americans were in the fifth month of a raucous debate regarding their own government's atomic energy policy. The debate had got under way shortly after Japan's surrender when President Truman asked Congress to formulate a national atomic policy. Stipulating only that the nature of atomic power was such that an absolute government monopoly of fissionable materials was imperative, the president left open an important question: Who should direct the country's atomic energy program, the military or a civilian agency? Observing that military control had succeeded spectacularly during the late war, leaders of the Army and Navy sought a continuation of military control. More to the point, military-naval leaders feared that a heady idealism about peace might influence a civilian agency to drop the country's nuclear guard. Comfortable with the prospect of continued military control, the White House lent support to the May-Johnson bill, introduced in Congress in October 1945, a measure that would leave control of atomic energy with the military.

Many Americans, including assorted educators and religious leaders, scientists and civil libertarians were aghast. Animated by a Jefferson-like distrust of generals and admirals, critics of the May-Johnson bill viewed military control of atomic energy as a threat to peace and democracy. Such sentiments struck a chord among congressional liberals, and in late 1945 Sen. Brien McMahon, Democrat of Connecticut, introduced legislation providing for an atomic control commission composed entirely of civilians. The McMahon bill drew an angry response, particularly from conservative members of the Military Affairs and Un-American Activities Committees of the House of Representatives, who feared that a civilian commission might be an easy mark for communist subversion.

At length, Sen. Arthur H. Vandenberg, Republican of Michigan, proposed appointment of a "military liaison committee" to consult with a civilian atomic energy commission; otherwise, McMahon's bill should remain intact. Vandenberg's compromise attracted sufficient support that the Atomic Energy Act achieved passage in the summer of 1946. The legislation provided for an AEC of four civilians, mandated a government monopoly of fissionable materials, gave the president exclusive authority to order the use of atomic weapons, and prohibited the passing of atomic information to foreign governments, even friendly ones. It also envisioned peaceful uses of the atom, and shortly after its establishment the AEC set up several divisions to work with educational and business institutions in turning atomic energy to medical and industrial purposes. (The functions and responsibilities of the AEC would pass to a new agency, the Nuclear Regulatory Commission, in 1974.)

Leaders in Washington, meanwhile, weighed the question of international control of atomic energy, a nettlesome question inasmuch as any agreement to control atomic energy throughout the world would doubtless require that the United States share its atomic secrets. Hearing out all sides on the question, President Truman in the autumn of 1945 told reporters that other powers would have to learn the secret of fabricating atomic weapons "on their own hook, just as we did." Still, the scientific equations for producing atomic explosions were widely understood, and nobody doubted that scientists and engineers in the Soviet Union and elsewhere would eventually figure out how to make atomic weapons. So leaders in Washington decided it was in the national interest that the United States take the initiative in working out a formula for the international control of atomic energy. The upshot was a plan presented in a speech in the gymnasium of Hunter College in New York in June 1946 by Bernard M. Baruch, a 75-year-old financier who was known as a counselor of presidents.

What came to be known as the Baruch Plan made clear that the United States was prepared to share its atomic secrets, discontinue the manufacture of atomic weapons, and destroy its stocks of such weapons—but not immediately. The United States would share its atomic secrets in stages, and for an unspecified period, while other nations were effectively prohibited from producing them, it would be at liberty to produce and maintain stocks of atomic warheads. Baruch's proposals striking no fire in the Kremlin, the Soviet delegate to the UN's AEC, Andrei Y. Gromyko, promptly countered the Baruch Plan by proposing an agreement that would prohibit the production of atomic bombs and provide for the destruction of existing stocks of such bombs. Gromyko also made it plain that the Soviet Union would not consent to international inspectors in its territory or any impairment of its right, as a permanent member of the UN's Security Council, to exercise a veto in matters pertaining to atomic energy. Gromyko's plan struck no fire in Washington.

Punctuating the futility of the quest to contain the atomic genie were goings-on in the Western Pacific during the month that followed the presenta-

July 1, 1946: In the first postwar test of nuclear weapons, an atomic bomb explodes over a flotilla of ships in the Bikini lagoon in the western Pacific.

tions by Baruch and Gromyko. In retrospect, those happenings appear ghastly. But in view of the fears and animosities that were swirling across the planet less than a year after conclusion of the global war, they were doubtless inevitable.

Their activities scarcely interrupted by the passing of the global war, the scientists and engineers who had fashioned America's atomic bomb, in early 1946, began preparations for a new test of atomic weapons. The site selected for the test was Bikini Island, 250 miles to the north of Kwajelein in the Marshall group. At length, 92 Japanese and obsolete American warships were anchored in the 25-mile Bikini lagoon. Then, on July 1, 1946, an Army Air Forces bomber released an atomic bomb that exploded above the flotilla. Only five of the ships were sunk. A few weeks later, a second bomb was exploded, this time beneath the water. That only a few ships sustained serious damage was irrelevant, for nearly every one of the target vessels was drenched with radioactive seawater, and according to a report by the Joint Chiefs of Staff, the "contaminated ships became radioactive stoves and would have burned all living things aboard them with invisible and painless but deadly radiation."

## SECURITY AFFAIRS

While weighing the question of control of atomic energy and sanctioning new tests of atomic weapons, leaders in Washington were determining the mission, strength, and composition of the country's armed forces. Historians have not accorded them high marks for their efforts. The reasons are transparent. Displaying what appears to have been inexcusable shortsightedness, nobody in high authority in Washington seemed to give serious thought to the possibility that the national interest might require U.S. participation in an armed conflict in which the stakes would not warrant a presidential decision to subject an enemy to atomic devastation. In a word, no leader apparently foresaw the possibility that the Washington government might feel constrained to project the country's armed forces into a so-called brushfire war in some peripheral area, say, the Korean peninsula. The overbearing assumption of the time was that any armed conflict involving the United States would be total in character and its outcome determined by the delivery of atomic bombs on the enemy, presumably the Soviet Union. Hence the country's conventional (that is, nonnuclear) forces, particularly those of the Army, were allowed to atrophy.

Meanwhile, America's military-naval establishment underwent a major reorganization that appeared long overdue. During the recent global war, competition between components of the country's armed forces, so many knowledgeable citizens contended, had increased the expense of conducting the war and affected combat efficiency. What was needed, some observers thought, was unification of those forces. But any suggestion that the armed forces be unified stirred fierce opposition, particularly among leaders of the Navy, for admirals feared that the Army would dominate a unified armed service, and the result might be elimination of the Marine Corps and discrimination against sea-based air power. The misgivings of the admirals aside, President

Truman, who was appalled by interservice rivalry and duplication, issued an order in August 1945 that the Army and Navy were to examine the question of how they might coordinate their activities. The result of the 17-month study was passage by Congress of the National Security Act of 1947.

The act actually proliferated the services, inasmuch as it established the Air Force as a branch independent of the Army and replaced the War Department with two new departments, those of the Army and the Air Force. But the secretaries of the new departments did not have cabinet status, as had the secretary of war, and the secretary of the navy lost his cabinet rank. In the interest of unification, or at least closer cooperation, the measure sanctioned a new superagency, the National Military Establishment (renamed the Department of Defense in 1949), headed by the secretary of defense. The secretary of defense *was* a member of the president's cabinet, and the secretaries of the army, navy, and air force reported to him. The legislation also formalized the institution of the Joint Chiefs of Staff, established by executive order during the war, and directed the service chiefs to work together in the preparation of defense plans and consideration of strategy.

The National Security Act gave birth to two additional bodies that would have large bearing on future events: the Central Intelligence Agency (CIA) and the National Security Council (NSC). The CIA assumed responsibility for collecting and evaluating intelligence data, a task hitherto performed sometimes haphazardly by a variety of agencies. Nobody in 1947 seemed to envision that the CIA would become involved in covert activities and as a result become a center of controversy. As for the NSC—which presently includes four statutory members, namely, the president, vice president, secretary of state, and secretary of defense, and two statutory advisers, the director of the CIA and chairman of the Joint Chiefs of Staff—its main purpose was to establish an official apparatus, well staffed and convenient to the president, for coordinating the thinking of the State Department and the National Military Establishment on major foreign policy questions. The NSC, so those who formulated it thought, would also give the president regular access to his chief foreign policy advisers, and indeed impose on him a fairly precise formula for dealing with matters touching the nation's security. A precise formula for dealing with national security matters, it was thought, would inhibit a president who, after the fashion of Roosevelt, might be inclined to make critical decisions without consulting diplomatic and military advisers—and, if circumstances required, reinforce an ineffectual chief executive.

## RECONVERSION

While dismantling and reorganizing their armed forces, Americans wrestled with the complexities of converting the national economy from one of war to one of peace. Reconversion quickly ran into a snag: a period of turbulence in labor-management relations. Observing that working people had made few wage demands during the war, unions insisted on raises in pay for their members. Uneasy about the consequences of the end of war production, business chieftains recoiled at the prospect of increased labor costs. The outcome, from the autumn of 1945 to the spring of 1946, was a succession of strikes in the automobile, steel, and other industries. The first wave of postwar work stoppages ended when management granted wage increases. But strikes by coal miners and railroad workers, to which President Truman responded by seizing coal mines and threatening to draft railroadmen into the Army, jolted the economy anew in the spring and autumn of 1946.

The labor picture brightened in 1947, and during the next few years labor-management relations tended to be tranquil. Wages went up, but management passed the costs on to consumers. Meanwhile, labor contracts underwent innovation. Wages became linked with the cost of living, so when prices went up wages followed. Many contracts provided company pensions to supplement Social Security retirement annuities, medical benefits for union members, and company-sponsored life insurance plans.

Further complicating reconversion was a collision between the president and the aforementioned conservative coalition in Congress. The collision came to pass when Truman, a few days after Japan's surrender, in September 1945, sent his first domestic message to Congress. Eventually known as the Fair Deal, the Truman program called for an extension of Social Security, national health insurance, increase in the minimum wage, slum clearance, new regional development projects patterned after the one in the Tennessee Valley, a full employment bill, and reorganization of the federal bureaucracy. Conservatives were dismayed. Alas, there was more. Truman also urged an extension of wartime price controls, believed by conservatives to be inhibiting production. Would prices go up following the elimination of controls? Temporarily perhaps. But, according to conservative calculations, increased production would intensify competition, and competition in turn would keep prices in line.

The battle over controls moved to a climax in the summer of 1946 when Truman asked Congress for an indefinite extension of the Office of Price Administration (OPA), the agency established during the war to keep inflation in check. Congress agreed to renew the OPA, but so emasculated its authority that the president vetoed the renewal legislation. Price controls ended two days later, and within a fortnight the country experienced its sharpest inflation since 1942. Almost in desperation, Congress voted a new bill to control prices and rents, signed by Truman with a warning that it would prove ineffectual. Events proved the president correct; the cost of living continued to inch upward.

Republicans and Democrats, meanwhile, had begun to deploy for the midterm election of 1946. Economic controls were an issue, and in view of popular weariness with wartime restrictions the issue worked to the advantage of the Republicans. Republicans, likewise, were able to exploit the annoyance that many voters felt as a result of labor disturbances, which according to Republicans were a consequence of the alleged coddling of labor by recent Democratic administrations. Another asset for Republicans was the increasing unpopularity of the president. Despite the fact that the citizenry had taken a generous view of Truman when Roosevelt's death propelled him into the White House in the spring of 1945, tens of millions of voters had concluded by the autumn of 1946 that he lacked the capacity to meet presidential responsibilities. Indeed, Truman appeared to be his party's chief liability as the electoral campaign got under way. Whatever the reasons, the outcome of the campaign was a Democratic disaster. For the first time since 1928, Republicans won control of both houses of Congress—and also ousted Democrats from several gubernatorial mansions.

Reconversion had other dimensions. Japan's surrender prompted demands for tax reductions, and with presidential approval Congress in the autumn of 1945 reduced taxes by $6 billion. In response to scattered concern that another depression might be in the offing, Congress in early 1946 passed the Full Employment Act, one of the few Fair Deal proposals to receive a sympathetic hearing on Capitol Hill. The measure committed the federal government to the maintenance of full employment, established the Council of Economic Advisers, and required that the president provide Congress with an annual report on the condition of the economy. Truman, meanwhile, set about to dispose of plants and facilities built by the government during the war, a $17-billion investment that by 1945 accounted for 20 percent of the country's industrial capacity. Noting that the U.S. Steel Corporation, for example, paid $47 million for a plant that had cost taxpayers $200 million, critics charged that sale of the plants constituted a massive giveaway of public property to big business. Defenders of the sales pointed to the jerry-built construction of many of the plants, the worn condition of machinery, and the expense of converting plants to the production of consumer goods.

Whatever the snags, reconversion resulted in no break in the prosperity that the global conflict had generated in the United States. Unemployment remained negligible. By latter-day standards, inflation was minimal. And in the five years that followed the war, the annual national output of goods and services (gross national product) advanced from $213 billion to $284 billion, national income from $181 billion to $241 billion. Even the country's oft-depressed farmers shared in the postwar prosperity, and tenancy, a longtime index of the condition of agriculture, reached its lowest point in the twentieth century.

What accounted for the continuing economic boom? The rampant demand of Americans for cars and houses, appliances and furniture, clothing, and God only knows what else was largely responsible. Inasmuch as a substantial part of the funds were used to purchase manufactured and agricultural commodities produced in the United States, appropriations by the Washington government for relief and reconstruction in the war-devastated countries provided another stimulus for the American economy.

## TRUMAN AND CONGRESS

While the national economy continued to prosper, Republicans in early 1947 took control of Capitol Hill. Truman was scarcely elated. Still, the new Congress acceded to another of the president's Fair Deal proposals by authorizing a commission to study the federal bureaucracy and make recommendations. To direct the investigation, Truman appointed former-President Herbert Hoover, and the study group became known as the Hoover Commission. The commission found much that was amiss in the bureaucracy: waste and duplication, inadequate staffing, antiquated accounting procedures. But the basic conclusion was that there were too many executive departments and agencies. Responding to the Hoover Commission's recommendations, Congress in 1949 passed the Reorganization Act, authorizing the president to submit plans for executive reorganization. The plans would go into effect automatically unless Congress specifically disapproved. Truman thereupon submitted 36 reorganization plans, to only one of which Congress objected. The most visible result was a substantial reduction in the number of federal departments and agencies.

Responding to a request by Truman, Congress also passed the Presidential Succession Act of 1947. Under existing legislation, the secretary of state, an appointed official, was next in line to become president after the vice president—and after him (or her?) other members of the cabinet. Truman thought the president should be an elected official, so the new legislation provided that the speaker of the House of Representatives and the president pro tempore of the Senate would have precedence over members of the cabinet in the presidential succession. Of less merit in Truman's view was the action whereby the Republican-controlled Eightieth Congress, also in 1947, submitted to the states a constitutional amendment limiting the president to two full terms, the unpopular incumbent excepted. Essentially a posthumous rebuke of Franklin Roosevelt, the only president to serve more than two terms, the Twenty-second Amendment achieved ratification in 1951.

Of more immediate moment, conservative leaders of the Eightieth Congress, sharing a popular view that unions had become too powerful and with excessive power had come irresponsibility, determined to move against organized labor, its membership rolls now including the names of 15 million men and women. The outcome was the Taft-Hartley Act of 1947, passed over Truman's veto with many votes to spare.

The Taft-Hartley measure outlawed the closed shop (a contract requiring that an individual join a union before he or she could get a job) and secondary boycotts, forbade strikes against the federal government and union contributions to political campaigns. It required that unions make annual statements on their finances, and compelled union leaders to take oaths that they were not communists. The law also required that a union give a 60-day notice in advance of a strike (thus eliminating the element of surprise in strike activity), and if the projected work stoppage would affect an entire industry or imperil the national health or safety, the "cooling-off" period could be extended to 80 days. In the extra 20 days, the National Labor Relations Board could poll employees by secret ballot to determine whether they wished to strike or accept management's "final offer" of settlement.

Denounced by organized labor as a "slave labor bill," the Taft-Hartley Act proved less bothersome to labor than expected. Indeed, it contributed to a strengthening of the labor movement in the United States, inasmuch as the

American Federation of Labor and Congress of Industrial Organizations, in part as a result of their hostility to the Taft-Hartley legislation, put aside feuds of the past and in 1955 merged into the AFL-CIO.

## "TO SECURE THESE RIGHTS"

Although conservatives who commanded the Eightieth Congress responded to demands that the power of organized labor be curtailed, they turned aside appeals that the authority of the national government be invoked to assist black citizens in their decades-old quest to achieve the proverbial promise of American life. A member of the conservative coalition, Sen. Richard B. Russell, Democrat of Georgia, caught a sentiment shared by tens of millions of white Americans, in the country's northern and western regions as well as the South, when in 1946 he declared, "We will resist to the bitter end, whatever the consequences, any measure or any movement that would have a tendency to bring about social equality and intermingling and amalgamation of the races." The conditions of life that prevailed among black Americans, in a word, failed to stir the consciences of Americans of the persuasion of the distinguished senator from Georgia.

Those conditions were generally abominable. Uprooted from the southern countryside in recent decades as a consequence of the mechanization of agriculture, a majority of blacks now dwelled in cities and towns, nearly all of them in exclusively black and often ramshackle neighborhoods in which loan sharks, numbers racketeers, and narcotics peddlers often thrived. All over the South, and in many other regions as well, black children attended all-black and almost invariably inferior schools, some of them little more than shacks presided over by teachers who were functionally illiterate, from which legions of them emerged as intellectual cripples. Most state universities in the South, not to mention the more reputable privately endowed centers of higher learning of the region, were closed to blacks.

The system of discrimination and segregation was indeed pervasive. State and local ordinances in the country's southern region kept blacks out of movie theaters and hotels, restaurants and swimming pools that were patronized by whites. Informal rules or customs accomplished the same purpose in other regions. Laws and ordinances across the South required blacks to quench their thirst at segregated drinking fountains and find relief in segregated rest rooms, ride at the rear of city buses and streetcars and find seating in "colored only" (and calculatedly less comfortable) sections of segregated or "Jim Crow" railway coaches. The charters of most craft unions of the AFL, as well as those of the railroad brotherhoods, contained "white only" clauses that effectively closed a wide variety of trades to blacks. Whether inhibited by union charters or not, countless white employers throughout the country categorically refused to consider job applications by blacks. Accordingly, great numbers of black citizens who were gainfully employed spent their days (or nights) sweeping streets, collecting garbage, cleaning rest rooms, or toiling as domestic servants.

The litany of disabilities suffered by blacks in the self-proclaimed citadel of democracy and equal opportunity, frankly, seemed endless. Black athletes were denied the opportunity to play major league baseball or professional football. Of larger import, blacks in all parts of the country were the victims of routine harassment by white law enforcement officials. If a black in a southern state was indicted for a crime, his or her fate was certain to be determined by an all-white jury. In most states of the onetime Confederacy, blacks were systematically denied the most basic right of citizens in a democratic society, namely, the right to vote. What if a black in the South sought to defy the racial caste system and exercise full rights as an American citizen? Unalterably committed to "the southern way of life," that is, the way of white supremacy and segregation, the typical white southerner had no tolerance for "uppity niggers." And if lynching had become unfashionable, there were other ways to keep assertive blacks "in their place": dismissal from jobs, eviction from rented dwellings, denial of credit.

Fortunately, black Americans found allies in their struggle for civil equality during the postwar years. Substantial numbers of their white compatriots came to understand that discrimination on account of race was a national scandal and that the time had come for America to honor its democratic ideals. Most were political liberals. Some were leaders of labor unions, others spokespeople from religious circles. But the most influential friend of black Americans in those years was the occupant of the mansion at 1600 Pennsylvania Avenue in Washington: Harry Truman, a man who had grown up in a segregated environment and as an adult taken racial discrimination more or less for granted.

Whatever his motives, the thirty-third president took up the cause of civil equality for black Americans. He asked Congress in 1946 to make the Fair Employment Practices Commission (FEPC), established by Roosevelt in 1941, a permanent agency. The conservative coalition prevented passage of legislation embodying the presidential request. Later that same year, Truman appointed a special Committee on Civil Rights to study the problem of discrimination in America and make recommendations. Made up of distinguished whites and blacks, the committee in 1947 issued a report entitled "To Secure These Rights" urging the government to move against racial injustice. Reinforced by the report, Truman in early 1948 sent Congress the most far-ranging request for civil rights legislation in the history of the republic. He sought a permanent Commission on Civil Rights and permanent FEPC, protection of the right to vote and protection against lynching, a strengthening of existing civil rights statutes, and prohibition of discrimination in interstate transportation facilities. As the president expected, his proposals got nowhere in the face of opposition by the conservative coalition.

Still, blacks registered a few gains in those years. Archbishop Joseph E. Ritter ordered desegregation of the Catholic school system of the archdiocese of St. Louis; scattered city and town councils passed antidiscrimination ordinances. A federal judge in 1947 ordered the Democratic party of South Caro-

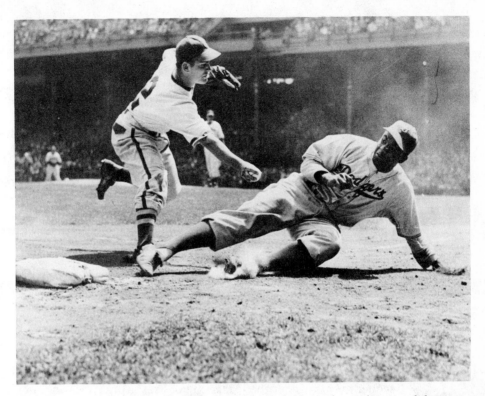

May 2, 1948: Major league baseball's first black player, Jackie Robinson, sliding into second base.

lina to permit blacks to vote in its primary elections. More dramatic was de-segregation of major league baseball when Jack Roosevelt "Jackie" Robinson in 1947 became the first baseman of the Brooklyn Dodgers. Ignoring racial slurs by players and fans of opposing teams, Robinson performed spectacularly, and opened the way to the big leagues for other black players, including the incomparable Willie Mays, who joined the New York Giants in 1951.

Almost unnoticed by most Americans were assorted happenings affecting other minority groups. The War Relocation Authority assisted the return to "normal outside communities" of scores of thousands of Japanese Americans who had been interned in relocation camps since 1942. The last of the internees departed the relocation center at Tule Lake, California, in early 1946. Meanwhile, federal courts issued a variety of decisions, and Congress passed legislation affecting Indian Americans. Congress in 1946, for example, established the Indian Claims Commission to facilitate the adjudication of claims by Indians for compensation resulting from the illegal seizure of their lands. Of comparable note were actions affecting Puerto Ricans, citizens of the United States since 1917.

## PUERTO RICO AND THE PHILIPPINES

Acquired by the United States in 1898 as a consequence of the Spanish-American War, Puerto Rico remained ridden by poverty and illiteracy, and in the view of some Puerto Ricans the island's regeneration required political independence. Responding to such sentiments, President Truman asked Congress to authorize a plebiscite allowing Puerto Ricans to indicate whether they preferred statehood for the island, independence, or commonwealth status. At length, in 1950, Congress approved a measure empowering Puerto Ricans to draft a constitution. In accord with the latter measure, a Puerto Rican assembly adopted a constitution that would make Puerto Rico a commonwealth of the United States. As a commonwealth, Puerto Rico would manage its own internal affairs, but the United States would manage its foreign relations and provide for its defense. The island's people and corporations would not be subject to federal taxation, and Puerto Ricans would continue to be free to migrate to the United States without restriction.

Bent on independence, a handful of Puerto Ricans set about to prevent a referendum on the new constitution. To that purpose, two of their number, on November 1, 1950, made a dramatic attempt to force their way into the Blair House in Washington, the temporary residence of the presidential family while the White House was undergoing renovation, to assassinate President Truman. The attack failed, as did the campaign to prevent the referendum. Approved overwhelmingly, the constitution became operative in 1950. In subsequent years, under the leadership of Pres. Muñoz Marín, Puerto Rico undertook Operation Bootstrap, and the outcome was improvement in the island's standard of living and a reduction of illiteracy among its people.

Meanwhile, in accord with a congressional act of 1934, the Philippines became an independent republic. The formal transfer of sovereignty in the islands took place on July 4, 1946, on the green crescent-shaped plateau overlooking Manila Bay. After Ambassador Paul V. McNutt read a proclamation by President Truman recognizing the independence of the Philippines, the Stars and Stripes was lowered from a flagstaff, the banner of the new republic raised. A band played the national anthems of both countries, artillerists fired a 21-gun salute, Gen. Douglas MacArthur, whose life and career had been intertwined with the Philippines, made a speech. The last speaker was Pres. Manual Roxas of the new republic. Observing that the flag of the United States had been lowered voluntarily, he announced, "In the hearts of millions of Filipinos, the Stars and Stripes flies more triumphantly than ever."

## ADVENT OF THE COLD WAR

Preoccupied with home affairs when the postwar era got under way, the people of the United States nonetheless had to contend with nettlesome problems in the realm of foreign affairs. In the preceding six or seven years, indeed, a transformation had come to pass in the matter of America's relations with the rest of the world. Technological developments, notably the advent of aircraft that could span oceans, and a dramatic shift in the international balance of power resulting from the destruction of Germany and Japan, the weakening of Britain and France, and the emergence of the United States and the Soviet Union as the premier powers of the world, had rendered impracticable a return by the United States to those halcyon times when it could isolate itself from the conflicts and controversies of the outer world and eschew international responsibilities whenever it saw fit. Illustrative of the transformation was the increase in the number of individuals employed by the State Department: from several hundred in 1938 to more than five thousand by 1946.

The concerns of the Washington government in foreign affairs as the postwar era began to unfold were myriad. They ranged from questions pertaining to the physical and economic restoration of war-battered nation-states to those pertaining to political arrangements in Germany, Japan, and Korea, not to mention civil strife in an array of countries, among them China, Greece, India, the Netherlands Indies, the Philippines, and Vietnam. But the focus of the concerns of the United States in the realm of foreign affairs during that period were what Americans had not the slightest doubt were the expansionist ambitions of the Soviet Union, the self-proclaimed bearer to the world of the gospel of Marx and Lenin.

In the aftermath of the Bolshevik Revolution of 1917, the United States had refused formal diplomatic ties with the fledgling Soviet state. At length, in 1933, the Washington government consented to diplomatic relations, but continued suckling by the Kremlin of communist revolutionaries in America and elsewhere, the manifest brutality of the regime of the dictator Stalin, and, ultimately, the Soviet Union's participation (with Germany) in the destruction of Poland and its aggression against Finland prompted a preponderance of Americans to view the Soviet state with undisguised contempt.

But then, in June 1941, the tyrant Hitler unleashed the armed might of Nazi Germany against the Soviet Union, and as the Red Army fell back toward Moscow the people of the United States pondered the consequences of a German conquest of the Stalinist empire. The probable consequences? Hitler would be master of the European "heartland" from the Atlantic to the Urals, a vast area whose human, industrial, and agricultural resources would, according to a time-honored geopolitical theory, make his Third Reich the dominant power of the world. Thus Americans acquiesced in a decision by leaders in Washington to throw support to the beleaguered Soviet Union, and as the months passed and the Red Army turned the tide of the war in Eastern Europe, most of them came to admire "our great Russian allies," as Gen. Dwight D. Eisenhower referred to them on that historic day (June 6, 1944) when United States, British, and Canadian troops stormed onto the beaches of Normandy. For their part, the Soviets consented to the UN Declaration of January 1942 proclaiming the right of national self-determination, that is, the right of all nations to choose their own form of government and manage their affairs without external interference. At the Yalta Conference of February 1945, the Soviets consented to the Declaration on Liberated Europe, a statement specifying free and unfettered elections and constitutional safeguards of freedom in liberated countries.

No fools, leaders of the United States understood that the Soviets did not share the American commitment to national self-determination—or the ideas of Americans regarding a world in which there would be no military alliances or balances of powers, one in which barriers to trade and travel would become almost nonexistent. They understood that Soviet leaders were animated by imperial ambitions that were not substantially different from those of their czarist predecessors; to wit, the Soviets sought hegemony in Eastern Europe, control of the Turkish straits, domination in Manchuria. But lest the Soviets negotiate a separate peace with Germany and leave the Western Allies in the lurch, as they had done in World War I in 1918, leaders in Washington kept their misgivings to themselves and continued their country's support of the Soviet military effort. They hoped, meanwhile, that contact with Americans might prompt the Soviets to modify their outlook, that is, put aside imperial ambitions—also the dream of assisting in the ideological conquest of the entire world by Marxism-Leninism—and support the establishment of a postwar world order along lines envisioned by Americans.

Scarcely had the war ended before it became manifest that the Soviets would not modify their outlook—that they had no intention, for example, of honoring their commitment to allow free and unfettered elections in Poland. On the contrary, it was transparent by the autumn of 1945 that they were converting Poland into a satellite state. It also became clear that they were bent on turning other countries occupied by the Red Army into satellites: Bulgaria, Czechoslovakia, Hungary, Romania. The latter states were so transformed from 1945 to 1948.

Meanwhile, in early 1946, the Kremlin organized the so-called Cominform, successor of the Comintern, which they had disbanded during the war in the interest of Allied harmony: an instrument for supporting communist revolutionaries across the world. In that same period, on February 9, 1946, Stalin delivered a militant speech at a meeting of communists in Moscow that would later be described as a veritable declaration of cold war. Elucidating the latter speech, the American chargé d'affaires in Moscow, George F. Kennan, cabled leaders in Washington that the Soviets would henceforth use every means at their disposal to infiltrate, divide, and weaken the West. Efforts to achieve a modus vivendi with them, he surmised, would prove chimerical. Events seemed to reinforce Kennan's analysis—first in Iran, then in Italy and Turkey.

To forestall Nazi activity in the historic Peacock Kingdom, British and Soviet forces had occupied Iran in 1941. To guard the main route by which the United States sent lend-lease supplies to the Soviet Union (by way of the Persian Gulf and across Iran), the United States sent a contingent of troops to Iran in 1942. A treaty with the Teheran government provided that the Allies would evacuate Iran within six months of the war's termination, and following Japan's surrender in the summer of 1945, the British and Americans withdrew their troops forthwith; Soviet troops remained in place. Indeed, the Soviets strengthened their forces in Iran, and before the end of 1945 were assisting separatist rebels in the country's northern region. Only when President Truman threatened to use force to defend Iran did the Soviets, in March 1946, consent to remove their troops.

Next, in the spring and summer of 1946, the Soviets supported demands by the Yugoslav government of the communist Josip Broz Tito that the city of Trieste and its environs, since 1919 a part of Italy, be ceded to Yugoslavia. As a result of another determined stand by Truman, the area became a "free territory," part of it administered by Britain and the United States, part by Yugoslavia. Of larger moment, the Soviets in that same period, using tactics of bluster and threat, pressed Turkey to accept "joint defense" of the Bosporus and Dardanelles. Control of the Turkish straits, of course, had been an age-old dream of Russians. Encouraged by the United States, the Turks turned aside Soviet blandishments.

Preoccupied by demobilization and reconversion, ordinary Americans in 1945 and 1946 took minimal note of what the Soviets were doing in Eastern Europe and elsewhere. They were inclined, morover, to resist any suggestion that the wartime Grand Alliance might not endure and that, on the contrary, the Western democracies might find it necessary to confront expansionist ambitions of the Soviet Union just as they had those of Nazi Germany and Imperial Japan. The depth of their inclination was revealed in March 1946 when Britain's wartime prime minister Winston Churchill delivered an address in a gymnasium on the campus of Westminster College in Fulton, Missouri. The illustrious Briton announced, "From Stettin in the Baltic to Trieste in the Adriatic, an Iron Curtain has descended across the [European] Continent." He then urged the United States and Britain to draw together in a political and military alliance in the face of the apparent Soviet threat to Western civilization. Although they would eventually accept Churchill's analysis and endorse the formation of a Western alliance, millions of Americans responded negatively to the ideas set out in the speech at Fulton. In their view, the Briton was consigning the fledgling UN to the scrap heap of history and proposing a return to the politics of alliance and confrontation that had produced so many wars in the past. So negative was the popular response to Churchill's speech, indeed, that President Truman felt compelled to deny he had read it in advance of its delivery—a denial that was palpably false.

At length, most Americans accepted the proposition that the United States and nation-states of similar orientation were in the grip of a cold war with the Soviet empire. Latter-day apologists of the behavior of the Soviets in the postwar years would call attention to the devastation and loss of life endured by the Soviet Union during World War II—between 10 and 20 million Soviet fighting people and civilians dead as a consequence of the German aggression—and conclude that justice was on the side of the Soviets in their determination to assert hegemony over the states on the western frontier of the Soviet Union, inasmuch as the Germans had used the territory of those states as a

springboard for their invasion. (Such considerations, it seems, scarcely justified Soviet behavior regarding Iran, Turkey, and Korea.) Offering almost no
supporting evidence, apologists also would argue that the United States opposed Soviet hegemony in Eastern Europe (and later opposed leftist insurgen-
cies in Vietnam, Central America, and elsewhere) because leaders in Washington, bent on maintaining an "open door" for American business enterprise
across the globe, calculated that governments presided over by Marxist-Leninists were apt to restrict or prohibit altogether the activities of capitalistic investors and traders.

Most Americans in the latter 1940s hooted—or seethed—when anybody
deigned to express such a tolerant view. In their perspective, the purpose of
the United States and the other democracies, if not the Soviet Union, in the
late war had been to rid the world of expansionist dictatorships and establish
the right of nations to order their affairs as they saw fit. Notwithstanding wartime pledges, most notably his consent to the Declaration on Liberated Europe, Stalin was apparently attempting to accomplish in Eastern Europe and
elsewhere what Hitler and his counterparts in Japan had attempted. To acquiesce in such goings-on, in the view of Americans, would constitute a betrayal
of the hundreds of thousands of their compatriots, not to mention millions of
men and women of other nationalities, who had forfeited their lives in the
global crusade for national self-determination and human dignity.

## TRUMAN DOCTRINE

The grim reality of the Cold War imprinted the consciousness of a preponderance of Americans for the first time when the Washington government responded to what it perceived to be twin crises in Greece and Turkey. Their
country exhausted by the recent war and their government edging toward
bankruptcy, the British in early 1947 advised the United States that Britain
could no longer shore up the existing regimes in Greece and Turkey. Officials
in Washington were thunderstruck, for at that time the royalist government
in Greece was under attack by communist insurgents who presumably took
orders from Moscow, while Turkey was feeling the hot breath of Soviet forces
deployed beyond its northern frontier. Without external reinforcement, Greece
and Turkey appeared likely to fall under domination of the Soviets, and that
in turn, so officials in Washington calculated, might clear the way for an extension of Soviet influence across the Middle East and northern Africa. To forestall such a catastrophic succession of events, President Truman on March
12, 1947, asked Congress for an emergency appropriation of $400 million to
reinforce the noncommunist governments of Greece and Turkey. After a two-
month debate, Congress voted the appropriation, and apparently as a consequence of American support—also the enterprise of a U.S. military advisory
group in Greece—the two countries managed to stay clear of the Soviet orbit.

As every student of the Cold War knows, Truman did not confine his remarks of March 12, 1947, to a request for funds for Greece and Turkey. He
also announced, "I believe it must be the policy of the United States to support

free peoples who are resisting attempted subjugation by armed minorities or by outside pressure." With those words, the thirty-third president enunciated the Truman Doctrine, a policy of global resistance to what most Americans believed was a veritable international communist conspiracy.

A short time later, in July 1947, the prestigious journal *Foreign Affairs* published an article by "Mr. X," later identified as George F. Kennan, an American diplomat and one of the country's foremost experts on Soviet affairs. Comparing the Soviet Union's recent thrust into Eastern Europe with the thirteenth-century migration of the Mongols, Kennan argued that the time had come for the United States and its democratic cohorts in the West to put the Soviets on notice that they had gone far enough. He made no suggestion that the West should strive to expel the Soviets from their recent conquests in Eastern Europe. On the contrary, he warned against provoking the Soviets by bluster or the issuance of impossible demands. Still, he argued, it was imperative that the Western democracies stand firm against further expansion by the Soviet state, or, to use language that would become fashionable, that the West "contain" Soviet power. Although it made no mention of a need to contain communist influence in countries far removed from the Soviet Union—a need, say, to move against communist insurgents in Latin America or Southeast Asia—Kennan's "X article" was widely thought to have provided an intellectual rationale for the Truman Doctrine. Meanwhile, in June 1947, the new secretary of state, George C. Marshall, in a commencement address at Harvard University, had announced a program recently worked out in the State Department that would be celebrated as the Marshall Plan.

## MARSHALL PLAN

By the autumn of 1946, Europe had made only minimal headway in its attempt to recover from the devastation of the late war. Then, in the winter of 1946–1947, snow, ice, and wind lashed the Continent, stalling transport facilities, forcing factories to close, dramatically increasing the level of personal suffering. The severe weather also assured a shortfall in Europe's wheat harvest in the coming autumn. Of the suffering and hardship in Europe, the correspondent Hanson W. Baldwin wrote in the *New York Times* in March 1947 that the United States was "the key to the destiny of tomorrow," and that Americans alone "may be able to avert the decline of Western Civilization" and "a reversion to nihilism and the Dark Ages." Alarmed, officials in Washington feared that Europeans outside the Soviet empire might look to communists for mitigation of their misery unless prosperity returned to their lives in the near future. The outcome was Marshall's address at Harvard.

Announcing that economic stability was a requisite for peace, the secretary pledged large-scale American assistance to Europe in its hour of distress. He denied that the assistance program he was proposing would be directed against any country or ideology, that is, the Soviet Union or communism. The objects of the program, he insisted, would be hunger and poverty, desperation and chaos. The secretary indeed defined his offer of aid as including "everything up to the Urals," which meant that the Soviet Union and its satellites would be at liberty to participate in the program and receive American assistance. (To the relief of officials in Washington, who feared that Soviet acquiescence might jeopardize congressional support for the program, the Soviets rejected Marshall's offer and compelled their satellites to do likewise.) At length, in December 1947, President Truman asked Congress to appropriate $17 billion to be distributed to the noncommunist countries of Europe over the next four years.

The Marshall program stirred vigorous debate across the United States. Somehow viewing it as an attack on the Soviet Union, former–Vice President Henry A. Wallace branded the program the "Martial Plan." Congressman Vito Marcantonio of New York, an unabashed advocate of the essentials of communism, proclaimed that the Marshall Plan had been fashioned "to safeguard and protect the expansion of Wall Street monopoly capital all over the world." Still, it was clear when Congress began to debate Truman's request in early 1948 that the Marshall program had strong support. Even Sen. Robert A. Taft, Republican of Ohio, announced that he would vote for it, despite a nagging fear that it might spread what he perceived to be the bankruptcy of Europe across the Atlantic to the United States. Then, in early 1948, Czech communists, with connivance of the Soviets, expelled democratic elements from the government in Prague, established a Stalinist dictatorship in what before World War II had been the most democratic country in East-Central Europe, and took Czechoslovakia behind the Iron Curtain. Spurred by the Czech tragedy, Congress in March 1948 passed the Economic Cooperation Act, the legislation that sanctioned the European Recovery Program (ERP), as the Marshall program was officially designated. In accord with Truman's request of the previous December, the measure pledged that over the next four years Congress would appropriate up to $17 billion for Europe's recovery, only $12 billion of which, as matters turned out, was actually needed.

The Economic Cooperation Administration (ECA), the agency set up to administer the ERP, quickly moved into gear, and over the next four years provided Europe with a substantial injection of capital. Great Britain received $2.8 billion, France $2.6 billion, West Germany $1.3 billion, Italy more than a billion, the Netherlands nearly a billion. Iceland received the least, $27 million. The results? If European resources actually accounted for between 80 and 90 percent of capital formation in Western Europe during the pristine years of the ERP, the Marshall funds provided the European nation-states with what one writer has described as "the critical margin" that made possible a dramatic economic recovery across large areas of Europe. As Michael J. Hogan has written in his prizewinning book on the Marshall Plan, the ERP "facilitated essential imports, eased production bottlenecks, encouraged higher rates of capital formation, and helped to suppress inflation, all of which led to gains in productivity, to improvements in trade, and to an era of social peace and prosperity more durable than any other in modern European history."

More concretely, Western Europe's industrial output by 1950 was up 45 percent over 1947, and by 1952 its industry was producing at a rate 200 percent higher than in 1938, the last year before World War II. To be sure, the benefits of the new prosperity tended to be distributed unevenly, hence millions of working people in Western Europe continued to support Communist parties, particularly in France and Italy. Moreover, as Hogan has demonstrated, the vision of American planners that the Marshall program would make Western Europe over in the image of its North American benefactor, that is, bring about an integrated West European economy akin to that which existed in the United States, one whose prosperity and stability would secure Western Europe against the threat of Sovietism and enable Western Europe to join the United States in a multilateral system of world trade, fell short of fulfillment. Still, the economic upsurge that took place in Western Europe nullified any immediate danger that communists might gain ascendancy in various of the countries of Western Europe. According to Hogan, indeed, "the Marshall Plan must be judged as one of the most successful peacetime foreign policies launched by the United States in this century."

## CRISIS IN BERLIN

Shortly before President Truman signed the legislation establishing the ERP in March 1948, a crisis boiled up in Germany, an occupied country in the years after World War II. Britain, France, and the United States were the occupiers of western Germany; the Soviet Union was the occupier of eastern Germany— save for the western half of the city of Berlin, which in accord with a wartime agreement was jointly occupied by forces of the Western powers. The trouble started when the Soviets began to harass motor and rail traffic that moved across their zone of occupation between western Germany and the Anglo-American-French sectors of Berlin, that is, West Berlin. Partial at first, the "Berlin blockade" became total in June of 1948.

What had prompted the blockade? The Soviets intimated that the blockade was a response to provocation by the Western powers. What provocation? Observing that the Soviets were turning their zone of occupation in East Germany into a Soviet satellite, and persuaded that the Soviets had no intention of cooperating in the establishment of a unified government for Germany on a basis of free elections, the United States and Britain had merged their zones of occupation into an embryonic West German state and given Germans extensive administrative responsibilities. (France brought its zone into the merger later on.) Next, the United States and Britain engineered a currency reform that seemed essential to West Germany's regeneration.

The reconstruction of a West Germany that was aligned with the Western democracies was the last thing the Soviets wanted to happen in Middle Europe. Their country having endured invasions by Germans during both world wars, the Soviets determined that Germany must never again become a first-rate power. A powerful Germany or even West Germany awaiting the appearance of a new Hitler was a prospect that leaders of the Soviet Union did not care to think about. Nor did they care to think about the prospect that a West Germany aligned with the Western democracies, if militarily impotent, might emerge as an economic powerhouse. Such a West Germany would doubtless

October 1948: German children watch C-54 Skymaster approach Tempelhof Airport during Berlin airlift.

stand as a barrier to the Kremlin's dream of turning all of Middle and Western Europe into a citadel of Marxism-Leninism.

Germany, of course, had been near the center of the myriad of problems dividing the Western democracies and the Kremlin since termination of the war in Europe. A major bone of contention had been the question of reparations payments by Germans to the Soviet Union. Remembering the devastation of vast reaches of their landscape wrought by the German invaders from 1941 to 1944, the Soviets demanded that the victors in the war compel the Germans to pay enormous reparations. Leaders of the West had no interest in extracting reparations for the Soviets in their zones of occupation in western Germany. So Western leaders reasoned, the Western powers would find it essential, given their commitment to West Germany's economic recovery, to pump capital funds of their own into West Germany to compensate for those it was losing via reparations payments. Thus the Western powers would, in fact, be footing the bill for regeneration of the Soviet Union. In light of recent Soviet behavior in Eastern Europe—also reckoning that the Soviets, because of their infamous collaboration with the Nazi regime from 1939 to 1941 were in no small measure to blame for their plight—leaders of the West were not inclined to call on their own taxpayers to ante up the funds for Soviet regeneration.

Reparations and other questions aside, the Soviets in the spring of 1948 rolled the dice in the matter of West Berlin. They apparently did so without fear that the outcome might be a new general war—and for the Soviet Union annihilation by America's nuclear bombs.

Recognizing that from the Soviet perspective the Anglo-American-French presence in West Berlin, 100 miles inside the Soviet zone of occupation in Germany, was at once an anomaly and an irritant, Western leaders nonetheless calculated that if they abandoned West Berlin in the face of Soviet pressure, the confidence of West Germans and other Europeans in the resolve of the Western democracies might prove fatal to the policy of containing the march of Soviet power and influence in the old Continent. Or as the occupant of the White House in Washington later wrote in his memoirs, "What was at stake in Berlin was . . . a struggle over Germany and, in a larger sense, over Europe." Hence Truman and other Western leaders determined that they must act.

To maintain the Anglo-American-French position in Berlin, and at the same time avoid an armed clash with the Soviets, Western leaders took up the idea of airlifting the necessities of life to West Berlin. Because the Soviets had previously guaranteed the Western powers access to West Berlin via specified air corridors—and because it clearly was in the interest of the Soviets to prevent the crisis from escalating into a war in which they might face nuclear devastation—Western leaders reckoned that the Soviets would not shoot down transports flying to and from West Berlin. Beginning in June 1948, therefore, hundreds of planes began shuttling food, coal, and other commodities to sustain West Berlin's 2 million inhabitants. After 321 days, in May 1949, the Soviets reopened the highways and railroads connecting West Berlin with West Germany.

For the Soviets, the affair was an unqualified disaster. The ingenious response to the Soviet challenge produced an outpouring of pro-Western enthusiasm throughout Europe, and instead of having their confidence in the United States and its allies shaken, West Germans and other Europeans were renewed in their faith in the resolve of the Western democracies to prevent any new Soviet expansion in Middle Europe. The Soviet defeat had other dimensions. The Berlin affair of 1948–1949 spurred the Western powers to get on with plans being formulated before the blockade to establish an independent West German state. Thus, in September 1949, the Federal Republic of Germany, its capital in the old Rhineland city of Bonn, came into existence. Equally serious from the Soviet perspective, the Berlin crisis was instrumental in bringing forth a Western military alliance of the very sort the Soviets had hoped to forestall: the North Atlantic Treaty Organization, put in effect in 1949.

## INDIA, INDONESIA, THE PHILIPPINES, AND JAPAN

Events of large import also were transpiring in other areas of the world. After months of negotiations punctuated by largely nonviolent protest, the government in London consented to relinquish authority in the Indian subcontinent. The outcome, in 1947, was the birth of two new nation-states, India and Pakistan. Tragically, the births were followed by communal violence that claimed the lives of 200,000 people—and in the spring of 1948 the life of Mohandas K. Gandhi, the longtime prophet of Indian independence. Two years after the appearance of independent India and Pakistan, in 1949, the Netherlands, prodded by the United States of America, recognized the independence of the United States of Indonesia (soon to be known as the Republic of Indonesia). In the new Republic of the Philippines, meanwhile, the communist-led Hukbalahap rebels, supported by tens of thousands of poverty-ridden peasants, sought to overthrow what they viewed as the oligarchic central government in Manila. Supplied with military equipment by the United States, the central government finally broke the power of the "Huks" in 1954.

Less publicized if no less important were goings-on in Japan, where General MacArthur exercised almost absolute authority. The general, in truth, functioned as a latter-day shōgun, that is, a behind-the-throne ruler of the Japanese nation. His public (but not private) demeanor cold and aloof, as befitted a shōgun, MacArthur never dined away from his residence (on the grounds of the U.S. embassy). He never appeared at parties or receptions or toured Japan. He never entertained Japanese dignitaries or paused to clasp hands with ordinary citizens. Face-to-face encounters with Japanese were confined to the emperor, the prime minister, and a handful of other officials. Cloaked in formality, such encounters invariably took place in MacArthur's office in the Dai Ichi (Number One) Building.

From the perspective of the United States, the general's performance was nothing short of brilliant. Under his tutelage, the Japanese rebuilt their battered cities, restored their industrial mechanism, executed a sweeping program of agrarian reform. They promulgated a constitution that provided for a parliamentary government whose representatives were freely elected by all adult citizens. The constitution guaranteed freedom of speech, assembly, and religion—also the right of citizens to own property, organize and bargain collectively, and enjoy equal educational opportunities. It proclaimed that Japan would never maintain armed forces and renounced war as a sovereign right of the Japanese nation. By 1951, when MacArthur bade farewell to Japan, the country's cities and railways and ports had been restored, the industrial mechanism was beginning to hum, and the new parliamentary government was firmly aligned with the government in Washington.

## PALESTINE

At the same time that MacArthur was overseeing the reconstruction of Japan, events of historic moment were transpiring in the Middle East where, as noted, Arabs were seething because of the determination of Zionists to establish a Jewish nation-state in Palestine, a longtime domain of Palestinian Arabs. Fated to cast a long shadow over the politics of the United States, not to mention the politics of the Middle East, over the next four decades and beyond, those events were rooted in the often tortured history of the Arab and Jewish peoples.

Arabs and Jews had lived in comparative peace in ancient Palestine until Jewish communities in the area disappeared in the eighth century A.D. Through the Middle Ages and into the modern era, Jews scattered across Europe, and substantial numbers of them eventually made their way to the New World. Sadly, they met rampant discrimination and persecution at the hands of Christians, who had apparently forgotten the directive of Jesus that his followers were to love their neighbors. At length, in the latter nineteenth century, a movement that came to be known as Zionism took form in Eastern Europe. Believing that Jews could find contentment and peace in the land of their ancestors, Zionists dreamed of establishing a national homeland for Jews in Palestine. They seemed almost oblivious to the fact that Palestine, by then a province of the Turkish empire, was now the homeland of hundreds of thousands of Palestinian Arabs.

The presence of Palestinians notwithstanding, Zionists began to trickle to Palestine in the closing decades of the nineteenth century. Then, during World War I, Turkey sided with Germany. Seizing the opportunity, the Zionists prevailed on Great Britain to declare that after the war it would "view with favor the establishment in Palestine of a national home for the Jewish people." When the League of Nations in 1920 mandated Palestine to Britain, the London government honored the foregoing declaration and opened Palestine to Jewish migration. Angry that the Paris Peace Conference of 1919 had ignored their appeals that Palestine be granted national independence and viewing Jewish migrants as interlopers, Palestinian Arabs were furious. The result was periodic terrorist attacks on Jews—to which Jews retaliated in kind. However resented by Arabs, Zionists continued to migrate to Palestine. World War II interrupted the migration, but as the global conflict moved to a climax, it became clear that Zionists, fired by the ghastly horror visited upon the Jewish people of Europe by Nazi Germany, intended to strive in the postwar period to organize a Jewish nation-state in Palestine. To counter the Zionists, Arabs organized the Arab League.

Still responsible for its administration, the British reached the end of their patience in Palestine in late 1946. Zionists were smuggling Jewish refugees into the country in defiance of British immigration quotas, Arabs and Jews were killing one another with increasing ferocity, and nobody—Arab, Jew, or outsider—had presented a formula for the political future of the area that promised peace. Administering Palestine, moreover, was expensive, and, as noted, British finances in the years after 1945 were precarious. So the government in London in the spring of 1947 turned over to the UN the task of working out a political arrangement for the country. At length, in the autumn of 1947, the General Assembly of the world organization approved a resolution—one that received the votes of both Soviet and American delegates—providing for the partition of Palestine into two independent states, one Arab, one Jewish. The two states were to function as a single economic unit, and the city of Jerusalem was to have a special status designed to protect the rights and interests of both Arabs and Jews. The government in London thereupon announced that British troops would withdraw from Palestine on May 15, 1948.

Zionists were ecstatic, Arabs furious. But then it appeared that the Washington government was reassessing its policy in the Middle East—and might prevail on the UN to reconsider its arrangement for Palestine. At that point, friends of Zionism in America, most of them Jews, bombarded the White House with letters, postcards, and telegrams urging that the United States stay firm in its support of the partition resolution. The Zionist campaign annoyed President Truman, who later wrote, "I do not think I ever had so much pressure and propaganda aimed at the White House as I had in this instance." If Truman was annoyed, officials in the State Department were troubled, and the president later recalled, "The Department of State's specialists on the Near East were, almost without exception, unfriendly to the idea of a Jewish state." The reason was not hard to discern. By supporting the establishment of a minuscule Jewish state in Palestine, the Washington government was certain to complicate its relations with an array of Arab states that reached from the Persian Gulf to the Mediterranean and across northern Africa, beneath the burning sands of several of which were vast pools of oil.

Still, it was the president who determined policy, and Truman, whatever his pique as a result of Zionist pressure, elected to support the establishment of a Jewish state in accord with the UN's partition resolution. As he later wrote, he determined to have no more nonsense from the "striped-pants boys" in the State Department. And so when Zionists, on May 15, 1948, declared the independence of Israel, the Washington government recognized the new state—within 11 minutes. Viewing the establishment of a little Jewish state in the Palestinian desert as right and proper—a sort of rough justice for Jews, who had endured so much abuse and discrimination through the centuries, the awful climax coming in the recent holocaust perpetrated by Hitler and his Nazi henchmen—a preponderance of Truman's compatriots approved of his decision.

Whatever the merits of the case for a Jewish state in the Middle East, Israel's declaration of independence signaled an attack on the new nation by Arab states on its frontiers. In the resultant war, one that Israel refers to as its War for Independence, the Israelis, who largely with funds provided by Jewish Americans were able to purchase guns, tanks, and planes (including Messerschmitt fighter planes of the defunct German *Luftwaffe*) in Czechoslovakia and elsewhere in the Soviet bloc, humbled their enemies at every turn. When the UN in 1949 arranged an uneasy armistice, Israel had enlarged its territory by 50 percent.

What happened to Palestinians who had lived in lands now absorbed by Israel? Some 700,000 fled to the West Bank, a part of Palestine occupied at the time of the armistice by Transjordan (present-day Jordan), and the Gaza Strip, a tiny area occupied by Egypt. Why did they leave? Palestinians insisted that Israelis forced them out at bayonet point—and there is no question that the Israeli army did indeed expel undisclosed numbers of Palestinians in territories it had seized. Israelis countered that most Palestinians, out of fright or hatred of Jews, simply abandoned their communities. Whatever their reasons for leaving the ancestral homeland, Palestinians found succor in squalid refugee

May 14, 1948: Prime Minister David Ben Gurion opens ceremony in which Israel declares independence.

camps maintained by the UN. The domiciles of great numbers of Palestinians down to the present day, the camps have stood as perpetual reminders of what Arabs perceive to be the evils of Zionism.

## RETROSPECT

Any scholar of history would be hard-pressed to identify a more exhilarating moment in the history of the United States than those months of spring and summer 1945 when the global war ground to a termination. The country had made a mighty contribution, one that Americans considered decisive, to the Allied victory over Nazi Germany, and almost singlehandedly crushed Imperial Japan. In that global crusade to rid the world of tyranny and guarantee the survival of liberty and democracy, its fighting men had fought bravely and effectively on land and sea and in the air, its workers and farmers had accomplished what Americans perceived to have been productive miracles by turning out mind-boggling quantities of what commentators in former times had referred to as the sinews of war. As the war unfolded, meanwhile, America's scientists and engineers had designed a succession of wondrous devices and instruments that substantially increased the clout of the national military-naval mechanism. And in the closing stages of the war, scientists of the now-fabled Manhattan Project had unleashed the fearsome power of nuclear energy, an achievement that, in addition to bringing the war to an abrupt and glorious end and ushering humankind into a new epoch, had for the time being at least assured the absolute primacy of American power.

From the perspective of the people of the United States, indeed, the "American Century" was in full blossom in the summer of 1945. What was the American Century? Coined by the magazine publisher Henry R. Luce, the term evoked an image of a prolonged period, one that would reach into the future as far as anybody could presently see, of American political, technological, and economic preeminence, one in which people across the face of the globe, conscious of the manifest superiority of American ideals and institutions, would strive as best they could to make their societies approximations of that of the North American utopia. It was an image that struck a chord with a people who for more than three centuries had perceived of their country as a New Isreal or promised land and themselves as a chosen people.

By 1948, the exhilaration felt by Americans in September 1945 had long since faded. It had faded in the face of political squabbling, labor turmoil, and racial tension, not to mention an hysterical search for communist subversives at home and, more importantly, collapse of the wartime Grand Alliance and onset of the Cold War abroad. Still, the national economic mechanism, having made the transition from war to peace was continuing to hum as the country approached mid-century. The hardships and miseries endured by scores of millions of Americans during the Great Depression of the 1930s were by now buried in sometimes bittersweet memory, and a preponderance of the citizenry was enjoying a level of prosperity that a dozen or so years before would have appeared to be an impossible dream. Of comparable moment, the United States continued to live as it had over most of its history in splendid security, for if the oceanic moats guarding its coasts were a bit less imposing as barriers to attack than formerly, it alone had The Bomb. The first bona fide superpower in the history of the world, it remained the only one. Thus the state or condition of the republic, if not as propitious as Americans would have liked, was from the perspective of most citizens, unless they happened to be black, Hispanic, Indian, or poor, not bad at all during the third year following the global war.

# Chapter
# 2

# A Time of Tribulation

*F*rom the perspective of Americans, 1948 was certainly a memorable year. The European Recovery Program got under way; the Western powers met the Soviet challenge in Berlin. The citizenry learned that on October 14, 1947, Capt. Charles E. "Chuck" Yeager of the Air Force had flown the Bell X-1 experimental airplane faster than the speed of sound. Jane Wyman (Mrs. Ronald Reagan) won an Academy Award as best actress of the year for her performance in the film *Johnny Belinda.* The thoroughbred colt Citation won racing's Triple Crown. The book *Sexual Behavior in the Human Male,* by Alfred C. Kinsey, W. B. Pomeroy, and C. E. Martin, became a bestseller. But the most memorable happening of 1948 was the re-election of Harry Truman to the presidency.

## ELECTION OF 1948

Having humbled the Democrats in the midterm election of 1946, Republicans were brimming with confidence as the presidential campaign of 1948 approached. Democrats, conversely, were dispirited and divided. A Gallup poll in April of 1948 indicated that only 36 percent of the citizenry approved of Truman's handling of the presidency. Truman's support of the aspirations of blacks had alienated legions of whites in the South, historically a bastion of the Democratic Party. His vigorous response to what he considered Soviet provocations had alienated ultraliberal Democrats, who insisted that the Soviet Union was not an expansionist power and would respond to an American policy shorn of militancy. Because Truman's chances of re-election appeared so bleak, many Democrats hoped that Gen. Dwight D. Eisenhower might be induced to carry their party's standard in the impending presidential campaign. But "Ike" made it clear that he would accept no political nomination in 1948. So when Democrats convened in Philadelphia in the summer of 1948, they nominated Truman for president and the venerable Sen. Alben W. Barkley of Kentucky for vice president.

Dismissing a rousing convention speech by Truman, most observers remained convinced that the Democrats were moving toward monstrous defeat. Reinforcing that conviction was the fact that delegates from Alabama and Mississippi had stalked from the Democratic convention when liberals led by Mayor Hubert H. Humphrey of Minneapolis secured acceptance of a platform statement committing the party to vigorous support of civil equality for racial minorities. Dissident southerners indeed organized the so-called Dixiecrat Party, held a one-day convention in Birmingham, and, cheered on by "rebel yells" and displays of Confederate flags, nominated Gov. J. Strom Thurmond of South Carolina for president. Meanwhile, ultraliberal Democrats were organizing the Progressive Party. Supported by the country's communists, the latter party was the creation of Henry A. Wallace, vice president from 1941 to 1945, secretary of commerce in 1945–1946—until Truman fired him following a speech in which he expressed views that ran counter to the administration's foreign policy. Wallace, of course, was the Progressive nominee for president.

In a raucous convention contested by conservative and moderate factions, Republicans had already bestowed their party's presidential nomination on the capable governor of New York, Thomas E. Dewey—whose name, Truman later reminded Democrats, rhymed with hooey. In the ensuing campaign, Dewey, a moderate who had lost to Roosevelt in the presidential contest of 1944, felt compelled to say nothing that might alienate Republican conservatives. In view of Truman's apparent unpopularity, moreover, he saw no need to lash out against his opponent. So Dewey, always immaculately groomed—resembling, some people thought, the figure of a bridegroom atop a wedding cake—kept his emotions in check, smiled profusely, spoke in platitudes.

If Dewey evaded controversy, Truman did not. Following the Democratic convention, he summoned the Eightieth Congress to assemble in special session, and when the Republican-controlled legislature declined to enact measures that he contended reflected pledges in the Republican platform, denounced the "do-nothing Eightieth Congress." He thereupon crisscrossed the country aboard a special train, pausing at innumerable "whistle-stops," railing against Republicans from the observation platform of his presidential car. Not infrequently, a voice in the crowd would shout, "Give 'em hell, Harry!" Grinning, the president would respond, "I'm goin' to." Truman reminded farmers that Republicans had been less than enthusiastic about subsidies for agriculture, and union members that the Republican-controlled Congress had passed the Taft-Hartley Act over his veto. He likewise became the first presidential candidate ever to make a concerted appeal to black voters, and took his campaign into New York's Harlem and Chicago's South Side.

Although tinged with demagoguery, Truman's tactics worked. Farmers, workers, and blacks rallied to his support. The Dixiecrats and Progressives attracted fewer voters than expected. So to the astonishment of nearly everybody, Truman scored a narrow victory. (Dewey later explained that after the election he felt akin to a man who had awakened to find himself in a coffin. Puzzled, the man asked himself, "If I am alive, why am I here? If I am dead, why do I have to go to the bathroom?")

## TRIBULATIONS OF TRUMAN

Still savoring his electoral triumph, Truman on January 6, 1949, rode up to the Capitol to deliver his annual State of the Union message. Skimming over foreign affairs, he made an impassioned appeal for congressional support of an array of initiatives in home affairs. He requested authority to control prices and rents, urged increases in the tax liabilities of corporations and the well-to-do. He asked Congress to repeal the Taft-Hartley Act, strengthen the antitrust laws, and "improve" the federal subsidy program for agriculture. He appealed for new regional development projects on the model of that in the Tennessee Valley and a St. Lawrence seaway; legislation that would enlarge the Social Security program, establish national health insurance, and provide federal assistance to schools; measures to clear slums, expand public housing, and enlarge the government's electric power program; passage of the civil rights legislation that he had proposed the previous year.

A fortnight later, on January 20, Truman celebrated his second inauguration. But if he thought Congress was apt to accept the verdict of voters in the recent election as a mandate to enact a program of innovation and reform such as he had outlined in the State of the Union address, he was fated to disappointment, for the conservative coalition of Republicans and southern Democrats continued to hold the balance of power on Capitol Hill. Only one Fair Deal proposal of consequence, accordingly, received congressional sanction during Truman's second term from 1949 to 1953. Pressed by the leaders of the country's burgeoning cities, Congress in 1949 passed the National Housing Act providing for the construction of 810,000 housing units for low-income families over a six-year period.

November 4, 1948: On the day after his re-election, President Truman displays an early edition of *The Chicago Tribune* erroneously reporting his defeat.

Most distressing was the conservative coalition's refusal to support initiatives to promote civil equality. That members of the party of Abraham Lincoln cooperated with descendants of onetime slaveowners to prevent passage of legislation to move descendants of former slaves toward full membership in the American democratic community was steeped in historical irony. Himself a descendant of supporters of the southern Confederacy, the president maneuvered as best he could without congressional support. He strengthened the civil rights section of the Justice Department and directed that the attorney general assist private parties in civil rights cases. He appointed the first black governor of the Virgin Islands, promoted two blacks to federal judgeships, directed that no defense contracts be awarded to firms practicing discrimination in employment. He moved against racial discrimination in federal agencies. Most important of all, he ordered the desegregation of the armed forces. He broke social taboos by inviting blacks to attend the inaugural reception and ball in January 1949.

If piqued by the refusal of Congress to accede to his Fair Deal proposals, Truman had other reasons for feeling frustrated in the months after his electoral triumph of autumn 1948. Of special moment, the national economy endured its first postwar recession. Steel output plummeted, farm income declined, unemployment increased from less than 2 percent to more than 3 percent.

Meanwhile, the country's armed forces became a center of a controversy, one that turned ultimately on the question of whether the Navy was to have a strategic mission in the atomic era. In a word, were the heavy bombers of the Air Force to have exclusive responsibility for delivering atomic warheads on an enemy in the event of a new general war? Or would carrier-based aircraft of the Navy also be outfitted to deliver a nuclear punch in the event the Cold War became hot? To carry out such a strategic mission, the Navy would need "super" aircraft carriers. But carriers were enormously expensive, and in the estimate of the Air Force enormously vulnerable. In view of the intercontinental range of the huge B-36 bombers that the Air Force was putting in service, moreover, or so partisans of the Air Force reasoned, carriers offered no strategic advantage.

The contentions of the Air Force aside, the Truman administration consented to construction of a supercarrier for the Navy, the USS *United States.* But scarcely had the keel of the giant vessel been put down, in the spring of 1949, when the secretary of defense ordered the project canceled. The upshot was "the revolt of the admirals." During the revolt, admirals and other partisans of the Navy unleashed a publicity barrage in which they castigated the B-36, a huge craft that was powered by six piston engines (mounted at the rear of the wings) and four jets. They argued that the B-36 (cruising speed, 370 miles an hour) was slow and ponderous, and would make an easy target for Soviet air defenses.

Whatever the merits of their arguments about the vulnerability of the B-36, the admirals did not get their way. Truman stayed with the decision of his secretary of defense—and relieved Adm. Lewis E. Denfield, the chief of naval operations, a seaman whose career had been long and distinguished. Still, the Navy's setback would prove transitory. In subsequent years, the Navy got its supercarriers, and with the advent of nuclear submarines armed with ballistic missiles the strategic mission of the Navy in a global showdown was assured.

Meanwhile, in the summer of 1949, an enterprising reporter caught a scent of scandal in the White House, and the trail led to Truman's longtime friend and military aide, Maj. Gen. Harry H. Vaughan, a man of rumpled demeanor whose barnyard humor gave the president temporary respites from the cares of state. It developed that Vaughan had received gifts, including deep freezers from individuals for whom he had done favors, for example, writing a "To Whom It May Concern" note on White House stationery observing that a businessman from Chicago was entitled to courtesies by American officials overseas. It also was alleged that a friend of Vaughan who had arranged a meeting of businesspeople with the general charged a fee of 5 percent of the value of any contract that might result from the meeting. In the view of critics, of course, Vaughan was guilty of having peddled influence; the general contended that he had committed no wrong when he put individuals who were seeking to do business with the government in contact with appropriate officials. As for the gifts, he insisted that they had been nothing more than expressions of friendship. Fiercely loyal to members of his official family, particularly those who were old cronies from Missouri, Truman supported Vaughan, and when asked during a press conference whether the general might be relieved, the president snapped, "He will not."

A year and a half later, in early 1951, alleged scandal in the Truman White House was again in the headlines, this time when a Senate subcommittee chaired by J. William Fulbright, Democrat of Arkansas, reported that influence emanating from the White House and the Democratic National Committee had affected the issuance of loans by the Reconstruction Finance Corporation (RFC), a lending agency of the federal government. Truman denounced the report as asinine, and characterized Fulbright, a former Rhodes Scholar and onetime president of the University of Arkansas, as "an overeducated s.o.b." (On a previous occasion, he had referred to Fulbright as Senator Halfbright.)

Fulbright thereupon opened public hearings on the matter, and it was quickly disclosed that an attorney who represented applicants for RFC loans had presented a mink coat valued at $8,500 to the husband of a White House stenographer. The implication was that the attorney had made the gift in return for favors extended by the stenographer's husband during his employment as an examiner by the federal lending agency. Otherwise, the hearings proved inconclusive, and no incumbent official was indicted as a result of the inquiry. Still, millions of Americans were persuaded that influence peddling was pervasive in the administration and that the president, by refusing to admit the truth, was behaving like the proverbial Missouri mule. Disgust resulting from Truman's behavior did not subside when the president, while on vacation at Key West, spent many hours playing poker, appointed Mayor William O'Dwyer of New York to be ambassador to Mexico although O'Dwyer had admitted to having appointed persons connected with organized crime to public office, and stood by his old friend William Boyle, the chairman of the Democratic National Committee, who reportedly received $8,000 from a company in St. Louis that had received a loan from the RFC after retaining Boyle as an attorney.

## LATIN AMERICA, POINT FOUR

If Truman had hoped to concentrate on home affairs during his second term in the White House, he found as the term got under way that dispatches from overseas continued to command much of his attention. A fair number of those dispatches emanated from U.S. embassies in Latin America, where unrest seemed rampant. Unrest, of course, was not a new phenomenon in Latin America. But with the onset of the Cold War, the region had become a source of increasing concern from the perspective of the United States, inasmuch as grinding poverty and hostility between socioeconomic classes appeared to make it a classic environment for the germination of communist ideas. Latin America, in truth, had been the focus of two notable diplomatic initiatives by the Washington government in recent years.

Although there was scant likelihood of a Soviet military thrust in Latin

America, the Washington government nonetheless pressed the other governments of the Americas to accept the principle of hemispheric solidarity, one that had long stirred the interest of North Americans. The outcome was the InterAmerican Treaty of Reciprocal Assistance, signed by representatives of 19 American governments at Rio de Janeiro in September 1947. The treaty bound each signatory to assist in meeting an armed attack against any country in the hemisphere, pending action by the UN.

Recognizing that the hemisphere's communists were apt to rely on subversion and guerrilla tactics to achieve their aims, leaders in Washington understood that the so-called Treaty of Rio did not meet the problem of how to keep communism in check in the Americas. Thus U.S. delegates at the Ninth International Conference of American States, which met at Bogotá in Colombia in the spring of 1948, pressed for a collective system for meeting problems relating to the security and well-being of the Western Hemisphere—including the problem of subversive and disruptive activities by communists. As if to underscore the need of such a system, a revolt, resulting in no small measure from communist agitation, broke out in Bogotá as the conference was getting under way, and within a few days several hundred people were slain and large parts of the city wrecked. When order returned, the delegates consented to a charter for the Organization of American States (OAS). Asserting that no state or group of states had a right to intervene directly or indirectly in the affairs of another, the charter outlined procedures for meeting political and economic problems in the hemisphere that North Americans hoped might prove useful in countering communist activities.

Latin Americans were only mildly interested in the Rio pact and the OAS. What they sought was extensive economic assistance by the United States. Their appeals for assistance on a large scale came to nothing. Persuaded that its principal challenges lay in Europe and Asia and conscious that its resources were limited, the Washington government advised Latin Americans that they would have to depend on their own resources and private investment by North American and European corporations and entrepreneurs to achieve regeneration. Meanwhile, communist influence continued to enlarge across the region, notably in Brazil, Chile, and Cuba.

Notwithstanding their government's failure to respond to the aspirations of Latin Americans, some thoughtful citizens of the North American superpower reasoned that if the United States was to carry out the purpose of the Truman Doctrine of containing communist influence around the globe, it was necessary that the Washington government try to cope with the problem of poverty in the underdeveloped world. Truman's response was the Point Four Program, announced in his inaugural address of January 1949. Point Four was to check communism in poverty-ridden countries by helping such countries to help themselves in achieving prosperity and stability. Because of the demands on American resources in Europe and elsewhere, the main export under Point Four would be American scientific and technical know-how. As matters turned out, more than a year went by before Congress acted on the president's proposal, and the first appropriation for Point Four was only $35 million, a pittance when measured against the dimension of the problem of poverty in the world.

In the first two years of the Point Four program, 30 Latin American, African, and Asian countries received assistance, in the main to improve health, agriculture, and transportation. Although Congress quadrupled the Point Four appropriation in 1952, the promise of the program never achieved fulfillment. Its national abundance notwithstanding, the United States did not have the wherewithal to underwrite the economy of every poor country in the world. As the Cold War dragged into the 1950s, moreover, Congress and the executive branch came under increasing pressure to earmark the bulk of foreign aid appropriations for military hardware. As a result, outlays for economic and technical assistance to underdeveloped areas declined.

## NATO

That Point Four—the name passed into oblivion following a reorganization of foreign assistance programs in 1953—failed to achieve its promise was understandable, inasmuch as most Americans considered assistance to underdeveloped countries to be of marginal importance in terms of the security of the United States. As for an alliance to contain Soviet military power in Europe, the perception of the people of the United States, at least by 1949, was markedly different. Most perceived such an alliance to be almost critical to the defense of the national homeland, not to mention the "Free World."

A first step in the formulation of an alliance of West European and North American nation-states was taken in early 1947 when Britain and France signed the Treaty of Dunkirk. The Dunkirk treaty pledged the signatories to unified action in the event either was threatened by a third power. The following year, Britain, France, and the Benelux countries (Belgium, the Netherlands, and Luxembourg), fearing a Soviet lunge westward, signed the Brussels Pact, a 50-year alliance binding each signatory to assist the other in case of attack by an outside power. Believing that West Europeans would need to feel secure from aggression from the Soviet bloc before they would throw themselves wholeheartedly into the European Recovery (Marshall) Program then taking form, leaders of the United States were delighted. Accordingly, President Truman lauded the alliance, and announced that he was sure the United States would help the signatories to carry out the alliance's aims. Such a statement indicated that the president was preparing the way for eventual American membership in the alliance—and so he was. For American participation, as everyone understood, was essential if any West European alliance was to have sufficient credibility to deter Soviet aggression.

Conscious of the national tradition against "entangling alliances," many Americans felt misgivings about the prospect that their country might become party to a European alliance. But the Soviet blockade of West Berlin, perceived by most Americans as a crude power maneuver by an expansionist and evil empire, virtually eliminated opposition in the United States to membership in an alliance with countries of what would come to be referred to as the North Atlantic community. In the same month that the blockade became total, June 1948, Senator Vandenberg of Michigan, a Republican architect of bipartisanship in foreign affairs, introduced a resolution calling for American association with such other regional and collective arrangements as were based on continuous self-help and mutual aid—an oblique way of saying that the United States should associate itself with the nations of the Brussels Pact. The resolution received overwhelming approval.

The Vandenberg resolution opened the way for negotiations that culminated in the North Atlantic Treaty, signed in April 1949 by representatives of Belgium, Canada, Denmark, France, Great Britain, Iceland, Italy, Luxembourg, the Netherlands, Portugal, and the United States. (Greece and Turkey would enter the alliance in 1952, West Germany in 1955, Spain in 1982.) In the United States, the treaty met only scattered opposition. Accordingly, in June 1949, it secured consent of the Senate by a vote of 82–13.

The heart of the North Atlantic Treaty announced that an armed attack against one or more of its parties would be considered an attack against them all, and that each member would assist the party or parties so attacked by taking such actions as it deemed necessary, including the use of armed force, "to restore and maintain the security of the North Atlantic area." But could the combined armies of the members of the alliance possibly stop an invasion by the Soviet juggernaut? Obviously not. How, then, was the alliance to achieve credibility? Answer: by virtue of the nuclear power of the United States. Should the Red Army invade Western Europe, the United States would unleash a nuclear attack on the Soviet empire—and according to the calculus of Western leaders, the fear of such a retaliatory attack would deter Soviet leaders from ordering an invasion. But could the United States be depended upon to make a nuclear response to Soviet aggression in Europe? Apparently it could. Because the United States would keep ground troops deployed in Western Europe, American troops would be engaged (and some of them killed) in the event of a Soviet invasion. The result would be war between the United States and the Soviet Union. In view of the manifest inferiority of its ground forces, the United States would have no choice than to conduct that war by smashing the Soviet Union with nuclear weapons.

## THE REVOLT OF TITO

Meanwhile, a rupture in relations between the Soviet dictator Stalin and Marshal Tito, the communist chieftain of Yugoslavia, had given the United States an unforeseen opportunity to assist in a rollback of the Iron Curtain in southeastern Europe. The rupture came to pass when Stalin, after failing to turn Yugoslavia into a Soviet satellite, in essence expelled Tito from the world communist movement.

Leaders in Washington did not quite know what to make of the Soviet-Yugoslav imbroglio, for defiance of the Soviet Union by another communist

## Cold War Europe in 1949–1950

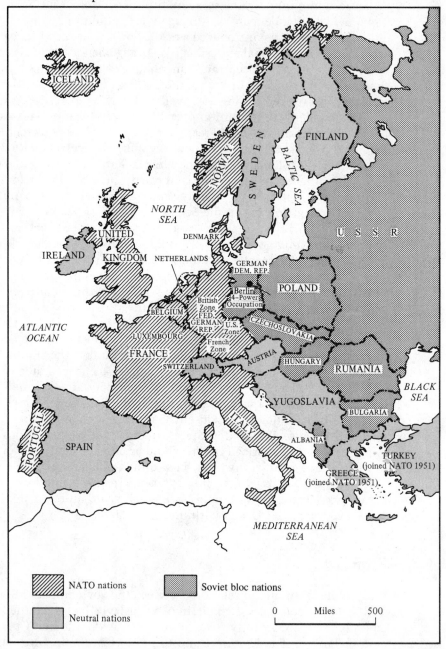

ICELAND

NORWAY

SWEDEN

FINLAND

BALTIC SEA

NORTH SEA

U S S R

UNITED KINGDOM

IRELAND

DENMARK

NETHERLANDS

GERMAN DEM. REP.

POLAND

Berlin
4–Power
Occupation

British Zone

FED.
GERMAN
REP.

U.S.
Zone

CZECHOSLOVAKIA

BELGIUM

ATLANTIC OCEAN

LUXEMBOURG

French
Zone

AUSTRIA

HUNGARY

RUMANIA

FRANCE

SWITZERLAND

BLACK SEA

YUGOSLAVIA

BULGARIA

PORTUGAL

SPAIN

ITALY

ALBANIA

TURKEY
(joined NATO 1951)

GREECE
(joined NATO 1951)

MEDITERRANEAN SEA

NATO nations

Soviet bloc nations

Neutral nations

0    Miles    500

state had hitherto seemed unthinkable. But then, in early 1949, they set about to help the Yugoslavs overcome the consequences of being cut off from intercourse with the Soviet Union and its satellites. Those steps did not receive unanimous endorsement across the United States. Many Americans calculated that the United States was engaged in a global crusade against communism, Tito was a communist, ergo it was an aberration for the Washington government to move to the assistance of Tito's regime. If such logic was hard to confute, leaders in Washington decided that it would be better if Yugoslavia was presided over by a communist regime that was independent of the Kremlin than by one that was under its domination. Over the next seven years, accordingly, the Washington government lent or granted well over a billion dollars to Yugoslavia.

As matters turned out, America's support of Tito did not necessarily assure permanent friendship with his regime. Eventually, after the death of Stalin in 1953, Tito and the new masters in the Kremlin smoothed over some of their differences, and in the latter 1950s relations between the United States and Yugoslavia cooled. Still, Yugoslavia did not slip behind the Iron Curtain, so the strategic and political gains resulting from the Truman administration's Yugoslav policy proved enduring.

## "LOSS" OF CHINA

Tito's revolt notwithstanding, Americans and their leaders continued to adhere to the maxim that Communist parties and movements across the globe were almost invariably under the direction of the Kremlin, and that any advance by communists anywhere constituted an extension of the Soviet empire. The most momentous expansion of what Americans perceived to be the Soviet empire took place when communists led by a ruthless philosopher-politician named Mao Zedong completed their conquest of China, the most populous nation on the face of the earth. The conquest was completed in December 1949 when Generalissimo Chiang Kai-shek, China's chief of state for more than two decades, led 1.5 million of his followers across the Formosa Strait to the island of Formosa (or Taiwan) where he established his "Free China" government.

Even before Chiang's retreat to Formosa, the United States had begun to reverberate to an acrimonious debate over America's responsibility for the "loss" of China to communism. One of those who spoke out was a 31-year-old Democratic congressman from Boston, John F. Kennedy, who in February 1949 charged that wrongheaded policies fashioned in the White House and State Department had opened the way for the communist triumph in China. "What our young men . . . saved [in World War II]," Kennedy declared, "our diplomats and our president have frittered away." On the other side was the voice of President Truman's fourth secretary of state, Dean G. Acheson. According to Acheson, the United States had provided large-scale military and economic assistance to Chiang, but because of corruption in his regime and his failure to redeem pledges of social and economic reform his popular support had melted away. The communists, Acheson said, had merely mounted a great national spirit of dissatisfaction and ridden it to victory and power. Which argument found a mark with the people of the United States in 1949–1950? Most Americans seemed to agree with Kennedy and other critics of Roosevelt-Truman policies that the United States had "sold Chiang Kai-shek down the river" to the communists.

In the mid-1930s, after a thrashing by Chiang's army, China's communists, now led by Mao, had made an epic "long march" to remote areas of northwestern China where they rebuilt their forces for the revolution that they professed to see in the future. Then, in 1937, Japan invaded China. While Chiang's army was in retreat, the communists returned to northeastern China, threw themselves into the struggle against the Japanese aggressors, and by the time of Japan's surrender in 1945 ruled tens of millions of Chinese. Meanwhile, in the closing days of the global conflict, the Soviets—who almost certainly would have made such a move without the urging of Roosevelt and concessions affirmed at Yalta—marched into Manchuria. They helped Mao and his followers consolidate authority in the huge province, and turned over to their Chinese comrades stocks of arms and ammunition captured from the Japanese. Otherwise, Soviet support of Mao was minimal, inasmuch as the

June 19, 1949: Mao Zedong and other communist leaders drafting plans for a new government on the eve of the communist victory in China.

Soviets, conscious of Russo-Chinese rivalries that reached well back into history, were not sure that a communist victory in China would be in their best interests.

As for leaders of the United States, they understood when the war in the Far East moved to its sudden termination in August 1945 that there would be a race between the followers of Chiang and Mao for control of the areas the Japanese would evacuate in China. To help Chiang get the better of the contest, American planes airlifted his soldiers to strategic points, and U.S. officials directed the emperor of Japan to order his armies in China to surrender only to representatives of Chiang's Nationalist regime. At the same time, American leaders arranged for the release of quantities of military equipment to Chiang, and agreed to continue to channel financial aid to his government. Between 1945 and 1949, indeed, the United States provided Chiang's government with some $2 billion in grants and credits.

Still, when fighting broke out between Nationalists and communists in the autumn of 1945, American leaders had scant hope that Chiang could win, and because of such pessimism urged Chiang to form a coalition government with Mao. To arrange a peace settlement and bring about a coalition government, President Truman in December 1945 dispatched Gen. George C. Marshall to China as a special ambassador. It asppeared for a time that the Marshall mission might succeed, for the Nationalists and communists in January 1946 agreed to a cease-fire. But the armistice broke down the following spring, and for the rest of the year civil war raged. As for a coalition government, that never came to pass. In any event, General Marshall returned to the United States in January 1947, his mission a failure.

Chiang's reputation, meanwhile, was slipping, in part because of popular outrage over graft in connection with relief supplies sent to China by the UN. Then, in 1947, Chiang launched his American-equipped armies against the communists in Manchuria. The communists repelled the attack, went over to the offensive, and by the end of 1948 had cleared the Nationalists from northeastern China. At the same time, the economy of Nationalist-controlled China collapsed, in part because of Chiang's refusal to risk his government's $300-million gold reserve to stabilize the wildly inflating Nationalist currency. All the while, Nationalist soldiers were flocking to the communist side, and several of Chiang's generals surrendered entire armies. With captured or surrendered American equipment, the communists pressed forward on all fronts, and by the spring of 1949 it was clear that Chiang was finished in China. The following December, the longtime Nationalist leader fled to Taiwan.

The "loss" of China came as a terrible shock to the people of the United States. Americans long had felt a special affection for the Chinese. But now the Chinese had fallen under the sway of communism—had become enemies. It was a catastrophe beyond measure, and left Americans at once sad and angry, and also frightened. Was it possible that the tide of history was indeed running in favor of communism?

## ADVENT OF McCARTHY

In that same period, Americans absorbed another shock when Alger Hiss, a onetime official in the State Department, was accused by a self-confessed former Soviet agent, Whittaker Chambers, of having passed secret government documents to a Soviet spy ring in the 1930s. The evidence against Hiss was impressive, and in early 1950 a jury found him guilty of having committed perjury when he denied under oath that he had passed the documents. How could Hiss, a member of a prominent family and graduate of Harvard, have betrayed his country?

While pondering the accusations against Hiss, Americans in September 1949 absorbed yet another shock: At least a half decade before scientists in American thought it possible, the Soviets had exploded a nuclear bomb. No longer could the United States rest secure in the knowledge that it alone had the doomsday weapon. It was as though the Soviet Union had trumped America's ace.

In response to the latter shock, President Truman addressed the question of whether the United States ought to perfect a thermonuclear or hydrogen bomb, many times more powerful than the atomic bomb. After weighing arguments that use of a weapon of such monstrous power would be immoral, hence it should never be built, he concluded that in the absence of a verifiable agreement committing all nations to refrain from fabricating hydrogen bombs, national security required that the United States produce them. The H-bomb project thereupon proceeded apace, and in the spring of 1951 scientists and technicians set off a small hydrogen bomb at Eniwetok Island in the Pacific and in the autumn of 1952 a much larger device. The results were mind-boggling.

Meanwhile, an obscure U.S. senator had flashed to prominence: Joseph R. McCarthy, Republican of Wisconsin. In search of an issue on which to base a campaign for re-election in 1952, McCarthy had hit on the idea of exposing alleged communist infiltration of the federal government. Red-baiting of course, was not a new phenomenon in America. Many Americans remembered "the Great Red Scare" of 1919–1920 and the rantings of the House Un-American Activities Committee (HUAC) in the 1930s. Following World War II, the HUAC had deployed against alleged communists and "fellow travelers" who it suspected had infiltrated the film industry of Hollywood. Of larger moment, as a result of the enterprise of a youthful congressman from California named Richard M. Nixon, the committee exposed Alger Hiss.

Indeed, it seemed in those years when the Cold War was taking form—and the Communist Party U.S.A. was defending every maneuver by the despicable Stalin—that the impulse to purge the country of communist influence was pervasive. Hitherto tolerant of communists, the CIO expelled 11 unions that it considered communist-dominated. Embarrassed that they, too, had taken a tolerant view of communists, political liberals organized Americans for Democratic Action to promote the principles of traditional American liberalism and guard the liberal movement against the subversive dogmas of communism. At the same time, the executive branch of the national government in Washington expanded and applied with renewed earnestness the so-called attorney general's list of subversive organizations, a relic of the Red Scare of 1919–1920. Then, in 1947, President Truman ordered the FBI and the Civil Service Commission to undertake a comprehensive investigation of all federal employees. As a result, the government dismissed 212 persons. The FBI, meanwhile, gathered evidence that leaders of the Communist Party U.S.A. had violated the Smith Act of 1940 by advocating the overthrow of the U.S. government. At length, in January 1949, the government brought 11 leaders of the party to trial, all 11 of whom were found guilty and sentenced to prison. Arguing that constitutional guarantees of freedom of speech and political activity offered no protection to conspirators who were plotting to destroy the country's constitutional system, the Supreme Court upheld the convictions in 1951.

Notwithstanding the Truman administration's campaign against subversion, many Americans continued to suspect that communists had managed to infiltrate the federal bureaucracy. Alger Hiss, after all, had been a federal official. Then, later in 1949, federal agents arrested Judith Coplon, a political analyst in the Justice Department, and accused her of providing Soviet agents with information on the FBI's counterespionage system. Next, in February 1950, British authorities arrested Klaus Fuchs, a nuclear physicist who had worked on the American atomic project, and charged him with having spied for the Soviets. From Fuchs, who quickly confessed, the trail led ultimately to Ethel and Julius Rosenberg, who had allegedly passed secret atomic data to the Soviet vice consul in New York City. Adjudged guilty, the Rosenbergs were sentenced to death. They died in New York's Sing Sing Prison in June 1953 after Pres. Dwight D. Eisenhower rejected impassioned appeals from around the world that he commute their sentences.

It was against the foregoing background of uncertainty, suspicion, and fear that Senator McCarthy set about to expose communist traitors in the federal government. He opened his campaign in February 1950 when he told a group of Republican ladies in Wheeling, West Virginia, that the State Department was riddled with communists. The speech drew little notice. But a few days later, at Salt Lake City, he charged that there were 57 card-carrying communists in the State Department. A few days later, he raised the figure to 81. At that point, he began to attract attention—and was pressed to identify the alleged communists. In response, on the evening of February 20, 1950, he presented his "cases" against alleged communists in the diplomatic service. It was one of the most bizarre performances in the annals of Congress. Shuffling papers, moving abruptly from one case to another, McCarthy was utterly incoherent, proved nothing, and prompted colleagues to agree with a prominent Republican that he must be some sort of nut. But the chaotic character of McCarthy's presentation tended to be lost on newspaper readers, millions of whom understood only that, according to the senator, communists were loose in the State Department.

Two days after his presentation, the Senate voted to investigate McCarthy's charges. Responsibility for the investigation would rest with a subcommittee headed by Millard Tydings, a conservative Democrat of Maryland. Hearings began in March 1950, and McCarthy's first case was that of a lawyer who, it turned out, had never worked for the State Department or any other agency of the federal government. And so it went. At length, McCarthy announced that he would stake everything on a single case and that the subject in the case was the top Soviet espionage agent in America. The "agent" turned out to be Owen Lattimore, a professor of political science at Johns Hopkins University who admired Mao Zedong, but apparently was no communist.

The Tydings Committee issued its report in July 1950, and the Democratic majority declared McCarthy's accusations groundless. The two Republican members contended that the investigation had not been sufficiently broad to exonerate the State Department of the charge that it was infiltrated by communists. The minority report notwithstanding, Democratic leaders felt confident that McCarthy was on the road to oblivion.

The Democrats were mistaken. Not only was McCarthy not on the road to oblivion, the "Second Red Scare" had not nearly run its course. Netting the votes of prominent liberals, the Internal Security (McCarran) Act passed through Congress in the autumn of 1950, then overcame a veto by President Truman. The legislation directed the Communist party and so-called communist front groups to label their propaganda, "Disseminated by a Communist organization." It provided that a member of the Communist party or a front organization could not receive a passport or secure employment in the federal bureaucracy or a defense plant; authorized the attorney general to apprehend and detain persons thought likely to commit sabotage or espionage; tightened espionage laws; extended the statute of limitations in spy cases from three years to ten. Two years later, in 1952, Congress passed the McCarran-Walter Immigration and Nationality Act over another veto by Truman. Included in the McCarran-Walter Act were provisions for denying entry to immigrants and deporting aliens who were deemed subversives or potential subversives.

Meanwhile, the fear of communist subversion reached into every state and locale. Because Henry Wadsworth Longfellow's Indian hero Hiawatha had tried to promote peace between Indian communities—and because communists continually organized what the news media described as peace offensives—Monogram pictures canceled plans for a film based on the Hiawatha story lest the company assist communist propaganda. School textbooks, particularly those in history and government, were scrutinized by school officials and assorted patriots, and those that failed to take what was deemed the proper stance regarding communism were banned from classrooms. State legislatures passed laws requiring state employees, including teachers in public schools and professors of state-supported colleges and universities, to sign oaths that they were not communists and were not affiliated with any communist-front organizations.

# CHALLENGE IN KOREA

While Senator Tydings's subcommittee was conducting its investigation of the charges raised by Senator McCarthy, events were unfolding in Northeast Asia that would have profound consequences for the United States. The communist regime of North Korea was assembling forces for an invasion of the noncommunist republic of South Korea. Then, in the predawn hours of June 25, 1950, North Korean infantrymen, supported by tanks and artillery, stormed forward.

As noted, Korea was a divided nation in the aftermath of the global war. The Soviet Union occupied the area to the north of the thirty-eighth parallel, the United States the area to the south. While the occupying powers quarreled over the question of a formula for unifying the two parts of the country under a single government, the Soviets set up a communist administration for northern Korea, its capital at P'yŏngyang, and placed that administration under the headship of a youthful communist, Kim Il-sung. In southern Korea, the Americans sanctioned a legislative assembly that came to be presided over by Syngman Rhee, an elderly and vigorously anticommunist Korean patriot.

Leaders in Washington in 1945–1946 felt increasing frustration in the matter of Korea. Communist-provoked disorders in the southern zone seemed out of control, and negotiations with the Soviets aimed at unifying the country had yielded nothing save recrimination. At length, the Joint Chiefs of Staff (JCS) urged the withdrawal of American troops from southern Korea. According to the JCS, Korea was of no strategic importance to the United States, and the troops could be put to better use elsewhere. Recognizing that an eventual communist takeover of all of Korea was apt to follow the withdrawal of American troops, the Truman administration was receptive to the arguments of the JCS. And so, to facilitate a graceful American exit from Korea, the United states in the autumn of 1947 prevailed on the UN to adopt a resolution calling for the establishment of a single government for Korea on the basis of free elections.

As anticipated, the Soviets refused to admit UN electoral commissioners to northern Korea, whereupon, in the spring of 1948, the commissioners oversaw elections in southern Korea. The outcome was establishment of the Republic of Korea (ROK), its capital at Seoul, and the election of Syngman Rhee to be its first president. A Supreme Assembly in P'yŏngyang at that point adopted a constitution for the Democratic People's Republic of Korea (DPRK) and designated Kim Il-sung to be its first premier. Both the ROK and DPRK claimed jurisdiction over the entire country. Recognizing that American troops provided his fledgling republic its best guarantee against an invasion by the forces of North Korea, President Rhee begged the Washington government to keep its troops deployed in South Korea, but to no avail. Leaving behind a military advisory group of five hundred men, the last American combat units sailed from South Korea in June 1949. Soviet troops had departed North Korea several months before.

The United States subsequently provided the ROK with military hardware; the military advisory group offered instruction and guidance. The United States also extended economic assistance. But what if Kim Il-sung should order North Korea's army across the parallel? The United States would stay clear of the resultant hostilities—and South Korea would doubtless fall to the communists. The Washington government's policy vis-à-vis Korea was no dark secret, and indeed its essence became public knowledge when Secretary of State Acheson, in a speech in early 1950, observed that South Korea was outside the American defensive perimeter in the Far East. Dismayed by the secretary's pronouncement, South Korean leaders appealed to the Washington government to extend its defensive line in the Far East to include South Korea. They appealed in vain. In that same time frame, that is, in early 1950, Kim Il-sung secured the consent of his mentor, Josef Stalin, to undertake an invasion of the South Korean republic. Like Kim, the Soviet tyrant had concluded that the United States would make no armed response to a North Korean thrust across the thirty-eighth parallel. As mentioned, Kim unleashed his army against South Korea on June 25, 1950.

Unbeknownst to Kim and Stalin, alas, the Truman administration had been reexamining its global policies. Of particular moment, or so it appears in retrospect, the State Department's Policy Planning Staff, in April 1950, had submitted a document, NSC 68, to the National Security Council. NSC 68 asserted that the Soviet Union, animated by a new fanatical faith, was seeking to impose absolute authority over the rest of the world. According to NSC 68: "The issues that face us are momentous, involving the fulfillment or destruction not only of this Republic but of civilization itself." NSC 68 did not state categorically that the United States ought to deploy its armed forces to meet aggressive moves by the Soviet Union or its satellites against one of the lesser noncommunist countries, say, South Korea. But it expressed the conviction that the Washington government should view any such moves with utmost seriousness. Asserted the document: "The assault on free institutions is world-wide now, and in the context of the present polarization of power a defeat of free institutions anywhere is a defeat everywhere."

Unfortunately, the United States, because it had allowed its conventional forces to deteriorate, had no choice at assorted pressure points across the world between capitulation to Soviet or Soviet-supported aggression and precipitating a global war. Or so thought the authors of NSC 68. The conclusion was transparent: The United States must build up its military strength as rapidly as possible. Wrote the authors of NSC 68: "It is necessary to have the military power to deter, if possible, Soviet expansion, and to defeat, if necessary, aggressive Soviet or Soviet-directed actions of a limited or total character." To counter limited Soviet actions, the United States needed to strengthen its conventional forces to a point where it was not so dependent on atomic weapons. To meet the threat of total war, the North American superpower should produce and stockpile thermonuclear weapons in the event they proved feasible.

NSC was an imposing document. It clearly reflected attitudes of the president and other American leaders regarding the Soviet Union. It also reflected a renewed determination by the Washington government to execute the policy enunciated in the Truman Doctrine of 1947, that is, the policy of global resistance to the expansionist impulses of "international communism."

As for Truman, he learned of the invasion of South Korea while spending a weekend at his home in Independence, Missouri. Flying back to Washington, he conferred with political and military advisers, and decided that the Soviets had prompted the attack. He also concluded that the credibility of the United States as the world's bulwark against what Americans perceived to be an aggressive Soviet empire required a determined response by the Washington government. In the absence of such a response, America's friends would have reason to doubt the viability of the commitment of the United States to contain the Soviet Union and its clients. More than that, the Soviets, like the Axis powers in the 1930s when appeased by the Western democracies, were apt to be emboldened to undertake new acts of aggression. So when it became clear that the South Koreans could not stop the invaders, Truman did precisely the opposite of what his administration had plainly indicated it would do in the event of a communist invasion of South Korea. He ordered U.S. military and naval forces to move to the defense of the ROK. Had the Soviets and North Koreans even remotely suspected that he might take such action in response to a communist thrust across the thirty-eighth parallel, they doubtless would have put aside any thoughts of a power move against the South Korean republic. (Truman also directed the Seventh Fleet to deploy in the Formosa Strait to prevent a communist invasion of Formosa—and likewise to prevent Chiang Kai-shek from complicating the situation in the Far East by attacking the communist-held mainland of China.) After the UN assumed at least titular command of the forces defending South Korea, 20 additional governments contributed combat or medical units to what was sometimes referred to as the world organization's "police action" in Northeast Asia.

As for the people of the United States, they overwhelmingly supported Truman's decision, taken without the formal consent of Congress, to dispatch American forces to Korea. Their support did not waver when the national government revived the military draft and recalled military and naval reservists to active duty. Nor did it waver in the face of crushing setbacks in the battle area.

Rushed from garrisons in Japan, where they had been poorly prepared for the rigors of combat, the first American ground troops in Korea were outnumbered and outgunned. But at length, after falling back through Taejŏn and Taegu and suffering heavy casualities, they and their South Korean comrades stiffened, reinforcements arrived, and by the first week in August of 1950 the North Korean offensive had ground to a halt at the southeastern tip of the peninsula—along the "Pusan perimeter." Meanwhile, the commander of what was officially designated the UN Command, General MacArthur, had drafted plans and assembled a force for what appeared (because of fearsome tides) a risky amphibious strike against Seoul, the enemy's strategic center in South Korea. According to his plan, the force, comprised of American marines and soldiers, would go ashore at Inch'ŏn, 20 miles west of Seoul on the Yellow Sea. Executed in mid-September 1950, the operation was a brilliant success. While

Korean War, 1950–1953

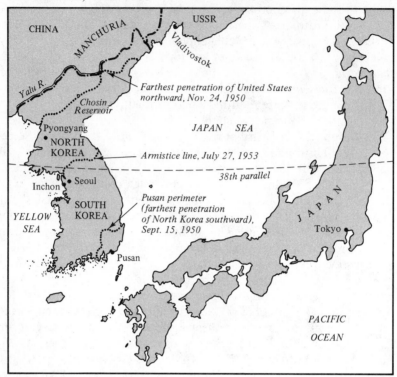

marines and and soldiers were liberating Seoul, UN forces broke out of the Pusan perimeter, and within days the North Koreans were retreating back over the thirty-eighth parallel. In an impressive ceremony near the end of September, MacArthur formally returned Seoul to President Rhee.

## OUT OF THE JAWS OF VICTORY

Leaders in Washington by now were wrestling with a new question: Should UN forces pursue the retreating North Koreans beyond the parallel and extend the authority of the ROK to all of Korea? Their impulse was that it would be nonsensical to pass up the present opportunity to unify the Korean nation under a noncommunist regime. But might a UN thrust into North Korea provoke China, the communist giant that lay beyond Korea's northern frontier? That question took on special urgency when the Chinese premier Chou En-lai announced that China would not "supinely tolerate the destruction of its neighbor by the imperialistic powers." Calculating that Chou was bluffing, leaders of the United States determined to continue the attack. The General Assembly of the UN sanctioned their decision.

By the second week in October, UN troops, mostly South Korean and American, were meeting minimal opposition as they pressed forward in North Korea. But then, in the last days of October, Chinese infantrymen made scattered contact with UN forces, then virtually faded from view. What were the Chinese up to? Surely leaders in Beijing did not suspect that UN forces might march across the Yalu into the Chinese province of Manchuria. Perhaps the Chinese were deploying to protect power stations in northernmost Korea that supplied electricity to Manchuria. Whatever was in the minds of leaders in Beijing, American leaders did not believe the Chinese were preparing a counterstroke against the UN Command. So UN forces continued to advance. On November 21, American battalions reached the Yalu; on the morning of November 24, MacArthur flew to Korea from Tokyo to preside over an offensive that he expected would terminate the war. Then it happened. On the evening of November 25, the Chinese, bugles blaring and cymbals clanging, smashed forward and turned the UN offensive into a headlong retreat.

Proclaiming that the UN Command faced "an entirely new war," MacArthur sought authority to send bombing planes against the enemy's air bases, staging areas, and supply lines in Manchuria. Intent on keeping the war con-

October 1950: U.S. Army troops advancing with minimal opposition in North Korea.

fined to the Korean peninsula, lest it escalate into World War III, his superiors denied him the authority he sought. When he continued to set out his thoughts to news correspondants, they forwarded him a presidential directive that military commanders were to make no public statements on political or military policy without obtaining clearance from Washington.

As UN forces continued to retreat, in mid-December 1950, Truman warned Americans that Soviet expansionism had placed the United States in grave danger, and to meet that danger he urged (in accord with NSC 68) a substantial buildup of American military and naval strength. Congress responded by voting an emergency appropriation of $20 billion for the armed forces. The result was a new burst of energy for the national economy. Although prices and wages inched upward and a steel strike in 1952 produced temporary economic disruption, the remaining 30 months of the Korean War were a time of unbridled prosperity in the United States.

Meanwhile, as 1950 turned to 1951, MacArthur renewed his appeal for authority to expand the war. He urged a campaign of aerial bombardment of China and a naval blockade of Chinese ports—also that forces of Chiang Kai-shek on Formosa be deployed in Korea. Still intent on keeping the war confined to Korea, lest it escalate into a general and perhaps global war, his superiors rejected his appeal.

At length, in January 1951, the communist offensive ground to a termination 50 miles below Seoul. Now under the field command of Lt. Gen. Matthew B. Ridgway, UN infantrymen, magnificently supported by artillery, tanks, and tactical aircraft, returned to the attack. By early March, they had recaptured Seoul, and were about to drive the enemy back over the thirty-eighth parallel into North Korea. Might they undertake a second attempt to expel communism from the peninsula and bring about the unification of Korea under the authority of the ROK? No way. After its forces had established a line of defense in the vicinity of the parallel, the UN would seek an armistice.

## THE GENERAL AND THE PRESIDENT

Alas, General MacArthur was bent on pressing forward and achieving the victory that had eluded him the previous autumn. Ignoring Truman's directive regarding public statements, he spelled out his views to news correspondents. And after learning that Truman was about to make a peace proposal, he issued, on March 24, 1951, an incredible statement threatening the Chinese with annihilation if they did not leave Korea. Because of the confusion generated by the general's broadside, Truman felt compelled to withhold his peace proposal. Then, on April 5, Rep. Joseph W. Martin, Jr., Republican of Massachusetts, read a letter he had received from MacArthur. The letter summarized the general's views about driving the communists from Korea, and concluded, "There is no substitute for victory." Five days later, on April 10, Truman relieved MacArthur of his various commands, replacing him with Ridgway.

Americans who remember 1951 are not apt to forget the popular response to Truman's action. Citizens from Maine to California expressed outrage that the president had sacked the architect of the Allied victory in the southwest Pacific during World War II and the bearer of democracy to conquered Japan. Of the president, whose approval rating had recently slipped to 28 percent, Senator McCarthy said; "The son of a bitch ought to be impeached." Many of McCarthy's compatriots agreed. *Life* published a picture of a grinning Sen. Richard M. Nixon holding a batch of telegrams urging Truman's impeachment. Students in California hanged the president in effigy; a woman in Maryland sent a telegram to the White House calling Truman a witling—after Western Union refused to transmit the word *moron*; and a man in Los Angeles told a television reporter that the country would not be in its present shape "if Harry Truman were alive." (The same man told the reporter that he was going out for a "Truman beer." "What kind of beer is that?" the reporter asked. "Just like any other kind," the man replied, "except it hasn't got a head.") A Gallup survey indicated that only 28 percent of the citizenry approved the president's action.

April 20, 1951: Recently dismissed from his various commands in the Far East by President Truman, General MacArthur acknowledges the cheers of throngs of admirers as his motorcade moves into Times Square from upper Broadway in New York City.

Following his relief from command, MacArthur, who had not set foot in the United States since 1937, was accorded an emotional farewell by millions of Japanese on departing Japan. He, his wife, and his young son received tumultuous receptions when their aircraft touched down in Honolulu, San Francisco, and Washington. Then, on April 19, MacArthur set out his views in an emotion-packed address before Congress. Recalling a line in an old barracks ballad that "old soldiers never die, they just fade away," he concluded by saying that like the old soldier in the ballad he would just fade away. Of course, he did not fade away, and further mob scenes played when the MacArthurs visited New York, Chicago, and Milwaukee. As for the president, he stayed in the background, emerging from his office and quarters only to throw out the first ball of the American League season at Griffith Stadium. But even the ballpark offered no escape from the national preoccupation of the moment: When Truman, a faint smile across his lips, prepared to make the toss a chorus of boos rolled out from the grandstand.

Meanwhile, Republican critics of Truman demanded a senatorial investigation of MacArthur's dismissal and the government's policy in the Far East. In view of the current enthusiasm for MacArthur, the Democratic-controlled Senate could scarcely turn aside their demand, and in the last week of April 1951 unanimously approved a resolution mandating a joint inquiry by the Armed Services and Foreign Relations Committees. The outcome, beginning in early May, was an eight-week grilling of MacArthur, Secretary of Defense George C. Marshall, the Joint Chiefs of Staff, Secretary of State Acheson, and several lesser individuals. Offering the most memorable utterance of the so-called MacArthur hearings was Gen. Omar N. Bradley, the chairman of the Joint Chiefs, who told the senators that the MacArthur strategy in the Far East "would involve us in the wrong war, at the wrong place, at the wrong time, and with the wrong enemy."

By the time the hearings droned to adjournment, on June 27, 1951, the issues that had prompted them seemed almost passé. The new reality was the prospect of a cease-fire in Korea, for on June 23 the Soviet ambassador to the UN, Jacob Malik, had proposed that the belligerents in Korea enter armistice negotiations. Suspecting a communist trick, leaders in Washington nonetheless found the Malik overture interesting. Thus, General Ridgway, on June 30, sent a message over the Armed Forces Radio network proposing armistice negotiations. A radio message from Beijing the following day suggested that such negotiations should take place at Kaesŏng, just below the thirty-eighth parallel along the western end of the battle line. Ridgway radioed approval of the Kaesŏng location on July 3; negotiations got under way on July 10.

## TALKING TRUCE, WAGING WAR

The cease-fire negotiations at Kaesŏng turned out to be a farce. The communists had prepared the negotiating site, which was to the rear of their defense line, and as cameras clicked the UN delegation was compelled to make its way to Kaesŏng in automobiles bearing white flags, indicating that the UN Command was surrendering. Inside the old teahouse that served as bargaining headquarters, the chief UN delegate was seated in a chair that was lower than that of his communist counterpart. And so it went. Clearly the communists were not searching for an early armistice. Still, because people across the world fervently wanted the negotiations to succeed, UN delegates allowed themselves to be subjected to interminable insults and harangues—until the latter part of August of 1951 when the communists broke off the talks after charging (falsely) that a UN plane had bombed the conference site.

Suspension of the truce talks signaled renewed activity on the battlefront. To straighten its line along the east-central segment of the front, UN forces pushed the communists off Bloody Ridge, cleared them from the Punch Bowl, expelled them from a succession of steep hills that came to be known as Heartbreak Ridge.

Frustrated on the battlefield, the communists, in October 1951, again indicated a willingness to discuss a truce. So armistice talks resumed, this time in a tent village at Panmunjŏm, a few miles from Kaesŏng. Progress was slow. Their discussions punctuated by insults, delegates wrangled over such issues as the location of an armistice line and policing a truce. By the spring of 1952, however, they had resolved all major issues save one: the repatriation of prisoners of war. Citing a rule of war hitherto endorsed by nearly all governments that prisoners (who it had been assumed would yearn to return to their homelands) were to be repatriated, the communists insisted that all POWs in Korea be sent home, against their wills if it came to that. Having discovered that more than fifty thousand prisoners in its compounds did not want to return to communist rule, the UN Command took the position that prisoners must be free to choose for themselves whether they would be repatriated. Because each side refused to budge on the POW issue, the Korean War dragged on for another 15 months.

Still, neither side was willing to accept the expense in blood of a new battlefield offensive, hence the war became stalemated—and attention remained fixed on Panmunjŏm, where negotiators continued to exchange insults and on occasion talk about a truce. Then, in October 1952, the UN Command broke off the armistice talks pending presentation by communists of "constructive proposals." Meanwhile, American troops died at a rate of about forty per week as they struggled for tactical advantage at such places as Pork Chop Hill, Old Baldy, and the Iron Triangle. UN aircraft and warships pulverized enemy targets behind the battle zone.

From the perspective of scores of thousands of young Americans who were deployed in Korea in 1952–1953, the war was without purpose. It seemed clear that the UN Command had no intention of organizing a new offensive to drive the enemy back to the Yalu, and troops found it hard to grasp the explanation that interminable patrols into no-man's-land, artillery and mortar duels, and attacks and counterattacks for a few barren hills were of large political importance. People back home in the United States were similarly frustrated; like soldiers in the battle area, they could not easily grasp the political argument for continuing a stalemated war. Many Americans, in truth, had lost their stomach for the war in the aftermath of China's entry in the conflict and the agonizing retreat of UN forces from North Korea in late 1950. Still, it never occurred to such Americans to organize protest demonstrations or accuse their leaders of pressing an immoral war. Young people did not mutilate draft cards or torch the Stars and Stripes or flaunt the banner of North Korea. It was against that background of frustration resulting from the war in Korea that the people of the United States prepared for the electoral campaign of 1952.

## ELECTION OF 1952

As they deployed for the electoral contest of 1952, Republicans determined to take maximum advantage of the citizenry's frustration in the matter of the Korean War. Recalling Secretary Acheson's speech of January 1950 in which he explained that Korea was outside the American defensive perimeter in the Far East, Republican orators and editorial writers proclaimed that the Truman administration had virtually invited the communists to commit aggression against South Korea. Thus the war, in the Republican view, could fairly be labeled "Mr. Truman's War."

If the policy of the Truman administration was to blame for the war in Korea, that policy, according to Republicans, reflected a tragic (and almost treasonous) failure by Democrats over the past decade to take a resolute stand against the communist menace. Or, as Republicans often asserted, Democrats had been "soft on communism." Republicans maintained that Democratic leaders of the national government had been inexcusably generous (or soft) in their dealings with the Soviets in the course of World War II. At Yalta, indeed, according to the Republican interpretation of recent history, a bemused and dying Roosevelt had handed over Eastern Europe to the Soviets and affirmed concessions that assured the victory of communism in China. Now, in the early 1950s, Democrats were content merely to "contain" the spread of communist influence and power. Republicans deplored containment as a negative and even immoral response to the menace presented by the Soviets and their communist ideology. Rather than simply contain communism, they sought to "roll back the Iron Curtain."

The alleged softness of Democrats in their approach to communism had other dimensions, so Republicans professed to believe. If many Republicans rejected the more outrageous charges issued by Senator McCarthy, most were persuaded that Alger Hiss and Judith Coplon were not the only communists (or "Reds") or fellow travelers (often referred to as "Pinks") who had penetrated the federal bureaucracy during the years of Democratic ascendancy in Washington. Republicans also determined to zero in on influence peddling in the Truman administration. But the issue of corruption transcended the White House. A special committee of the Senate headed by Estes Kefauver, a liberal Democrat of Tennessee, had investigated organized crime in 1950–1951, and in public hearings, many of them televised, evidence was disclosed that Democratic "machines" in several large cities were connected with organized racketeers.

Whom would Republicans nominate for president in 1952? The conservative faction of the Grand Old Party (GOP) was bent on delivering the nomination to Sen. Robert A. Taft of Ohio, widely referred to as "Mr. Republican," a son of former-President William Howard Taft. Moderate Republicans cringed at the prospect that Taft might become the GOP standard-bearer. They perceived of Taft as a Neanderthal conservative and America-firster (or isolationist) who would strive to return the country to the halcyon days of Calvin Coolidge and Herbert Hoover when the federal government accepted few responsibilities for maintaining the welfare of the citizenry and kept a low profile in international politics. Such a return, they believed, would be calamitous. Other Republicans simply believed that Taft, an uncharismatic man whose ideas seemed out of touch with those of the mainstream of the national electorate, would take Republicans to defeat in the autumn election.

To counter Taft, moderate Republicans, and also Republicans whose overbearing interest was victory on Election Day, sought the nomination of General Eisenhower, a soldier who had stayed clear of politics—who had never said publicly whether he was a Democrat or a Republican. Since late 1950 the commander of NATO forces in Europe, Eisenhower was, of course, a bona fide national hero whom most Americans referred to affectionately as "Ike." He had an infectious grin, and appeared to entertain ideas that were akin to those of the moderate faction of the GOP. Persuaded by Republican moderates that only he could prevent the nomination of Taft, whose views in matters of foreign affairs he deplored, Eisenhower did not protest when a prominent moderate disclosed in early 1952 that Ike was, in fact, a Republican. Next, after voters had accorded him a succession of victories in primary elections, he resigned his NATO command and returned to the United States to campaign for the nomination. At the Republican national convention in Chicago in July 1952, following a bruising contest over the seating of delegates from southern states, the 62-year-old Eisenhower won the nomination on the first ballot. For vice president the delegates, choosing from a list of names provided by the general, turned to 39-year-old Richard Nixon, whose youth would offset what was considered Eisenhower's advanced age. Nixon's reputation as a militant anticommunist, moreover, would appeal to admirers of Senator McCarthy.

Meanwhile, in March 1952, Harry Truman announced that he would not seek another term in the White House. Thus delegates to the Democratic national convention in Chicago the following summer nominated Gov. Adlai E. Stevenson of Illinois for president. To appease the party's southern faction, the delegates, at Stevenson's request, nominated Sen. John J. Sparkman of Alabama for vice president.

Shortly after serious campaigning got under way, in September 1952, Democratic hopes soared when it was disclosed that Senator Nixon had been the beneficiary of a special fund collected by several millionaires in California for the purpose of offsetting the expense of meeting senatorial responsibilities. Millions of citizens were outraged—reckoned that Nixon had peddled his in-

September 23, 1952: Beleaguered vice presidential candidate Richard Nixon explaining "expense fund" on national television.

fluence after the fashion of "the Missouri Gang" in the White House. And for a time it appeared that Eisenhower might feel compelled to ask Nixon for his resignation from the Republican ticket. But the electorate responded sympathetically when Nixon defended his behavior in a carefully staged television address—the famous "Checkers speech," so called because of the candidate's reference to the Nixon family dog, Checkers. Nixon thus survived what he would later style as one of a succession of crises in his political career.

Otherwise, the campaign was a disaster from the perspective of Democrats, brightened only by the eloquence and wit of Stevenson. Highlighted by Truman's seizure of the mills, four months of labor turmoil in the steel industry in the spring and summer of 1952 had further aroused voters against the Democrats. And for all of his well-turned phrases and witticisms, Stevenson proved no match for Eisenhower, a national hero and veritable symbol of integrity and decency in the estimate of most Americans. Nor was Stevenson able to cope with the Republican contention that his was the party of "Korea, communism, and corruption"—or $K_1C_2$, in the language of some Republicans.

The central issue, of course, was Korea, and Eisenhower asserted in mid-September that the United States was embroiled in war in Korea because the Truman administration had allowed America to become weak—also because it had abandoned China to the communists. Then, as the campaign was moving to a climax, the general electrified millions of his compatriots when he announced that the first task of a new Republican administration would be to bring the war in Korea to an early and honorable end. "That job requires a personal trip to Korea. . . . I shall make the trip. . . . I shall go to Korea."

Less than a fortnight later, voters gave Eisenhower a landslide victory over Stevenson, and returned Republican majorities to both houses of Congress. (Two days after the election, on November 6, 1952, another event of large moment transpired: President Truman issued a secret directive establishing the National Security Agency [NSA] to protect American codes and communications, break the codes of other governments, and gather information. Relying mainly on electronic devices, the NSA would eventually surpass the CIA in importance as an agency for gathering intelligence—and would remain so secret that only a handful of Americans would know of its existence before the 1970s.)

Few Americans, even among those who had marked ballots for Stevenson, felt distraught by the outcome of the election. Nearly everybody in the republic—Harry Truman a notable exception—genuinely liked Ike.

## IKE

Born in Denison, Texas, in 1890, Eisenhower had grown up in Abilene, Kansas, graduated from high school, and entered the U.S. Military Academy at West Point. Commissioned a second lieutenant in 1915, he was assigned to Fort Sam Houston in Texas. During America's participation in the Great War in 1917–1918, he served as an instructor at assorted training camps in the United States. After the war, he did a tour of duty in Panama, and in 1932 became an aide to the Army's chief of staff, Gen. Douglas MacArthur. He accompanied MacArthur to the Philippines to help build a Filipino army, and returned to the United States in 1938.

Eisenhower received promotion to brigadier general as a consequence of his performance in the Army's maneuvers in Louisiana in 1941, and following the Japanese attack on Pearl Harbor was summoned to Washington to help plan strategy for the war in the Pacific. But then the Army's chief of staff, General Marshall, impressed by Eisenhower's tact and organizational skills, gave him responsibility for developing plans for an eventual Allied invasion of Axis-occupied Europe. Next, in June 1942, Marshall made him commanding general of the European Theater of Operations, advancing him over more than 350 senior officers. The first major undertaking of the new command was Operation Torch, the Allied invasion of North Africa, executed in the autumn of 1942. Eisenhower commanded the successful invasions of Sicily and Italy in the summer of 1943, whereupon President Roosevelt decided that he should oversee Operation Overlord, the attack on Hitler's *Festung Europa,* the greatest amphibious maneuver in the history of warfare, carried out in June 1944.

Shortly after surrender of the Axis, in 1945, President Truman recalled Eisenhower from Europe and made him chief of staff of the Army. While presiding over the Army's demobilization, Ike composed a memoir of the recent war, *Crusade in Europe.* Published in 1948, the book was an instant bestseller. Turning aside overtures that he enter politics, Eisenhower left the Army in 1948 to take over the the presidency of Columbia University. The routine of campus administration bored him, so he was pleased in late 1950 when Truman asked him to return to active duty in the Army and assume command of the forces of NATO. Hardly had he settled in at NATO headquarters in Paris before a stream of moderate Republicans began to arrive to urge him to seek the GOP nomination for president.

Like most public men and women, Eisenhower did not conform exactly with the public's perception of him. His boyish grin and grandfatherly demeanor notwithstanding, he had a volcanic temper, and when aroused was not above issuing a stream of invective liberally punctuated by profanity. If the memoir by his wartime aide in North Africa and Britain, Kay Summersby, is to be believed, his relationship with his wife had not always been tender and harmonious. Still, he was, as Americans perceived him to be, a man of integrity. Like Truman, whom he came to despise in the course of the electoral campaign of 1952, he was without guile. Unlike his onetime mentor General MacArthur, he was neither vain nor pretentious.

## ARMISTICE IN KOREA

How Eisenhower, not brilliant but certainly bright, would perform as president remained to be seen at the time of his election in early November of 1952. But in the recent campaign he had pledged to go to Korea, so at the end of November he boarded a four-engine Constellation and set out for the ancient "Land of the Morning Calm." During his 72-hour sojourn in Korea, he conferred with American commanders, reviewed troops near the battlefront, visited wounded soldiers. He limited his contact with the South Korean president Syngman Rhee to one hour.

The trip was not without consequence, for it reinforced Eisenhower in his conviction that the United States and its allies could not stand indefinitely on a static front and continue to accept casualties without any visible result. "Small attacks on small hills," he later observed in his memoirs, "would not end wars." A few weeks after taking the presidential oath, accordingly, in February 1953, he discreetly advised the communists that if progress toward terminating the war was not soon forthcoming, the United States intended to move decisively and without inhibition in its use of weapons, and would no longer feel constrained to confine hostilities to the Korean peninsula. The new president, in a word, was threatening to hit the enemy with nuclear weapons and to carry the war, as MacArthur had urged two years before, to the territory

December 1952: President-elect Eisenhower lunches with troops during his 72-hour visit to Korea.

of China. A short time later, in early March of 1953, the Soviet dictator Stalin died, and while consolidating power in the Kremlin, the new Soviet leaders appeared to seek a reduction of tensions across the world.

To what extent the North Koreans and Chinese were moved by Eisenhower's threat and pressure by the new leaders in Moscow is impossible to say. But in April 1953, they consented to a proposal advanced by the current commander of UN operations in Korea, Gen. Mark W. Clark, to exchange sick and wounded prisoners. The result was Operation Little Switch. Next, the communists indicated that they were at last prepared to accept the substance of the UN position regarding the repatriation of POWs. Shortly thereafter, on April 26, 1953, negotiations resumed at Panmunjŏm, and over the next few weeks negotiators formulated final arrangements for a cease-fire.

Only one obstacle remained: the government of South Korea. President Rhee and many South Koreans dreamed of organizing a new battlefield offensive that would result in the expulsion of communism from Korea and unification of the country under the authority of the ROK. And when Rhee arbitrarily released thousands of North Korean POWs from South Korean compounds, thus making it impossible for communist emissaries to try to persuade them to return home in accord with the repatriation agreement recently worked out at Panmunjŏm, it appeared that the projected cease-fire agreement might be in jeopardy. Angry over the release of the prisoners, Eisenhower advised Rhee that the United States and the other UN partners were determined to terminate the war along the present battle line, and would lend no support to a renewed offensive. To assuage and reassure the South Koreans, however, he indicated that the United States would continue to provide economic and military assistance to the ROK, and enter into a mutual security pact with Rhee's government. The South Korean president thereupon gave his grudging sanction to the armistice agreement.

At length, on July 27, 1953, after the communists had made a final attack on UN defenses to give the appearance that they had ended the war on a note of triumph, the negotiators at Panmunjŏm put their hands to an armistice document. The Korean War thus passed into history. It had claimed the lives of an estimated 2 million military-naval personnel and civilians. American deaths in the conflict totaled 54,246: 33,629 U.S. soldiers, marines, airmen, and seamen KIA (killed in action), 20,617 dead of accidents and disease. Although leaving large areas of the Korean peninsula devastated and the urban areas of North Korea utterly flattened (a result of indiscriminate bombing raids ordered by the UN Command), the war had rescued South Korea from the clutches of Kim Il-sung's Stalinist tyranny. It had reinforced the determination of the United States to contain the communist scourge in the Far East. As a result, the Washington government had made itself the protector of Formosa, accelerated its assistance to the French and their noncommunist Vietnamese allies in Vietnam, and, in 1951, negotiated a peace treaty with the Japanese that made Japan its ally. In that same year, it negotiated mutual security pacts with the Philippines and (the "ANZUS" pact) with Australia and New Zealand. Finally, the war, while energizing the American economy, offered the people of the United States a new lesson in the national cost of being a super-powerful guardian of "the free world," as well as a beginning lesson in the vagaries and frustrations of brushfire conflicts in distant areas of the globe.

## RETROSPECT

If Americans went about their lives, day in and day out, pretty much as they always had—experienced the usual joys and sorrows, successes and failures—the years of Harry Truman's second term in the White House did not comprise one of the happier times in the annals of their republic.

The citizenry had little confidence in national leaders, particularly the occupant of the Oval Office, whose re-election to the presidency in 1948 it intensely came to regret. Scarcely any American in those years, it seems fair to say, had the remotest inkling that historical scholars in decades to come would be almost unanimous in adjudging Harry Truman a near-great or even great president. At one point in the second term, indeed, Truman's popular approval rating according to opinion polls sank to 23 percent, several points lower than Richard Nixon would record in 1974 at the time of his resignation from the presidency in disgrace. The popular view at the time was that at heart Truman was a hack politician who had never transcended habits or perceptions acquired in the days when he was a cog in the Pendergast machine in Kansas City. Worse, the president was not very bright, or so it was widely thought. "To err is Truman," Americans used to say.

Of larger moment, Americans from 1949 to 1953 were tormented by the threat of communism, both at home and across the world. Great numbers of them were persuaded that loose in the country were legions of communists or communist sympathizers who were "boring from within" to bring down traditional political and socioeconomic institutions and turn the United States into a citadel of Marxism-Leninism and perhaps a satellite of the Kremlin. Such Americans were genuinely frightened when Joe McCarthy proclaimed that the federal bureaucracy was riddled with communists. And they experienced feelings of dismay tinctured with shock when the Soviets exploded a nuclear bomb—and for the first time since the War of 1812 brought the United States under the gun of a powerful enemy, a shattering development in the perspective of a people who for 135 years had felt totally secure behind oceanic barriers. They likewise felt dismay and surprise when the tide of communism rolled across China, the homeland of a quarter of the people of the earth. And they felt dismay if not shock again when their crusade in Korea turned into a frustrating stalemate.

Still, better days were in the offing, for the electorate in the autumn of 1952 had chosen a veritable symbol of victory and traditional virtues to preside over the destiny of the republic. Just as Ike had marshaled great armies and guided them in a triumphal crusade against the vilest of enemies from 1942 to 1945, so would he now marshal the energies of the people of the United States and lead them in a crusade to rid the country of communists and communist (equated by many citizens with liberal) ideas and stay the tide of communism across the world.

# Chapter
# 3

---

# Holding the Line

Six months before hostilities ended in Korea, on January 20, 1953, President-elect and Mrs. Eisenhower had an early breakfast, attended a special service at the National Presbyterian Church, then made their way to the White House. Because of lingering bitterness resulting from remarks uttered by Truman during the recent electoral campaign, the Eisenhowers forewent the customary preinauguration social formalities inside the White House, and instead met President and Mrs. Truman under the portico of the executive mansion. Thereupon the president and president-elect, side by side, motored up Pennsylvania Avenue, their ladies following in a second limousine. On a platform atop the east steps of the Capitol, Eisenhower repeated the presidential oath, then delivered his inaugural address. After the ceremonies at the Capitol, the Eisenhowers and Trumans parted. His wife at his side, the new president, flashing his famous grin, waving to the throngs of people lining the thoroughfares, moved off to a reviewing stand near the White House to watch the inaugural parade. Later in the day, the former president and his wife boarded the Baltimore & Ohio Railroad's National Limited for the trip back to Independence and retirement.

## IKE THE CONSERVATIVE

Although the new chief executive was generally perceived as a moderate Republican, nine of the ten members of his cabinet were wealthy businessmen of conservative orientation. And in home affairs Eisenhower certainly—in the words of Arthur Larson, a member of his administration—"started from a rather simplistic conservative base." Which meant that he was much concerned by what he perceived to be the problem of maintaining the fiscal integrity of the federal government, had uncompromising faith in the system of free enterprise, and had no interest in sallying forth as a new champion of the welfare or guarantor or social service state. As time passed, he became increasingly confirmed in his conservatism, and commented in 1956 that the late Senator Taft, an idol of conservatives, had in fact been less conservative than he in matters of home affairs.

As a conservative, Eisenhower determined to reduce government spending, balance the federal budget, and curb inflation. Reducing spending and balancing the budget proved difficult. Interest payments on the national debt had to be made, veterans and Social Security benefits funded, an effective military-naval establishment maintained. Assistance to the country's friends overseas, in the president's view, had to be continued. Accordingly, the budget achieved balance only three times during Eisenhower's eight years in the White House, and the deficit in 1958, $12 billion, was the largest peacetime deficit to that time. Figures pertaining to inflation were more satisfying. Limits on federal spending and "tight money" (the policy of attracting investment funds into the Treasury by offering high interest rates on government bonds) were the tools for countering inflation. The tools appeared effective. Prices remained stable during the first three years, increased 3 percent in 1956, then moved up at a rate of less than 2 percent per year over the last four years of the Eisenhower presidency.

The thirty-fourth president, in truth, manifested his conservatism in myriad ways. He approved a substantial tax cut, particularly for businesses, and supported legislation reducing subsidies to farmers. Two years later, in 1956, he vetoed a measure sponsored by Democrats, who had regained control of Congress as a result of the election of 1954, which would have returned farm subsidies to the pre-1954 level. (A hostile reaction in the farm belt compelled him to approve the Soil Bank Act of 1956 providing payments to farmers who agreed to reduce the acres on which they normally cultivated "basic" crops, as well as those who agreed to use part of their land for conservation purposes.) He declined to support proposed amendments to the Taft-Hartley Act. And in the aftermath of disclosures that union officials had used union funds to finance gambling ventures and prostitution, and that the president of the teamsters' union had used teamster funds to invest in the stock market, he signed a measure in 1958 requiring unions to account publicly for welfare and pension funds and another in 1959 providing additional safeguards for union funds, guaranteeing union members the right to elect leaders by secret ballot, and strengthening the Taft-Hartley Act's provisions against secondary boycotts and illegal picketing.

In the first months of his presidency, Eisenhower approved the Submerged Lands Act, similar to legislation Truman had vetoed the year before, granting coastal states title to land and resources immediately off their shores. Liberals had long contended that offshore lands belonged to the entire nation—and indeed Eisenhower signed a companion measure proclaiming that the federal government had jurisdiction over the seabed and subsoil of the continental shelf that lay beyond the coastal tidelands. He favored legislation that would exempt from federal regulation natural gas entering interstate pipelines.

Contending that expenditures for expanding the Tennessee Valley Authority (TVA) would require "taxing the whole country to provide cheap power to the Tennessee Valley and allow it to siphon off industry from other areas," Eisenhower rejected appeals for funds with which to enlarge the TVA. Rather than enlarge TVA's facilities to meet the expanding requirements of the Atomic Energy Commission, indeed, the administration negotiated a contract with private utility companies to build a generating plant to provide the city of Memphis with electricity. Relieved of responsibilities at Memphis, the TVA could meet the needs of atomic energy installations in the region. (When Memphis elected to build its own generating plant, the administration canceled the so-called Dixon-Yates contract.)

Turning aside appeals by liberals that the government build a high-level dam at Hell's Canyon, a deep gorge on the Snake River along the Idaho-Oregon boundary, to provide electricity and facilitate irrigation over a wide area, the Eisenhower administration granted a license to the Idaho Power Company to build three low-level dams in the region. Rejecting the argument of liberals that atomic energy should remain a public resource, Eisenhower supported a provision in the Atomic Energy Act of 1954 authorizing the AEC to issue licenses to private power companies to build nuclear reactors for the generation of electricity.

## IKE THE MODERATE

Still, Eisenhower was not uncompromising in his conservatism. He authorized establishment in 1953 of the Department of Health, Education, and Welfare to coordinate and supervise an array of federal programs. He signed legislation that enlarged Social Security benefits and brought an additional 10 million citizens, including farmers, clergymen, and physicians, into the Social Security system. He approved the Housing Act of 1955 that liberalized terms of loans for private housing construction that were insured by the Federal Housing Administration (FHA) and empowered the FHA to insure loans for the renovation of older dwellings. Rejecting appeals by conservatives for tariff protection against imports, Eisenhower gave unflagging support to legislation to extend the reciprocal trade program. He approved an increase in the federal minimum wage standard.

Shortly after Eisenhower entered the White House, a special Commission on Health Needs of the Nation recommended a federal insurance program to help citizens meet medical expenses. When the American Medical Association (AMA) protested that such a program would be a harbinger of socialized medicine in the country, the president proposed a federally financed "reinsurance" fund to encourage private and nonprofit health insurance organizations to offer broader coverage. To no avail: The AMA again raised the fear of socialized medicine, and its arguments found their mark with the conservative coalition on Capitol Hill. In the latter part of the Eisenhower presidency, congressional liberals proposed incorporation of a program of medical insurance for the elderly in the Social Security system. In the face of opposition by the AMA, the "medicare" proposal got nowhere. Still, Eisenhower, conceding that medical expenses were a serious problem for many elderly citizens, endorsed the Kerr-Mills Act of 1960 granting federal funds to states for use in medical assistance programs for elderly citizens who were indigent.

Because of a sharply increased birthrate in recent years, the United States during the time of the Eisenhower presidency faced a shortage of teachers and classrooms, and in the view of many observers only the federal government had the requisite resources to meet the problem. But proposals for federal aid to education stirred sharp opposition. As for Eisenhower, he moved cautiously, but did persuade Congress in 1953 to authorize federal grants to assist in school construction in "impacted areas" where defense industry and military installations had produced an abnormal growth of population.

The thirty-fourth president approved the Refugee Act of 1953 allowing admission into the country of 200,000 political refugees, most of them people fleeing communism and displaced persons. He signed a measure in 1957 authorizing the admission of an additional 60,000 immigrants annually, granting entry to orphans adopted by American citizens, authorizing the admission of 50 diplomats and 1,500 scientists and technicians who might be of help in America's infant ballistic missile program.

Eisenhower in 1954 approved legislation establishing the Air Force Academy, and signed measures in 1958 and 1959, respectively, approving the admission of Alaska and Hawaii as states in the Federal Union. When it became clear that neither private enterprise nor state or local authorities could provide the requisite financing, he approved legislation in 1956 appropriating $760 million for the Upper Colorado River Irrigation and Reclamation Project. He prevailed on Congress in 1954 to authorize joint construction with Canada of a St. Lawrence seaway. (Completed in 1959, the seaway became an important route for non-ocean-going ships, or "lakers," transporting such bulky commodities as grain and iron ore. But in large measure because its narrow locks and in some places shallow water cannot accommodate the huge ocean freighters, or "salties," that have come into service since 1959, it has not come close to fulfilling the expectations of its Canadian and American proponents in 1954.) And at his behest, Congress in 1956 passed the Federal Aid Highway Act authorizing expenditure of more than $27 billion over 16 years for the construction of nearly 42,000 miles of interstate highways. Eisenhower, meanwhile, contributed to the demise of Senator McCarthy, widely admired by Republican conservatives.

## DEMISE OF McCARTHY

The aforementioned majority report of the Tydings subcommittee gave no pause to Joe McCarthy. Nor did it diminish his standing among millions of his compatriots. McCarthy, indeed, was instrumental in bringing about the defeat in the election of 1950 of several Democratic senators, including Millard Tydings. He received an enthusiastic ovation when he appeared at the Republican national convention of 1952. As for Eisenhower, he felt contempt for McCarthy, the more so in light of the senator's vilification of General Marshall in an outrageous statement released in June 1951. And during a campaign trip by rail across Wisconsin in 1952, he planned, while McCarthy stood at his side, to make a statement praising Marshall. Aides unfortunately persuaded him to delete the statement from his remarks.

Reelected in 1952, McCarthy became chairman of the subcommittee of the Senate's Committee on Government Operations in the Eighty-second Congress. An early object of the subcommittee's endeavors was the Voice of America (VOA), an overseas information and propaganda agency. When McCarthy announced that VOA libraries contained subversive literature, Eisenhower expressed contempt for "book burners." Still, the president proceeded cautiously. In his words, he did not wish "to get in the gutter with that guy." He concluded, moreover, that in time McCarthy would bring about his own demise.

McCarthy doubtless thought otherwise, and when Eisenhower appointed the career diplomat Charles E. Bohlen to be America's ambassador to the Soviet Union, McCarthy denounced Bohlen as a security risk. He next generated headlines when he accused the Army of laxity in the matter of keeping itself free of subversives. The basis for the charge? A dentist named Irving Peress, stationed at Fort Monmouth, New Jersey, had been promoted from captain to major. According to McCarthy, Peress was a security risk. Responsible for the promotion of Peress was Brig. Ralph Zwicker, the commander at Fort Monmouth, a hero of World War II. During an interrogation of Zwicker, McCarthy declared, "You are a disgrace to the uniform. You are shielding communist conspirators. You're ignorant."

The Eisenhower administration at that point determined to stand up to McCarthy. Its tactic was to draw attention to two members of McCarthy's staff, Roy Cohn and G. David Schine. As chief counsel of McCarthy's subcommittee, according to the secretary of the Army, Cohn had demanded preferen-

May 3, 1954: Senator McCarthy and Committee Counsel Roy Cohn during the Army-McCarthy hearings.

tial treatment for Schine after Schine was drafted into the military service. McCarthy retorted that the secretary was employing smear tactics.

The outcome, in spring of 1954, was the "Army–McCarthy hearings." The testimony and evidence offered during the hearings provided scant illumination of the points at issue. But large numbers of Americans, following the proceedings via television, were appalled by McCarthy's crude and seemingly irresponsible behavior. Next, several months later, a special Senate committee recommended that McCarthy be censured for conduct that tended to bring the Senate into disrepute. By a vote of 67–22, in December 1954, the Senate censured McCarthy. Eisenhower publicly commended the Senate for its action. The result was a dramatic erosion of McCarthy's popular support. (Less than three years later, the senator died, apparently of hepatitic infection aggravated by alcoholism. He was 47 years old.)

Americans nonetheless continued to worry about communist subversion. Because in former years he had associated with communists and fellow travelers, and was thus considered a security risk, the AEC in 1954 lifted the security clearance of J. Robert Oppenheimer, the nuclear physicist who had presided over development of the atomic bomb. In the following year, 1955, Congress passed the Communist Control Act depriving the Communist Party U.S.A. of rights, privileges, and immunities normally extended to legal bodies. Meanwhile, the Eisenhower administration took a tolerant view of the techniques employed by the Federal Bureau of Investigation (FBI), headed by J. Edgar Hoover, in its search for communist subversives: illegal wiretaps, mail-openings, break-ins. And in 1958, Robert H. W. Welch, Jr., a wealthy candy maker from New England, founded the John Birch Society, named for an American intelligence officer who was killed in China near the end of World War II and who was, according to Welch, the first casualty of the Cold War. Vehemently anticommunist (and ultraconservative), the society eventually claimed 100,000 members. It opened hundreds of bookstores that disseminated literature propounding its views, scrutinized school curricula and textbooks for evidence that they promoted communism, assailed political and judicial personages whom it considered supportive of communist ideology. (At one point, Welch described President Eisenhower as a "dedicated, conscious agent of the communist conspiracy.")

## COPING WITH THE KREMLIN

Historians have observed that, however divided on questions of home affairs, the people of the United States during the first two decades after World War II arrived at something approximating a consensus regarding the foreign affairs of their superpowerful republic. The accuracy of that observation is beyond dispute. A preponderance of Americans in the years 1945–1964 clearly agreed that the great overbearing reality in the realm of foreign affairs was the Cold War and that the United States must meet the challenge to its security and interests, not to mention its professed values, presented by what nearly every American believed without reservation was an aggressive and treacherous Soviet empire. Still, Americans were not always in total agreement during those years on the question of how the United States ought to go about the task of meeting the Soviet challenge. And on occasion they gave vigorous expression to their disagreement. Most notably perhaps, Republican orators during the electoral campaign of 1952 assailed the policy, inaugurated during the Truman presidency, of striving to contain the power and influence of the Soviet empire within its existing boundaries, and denounced containment as a negative approach to the Soviet menace. Republican orators intimated, moreover, that containment was downright immoral, inasmuch as it appeared to recognize the legitimacy, or at least the permanency, of the recent conquest of Eastern Europe and China by communists. Hence the United States should not be content with merely containing Soviet power and influence. Rather, it should adopt policies calculated to roll back the Iron Curtain and liberate the "captive peoples" of Eastern Europe (also policies aimed at lifting the burden of communism from the long-suffering people of China).

Shortly after Eisenhower took the presidential oath, in early 1953, the new secretary of state, John Foster Dulles, a self-assured and unctuous man, announced that the new administration would take an aggressive stance vis-à-vis communists. He assured the captive peoples of Eastern Europe, "You can count on us." The policy of liberating captive peoples, alas, proved nothing more than a pious hope. When anti-Soviet riots shattered the calm of East Germany in June 1953, Eisenhower announced that the Washington government would not intervene. When Hungary's "Freedom Fighters" rose up against Sovietism in the autumn of 1956, they received no assistance from the United States.

The government in Washington, meanwhile, sought to take the measure of the new leadership in the Kremlin, which comprised, in the first year or so after Stalin's death, a five-member presidium of the Council of Ministers headed by Georgi M. Malenkov. The first signs were hopeful, for the new Soviet leaders seemed to take a conciliatory stand toward the West. Still, leaders in Washington elected to hedge their bets. They continued to build up the country's nuclear striking force, the more so after Malenkov announced in August 1953 that Soviet scientists had exploded a hydrogen bomb. They sanctioned a new series of tests of American H-bombs, conducted near Bikini Island in March and April of 1954. They determined to strengthen the defense of Western Europe, and to that end, in 1953, reached an agreement with the dictator Franco authorizing American air bases in Spain. Libya sanctioned a U.S. air base near Tripoli in 1954. More important, the Washington government, brushing aside misgivings harbored by the French, engineered entry in NATO in 1955 of the fledgling West German republic. For their part, Soviet leaders continued to exhibit a spirit of restraint and conciliation. Of special note, they agreed in 1955 to a treaty reestablishing Austria, jointly occupied since World War II by Britain, the Soviet Union, and the United States, as an independent state, and committing the Vienna government to a policy of neutrality vis-à-vis the Soviet empire and the West.

In that period of apparent thaw in the Cold War, Eisenhower thought the time opportune to make an overture aimed at curtailing the accumulation by the superpowers of ever-larger stocks of nuclear weapons. He understood, of course, that initiatives by the Truman administration to achieve nuclear disarmament had floundered on the issue of on-site inspection. The Washington government simply insisted that any arms control agreement must include provisions allowing ongoing inspection of the nuclear facilities and military installations of the signatories; the Soviets had categorically refused to consider such provisions. Eisenhower thus determined to offer a proposal that would sidestep the issue of on-site inspection. Specifically, in an address at the UN in December 1953, he proposed that the power of the atom be harnessed "to serve the peaceful uses of mankind." What he had in mind was that the nuclear powers would turn over atomic materials to a new UN agency that would oversee their use in peaceful enterprises across the world. The diversion of nuclear materials from the production of bombs, the president calculated, would bring a deceleration of the "arms race," while cooperation in ventures to turn the power of the atom to enterprises of peace might produce a climate of trust among the nuclear powers that would make possible an agreement to eliminate the doomsday weapons.

Although the Soviets betrayed scant interest in "atoms for peace," President Eisenhower in early 1955 became the object of appeals from around the world that he participate in a new summit conference involving leaders of the other Western powers and those of the Soviet Union for the purpose of reducing global tensions. As one who had minimal faith in summitry, Ike responded coolly, but then decided that if a summit meeting offered any chance, however remote, of promoting peace, such a meeting must take place. Plans jelled quickly when he disclosed his willingness to participate in a summit meeting, and in July 1955 he repaired to Geneva for a new exercise in summitry with Prime Minister Anthony Eden of Great Britain, Premier Edgar Faure of France, and the new chieftains of the Soviet Union, Nikolai Bulganin and Nikita Khrushchev.

An atmosphere of friendliness prevailed during the five-day conference, and the conferees frequently smiled and shook hands as movie cameras whirred and flashbulbs popped. Rather quickly, though, it became clear that the issues separating the Western powers and the Soviet Union would not yield to good fellowship and informal conversation. Then, as the meeting was about to close, Eisenhower startled the other conferees and sent a wave of excitement across the world when he made a dramatic proposal for "open skies." Should they accept the proposal, the major powers would supply each other with complete blueprints of military establishments and allow unlimited inspection of their territories by unarmed aircraft. According to the president's logic, no signatory of an open skies agreement would be able to assemble forces for a surprise attack if its territory was subjected to continuing aerial surveillance. At length, in 1957, the Soviets disclosed that they would have nothing to do with open skies.

Despite the fact that it resulted in no agreements of substance, the summit conference of 1955 generated much comment about an impulse to conciliation and accommodation that presumably had come to animate the adversaries in the Cold War—a "spirit of Geneva." That a new spirit was animating leaders in the Kremlin seemed manifest in the spring of 1956 when news filtered out of the Soviet Union of a remarkable speech the previous February by Nikita Khrushchev, who had emerged as the dominant member of the Soviet hierarchy. Addressing a secret congress of the Communist party, Khrushchev assailed the brutality and alleged blunders of the late dictator Stalin. And while insisting that communism would eventually triumph over capitalism, he declared that the Soviet Union sought to cooperate with the United States in the interest of peace. Khrushchev had officially thrown the principles of Stalinism to the scrap heap of history, or so it seemed.

But then, in October and November 1956, Hungarian workers, students, and intellectuals rose up in violent protest against the oppressive policies of the communist regime in Budapest. When it became clear that the insurgents were bent on ridding their country of communism, not just oppressive policies, leaders in Moscow ordered armored columns of the Red Army to the Hungarian capital, put down the Freedom Fighters in a sea of blood, and returned Hungary to the status of a docile satellite of the Soviet Union. Next, in late 1958, the Soviets provoked a new crisis in Berlin.

The latest chapter in the seemingly interminable controversy over Berlin began when Khrushchev demanded that West Berlin be handed over to the German Democratic Republic (East Germany), a satellite of the Soviet Union, or turned into an international free city. Unless the West accepted one of the alternatives by May 1959, he would at that time turn over control of the access routes linking West Germany with West Berlin to the government of East Germany, one that was scorned by the Western powers.

September 15, 1959: President Eisenhower and Premier Khrushchev during ceremony at Andrews Air Force Base on the Soviet chieftain's arrival in United States for state visit.

Declining to flinch in the face of Khrushchev's bluster, President Eisenhower stated that the United States would be party to no agreement that would hand over West Berlin to what he described as hostile domination. Might his stance result in an armed clash and perhaps a nuclear nightmare? Eisenhower did not think it would. As he later wrote in his memoirs, "Foster Dulles and I put less credibility in Khrushchev's threat to move in the following May than he possibly expected." At length, the day of the deadline, May 27, 1959, arrived. Khrushchev did nothing. Or as Eisenhower later recalled in his memoirs: "The day came and went—a day lost in history." At that point, relations between the Kremlin and the West underwent one of their intermittent thaws, and in the summer of 1959 President Eisenhower invited Khrushchev to travel to the United States, tour the country, and meet informally with him to talk over Soviet-American problems. Khrushchev accepted the invitation.

Khrushchev arrived in the United States in September 1959, was greeted at Andrews Air Force Base by the president, given a sightseeing tour of Washington by helicopter. He was the guest of honor at a state dinner in the White House. Next, he went on a ten-day tour of the United States. He visited the grave of former-President Roosevelt at Hyde Park, tramped through fields of hybrid corn in Iowa, visited a plant that produced intercontinental ballistic missiles, inspected a steel mill in Pittsburgh. Typically, Khrushchev, a rotund man, abounded with energy and usually exuded good humor. As for the people of America who turned out to see the Soviet chieftain, most were courteous if restrained. Climaxing the visit was a two-day meeting between Khrushchev and Eisenhower at the latter's hideaway, Camp David, Maryland. The two leaders talked amicably, agreed that policies of peaceful coexistence were mandatory, and intimated that it might be a good idea if leaders of the major powers held another summit conference. Finally, the Soviet leader reiterated an invitation made earlier to Eisenhower to visit the Soviet Union during the coming year.

The Khrushchev visit apparently had been a huge success. People across the world began to ponder the "spirit of Camp David," which like the spirit of Geneva a few years before presumably signaled a relaxation of East-West tensions and perhaps an end to the Cold War.

## CHINA

During the political campaign of 1952, Republican orators castigated the Democratic administration for having "leashed" Generalissimo Chiang Kai-shek since the onset of the Korean War by deploying the Seventh Fleet in the Formosa Strait. Those orators pledged that if Republicans regained the White House they would unleash Chiang, who, it was intimated, would then return to the mainland, rally the Chinese people to his Nationalist standard, and sweep Mao Zedong and the communists from power. People who seriously believed that Chiang had the wherewithal to execute such a counter-revolution might well have been suspected of believing in the tooth fairy.

Professing to believe that the people of China would fall in behind Chiang if he could get back to the mainland, many Americans were pleased when President Eisenhower in early 1953 removed the Seventh Fleet from the Formosa Strait, that is, unleashed Chiang Kai-shek. The unleashed generalissimo, of course, made no move to return to the mainland. Still, the Eisenhower administration, persuaded that the United States must sustain Chiang and turn Formosa into a bastion of containment in the Far East, negotiated a mutual security treaty with the Nationalist government in Taipei in 1954. By the treaty, the United States promised to resist any attack on Formosa or the Pescadores; Chiang authorized American bases in his territory and promised that he would undertake no military operations against mainland China without the consent of the United States.

Then, in 1955, the communists began to threaten an invasion of two Nationalist-held rocks that jutted out of the Formosa Strait: Quemoy and Matsu, the only conceivable value of which was psychological. Incredibly, or so it seems in retrospect, President Eisenhower warned that the United States was prepared to resist a communist move against the tiny islands, neither of which was covered by the treaty of 1954. To reinforce the presidential warning, Congress approved the Formosa Resolution sanctioning the deployment of American forces to prevent Quemoy and Matsu from falling to the communists. Fortunately, the communists undertook no invasion of the Nationalist outposts, and Secretary Dulles probably exaggerated when he later wrote that the United States and China had stood on "the brink of war" in 1955. But three years later, in 1958, a communist invasion of Quemoy and Matsu again appeared imminent, whereupon Eisenhower, in accord with the Formosa Resolution, ordered American warships to deploy around the two islets. Fortunately, no communist shells fell on American ships, and leaders in Beijing elected not to risk a confrontation with the North American superpower by executing its latest invasion threat.

The Eisenhower administration, meanwhile, stayed firm in the policy of refusing to recognize the legitimacy of the government in Beijing. By ostracizing the Beijing regime, the United States hoped to weaken it and perhaps contribute to its demise. Another consideration was the political climate in the United States. Any move to recognize the legitimacy of the communist government of China, establish normal diplomatic relations with it, and tolerate its entry in the UN was certain to stir the passions of many Americans who admired Chiang as a genuine Chinese hero and despised Mao as a personification of evil.

## VIETNAM

Another area of the Far East that commanded the attention of the Washington government during the 1950s was Southeast Asia, a vast area of more than 200 million people that was rich in rubber, tin, manganese, rice, and oil. It was an area which, when the Japanese set about to take it over in 1940–1941, had prompted a response in Washington that in turn resulted in Japan's decision to attack Pearl Harbor and the Philippines. Communists were active in the area at the dawn of the 1950s, particularly in Malaya and Vietnam. In Malaya, a British colony, it appeared that the British would be able to take the measure of the communists. But in Vietnam, a part of the French colony of Indochina, the French seemed to be losing their struggle to put down insurgents led by the communist Ho Chi Minh.

On the outbreak of hostilities between the French and the forces of Ho in late 1946, Americans tended to be indifferent. But when the United States became caught up in the Cold War, which Americans perceived as a struggle to the death between "the free world" and international communism, Americans concluded that the French were fighting the good fight against the international communist conspiracy. Mao Zedong's triumph in China sharpened America's interest in Vietnam, and Secretary of State Acheson announced in the spring of 1950 that the United States would provide economic and military assistance to the French and their anticommunist Vietnamese allies in the war against Ho's Vietminh. North Korea's invasion of South Korea took place a few weeks later, and the outcome was increased determination by the Washington government to assist the French in Indochina. The United States by 1953 was shouldering more than a third of the expense of the French campaign.

Then, in the spring of 1954, the Vietminh trapped several thousand French soldiers at the hamlet of Dien Bien Phu in northwestern Vietnam. Dien Bien Phu had no large strategic importance, and the French troops who were deployed in its environs comprised only a fraction of the French forces in Vietnam. But it soon became apparent that if Dien Bien Phu fell to the Vietminh the morale of the French—back home in France—would crack, and the government in Paris would feel compelled to accept a settlement of the war on terms favorable to the Vietminh.

As Ho's forces continued to besiege the French garrison at Dien Bien Phu, in April 1954, President Eisenhower expounded a "domino theory": If the communists knocked over Vietnam, the other colonies and countries of the area—Laos, Cambodia, Thailand, Malaya, Indonesia, the Philippines—would likely fall, one by one, under communist domination. Gaining control of Southeast Asia's human and material resources would, of course, immeasurably strengthen the international communist conspiracy. From the foregoing assumption derived an inevitable question: Should the United States, as it had in Korea, send armed forces to save Vietnam and, ultimately, Southeast Asia from the grasp of communism? Eisenhower weighed that question—and seriously considered ordering strikes by American bombing planes to help the French garrison at Dien Bien Phu break the communist encirclement. At length, he decided to do nothing, and on May 7, 1954, the 12,000-man French garrison at Dien Bien Phu stacked arms and surrendered.

Even before the fall of Dien Bien Phu, representatives of several countries, including France, Great Britain, the People's Republic of China, the Soviet

Union, and the United States, had assembled in Geneva to consider problems relating to the Far East. To the dismay of the Vietminh, a resultant agreement in June 1954 provided that hostilities would cease across Indochina and that forces of the Vietminh would evacuate Cambodia and Laos. The government of Ho Chi Minh's Democratic Republic of Vietnam would administer Vietnam to the north of the seventeenth parallel. That of the National State of Vietnam, sanctioned by the French in 1949 and headed by the onetime emperor of Vietnam (and collaborator with the Japanese) Bao Dai, would administer the part of the country to the south of that line. For three hundred days, there would be freedom of movement for all persons wishing to make their way from one part of the divided country to the other. After two years, in July 1956, representatives of the Democratic Republic of Vietnam and the National State of Vietnam would arrange elections that would result in the establishment of a single government for the entire country.

Only that part of the agreement pertaining to a cease-fire was committed to signed documents; the rest received the oral endorsement of the participants—the United States and the National State of Vietnam excepted. The Washington government pledged only that it would "not use force to disturb the settlement."

However disappointed by the Geneva settlement, the Vietminh were confident that because of Ho's stature as a national hero, and also because of their expertise in the arts of persuasion and intimidation, they would win the elections to be held in 1956 and, accordingly, take control of all of Vietnam. Ho and his comrades were unduly optimistic. The government in Saigon, guided by Bao Dai's premier Ngo Dinh Diem, a bona fide Vietnamese patriot, a Roman Catholic, and an implacable foe of communism, determined to do everything in its power to prevent the communists from gaining control of South Vietnam. Equally important, leaders in Washington had decided that the United States must step up its efforts to contain communism in Southeast Asia.

Despite its reluctance to move to the assistance of the French at Dien Bien Phu, the Eisenhower administration continued to adhere to the domino theory, and also to view Southeast Asia as an area of critical importance in Cold War calculations. Accordingly, it prevailed on Australia, Britain, France, New Zealand, the Philippines, Pakistan, and Thailand to join with the United States in the Southeast Asia Treaty Organization (SEATO). In the event of an attack on any of the SEATO partners—or an attack on Cambodia, Laos, or South Vietnam—the attack was to be considered a threat to the security of all, whereupon each partner would act to meet the common danger in accord with its constitutional processes. In the event of aggression by subversion, the partners would agree on common measures to meet the problem. Viewed in some quarters as a Southeast Asian counterpart of NATO, SEATO never became an effective instrument for containing communist influence and power in Southeast Asia.

Meanwhile, the government in Saigon was establishing its authority across most of Vietnam below the seventeenth parallel. Then, in 1955, Diem overwhelmed Bao Dai in an election to determine which of the two would be South Vietnam's head of state. Whereupon he proclaimed South Vietnam a republic and himself its first president. The following year, 1956, Diem, encouraged by the United States, made it clear that he would permit no elections in South Vietnam in accord with the Geneva agreement of 1954, then set about to strengthen his authority and broaden his popular support. Assisted by the United States, he reformed and reequipped the South Vietnamese army and enhanced the effectiveness of the national police. Economic and technical problems proved more nettlesome, but with American help the Saigon government made headway in those areas as well.

During those same years, Ho Chi Minh and his comrades in Hanoi set about to consolidate authority in North Vietnam, and to that purpose employed conventional communist tactics of terror, forced confessions, and midnight arrests. Some observers have estimated that during the 1950s Ho's execution squads liquidated upward of 100,000 "feudalists" and "reactionaries." At the same time, virtually every citizen above the age of six was compelled to enroll in a communist cell that conducted indoctrination sessions and urged members to report acquaintances and friends—even parents—who might be guilty of reactionary thought or behavior. The press and schools came under rigid government control, and intellectuals who deigned to criticize the regime were forced to make public apologies and in many instances sent off to forced labor camps.

Persuaded that they had been cheated of the rightful fruits of their victory over the French when national elections failed to take place, the communists nonetheless felt confident that Diem's regime would fall of its own ineptitude and they would then pick up the pieces. It appeared by 1958, however, that Diem, in part because of modest attempts to bring about social and economic reform, was continuing to gain popular support across South Vietnam, and the oft-predicted collapse of his government was not imminent. Whereupon the communists switched tactics: Instead of standing by and waiting for Diem's government to topple, they determined to give it a vigorous shove. Thus they launched a guerrilla campaign aimed at undermining Diem's authority, a mark of which was terrorist attacks against supporters of the Saigon government, particularly village chieftains. They also set about to wreck Diem's modest program of land reform. Finally, in 1958, they organized the National Liberation Front (or Vietcong) to oversee the campaign of disruption in South Vietnam.

Diem, unfortunately, did not respond to the communist campaign by accelerating his program of domestic reform and enlarging the base of his regime. On the contrary, he permitted the reform program to lapse, resorted increasingly to tactics of repression, and allowed his regime to remain a narrow oligarchy presided over by his relatives and cronies, a preoccupation of whom appeared to be personal enrichment at the expense of the long-suffering South Vietnamese citizenry. Such a response was an ill omen for both Diem and the fledgling republic of South Vietnam.

## ELECTION OF 1956

Two months after the summit conference at Geneva, on September 24, 1955, while on vacation in Colorado, President Eisenhower suffered a heart attack, and for seven weeks was a patient in an Army hospital near Denver. Would the heart attack prevent the president from seeking another term in the White House? Fortunately, Ike's convalescence proceeded without incident, and in mid-February 1956 he announced that he would accept re-election. But then, on June 8, 1956, he suffered an attack of ileitis, an inflammation of the lower portion of the small intestine. An emergency operation corrected the problem, and the president, looking old and wan, apparently gave no thought to withdrawing from the electoral contest.

Several weeks later, in mid-August 1956, Democratic delegates gathered at their national convention in Chicago and nominated Adlai Stevenson for president. Stevenson then left it entirely to the delegates to nominate his vice presidential running mate, and in a spirited afternoon the delegates accorded the nomination to Sen. Estes Kefauver of Tennessee. But the man who made the largest impression on delegates, and also a national television audience, was the youthful senator from Massachusetts, John F. Kennedy, who exuded charm and good humor after losing the vice presidential nomination to Kefauver by an eyelash. Convening in San Francisco the following week, Republican delegates renominated Eisenhower and Nixon.

That the Eisenhower-Nixon ticket would emerge triumphant on election day was apparent from the outset of the campaign, and when they marked ballots in early November, voters gave Eisenhower and Nixon 35 million votes, Stevenson and Kefauver 26 million. The margin in the Electoral College was 457–74. Although Democrats would retain majorities in both houses of the new Congress, it was clear that the conservative coalition of southern Democrats and Republicans would continue to hold the balance of power on Capitol Hill.

## "MY FEET HURT"

A few weeks before President Eisenhower suffered his heart attack, in August 1955, a youth who was fishing in the Tallahatchie River in Mississippi observed two feet protruding above the water. The feet belonged to a body that was anchored to an 80-pound cotton-gin fan. The body had been hideously battered, and all that one could say for certain was that it was human and male. But on a finger was a ring that belonged to Emmett "Bobo" Till, a 14-year-old black youth who recently had traveled south from his home in Chicago to visit relatives in the lush delta area of southern Mississippi. What happened to Emmett Till, a brash and swaggering youth, is no great mystery. To impress youthful relatives and friends, he asked a white woman, who with her husband operated a rural store, for a date, and while his startled companions were hustling him away from the store, he executed what was later described as a wolf whistle. On learning of the incident, the woman's husband and his half brother abducted Till, beat him, and the half brother shot him to death. A short time later, authorities in Tallahatchie County arrested the two men, a grand jury indicted them for murder, and at length a trial got under way in the town of Sumner. What transpired was a farce. As William Bradford Huie, a white native of Alabama, later wrote in his book *Wolf Whistle* (1959), nobody doubted the guilt of the defendants, but there was never the slightest doubt that the all-male, all-white jury would set them free. And so it came to pass.

The brutal murder of Emmett Till and acquittal of his killers caused large numbers of Americans, white as well as black, to wonder anew whether the United States, the self-proclaimed citadel of "freedom and justice for all," would ever be free of the awful burden it continued to bear as a result of more than three centuries of gross and unrelenting abuse of Americans of African descent. But on the afternoon of December 1, 1955, some three months after the lynching of "Bobo" Till, an incident in Montgomery, Alabama, touched off events that prompted many whites and blacks to conclude that headway was indeed possible in the crusade to lift the foregoing burden.

The first day of December of 1955 was a warm one in the Alabama capital, and when Rosa Parks, a petite and soft-spoken woman of dark skin who was employed in a downtown department store, boarded the Cleveland Avenue bus she was tired and her feet ached. As prescribed by law, she moved to the rear of the bus, normally reserved for black passengers, and sat down. But the bus was crowded, and several white passengers, unable to find seats in the front, or white section, of the segregated conveyance, were standing in the aisle. Noting the plight of the white passengers, the driver of the bus made his way to the rear of the vehicle and ordered Parks and three other blacks to surrender their seats. When Parks refused to move, the driver summoned police. There was no commotion, no black passengers spoke out in support of Parks, and when the police arrived she went away peaceably. Driven to a police station, she was charged with having disturbed the peace.

Rosa Parks had not intended a display of defiance when she boarded the Cleveland Avenue bus. She later explained that she decided on impulse to keep her seat for the simple reason that "my feet hurt." Whatever her intention, word of the incident spread quickly among the black citizenry of Montgomery, and by nightfall blacks were astir. How might blacks show their indignation? A group of leaders that included the Rev. Martin Luther King, Jr., decided that they ought to observe a one-day boycott of city buses. On the day of the boycott, December 5, nearly 100 percent of the city's blacks declined to ride the buses. Elated, black leaders determined that the boycott should continue indefinitely. They also organized the Montgomery Improvement Association (MIA) to direct the boycott and elected King the association's president. That evening, at a rally at the Holt Street Baptist Church, King, urging his auditors to love their enemies, insisted that Montgomery's blacks must protest nonviolently.

Meetings between city officials and black leaders coming to nothing, the boycott continued for month after month, and to provide transportation for

February 1956: Deputy sheriff fingerprinting Rosa Parks at the time of the
Montgomery bus boycott.

black citizens the MIA organized a huge carpool. Funds for the purchase of
new station wagons for the carpool arrived from the national headquarters of
the National Association for the Advancement of Colored People (NAACP)
and the United Automobile Workers. A rally at Madison Square Garden in
New York attended by Eleanor Roosevelt, Sammy Davis, Jr., and other celebri-
ties, including Rosa Parks and King, brought in additional funds. Ordinary people from as far away as Britain and India sent donations. Still, white segregationists in Montgomery seemed no less determined than blacks to stand their
ground. To counter the boycott, white authorities arrested King and other
black leaders, and charged them with violating Alabama's antiboycott statute.
King and the others were found guilty and fined. An unidentified person hurled
a bomb on the front porch of King's house. (King arrived shortly after the explosion and appealed to angry blacks to keep their tempers in check: "We must
love our white brothers no matter what they do to us.") White businesspeople
fired black employees, and white families discharged black domestic servants
who supported the boycott.

It appeared in the autumn of 1956, indeed, that the boycott was about to collapse when city authorities undertook to enjoin the carpool as a public nuisance and an unlicensed enterprise. But then the Supreme Court in Washington issued its ruling in the matter of a suit challenging the constitutionality of state and local laws in Alabama requiring the segregation of passengers on buses. The high court upheld a decision by a special U.S. District Court that the laws were unconstitutional. On receiving a proper order, authorities of Montgomery on December 21, 1956, ordered desegregation of the city's buses. The boycott was thereupon terminated. It had lasted for 382 days.

In the following month, January 1957, black leaders of ten southern states convened in Atlanta and organized the Southern Christian Leadership Conference (SCLC) to press the campaign for civil equality for black Americans. They agreed that the SCLC would employ methods similar to those used in the Montgomery bus boycott, and they chose Martin Luther King, Jr., to lead the new organization.

## KING

Born in Atlanta on January 15, 1929, Martin Luther King, Jr., experienced a comfortable and happy childhood. He was a good student, attended Morehouse College, and in 1948 received a bachelor of divinity degree from Crozer Theological Seminary in Pennsylvania. While at Crozer, he became immersed in the ideas of Mohandas K. Gandhi, the late leader of India's independence movement who had urged his followers to embrace tactics of nonviolence, civil disobedience, and passive resistance. Shortly after undertaking graduate studies at Boston University that would result in a Ph.D., King married Coretta Scott, and in 1954 accepted appointment as pastor of the Dexter Avenue Baptist Church in Montgomery, Alabama. On assuming his pastorate, he organized a social and political action committee to help parishioners meet problems deriving from racial discrimination. He also encouraged them to try to become registered voters and take part in the activities of the NAACP. Then, as noted, King achieved international celebrity as a consequence of his leadership of the Montgomery bus boycott. In the years that followed, he made hundreds of speeches. He attended the independence celebration of the new African republic of Ghana in 1957. His first book, *Stride Toward Freedom*, appeared in 1958. He realized a dream of several years when he visited India, the homeland of Gandhi. Meanwhile, King observed that the Nation of Islam—or Muslim sect—was enlarging its membership and influence. The Black Muslims disturbed King.

A mysterious black man known as Wali D. Fard, who taught that God or Allah was black and that whites were devils, established the first temple or mosque of the Black Muslims in Detroit in 1931. Scorning Christianity as a religion of white oppressors, Fard and his followers rested their faith on their own interpretation of the teachings of the Prophet Muhammad. When Fard disappeared in 1934, the Muslims passed under the leadership of Elijah Muhammad (he had replaced his "slave name" of Poole with the proper Muslim name of Muhammad). Under the title of Messenger of Allah, Elijah Muhammad insisted that members of the Nation of Islam live in accord with a puritanical code of personal morality and a rigid work ethic. He taught that in a future Battle of Armageddon the white race would be destroyed and the black left to reign over the world in peace and harmony. In the meantime, Black Muslims were to immerse themselves in study, and reinforce and protect one another. They were to carry no weapons and resort to violence only if attacked. If Elijah Muhammad's message resulted in few conversions to the Nation of Islam in the 1930s and early 1940s, it found a response among increasing numbers of frustrated and angry blacks in the years after World War II, and by the 1950s perhaps a hundred thousand blacks were enrolled in Black Muslim congregations that had appeared in most of the country's principal cities. Contemptuous of the movement to achieve racial integration in America, Black Muslims demanded that the federal government organize a separate state in which black people could live in isolation from the country's white-dominated society.

Rejecting Muslim arguments in support of black separatism, Martin Luther King determined to accelerate the nonviolent crusade aimed at moving blacks into the mainstream of American life. To that purpose, he decided that he must move to Atlanta, location of the headquarters of the SCLC. And so in 1960 he returned to the city of his birth, where he assumed closer direction of the SCLC, and also became copastor with his father of the Ebenezer Baptist Church.

Notwithstanding his emergence over the past half-decade as the country's most influential spokesperson of the aspirations of black citizens, King was not without weaknesses and shortcomings. By his own admission, he ate too much. Evidence accumulated in later years indicated that he had a fondness for intimate relations with women other than his wife. He was a haphazard administrator. And it has been argued that he was not a bona fide intellectual. As the disappointing outcome of his attempt in 1961 to advance the civil liberties of black people in Albany, Georgia, would demonstrate, his judgment was not flawless. Still, he was a man of transparent insight, sensitivity, and courage. He also had an unprecedented gift for verbalizing the frustrations and weariness of millions of African Americans. In a book entitled *The Negro Revolt*, published in 1962, the black journalist Louis E. Lomax wrote: "King is the foremost interpreter of the Negro's tiredness in terms which the mass Negro can understand and respond to. This is the magic about King's many speaking engagements; in some instinctive way he helps Negroes understand how they themselves feel and why they feel as they do; and he is the first Negro minister I ever heard who can reduce the Negro matter to a spiritual matter and yet inspire the people to seek a solution on this side of the Jordan, not in the life beyond."[1]

---

[1]Louis E. Lomax, *The Negro Revolt*, New York: Harper & Row, Publishers, Inc., 1962, p. 91.

## IKE, THE SUPREME COURT, AND CIVIL RIGHTS

One American who did not hold Martin Luther King, Jr., or his crusade on behalf of equal rights for black citizens in particularly high esteem was Dwight D. Eisenhower, a man who had never felt uncomfortable with the Army's practice of racial segregation and discrimination during his long military career. Still, Eisenhower took a variety of initiatives in the area of civil rights after repeating the presidential oath in early 1953. Those initiatives soon yielded results. Schools on military and naval reservations were desegregated, as were hospitals of the Veterans Administration, and by the end of 1953 the last vestiges of segregation had nearly disappeared in the armed forces. Beginning in 1954, all federal contracts included clauses prohibiting contractors from practicing segregation and discrimination. Ike persuaded owners of movie houses in the District of Columbia to terminate segregationist policies. Hotels and restaurants in the federal city that hitherto had served only whites responded to his gentle appeals and opened their doors to blacks. Emissaries of the administration persuaded the Capitol Transit Company to end discrimination in employment. Then, in 1954, the Supreme Court, now presided over by Chief Justice Earl Warren, whom Eisenhower had appointed to the high bench in 1953, issued its decision in the case of *Brown* v. *Board of Education of Topeka.*

Observing the manifest inferiority of the "colored" schools that black children, particularly in the South, were compelled to attend, critics of segregation had long argued that laws and ordinances requiring segregated public schools violated the equal protection clause of the Fourteenth Amendment to the Constitution. Many decades before, the Supreme Court had decided otherwise. In its decision in the case of *Plessy* v. *Ferguson,* issued in 1896, the high court ruled that state laws requiring segregated public facilities did not contravene the Fourteenth Amendment provided such facilities were of equal quality. The court thus spelled out a doctrine of "separate but equal."

The separate but equal doctrine proved a farce: Schools and other facilities, particularly (but not exclusively) in the South, remained rigidly segregated but blatantly unequal. Recognizing that the American dream of a life of prosperity and dignity would always be beyond the reach of most of their people until they achieved equality of opportunity in education, black leaders in the 1930s and 1940s began to speak out against segregated schools, and in a few states, including Kentucky, Missouri, and Oklahoma, they made headway in cracking barriers that prevented blacks from gaining admission to colleges, universities, and professional schools. But into the 1950s the system of racial segregation remained intact in elementary and secondary schools in many states. The result was a flurry of lawsuits challenging the logic of the *Plessy* decision.

Then, on May 17, 1954, the Supreme Court unanimously ruled in the *Brown* case that laws mandating segregation in public schools violated the federal Constitution. It mattered not that separate schools might be of equal quality, for in the court's opinion, "Separate educational facilities are inherently unequal." Therefore, the justices asserted, "We hold that the plaintiffs . . . are deprived of the equal protection of laws guaranteed by the Fourteenth

Amendment." (The court followed up the *Brown* decision between 1954 and 1956 by voiding segregation in tax-supported graduate schools, colleges, and universities; in public housing projects and public parks; on public playgrounds and golf courses, and on intrastate buses.) In the spring of 1955, the court directed federal district courts to require compliance with its decision in the *Brown* case "with all deliberate speed."

In the states of the onetime Confederacy, where racial segregation was a pillar of "the southern way of life," the response of whites to the *Brown* decision tended to be angry. An editor in Jackson, Mississippi, caught a popular sentiment in the former Confederate states when he denounced the decision as "the worst thing that has happened to the South since the carpetbaggers and scalawags took charge of our civil government [after the Civil War]." Eighty-one members of Congress from the South in 1956 signed "the Southern Manifesto" proclaiming that in the *Brown* ruling the justices of the Supreme court had "substituted their personal political and social ideas for the established law of the land."

White southerners did more than protest. Resurrecting the hoary doctrine of nullification, the legislature of Georgia declared that the *Brown* decision was "null, void and of no effect within the state." The government of Virginia set about to transform the state's public schools into state-supported "private" schools. (Subsequent judgments by the federal courts enjoined Virginia from abolishing its public schools and using public funds to support nonpublic schools.) Meanwhile, the Ku Klux Klan experienced a renaissance, particularly in Alabama, Florida, Georgia, and South Carolina, and the result was a new outbreak of cross burnings and torchlight rallies, bombings and beatings. Usually eschewing violence, newly organized white citizens' councils applied economic pressure in defense of segregation. If a white businessman seemed "soft" on segregation, the local citizens' council might direct whites to boycott his place of business and perhaps persuade the local bank to deny him further credit. If a black man indicated that he planned to enroll his children in the local white school, the council might arrange to have him dismissed from his job. Because of white hostility to the *Brown* decision, only token integration had taken place by 1960 in the public schools of Arkansas, Florida, Louisiana, North Carolina, Tennessee, Texas, and Virginia, and none at all in those of Alabama, Georgia, Mississippi, and South Carolina.

As for President Eisenhower, he thought poorly of the *Brown* decision—he told presidential assistant Arthur Larson, "I personally think the decision was wrong."[2] Another member of his administration, Emmet John Hughes, recalled him as having said, "I am convinced that the Supreme Court decision *set back* progress in the South *at least fifteen years*. . . . It's all very well to talk about school integration—if you remember you may be also talking about social *disintegration*. Feelings are deep on this, especially where children are involved. . . . We can't demand *perfection* in these moral questions. All we can

[2]Arthur Larson, *Eisenhower: The President Nobody Knew* (New York: Charles Scribner's Sons, 1968), p. 124.

do is keep working toward a goal and keep it high. And the fellow who tries to tell me that you can do these things by *force* is just plain nuts."[3] Whatever his private thoughts about the *Brown* decision, Eisenhower responded forcefully when the issue of school integration touched off a civil crisis in Little Rock, Arkansas, in 1957.

The Little Rock affair began to unfold in September 1957 when nine young blacks, in accord with a plan prepared by the local school board and endorsed by a federal district judge, prepared to enroll in Little Rock's Central High School. Segregationists were incensed, and Gov. Orval Faubus ordered troops of the Arkansas National Guard to deploy around the school building—not to protect the black students but to prevent them from entering. When the federal district judge who had endorsed the integration plan gave Faubus ten days to explain why he was acting in defiance of the decree ordering the integration of Central High School, the governor flew off to confer with President Eisenhower, who was vacationing at Newport, Rhode Island. Following the meeting with the president, Faubus agreed to withdraw the national guardsmen. Whereupon, on September 23, the nine black students were secretly ushered into the school, a happening that touched off the mob violence predicted by Faubus—and which, in the view of integrationists, was largely a result of the governor's inflammatory statements.

His patience exhausted, Eisenhower in a radio and TV address denounced "the disgraceful occurrence" in Little Rock, then issued a proclamation directing all persons "to cease and desist therefrom" their opposition to federal court orders and mobs "to disperse forthwith." When hundreds of segregationists, in apparent defiance of the presidential directive, again gathered outside Central High School, Eisenhower dispatched Army paratroops to the scene, and as soldiers patrolled inside and outside the building the nine black students entered the school and attended classes. As for Faubus, he denounced "the military occupation" of Arkansas, and when a segregationist suffered a slight cut as a result of contact with a federal bayonet the governor proclaimed that "cold, naked, unsheathed knives" were spilling the "warm and red blood of patriotic American citizens." At length, the situation calmed, and in December 1957 most of the troops departed the premises of Central High School. Meanwhile, in September 1957, President Eisenhower signed the first civil rights legislation consented to by Congress since 1875.

If not inclined to propose far-ranging measures after the fashion of Harry Truman, Eisenhower was willing to ask Congress to approve measures designed to achieve modest advances in the area of civil rights. The Civil Rights Act of 1957 was such a measure. It provided for a permanent Civil Rights Commission and appointment of an assistant attorney general to supervise the civil rights activities of the Justice Department. Of larger moment, or so it seemed in 1957, it authorized the Justice Department to issue injunctions when it determined that state or local authorities had denied citizens the right to vote.

---

[3]Emmet John Hughes, *The Ordeal of Power: A Political Memoir of the Eisenhower Years* (New York: Atheneum, 1975), p. 201.

The Civil Rights Commission reported in 1959 that the civil rights legislation of 1957 had failed to break down barriers preventing black citizens of the lower South from becoming voters, and observed that only 5 percent of the black citizens of voting age in Mississippi were registered to vote. To meet the problem, the commission urged new legislation that would permit the president to appoint special registrars endowed with the authority to register all qualified blacks as voters. Opposed to direct federal intervention in local electoral affairs, the Eisenhower administration made no response to the commission's recommendation.

Still, the administration concluded that further legislation in the area of voting rights was necessary, and the outcome was the Civil Rights Act of 1960. The new statute provided that *if* the Justice Department won a suit to require local registrars to register blacks as voters, it could then ask a federal court to make an additional finding that blacks had been prevented from voting because of a pattern of discrimination. *If* the court agreed with the Justice Department's contention, it would appoint referees who—*if* they found that voting discrimination persisted—could put qualified black citizens on voting rolls. During debate on the foregoing measure, Senator Sparkman of Alabama boasted that "the effects of the legislation will be negligible." Events proved the senator correct. Into the early 1960s, white southerners, by legal ruses and outright intimidation, continued to prevent large numbers of black citizens from registering and voting.

## ROCKETS AND OUTER SPACE

The quest of black Americans to achieve civil equality was, of course, only one of a long list of questions that commanded the attention of President Eisenhower. Another was defense, and closely related to defense was the exploration of outer space.

A few months after Germany's surrender, in September 1945, the Army brought to the United States 119 German scientists and engineers who, in the latter stages of the global war, had developed the fearsome V-2 rocket. One of the Germans was Wernher von Braun. The Germans were set to work on a guided missile program at Fort Bliss, Texas—a program subsequently moved to the Redstone Arsenal at Huntsville, Alabama. Tests resulting from the enterprise of the Germans and their American colleagues took place at the White Sands Proving Ground in New Mexico, and after the move to Huntsville at Cape Canaveral, Florida. The Air Force, meanwhile, sought to develop a long-range cruise-type missile.

The scientists and engineers who were striving to perfect rocket-powered missiles for the United States toiled with minimal support by the Washington government. Indeed, the federal budget in 1953 provided only a million dollars for missile development. But then, in 1954–1955, intelligence data disclosed that the Soviets, who also had secured the services of German rocket experts at the end of World War II, might soon deploy an operational ballistic missile system. Whereupon Eisenhower ordered the Defense Department to give top priority to America's missile program. Less than three years later, accordingly, in the spring of 1958, Army units in Germany received Redstone missiles that were capable of delivering nuclear warheads on targets up to 100 miles distant. Later that year, the Air Force took delivery of the first Jupiter intermediate-range (1,600 miles) ballistic missiles, 60 of which were deployed in Turkey and Italy.

The Air Force, meanwhile, pressed development of an intercontinental ballistic missile (ICBM), that is, one having a range of 4,000 miles and more, and by 1960 it and its civilian contractors had perfected liquid-propellant Atlas and Titan ICBMs, giant missiles—the Titan 2 reached a height of 103 feet when deployed in an underground silo—that, respectively, could strike targets 9,000 and 7,000 miles distant. The solid-fuel Minuteman, only 56 feet in length but capable of flying 7,000 miles, became operational in 1961. By the end of 1962, the Air Force had deployed 284 ICBMs at bases in Arizona, Arkansas, Kansas, and elsewhere.

Of comparable import was a missile program undertaken by the Navy. As a result of an enterprise directed by Adm. Hyman G. Rickover, the Navy in 1954 launched the first nuclear-powered submarine, the USS *Nautilus*, then set about to perfect a missile that could be launched from under water. The outcome was the Polaris program, and construction of the first Polaris submarines, *George Washington, Ethan Allen*, and *Patrick Henry*, got under way in 1958. Commissioned in 1959, the *George Washington* made the first submerged launch of a Polaris test vehicle in the summer of 1960. By 1966, the Navy was operating 41 Polaris-class submarines whose solid-fuel missiles could reach targets at distances of 1,400 to 2,900 miles.

In those same years, scientists and engineers had begun to ponder the possibility of using military rockets to put artificial satellites in orbit around the earth. They surmised that satellites packed with instruments could yield a bonanza of scientific data. Interest in earth satellites enlarged in the autumn of 1954 when scientists representing 40 nations assembled in Rome to formulate plans for an International Geophysical Year, to be observed in 1957–1958, during which scientists would make the first coordinated study ever of the earth and its atmosphere. To enable scientists to study radiation, the density of the earth's upper atmosphere, the composition of the earth's crust, and the precise shape of the earth, the scientists at Rome urged participating countries to undertake programs to launch earth satellites. The following spring, Radio Moscow reported that Soviet scientists were planning to put satellites in orbit. Two months later, the White House let it be known that President Eisenhower had agreed to support an American satellite project.

After extensive discussion, the Defense Department decided that the Navy's Vanguard rocket would be the launch vehicle for America's first earth satellite, a grapefruit-size sphere weighing less than four pounds. Few people in America foresaw that an important propaganda advantage would accrue to the country that put the first satellite in orbit, hence little sense of urgency animated Project Vanguard. Then, on October 5, 1957, the Soviets, using a giant ICBM, put a satellite weighing an incredible 184 pounds in orbit around the earth. They called the satellite *Sputnik.*

People across the world were thunderstruck by the Soviet achievement, and most Americans, dismissing Eisenhower's assertion that *Sputnik* had not increased his sense of apprehension "one iota," felt chagrin tinctured with dismay. The response of great numbers of Americans, frankly, bordered on the hysterical. Many concluded that the Soviet spectacular in space proved that the United States had fallen behind the Soviet Union in critical areas of science and technology, and if it failed to undertake a crash program to enhance education in those areas would one day find itself at the mercy of the Kremlin. Or as Ike later recalled in his memoirs, "Some alarmed citizens . . . were urging vastly increased spending and wholesale revision of our schools so as to turn nearly every student into a scientist or engineer as quickly as possible."

Responding to popular concern, Eisenhower sent a special message on education to Congress. The outcome, in September 1958, was the National Defense Education Act. The legislation authorized low-interest loans for deserving college and university students; grants to improve instruction in science, mathematics, and modern foreign languages in the public schools; graduate fellowships for prospective college and university teachers; grants to enhance guidance counseling in the public schools; and grants for vocational training programs for students who did not opt for college.

Meanwhile, on November 3, 1957, the Soviets launched *Sputnik II*, a satellite that weighed a mind-boggling 1,100 pounds and carried a dog named Laika. Three weeks later, on November 26, President Eisenhower suffered a mild stroke. Then, on December 6, the Navy set about to launch the first American satellite from Cape Canaveral into orbit around the earth. The outcome was a national humiliation. Belching flame and smoke, the Vanguard rocket rose 4 feet, settled awkwardly back on its launching pad, and exploded in a spectacular fireball. Cynics had a field day at America's expense, rechristening the grounded satellite *Stallnik, Flopnik, Dudnik, Puffnik, Phutnik, Oopsnik, Goofnik, Kaputnik,* and *Sputternik.* Soviet diplomats at the UN suggested that the United States apply for Soviet technical assistance to backward nations.

Fortunately, von Braun, his fellow German émigrés, and their American colleagues had continued work on the Jupiter C rocket, actually a cluster of rockets that Navy technicians had referred to as "cluster's last stand," and in the aftermath of the Vanguard fiasco pressed ahead with plans to use the Jupiter C to put a satellite in orbit. At length, everything was set. And on the evening of January 31, 1958, a Jupiter C rocket, an 18-pound satellite of cylindrical shape mounted at its tip, executed a perfect liftoff at Cape Canaveral. Alas, for more than fifty minutes it was not known whether the satellite, *Explorer I*, had achieved orbit, and von Braun, monitoring events from the Pentagon outside Washington, became increasingly nervous. But then the director of the Army Ballistic Missile Agency at Cape Canaveral, on receiving a message from a tracking station at Earthquake Valley in California, reported, "Earthquake Valley has the bird." Staring at his watch, von Braun observed, "She is eight minutes late. Interesting."

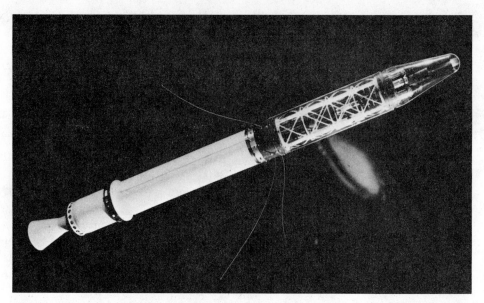

January 31, 1958: A model of Explorer I, the first U.S. satellite to orbit the earth.

The "beep, beep" emitted by a tiny radio transmitter aboard *Explorer I* filled Americans with a sense of satisfaction—and, more importantly perhaps, a sense of relief that the United States had at last placed a satellite, however diminutive in comparsion with vehicles put up by the Soviets, in orbit about the earth.

After a second launching failure, the Navy in March 1958 put a Vanguard satellite in an unusually stable orbit, and the tiny radio aboard the 3.25-pound craft transmitted a treasure trove of scientific information back to earth over the next six years. Then, the following July, Congress passed legislation establishing the National Aeronautical and Space Administration (NASA) to assume responsibility for all of the country's space activities "except those projects primarily associated with military requirements." Even though the giant rockets of the Soviet Union continued to put larger payloads in space—and in September 1959 sent *Lunik II* crashing to the surface of the moon—NASA over the next few years administered a succession of launches of space vehicles. Of particular note were five deep probes into outer space, one of which sent a satellite into orbit around the sun, and the launching in 1962 of *Echo I*, a spherical balloon 100 feet in diameter that bounced radio messages back to earth as it orbited the planet.

Meanwhile, scientists, engineers, and others had begun to speculate about the possibility of putting humans in orbit aboard space vehicles and returning them safely to earth. At length, shortly after its establishment in 1958, NASA inaugurated a man-in-space program designated Project Mercury, and the following year selected seven men from the armed forces to be the country's first astronauts. In 1960, von Braun and the German émigrés and Americans under his direction were transferred from the Army to NASA, and a substantial segment of the Redstone Arsenal became the George C. Marshall Space Flight Center. Von Braun and his colleagues thereupon pressed development of the Saturn family of nonmilitary rockets that would become the country's first genuine engines for exploring outer space.

Few Americans spoke out against the national program of space exploration, frightfully expensive though it was, for most citizens accepted the argument that scientific and intelligence data gathered by satellites and the technological advances the program was yielding—more powerful rockets, sophisticated guidance systems, miniaturized circuitry—were essential if the United States was to maintain its ability to defend itself against the Soviet Union. Still, some Americans contended in the 1950s that the country had become so preoccupied with preparing for a nuclear showdown with its rival superpower that it was tolerating a dangerous deterioration of conventional essentially (non-nuclear) armed forces.

At the time he entered the White House in 1953, President Eisenhower was persuaded that the people of the United States would not tolerate a succession of limited or brushfire wars akin to that presently being fought in Korea. He also was bent on reducing federal spending and bringing the federal budget into balance. Any meaningful reduction of federal spending, of course, would require reduced appropriations for the armed forces. So a central question facing the new administration was the following: How might it maintain a military-naval establishment that could guard the nation and enable the Washington government to protect American interests and honor commitments while consuming less of the federal income? The answer became a policy of "massive retaliation."

In accord with the policy of massive retaliation, the United States would concentrate on building a fearsome arsenal of nuclear warheads. Because nuclear weapons systems, relative to their destructive power, were less expensive to build and maintain than conventional forces, the result would be savings in outlays for defense—"a bigger bang for a buck." The country's nuclear force would be of such dimension that the nuclear force of no aggressor, translated the Soviet Union, would have the capacity to destroy it in a surprise attack. Which meant that in the aftermath of a surprise attack upon its nuclear arsenal, the United States would have the retaliatory capacity to inflict unacceptable damage on the aggressor. According to the calculus that underpinned massive retaliation, therefore, America's fearsome nuclear force would, in fact, deter a nuclear showdown between the superpowers.

As had been assumed from the inception of NATO in 1949, the United States also would unleash its nuclear power in the event of an invasion of the territory of its allies in Europe. But what if the Soviet Union or one of its clients should undertake an invasion of the territory of a non-NATO ally or friend of the United States in the manner of North Korea's strike over the thirty-eighth parallel in 1950? In accord with the policy of massive retaliation, the United States would not respond, as it had in Korea, by dispatching conventional forces to stay the tide of aggression. Rather, it would seriously consider launching its nuclear-laden intercontinental bombing planes (and, later, rocket-powered missiles) against the perpetrators of aggression. The result? Eisenhower and his advisers reckoned that the risk of massive nuclear retaliation would also deter aggressors who might contemplate an attack by conventional forces against some peripheral area of the noncommunist world.

But would a president order nuclear retaliation against an aggressor in a peripheral area of the world? Assorted critics doubted that he would. Only in the unlikely event that the security interests of the United States were directly and immediately threatened, they thought, would a president sanction the use of nuclear weapons. Hence the United States, its conventional forces having been allowed to deteriorate, would be powerless to engage in limited or brushfire wars. Thus there was little to prevent the communists from nibbling away at the noncommunist world at uncounted points across the globe. Whatever its merit, the foregoing argument made no apparent impression on Eisenhower. The president stood by massive retaliation, a policy that resulted in a reduction of spending for defense from $46 billion in 1954 to $40 billion in 1956—and left the country's conventional forces relatively small and weak.

## MIDDLE EAST

While pondering an array of domestic and foreign concerns, President Eisenhower found it necessary to think about the Middle East—especially about its oil, for in the aftermath of the global war, American oil companies had become increasingly active in the Middle East. Because domestic production met a preponderance of America's petroleum requirements at that time, most of the crude extracted in the Middle East by American corporations found its way up through the Red Sea and Suez Canal to Western and Southern Europe. The result was enormous profits for the American companies. But the profits of American companies were not the only concern of officials in Washington by the turn of the 1950s, when they pondered the Middle East's oil. What if the Kremlin should set about to extend its influence in the area? The fall of a substantial part of the region to Soviet domination would be devastating in terms of America's strategic interests, inasmuch as the country's allies in NATO were heavily dependent on Middle Eastern oil. Unfortunately, American policy in the Middle East carried a heavy burden: The populations of all of the region's oil-producing countries save Iran were predominantly Arab, and Arabs everywhere continued to resent the part taken by the United States in the establishment of Israel in what for more than a millennium had been the Arab domain of Palestine. To placate various of the Arab states, the Truman administration arranged secret subsidies.

Then, in 1951, trouble flared in Iran when Prime Minister Mohammed Mossadeq, a frail patriot who had a rare capacity to stir the emotions of ordinary Iranians, ordered the nationalization of the oil fields and refineries of the British-owned Anglo-Iranian Oil Company. Whereupon the British persuaded the international companies that controlled the distribution of petroleum to cut Iran out of the world market. The Iranian economy, as a consequence, was seriously depressed by the time Eisenhower moved into the White House, and when the new American president turned aside an appeal by Mossadeq for economic assistance the Iranian prime minister, in July 1953, dissolved the country's parliament, received a trade mission from the Soviet Union, and accepted support by Iran's communist party.

Suspecting that Iran might be falling under Soviet domination, Eisenhower authorized the CIA to arrange the removal of Mossadeq from power. The CIA thereupon sent Kermit Roosevelt, a grandson of Theodore Roosevelt, to Teheran, where Roosevelt engineered what one CIA operative later described as "a real James Bond operation." After securing the support of leaders of the Iranian army, Roosevelt hired a veritable mob to take to the streets to demonstrate against Mossadeq, and in the resultant disorder an indeterminate number of Iranians lost their lives. But after some anxious moments, during which Shah Mohammad Reza Pahlavi, little more than a figurehead since his accession to the Peacock Throne in 1941, fled the country, the Iranian army imprisoned Mossadeq. The shah then returned to Teheran and established himself as the unchallenged ruler of the country, the United States extended $45 million in economic assistance to his government, and Eisenhower secretly bestowed a National Security Medal on Roosevelt.

In the year following Mossadeq's downfall, 1954, Turkey and Pakistan signed the Baghdad Pact, an alliance whose underlying purpose was to establish a united front vis-à-vis the Soviet Union. The alliance was redesignated the Middle East Treaty Organization (METO) in 1955 when Britain, Iraq, and Iran joined. Although pledging support, the United States declined to join METO lest it offend Egypt, the nation through whose territory passed the Suez Canal, increasingly a focal point of American policy in the Middle East.

In the latter 1940s, Egypt had limped along under the rule of King Farouk, a fat, luxury-loving monarch. Then, in 1952, a clique of army officers that included Lt. Col. Gamal Abdel Nasser overthrew Farouk and sent him packing, to exile in Europe. Two years later, in 1954, Nasser emerged as the president of the military government, and indeed became a veritable dictator. Nasser's goals? In addition to revitalizing Egypt, he wanted to bring unity to the Arab peoples of North Africa and the Middle East to enable them to make a concerted assault on their common problems of poverty and ignorance, and their common enemies, the Israelis. The nerve center of a unified Arab world would be Egypt, its leader Nasser.

The United States initially took a tolerant view of Nasser's rule in Egypt. But then, in 1955, relations between the Washington and Cairo governments began to turn sour. Nasser blamed the United States for a sharp decline in the world price of cotton that struck hard at the Egyptian economy. Next, he forged a deal with the Soviet Union whereby the Soviets agreed to buy Egyptian cotton in exchange for Soviet armaments.

A short time later, Nasser announced plans for a huge dam and hydroelectric power station at Aswan, on the Nile some 800 miles upstream from Cairo.

In addition to providing cheap electricity, such a dam would enable Egypt, by irrigation, to enlarge by 50 percent the square miles of land under cultivation. There was, unfortunately, a problem: money. To meet his financial problems, Nasser turned to the West, and the United States and Britain promptly agreed to lend Egypt a large sum for the Aswan enterprise. But then Nasser encouraged terrorist raids against Israel, urged rebels in Algeria to step up activities against their French overseers, and all the while seemed to be drawing closer to the Soviet Union. The United States and Britain, accordingly, stalled on the pledge of support for the Aswan project, prompting Nasser to advise leaders in Washington that if the Aswan funds were not soon forthcoming Egypt would secure the requisite funding from the Soviet Union. Then, on July 19, 1956, Secretary of State Dulles notified the Egyptians that the United States had changed its mind and would not support the Aswan Dam project. From London, the Egyptians received similar notification.

The pot now began to boil in Egypt. Denouncing the United States, praising the Soviet Union, and declaring that Egypt would never beg for a loan, Nasser, on July 26, 1956, nationalized the Suez Canal, hitherto a property of the Suez Canal Company, a majority of whose stockholders were British. He announced that his government would divert revenues earned from operating the waterway to the Aswan Dam project. Their national spirit stirred by Nasser's bold action, the people of Egypt, who until recently had chafed under many decades of British domination, were deliriously happy. As for the Eisenhower administration in Washington, it indicated that its only concern was efficient operation of the canal. Bent on deriving revenue from the canal, Nasser would surely strive to keep it operating efficiently.

Officials in London and Paris took a different view. They perceived Nasser as an adventurer who threatened a variety of British and French interests across North Africa and the Middle East. Such perceptions prompted Prime Minister Anthony Eden and Premier Christian Pineau to conclude that sooner or later their governments would have to deal forcefully with Nasser, and, given the pretext offered by his seizure of the canal, now was an opportune time to do so. Thus, while diplomatic fencing continued, Britain and France began to prepare for a military showdown with Egypt. Likewise preparing for hostilities was Israel, whose leaders viewed Nasser as an enduring threat to Israel's security.

Then, on October 29, 1956, as the electoral campaign in the United States was grinding to a climax and people across the world were looking on with a mixture of amazement and horror while the Soviets put down the anticommunist rebellion in Hungary, the Israelis sent forces plunging into Egypt, and in a dazzling display of speed and maneuver those forces swept across the Sinai peninsula to the east bank of the Suez Canal. The government in Washington was aghast. If not stopped immediately, American leaders feared, the Israeli-Egyptian hostilities might escalate into a much larger conflict. The United States thus introduced a resolution in the Security Council of the UN urging all members to avoid the use of force in Egypt and demanding that the Israelis withdraw from Egyptian territory. To no avail; the British and French vetoed the resolution. Next, on the following day, British and French bombing planes roared over Cairo, and transports flying the Union Jack of Britain and Tricolor of France unloaded thousands of troops in Egypt.

To nobody's surprise, Arab states and countries that recently had thrown off the yoke of colonialism expressed outrage. Even the Soviets, their hands dripping with the blood of Hungary's Freedom Fighters, denounced the attack. But what leaders in London, Paris, and Tel Aviv had not expected were the expressions of outrage that emanated from the United States. Sharing the sentiments of his compatriots, Eisenhower directed the U.S. delegation at the UN to introduce a resolution demanding an immediate cease-fire in Egypt. The resolution won overwhelming approval. Assailed by foe and friend alike—also under increasing attack by their own populations—the governments of Britain and France buckled, and on November 6 gave up their military adventure in Egypt. The government of Israel had little choice than to do likewise.

The righteous response of their government in the face of what they perceived to be aggression by its allies and friends exhilarated most Americans. Then, in January 1957, the president announced the "Eisenhower Doctrine." A response to efforts by the Kremlin to enlarge Soviet influence in the Middle East in the aftermath of the Suez crisis, the Eisenhower Doctrine proclaimed that the United States would provide economic and military assistance to countries in the Middle East, and in the event any country in the area came under overt attack by the forces of "international communism" the United States might intervene with military and naval forces. A short time later, Congress overwhelmingly endorsed the Eisenhower Doctrine, and voted $200 million for economic and military assistance to the countries of the Middle East.

Several months after Eisenhower proclaimed his doctrine, a procommunist faction took control of the government of Syria, and in the following year Syria joined Egypt and Yemen to form the United Arab Republic. Establishment of the UAR seemed a long step toward fulfillment of Colonel Nasser's dream of unifying the Arab world. The more so in light of Nasser's pro-Soviet orientation, that dream seemed to bode ill for the United States and its friends.

Then in the summer of 1958, a new crisis boiled up in the Middle East. The trouble began when anti-Western conspirators murdered King Faisal, Iraq's youthful pro-Western monarch. It was clear that the new government would take Iraq out of METO, and it appeared that the Soviets might have a new center of influence in the Middle East and the UAR a new member state. Panic thereupon seized the pro-Western governments of Lebanon and Jordan. Pro-Nasser elements were active in the two countries, and both Pres. Camille Chamoun of Lebanon and King Hussein of Jordan feared repetition of the recent coup in Iraq. To brace their governments against such an outcome, Chamoun turned to the United States, Hussein to Britain. The governments in Washington and London responded immediately. President Eisenhower dispatched several thousand marines and paratroops to stabilize the situation in Lebanon; the British sent a force of paratroops to Jordan.

Ominous rumblings thereupon emanated from the Kremlin. But the danger of a Soviet move passed when it became clear that the United States and

Britain would not press their interventions beyond Lebanon and Jordan. The United States, meanwhile, had placed the issue before the UN, and at length an agreement emerged. The Arab states, including the UAR, pledged noninterference in each other's affairs, the secretary-general of the UN promised to send observers to Lebanon and Jordan, and the United States and Britain agreed to withdraw their troops.

The return of tranquility to Lebanon did not signal the passing of American concerns in the Middle East. Nasser announced in late 1958 that the Soviets would lend $100 million for construction of the Aswan Dam, Iraq withdrew from METO, the Israeli-Arab feud continued. Still, the new regime in Iraq kept its distance from both the Soviet Union and the UAR, and before the expiration of Ike's term had established satisfactory relations with the United States.

## GUATEMALA

Another area of the outer world that commanded the attention of President Eisenhower was Latin America, and in the summer of 1953, he sent his younger brother Milton, a distinguished academician, on a "fact-finding" mission to the region. After visiting ten countries, Milton Eisenhower reported that conditions were worsening in Latin America. How might the trend be reversed and the region brought to prosperity? What Latin America needed most of all, Eisenhower thought, was a massive injection of capital by corporations and entrepreneurs of North America and Europe. Meanwhile, what appeared to leaders in Washington to be a bona fide communist threat had taken form in the Central American republic of Guatemala, a poverty-ridden country of nearly 3 million people whose economy was dominated by foreign corporations, notably the United Fruit Company.

Shortly after Eisenhower entered the White House, in February 1953, the president of Guatemala, Jacobo Arbenz Guzmán, a onetime army officer who had won election to the Guatemalan presidency in 1951, announced that the government in Guatemala City intended to take over 225,000 acres of uncultivated land belonging to the United Fruit Company and distribute it to peasants. By way of compensation, the company would receive $600,000, a woefully inadequate sum in the view of the Washington government, but the value of the property as reported for tax purposes. Almost overnight, as a consequence, Guatemala caught the attention of leaders of the United States.

Officials in Washington had been aware for some time that the Arbenz regime, which had endorsed the outrageous charge put forth by communists that the United States had waged germ warfare in Korea, included an assortment of avowed Marxists. Now the regime was nationalizing property owned by foreign capitalists. Equally ominous were reports that the regime was using conventional communist tactics of intimidation and even murder to silence domestic critics, and was conspiring to foment unrest in neighboring countries. Clearly, leaders in Washington concluded, Guatemala had fallen under domination of the international communist conspiracy. What would be the outcome if Guatemala remained in the grip of communists? The Soviets would have a base in Central America from which they could subvert other countries of the region, perhaps even Mexico. Exclaimed Eisenhower during a cabinet meeting, "My God, just think what it would mean to us if Mexico went communist!"

Then, in May 1954, a Swedish freighter delivered to Guatemala a shipment of small artillery pieces and small arms of Czech origin. Secretary of State Dulles denounced the shipment as a violation of the Monroe Doctrine, the chairman of the Senate Foreign Relations Committee described it as "part of the master plan of world communism," and the Senate adopted a resolution, by a vote of 69–1, describing what was happening in Guatemala as an example of "Soviet interference" and "external aggression." Eisenhower thereupon directed that 50 tons of weapons and ammunition be airlifted to Guatemala's neighbors, Honduras and Nicaragua, both of them under the iron-fisted rule of anticommunist dictators. He ordered a naval blockade of Guatemala, and prevailed on the OAS to approve a resolution condemning the control of any government in the Western Hemisphere by the international communist movement.

The CIA, meanwhile, had begun to train a force of noncommunist Guatemalans in neighboring Honduras and on an island off Guatemala's coast. To command the force, the CIA selected Col. Carlos Castillo Armas of Guatemala's regular army. The CIA also arranged air drops of munitions to opponents of the Arbenz regime inside Guatemala.

At length, a minuscule force of fewer than two hundred CIA-trained Guatemalans crossed the border from Honduras to Guatemala. The regular army of Guatemala offered no resistance. Supporting the rebel movement were three obsolete aircraft, based in Nicaragua and flown by CIA pilots, which buzzed and bombed Guatemala City. At that point, Arbenz appealed to the UN Security Council to consider the situation in Guatemala. What he sought was a resolution condemning North American interference in his country. The U.S. ambassador to the UN, Henry Cabot Lodge, Jr., denied that his government was involved in any way in the fighting in Guatemala—and the situation in Guatemala stayed off the Security Council's agenda.

Eisenhower, meanwhile, ordered the CIA to dispatch additional arms and aircraft to the rebels' force in Guatemala. (Nicaragua's infamous dictator Debayle Anastasio Somoza was the conduit for providing the planes.) Whereupon the Arbenz government, abandoned by the army as well as the presumably procommunist labor unions, collapsed. After Arbenz fled to Eastern Europe, the rebel commander Colonel Castillo arrived in Guatemala City aboard a plane of the U.S. embassy to organize a military junta to administer the country. The junta promptly restored the expropriated lands of the United Fruit Company and abolished taxes on the dividends of foreign investors. The Washington government arranged to assist Guatemala in the amount of approximately $45 million a year. And Castillo, who subsequently assumed dictatorial control of the government, established one of the most repressive regimes in the Western Hemisphere.

Four years after Castillo's accession to power in Guatemala, in the spring of 1958, Eisenhower sent Vice President Nixon on a goodwill tour of Latin America. The trip turned into a nightmare. In Peru and Venezuela, the vice president was jeered and heckled, made the target of eggs and fruit, even spat upon. In Caracas, the windows of his limousine were smashed. For his part, Nixon kept his cool, and won widespread acclaim for courage and patience. The people of the United States, of course, were shocked and outraged. They also were alarmed. As a result, Congress in 1959 voted increased funds for economic assistance to Latin America, and the Eisenhower administration took new steps to encourage private investment in the area. North America's renewed interest in Latin America met a favorable response, and when Ike toured the region in early 1960 he was warmly received in every city he visited. Meanwhile, happenings of great import were taking place in Cuba, the fabled "Pearl of the Antilles."

## CUBA

Because it was a pleasure mecca for wealthy North Americans and was able to sell its cigars, rum, and sugar in the United States, Cuba in the aftermath of the global war enjoyed a higher level of prosperity than most nation-states of Latin America. Compared with its superpowerful neighbor to the north, of course, it appeared poor and backward. Why was Cuba poor and backward? In part because of political turmoil and rule by corrupt and repressive dictators—also, in the perspective of most Cubans, because of meddling by the government in Washington and the fact that many of Cuba's economic resources were controlled by North American corporations and entrepreneurs who carted off profits to the United States.

Whatever its origin, Cuba's misfortune did not diminish in 1952 when Fulgencio Batista, a onetime army sergeant who had commanded Cuba's government intermittently since 1933, engineered a coup that returned him to power in Havana. Batista's goal? Mainly, it appeared, to control the national bureaucracy for the monetary benefit of his family and entourage. When Batista failed to redeem promises of general elections made at the time he took power, many Cubans became restive, and to keep such restiveness in check he invoked the conventional instruments of tyrants: intimidation, midnight arrests, torture, murder. To its discredit, the Washington government tended to ignore the depredations and brutalities of Batista, who was keeping order in Cuba—and, more importantly, stood forth as a bulwark against communism in the Caribbean.

Great numbers of Cubans, needless to say, detested Batista and his regime, among them a dreamy youth named Fidel Castro, the son of a well-to-do planter and a graduate of the Havana Law School, who on July 26, 1953, led fellow malcontents in a quixotic attack on an army barracks in southeastern Cuba. The leader of the foregoing misadventure found himself behind bars. On his release from jail in 1955, Castro made his way to Mexico where he organized a minuscule guerrilla force comprised largely of young Cuban dissidents. He and his intrepid band in late 1956 entered Oriente Province in eastern Cuba, and there, in the Sierra Maestra mountains, evaded capture by Batista's soldiers, raided government installations, and organized an anti-Batista underground in Cuba's urban areas. Promises that the success of his insurgency would result in far-ranging social reforms and a democratic government on the basis of free elections brought Castro wide support among Cuba's intellectuals, students, and peasants. As for Batista, he responded to the Castro insurgency by launching an indiscriminate campaign of harassment and murder that outraged many of Cuba's professional people.

Meanwhile the Washington government began to reevaluate its relations with Batista's regime. And when Batista violated a military assistance agreement by using American-equipped troops to crush an uprising at a naval base, the Eisenhower administration in early 1958 suspended arms shipments to his government. All the while, the CIA and FBI maintained contact with Castro, and the Washington government made no more than a halfhearted effort to

April 19, 1959: Prime Minister Castro and Vice President Nixon shake hands after meeting behind closed doors in Washington.

prevent the illegal shipment of arms from the United States to the Castro guerrillas.

The end of Cuba's current civil strife was in sight by the autumn of 1958. Castro had secured the eastern half of the island, and Batista's demoralized army had about given up the struggle. At length, on January 1, 1959, a fortnight after the U.S. ambassador in Havana had urged him to retire, Batista fled the country. A few days later, the bearded Castro, outfitted in a green fatigue uniform and chomping on a cigar, paraded along the thoroughfares of the capital while hundreds of thousands of deliriously happy Cubans cheered and strewed his path with flowers.

Most people in the United States seemed pleased. Some of Batista's followers, it was true, were warning that Castro was a communist, but North Americans were inclined to dismiss such warnings as the ravings of vanquished tyrants. Was it not true that many of Castro's partisans wore Roman Catholic religious medals? Was it not true that Cuba's Communist party had fallen in behind Castro only when it became clear that he was winning his struggle with Batista? Had Castro not repeatedly pledged support of democratic processes? In the perspective of most North Americans, then, "Fidel" was a fine-humored patriot who would bring democracy and renewal to what the Spaniards had termed "the Ever-Faithful Isle." Putting aside suspicions that communists had in fact penetrated the Castro movement, officials in Washington signaled an interest in establishing friendly relations with the new regime in Havana, and as a measure of their government's good intentions indicated a willingness to extend financial assistance to the Castro regime.

When in subsequent weeks that regime put alleged criminals of the Batista era on trial, the optimism of North Americans began to diminish—and the National Security Council secretly began to weigh the prospect of trying to arrange Castro's overthrow. Conducted in a sports arena in Havana that was packed with Castro partisans, the trials were a farce. While the partisans cheered and stamped their feet and whistled, Castro's fatigue-clad functionaries meted out kangaroo justice. Death by firing squad was the fate of many of those adjudged guilty. When Castro traveled to the United States in May 1959 to address the American Society of Newspaper Editors, he defended the trials and, countering accusations by many Cubans who recently had fled the island and taken up residence in the United States, insisted that communism was making no headway in Cuba. On the latter point, increasing numbers of North Americans were dubious. After talking for three hours with the self-styled "maximum leader," Vice President Nixon—filling in for Eisenhower, who refused to meet with Castro—reported to the CIA that Castro was "either incredibly naive about communism or under communist discipline."

Castro, meanwhile, had fashioned plans to nationalize oil refineries, sugar plantations, and other properties owned by foreign corporations, most of them North American. The United States had long taken the position that a government had every right to nationalize private property—provided it made prompt and fair compensation to the former owners. Despite assurances to the contrary during his aforementioned visit to the United States, Castro soon made it plain that his regime would not compensate North American and other capitalists whose properties it had expropriated. Next, Castro undertook a noisy campaign of anti-Americanism, and before throngs of cheering partisans issued harangues in which he blamed the United States for nearly every ill that had befallen Cuba over the past 60 years.

Equally serious in the estimate of North Americans, Castro by the summer of 1959 was purging anticommunists from his regime and replacing them with avowed Marxist-Leninists. Clearly, he had not the slightest intention of arranging the free elections he had so frequently promised. At the same time, he was becoming increasingly chummy with leaders in the Kremlin. Making Castro's drift toward communism particularly ominous, in the view of the Washington government, was his oft-repeated declaration that he intended to be the bearer of revolution to the rest of Latin America. During his first six months in power, indeed, the maximum leader encouraged revolutionary activity in the Dominican Republic, Haiti, Nicaragua, and Panama. That activity had come to nothing, but with support of the Soviet Union, leaders in Washington surmised, future attempts to topple existing noncommunist regimes might prove more successful.

The outcome was predictable. The Washington government cut back the quota of sugar that Cuba could sell in the United States, then eliminated Cuba's quota entirely. Next, in January 1961, in the last weeks of the Eisenhower presidency, the United States severed diplomatic relations with the Castro regime.

## RETROSPECT

The historian Charles C. Alexander, in his book *Holding the Line: The Eisenhower Era, 1952–1961* (1975) perceived the presidency of Dwight D. Eisenhower as one that was content to "hold the line" in both home affairs and foreign affairs. His perception is compelling. If Republican spokespeople over the previous two decades had routinely denounced "the welfare state" philosophy that Franklin Roosevelt and the New Dealers had fastened on the republic in the 1930s, Eisenhower betrayed no interest whatever in turning back the clock to those days before Roosevelt engineered what many Americans have described as "the New Deal Revolution." Ike, to be sure, had no inclination to appreciably enlarge the welfare (or guarantor or social service) state. But he had no inclination to contract it either. He was content to hold the line, likewise, in foreign affairs. In the opening years of the 1950s, and particularly during the electoral campaign of 1952, Republican orators had routinely lambasted the Truman administration's policy of containing the influence and power of the Soviet empire—had spoken of rolling back the Iron Curtain and liberating the "captive peoples" of Eastern Europe, as well as those of China. Containment, they insisted, was a negative and even dishonorable policy. On assuming the presidency in 1953, Eisenhower elected to ignore the fiery rhetoric of Republican partisans. He continued and indeed reinforced the policy of containment. In Charles Alexander's phrase, he determined to hold the line.

Scholars of history in recent years have tended to take a generous view of the Eisenhower presidency and its policy of holding the line, particularly in foreign affairs. Arguably, their generosity has been somewhat excessive. The Eisenhower administration was halfhearted at best in its approach to the scandal of discrimination on account of race in the self-proclaimed citadel of democracy and justice and equal opportunity. And a variety of other problems, for example, poverty in the midst of unparalleled abundance, pollution of the natural environment, and the abuse of consumers scarcely touched the consciousness of Ike and the men, nearly all of them wealthy titans of big business, to whom he looked for advice and reinforcement. Eisenhower had no qualms about using the CIA to conduct covert operations aimed at destabilizing countries with which the United States was presumably at peace. Indeed, according to the historian Stephen E. Ambrose, the CIA, under the direction and orders of Ike, became "one of America's chief weapons in the Cold War." Still, as his apologists observe, Eisenhower took care to prevent the Cold War from breaking open into a nuclear holocaust. And in the words of the historian Robert A. Divine, he demonstrated "admirable restraint" in keeping the country clear of military adventures in faraway areas of the world. Most importantly, scholars of recent times have thought, Eisenhower resisted the temptation to project American military-naval power into the cauldron of Vietnam— a temptation that his successors in the White House, to the immeasurable misfortune of the republic, failed to resist.

# Chapter
# 4

---

# A Pulsating Society

*D*uring the decade and a half after World War II, the people of the United States kept watch on the doings of the government in Washington and worried about "the international communist conspiracy." But day in and day out, year in and year out, they spent comparatively few of their waking moments immersed in thought about the national government's approaches to the economy and civil rights, the Cold War and space exploration. Rather, they concentrated on their personal lives—their individual quests for happiness and fulfillment and security. And as any social historian will insist, the way in which scores of millions of Americans went about the task of daily living— what they accomplished individually and collectively—has as much to say to succeeding generations about the condition of the North American superpower as it passed across the decade and a half following the global war as do the myriad activities and policies of the government in Washington.

## CHANGING DEMOGRAPHICS

During the 15 years that followed World War II, the population of the United States expanded prodigiously, from 140 million in 1945 to 178.4 million in 1960. That expansion was attributable in part to a declining death rate, from 10.6 per thousand in 1945 to 9.5 in 1960, and to the arrival in the country of between 3 and 4 million immigrants (1.8 million Europeans, about 155,000 Asians, and perhaps 2.5 million Canadians and inhabitants of other countries of the Western Hemisphere). But most of the expansion resulted from a "baby boom."

Why the typical young married couple in the United States during the years 1945 to 1960 determined to produce a child or two more than their parents (but one or two fewer than their grandparents) has been a subject of extensive speculation. Foremost no doubt, young couples tended to think children affordable, largely because the national economy was functioning at full throttle. Unlike most newlyweds of the succeeding generation, moreover, the typical young couple of the postwar years was not particularly inclined to postpone the enterprise of parenting until it gained title to a new car (or two), purchased a house, and enjoyed several years of relatively unencumbered living. Then during that period before the movement to achieve "women's liberation" gathered momentum, most young married women appeared to have little quarrel with the proposition that they could find personal fulfillment and contentment as housewives and mothers—were less inclined than their daughters would be in the 1970s and 1980s to aspire to employment and careers outside the household—hence were less inclined to view children as encumbrances. But most important perhaps, millions of young marrieds from 1945 to 1960 simply appeared to think that the ideal family should have three or four children rather than the two or three that their parents had been inclined to consider the ideal.

Whatever the explanation, births per thousand people in the United States advanced from 20.4 in 1945 to 24.1 in 1950 to 25.0 in 1957, then slipped to 23.7 in 1960. (The rate had been 30.1 in 1910 and 18.7 in 1935, and would be 15.5 in 1983.) More to the point, nearly 58 million Americans were born during the period from 1945 to 1960; some 22 million died. The outcome of the soaring birthrate and a declining death rate—also the arrival in the country of between 3 and 4 million legal and illegal immigrants—was a net increase in the national population between 1945 and 1960 of roughly 39 million.

Another outcome of the baby boom of 1945–1960 was a substantial increase in the number of Americans who were 14 years of age or younger: from 33.5 million (23 percent of the total population) in 1945 to 56 million (31 percent of the total) by 1960. The social consequences of the baby boom, of course, were momentous. The boom fueled the economy, inasmuch as the surging population generated new demand for uncounted commodities—diapers, baby food, children's clothing and shoes, children's furniture, toys—and services,notably medical. As the young citizens reached school age, communities across the entire republic found themselves pressed to provide additional class-rooms and teachers. (Enrollment in kindergartens and elementary and secondary schools burgeoned from 28 million in 1950 to 42 million in 1960.) When the children of the baby boom reached adolescence and young adulthood in the 1960s, their sheer numbers accentuated the effect of the restlessness, rebelliousness, and assertiveness that animated great numbers of young Americans during that tumultuous decade. And when they entered the traditional child-producing years, in the latter 1960s and 1970s, and decided that they did not choose to produce as many children as their parents had produced, the entire economy felt the effect.

If the numbers of Americans who were very young (14 years of age and younger) increased dramatically during the decade and a half after World War II, so did the numbers of those who were very old. Why? Largely, it would seem, because of improved nutrition and impressive advances in the quality of health care in the United States. In any event, citizens of age 75 and older numbered 2.6 million in 1940, 5.5 million in 1960. Those figures inevitably raised an array of questions relating to the elderly—or, as they came to be referred to, senior citizens. Could the Social Security system provide adequate support for the increasing numbers of citizens who survived for many years after retirement? What was to be done about the increasing numbers of elderly people who did not require hospitalization but were too ill or infirm to take care of themselves? Increasingly, the answer to the latter question was that elderly people could find refuge in nursing homes, dispensers of health care that were unknown in most communities of the republic before the global war.

Meanwhile, as it had from the founding of the republic in the 1770s, the balance of the national population continued to shift westward—also slightly southward, in the direction of Texas and California. No state, in truth, came close to matching the population increase recorded during the postwar era by California: from 10.5 million in 1950 to 15.7 million in 1960. And it was clear that the Golden State of California would soon displace the Empire State of New York (population in 1960: 16.7 million) as the most populous state of the republic.

Did impressive growth in population in California and Texas (also in Arizona and Florida) signal a population decline in the historic industrial heartland of the country (the area that in decades to come would be referred to as the Rush Belt)? It did not. Displaced by the continuing mechanization of agriculture and depression in the coalfields (as railroads shifted from steam to diesel motive power and householders from coal to oil and natural gas for heating), a veritable army of small-town and rural people from Kentucky, Tennessee, West Virginia, and elsewhere found its way northward across the Ohio

River where automobile plants, steel mills, and other industrial enterprises, not yet devastated by competitive gales that within a decade or so would swirl over the republic from Western Europe and Japan, were operating at full tilt. Accordingly, the population of the region identified by the U.S. Bureau of the Census as the East North Central (Illinois, Indiana, Michigan, Ohio, and Wisconsin), experienced substantial growth—from 30.3 million in 1950 to 36.2 million in 1960.

The population of the United States became increasingly urban during the decade and a half following World War II. In 1950, some 96.4 million Americans, or 63 percent, lived in areas defined by the U.S. Bureau of the Census as urban (essentially incorporated towns of 2,500 or more inhabitants), 54.2 million in rural areas. Ten years later, in 1960, 125.2 million, or 70 percent, lived in urban areas, 54.0 million in the countryside. Their populations scarcely changing (7.7 million and 3.5 million, respectively, in 1960), New York and Chicago remained the first and second cities in terms of population. Los Angeles, the third largest city of the country, experienced a growth in population from 1.9 million in 1950 to 2.4 million in 1960. Among cities recording particularly impressive increases in population between 1950 and 1960 were Atlanta (from 331,314 to 487,455), Dallas (434,462 to 679,684), Houston (596,163 to 938,219), San Diego (334,387 to 573,224), and Tampa (124,681 to 274,970). Meanwhile, great numbers of urban dwellers took up residence in suburbs during these years.

Suburbs were scarcely a new phenomenon. The village of Brooklyn appeared in the 1820s as a suburban community where New Yorkers could escape the noise and confusion of Manhattan and enjoy something approximating a union of urbanity and rusticity. Still, it was not until the closing decades of the nineteenth century, when electric traction provided cheap and rapid transportation, that large numbers of urban dwellers found it practicable to migrate from inner cities to suburbs. The movement to suburbs accelerated during the 1920s when millions of urban dwellers acquired automobiles. Indeed, more than 70 percent of the new houses that were constructed in the large urban areas of the republic during the 1920s and 1930s were built in suburbs.

A variety of considerations prompted the rush to the suburbs in the aftermath of the global war. As in former times, many urban dwellers simply wanted to escape the noise and confusion of inner cities—wanted to achieve that fabled union of urbanity and rusticity. Others exited the inner cores of cities as poor whites and blacks, many of them in flight from the rural areas of the South, moved in. Still others took up residence in suburbs because new and comfortable houses at affordable prices were more readily available in suburban areas. Such was the case because housing developers found that only in suburban areas could they purchase large parcels of land at realistic prices, and because lending agencies, including the Federal Housing Administration, considered loans for the construction of houses in suburbs to be safer investments than loans for the construction of residential properties in inner cities.

## A BOOMING AND CHANGING ECONOMY

Meanwhile, the economy of the United States was booming. Why was it booming? As already noted, the rampant determination of seemingly the entire American population to divest itself of savings accumulated during the global war in order to buy a whole array of commodities that had been unavailable from 1942 to 1945 fueled the national economy. Investment on a grand scale by the country's corporations and entrepreneurs likewise stimulated economic growth, as did a continued high level of spending by the government in Washington.

Still, the great postwar prosperity transcended savings and investment and spending. Just as Americans achieved an oft-discussed consensus in the matter of foreign policy during the years after World War II, they also achieved a socioeconomic consensus. It was a consensus born of the years of the late war when a great partnership of government and business had managed and driven the national economy in the interest of victory over the Axis aggressors. As the columnist Robert Samuelson wrote in *Newsweek* in 1985, "Private enterprise would remain responsible for producing our wealth, but government would promote and police economic growth to eliminate instability and protect victims of economic change." The consequence of that consensus was a new political climate in which the confidence of the citizenry in the viability and essential justice of the socioeconomic system remained high and (after the first year or so following the war) labor strife was kept to a minimum. That climate was conducive to a level of economic performance that had never been approached in the United States or anywhere else in the world over a comparable period.

Random statistics illustrate the country's economic vitality during the decade and a half after the global war. The gross national product in constant (1954) dollars advanced from $2,096 per capita in 1950 to $2,536 in 1960, disposable personal income from $1,523 to $1,758. Gross national savings went from $78.5 billion in 1950 to $119.4 billion in 1960, gross national investment from $78.0 billion to $117.4 billion. The total assets of American corporations increased from $598 billion in 1950 to $1.2 trillion in 1960. Registrations of private automobiles in the United States totaled 25.7 million in 1945, 40.3 in 1950, 61.6 in 1960. The generation of electricity increased from 179.9 kilowatt-hours in 1945 to 841.6 million in 1960. The percentage of the national work force that was unemployed at any given time remained low. After a sharp increase from 57.9 in 1945 to 87.9 in 1948, the wholesale price index advanced moderately to 96.2 in 1956 and to 100.7 in 1960.

Economic growth and prosperity were accompanied by changes in nearly every aspect of the economic life of the North American superpower. There was far-ranging change in agriculture. Of particular note was the absorption of hundreds of thousands of small farms by larger operators. If total farm acreage enlarged, from 1.0 billion in 1940 to 1.12 billion in 1959, the total number of farms in the United States declined from 6.0 million in 1940 to 3.7 million in 1959. The number of individuals who were actively engaged in agriculture likewise declined, from 8.5 million in 1945 to 5.7 million in 1960, the country's farm population (not to be confused with the rural population) from 17.5 percent of the total population in 1945 to 8.7 percent in 1960. Deliberately restricted in the interest of higher prices and incomes, the total output of farm commodities in the United States nonetheless increased. What transpired, of course, was a monumental advance in productivity in the farm belt. The principal sources of that advance were (1) the continuing mechanization of agriculture, (2) a biological revolution that resulted in the perfection of new hybrid strains of corn and other crops and important advances in animal nutrition and plant and animal breeding, and (3) a chemical revolution that was marked by a dramatic expansion of the use of fertilizers, insecticides, herbicides, and fungicides. After the global war, in truth, American farmers increasingly became agribusinesspeople who, in addition to understanding the new scientific verities of agriculture, knew how to manage capital and market commodities to maximum advantage.

## RAILROADS AND AIRLINES

The capacity to move commodities and people from one locale or region of the country to another efficiently and at low cost, as students learn in beginning economics courses, is essential to the life of a modern industrial society. Certainly, efficient and low-cost transportation had been critical to the transformation of the United States during the decades following 1850 from a struggling agrarian republic to the premier industrial power of the world. It also had been critical to the success of the United States in bringing its enemies to defeat during the late global conflict.

As they had been for several generations, railroads remained America's principal long-distance haulers of freight during World War II, and in 1945 carried 736 million ton-miles of intercity cargo, or 68 percent of the national total. Motor trucks, by comparison, carried 67 million ton-miles of intercity freight in 1945, or 6.24 percent of the national total. During the decade and a half after the war, the railroads speeded operations by retiring all of their remaining steam locomotives and replacing them with more powerful and efficient diesel-electric motive power. They modernized yard facilities, put down new and heavier rail, bought scores of thousands of new freight cars, inaugurated a variety of new services, including "piggy-back" (the shipment of loaded semitrailers aboard flat cars).

Still, the railroads found it increasingly difficult to meet the competition of motor carriers, except for shipments of coal, grain, and other bulky commodities. Because they were not bound to rails and did not have to work their way through complicated terminals when moving cross-country, trucks were often able to provide shippers with faster and more reliable service. In any event, the percentage of intercity freight handled by railroads slipped perceptibly during the postwar era. In 1960, railroads hauled 594 million ton-miles of freight, or 44 percent of the national total, trucks 297 ton-miles, or 22.2 percent. Inland waterways (16.4 percent) and oil pipelines (17.3 percent) carried nearly all of the remainder.

During the war, when new cars and tires were unobtainable and gasoline strictly rationed, railroads also carried impressive numbers of intercity passengers. Optimistic about the future of passenger traffic, the railroads in the years following the war reequipped their premier passenger trains—Twentieth-Century Limited, Orange Blossom Special, Super Chief—with luxurious coaches and parlor cars, roomettes and observation lounges. They inaugurated an array of new streamliners, the most heralded of which was the California Zephyr, its schedule between Chicago and San Francisco arranged to afford passengers spectacular daytime views of the Rockies and Sierra Nevadas from "vista-dome" coaches.

Alas, it was soon apparent that the train, however luxurious, could never persuade sufficient numbers of travelers to leave their automobiles at home and thus enable more than a handful of the magnificent limiteds to maintain profitability. Statistics provided proof. In 1950, railroads carried only 6.8 percent of the country's intercity passengers, automobiles 85.1 percent. Still, the railroads seemed reluctant to face up to reality, and in the latter 1950s several of them experimented with revolutionary ultralightweight equipment that they hoped might somehow turn passenger train losses into profits. To no avail: The decline of the passenger train continued, and in 1960 the railroads carried only 2.8 percent of the country's intercity travelers.

As the passenger train went into eclipse, the commercial airliner emerged as the country's most glamorous mode of intercity transport. Apart from its incomparable speed, the airliner had several advantages in its competition with the passenger train. One was the attitude of management. The principal source of earnings for railroads was the carriage of freight, and many railroadmen had long looked on the passenger train as an encumbrance—an attitude that sometimes became apparent in the dispatching of trains and treatment of passengers. By contrast, the goodwill of passengers was a veritable obsession of the airlines. Air carriers, moreover, were the beneficiaries of weather and traffic-control services provided by the federal government and also direct subsidies (more than $75 million in 1953). They benefited from the conviction of urban officials across the country that the prosperity and growth of their communities required taxpayers to ante up enormous sums of money for the construction of magnificent air terminals. Railroads received no comparable public support. Airlines likewise benefited from the attitude of the federal agencies, the Civil Aeronautics Board (CAB), Civil Aeronautics Administration (CAA), and (after 1958) the Federal Aviation Agency (FAA), charged with overseeing their activities. The CAB, CAA, and then the FAA (a superagency that absorbed the CAB and CAA) operated on the premise that it was their function to encourage and promote the commercial airline industry. The Interstate Commerce Commission, conversely, had historically taken the view that its role vis-à-vis the railroads was to prevent the railroads from abusing the public interest.

Meanwhile, the airlines of the United States put in service larger and faster aircraft. They introduced the Douglas DC-6 in 1946, a successor to the venerable twin-engine DC-3 (first flown in 1935, the world's first modern airliner). The four piston engines of the DC-6 could propel up to 58 passengers through the skies at more than 300 miles per hour. The equally impressive Lockheed Constellation entered commercial service the following year, the Super Constellation (capable of accommodating up to 88 passengers and flying at a speed of 374 miles an hour) and the DC-7 in the early 1950s. The British flew the first turbojet airliner in 1949, the De Havilland Comet, two of which broke apart in flight after being put in transoceanic service. The Comet could fly at a speed of 500 miles an hour. The first American-built jets, the Boeing 707 and Douglas DC-8, took to the air in the latter 1950s. Each craft was capable of transporting 150 passengers on nonstop flights of 5,000 miles at speeds of 550 miles an hour. The formal entry of the United States in the commercial jet age took place on October 26, 1958, when a 707, its cabin filled with paying passengers, winged across the Atlantic. That flight signaled the demise of regularly scheduled operations by transatlantic ocean liners, the swiftest of which was the SS *United States*, a magnificent vessel that had been christened at Newport News in 1951.

Although two or more airliners went down nearly every year in the United States—109 people perished in such crashes in 1950, 363 in 1960—travelers increasingly lost their fear of flying. They also found the unmatched speed of the commercial airliners increasingly attractive. Accordingly, America's air carriers flew 30.5 billion domestic passenger-miles in 1960, compared with 3.3 billion in 1945 and 8.0 billion in 1950. They flew 8.3 billion international passenger-miles in 1960, compared with 448 million in 1945 and 2.2 billion in 1950. At that, the airlines accounted for only 4.46 percent of the country's intercity passenger traffic in 1960.

## AUTOMOBILES

The motor car, of course, remained the principal means by which Americans moved from one town or city to another—or made their way across urban areas and about the countryside. Like nothing else, it symbolized the affluence and dynamism of the sprawling superpower's pulsating urban-industrial civilization. Commentators on that civilization often alluded to the decades-old "love affair" between Americans and their cars. Indeed, a favorite pastime of legions of Americans was car watching—keeping abreast of the latest developments in automotive engineering and design. Such Americans took in auto shows in the major cities, savored the pages of *Motor Trend* and other popular car magazines, talked endlessly among themselves about engines and transmissions, body styles and handling characteristics.

Save for the innovative models turned out by Studebaker and the industry's newcomer, the Kaiser Corporation, the cars of 1946–1947 were essentially unchanged from those of 1941–1942. But within a couple of years, the cars of old-line manufacturers began to shed their prewar appearances, and in some instances, the changes were spectacular. The Nash of 1948, for example, featured skirts on the front as well as the rear fender panels, the Hudson of that same year, a recessed floor that gave it the lowest center of gravity of any American-built automobile. Wraparound windshields were the styling rage of the industry in 1954–1955; rear fender panels in the configuration of fins, featured on the Cadillac and Chrysler Imperial as well as lesser models for a couple of seasons in the latter 1950s, were another. Manufacturers improved the appearance and comfort of station wagons (whose increasing popularity in the latter 1950s may have owed as much to the baby boom and the migration of millions of Americans to suburbs as to better looks).

Of larger moment were developments in automotive engineering. The years following the global war brought rapid development of the automatic transmission. Power steering appeared in production models of American cars in 1951, power brakes and the four-barrel carburetor (yielding improved volumetric efficiency or breathing ability at high speeds) in 1952. Engines became more powerful until, in 1958, the Ford Motor Company brought the "horsepower race" to a climax when it equipped all new Lincolns and Continentals and some Mercurys with 400-horsepower motors. In the interest of power and efficiency, overhead-valve power plants displaced those of the L-head genre. V-8's displaced straight 8's. Air conditioners became available as optional equipment on several models in 1953. Ford and Chrysler introduced seat belts in 1956; Chrysler installed the first alternators (instead of generators) in production cars in 1960.

The pulses of few car enthusiasts beat faster in the latter 1940s when Kaiser introduced the Henry J, a minuscule and utilitarian conveyance that in a later time would have been designated a subcompact. Slightly more interesting were the somewhat larger "compacts" that found a market among a coterie of economy-minded motorists through the 1950s: Nash Rambler, Studebaker Lark, Plymouth Valiant, Ford Falcon. But what turned the heads of genuine car lovers were such creations as the Ford Thunderbird and Chevrolet Corvette, introduced in the mid-1950s, small sports cars that were destined to become American classics, and the long and powerful Continental Mark II, introduced in 1955 and likewise destined to become a classic (and which was shipped from the factory in a fleece-lined plastic covering). Enthusiasts also responded to the rear-engine (and ill-starred) Chevrolet Corvair, introduced in 1959.

Aficionados took note of the advent and passing of assorted automotive nameplates. The nameplates of Kaiser and Frazer appeared in 1946. The latter disappeared after a couple of seasons. The entrepreneur Preston Tucker generated reams of publicity in the summer of 1947 when he displayed a prototype of a racy rear-engine sedan, the Tucker Torpedo, which he intended to mass-produce. Unfortunately, his company folded before it could turn out even a handful of cars. A merger of the ailing Kaiser Motor Company and Willys Motors in 1953 failed to rescue the nameplates of Kaiser and Willys from the scrap heap of history. A merger of Nash-Kelvinator Corporation and the Hudson Motor Car Company in 1954 establishing the American Motors Corporation resulted (in 1957) in the demise of the time-honored nameplates of Nash and Hudson. A merger of the struggling Studebaker Corporation and the Packard Motor Car Company, also in 1954, gave the nameplates of Studebaker and Packard a reprieve, but they, too, had passed into oblivion by the mid-1960s. After an unprecedented publicity campaign, the Ford Motor Company introduced its Edsel in 1957. Initially marked by a vertical grille, the Edsel became a national laughingstock and was discontinued after three seasons.

## PLASTICS AND ELECTRONICS

The years following World War II, as noted, were a time of impressive economic growth in the United States. Making a powerful contribution to that growth, of course, were the country's booming manufacturing industries, among them plastics and electronics. The latter industries, in truth, literally "took off" during the decade and a half after the global conflict.

Moldable materials produced from natural or synthetic substances (notably chemicals derived from air, coal, petroleum, and water), plastics trace their origin to the year 1869 when John Wesley Hyatt of Starkey, New York, striving to perfect a synthetic billiard ball, invented celluloid. In the first years of the twentieth century, Leo Baekeland discovered the phenol-formaldehyde resin that came to be known as bakelite, and from that discovery derived a variety of new plastics and processing techniques. Still, plastics were essentially a scientific curiosity down to the time of America's entry in World War II, when chemists sought synthetic replacements for natural materials, particularly rubber, which because of the war had become unobtainable. One type of plastic material, polyethylene, was developed during the war to meet the stringent insulating requirements of radar.

Because plastics could be produced with an assortment of properties (electrical insulation capacity, flexibility, rigidity, dimensional stability, transparency, opacity, and strength), they found an incredible array of nonmilitary applications in the aftermath of the war. Those applications included the manufacture of airplane canopies, appliance housings, automobile components (including dashboards, ignition parts, steering wheels, taillights, trim, and upholstery), beads, camera cases, clothing hangers, electrical insulation, garden hose, helmets, ladies' shoe heels, molded gears, pipe for farm, mine, and home uses, protective wrapping for foods, refrigerator door liners, shower curtains, toothbrush handles, toys, typewriter cases, wall and floor tile, washing machine agitators, wearing apparel. Negligible in 1940, the output of plastics in the United States by 1959 exceeded 4 billion pounds.

There was impressive growth during the postwar years of industries that manufactured and marketed electron devices, that is, devices whose operations depend on the emission of electrons from solids and liquids and on the controlled motions of those electrons. Of particular moment was the rampant growth of the segment of the electronics industry that produced and distributed television broadcasting equipment and receiving sets.

The essential principles of electronic television were proposed as early as 1908, and the first phototube was introduced in 1914. Eleven years later, in April of 1925, an obscure Scotsman, John Logie Baird, having set up his equipment in two rooms on an upper floor of a department store in the west end of London, demonstrated that it was possible to transmit moving images from one point to another. Three years later, in 1928, station WGY in Schenectady, New York, inaugurated regular television broadcasts. Other stations experimented with television broadcasting in subsequent years, but until Vladimir K. Zworykin perfected an all-electronic TV system (1936) the quality of picture reproduction was poor. Automatic relay stations to transmit television beyond its natural range went into operation in 1940, and in that year the Republican national convention in Philadelphia was televised to New York via coaxial cable.

Television development in the United States languished during the years of the country's involvement in World War II. Then, after 1945, the application to pulse and video techniques and microwave communication of the wartime development and refinement of radar circuitry enabled the fledgling television industry to resolve a variety of problems, most importantly that presented by the short range of television broadcasts. Whereupon the industry began to enlarge—and after 1950 seemed to explode. Manufacturers found themselves awash with orders for broadcasting equipment for new TV stations. (Six television stations had been on the air in the United States and its territories in 1945; 97 were broadcasting in 1950; 517 in 1960.) The factories of such giants of the industry as RCA and Zenith operated day and night to meet the burgeoning demand for television receiving sets. (More than 3.8 million American households had TV sets in 1950, 45.7 million in 1960.)

## COMPUTERS

If the years following World War II were a time of economic expansion and change in the United States, they also were a time of impressive technological and scientific achievement (some of it already considered). No such achievement was of more far-reaching import perhaps than perfection of the electronic digital computer.

Historians have traced the origins of the modern computer to that time in the distant past when unknown and unheralded people, having come to an understanding of numbers, began to use sticks, pebbles, and their fingers for counting. Then, around 3000 B.C., some enterprising individual hit on the idea of stringing beads on strands (or inserting them in slots) that were secured within a rigid wooden frame. Thus was born the abacus, for the next five thousand years humankind's most successful computer. Many centuries later, in A.D. 1623, a German, Wilhelm Schickard, fashioned a crude machine that could add and subtract and with manual assistance multiply and divide. Of larger moment were the efforts in the 1820s and 1830s of an irascible Englishman, Charles Babbage, who designed and set about to build an amazingly sophisticated calculating machine that would have a "store" or memory and even print answers on specially engraved copperplates. Unfortunately, the machine technology of the time was not sufficiently advanced to make possible the realization of Babbage's ideas, some of them essential to computer design in the present day. Largely to facilitate the task of tabulating data collected by the U.S. Bureau of the Census, Herman Hollerith in the 1880s perfected a punch-card sorter that has been described as a forerunner of the modern digital computer.

Through the early decades of the twentieth century, various scientists, mathematicians, and engineers quietly labored to fashion more efficient computing devices, and during World War II the physicist Vannevar Bush and others produced analog computers, or "differential analyzers," that proved useful in solving mathematical equations relating to aircraft design and ballistics problems. In the words of the writer D. S. Halacy, Jr., an analog computer is "a laboratory model of a physical system which may be studied and measured to learn certain implicit facts." (Clocks and speedometers are analog devices.)

Meanwhile, a group of scientists and engineers headed by the physicist Howard H. Aiken of Harvard and Clair D. Lake of the International Business Machines Corporation had set about to produce an electromechanical digital computer, that is, a counting device whose on-off circuit switches parallel the yes-no paradigm that makes logical thinking possible. The Aiken-Lake group completed the Harvard-IBM Mark I device in 1944. But the flowering of electronics in that very period was fated to doom electromechanical computers to extinction. Indeed, it was in December 1945 that a group of scientists and engineers directed by John P. Eckert, Jr., and John W. Mauchly of the University of Pennsylvania produced the world's first electronic digital computer, the ENIAC (Electro Numerical Integrator and Computer). A veritable behemoth, at least when compared with later generations of computers, ENIAC contained 18,000 vacuum tubes and 6,000 switches, was 100 feet long and 10 feet high, and weighed 30 tons.

Its sheer bulk, and also its lack of reliability, restricted the utility of ENIAC, but then, in 1948, a research group at the Bell Telephone Laboratory, headed by William P. Shockley (who subsequently received the Nobel Prize for physics), produced the transistor, a solid-state electronic device composed of semiconductor material (for example, silicon) that controls the flow of electrical current without the use of a vacuum. As the writer Geoffrey Perrett later noted, the transistor would prove "the ideal replacement for the fragile, cumbersome vacuum tubes which had made ENIAC so unreliable and so elephantine." (By the end of the 1950s, in truth, engineers were able to arrange dozens of transistors in an integrated circuit on a single silicon chip that was smaller than the eye of a sewing needle.) The transistor, then, made possible a dramatic shrinking of the dimensions of computers and a dramatic increase in their reliability.

As they became smaller and more reliable (also more powerful), computers found increased utility. The Los Alamos Atomic Energy Laboratory in 1948 used an IBM computer to solve a problem involving some 9 million mathematical operations that would have required skilled mathematicians an estimated 1,500 years to solve. The computer solved the problem in 150 hours. A MANIAC computer designed by the brilliant Hungarian émigré John Louis von Neumann hastened development of America's hydrogen bomb. The U.S. Bureau of the Census purchased a UNIVAC I in 1951 to take over the onerous chore of processing census data. Operating almost without pause, the bureau's computer performed 510 billion mathematical calculations during the next ten years. The omnipresence of computers by 1961 prompted the American Bar Association and the American Law Institute to proclaim that the computer was fated to cast its "automated shadow on every phase of society."

The institute's pronouncement does not appear exaggerated. In 1961, agencies of the federal government, including the Atomic Energy Commission, Department of Commerce, Department of Defense, Federal Aviation Agency, NASA, and the Post Office, were operating eight hundred large computers. The armed forces were using computers to simulate war games, evaluate the quality of ammunition, control the missiles and aircraft of the complex warning system designed to protect the country from surprise attack, control the flight of bombing planes and ballistic missiles, and navigate submarines. Computers had become the indispensable tools of air traffic controllers and meteorologists, not to mention the men and women of the country's fledgling space program. In 1954, the General Electric Company had installed the first large-scale computer, a UNIVAC, for its business data processing, an event that the editors of the *Harvard Business Review* thought future historians might view as marking the beginning of the second industrial revolution. By 1961, businesses in the United States were operating some six thousand large computers. Banks and insurance companies were the prime users of the devices, but by the start of the 1960s department stores and supermarket chains were experimenting with computers, particularly for the purposes of ordering and inventory management. Computers were scheduling hotel and airline reservations, handling the accounts of the hotel industry, controlling the stocks of spare parts of airlines. Engineers and industrialists were using them to design bridges and highways, analyze variables in the production of gasoline, and control the operations of steel mills.

## MEDICAL AND BIOLOGICAL SCIENCE

While some people were building more sophisticated computers, others were pushing back the frontiers of medical science. Most importantly perhaps, researchers perfected new antibiotics, that is, chemical substances capable of destroying or inhibiting the growth of bacteria and other microorganisms.

It was in 1928 that an obscure Englishman, Alexander Fleming, observed that a mold, having gained access to a culture plate, had devastated colonies of staphylococcus that he had been cultivating. He identified the mold as *Penicillium notatum*, then discovered that the mold produces a substance which dramatically inhibits the growth of the organisms that cause a range of infectious diseases. He named the latter substance penicillin. Interestingly, Fleming's historic discovery failed to stir much interest among medical researchers for nearly a decade—until a group of scientists at Oxford University in Great Britain headed by Howard W. Florey undertook to study penicillin. Then, in 1941, the drug was demonstrated to be effective when administered to an Oxford policeman who was dying of septicemia. A short time later, the production of penicillin was begun in the United States (and a more productive species of the substance obtained from a rotting cantaloupe found in a market in Peoria, Illinois). Although there was scarcely enough penicillin available in the entire world in 1942 to treat a hundred patients, the United States by the end of 1943 was producing sufficient quantities of the drug to meet the needs of its armed forces and those of its allies, and by 1945, the needs of its civil population. In the words of the historians of medicine James Bordley III and A. McGehee Harvey, "No events of the twentieth century have had such a resounding impact upon both medical science and practical medical therapy as the introduction of penicillin and related agents."

As for related agents, the Ukranian émigré Selman A. Waksman, toiling in a laboratory at Rutgers University in New Jersey in 1943, discovered streptomycin. For his enterprise, Waksman would receive a Nobel Prize in 1952. Streptomycin proved particularly effective in the treatment of tuberculosis, the infamous "great white plague" that a half century before had annually claimed the lives of more Americans than any other disease. Hitherto consigned to sanatoriums for prolonged rest, victims of tuberculosis now were treated with streptomycin. Equally effective against TB, but less toxic, was isoniazid, successfully tested by E. R. Squibb and Sons and the Hoffman-La Roche research laboratories in 1951. Meanwhile, in 1947, researchers of Parke, Davis and Company had brought forth Chloromycetin, a "broad-spectrum" antibiotic that quickly proved its effectiveness during typhus epidemics in South America and the Malay Peninsula. In 1947, Benjamin M. Duggar, a retired botany professor at the University of Wisconsin, produced Aureomycin, another broad-spectrum antibiotic. Effective against the organisms that caused more than a hundred diseases, Aureomycin soon became the antibiotic that physicians prescribed most frequently.

Antibiotics were not the only new drugs that proved effective against various of the maladies that afflicted humankind. In the mid-1940s, researchers in the United States improved the antihistamine drugs recently brought forth by French investigators, and in 1946 introduced Benadryl and Pyribenzamine, both of which proved effective against food sensitivities, hay fever, and asthma. In 1948, Leslie N. Gay, chief of the allergy clinic at Johns Hopkins University in Baltimore, prescribed the new drug Dramamine in treating the hives of a woman patient. The woman reported that the drug had failed to cure her hives but seemed to prevent motion sickness. Subsequent tests established that motion sickness could indeed be prevented by the ingestion of Dramamine. In 1949, E. C. Kendall of the Mayo Clinic in Rochester, Minnesota, demonstrated the effectiveness of the adrenal steroid cortisone in the treatment of rheumatoid arthritis. In 1952, Francis Boyer introduced the tranquilizer Thorazine, a drug that immediately proved effective in the treatment of psychoneurotic behavior. In 1956, Smith Kline and French Laboratories introduced the tranquilizer Compazine. New anticonvulsants and antispasmodics offered benefit to victims of Parkinson's disease and epilepsy.

The achievements of medical researchers during the postwar years were indeed phenomenal. In the latter 1940s, a group headed by John P. Merrill of the Peter Bent Brigham Hospital in Boston improved the artificial kidney, developed by the Dutch physician William J. Kolff a few years before and essential to the technique of renal dialysis. In the mid-1940s, Helen B. Taussig and Alfred Blalock of Johns Hopkins Hospital in Baltimore perfected an operation to increase the blood flow to the lungs of so-called blue babies. In 1948, Charles Bailey of the Peter Bent Brigham Hospital performed a successful operation to resolve problems resulting from scarring of the mitral valve of a patient's heart. In 1952, Charles Hufnagel of the Georgetown University Medical Center in Washington inserted an artificial valve in the heart of a patient. An array of researchers, meanwhile, were striving to identify the causes of the many varieties of cancer—and during the 1950s determined that cigarette smoking was in no small measure responsible for the increasing incidence of cancer of the lung. Other researchers concentrated on the early diagnosis and treatment of cancer. There were refinements of the method of diagnosing uterine cancer by the vaginal, or "Pap," smear, a procedure perfected during the early 1940s by George N. Papanicolaou. There were new surgical techniques and impressive improvements in the techniques of radiation therapy. There was a dramatic increase in the use of chemicals as therapeutic agents in the battle against cancer. Chemotherapy resulted in cures in a high percentage of cases of choriocarcinoma and remissions for victims of leukemia. Against most cancers, unfortunately, it proved only marginally effective. There were notable improvements in the surgical techniques employed to relieve backache and other pains caused by herniation of the cartilaginous disc between the vertebrae. In the latter 1940s, eye surgeons perfected the procedure whereby a healthy cornea is transplanted from the eye of a deceased donor to a patient whose cornea has become scarred, cloudy, or distorted, and who, as a result—in addition to being visually impaired—may face a threat of blindness. In the 1950s, researchers working under the direction of Gregory Pincus developed norethynodrel, which in 1960 went on the market as an oral contraceptive.

Because millions of Americans thought contraception sinful, medical researchers had taken little interest in improving contraceptive techniques. Still, assorted researchers (some of them working in the field of veterinary medicine) had made discoveries and observations establishing that the administration of ovarian hormones to laboratory animals prevented ovulation. And in 1945, Fuller Albright of Massachusetts General Hospital wrote of the potential of ovulation-inhibiting doses of estrogen for achieving contraception. Then, in 1950, the longtime feminist and champion of birth control Margaret Sanger enlisted the assistance of Pincus, a reproductive biologist at the Worcester Foundation in Massachusetts. Intimating that they were working on a compound to counter infertility in women, Pincus and his associates moved forward with their research and by 1954 had developed norethynodrel. In 1957, the G. D. Searle Company began to market norethynodrel—as a fertility drug, not a birth control pill. But at length, in 1960, various pharmaceutical firms began to actively promote norethynodrel as an oral contraceptive.

Unquestionably the most heralded achievement in the field of medical science in the years after World War II was that presided over by Jonas Edward Salk. Born in New York City in 1914, the son of a garment worker, Salk had graduated from a high school for exceptional students and received a bachelor's degree from the City College of New York in 1934 and a medical degree from New York University in 1939. A fellowship in epidemiology in 1942 took him to the University of Michigan where he did research on the influenza virus and helped develop commercial vaccines to counter influenza. After joining the staff of the University of Pittsburgh in 1947, he continued his work on viruses and, funded by the March of Dimes of the National Foundation for Infantile Paralysis, became the director of a study of polio viruses.

For as long as anybody could remember, poliomyelitis had claimed the lives of thousands of people across the world each year and left hundreds of thousands crippled for life. Children were the principle victims, but polio also struck adults, for example, Franklin D. Roosevelt, who was stricken at age 39

April 1955: Expressing varying emotions, children receive injections of the antipolio vaccine.

in 1921. Then, in 1953, Salk disclosed that a vaccine developed by him and his associates had proved experimentally successful in combating the dreaded disease. The National Foundation for Infantile Paralysis thereupon undertook an elaborate field trial involving upward of a million children to determine whether the vaccine could, in fact, protect children against polio under normal conditions of exposure to the disease. At length, in April of 1955, the foundation released its report: The "Salk vaccine" was at once safe and effective.

Of comparable moment perhaps, if scarcely noticed by the public at large, was the achievement of the Briton Francis H. C. Crick and the American James D. Watson, who disclosed in 1953 that, as a result of their studies at Cambridge University in Great Britain, they had identified the structure of the DNA molecule, an essential component in all living matter—the molecule that contains the genetic code and transmits the hereditary pattern. By unraveling the biochemical basis of life and reproduction, Crick and Watson had made one of the most portentous discoveries in the history of the human race, inasmuch as it opened extraordinary possibilities, for good or ill, in the field of genetic engineering.

Meanwhile, millions of Americans were outraged by a campaign, undertaken in the latter 1940s and staunchly supported by the American Dental Association, to add fluorine compounds (or fluorides) to community water supplies at a ratio of one part of fluorine to a million parts of water for the purpose of preventing tooth decay. The dental effects of fluorination had been discovered in 1927 after several communities in New Jersey began to be supplied with water containing minute quantities of fluorine. Residents of the communities were shown to have experienced a marked decline in the incidence of tooth decay. Still, legions of Americans resisted the post–World War II campaign to add fluorine to water supplies. Many of them viewed fluorine, defined in the dictionary as "a corrosive, poisonous, pale greenish-yellow gaseous chemical element," as a poison. Not a few Americans, moreover, suspected that the campaign to add fluorine to water supplies was a communist-orchestrated plot to weaken the minds and spirits and break the health of the people of the United States. Opposition notwithstanding, nearly 35 million people across the country were drinking fluorinated (or fluoridated) water by 1960.

## ARCHITECTURE

At the same time that citizens were weighing the pros and cons of fluorinated water, the country's architects were designing houses and apartments, office buildings and shopping centers, supermarkets and drive-in theaters, schools and hospitals, churches and synagogues that touched the consciousness of every American. Of special note in the aftermath of the global war, increased building costs compelled architects to design buildings that were often described as simple and direct. Characterized by large windows and pitched roofs, the single-story "ranch-style" structure became a preferred design for new houses. Simplicity of design also characterized new commercial and government buildings. New schools tended to be one- or two-story structures that abounded with large windows and on the interior were awash with bright colors.

What did Americans of the time tend to think of the enterprise of their architects? Not much. Particularly when assessing larger structures, most of them designed in accord with the formal "international style" developed in Germany during the 1930s—for example, the UN headquarters in New York—they were inclined to view the straight-edge, functional designs of contemporary architects as cold and forbidding and (what was worse) ugly. Foremost among those architects of the international style whose work was an object of widespread criticism was Ludwig Mies van der Rohe (known as Mies), an immigrant from Germany who designed the squat, box-shaped buildings of the Illinois Institute of Technology, a succession of glass towers on Lake Shore Drive in Chicago, and the slim and elegant Seagram Building in New York. Still, a few architects ventured away from the international style, among them the legendary Frank Lloyd Wright, who until his death in 1959 at age 90 remained the country's most renowned architect, and the result was such innovative designs as those of the buildings of the U.S. Air Force Academy in Colorado; the First Presbyterian Church in Stamford, Connecticut (a structure of old wood and glass in the shape of a stylized fish whose interior seemed aglow with subdued color); and the elaborate Price Tower (designed by Wright) in Bartlesville, Oklahoma.

## CRIME

The contours of houses and office buildings, schools and hospitals may touch the consciousness of every American, but the work of architects is not an enterprise that often stirs the meditations of the typical American. The typical American is far more apt to contemplate the enterprise of criminals. Criminal activity, after all, is eminently fascinating. It also threatens the property and even the person of nearly every citizen.

If statistics relating to criminal activity across the country during any period are of dubious reliability, inasmuch as they are derived from reports by thousands of local law enforcement agencies of varying efficiency, it seems clear that the rate of crime in the United States, following a modest decline in the immediate aftermath of the global war, underwent a steady increase thereafter. Figures assembled by various sources disclosed increases in the incidence of murders and aggravated assaults, armed robberies and thefts. There was an increase in white-collar crime—in most instances, stealing from one's employer. While serving as assistant treasurer of the Commonwealth Building and Loan Association of Norfolk, Minnie Clark Mangum, for example, embezzled $3 million during the 1950s, most of which she gave to friends, relatives, and her favorite charities. There also took place after the war an astonishing increase in juvenile crime, and by the middle 1950s juvenile courts were convicting upward of a half-million children and teenagers each year. Undisclosed numbers of juvenile offenders were members of gangs, most of them spawned in slum areas of such cities as New York, Chicago, and Los Angeles. In addition to executing thefts and armed robberies and rapes, juvenile gangs armed with zip guns and switchblades, lengths of chain and pieces of pipe, axes and crowbars, made war on one another, sometimes with deadly results. And on occasion, gangs tortured and even murdered victims for what appeared to be the mere hell of doing it, as in Brooklyn in 1954 when members of a gang burned the soles of a man's feet with lighted cigarettes, then slowly drowned him.

The increase in juvenile crime dismayed and in many urban areas frightened law-abiding citizens. But Americans of the postwar era appeared to find greater fascination in the enterprise of "organized crime." Structured criminal organizations presided over by unscupulous individuals who posed as legitimate businesspeople were scarcely a new phenomenon in the United States. They had flourished in the decade and a half after World War I, during the time of national prohibition, when they provided their thirsty compatriots with illegal booze. The passing of prohibition in 1933 scarcely gave them pause, inasmuch as millions of citizens, most of whom doubtless perceived of themselves as law-respecting, were inveterate consumers of a variety of illegal commodities and services that criminal organizations were capable of providing: narcotics, pornography, prostitution, and (most importantly) opportunities to gamble. Other sources of revenue included loan-sharking, blackmail, and "protection," that is, the extortion of money from legitimate businesses, for example, dry-cleaning establishments and auto-repair shops, by threatening bodily harm to proprietors or damage to their places of business. Mobsters operated car-theft rings and bought and sold stolen merchandise. In the years following the global war, they discovered yet another lucrative enterprise: labor racketeering. After infiltrating such unions as those representing truckers and longshoremen, mobsters brokered contracts between employers and the unions to head off costly strikes—in return for payoffs to themselves. Of larger moment, they conspired with corrupt labor chieftains to invest union pension and welfare funds in assorted mob enterprises, many of them legitimate.

The legal enterprises in which criminal organizations invested their ill-gotten profits included retail firms, restaurants and bars, jukebox distributorships and bowling alleys, hotels and parking lots, trucking companies and food supply companies. At the close of World War II, the organization headed by the notorious Benjamin Siegel (known as "Bugsy" because of his habit of throwing temper tantrums when agitated) erected the lavish Flamingo Hotel in Las Vegas, at the time a rather sleepy desert community of fewer than 20,000 people. When the Flamingo's casino began to yield impressive returns, other mobsters (and a few legitimate entrepreneurs) emulated Siegel, and by 1960 Las Vegas was a glittering mecca for gamblers and pleasure seekers whose population had soared beyond 60,000. Meanwhile, particularly during the 1950s, the mobs invested extensively in an array of small recording companies.

What if a competitor sought to encroach what a criminal organization regarded as its exclusive territory (or "turf")? The organization might dispatch the competitor's leader or some of its functionaries in a hail of bullets. Bugsy Siegel was so dispatched in 1949 while sitting on a couch and reading a newspaper in the home of a friend in Beverly Hills. The infamous head of "Murder, Incorporated," Albert Anastasia, was gunned down in 1957 in the barbershop of the Park-Sheraton Hotel in New York—while lying back in a barber's chair, his head shrouded in steaming towels. To keep the law at bay, the mobs routinely bribed police officers and other public officials.

After World War II, Americans became increasingly conscious of organized, or syndicated, crime. They usually referred to criminal organizations as the Mafia, the name long applied to the criminal syndicate in Sicily. It was a misleading term, inasmuch as it intimated that a preponderance of the country's organized criminals were of Sicilian or at least Italian origin and that syndicated criminal activity in the United States was under the direction of a monolithic organization. Many mobsters were indeed of Italian descent, but many were not. Some were of Irish extraction, others of Jewish, still others of Chinese. As for a monolithic organization, nothing of the sort existed. Rather, hundreds of criminal organizations, most of them comprising a comparative handful of mobsters (who toiled long hours and realized modest returns), functioned more or less independently in every part of the republic. To be sure, the five Cosa Nostra (or Mafia) "families" in New York City, along with nineteen or so families in other cities, formed a commission comprising about a dozen "Dons" and "Bosses" to arbitrate disputes and formulate general policy. But the commission exercised about as much authority over organized crime in the United States as the UN exercised over the political affairs of the world. Only occasionally was the commission able to settle a dispute or establish a policy that the families would respect for any length of time.

Increased public awareness of its activities notwithstanding, organized crime suffered no important reverses between 1945 and 1960. Because of the ability of leaders of criminal organizations to insulate themselves from day-to-day operations of their illegal enterprises, it was hard to gather evidence against them. Moreover, the director of the FBI, J. Edgar Hoover, his attention fixed on communist subversion, took little interest in trying to gather evidence against the mob. Ultimately, of course, it was the willingness of tens of millions of ordinary citizens to pay out billions of dollars each year for the commodities and services provided by criminal organizations that enabled the mobsters to stay in business.

## THE FAMILY

However fascinated by the enterprise of mobsters, a preponderance of the people of the United States in the years 1945–1960 continued to hold traditional values in high esteem, particularly those associated with the nuclear family. Hence they tended to look with dismay on statistics disclosing that illegitimate births by white mothers in the United States advanced from 56.4 per thousand live births in 1945 to 82.5 in 1960, by nonwhite mothers from 60.9

to 141.8. But they found satisfaction in figures disclosing that Americans were divorcing less frequently than they had during the preceding decade or so. What they thought about other changes that were taking place in the family life of the republic is hard to say.

To meet family needs (and wants), increasing numbers of mothers of children under the age of 18 were "gainfully employed" during the postwar years: 4.1 million in 1948, 7.5 million in 1958. As a consequence, according to various studies, fathers increasingly involved themselves in caring for children and managing households. Although producing a child or two more than their parents had produced, the typical married couple appeared more apt to use contraception, the more so since state and federal laws restricting the transportation and dispensation of such devices generally went unenforced. As fate would have it, the usual methods of contraception often proved unreliable, and the result was the birth of great numbers of "unplanned" babies, inasmuch as a preponderance of Americans at that time recoiled at the thought of aborting an embryo or fetus, which remained illegal in any case, except (in several states) when the life of the mother was determined to be at risk. Then, in 1960, a new type of contraceptive, the birth control pill, went on sale. The pill for the first time offered a method of contraception that was almost 100 percent effective.

Parents, meanwhile, considered strategies for rearing children, and in the postwar era millions of them weighed the writings of Benjamin Spock, a pediatrician who suggested that parents should impose few restraints on children, shower them with affection, and encourage them to develop their individual personalities. When legions of young people during the 1960s rebelled against the values of their parents and, in the view of older Americans, became generally obnoxious, some critics placed much of the blame on Dr. Spock. Had they been subjected to more discipline in their formative years, so critics maintained, the children-turned-young adults would be less inclined to rebellion. Such a conclusion rested on the assumption that parents were largely responsible for forming the values and patterns of behavior of children. But even as parents were applying the maxims of Dr. Spock, in the 1950s scattered studies were suggesting that peer group pressure and the entertainment media, particularly television, were in fact more important than parents in shaping youthful values and behavior.

## EDUCATION

An overriding concern in most families was schooling for children, and the years following World War II were a time of ferment in American education. As already noted, the country's schools found themselves caught up in the postwar search for communist subversion and in the struggle for civil equality, while shortages of classrooms and teachers resulting from the baby boom prompted a national debate over the merits of assistance to education by the federal government.

Enrollments in the country's colleges and universities dramatically increased during the period, from 1.4 million in 1940 to 2.6 million in 1950 to 3.2 million in 1960. Such increases resulted from a variety of circumstances. Of particular note, large numbers of veterans of the armed forces enrolled in colleges and universities in accord with provisions of the Servicemen's Readjustment Act of 1944, the so-called GI Bill of Rights, which offered subsistence allowances and payments of tuition and allowances for books and supplies. Subsequent legislation, Public Law 550, provided monthly payments to veterans of the years of the Korean War who were enrolled in colleges and universities. Almost a third of the students enrolled in colleges in 1949–1950 were verterans, and during the entire period 7.8 million veterans received educational benefits under the GI bills at a cost to taxpayers of $14.5 billion. Colleges and university enrollments also expanded because higher education became affordable to increasing numbers of Americans during that period of economic prosperity.

Of comparable moment was the long-running debate over the objectives and quality of elementary and secondary education in the United States. It was a debate that centered on the merits of "progressive education."

Reacting against an educational system that emphasized memorization, drill, and discipline, educators of the progressive genre began to argue in the early years of the twentieth century that children should be encouraged to develop according to their peculiar talents, to assert their individuality, and to acquire skills that would enable them to adjust to all manner of life situations. Schoolchildren, in a word, should undertake individual projects, express themselves creatively through the arts, go on field trips. Since most would never enroll in colleges or universities, they should have the opportunity to take courses in homemaking and typing, woodworking and auto mechanics, agriculture and mechanical drawing. Such ideas made perfect sense in the estimate of nearly every educator in America by the 1920s, and at the end of World War II progressive education stood almost unchallenged.

Challenge was in the offing, and beginning in the late 1940s progressive education began to come under unrelenting attack. According to critics, progressive educators had lost sight of the fact that the primary function of schools was to encourage intellectual growth. Intensive work in basic subjects, the critics maintained, should be the preoccupation of the schools. Of the critics, none stirred as much debate as Arthur Bestor, a historian at the University of Illinois, whose book *Educational Wastelands* appeared in 1953. Arguing that the essential purpose of education was "the deliberate cultivation of the ability to think," Bestor argued that every student should be immersed in a variety of intellectual disciplines, including mathematics, science, language, and history. Another critic was Vice Adm. Hyman G. Rickover of the Navy, who assailed "life-adjustment" education and contended that educators were placing the country's security in jeopardy by failing to stress intellectual competence. "The future belongs to the best-educated nation," Rickover asserted. America's rival in the contest for future preeminence, of course, was the Soviet Union. "Russian engineering and scientific development constitute a threat to our military power. . . . There can be no second place in a contest with Russia and there will be no second chance if we lose."

James B. Conant, a distinguished physicist, onetime president of Harvard, and more recently the U.S. ambassador to West Germany, entered the debate in 1959 with a book entitled *The American High School*. Like Rickover and others, he was a "Cold Warrior" who feared the Soviet impulse to conquest, and thus argued that for "the sake of the nation" bright students should undertake demanding programs of study. But he contended that there was nothing inherently wrong with the comprehensive high school that had resulted from the ideas of progressive educationists. The achievement of intellectual quality was possible in the comprehensive high school, he believed, mainly by eliminating very small secondary schools and requiring all students to complete a core of courses in English, mathematics, science, and social studies. As one might expect, educators proved more receptive to the arguments of Conant than to those of more vehement critics such as Bestor and Rickover.

## RELIGION AND REASSURANCE

Whereas education was a preoccupation of large numbers of Americans during the period from 1945 to 1960, religion was a preoccupation of many others. Indeed, religion experienced something akin to a golden era in the United States during the decade and a half after the global war. Some observers found an explanation in anxieties resulting from the threat of nuclear annihilation that now hung over the planet. Whatever the explanation, membership in religious organizations continued to enlarge. Some 86.8 million Americans, or 57 percent of the national population, claimed membership in churches or synagogues in 1950, 114.4 million (64 percent) in 1960. Asked to enumerate the types of news stories that readers would most like to encounter in their daily papers, editors of 51 of the country's largest newspapers surmised in 1950 that readers would most like to read that the Stalinist dictatorship had collapsed, war had been permanently abolished, and scientists had found a cure for cancer. After that, they thought, the people of the United States would most like to read that Jesus of Nazareth had returned to earth and that science had proved the existence of life after death. Eighty-one percent of the respondents to a Gallup poll in 1957 affirmed that "religion can answer all or most of today's problems."

Evidence of the esteem in which Americans of the postwar era held religion was indeed pervasive. Church buildings and parochial schools (mostly Catholic) proliferated. New religious denominations appeared, including the Church of the Nazarene, Churches of God, and Pentecostal Assemblies. Enrollment in colleges and universities having religious affiliations burgeoned. The "crusades" of a youthful Baptist minister from North Carolina, Billy Graham, drew huge audiences, and a poll of Americans in the mid-1950s disclosed that Graham was one of the most admired men in the country. The books and radio talks and, at length, television homilies of Monsignor Fulton J. Sheen

June 19, 1960: The evangelist Billy Graham opens his National Capital Crusade before an overflow audience in Griffith Stadium in Washington, the home park of baseball's Washington Senators.

appealed, to millions of Americans of nearly all religious persuasions, and in 1954 Sheen, a man of rare theatrical talent as well as wit and intellect, was named television's "man of the year." The revised standard version of the Bible ranked second on the bestseller list in 1952, and novels and nonfiction books having religious themes were likewise bestsellers: Lloyd C. Douglas's *The Big Fisherman* (1949) and *The Robe* (1953), Henry Morton Robinson's *The*

*Cardinal* (1950), and Catherine Marshall's *A Man Called Peter* (1953). Films adapted from the foregoing books, as well as others constructed around religious themes, were box-office successes. Indeed, *The Ten Commandments*, released by Paramount Pictures in 1957, yielded the largest financial return of any film to that time. Congress, meanwhile, responded to the religious impulses of the citizenry by inserting the words "under God" in the pledge of national allegiance.

While millions of Americans sought reinforcement in religion, uncounted others sought it in what has been termed the cult of reassurance. The premier spokesman of the latter cult was the Presbyterian minister Norman Vincent Peale, whose books *A Guide to Confident Living* (1949) and *The Power of Positive Thinking* (1952) sold millions of copies. Presented on radio and television as well as in books and articles, Peale's message was that negative thinking rather than the forces and institutions of society was the main cause of anxiety and frustration. It was a message that met a wide response in a time when great numbers of Americans were taking a strong interest in psychological explanations and techniques as well as religion—when people sprinkled conversation with such terms as *neurosis* and *maladjustment*, authors and film producers accentuated the compulsions and complexes of characters, and magazines offered a plethora of self-analysis quizzes and psychological counsel.

## TELEVISION AND MOTION PICTURES

As in every era, Americans of the postwar years sought release as well as reassurance. Particularly in nonworking hours, therefore, they flocked to taverns and nightclubs, American Legion posts and the club rooms of Elks and Moose lodges, bowling alleys and golf courses. They hunted and fished, gambled and went on vacations (for example, to Disneyland, the elaborate and, in the view of many visitors, magical theme park that opened near Anaheim in 1955). They read magazines: *Life, Look, Reader's Digest,* and *Saturday Evening Post,* the big four among popular periodicals of the postwar years. They watched television.

As already noted, the growth of television in postwar America was nothing short of phenomenal. Not that television in its pristine years was free of problems. The typical outdoor antennas in that time before cable TV could not pick up the signals of broadcasting stations that were more than 60 or 70 miles distant. The screens of the early receiving sets were small, and the black-and-white images they provided often fuzzy. Problems notwithstanding, the people of the country responded to television with unabashed enthusiasm. As a result, the big-name radio shows of the broadcasting networks left the air one by one, sometimes to be transformed into television programs. Radio thereupon became largely a preserve of local disc jockeys and purveyors of local news and sporting reports. (At that, the number of radio stations, a preponderance of them situated in small towns, increased from 936 in 1945 to 4,611 in 1960.)

Mesmerized by "Howdy Doody" and "I Love Lucy," "Milton Berle" and "Gun-smoke," not to mention the news commentaries of Edward R. Murrow and live coverage of the World Series and national political conventions, few Americans lamented the decline of network radio. Like radio, of course, television depended on advertising revenues, and corporate advertisers discovered at the outset of the television era that no other medium could match television's combination of audio and visual appeals. Advertisers thus expended $171 million for television commercials in 1950, $1.5 billion in 1960.

Only one dark cloud crossed television's horizon in the period: the notorious quiz scandals. But the scandals brought only temporary embarrassment. They came to light in 1959 when it was disclosed that producers had rigged quiz contests on such enormously popular big-prize shows as NBC-TV's "21" and CBS-TV's "64,000 Dollar Question." A high point in the process of disclosure occurred when Charles Van Doren, a handsome and articulate member of a prominent and intellectually renowed family who had won $129,000 on "21," admitted to a congressional investigating committee that the producer had provided him with both questions and answers in advance of his 14 weekly appearances on the show and instructed him to grimace and hesitate in the interest of building suspense.

Inevitably, television had enormous implications for the motion picture industry. Unlike radio, which the latter industry had never viewed as much of a threat to its prosperity, television offered moving images as well as sound, just like the movies. Millions of Americans at the dawn of the television era, indeed, perceived of the television set in the main as a wondrous device that enabled them to experience movielike entertainment in the comfort of their own living rooms and without the requirement of paying admissions charges.

In the years that immediately followed the war, Americans continued to crowd into motion picture theaters in record numbers to experience such award-winning films as *Gentleman's Agreement* (1946) and *All the King's Men* (1948). But it was clear by 1950 that television represented a genuine threat to the motion picture industry, for increasing numbers of moviegoers were opting to stay at home and watch TV rather than go out to the movies. Weekly attendance thus began to slip. But the industry responded to the challenge. While turning out fewer films than in former years, those that it did turn out tended to be of higher quality, for example, *The African Queen* (1950), *Around the World in Eighty Days* (1957), and *Bridge on the River Kwai* (1958). It introduced Cinerama, Todd A-O, VistaVision, and CinemaScope, each of which projected images across a wide screen. It experimented with three-dimensional films and encouraged the growth of that postwar phenomenon, the drive-in theater, of special appeal to automobile-oriented teenagers and young adults. If weekly attendance at the movies never reached the 50 or so million people of the years immediately following the global war, it had advanced by the latter 1950s beyond 45 million, up several million from the early 1950s. Meanwhile, the motion picture industry gave up its struggle to keep old movies off the TV tube, and in the latter 1950s the owners of old films closed several deals with television broadcasters. More than that, the film makers set about to produce a new genre of motion picture: the made-for-television movie.

## NEWSPAPERS, BOOKS, DRAMA

Less affected by television was the newspaper industry. Newspaper provided far more news and analysis than television regarding domestic politics, relations with the Soviet empire, and the conflict in Korea—also about the romance and marriage of Princess Elizabeth of Great Britain in 1947; the transformation of a onetime army private, 26-year-old George W. Jorgensen to the "blond beauty" Christine Jorgensen following six surgeries and two thousand hormone injections in a hospital in Copenhagen in 1952; and the execution at San Quentin in 1960 of Caryl Chessman, the so-called red-light bandit who had written the best-selling review of his own criminal career, *Cell 2455 Death Row*. In the pages of newspapers, people could peruse the insightful columns of Walter Lippmann, sometimes referred to as the national conscience, weigh the commentaries of newspaper editors, pore over myriad stories emanating from the world of sports. On the comic pages, they could follow the adventures of Steve Canyon and Dick Tracy, the whimsy of Li'l Abner and Pogo, and (in what were sometimes referred to as the "soap opera" comic strips) the doings of Rex Morgan and Mary Worth. In any event, the average daily circulation of the country's newspapers, not to mention advertising revenues, increased steadily during the postwar period. Still, intermittent strikes and escalating costs of newsprint and new equipment forced the merger of many competing newspapers and the demise of such well-known dailies as the Boston *Post*, Brooklyn *Eagle*, and St. Louis *Star-Times*.

Nor did television appear to have an adverse effect on the sale of books. Americans bought books by the tens of millions in 1945–1960. In particular they bought paperbacks, introduced in the American market in 1939 by Pocket Books. Their favorites were mystery fiction, and the most popular mysteries were those by Erle Stanley Gardner and Mickey Spillane (the latter of whose yarns featured the adventures of the violence-prone and sexually uninhibited detective Mike Hammer). Still, the best-selling book of the postwar years was Grace Metalious's steamy novel *Peyton Place* (1956), which eventually sold some 10 million copies, 95 percent of them in paperback.

In the estimate of most critics, of course, *Peyton Place* was not an outstanding piece of literature. Unfortunately, one could say the same about nearly every other novel published during the period. The better novelists certainly were competent, and Americans did not want for well-crafted and stimulating novels to read, for example, James Jones's *From Here to Eternity* (1948), Ernest Hemingway's *The Old Man and the Sea* (1952), and James Baldwin's *Go Tell It on the Mountain* (1953). But only Norman Mailer's terrifying account of men in battle, *The Naked and the Dead* (1948), won much critical acclaim. In part because the enterprise of novelists fell short of expectations—but more importantly because of the voracious appetites of Americans of the period for facts and practical guidance—sales of nonfiction books, including gardening manuals and cookbooks, marriage handbooks and psychological guides, histories and biographies, eventually surpassed those of books that offered fictional themes.

As with the country's novelists, so with its playwrights: Other than Tennessee Williams's *A Street Named Desire* (1947) and Arthur Miller's *Death of a Salesman* (1949), few new plays of the period excited drama critics. Serious music seemed to fare better, and critics detected a new maturity in the music being written in the United States and performed on its concert stages. Americans appeared to take new interest in choral music, opera, and ballet. But it was musical comedy that generated the most excitement in the years after the war, and enthusiastic audiences crowded into theaters to experience such hits as *Annie Get Your Gun, Carousel, The King and I, Kiss Me Kate,* and *South Pacific.*

## ROCK 'N' ROLL

The most ardent listeners of music were teenagers and young adults, and only a comparative handful of them cared much for classical music or even musical comedy. Particularly in the early postwar years, their tastes ran to the jazz and swing sounds of such big bands as those of Benny Goodman and Harry James and the mellow offerings of such vocalists as Bing Crosby and Frank Sinatra, Dinah Shore and Patti Page. Some of them responded to the country melodies crafted by the incomparable Hank Williams and the mellow voice of the Grand Ole Opry star Red Foley. But then, in the early 1950s, the musical tastes of tens of millions of young Americans began to change.

It was in 1953 that an obscure disc jockey in Cleveland named Alan Freed inaugurated "Moondog's Rock and Roll Party," during which he played rhythm-and-blues records by black performers for radio audiences that consisted in the main of white teenagers. The tempo, heavy beat, and frenetic vocal styles of the rhythm-and-blues music met an enthusiastic response among Freed's young white listeners. But Freed did not refer to the music he was playing as rhythm-and-blues. Conscious that the term rhythm-and-blues had racial connotations, he referred to it as rock 'n' roll, a variant of phrases that had appeared in lyrics of rhythm-and-blues music and was sexually allusive, as in "rock me, roll me, all night long."

Whatever the origins of the music that Freed was playing, recording companies quickly took note of his success, and thereupon signed white performers to more or less copy rhythm-and-blues records by blacks (for example, Little Richard) and then to record new songs that represented an amalgam of rhythm-and-blues and country-western or hillbilly sounds. The first bona fide rock 'n' roll hit was "Crazy Man, Crazy," recorded by Bill Haley and His Comets in 1953. Recorded by Haley and his group the following year, "Shake, Rattle and Roll" and "Rock Around the Clock," the latter of which was the theme of the hit film *Blackboard Jungle,* were even more popular.

A pronounced beat and the sounds of amplified guitars characterized early rock 'n' roll. The music tended to be raucous, uninhibited, sensual. Its lyrics expressed independence, disdain for conventionality, unabashed sexuality—also insecurity, pain, violence. Performers convulsed their bodies, flailed their arms, kicked their legs. They frequently shouted the lyrics of their songs. Like

June 1956: Described in a press release as 'one of the newer song stylists,' Elvis Presley performs in Long Beach.

the portrayal by the actor James Dean in the widely acclaimed film *Rebel Without a Cause,* rock 'n' roll seemed to catch the restlessness and spirit of rebellion against accepted norms of behavior and orthodox values that were beginning to animate increasing numbers of young Americans. Indeed, rock 'n' roll was the first musical form in the American experience to be aimed almost exclusively at younger citizens. And what did older Americans think of the new music? Viewing it as vulgar, animalistic, coarse, nauseating, degenerate, riotous, moronic, uncultured, and subversive of good morals, they almost universally despised it.

Within a few years, the hostility that Americans who were past 30 felt for rock 'n' roll appeared to decline. Responsible in part for that decline was Elvis Presley, a youthful truck driver of Memphis who catapulted to prominence in the mid-1950s when he recorded "Heartbreak Hotel" and "You Ain't Nuthin' But a Hound Dog."

Immersed from childhood in country or hillbilly music, Presley had taken to listening to rhythm-and-blues recordings that were broadcast over radio stations catering to the tastes of predominantly black audiences. Out of that experience, he fashioned a style that some aficionados referred to as rockabilly, most people as rock 'n' roll. Exuding sensuality, Presley wore long sideburns and tight-fitting pants, wriggled his hips, and leered at audiences. But his voice was rich and talent manifest. Moreover, he doted on his parents—and by the end of the 1950s was recording gospel songs and sentimental ballads as well as rock 'n' roll pieces. He thus came to be tolerated if not enthusiastically embraced by large numbers of older Americans, and as a result played an important part in easing rock 'n' roll into the cultural mainstream.

## SPORTS

Spectator sports had been an obsession of uncounted Americans, particularly men, for several generations. And such sporting performers as Babe Ruth, Jack Dempsey, and Red Grange had become bona fide folk heroes in the United States. No less than in former times, spectator sports remained an obsession of uncounted Americans, particularly men, during the decade and a half following World War II.

Boxing enthusiasts witnessed the decline of the incomparable heavyweight champion Joe Louis in the latter 1940s and the advent (and decline) during the 1950s of another premier heavyweight champion, Rocky Marciano. Other fighters of renown were the middleweight Tony Zale and the featherweight Willie Pep. But the outstanding performer of the period was the peerless middleweight and welterweight "Sugar Ray" Robinson, considered by some veteran observers of the sport to be the finest fighter "pound for pound" ever to step into a boxing ring.

Golf had an array of memorable performers, including Patty Berg and Louise Suggs—also Mildred "Babe" Didrickson Zaharias, generally regarded as the best female athlete that America had produced. The latter 1950s witnessed the emergence of Arnold Palmer, who won the Masters tournament in 1958 and 1960, and a brilliant amateur, Jack Nicklaus. But the premier golfer of the period was 140-pound Ben Hogan, who at the time of his retirement from the professional tour in 1955 had won more major tournaments than any performer to that time. Jack Kramer, Pancho Gonzales, and Vic Sexias were the brightest stars in men's tennis. The most renowned of the women performers was Maureen "Little Mo" Connolly, who at the age of 18 in 1953 won all four major singles championships—the Australian, British, French, and American.

Thoroughbred racing lost none of its appeal—indeed attendance at horse tracks steadily increased. The premier thoroughbreds of the period were Assault, Armed, Citation, Native Dancer, and Nashua, the premier jockeys Eddie Arcaro, Johnny Longdon, and Bill Shoemaker. Motor racing also attracted legions of paying customers. Among the most daring drivers in open-cockpit racing were Mauri Rose and Bill Vukovich, the latter of whom lost his life in a fiery crash at Indianapolis in 1955. A new phenomenon in the postwar era was stock-car racing. For a couple of seasons in the early 1950s, the stock-car circuit was dominated by a single make of car to an extent that has remained unrivaled: the Hudson Hornet, powered by an L-head six-cylinder engine.

Led by such performers as the sprinters Harrison Dillard and Mel Patton and the decathlon champion Bob Mathias, U.S. athletes dominated the summer Olympic games in London in 1948. Four years later, in 1952 at Helsinki, athletes representing the United States again accumulated the most points during the summer games, although those representing the Soviet Union were a strong second. At the summer games in Melbourne in 1956, Soviet athletes accumulated 722 points to 593 for those of the United States. Only in men's track and field and basketball did Americans predominate. At Rome in 1960, the Soviets did even better, accumulating 807.5 points to 564.5 for the Americans. Still, the American sprinter Wilma Rudolph, a partial invalid as a child, won three gold medals, Cassius M. Clay won the light-heavyweight boxing championship, and the U.S. basketball squad, in the estimate of some observers the best amateur basketball team assembled to that time, rolled over all of its opponents. Only in men and women's figure skating did Americans have much to show for their efforts in the winter Olympics. Tenley Albright, for example, won the gold medal in women's figure skating in 1956, the diminutive Carol Heiss, in 1960.

Despite almost total domination by two teams, the Detroit Red Wings (who won seven consecutive National Hockey League championships between 1949 and 1955) and the Montreal Canadiens, professional ice hockey won legions of new enthusiasts during the postwar period. High school, college, and professional basketball also flourished. The most successful college team of the period—if one measures success in terms of victories achieved on the playing floor—were the Wildcats of the University of Kentucky, coached by the legendary Adolph Rupp. The Cats won National Collegiate Athletic Association championships in 1948, 1949, 1951, and 1958. Unfortunately, several of their players, as well as players of teams representing Bradley University, the City College of New York, Long Island University, Manhattan College, New York University, and the University of Toledo were implicated in a point-fixing scandal in 1951. In professional basketball, the National Basketball Association was formed in 1949, and during the league's pristine years the Minneapolis Lakers, led by George Mikan, were the dominant team. By the end of the 1950s, the Boston Celtics, coached by Arnold "Red" Auerbach and led by 6-foot-10-inch Bill Russell, had emerged as a professional basketball power.

The traditional "national pastime," major league baseball offered its fans an array of superlative players during the decade and a half after World War II, among them Ted Williams of the Red Sox and Stan Musial of the Cardinals, Willie Mays of the Giants and Warren Spahn of the Braves. The time-honored game also produced many memorable moments, including the perfect game pitched by Don Larsen of the Yankees in the World Series of 1956 and the dramatic home run by Bobby Thomson in 1951 that brought a National League championship to the Giants. While generating memorable moments, major league baseball, as previously mentioned, put aside its infamous color line that had prohibited black players from competing. It also changed its half-century configuration of franchises when the Boston Braves moved to Milwaukee in 1953, the St. Louis Browns to Baltimore (where they became the Orioles) in

1954, and the Brooklyn Dodgers and New York Giants to Los Angeles and San Francisco, respectively, in 1958.

Baseball produced an array of heroes and memorable moments, but football was the professional sport that experienced the most impressive increase in popularity in the postwar era. Television was in no small measure responsible. Because much of its action at any given moment centered on a comparatively small part of the playing field, football was remarkably suited to television. With its mixture of machinelike precision and controlled mayhem, moreover, pro football also appealed to that same impulse to masculinity that prompted millions of adult males of the period to savor Mickey Spillane novels and smoke Marlboro cigarettes. For whatever reason, the sport prospered, and among sports enthusiasts the names Otto Graham and Johnny Unitas became almost as well known as Ted Williams and Stan Musial.

The increasing popularity of professional football did not diminish the appeal of the collegiate game. College football's appeal was easily understood, for scarcely any other sporting activity could match the color, pageantry, and excitement of a college football game on a sunny Saturday afternoon in the autumn—especially one involving Army or Notre Dame, Michigan or Oklahoma, Louisiana State or UCLA, schools whose teams established reputations as veritable powerhouses at one time or another during the years following World War II.

## CRITICS OF AMERICAN SOCIETY

Although a preponderance of Americans during the period thought the essential condition of the national society just fine, some of their compatriots believed otherwise. Among the latter were assorted individuals who assailed what they perceived to be the decadence or at least the shortcomings of the fabled citadel of freedom, democracy, and opportunity.

While young Americans continued to die in Korea and Eisenhower and Stevenson campaigned for the presidency in the autumn of 1952, Charles Scribner's Sons published a novel by the youthful writer John Chellon Holmes entitled *Go*. It was not a major publishing event. Drawn from the author's experiences and observations in the bohemian colony of Greenwich Village in New York, *Go* sold fewer than three thousand copies and received scant literary attention. But at several points in the novel the author invoked the term *Beat Generation*, translated exhausted generation, and in subsequent years, when Americans became conscious of "beatniks," Holmes's book was widely referred to as the first novel of the Beat Generation.

Their numbers never exceeding a few thousand, beatniks were social dropouts who professed contempt for the conventions, values, and institutions of society at large, that is, the society of the "squares." Caught up in a mindless quest for material comfort and social status, squares, according to beatniks, were intellectually and spiritually vacant, their society decadent and without purpose or joy. Beatniks scorned the moral and ethical precepts of Christianity, which they perceived to be at the root of most of the ills of Western society. They derided all agents of authority, particularly the government and police, and felt only contempt for displays of patriotism. They ridiculed the work ethic, hence eschewed regular employment, and tended to be apolitical and generally indifferent to the problems of the larger society. They sought personal release and, so they maintained, purification and illumination.

The mecca of the Beat Generation by the mid-1950s had become the North Beach section of San Francisco, where beatniks crowded into antiquated and sometimes run-down apartments, which they referred to as "pads." Furnishings in the typical pad were contrivedly sparse: perhaps a mattress, a table and lamp, some bells and bamboo curtains, a wine bottle or two suspended from the ceiling. Beatniks seldom bathed. The men usually wore sandals or went barefooted and grew beards, the women let their hair grow long and straight and wore jeans and sweaters. Jazz music and indiscriminate sexual activity were central to their lifestyle. They contended that spontaneity was the premier value in personal relations and creative activities, and professed to seek a more perfect appreciation of what they referred to as higher reality by spacing out on drugs, particularly marijuana. They spiced their conversation with obscenities, and delighted in provoking or scandalizing squares by flaunting their views and lifestyle. They cultivated Eastern mysticism, notably Zen Buddhism, which they believed offered a philosophic justification for their refusal to seek gainful employment and for their sometimes raucous demonstrations against the values and institutions of the squares.

Beatniks liked to gather in coffeehouses to listen to beatnik poetry read to the accompaniment of progressive jazz. Sprinkled with obscenities, the poems usually juxtaposed seemingly unrelated images and often were oriented toward eroticism. A purpose of the poets was to liberate poetry from what they perceived to be academic artificiality, and the result was cut-up and disjointed verse that nonbeatniks often found chaotic. The most acclaimed poet of the Beat Generation was Allen Ginsburg, whose best piece, *Howl*, appeared in 1956. The best-known novelist was Jack Kerouac, whose book *On the Road* (1955) conveyed the author's view of what he perceived to be the emptiness of life in the contemporary United States by narrating the travels and experiences of a youthful drifter.

Beatniks were not the only critics of American society in the decade and a half after World War II. Nor were they the most influential. Far more attention, for example, was lavished on William H. Whyte's book *The Organization Man* (1956) than on Kerouac's *On the Road*. Drawing on theories set out in the sociological treatise by David Riesman, *The Lonely Crowd: A Study of the Changing American Character* (1950), Whyte contended that Americans in recent times had increasingly subordinated themselves to the interests and the ethos of big organizations (corporations, the government, universities, labor unions) that promised security and high standards of living. By so doing, he thought, they had forfeited the commitment to individual initiative, thrift, and competition which, in his view, had animated earlier generations of Americans and resulted in the phenomenal expansion and development of the nation.

Another social critic of the period who attracted wide attention was the journalist Vance O. Packard. In *The Hidden Persuaders* (1957), Packard examined the motivational research that undergirded current advertising campaigns. He observed, for example, that motivational research had prompted the conclusion that the advertising campaign in support of Marlboro cigarettes, resting as it did on feminine appeals, was sexually maladjusted, whereupon the campaign was revised to associate the Marlboro brand with masculinity—and as a result the sales of Marlboros skyrocketed. By scientifically catering to the irrational, Packard believed, advertisers and other manipulators were contributing to the establishment of a progressively less rational society. In *The Status Seekers* (1959), he complained of increasing social stratification as millions of Americans strained to surround themselves with visible evidence of the superior rank in society to which they believed themselves entitled. As a consequence, he thought, opportunities for upward mobility in the United States were undergoing an unfortunate constriction. In *The Waste Makers* (1960), he argued that consumption for the sake of consumption had come to be exalted as a virtue and that early "product death" in the interest of consumption (and of course profit) had become a watchword in America's manufacturing industries.

Of larger influence was the volume by the Harvard economist John Kenneth Galbraith, *The Affluent Society* (1958). Anticipating Packard's third volume, Galbraith assailed what he thought was the uncontrolled production of superfluous commodities. Producing beyond the level of reasonable need, he contended, required the creation of artificial markets and led to the absurdity of urging people to buy commodities that they neither wanted nor needed in order that fellow citizens might continue to be paid for producing the unwanted and unneeded commodities. While production had thus increased, he went on, public services had failed to keep pace with the needs of society. Galbraith also addressed the problem of poverty in affluent America. Recalling the words of William Pitt, Britain's Great Commoner of the eighteenth century, that poverty was no disgrace but was damned annoying, he wrote, "In the contemporary United States it is not annoying but it is a disgrace."

## RETROSPECT

Various of the complaints registered by beatniks and other critics regarding the pulsating society of the United States during the decade and a half after the global war were arguably on the mark. As the beatniks and other critics contended, most Americans in those years probably were unduly preoccupied by a sometimes vacuous quest for material comfort and will to consume the baubles and savor the myriad pleasures and diversions that their rampant affluence brought within reach. As latter-day critics have observed, a preponderance of the citizenry of the United States in the postwar era appeared almost impervious to the scandal of abuse and discrimination endured by millions of citizens on account of race in what a great majority of Americans believed without reservation to be a land of unparalleled liberty, justice, and opportunity. Most citizens of the North American superpower during the years 1945–1960, moreover, were nearly blind to the grinding poverty and resultant despair that gripped perhaps one-fifth of their compatriots, who resided in what the social critic Michael Harrington a few years later would identify as "the Other America," that is, the America of privation and slums, a part of the great and prosperous republic that seldom passed the vision or touched the consciousness of the great preponderance of its affluent citizens. Nor were many Americans of those years sensitive to a variety of other problems confronting their prosperous and pulsating society that would become apparent in the years to come: rampant discrimination against women—in education, in the law, in the workplace, in education, in the professions, not to mention in the typical American household; blatant pollution and even destruction of the natural environment by ordinary citizens as well as by corporations and agencies of government, national as well as local; widespread abuse of consumers by corporations and entrepreneurs who produced and marketed goods and services.

Still, for scores of millions of Americans, the years 1945–1960 were good years, to borrow the term applied by the writer Walter Lord to the first thirteen or so years of the twentieth century in the United States, notwithstanding assorted anxieties and frustrations wrought by the Cold War and a hot war in Korea, the abiding threat of nuclear annihilation, the rantings of Joe McCarthy and partisans of the John Birch Society, the depredations of the Mafia and legions of lesser criminals, and the stirrings of black citizens who had become weary of abuse and discrimination and yearned to enter the mainstream of the national life. Encountering only minor recessions, the national economy expanded steadily. Their myriad machines emitting a cacophony of shrieks and clangs and hisses, the country's manufacturing industries boomed during the postwar era, and it crossed the minds of few if any Americans that manufacturers in Western Europe, Japan, and elsewhere might one day become so proficient and aggressive that they would challenge the supremacy of American manufacturers in the United States itself, not to mention across the face of the planet. New industries, meanwhile, offered bright new opportunities for employment and profits.

Sharing in the national abundance on a scale that was unprecedented, tens of millions of ordinary citizens could fulfill dreams of owning homes and buying new cars. They could travel about their continental republic as they never had before, in their own cars or aboard streamlined and luxurious trains or sleek and swift airliners. Large numbers of them traveled abroad, as passengers on luxurious ocean liners or new transoceanic aircraft. The new gadget television opened new vistas of entertainment for scores of millions of Americans, the poor as well as the affluent. And if one tired of the tube, there were quality movies, books, and stage productions to savor. Thanks to the new antibiotic drugs and the Salk vaccine, the scourge of infection and disease appeared far less menacing than formerly.

Americans had lived in worse times. Indeed, from the perspective of scores of millions of citizens of the United States who had suffered genuine privation during the Great Depression of the 1930s and patiently endured the shortages of consumer goods and other annoyances during the global war but now were wallowing in affluence, the 15 years that followed the global war were more than good. They were golden.

# Chapter
# 5

# The Torch Is Passed

$A$t the dawn of 1960, Pres. Dwight D. Eisenhower pondered with optimism what was certain to be the final year of his public life. Most of all, he hoped that he might prevail on the leaders of Britain, France, West Germany, and the Soviet Union, during a summit conference that was scheduled to take place in Paris in the spring, to accept a disarmament treaty—an historic accomplishment that would provide a capstone to his half century of public service. When Khrushchev in early 1960 reiterated his demand that West Berlin be made an "international free city," a ploy that Western leaders believed was intended to facilitate a communist takeover of West Berlin, Eisenhower's hope that the impending summit conference would yield a disarmament treaty and inaugurate a dramatic winding down of the Cold War declined. Still, he determined to do whatever he could to further the cause of peace when Pres. Charles de Gaulle of France called the summit meeting to order.

Then, on May 5, 1960, 11 days before the summit conference was to begin, Khrushchev announced that the Soviets had shot down a U.S. aircraft inside Soviet territory. The plane was a high-flying U-2—one of several U-2s that had been flying over the Soviet Union during the past four years and with powerful cameras photographing industrial and military installations. After the State Department, hoping the pilot of the downed U-2 was dead, had put out a "cover story" that an American weather research plane may have strayed over the Soviet border and crashed, Khrushchev produced chunks of the plane and, worse, the pilot, Francis Gary Powers, who was very much alive—and who readily admitted that he had been on a spy mission. The State Department thereupon put out a statement that no official in Washington (namely, Eisenhower) had sanctioned the ill-starred flight of the U-2. Recognizing that the latter statement intimated that Ike was not in charge of his own administration, the state Department put out a third statement, this one leaving no doubt that responsibility for spy flights rested with the president.

A few days later, Eisenhower, looking old and depressed, flew to Paris. What followed was the most humiliating episode of his long career. Hardly

August 17, 1960: Francis Gary Powers in the dock in Moscow's Hall of Mirrors during his trial on espionage charges.

had the conference got under way before Khrushchev was on his feet, shouting and shaking his fists, demanding that Eisenhower order a halt to spy flights and apologize for previous flights. The president had already announced termination of U-2 flights over the Soviet Union, but he categorically refused to apologize. In the absence of an apology, Khrushchev would not negotiate. Thus ended Eisenhower's bright hopes of a few months before, although it is clear in retrospect that those hopes had been quite unrealistic. It is almost inconceivable that the summit conference might have yielded even a tentative disarmament agreement and heralded an end to the Cold War.

## ELECTION OF 1960

At the time of the debacle in Paris, the contest to determine who would succeed Eisenhower in the White House had moved into high gear. If Gov. Nelson A. Rockefeller of New York refused to give up his quest for the Republican nomination, it was clear by May of 1950 that Vice Pres. Richard Nixon would carry the standard of the GOP during the autumn campaign. John F. Kennedy, a youthful and charismatic senator of Massachusetts, was the leading contender for the Democratic presidential nomination.

Although the 43-year-old Kennedy had won a succession of primary elections, most importantly in Wisconsin and West Virginia, he did not yet have a lock on the nomination by mid-May of 1960. Some Democrats thought him too young to be president. Liberals doubted his commitment to the party's longtime liberal principles. And many Democrats suspected that his Catholic religious faith would assure his defeat in the autumn election should he win the nomination in the summer. Thus he faced an assortment of rivals, the most formidable of whom was Sen. Lyndon B. Johnson of Texas, the Democratic leader in the upper chamber of the national legislature. It mattered not. When delegates convened in Los Angeles in July, Kennedy won the nomination on the first ballot, then, in a move that stunned many of his partisans, designated Johnson to be his vice presidential running mate. A few weeks later, in Chicago, the Republicans nominated Nixon for president and Henry Cabot Lodge, Jr., for vice president.

As every American who has even a passing interest in presidential politics knows, the high points of the Kennedy-Nixon contest were four televised "debates" between the two candidates. During the personal confrontations, Kennedy cast a more appealing image than Nixon. More than that, he appeared at least as knowledgeable as his rival, hence was able to counter the Republican argument that Nixon's experience in the Eisenhower administration had given the vice president special insight into the problems facing the republic. A phone call to the wife of Martin Luther King, Jr., following the arrest of the civil rights leader during a demonstration in Georgia, prompted black voters to rally behind Kennedy.

On November 6, 1960, the electorate rendered its verdict. According to the official count, the Democratic ticket edged the Republican by a mere

October 7, 1960: John Kennedy and Richard Nixon answer questions during nationally televised debate.

112,000 votes. (The Democratic margin in the Electoral College was 303–219.) But was the count honest? Persuaded that the Democrats had stolen thousands of votes, particularly in Illinois and Texas, Nixon was sure that it was not. But lest the national government be snarled for months until the courts resolved the question of who was to be president, he chose to make no challenge to Kennedy's election, arguably one of the most high-minded decisions by an American political figure in modern times. As for Congress, the conservative coalition of southern Democrats and Republicans would continue to reign supreme on Capitol Hill.

Three days before turning over the presidency to Kennedy, on January 17, 1961, President Eisenhower went before television cameras and delivered a farewell address to his compatriots. Save for that by George Washington in 1796, no farewell statement by an outgoing chief executive has left such an impression on the people of the United States. After asserting that the United States was locked in a deadly struggle with an atheistic and ruthless adversary that required the maintenance of a powerful military-naval establishment, he warned, "We must guard against the acquisition of unwarranted influence . . . by the military-industrial complex." Americans, the thirty-fourth president went on, "must never let the weight of this combination endanger our liberties or democratic processes." He observed that the country's scientists and engineers were increasingly functioning at the direction of the federal government.

"The prospects of domination of the nation's scholars by Federal employment, project allocations, and the power of money is ever present—and is gravely to be regarded." Ike, in a word, feared that public policy might become the captive of what he described as a scientific-technological elite. He told his compatriots that "disarmament with mutual honor and confidence is a continuing imperative," and confessed that he was putting down his responsibilities in the field of disarmament with a profound sense of disappointment. "As one who has witnessed the horror and the lingering sadness of war—as one who knows that another war could utterly destroy this civilization which has been so slowly and painfully built over two thousand years—I wish I could say tonight that a lasting peace is in sight."

However moving and even profound the words of Eisenhower, those days of early 1961 belonged to Kennedy, and on January 20, a frigid day in Washington, JFK took the presidential oath on a platform built atop the east steps of the Capitol, then gave a rousing oration in which he proclaimed, "The torch has been passed to a new generation of Americans, born in this century, tempered by war, disciplined by a hard and bitter peace, proud of our ancient heritage, and unwilling to witness or permit the slow undoing of those human rights to which this nation has always been committed, and to which we are committed today at home and around the world." Thus began a presidency that would survive for 1,036 days.

## JOHN F. KENNEDY

Born in Brookline, Massachusetts, in 1917, John F. Kennedy grew up as a member of a wealthy and gregarious Irish-Catholic family, attended the exclusive Choate preparatory school in Connecticut, and while a student at Harvard wrote a provocative book entitled *Why England Slept* (an analysis of British and French appeasement of Hitler during the Czech crisis of 1938). He graduated from Harvard with honors in 1940, accepted a commission in the Navy in the autumn of 1941, commanded a PT (patrol-torpedo) boat in the southwest Pacific in 1943, and was decorated for heroism for his efforts to save surviving members of his crew after a Japanese destroyer rammed his boat. Following the war, in 1946, he won election to the House of Representatives in Washington, in 1952 unseated the incumbent Republican senator Henry Cabot Lodge, Jr., and in 1953 married the attractive and socially prominent Jacqueline Bouvier. After recuperating from a delicate back operation that nearly claimed his life, he won a Pulitzer Prize for authorship of the best-selling book *Profiles in Courage* (largely written, in fact, by members of his staff), in 1958 won reelection to the Senate by an overwhelming margin, and in 1960 won the presidency.

The public persona of "Jack" Kennedy certainly captivated millions of his compatriots. Small wonder, for Kennedy was urbane and witty, articulate and poised, had a puckish sense of humor and an unsurpassed zest for life. He took care to show respect for artistic accomplishment, and liked to quote philoso-

January 20, 1961: After repeating the presidential oath, John F. Kennedy delivers his inaugural address.

phers and poets. If manifestly bright, he was nonetheless an eminently practical man who scorned abstractions and empty slogans.

Still, appearances were deceptive. Unbeknownst to most Americans, he suffered from Addison's disease, a malady of the suprarenal glands that causes anemia, and required daily dosages of cortisone. Until he set his sights on the presidency in the latter 1950s, he had seldom taken legislative responsibilities seriously. He was sexually promiscuous. While a youthful intelligence officer in the Navy during the war, he had an affair with a Danish beauty who had

associated with Hitler and other ranking Nazis, a matter of considerable interest to the FBI. His pursuit of beautiful women did not stop after his marriage—
and would not stop after he entered the White House. During the time he was
president, indeed, he had liaisons in the executive mansion itself. His commitment to Catholic religious principles was quite superficial. And his marriage
was troubled from its inception. At length, in the latter 1950s, his wife considered divorce, only to be persuaded to stay with him in the interest of his presidential ambition.

## ON A NEW FRONTIER?

In his speech accepting his party's nomination for president in the summer
of 1960, John Kennedy stirred millions of his compatriots when he spoke of
challenging a "new frontier" of unknown opportunities and unfulfilled hopes.
But when he repeated the presidential oath on that cold day in January 1961,
his first challenge was an economic recession—one that had contributed to
his electoral victory over Richard Nixon the previous autumn.

To counter the recession, the new president took a variety of initiatives.
He directed federal agencies to accelerate building programs and authorized
increased allotments of surplus food to the poor. He persuaded Congress to
pass the Area Redevelopment Act authorizing grants and loans to communities that faced persistent economic distress (for example, in the Appalachian
Mountains) and funds for vocational retraining for citizens who were unemployed. He persuaded Congress to increase the minimum wage and amend the
Social Security law to authorize payments for the care of the children of unemployed parents, enable male citizens to begin receiving retirement benefits at
age 62, and raise the maximum benefit for old-age pensioners. For reasons that
had little to do with Kennedy's initiatives, the economy rebounded in the
spring of 1961, and the outcome was one of the sharpest economic recoveries
in the country's history.

However prosperous, the economy was never far from Kennedy's thoughts,
and in the spring of 1962, the president responded with undisguised anger
when the steel industry raised the price of steel—shortly after his administration had prevailed on the U.S. Steel Workers to put aside demands for an infla-
tionary wage increase. Tongue-lashed by the president and threatened with
antitrust action by the Justice Department, the steel companies rolled back
the price increase. The imbroglio with the steelmakers reinforced a perception
of many businesspeople that Kennedy was antibusiness. Some businesspeople
revised their view when the president, turning aside arguments of Democratic
liberals, determined that a privately owned corporation should operate Telstar,
a communications satellite system that would relay television broadcasts and
telephone and telegraph messages across the world. Others revised their view
when, after a sharp decline in stock prices in the spring and summer of 1962
appeared to signal a new recession, Kennedy proposed initiatives to stimulate
business activity.

Kennedy meanwhile labored in behalf of trade expansion and sought to cope with problems relating to agriculture and labor. The trade expansion program derived from his determination to come to grips with the increasing imbalance of his country's trade with the European Economic Community (or Common Market), an association of France, West Germany, and the Benelux countries that had taken form in 1957. The imbalance was largely a result of the Common Market's tariff barriers against imports from nonmember countries. Kennedy also believed that the emergence of the Common Market as a fiercely competitive trading bloc, arrayed against Great Britain and Canada as well as the United States, was having a divisive effect on the NATO alliance. The outcome, in the autumn of 1962, was congressional approval of the Trade Expansion Act, bestowing on the president wide authority to negotiate tariff reductions with other countries, particularly those of Western Europe, and to increase tariffs if he thought it necessary.

The overbearing agricultural problem confronting Kennedy was the huge expense of storing farm commodities that had passed—and were continuing to pass—to the ownership of the federal government in accord with the farm subsidy program. To meet the problem, he resorted to a variety of expedients. He reinstituted the Food Stamp program of the 1930s whereby destitute individuals could obtain stamps that they could use in lieu of cash for the purchase of food, and ordered that food be distributed to several million poor Americans. Reviving the dormant Food for Peace program that had originated (and languished) in the time of Eisenhower, he arranged the distribution of great quantities of America's surplus food to countries of the Third World whose peoples were enduring hunger and malnutrition. He signed legislation enacted by Congress for cutbacks in the production of wheat and feed grains and the withdrawal of land from cultivation under long-term contracts.

Regarding labor, Kennedy permitted his brother, Attorney General Robert F. Kennedy, to move against James R. Hoffa, the stocky tough-talking president of the International Brotherhood of Teamsters, considered by the president and millions of other Americans to be the country's most unsavory labor chieftain. The outcome was a prison term for Hoffa. To help unemployed working people to acquire marketable skills, Kennedy persuaded Congress in 1963 to pass the Manpower Development and Training Act to provide special vocational training for citizens who were out of work. But he offered no support when the railroad brotherhoods threatened a strike in the face of demands by the railroads that they be allowed to eliminate the jobs of 45,000 locomotive firemen whose responsibilities had become largely redundant with the advent of diesel-electric motive power. Instead, he signed legislation imposing compulsory arbitration on the disputants. In the following year, 1964, arbiters ruled that companies could operate diesel-electrics in freight and switching service without firemen.

Although the conservative coalition that commanded Capitol Hill sanctioned what appeared to be liberal-style initiatives by Kennedy to stimulate the economy and provide a modicum of relief for the victims of economic distress, it responded negatively to other presidential initiatives that seemed to bear a liberal mark—for example, to his request for legislation to close "loopholes" that enabled individuals, usually those who were wealthy, and corporations to reduce or eliminate altogether their tax liabilities. Kennedy's request for $3 billion to increase the salaries of public school teachers and fund the construction of public school buildings got nowhere. The same fate befell his request for congressional enactment of legislation establishing Medicare. The conservative coalition also turned aside his request for legislation to establish a Department of Urban Affairs, in part because he offended the sensibilities of southern members of Congress when he announced that he would nominate Robert C. Weaver, a black, to be the first secretary of urban affairs.

Still, Congress endorsed Kennedy's request that it extend the National Defense Education Act of 1958, as well as earlier legislation that provided federal assistance to school districts in "impacted areas" in which the presence of federal installations had swollen school populations. The president prevailed on Congress to approve legislation appropriating $175 million to help medical schools to enlarge faculties and another $61 million from which students of medicine, osteopathy, and dentistry could borrow at low rates of interest. He persuaded Congress to appropriate nearly a half-billion dollars to combat mental illness and retardation. Reinforced by a popular outcry resulting from the birth without arms or legs of a number of babies whose mothers, during pregnancy, had taken the sleep-inducing drug thalidomide, he secured passage of the Drug Industry Act of 1962 that tightened federal controls over the manufacture and sale of drugs. At his behest, Congress passed the Vaccination Assistance Act of 1962 appropriating $25 million to assist states and communities to carry out intensive vaccination programs to protect their populations, particularly preschool children, against polio, diphtheria, whooping cough, and tetanus. Also at his behest, Congress consented to the Housing Act of 1961 appropriating $4.9 billion for construction of "middle-income" houses, loans to elderly citizens for the purchase of houses, urban renewal programs, construction of new mass transportation facilities, loans for the construction of hospitals and college dormitories, and loans to citizens in rural areas for the purchase and improvement of houses. It approved the Clean Air Act of 1963 to control and prevent air pollution.

Not all initiatives by the Kennedy administration were directed toward the legislative branch of the national government. At least one initiative of incalculable import was directed toward the judicial branch, and the Supreme Court responded in 1962 by handing down a historic decision in the case of *Baker* v. *Carr*. The issue in the case, brought before the high court by the president's brother, the attorney general, was the refusal of the lower house of the legislature of Tennessee to reapportion itself in accord with shifting patterns of population. In a word, despite the extensive growth of Tennessee's urban areas, legislative districts remained drawn as in the time when a preponderance of the population lived in small towns and the countryside, hence the legislature continued to be dominated by the representatives of rural citizens. The Supreme Court ruled in *Baker* v. *Carr* that federal courts had authority to require state legislatures to apportion themselves in accord with actual distributions of population. Within a short time, as a result, suits demanding reapportionment of legislative districts were filed in more than twenty states, and it appeared that the day of small-town rural domination of state governments to the detriment of cities was about to end.

## CIVIL RIGHTS

*Baker* v. *Carr* was an historic decision, and students of government, not to mention those urban dwellers who grasped its importance, hailed the reapportionment of state legislatures that the decision portended. But great numbers of citizens believed the accelerating movement aimed at achieving civil equality for what in subsequent years would be widely identified as the country's black underclass was of far greater moment. The logic underpinning their belief is hard to confute.

Their expectations regarding their place in the national society having been heightened as a result of modest advances in the area of civil rights during the 1950s, black Americans were manifestly restless at the dawn of the 1960s. Many blacks, moreover, were eschewing the time-honored tactics of the NAACP—tactics resting on an assumption that the federal courts and Congress offered the surest vehicles for achieving civil liberties. Inspired by the bus boycott in Montgomery, Alabama, in 1955–1956, such blacks suspected that massive nonviolent protest offered a more effective means of breaking down the walls of segregation and unequal treatment. Some of them tried the new tactics for the first time during the "sit-ins" of 1960. The sit-ins began when four black students, denied service at a segregated lunch counter in Greensboro, North Carolina, elected to stay seated until the counter closed. Before long, blacks had organized more than eight hundred sit-ins to protest discrimination in every state of the South and also in Illinois, Ohio, and Nevada. As a result of the sit-ins, restaurants in at least eight major cities were desegregated, whites became increasingly conscious of the frustration of their black compatriots, and large numbers of blacks became persuaded of the merits of the tactics of civil disobedience.

At the time of the sit-ins, John F. Kennedy was pressing his campaign for the presidency. Since Kennedy had never been in the front rank of congressional crusaders for civil rights, most black leaders hoped that Adlai Stevenson or Hubert Humphrey would win the Democratic nomination for president. Aware that he had not struck fire with blacks, Kennedy insisted that the Democratic party adopt a strong platform statement on behalf of civil rights at its national convention in the summer of 1960 and, after securing the presidential nomination, set about to gain the allegiance of black voters. He spoke out in favor of legislation that would guarantee blacks of states of the onetime Confederacy the right to vote, urged federal action to widen the employment opportunities of blacks, promised that if elected he would increase the number of blacks in the federal service. He declared that "by a stroke of the pen" President Eisenhower could eliminate discrimination in federally financed housing, and thus implicitly pledged that if elected he would promptly take pen in hand and make that stroke. As previously noted, when Martin Luther King, Jr., was arrested during a protest demonstration at the height of the electoral campaign, Kennedy expressed concern for the civil rights leader in a telephone call to Mrs. King. Kennedy's enterprise was rewarded, for on election day more than 70 percent of black voters pulled levers or marked ballots for the Kennedy-Johnson ticket. Those votes provided the ticket its margin of victory in Illinois, Michigan, Texas, South Carolina, and possibly Louisiana, and without the electoral votes of the latter states Kennedy and Johnson would have lost the election.

Fearing that if he pressed Congress to pass civil rights legislation, or if he made that much-remarked stroke of the pen, he would jeopardize other social and economic initiatives of importance to blacks as well as whites, Kennedy did not make haste to redeem all of his campaign pledges regarding civil rights when he moved into the White House. Black leaders expressed disappointment.

Still, the president was not totally quiescent in the matter of civil rights. He issued an executive order prohibiting racial discrimination in federal employment, and made a special effort to appoint blacks to high positions in the federal bureaucracy, the foreign service, and the federal judiciary. He set up the President's Committee on Equal Employment Opportunity to urge businesses to eliminate discriminatory practices and elevate blacks to positions of responsibility. He publicly denounced racial discrimination and segregation, and needled white proponents of civil rights who retained memberships in social clubs that refused to admit blacks as members. More important perhaps, he gave his brother "Bobby" free reign to use the authority of the Justice Department on behalf of civil rights. The younger Kennedy, accordingly, increased the number of black attorneys in the department, appointed the first blacks to be U.S. attorneys, and enlarged the staff of the department's Civil Rights Division. He and his assistants helped to bring about the peaceful integration of public schools in several southern cities. They sought court action to reopen the public schools of Prince Edward County, Virginia, which authorities had closed to prevent integration. Using powers granted by the Civil Rights Acts of 1957 and 1960, Attorney General Kennedy filed suits to eliminate obstacles to voting by blacks in southern states, then organized a campaign to persuade blacks to put aside fear and apathy and get their names on voting registers. Attorney General Kennedy also intervened in behalf of blacks during "the freedom rides."

Shortly after John Kennedy became president, in early 1961, James Farmer of the Congress of Racial Equality announced that his organization would conduct what he described as freedom rides through the South to test racial discrimination in interstate bus terminals. Accordingly, in May of 1961, seven black and six white freedom riders boarded a bus in Washington, destination: New Orleans. In Virginia, the Carolinas, and Georgia, the riders on occasion found facilities closed when they arrived. At times they were taunted by local whites, and on two occasions members of the group were arrested but later released. Then, as they approached Anniston, Alabama, a white mob attacked a Greyhound bus in which part of the group was traveling. Angry whites slashed tires, and somebody hurled an incendiary device through a window. The bus quickly became an inferno. Fortunately, all of the passengers managed to escape the burning bus with only minor injuries. Later, in Birmingham, freedom riders aboard a second bus were assaulted as they debarked, and one member of the group sustained injuries that required 50 stitches. Ignoring warnings of trouble communicated by the Justice Department, white authorities in Alabama had done nothing to forestall the outrages in Anniston and Birmingham. Nor did they subsequently arrest any of the perpetrators of the outrages.

Other groups of freedom riders were by now moving toward Alabama, and when it became clear that white officials would not protect them Attorney General Kennedy dispatched six hundred deputy federal marshals to the state. His action prompted Gov. John Patterson to complain that Alabama was being invaded. The presence of the marshals notwithstanding, violence flared off and on for another fortnight in Alabama, and also in Mississippi, as freedom rides continued. Adding to the confusion was a "hate bus" sent southward by the American Nazi Party, a minuscule organization made up in the main of social misfits who wore Nazi-style uniforms, exchanged Nazi salutes, and proclaimed the dogma of white supremacy. But then, toward the end of May 1961, calm more or less returned to the cotton belt.

Despite the New Frontier administration's forthright response to the outrages against freedom riders, President Kennedy's performance in the area of civil rights continued to dismay black leaders. The leaders were particularly disappointed that the president had not made that stroke of the pen to eliminate discrimination in federally financed housing and had not asked Congress for new civil rights legislation. Their sentiments underwent no apparent change in August of 1962 when Congress, responding to Kennedy's urging, approved a constitutional amendment asserting that failure to pay a poll tax or any other tax could not render an individual ineligible to vote in federal elections. The payment of poll taxes, which large numbers of poor blacks could ill afford, was a requisite for voting in five southern states, and indeed the poll tax had been fashioned many decades before as a device to keep black citizens from exercising the franchise. The amendment, the twenty-fourth, achieved ratification in 1964.

Scarcely had the freedom rides passed from the public consciousness before Americans, in September 1962, were enduring the trauma of a new outbreak of racial violence. The trouble developed when a black Mississippian and veteran of the Air Force, James H. Meredith, supported by a federal court order, sought to enroll in the all-white University of Mississippi, only to find his path blocked by Gov. Ross Barnett. Reinforcing Barnett were white students who marched about the Ole Miss campus in Oxford, Mississippi, singing "Glory, Glory Segregation." Despite appeals by Attorney General Kennedy, and also a new court order enjoining officials in Mississippi to refrain from interfering with Meredith's registration, Barnett prevented a second attempt by Meredith to enroll at the university. The governor again had the support of a white mob that shouted, "Nigger, go home!" and punctuated proceedings with Confederate yells. At length, President Kennedy, to meet wholesale violence if it erupted on the campus, federalized the Mississippi National Guard, whereupon Barnett agreed that Meredith could register. Accordingly, as the sun was going down on September 30, 1962, Meredith, accompanied by federal marshals, made his way to the campus and settled in a dormitory room. He was scheduled to register on the morrow.

That evening, President Kennedy went before television cameras and explained why, to get a black man enrolled in a university, he had mobilized the power of the federal government. He concluded by appealing to the students of Ole Miss to uphold "the honor of your university." Ole Miss students jeered and hooted. Next, the campus erupted. Whites, some of them armed, stepped up an attack on federal marshals that had begun before Kennedy's address. During the melee, hundreds of people were injured and two men killed. But then troops of the Mississippi National Guard—also Army paratroops—arrived and the battle ended. Meredith registered the next morning, and notwithstanding the presence of marshals, the hostility of fellow students, and threats to his family, received a diploma in 1963. Before long, moreover, the barriers of segregation were falling at hitherto all-white colleges and universities across the entire South.

A short time after "the battle of Oxford," in late 1962, Kennedy at last made the much-discussed stroke of the pen when he signed an executive order prohibiting discrimination in housing owned or insured by the federal government. Then, in February 1963, the president, after reciting the evil consequences of racial discrimination and proclaiming that "above all, it is wrong," asked Congress for new civil rights legislation. Intended to strengthen existing voting laws and help schools to desegregate, the measure that he requested failed to stir much enthusiasm among black leaders. Those leaders wanted legislation that would prohibit discrimination in employment and discrimination by businesses, for example, hotels and restaurants and places of entertainment, that solicited the patronage of the general public. Kennedy's civil rights proposal stirred even less enthusiasm in Congress, not because it was overly cautious, but because in the estimate of the conservative coalition it went too far. Accordingly, it quickly bogged down on Capitol Hill.

While Kennedy's civil rights proposals were languishing in Congress, the country faced a new racial crisis. The troubled flared when blacks, led by Martin Luther King, Jr., began to march in the streets and stage sit-ins to protest discrimination in employment and discriminatory practices by merchants and restaurateurs in Birmingham, Alabama. Predictably, the protesters collided with the white citizenry. They also collided with Police Commissioner Eugene "Bull" Connor, a combative man who was bent on making life as uncomfortable as possible for those who would upset the traditional folkways of Birmingham. In the days and weeks that followed, the blacks and their white allies were taunted by obscenities, assaulted with rocks and bottles, and hauled off to Connor's jails by the hundreds. Then, on May 3, 1963, authorities turned high-pressure fire hoses on protest marchers, while Connor's police confronted them with snarling, salivating German shepherd dogs. During the ensuing rumble, a photographer snapped a picture of a dog, its teeth bared, lunging at a black demonstrator. The photo soon was flashing across the entire world.

At length, authorities in Birmingham and protest leaders, largely as a result of mediation by emissaries of the White House, agreed to a truce. Whereupon an uneasy calm settled over the Alabama metropolis. But then, toward the end of May of 1963, national attention again centered on Alabama, this time when Gov. George C. Wallace, by deploying himself in front of the administration building, personally prevented two black Alabamians, both of them supported by orders of a federal court, from enrolling at the University of Alabama.

Back in 1956, the 26-year-old daughter of a black tenant farmer, Autherine J. Lucy, armed with a court order, had enrolled at that same university. Large numbers of white students, not to mention uncounted white Alabamians, were incensed. Singing "Dixie," students paraded about the campus shouting "To hell with Autherine!" and "Keep 'Bama white!" They burned a Ku Klux-style cross in front of the house of the president. Another mob hurled stones and eggs at an automobile that was delivering the black student to a class. The board of trustees thereupon suspended Lucy—"for your safety"—and then expelled her when she brought suit against the university. Now, seven years later, in 1963, two more black Alabamians set about to enroll at the University of Alabama.

The outcome would be different this time. On learning of Governor Wallace's "stand in the schoolhouse door," President Kennedy federalized the Alabama National Guard—and made it clear that he would tolerate no defiance by Alabama's civil authorities. Persuaded by the determination of the president, Wallace judiciously absented himself from the campus at Tuscaloosa when the blacks made their second attempt to register. In a television address that same evening, Kennedy related the events in Tuscaloosa. Making the most eloquent appeal for the elimination of second-class citizenship in the annals of the presidency to that time, he declared, "The rights of every man are diminished when the rights of one man are threatened." Still, triumph in the area of civil rights was inevitably tinctured by tragedy, or so it seemed, for later that same night Medgar Evers, the director of the NAACP in Mississippi, was shot to death in front of his house in Jackson, Mississippi.

A fortnight later, in June 1963, Kennedy sent a new civil rights message to Congress in which he asked for legislation that went beyond the measure he had requested the previous February. Included in the updated proposal were provisions to guarantee equal treatment for all citizens by businesses soliciting the patronage of the general public, that is, equal accommodations in what were considered public facilities. Other provisions would allow the attorney general to initiate suits to desegregate public schools, eliminate discrimination in employment, and permit the federal government to withhold funds from programs and activities in which racial discrimination existed. Not since

Harry Truman in 1948 had a president asked Congress to approve civil rights legislation of comparable reach, and black leaders promptly began to search for means of applying pressure on Congress to secure its passage. Out of the search emerged the idea of a massive "march on Washington" by civil rights activists. Fearing that Congress might view a march as a form of intimidation, Kennedy had scant enthusiasm for the idea, but gave his endorsement when black leaders pledged that the march would be peaceful and agreed that marchers would assemble around the Lincoln Memorial rather than Capitol Hill.

The outcome, on August 28, 1963, was one of the most memorable happenings of the 1960s. Not a hundred thousand people as had been expected but a quarter million, of all ages and races, creeds and religions, by car and bus, train and plane, cascaded into the national capital. The weather was perfect, warm and sunny, and in a spirit that was remarkably free of rancor the marchers, chanting and singing, wound through the streets of the federal city, and eventually gathered in a giant assemblage around the Lincoln Memorial. After several leaders of the civil rights crusade had addressed the throng, there came the climactic moment: Martin Luther King, Jr., who more than any other individual symbolized the black American's quest for equal justice and equal opportunity, made his way to the rostrum, and in tones and a cadence that captured the agony and hope of uncounted generations of black people in America told his auditors that he had a dream. "Even though we face the difficulties of today and tomorrow, I still have a dream. . . . I have a dream that on the red

August 28, 1963: Blacks display signs spelling out their aspirations and demands during the celebrated "March on Washington."

hills of Georgia the sons of former slaves and the sons of former slaveowners will be able to sit together at the table of brotherhood. . . . I have a dream that one day every valley shall be exalted, every hill and mountain shall be made low, the rough places will be made plain, and the crooked places will be made straight, and the glory of the Lord shall be revealed and all flesh shall see it together." That evening, as dusk settled over Washington, the marchers departed as they had come, in a spirit of peace and brotherhood. Unfortunately, the march made no notable impression on the conservative coalition in Congress. When the Kennedy administration ended less than three months later, the civil rights bill remained mired in the judiciary committees of the House and Senate to which it had been referred for consideration (and, of course, was not apt to come up for a final vote until the committees reported it to the full membership of the respective chambers of the national legislature).

## OUTER SPACE

That the movement to guarantee equal justice and opportunity for black Americans made slow headway during his presidency was a source of acute disappointment to John F. Kennedy. But the progress recorded by the program to put U.S. astronauts in outer space warmed the heart of the thirty-fifth chief executive, for the latter program was an unqualified success.

At the time Kennedy entered the White House, NASA was proceeding with plans to launch the Mercury astronauts into space. Then, in April 1961, the news flashed around the world that Yuri A. Gagarin of the Soviet Union had ridden a 5-ton spacecraft into the heavens—and, more than that, been put in orbit around the earth. America's first man-in-space venture was to be a suborbital mission, a rather unimposing enterprise compared with that involving Gagarin. However unimposing his mission, Americans responded enthusiastically when Lt. Comdr. Alan B. Shepard of the Navy, less than a month after Gargarin's flight, was sealed into a spacecraft designated *Freedom 7* and launched from Cape Canaveral on a 15-minute flight that took him to an altitude of 116.5 miles and down the Atlantic test range 302 miles.

Three weeks after Shepard's flight, President Kennedy, speaking to a joint session of Congress, urged Americans to commit themselves "to achieving the goal before this decade is out of landing a man on the moon and returning him safely to earth." But then, in August 1961, a few weeks after Capt. Virgil I. "Gus" Grissom of the Air Force, in *Liberty Bell 7*, had completed a suborbital mission similar to that of Shepard, America's pride suffered a new jolt: The Soviet cosmonaut Maj. Gherman S. Titov orbited the earth an incredible 18 times.

NASA thereupon accelerated plans to put a U.S. astronaut in earth orbit, and designated Lt. Col. John H. Glenn, Jr., of the Marine Corps, affable and handsome, to be the astronaut. At length, on the morning of February 20, 1962, Glenn slipped into *Friendship 7*—the "7" included in the spacecraft's name in recognition of the seven Mercury astronauts—and several hours later, while tens of millions of his compatriots observed the proceedings via TV, the service tower was rolled away, leaving the white Atlas-Mercury rocket standing alone, gleaming in the morning sunlight. Then, at 9:46 A.M., the matter-of-fact voice of Lt. Col. John A. "Shorty" Powers, "the voice of Mercury Control," intoned: "We are at T minus 19 seconds. T minus 10 seconds, 8, 7, 6, 5, 4, 3, 2, 1, 0. Ignition." Within seconds, the streaking Atlas-Mercury and its payload *Friendship 7* had vanished into the heavens. Four hours, 55 minutes, and 10 seconds after liftoff, Glenn's spacecraft, after three orbits of the earth, splashed down in the Atlantic. Not since Charles Lindbergh's epic transatlantic flight of 1927 had Americans felt such a sense of exhilaration. Or so it appeared.

Three months later, in May 1962, Lt. Comdr. Malcolm Scott Carpenter of the Navy, in *Aurora 7*, duplicated Glenn's three-orbit mission. But then American pride suffered yet another jolt: The Soviets in August 1962 sent two spaceships into orbit at the same time, one of which orbited the earth 48 times, the other 64. If boggled by the power of Soviet rockets, Americans nonetheless took satisfaction in October 1962 when Comdr. Walter M. Schirra, Jr., of the Navy, in *Sigma 7*, made 6 revolutions of the earth and in May 1963 when Capt. Leroy Gordon Cooper of the Air Force, in *Faith 7*, made 22.

Manned spaceflights may have captured the popular imagination, but from the perspective of science an unmanned flight in 1962 was at least as important. The flight got under way in late August when an Atlas rocket propelled a 447-pound instrument-laden spacecraft designated *Mariner 2* into orbit. After *Mariner 2* had made one revolution of the earth, controllers at Cape Canaveral manipulated buttons that sent the craft rocketing in the direction of Venus, a misty planet about the size of the earth that long had enchanted earthlings. One hundred and nine days later, in mid-December 1962, the spacecraft flew past Venus at a distance of 21,598 miles. The sophisticated instruments aboard *Mariner 2* disclosed that Venus, whatever its place in the legends and dreams of earth people, was a veritable "hell in heaven," a dry and lifeless sphere on which temperatures reached 800°F.

## IN A DANGEROUS WORLD

The spectacular achievements of the U.S. space program exhilarated most Americans during the early 1960s. And President Kennedy assuredly shared that sense of exhilaration. But the thirty-fifth chief executive understood full well that history's verdict on the Kennedy presidency was not apt to turn on successes and failures recorded by the space program. Rather, it would likely turn on the successes and failures recorded by his administration in the area of world affairs.

The international political environment had undergone extensive changes over the past dozen years. Of special note, the dominance of the superpowers vis-à-vis their allies and clients had declined since the early years of the Cold War. Whatever the purposes of their masters in the Kremlin, leaders of the satellite states of Eastern Europe wanted better relations and increased trade with the West. More notable perhaps, Mao Zedong's regime in China was becoming increasingly impatient with what it considered the caution and lack of revolutionary zeal of the leadership in Moscow. The Chinese, likewise, resented Soviet rule or domination in territories that they believed were rightful parts of China. Meanwhile, the states of Western Europe, their economies regenerated, felt less dependent on and hence less subservient to the United States than in former years. Now led by the willful Charles de Gaulle, France in particular seemed bent on charting its own course in international affairs. Another change of large import: An array of newly independent nation-states had appeared, most of them as a result of the collapse of the colonial empires in Africa and Asia of the onetime powers of Europe (and many more would appear over the next quarter century—in the Caribbean and Western Pacific as well as in Africa and Asia).

Still, Kennedy believed the Cold War remained the great overbearing reality in international affairs, for he shared the conviction of Truman and Eisenhower that America and the rest of "the free world" were in the grip of a titanic struggle to contain the expansionist impulses of the Soviet Union and various of its clients. His inaugural address, indeed, was a veritable call to arms—an appeal that his compatriots stay the course in the Cold War struggle until the Marxist-Leninist monster had been tamed. Declared the youthful chief executive, "Let every nation know, whether it wishes us well or ill, that we shall pay any price, bear any burden, meet any hardship, support any friend, oppose any foe to assure the survival and success of liberty."

It was axiomatic, Kennedy believed, that if Americans were to assure the survival and success of liberty in the dangerous world of the 1960s, they must have a powerful military-naval establishment. Most importantly, it was mandatory that the United States maintain an arsenal of nuclear weapons of such destructive capacity that its principal antagonist in world affairs, the Soviet Union, would not dare risk a nuclear confrontation with its rival superpower, say, by undertaking an invasion of Western Europe. Reduced to essentials, the United States must maintain a nuclear force of such dimension and diversity that the Soviets could not hope to neutralize it in a surprise nuclear attack of their own—that American missiles and strategic bombers would survive such an attack in sufficient numbers to enable the United States to retaliate by inflicting destruction on a scale that the Soviets would consider unacceptable.

Outwardly, Kennedy's nuclear strategy appeared identical to the "massive retaliation" strategy of Eisenhower. But there was, in fact, a notable difference. Bothered by the extent of the death and destruction that would result from massive and indiscriminate retaliation during a nuclear showdown, the Kennedy administration adopted a new strategy, referred to in the lexicon of nuclear strategists as counterforce. In the event the United States felt compelled to make a nuclear strike against the Soviet Union, say, in retaliation for a surprise attack against its own territory or a Soviet invasion of Western Europe, it would not necessarily resort to a massive and indiscriminate attack. If circumstances seemed to warrant, it would send its missiles and bombing planes winging toward Soviet military installations only. In its first strike, in a word, the United States would spare Soviet cities. The idea was to leave open some options that would make possible the termination of the war by means other than total destruction. Only as a last resort, therefore, would the United States set about to destroy the enemy's society.

Implementation of the counterforce strategy, of course, would require a huge nuclear arsenal, one of such dimension that it could survive a surprise attack by the Soviet Union and retaliate effectively against nuclear forces the Soviets had held in reserve—or, if it came to that, against Soviet cities. Thus the Kennedy administration set about to increase the number of ICBMs in the country's nuclear arsenal from 600 to 1,000. Solid-fuel *Minutemen* would provide the core of the enlarged ICBM force. It also set about to increase the number of nuclear submarines from 29 to 41. The 41 undersea boats would carry 656 submarine-launched ballistic missiles (SLBMs).

Still, the New Frontiersmen sought a military-naval force of sufficient power and diversity that the Washington government could respond effectively to any brushfire threat, or perhaps a probing adventure by Soviet or satellite forces in Europe, without resorting to nuclear weapons. In the words of Secretary of Defense Robert S. McNamara, "We believe in a policy of controlled, flexible response where the military force of the United States would become a finely tuned instrument of national policy, versatile enough to meet with appropriate force the full spectrum of possible threats to our national security from guerrilla subversion to all-out war."

Kennedy and McNamara, accordingly, set about to enhance the ability of America's armed forces to wage non-nuclear or conventional war. They approved the modernization of naval aviation and authorized the Navy to maintain 24 aircraft carriers, sanctioned improvement of the capacity of the Marine Corps to conduct amphibious operations. They oversaw expansion of the Army's combat divisions from 11 to 16, and directed the Army to increase its firepower and mobility. McNamara fashioned Strike Command, an organization that joined the Army's two airborne divisions with the Air Force's Tactical Air Command and Military Airlift Command. He approved the procurement of large strategic transport planes for the latter command and additional helicopters for all Army divisions.

Meanwhile, Kennedy and McNamara pondered the question of how to counter attempts by communists to extend their authority and influence by terror, intimidation, and subversion—by "unconventional war" that, in the words of the historian Russell F. Weigley, was "often just below or just above the threshold of what Westerners were accustomed to recognize as war." The communists referred to unconventional campaigns such as they had waged in the Philippines and Malaya and presently were conducting in Indochina as "wars of national liberation," and shortly before Kennedy assumed the presidency Nikita Khrushchev proclaimed Soviet support of wars of that type.

When they weighed the question of unconventional war, Kennedy and McNamara were inclined to think that it would be a mistake to commit American conventional forces of an appreciable dimension to a conflict of that sort. The firepower of such forces, they reckoned, would be of minimal value in unconventional or guerrilla warfare. Moreover, as Russell Weigley has observed, the alien presence of large numbers of American troops might simply aggravate the political discontent and economic dislocation on which the insurgency subsisted. But Kennedy and McNamara believed the United States did not lack the wherewithal to influence the combat in an unconventional war. That wherewithal could be provided by the Army's Special Forces.

The mission of the Special Forces when organized in the 1950s had been to operate behind enemy lines in the aftermath of a nuclear exchange. But Kennedy and McNamara decided that the Special Forces, numbering about a thousand men in 1961, should concentrate on the task of influencing unconventional or guerrilla (or irregular) conflicts such as the one presently unfolding in Indochina, in the main by advising and encouraging government troops who were striving to take the measure of insurgents. The men of the Special Forces would learn local languages and dialects. They would be expert parachutists—and also experts in weapons and demolitions and hand-to-hand combat. Over the objections of ranking officers of the Army, who tended to take a critical view of elitist forces, Kennedy authorized the troops of the Special Forces to wear green berets, and henceforth they were known as the Green Berets. By 1966, the Green Berets numbered more than ten thousand.

## THE THIRD WORLD

If President Kennedy believed the overbearing reality in world affairs was the Cold War, he also believed that in no small measure the focus of that war had shifted from Europe to the Third World, that is, to an array of underdeveloped countries of Africa, Asia, and Latin America that girdled the globe to the south of Europe, the Soviet Union, and the United States. Administering many (perhaps most) Third World countries were governments that were weak and inefficient, in some instances notoriously corrupt and repressive. Ravaged by disease and malnutrition, illiterate or at best semiliterate, populations tended to be mired in poverty. In such circumstances, Kennedy reckoned, the people of Third World countries might prove—indeed, in some instances had proved—susceptible to the appeals of communism. Communism offered a simplistic analysis of their plight and, more important, a quick resolution of their problems. Accordingly, the thirty-fifth president declared in his inaugural address, "To those people in the huts and villages of half the globe struggling to break the bonds of mass misery, we pledge our best efforts to help them help themselves. . . . If a free society cannot help the many who are poor, it cannot save the few who are rich."

The most obvious vehicle for assisting the countries of the Third World—one that Kennedy determined to utilize—was the foreign aid program, the centerpieces of which were grants and low-interest loans. Unfortunately, congressional appropriations for foreign aid from 1961 to 1963 fell far short of the president's requests. Kennedy, meanwhile, sought other opportunities for assisting poor countries. Such an opportunity, he thought, was offered by Ameri-

March 1965: Peace Corpswoman Ann Aukerman Moore of Alexandria, Ohio, administers vitamins to a baby boy in Togo in West Africa.

ca's stocks of surplus food. So he revitalized the dormant Food for Peace Program, and by 1964 the program had provided such commodities as cornmeal, flour, powdered milk, and edible oils to more than 100 million people in 114 countries and territories. The largest single recipient was Algeria, threatened by mass starvation during the winter of 1962–1963.

Another opportunity for helping peoples of the Third World, Kennedy thought, was afforded by the idealism and spirit of self-sacrifice of a segment of the American population, much of it made up of young people who had recently graduated or were about to graduate from colleges and universities. The outcome was the Peace Corps, approved by Congress with a manifest absence of enthusiasm in 1961. By 1963, some 5,000 Peace Corps volunteers, including teachers and civil engineers, agronomists and medical doctors, were toiling in 46 countries in Latin America, Africa, the Middle East, Central Asia, Southeast Asia, andthe Western Pacific. Critics observed that the volunteers, notwithstanding their dedication and high sense of mission, could not begin to resolve the staggering economic and social problems of the Third World. Still, most Americans appeared to think the Peace Corps eminently worthwhile. Accordingly, Congress in 1963, at the same time that it was slashing the president's foreign aid request, dramatically increased the appropriation for the Peace Corps.

If all of the Third World stirred the concern and compassion of President Kennedy, the part of that globe-girdling territory that, in his estimate, was most important in terms of the interests and security of the United States was Latin America, where 2 percent of the population owned more than 50 percent of the wealth, including most of the land, and breadwinners of tens of millions of poor families spent their days scrounging about cities in search of odd jobs or toiling in the blistering sun on sugar or coffee plantations or in banana fields for a few pesos. At night, Latin America's poor found shelter in rat-infested tenements and cardboard and tin shacks in urban slums and in crude huts in squalid villages in the countryside. Regular medical attention or schooling? For most of Latin America's poor, those were dreams. Reality consisted of pain and hunger, disease and ignorance.

To help Latin Americans meet their problems, and also to weaken the appeal of totalitarian communism, particularly as preached by Fidel Castro, Kennedy in March 1961 announced the Alliance for Progress whereby the United States, in cooperation with the governments of Latin America, would address those problems. Several months later, the Washington government put up a billion dollars in support of the alliance; Latin American governments set up commissions and boards to implement its goals. And before long, North Americans were reading reports extolling reforms and enlarged educational opportunities in Latin America. But after a couple of years, enthusiasm for the alliance began to weaken, and by the end of the 1960s nearly everyone conceded that the Alliance for Progress had failed.

What had gone wrong? Everything, or so it seemed. The oligarchic governments that reigned unchallenged throughout much of Latin America took no interest in redistributing wealth. Latin America's soaring birthrate nullified economic gains. North American entrepreneurs and corporations had declined to invest in Latin America on a scale that was essential if the alliance was to achieve its objectives. Meanwhile, the Congress in Washington steadily reduced appropriations for the Alliance for Progress—to a mere $336 million in 1968. (The Washington government made its final disbursement of funds for the alliance in 1973.)

## BAY OF PIGS

At the same time, in March 1961, that President Kennedy announced the Alliance for Progress, a central purpose of which was to contain "Castroism," his administration was weighing plans for a more direct strike against the influence of Cuba's bearded revolutionary. The plans had begun to take form a year before, in March 1961, when President Eisenhower—aware that large numbers of Cubans who had fled the Pearl of the Antilles and settled in the United States, mainly in Florida, were aching for a chance to contribute to the demise of Cuba's self-styled maximum leader—authorized the CIA to organize a minuscule military force comprised of the most militant Cuban exiles for possible military action against the Castro regime. By the summer of 1960, several hundred Cubans were undergoing training by CIA agents and U.S. military personnel in jungle clearings in Guatemala.

The CIA, meanwhile, was considering other actions against Castro, including attempts to undermine his charismatic appeal. One possibility was to induce the maximum leader, just before he delivered a speech, to smoke a cigar laced with a chemical that would result in temporary disorientation. Another was to have his shoes dusted with a strong depilatory that it was thought would make his beard fall out. More ominous, the agency set about to arrange Castro's assassination. To that purpose, in the summer of 1960, a box of Castro's favorite brand of cigars was treated with lethal poison and subsequently sent to Havana. Whether an attempt was made to pass the cigars to Castro remains unclear. Also in the summer of 1960, the CIA set about to enlist members of the criminal underworld—the Mafia—to help arrange the demise of the Cuban dictator. The agency made contact with an underworld figure whose gambling operations in Havana had been closed after Castro's accession to power, and he in turn brought other hoodlums into the conspiracy. At length, in early 1961, the CIA delivered a batch of poison pills to Cuba with the intent that a waiter would drop one in Castro's drink while the maximum leader was dining at a restaurant in Havana. What, if anything, Ike may have known about such goings-on likewise remains unclear.

As for John Kennedy, he complained in the course of his campaign for the presidency in 1960, that anti-Castro "fighters for freedom" in the United States had received virtually no support by the Washington government. Then, following his victory in the presidential balloting, he learned of the force of Cuban exiles that the CIA had assembled in Guatemala—also that the CIA was working out plans for an invasion of Castro's island fortress. So the scenario went, a rebel invasion would trigger a rebellion among Cuba's "masses," who it was presumed were fed up with Castroism and would leap at the opportunity to rid themselves of the bearded tyrant. Given the support of the Cuban people and the ineptitude of the buffoon Castro, the scenario concluded, the invasion-inspired uprising was almost certain to succeed.

A few weeks after he repeated the presidential oath, in March 1961, Kennedy and members of his administration got down to the business of weighing the merits of the CIA scenario. Unfortunately, neither the president nor other New Frontiersmen made any serious effort to counter the CIA's arguments in support of an invasion of Cuba by the exile "army." At length, following a climactic discussion in the Cabinet Room on the evening of April 4, 1961, Kennedy made his decision: The invasion would be undertaken. But he made it clear that under no circumstances would he commit U.S. military and naval forces to assure the success of the operation. The exiles, in a word, would be put ashore; thereafter, they would be on their own.

The first blow against Castro's island fell in the early hours of April 15 when two antiquated B-26 bombing planes, disguised with the insignia of Castro's air force, took off from an airstrip in Nicaragua, flew northward over the Caribbean, and swooped down on airfields in Cuba. After failing to achieve their objective of knocking out Castro's tiny air arm, the bombers roared to Florida where, on landing, their crewmen claimed that they were Castro's fliers and were defecting to the United States.

The exile army, meanwhile, had evacuated the camps in Guatemala, boarded a flotilla of cargo ships and landing craft at a port in Nicaragua, and by the night of April 16 was moving across the Caribbean, destination: the Bay of Pigs on the lightly defended south coast of Cuba. At 1:00 A.M. on April 17, their activities accompanied by the bellowing of alligators and rustling of tropical birds, the exile soldiers disembarked and moved inland. They proceeded without opposition—but not for long.

By daybreak, Cuba's maximum leader, whose agents had advised him that the long-expected invasion by the exile army was imminent, had learned of the landing, and in that hour of crisis demonstrated that he was not the buffoon that operatives of the CIA had thought him to be. With coolness and efficiency, Castro issued orders that alerted his quarter-million-man army and sent advanced units racing toward the Bay of Pigs. He directed his secret police to round up individuals suspected of being hostile to the regime. Then, at 6:45 A.M., one of the six warplanes of his air force sent rockets crashing into the cargo ship *Houston* which, in addition to the usual supplies, carried most of the exile army's communications equipment. When the *Houston* ran aground on a sandpit 2 miles from shore, its cargo was lost to the invaders.

Before the passage of many hours, it was clear that Operation Pluto was going nowhere. Why? Because the action at the Bay of Pigs had failed to set off a popular uprising against Castro. The assumption that such an uprising would follow the invasion by the exile army had, of course, been the keystone of Pluto, for the 1,500-man exile army, standing alone, could not possibly cope with Castro's army of a quarter-million men. By the second morning of the invasion, in any event, Castro's soldiers, spearheaded by Soviet-built T-34 tanks, had surrounded the exile force, and his jet-powered aircraft were zooming back and forth overhead, spraying it with bullets and rockets. In Washington, meanwhile, a pall of gloom had settled over the White House. But to the dismay of the CIA, which had assumed that Kennedy, despite his professed determination to keep U.S. forces clear of the fighting, would not stand by and allow the operation to fail, the president turned aside appeals by various officials of the intelligence and defense establishments that he try to salvage the operation by ordering strikes against Castro's forces by carrier-based aircraft of the Navy.

The rest was anticlimactic. Effectively supported from the air, Castro's soldiers methodically closed in about the invaders, and after four days the battle was over. Some three hundred of the exile warriors had died, and, inasmuch as nobody had thought to work out a plan for evacuating the exile force in the event the operation failed, twelve hundred were captured. Thus ended what the writer Theodore Draper subsequently described as one of those rare episodes in history, to wit, a perfect failure—an operation in which everything that could go wrong did go wrong.

At the same time that Castro's partisans in Cuba were celebrating the surrender of the tattered remnants of the exile army, the Washington government was absorbing unparalleled criticism from around the world. And from his compatriots, President Kennedy came under attack on the one hand because he had permitted the United States to become involved in such a dubious operation as Pluto, and on the other because he had not invoked the country's military might to assure success of the invasion—which criticism prompted the president to remark, "Victory has a hundred fathers and defeat is an orphan."

Still, neither the CIA nor Kennedy gave up the hope of eliminating Cuba's communist dictator. The intelligence agency in the spring of 1962 reactivated plans to assassinate Castro. It reestablished contact with underworld figures, including Sam Giancana, whose friend Judith Campbell was having extramarital liaisons with President Kennedy in the White House at that very time. The poison pill remained the preferred method of getting rid of the maximum leader, although the CIA explored other ideas, for example, depositing a seashell rigged with explosives in an area where Castro frequently went skin diving. The agency, meanwhile, was dealing with a highly placed Cuban official referred to as AM/LASH who enjoyed the confidence of Castro. It prepared a ballpoint pen rigged with a poisoned hypodermic needle with which it hoped AM/LASH might jab the Cuban premier. It provided AM/LASH with a silencer-equipped pistol and highly concentrated explosives with which to make a bomb. Nothing, of course, came of the assorted schemes to assassinate Castro, and in June 1965, during the presidential administration of Lyndon B. Johnson, the CIA terminated contact with AM/LASH.

To what extent President Kennedy was kept informed of the CIA's covert enterprises aimed at killing Castro remains unclear. But in the autumn of 1961 he gave his sanction to Operation Mongoose, a covert operation by which the United States would help Cubans to overthrow the Castro regime. Its managers pressed for results by the president's brother Robert, Mongoose accomplished little. It gathered some intelligence data and conducted a sabotage operation against a Cuban copper mine. Then, in the autumn of 1962, it was terminated.

## LAOS

At the same time that he was weighing the merits of Operation Pluto, during the first months of his tenure in the White House, President Kennedy was also wrestling with the question of what his New Frontier administration ought to do about Laos, a poor and sparsely populated land of jungles and mountains in Southeast Asia that seemed threatened by a communist takeover. Like Eisenhower, Kennedy regarded Laos as a "domino," which if knocked over by the communists was apt to send the rest of the nation-states of Southeast Asia falling to communism, one after the other—after the fashion of a row of dominoes. But unlike Eisenhowever, he was not bent on making Laos a bastion of anticommunism. Rather, he sought the neutralization of the ancient and somnolent kingdom under the leadership of Prince Souvana Phouma. So he set about to persuade the militant communist faction in Laos, the Pathet Lao, and its friends in Moscow, Beijing, and Hanoi that the United States would not acquiesce in a communist takeover of Laos. To that purpose, he moved the Seventh Fleet into the South China Sea, alerted U.S. troops in Okinawa, and ordered five hundred marines to Thailand, Laos's neighbor to the west.

Kennedy's show of force appeared effective, for in May 1961 the Pathet Lao, pressed by the Soviets, accepted a cease-fire—which it subsequently violated repeatedly—and in July 1962 delegates representing China, the Soviet Union, the United States, and 11 other countries met at Geneva and pledged to uphold the independence and neutrality of Laos.

Tragically, the agony of Laos was not over. The Pathet Lao refused to take up portfolios in a coalition government, China and the Soviet Union continued to provide the communist faction with military assistance, and North Vietnam, in open violation of the recent Geneva accord, kept several thousand soldiers deployed in Laos to support the Pathet Lao. The North Vietnamese further violated Laotian neutrality by dispatching troops and supplies southward to reinforce communist insurgents in South Vietnam by way of the so-called Ho Chi Minh Trail—in truth, an assortment of trails—that meandered from the southern region of North Vietnam through southeastern Laos and into South Vietnam. The United States responded to the refusal of the communists to respect the neutrality of Laos by providing (via the CIA) covert military assistance and guidance to the central government in Vientiane, and, beginning in 1965, by raining bombs down on the Ho Chi Minh Trail.

Ground fighting in Laos, meanwhile, flared off and on. Employing conventional infantry tactics, the Royal Laotian Army would periodically mount an attack on the strategic Plain of Jars in central Laos; the Pathet Lao would counterattack. Then, in 1969, the scale of fighting in Laos dramatically increased, and for a time government forces, supported by American fighter-bombers based in Thailand, pushed the Pathet Lao back. Not for long. Reinforced by fifty thousand seasoned soldiers of North Vietnam, the Pathet Lao by the spring of 1970 had turned the tide, expelled government troops from the Plain of Jars, and seemed on the verge of taking over the entire country. The American response? Their ideas about participating in faraway brushfire wars having undergone radical change since those days of the early 1960s when President Kennedy hinted that he might deploy American troops to keep Laos out of the clutches of the communists, the people of the United States recoiled at the prospect of American troops fighting in Laos. Indeed the administration of Pres. Richard Nixon felt compelled to emphasize that under no circumstances would it send U.S. ground troops into the country.

## VIETNAM

Intertwined with the problem of Laos, of course, was that of South Vietnam, in the view of President Kennedy and millions of his compatriots another of Southeast Asia's dominoes. Because its people were far more numerous than the Laotians (15 million to 2 million) and more aggressive in spirit, South Vietnam, indeed, appeared manifestly more important in terms of the domino theory than Laos. Well before the passage of Kennedy's first year in the White House, accordingly, South Vietnam had returned to the center of the Washington government's strategic calculations regarding Southeast Asia.

If Vietcong (VC) guerrillas, directed and supplied by Ho Chi Minh's regime in Hanoi, were gathering strength across South Vietnam, President Ngo Dinh Diem's government appeared in no immediate danger at the time John Kennedy repeated the presidential oath in Washington. But when, in September 1961, the VC seized a provincial capital and beheaded the governor, the morale of political and military leaders in Saigon slipped perceptibly. Whereupon Kennedy, in October 1961, sent Gen. Maxwell D. Taylor of the Army and Walt Whitman Rostow of the White House staff on a "fact-finding" mission to Vietnam. After a two-week tour of South Vietnam, Taylor and Rostow reported that the situation in the country, from the perspective of American interests, was indeed precarious, but with increased advice and support by the United States, including perhaps the deployment of as many as ten thousand American troops in South Vietnam, the noncommunists stood a reasonable chance of emerging triumphant in their struggle against the followers of Ho Chi Minh.

President Kennedy read the Taylor-Rostow report with interest, was pleased that his two emissaries did not consider the noncommunist cause in South Vietnam hopeless, and liked the idea of helping the Saigon government and the Army of the Republic of Vietnam (ARVN) by advising them more closely. The president, on the other hand, took a critical view of dramatically increasing the number of U.S. military personnel in South Vietnam. As he explained privately, sending troops was akin to taking a drink: "The effect wears off, and you have to take another." He concluded, moreover, that in the last analysis the South Vietnamese would have to win or lose the war for themselves, that turning the struggle into an American war, that is, a white man's war, would be to invite certain defeat. Still, as the historian Arthur M. Schlesinger, Jr., has written, Kennedy felt compelled to take a drink by increasing the number of American military "advisers" in South Vietnam. And, Schlesinger continued, "More drinks were still to come." At the end of 1961, Kennedy's first year in the White House, 1,300 American military personnel were in Vietnam, by the end of 1962 nearly 10,000, and at the time the Kennedy administration ended, in November 1963, about 16,000.

At the same time that the United States was escalating its military involvement in Vietnam, in 1962, the Diem government inaugurated a "strategic hamlet" program whereby peasants in areas in which the Vietcong were particularly active were assembled in hamlets surrounded by moats and fences constructed of bamboo stakes and guarded by armed soldiers. The strategic hamlet, so the theory went, would secure peasants against raids by VC terrorists and also serve as an agent of assorted services, for example, medical care and educational activities, thus binding peasants to the Saigon government. Equally important, the strategic hamlets would isolate Vietcong guerrillas from those peasants who out of loyalty to their cause or fear of reprisals were inclined to provide them with the necessities of life and afford them protection.

The strategic hamlet program quickly faltered. Longing to return to their own villages, many peasants simply hated life in the hamlets, the more so when the VC overran several of them. Meanwhile, the VC, reinforced by personnel and equipment dispatched southward from North Vietnam, regained the initiative in the fighting in the countryside after a short period of aggressive action by the ARVN. Following a trip to Vietnam in late 1962, Secretary of Defense McNamara nonetheless declared "Every quantitative measurement we have shows we're winning this war." And in his State of the Union address of January 1963, President Kennedy asserted, "The spearpoint of aggression has been blunted in South Vietnam."

Kennedy clearly misspoke, as a one-day battle in the Mekong Delta a few weeks before, on January 2, 1963, should have demonstrated conclusively to him and other leaders in Washington. In that action, three battalions of ARVN, advised by Americans, supported by artillery, fighter-bombers, and helicopters, and equipped with amphibious armored personnel carriers and flame-throwers, failed ignominiously (largely because of sheer cowardice) when they attacked a single battalion of lightly armed Vietcong near the hamlet of Ap Bac. Indeed, the action at Ap Bac, incredibly labeled a victory by ranking U.S. officers in Saigon, was an unmitigated disaster for the Saigon government and its partisans, and in the estimate of the writer Neil Sheehan was "a decisive battle for . . . the Vietnamese Revolution," one that should have proved to leaders of the United States once and for all that the corruption-ridden Saigon government and its inept army were beyond redemption.

Whatever the significance of the battle of Ap Bac, events in South Vietnam took a dramatic turn for the worse in the spring and summer of 1963, at least in the perspective of the United States. The trouble began when two politically active Buddhist monks undertook a campaign of vilification against President Diem. The two monks and their followers charged that Diem, a Roman Catholic, had appointed Catholics to most of the responsible positions in his government and in other ways favored Catholicism, the religious faith of a small minority of the South Vietnamese population, and discriminated against Buddhism, a faith for which a substantial percentage of the national population felt a measure of affinity. The upshot was Buddhist-inspired street demonstrations against the Diem regime in Saigon and elsewhere. Next, in May 1963, Buddhists requested government permission to fly Buddhist flags during celebrations commemorating the 2,587th birthday of Gautama Buddha. Permission was denied. Whereupon Buddhists in the ancient coastal city of Hué, a center of Buddhist culture, organized an unusually hostile demonstration against the Saigon government. Apparently seized by panic, government police who had been deployed to keep order during the demonstration opened fire. When the shooting stopped, 12 demonstrators lay dead in the street.

A few weeks later, on June 11, a thousand Buddhist monks and nuns paraded through Saigon, stopped at a main intersection, and gathered around an elderly monk, or *bonze,* named Thich Quang Duc, who, fingering a rosary of acorns, was squatting in the middle of the street. Two monks then stepped forward and doused Quang Duc with 5 gallons of gasoline. Next, the elderly man, muttering, "I return to the eternal Buddha," struck a match and touched it to his saffron robe. As the flames roared and black smoke billowed, monks and nuns chanted, people wept. After ten minutes, the charred body of Quang Duc fell back against the pavement.

Word of Quang Duc's self-inflicted martyrdom swept across South Vietnam and sparked new hostility to the Diem regime. To placate his critics, Diem released Buddhist prisoners and lifted restrictions on the display of Buddhist flags. His action was too late. There were more street demonstrations— and more self-immolations. Then, on a hot evening in late August, a few days after Diem had assured the U.S. ambassador that there would be no further action against the Buddhists, South Vietnamese police and elements of the ARVN stormed Buddhist pagodas in Saigon, Hué, and other cities, dragged fourteen hundred kicking and screaming monks and nuns into the streets, and carted them off to jail. Diem charged that the monks and nuns were communists in disguise.

At that point, a group of generals of the South Vietnamese army opened secret communications with American officials. The generals wanted to know how the Washington government was apt to respond if they arranged the overthrow of Diem's government. The new American ambassador in Saigon, Henry Cabot Lodge, Jr., let them know that the United States would do nothing to assist a coup but would support a new government provided it appeared to have a reasonable chance of bringing stability to the country. Then, on August 31, the generals informed the Americans that they had put aside the plan to get rid of Diem's government.

Inasmuch as the Kennedy administration had no intention of adopting a policy, say, a termination of U.S. economic and military aid to the government in Saigon that would, in effect, hand over South Vietnam to the communists, there seemed nothing left to do than to continue to support Diem while pressing him to placate the Buddhists and reform his government. To the latter purpose, the Washington government suspended a monthly payment of $250,000 to support South Vietnam's "special forces," a commercial import program that netted South Vietnam $100 million annually, and a surplus commodity program involving the shipment of rice, milk, and tobacco to the country that brought in an additional $25 million a year. Diem ignored the American pressure. Then, in early October, leaders in Washington learned that ARVN generals had revived the conspiracy to overthrow Diem. Communicating through the CIA and Ambassador Lodge, they informed the conspirators that the U.S. position regarding a coup against Diem, set out at the end of August, remained unchanged.

Heavy with tension, Saigon by the end of October 1963 was awash with rumors that a coup was imminent. Then, at 1:30 P.M. on November 1, mutinous troops surrounded the presidential palace; others captured the police headquarters and radio station. Tapes proclaiming a revolution were put on the air. But Diem and his notorious brother and confidant, Ngo Dinh Nhu, ensconced in an air-conditioned cellar of the palace, were confident that they would survive the coup, and thus rejected an appeal by the conspirators that they surrender. Next, at about three o'clock, Diem put in a telephone call to a leader of the coup. He wanted a conference with his mutinous generals. Conscious of Diem's persuasive talents, the generals refused a conference. At 4:30 P.M., the president telephoned Lodge. He wanted to know the attitude of the United States regarding the events that were unfolding. Lodge was evasive. A short time later, the conspirators, in a phone conversation, promised that Diem and Nhu would be allowed to leave the country if they surrendered. Diem turned aside the offer. Instead, using a private radio transmitter, he sought the assistance of province chiefs and various organizations that he believed remained loyal to him. His appeal brought no response.

At length, around eight o'clock in the evening, Diem and Nhu escaped the palace by a secret passage and made their way by Land-Rover to a villa in the Chinese suburb of Cholon. Unaware that the Ngo brothers had departed, the conspirators launched two artillery-supported attacks on the palace, only to be repulsed by guard units still loyal to Diem. Then, at 5:00 A.M. on November 2, they attacked again, and after 45 minutes stormed into and set about to loot the palace. While the looters were going about their business, at approximately 6:00 A.M., Diem phoned a leader of the conspiracy and advised him that he and Nhu were at the Church of St. Francis Xavier in Cholon and were prepared to surrender unconditionally. Within an hour, an armored personnel carrier rolled up in front of the church, and the Ngo brothers calmly entered the vehicle. Acting without consent of the leaders of the conspiracy, a major and a captain thereupon sprayed the two men with bullets fired from an automatic weapon and the captain stabbed the corpses repeatedly with a knife.

Most residents of Saigon were jubilant, or so it appeared. People of all ages paraded through the streets of the capital by the thousands, shouting and singing, defacing portraits of the fallen president. In the countryside, the writer Stanley Karnow has noted in his book *Vietnam: A History* (1983), some peasants destroyed their strategic hamlets. Political prisoners emerged from jails. At the U.S. embassy, Ambassador Lodge was manifestly pleased.

In the Oval Office in faraway Washington the response was different. Assuredly not disappointed that Diem's regime had fallen, President Kennedy was mortified by the murder of Diem and his brother. General Taylor later recalled that on learning of the killings, "He leaped to his feet and rushed from the room with a look of shock and dismay on his face which I had never seen before." Three weeks later, Kennedy would have his own rendezvous with an assassin.

## AFRICA

Another area of the Third World that commanded the attention of President Kennedy was Africa. The fabled Dark Continent was scarcely a new interest of the youthful chief executive.

During his last years in the Senate, while chairman of the African Subcommittee of the Foreign Relations Committee, Kennedy had made repeated references to Africa in his public comments, and lamented, "We [Americans] have lost ground in Africa because we have neglected and ignored the aspirations of the African people." Then, after his election to the presidency, he appointed former-Governor G. Mennen Williams of Michigan, a liberal who for many years had been in the front rank of the civil rights movement in the United States, to be assistant secretary of state for African affairs—"a position of responsibility," the president-elect said with some exaggeration, "second to none in the new administration." Upon entering the executive mansion, he gave Williams, who quickly became immensely popular among black Africans, unstinting support, and rallied to his defense when he came under criticism. During a visit to Nairobi in East Africa, for example, the assistant secretary touched off a minor tempest by remarking that Africa was for the Africans. Asked about Williams's remark during a press conference, the president responded, "I don't know who else Africa should be for." Kennedy, meanwhile, took care to appoint people of ability to be ambassadors to the new African states. And when a succession of African leaders called at the White House, the youthful chief executive treated them with dignity and, equally important, was able to persuade them that he and his administration were genuinely interested in Africa and its problems. Unfortunately, a full-dress crisis was boiling in Africa, specifically in the Congo, when Kennedy moved into the White House.

Confusion and disorder seized what hitherto had been the Belgian Congo when, in 1960, the government in Brussels recognized its independence and several provinces, including Katanga, a mineral-rich area without which the Congolese state stood little chance to survive, announced their secession from the Republic of the Congo. In desperation, Prime Minister Patrice Lumumba cabled the UN for help, and the Security Council voted to send a peacekeeping force to the troubled country. Lumumba also appealed to Premier Khrushchev in Moscow, and the Soviet leader agreed to dispatch arms and "technical assistance" to Lumumba's regime. Whereupon, in September 1960, Pres. Joseph Kasavubu, vigorously opposed to a strong Soviet presence in the country, dismissed Lumumba and closed the Soviet and Czech embassies. The charismatic Lumumba then fled to the interior of the country, to Stanleyville, where with Soviet support he set about to organize his followers for an attempt to return to power. At that point, in the autumn of 1960, the CIA directed two of its agents to arrange Lumumba's assassination. It sent some poisons to the Congo, and the two agents took exploratory steps aimed at gaining access to Lumumba. But before they could act, Lumumba was captured by Kasavubu's agents, turned over to Moise Tshombe, the leader of the rebellious Katanga province, and a short time later murdered by Katanga tribesmen.

Infuriated by the turn of events in the Congo, Khrushchev denounced the UN peacekeeping effort in the country and opened a campaign of personal abuse against the UN's secretary-general, Dag Hammarskjöld of Sweden. Meanwhile, in January 1961, Kennedy took the reins of executive authority in Washington, and at the same time that he was wrestling with the problems of Laos and Cuba set about to obstruct further Soviet penetration of the Congo. Inasmuch as Soviet success appeared to depend on continuing turmoil and division in the country and eventual collapse of the central government in Leopoldville, Kennedy determined, by giving maximum support to the UN peacekeeping operation, to work for an end to hostilities in the Congo and restoration of the authority of the central government over the entire country. The president's policy did not yield immediate results, but at length, in 1962, UN forces gained the upper hand in Katanga, Tshombe's resistance collapsed, and the Katanga secession ended.

Thus passed the crisis in the Congo. If stupefying problems continued to plague the new nation-state, peace nonetheless had returned to Central Africa, the Republic of the Congo (later Zaire) was given a chance to survive, and the Kremlin had been foiled in its attempt to make the Congo a base of Soviet influence.

## CRISIS IN BERLIN

While campaigning for president in 1960, John Kennedy understood that foiling maneuvers by the Kremlin aimed at extending Soviet influence and power, and at the same time avoiding a nuclear showdown with his country's superpowerful rival, would be a great overbearing challenge confronting a Kennedy presidency. Scarcely had he settled into the White House, in early 1961, before that challenge confronted him head-on: Nikita Khrushchev announced that Britain, France, and the United States must accept a new arrangement for West Berlin; otherwise, the Kremlin would sign a treaty with the satellite government of East Germany and hand over to the East Germans control of the access routes connecting West Germany with West Berlin. In the latter event, the Western powers would be left with two alternatives if they remained bent on maintaining their position in West Berlin. They could negotiate an agreement with the East German government, whose legitimacy they hitherto had refused to recognize, to keep open the access routes—and thus grant at least tacit recognition to the East German regime. Or they could force their way across East Germany, an action that might produce a nuclear confrontation between the superpowers, inasmuch as Khrushchev had made it clear that the Soviets intended to back the East Germans to the hilt. What sort of arrangement in West Berlin were the Soviets apt to consider satisfactory? As in the past, leaders in the Kremlin apparently wanted to make West Berlin (but not East Berlin) an international free city, a step that Western leaders calculated would amount to nothing less than a prelude to a communist takeover of the noncommunist half of Berlin.

In large measure to impress on the Soviets that the Western powers had no intention of negotiating with the East Germans or surrendering West Berlin to their tender mercies, Kennedy arranged a face-to face meeting with Khrushchev. For Kennedy, the meeting, which took place in Vienna in June 1961, proved an exercise in frustration. Apparently testing the nerves of the youthful president, Khrushchev was rude, intransigent, and threatening. (After the first day of discussions, Kennedy asked Llewellyn Thompson, the U.S. ambassador to the Soviet Union, "Is it always like this?" Replied Thompson, "Par for the course.")

Back in Washington, Kennedy quietly warned the Soviets against underestimating the resolve of the West to resist a new Soviet power maneuver in Berlin. With an absence of histrionics, he thereupon set about to increase the state of readiness of America's armed forces—and took care to let the Soviets know what he was doing. At the same time, he asked Congress for authority to summon a quarter-million Army, Navy, and Air Force reservists to active duty. Congress granted the authority on August 1. Then, shortly after midnight on August 13, East German soldiers and police closed most of the crossing points between East and West Berlin. Four days later, the East Germans began constructing the infamous Berlin Wall. The purpose of the wall? To plug a gap in the Iron Curtain and stop the flow of people to the West, particularly artisans, scientists, and technicians, whose expertise and skills the communist empire could ill afford to lose. Whatever its purpose, people across the noncommunist world viewed the wall as an abomination.

The next development of what would become known as the Berlin crisis of 1961 came to pass on the last day of August when the Soviets announced termination of an informal moratorium on nuclear testing that the superpowers had observed over the past several years, and boasted of their ability to hit any spot on earth with weapons presently in their nuclear arsenal. Whereupon people across the United States began to ponder a crash program to build shelters to protect citizens from radioactive fallout in the event of a nuclear war. Meanwhile, East German police and soldiers made their special contribution to the tension when they gunned down several of their compatriots who, in desperation, tried to escape to the West before the wall's completion.

Then, in October 1961, the dark cloud that had hung over the world in recent months disappeared: Khrushchev announced that he would not sign a treaty with East Germany at the present time. Although the latest crisis over Berlin now belonged to history, the divided city continued to receive close attention by leaders of the United States. And to demonstrate his country's abiding interest in the city, and also its resolve to keep the western sectors free of communist rule, President Kennedy, in the summer of 1963, flew to West Berlin. He visited the wall, told West Berliners that America "will risk its cities to defend yours because we need your freedom to protect ours," and thrilled West Berliners (indeed nearly all West Germans) by proclaiming, "Ich bin ein Berliner."

## MISSILE CRISIS

A year after the passing of the crisis in Berlin, in the autumn of 1962, Kennedy faced a new crisis involving the Soviet Union, this time in Cuba. The crisis began to unfold when a U-2 spy plane, in mid-October, returned from a reconnaissance flight over Cuba with photographs disclosing that launching pads for ballistic missiles were under construction on Castro's island. By whom? Without doubt, the Soviets.

According to the calculus of leaders in Washington, the Soviets had two objectives. First, they intended to substantially increase the striking power of missiles targeted on the United States. By thus shifting the balance of nuclear power, they would place themselves in a stronger position when wrestling with the Americans over such issues as the future of West Berlin. Second, they hoped to undermine the faith of America's allies that in a showdown the North American superpower would honor commitments to move to their defense. For if the United States would stand by and tolerate a power maneuver in their own part of the world that dramatically raised the capacity of the Soviets to threaten American security, why should the allies have great confidence that leaders in Washington would respond forcibly to threats to their security?

Recalling recent assurances by Premier Khrushchev that the Soviets would not install offensive weapons in Castro's island, President Kennedy was furious. And he was determined to act. But what kind of action? Various of his advisers proposed that he send U.S. bombing planes against the missile sites. Kennedy thought poorly of the proposal. Inasmuch as air strikes would claim the lives of Soviet personnel, leaders in the Kremlin would likely feel compelled to order an equally provocative response, and the outcome might be a nuclear confrontation. A better alternative, Kennedy decided, would be imposition of a naval blockade about Cuba to prevent the Soviets from shipping additional missiles to the island and hopefully persuade them to withdraw those that already were there. A blockade—or "quarantine"—would also allow leaders in the Kremlin several days to ponder what was happening in the Caribbean, and, as a consequence, terminate with minimal loss of prestige their current adventure in Cuba. If the Soviets tried to send ships laden with missiles through the naval barrier and continued work at the missile sites, the United States, in Kennedy's view, would have no choice: It would have to dispatch bombing planes against the sites and perhaps undertake an invasion of Cuba.

The more he thought about it, the better Kennedy liked the idea of a block-ade, and on Monday, October 22, he ordered blockading ships to Cuban waters. He also ordered amphibious forces to assemble in Florida for a possible inva-sion of Castro's island fortress. That evening, the youthful president went be-fore television cameras and told his compatriots what the Soviets were up to in Cuba and what the Washington government was doing about it. To borrow a tennis metaphor, the ball was now in the court of the Soviets, and over the next three days nobody could say for sure how they intended to respond. Mean-while, work at the missile sites continued, and out in the Atlantic 20 Soviet freighters, some of them probably transporting missiles, were steaming toward Cuba. People across the world looked on with amazement mixed with horror, for it appeared that the superpowers were actually teetering on the brink of nuclear war.

Then, on Friday, October 26, the Soviets hinted that they would withdraw the missiles from Cuba if the United States would terminate the blockade and pledge to undertake no invasion of Cuba. Kennedy promptly indicated accep-tance of such a deal. The great missile crisis appeared to have ended. But then, the following day (Saturday), Khrushchev raised the ante, in a manner of speak-ing, by demanding that the United States also remove the fifteen Jupiter inter-mediate-range ballistic missiles (IRBMs) that it had deployed in Turkey in 1961. Because the liquid-fueled Jupiters would require hours of preparation before they could be fired and were quite inaccurate, Kennedy had already con-sidered removing them from Turkey. Still, he determined to establish no prec-edent whereby the United States would make concessions whenever the Sovi-ets provoked a crisis. More than that, he reckoned that an apparent weakening of the defenses of a NATO ally (in this instance, Turkey) to get Soviet missiles out of Cuba would devastate the confidence of the NATO allies in the reliabil-ity and resolve of the United States—that, as the British prime minister Harold Macmillan later wrote, the NATO allies "would feel that to avoid the Cuban threat the U.S. . . . had bargained away their protection." So the president, on the suggestion of his brother Bobby, ignored Khrushchev's Saturday communi-cation and responded affirmatively to that of Friday—the one indicating that the Soviets would withdraw the missiles from Cuba in return for termination of the blockade and a pledge that the United States would make no invasion of Cuba. (Although, in a secret meeting on that same evening with the Soviet ambassador in Washington, Anatoly Dobrynin, Robert Kennedy intimated that the United States would probably remove the Jupiters from Turkey fol-lowing an appropriate lapse of time.)

The next day, Sunday, October 28, a beautiful autumn day in Washington, Kennedy read a cable dispatched by Khrushchev advising that work at the mis-sile sites would end and the missiles would be shipped back to the Soviet Union. In a television address that evening, Kennedy spoke of Khrushchev's "statesmanlike decision." When Fidel Castro, the forgotten head of state dur-ing the crisis, threatened to drop a clod in the churn by announcing that he would not allow the on-the-ground inspection of the missile sites that the Washington government had insisted upon, Kennedy, having caught a glimpse of Armageddon in recent days, remained calm. Persuaded that U-2 spy planes and other aircraft could provide adequate surveillance of the sites, he declined to press the point of on-the-ground inspection. (U.S. aircraft and ships were subsequently permitted to make visual "alongside" inspection of missiles that were lashed to the decks of Soviet ships departing Cuba for their homeland.) Thus passed the most frightening crisis that the world has faced since World War II.

Various partisans of President Kennedy have agreed with the assessment later offered by Richard Nixon, to wit, that Kennedy's performance during the Cuban missile crisis constituted the youthful president's "finest hour" in the White House. Other observers and students of the missile crisis have taken a less exalted view. Some critics have raised the questions: What if Khrushchev had not yielded, that is, had held firm in his demand that as a price for removing Soviet missiles from Cuba the United States must remove the Jupiters from Turkey? Would Kennedy have actually risked the horror of nuclear war to avoid a quid pro quo bargain with the Soviets in the matter of the missiles? To have risked a nuclear holocaust that mere removal of the obsolete Jupiters from Turkey could have prevented, such critics have thought, bordered on criminal irresponsibility. (In a remarkable statement prepared in 1987, Kennedy's secretary of state, Dean Rusk, asserted that Kennedy had in fact instructed him to prepare the groundwork for making an offer whereby the United States would remove the Jupiters from Turkey if Khrushchev's reply to his communication of October 27 was negative. To make it appear as a proposal generated by the UN, Secretary General U Thant of the world organization would issue a statement that had been drafted in Washington urging the United States to remove the Jupiters from Turkey and the Soviets to remove their SS-4s and SS-5s from Cuba.) Other critics, mainly Americans of conservative political persuasion, have taken Kennedy to task for having acceded to Khrushchev's demand that, as a price for removal of the Soviet missiles from Cuba, the United States pledge to refrain from invading Castro's bastion of communism. As a result of that pledge, they contend, the United States was prevented from ever ridding—or even threatening to rid—the hemisphere of the Castro menace.

Later-day assessments aside, in the aftermath of the missile crisis, the Cold War underwent one of its periodic "thaws." Perhaps sobered by the experience of having approached the abyss of nuclear war, leaders in Washington and Moscow appeared to think less about confrontation and more about "peaceful coexistence." So when crop failures threatened the Soviet Union with severe food shortages, in the autumn of 1963, President Kennedy responded to an appeal by the Kremlin and, over the objections of various of his compatriots who opposed any action that smacked of assistance to communists, approved the sale to the Soviets of American wheat valued at $250 million. A few months before the wheat sale, in the summer of 1963, the governments in Washington and Moscow agreed to set up a direct telephone system (a "hot line") between the two capitals to permit instant communication during times of crisis. Of larger moment, representatives of the two superpowers (and also those of Britain), in August 1963 put their hands to a treaty pledging that their governments would sanction no further nuclear tests in the atmosphere, in outer space, or under water. Henceforth, in a word, the signatories of the "test ban" would conduct all nuclear tests underground. The Senate in Washington consented to the treaty the following month. An additional 99 governments subsequently signed the treaty. Those of France and China, unfortunately, did not. Bent on becoming nuclear powers, the latter two states were persuaded that they would need to conduct atmospheric tests if they were to achieve their purposes.

## DALLAS

Taking for granted that he would seek a second term in the White House, President Kennedy meanwhile was giving increasing thought to the electoral contest of 1964. And it was for the purpose of urging the feuding factions of the Democratic Party in the Lone Star state to put aside differences and work together, at least through 1964, that Kennedy, in the autumn of 1963, decided to make a trip to Texas. On the morning of November 21, accordingly, the president and Mrs. Kennedy walked onto the lawn of the White House, zoomed over the capital in a helicopter to Andrews Air Force Base, and boarded Air Force One, the white-and-blue Boeing 707 that was the chief executive's official plane. Within minutes, the presidential couple was winging through the sky in a southwesterly direction, destination: San Antonio.

After the president dedicated an aerospace medical center, he and his entourage flew to Houston where Kennedy attended a dinner in honor of Rep. Albert Thomas, and after that to Fort Worth where the presidential party spent the night in the Hotel Texas. The following morning, November 22, Kennedy, seemingly refreshed and in high humor, walked across the street to a parking lot where he shook hands and exchanged pleasantries with a gathering of people, most of them presumably Texans. A short time later, he was the guest of honor at a breakfast sponsored by the Fort Worth Chamber of Commerce. Dressed in a bluish-gray suit, a white shirt with gray stripes, and a dark blue tie, the president laughed when his hosts presented him with a "cow country" hat (but declined to put it on), joined the 2,500 guests in a standing ovation when Mrs. Kennedy, radiant in a pink suit and matching pillbox hat, made a belated entrance to the dining room, and during after-breakfast remarks observed, "We live in a very dangerous and uncertain world." He and his entourage thereupon returned to the airport, boarded Air Force One, and took off for the short flight to Dallas. The big jet touched down at Love Field outside Dallas at 11:30 A.M.

Following his wife, the president emerged from the plane, fidgeted with his necktie, tried vainly to put his unruly hair in place. After the ritual of exchanging greetings with local dignitaries, and several minutes of handshaking and chatting with well-wishers who were restrained by a low chain-link fence, the presidential couple joined Governor and Mrs. John B. Connally in a limousine that was to take them through downtown Dallas and thence to the Trade Mart where the president was scheduled to deliver a luncheon speech. Because the day was bright and sunny, and also because Kennedy did not want to obstruct the view of citizens who wished to see the president, secret service agents did not put the limousine's "bubble top" in place.

At length, at 12:21 P.M., the presidential motorcade, now moving at a crawl, turned left onto Elm Street. The people lining the steet were cheering and waving, and when Mrs. Connally turned to Kennedy and remarked, "No one can say Dallas doesn't love and respect you, Mr. President," the chief executive replied, "You sure can't." At that point, the motorcade was slowly making its way past the Texas School Book Depository, a seven-story building of red brick that appeared almost shabby in comparison with the gleaming architectural creations of downtown Dallas.

However unimposing the School Book Depository might appear, its sixth floor was providing a perch for Lee Harvey Oswald, a sharp-faced onetime marine of 24 who had returned to the United States after renouncing his American citizenship and living for a time in the Soviet Union. And when the presidential limousine passed beneath the window behind which he had deployed himself, Oswald propped a carbine of Italian manufacture on a stack of empty cartons, caught the image of the president in the cross hairs of the weapon's telescopic sight, and just as he had been taught to do while in the Marine Corps, squeezed the trigger—once, twice, three times. On May 29, 1964, John F. Kennedy would have celebrated his forty-seventh birthday.

## RETROSPECT

Tens of millions of American were delighted when on January 20, 1961, the grandfatherly Eisenhower passed the torch of national leadership to the youthful Kennedy. Inspired by the Broadway musical *Camelot* depicting the romantic adventures of the legendary King Arthur and a galaxy of courageous knights and beautiful ladies, many of them would come to view Kennedy as a sort of twentieth-century Arthur who was restoring idealism and grace and an appreciation of beauty to the realm. Indeed, people fell to referring to the Kennedy White House as Camelot, the palace and court of the good King Arthur. Later, during the mid-1970s, Americans learned of the philandering of the thirty-fifth president—of extramarital liaisons within the hallowed walls of the executive mansion itself. Feeling dismay and disgust tinctured with disappointment and profound sadness, millions of them stopped thinking of Kennedy as a modern-day King Arthur and his White House as Camelot.

His personal behavior aside, Kennedy made a large imprint on national affairs during his abbreviated presidency. Despite the fact that the national economy reached new levels of prosperity at the time of his tenure in the Oval Office, tens of millions of Americans continued to be poor, and in the years 1961–1963 a national administration for the first time since the Great Depression of the 1930s addressed, however haltingly, the anomaly and scandal of poverty in the midst of unparalleled abundance. Kennedy's administration mobilized its resources as had no other to that time in behalf of the crusade for civil equality for racial minorities, fought what many Americans believed was the good fight for Medicare and federal assistance to schools, gave unstinting support to the national endeavor to explore the reaches of outer space. It relieved the hunger of hundreds of thousands and perhaps millions of people in various corners of the world, and offered thousands of young Americans an opportunity to give substance to idealistic impulses.

The Kennedy administration revised the country's nuclear strategy while presiding over a substantial buildup of its nuclear arsenal and a strengthening of its conventional military-naval forces. It sanctioned dubious covert ventures by the CIA, tolerated equally dubious activity against American citizens by the FBI, and continued the Washington government's tacit alliance with such repressive regimes as that of the infamous Anastasio Somoza Debayle in Nicaragua. It authorized the idiotic venture at the Bay of Pigs and bore at least partial responsibility for a diplomatic success in Central Africa. It viewed the anguish of the Third World with greater sympathy than any administration in Washington before or since (that of Jimmy Carter excepted perhaps). It escalated U.S. involvement in the interminable conflict in Vietnam, stood up to the Soviets in the matter of West Berlin, stared them down during the Cuban missile crisis.

How have historical scholars tended to assess Kennedy the president? Several hundred of those polled in 1982 by the historians Robert K. Murray and Tim H. Blessing ranked him thirteenth among the 39 men who had held the presidential office to 1981. They classified him as an "above average" chief executive.

# Chapter
# 6

---

# The Tragedy of
# Lyndon Johnson

*H*is face drawn, the thirty-sixth president of the United States repeated
the oath of office in the cabin of Air Force One, still parked at Love Field
outside Dallas. To his right stood his wife, to his left the wife of the slain
president, her pink dress splattered with blood, her expression one of horror
mingled with disbelief. In a compartment in the rear of the aircraft rested a
casket containing the mortal remains of John F. Kennedy. Within minutes of
the oath taking, the big plane was streaking through the heavens, destination:
the national capital. Via television, scores of millions of stunned Americans
witnessed its arrival at Andrews Air Force Base—watched as the casket, Mrs.
Kennedy at its side, was lowered from the plane and placed in a hearse,
watched and listened as the new president made a brief and dignified statement.

# LBJ

Born in Blanco County, Texas, in 1908, Lyndon Johnson grew up in Johnson City, Texas, attended Southwest State Teachers College in San Marcos, Texas, taught school for two years. Fascinated by politics, he found employment as secretary for a Texas congressman. In 1934, he married Claudia Alta "Lady Bird" Taylor, a shy and intelligent graduate of the University of Texas who would, on coming into a substantial inheritance, buy a radio station in Austin, Texas, which the Johnsons would parlay into a multimillion-dollar fortune. In 1935, Pres. Franklin D. Roosevelt appointed Johnson to direct the program of the National Youth Administration in Texas, in which capacity he organized an array of projects that gave employment to thousands of young Texans during that time of economic depression. In 1937, on the death of the congressman of his home district, he won election to the national House of Representatives, won re-election in 1938 and 1940, lost a campaign for election to the Senate in 1941. A lieutenant commander in the naval reserve, he was summoned to active duty in the Navy in early 1942, and was awarded a Silver Star

November 22, 1963: Flanked by his wife and the widow of the late President Kennedy, Lyndon Johnson repeats presidential oath in the cabin of Air Force One.

for "gallantry in action" by Gen. Douglas MacArthur after a B-26 bombing plane in which he was a mere passenger came under attack by Japanese fighter planes during a mission over New Guinea. A short time later, Roosevelt ordered Johnson and all other members of Congress who had gone on active duty in the armed forces to return to Washington.

Reelected to the House in 1942, 1944, and 1946, Johnson won election to the Senate in 1948. During his first term, his Democratic colleagues elected him their leader, and when the Democrats regained control of the Senate in 1955 he became the Senate majority leader. In his new role, he seemed akin to a volcano that was about to erupt at any moment as he strode the corridors and cloakrooms of the Senate Office Building and Capitol, chain-smoking cigarettes, barking out orders to aides, buttonholing and cajoling fellow senators. Then, in the summer of 1955, he suffered a near-fatal heart attack, but after six months of rest was back in the Senate and operating at his former pace.

Johnson determined to seek the presidency in 1960, but because Democratic liberals perceived him as one who would go to any length to protect the oil and natural gas interests of his home state and never press meaningful legislation aimed at securing the civil rights of blacks or support liberal initiatives, for example, medical care for the elderly under the Social Security system, he really stood no chance of achieving his goal. But on winning the presidential nomination, John F. Kennedy, apparently as a gesture of respect, invited Johnson to be his vice presidential running mate. To his surprise and apparent chagrin, Johnson accepted. The Kennedy-Johnson ticket of course won a narrow victory on Election Day the following November.

As vice president, Johnson's responsibilities were largely ceremonial. Moreover, if the president respected him, other New Frontiersmen, including the president's brother Bobby, made no attempt to disguise their contempt for him, and privately ridiculed his Texas accent and what they perceived to be his "corn pone" manners. Thus Johnson, at once vain and proud, was generally unhappy in the vice presidency. Or as the writer Theodore H. White later recalled, "Chafing in inaction when his nature yearned to act, conscious of indignities real and imagined, Johnson went through three years of slow burn."

Then, on November 22, 1963, Lyndon B. Johnson—manifestly bright (but in the view of some observers lacking intellectual sophistication), sensitive, beset by insecurities, arrogant, overbearing, crude, earthy, profane, charming (when he felt the urge to be), bursting with energy, totally preoccupied by the craft of politics, more animated by essential Christian principles than was popularly understood (particularly by that principle regarding the Christian's responsibility to do good for the downtrodden and unfortunate)—became the president of the United States.

## JOHNSON TAKES CHARGE

The people of the United States were in a state of collective shock when Lyndon Johnson assumed responsibilities of national leadership on November 22, 1963. Many of them were questioning the viability of the country's basic institutions and values. But almost overnight their nerves were settled and their confidence restored, for the new chief executive, moving calmly and resolutely, took a firm grip on the instruments of national power.

An initial task confronting Johnson was resolution of the question that was bedeviling millions of Americans: Did Lee Harvey Oswald act alone and on his own initiative when he aimed his rifle at President Kennedy? Accordingly, the new chief executive appointed a blue-ribbon commission headed by Chief Justice Earl Warren (one of the commission's members was a future president, Rep. Gerald R. Ford) to investigate the presidential assassination. Complicating the task of the Warren Commission was the fact that Oswald, captured by police in a suburban movie theater in Dallas a couple of hours after the events in the vicinity of the schoolbook depository, was shot to death two days later by Jack Ruby, the owner of a sleazy nightclub, while being led through the Dallas police headquarters. After scrutinizing reams of documents and taking the testimony of scores of witnesses, the commission concluded that Oswald, an angry and frustrated misfit, had acted entirely alone. In a word, he was not party to a larger conspiracy.

The new president, meanwhile, set about to secure congressional consent to his late predecessor's legislative program, and decided that his first priority would be enactment of a measure to stimulate the national economy, which had shown signs of sluggishness in recent months, by reducing personal and corporate income taxes. The measure had already passed the House of Representatives, but appeared hopelessly stalled in the Finance Committee of the Senate. So Johnson cajoled Sen. Harry Flood Byrd of Virginia, a conservative Democrat who was chairman of the latter committee, to allow the measure to reach the floor of the upper chamber. Avowing his determination to vote against the tax cut, Byrd at length allowed the bill to exit his committee. Next, in the words of the historian and onetime White House assistant Eric F. Goldman, Johnson "practiced every form of arm-twisting known to political osteopathy" to muster the votes needed to get the legislation through the Senate. His enterprise met success, and in February of 1964 the president, beaming with satisfaction, signed the tax-reduction measure. During the signing ceremony, he even praised Byrd—"no doubt the only bill-signing ceremony," Goldman later wrote, "at which a President had lauded a congressman who voted against the legislation."

Johnson, the Texan who liberals had once thought felt no commitment to civil equality, now determined to persuade Congress to approve the civil rights package put before it in June 1961 by President Kennedy. Might he make compromises, say, on the emotion-charged "public accommodations" section, that is, the section prohibiting discrimination on account of race in hotels, restaurants, theaters, and other places of business purporting to serve the general public? He made it plain that he would not. During a conversation with a friend, he allegedly recalled that former-Vice President John Nance Garner of Texas had been a great poker player, and "He told me once that there comes a time in every game when a man has to put in all his stack." Said the president, "Well, I'm shoving in all my stack on the civil rights bill."

Moving the civil rights bill through the House of Representative presented no difficulty, and in February 1964 the legislation won overwhelming approval in the lower chamber of Congress. But in the upper chamber, 18 members representing states of the onetime Confederacy were bent on doing everything possible to prevent the measure from coming to a vote, for it was transparent that if given an opportunity to vote, a substantial majority of senators would give it their consent.

The southerners first sought to have the bill sent to the Senate Judiciary Committee headed by James O. Eastland of Mississippi, a veteran segregationist who had assisted in the destruction of a variety of civil rights proposals over the years. Eastland, they were sure, would be able to prevent the measure from ever reaching the Senate floor. But unlike in former times, the proponents of civil rights legislation were no less determined and organized than the southerners. Accordingly, Senate Majority Leader Mike Mansfield of Montana was able to steer the measure around Eastland's committee. Undaunted, the southerners, taking advantage of the Senate's rule allowing unlimited debate, mounted what turned out to be the longest filibuster in the history of the upper chamber. Day after day—for three months—the southern senators droned on about the alleged unconstitutionality of the civil rights bill, the alleged evils of "mongrelization" of the races, and numerous other topics that related only vaguely if at all to the issues at hand.

The filibuster did not yield the traditional result, to wit, an early surrender by proponents of civil equality. Led by Mansfield, Hubert Humphrey, and Thomas H. Kuchel, Republican of California, supporters of the legislation refused to be worn down by the southern talkathon, made certain that they were adequately represented on the floor of the Senate at all times, and used every parliamentary tactic available to harass the filibusterers. President Johnson, meanwhile, brought to bear the power of the executive office to weaken the filibuster and his legendary powers of persuasion to build support for the bill.

Still, there seemed only one way to break the filibuster: by taking advantage of a relatively new Senate rule by which debate could be terminated and a vote taken if three-fourths of the members voted to invoke cloture. Securing the requisite votes, proponents of civil equality understood, would be no easy matter, for a fair number of conservative Republicans of the North and West were only slightly more enthusiastic about civil rights legislation than the southern filibusterers. There was, in truth, only one way to win over the requisite number of conservative Republicans to invoke cloture: persuade their premier spokesman, and also the Republican minority leader in the Senate, Everett McKinley Dirksen, the grandiloquent legislator of Illinois whose mellifluous tones and embellished phrases had prompted news people to refer to him as "the wizard of ooze."

To win him over, President Johnson invited Dirksen to the White House for several long discussions. As for Dirksen, he was, in Goldman's words, magisterial, and Goldman later quoted him as pontificating at one point, "I trust that the time will never come in my public career when the waters of partisanship will flow so swift and so deep as to obscure my estimate of the national interest. I trust I can disenthrall myself from all bias, and see clearly and cleanly what the issue is and then render an independent judgment." At length, the senator saw the national interest, to wit, that the country needed the civil rights bill, and helped work out minor amendments that made the legislation more palatable to his conservative colleagues. Whereupon cloture was invoked, and by a vote of 73–27 the measure secured approval of the Senate.

After the House had consented to the upper chamber's amendments, on July 2, 1964, President Johnson, his countenance again beaming with satisfaction, signed the Civil Rights Act of 1964. The most far-reaching civil rights legislation ever enacted in the United States, the measure prohibited discrimination on account of race in hotels, restaurants, theaters, and other places of "public accommodation"; authorized the attorney general to initiate suits or otherwise intervene on behalf of victims of discrimination; forbade both employers and labor unions from practicing racial discrimination (and thus struck down the "white only" charters of numerous labor organizations); allowed the withholding of federal funds from projects in which racial discrimination persisted; and forbade the application of different standards of eligibility to whites and blacks who wished to register and vote.

Meanwhile, Johnson had determined to strike hard and fast against the demon of poverty in the world's most affluent society—to eliminate a staggering social waste that was once a national scandal and a drag on the national economy, and defuse the poverty-rooted anger and frustration that in his first year in the White House would produce disturbances in the black ghettos of Chicago, Jersey City, New York, and Rochester. In his State of the Union address of January 1964, accordingly, he announced, "This administration here and now declares unconditional war" on poverty. Two months later, he sent Congress a message in which he requested an appropriation of nearly a billion dollars to finance that war, and proclaimed, "The president of the United States is president of all the people in every section of the country. But this office holds a special responsibility to the distressed and disinherited, the hungry and the hopeless of this abundant nation."

Johnson's so-called economic opportunity measure passed through the Senate with minimal debate, and supporters of the legislation felt optimistic that it would soon secure passage in the House, the more so when the conservative congressman Phil M. Landrum, Democrat of Georgia, argued that, contrary to the popular perception that the economic opportunity bill was liberal, it was, in fact, essentially conservative. If the problem of poverty was not resolved, Landrum reasoned, the poor were apt to rise up and tear apart the existing socioeconomic structure of the republic. "We are dealing with social dynamite," he shouted in one of the more compelling orations delivered in Congress in recent times. But most members of the conservative coalition on Capitol Hill did not accept Landrum's logic, and before long it was evident that the economic opportunity legislation was in serious trouble. Whereupon Johnson moved into action. Using his favorite instrument, namely the telephone, he cajoled reluctant and recalcitrant members of Congress, and also put pressure on them via influential residents of their home states. The presidential arm-twisting proved effective, the measure secured passage, and on August 20, 1964, in the Rose Garden of the White House, Johnson signed the Economic Opportunity Act.

The economic opportunity legislation provided for the establishment of rural conservation camps and urban training centers to help 40,000 school dropouts to obtain job training; work-training programs to enable 200,000 boys and girls to stay in school by providing them with part-time employment; part-time jobs to help 140,000 college and university students to stay in school; federal funds to urban and rural communities to help them counter poverty and illiteracy; loans to farmers to help them improve their land; loans to small businesses to encourage them to hire the chronically unemployed; and job-training programs for heads of families who were on welfare rolls. To coordinate the federal antipoverty program, it established the Office of Economic Opportunity.

If the tax cut, the Civil Rights Act, and the Economic Opportunity Act were the premier achievements, Johnson realized other successes during his first year in the Oval Office. He prevailed on Congress to establish a 9-million-acre wilderness preserve from government-owned lands; enact a housing bill providing for the construction of 35,000 low-rent housing units for poor families; approve a measure whereby the federal government would help cities to improve and expand public transport facilities; appropriate $400 million to continue federal aid to schools in "impacted areas"; extend the National Defense Education Act of 1958; and amend the latter measure to provide support for instruction in the humanities (including history) as well as science, mathematics, and modern languages.

## PANAMA

At the same time that he was maneuvering legislative proposals through Congress, in 1964, President Johnson was striving to cope with a variety of diplomatic problems, one of them originating in Panama. Although a small nation-state of fewer than 1.5 million people, Panama loomed large in the strategic calculations of the United States, for across its isthmian territory meandered the Panama Canal, the 51-mile waterway that connected (and continues to connect) the Caribbean Sea and Pacific Ocean. Essential to the efficient operation of the U.S. Navy, the canal also provided easy passage each year for thousands of commercial vessels, about 10 percent of which flew the Stars and Stripes. The canal, of course, was the property of the United States, and passed through the Canal Zone, a 10-mile-wide strip of land that Panama had leased in perpetuity to the United States in 1903. Living and working in the Canal Zone in 1964 were some forty thousand American civilian and military-naval personnel.

The seeds of trouble had been present in Panama, a country that was ridden with poverty, for a long time. Although the United States, in 1955, had raised the annuity that it paid to Panama for lease of the Canal Zone from $250,000 to $1.9 million, many Panamanians believed their government was not receiving a fair share of the returns from operation of the international waterway that passed through their isthmian republic. Panamanian nationalists had other grievances. They thought North Americans behaved as though the Canal Zone were a colony of the United States and not a sovereign part of the Republic of Panama. They resented the fact that the best jobs in connection with operation of the canal were the preserve of North Americans who, in turn, often treated Panamanians with contempt and enjoyed a standard of living that stood out in stark contrast with that of most Panmanians. As for the trouble of 1964, it was the consequence of a smoldering quarrel over the flying of flags in the Canal Zone.

To demonstrate that the Canal Zone was indeed a part of the Panamanian nation, President Eisenhower had decreed in 1959 that the Panamanian flag should fly alongside the Stars and Stripes throughout the Canal Zone. But the sight of the Panamanian banner fluttering next to Old Glory in front of their schools offended the sensibilities of North American students, whereupon the Washington government, in 1963, ruled that no flags at all should be displayed in front of schools in the zone. Their sensibilities still offended, a group of North American students in Balboa raised the Stars and Stripes in front of their school anyhow. That action prompted Panamanian nationalists to force their way into the zone, burn buildings, destroy automobiles, and assault several "gringos." Order returned only when U.S. troops intervened. At that point, Pres. Roberto Chiari broke diplomatic relations with the United States, demanded that the Hay-Bunau-Varilla Treaty of 1903 (by which the United States had acquired its lease of the Canal Zone) be renegotiated, and hinted that Panama might insist on nationalizing the Panama Canal. He also charged the United States with aggression, and placed the issue before the UN and the Organization of American States.

If Chiari's action exhilarated his compatriots, it caused President Johnson to bristle. Observing that Panama was no larger than St. Louis, LBJ made it clear that he had no intention of knuckling under to the Panamanians—lest nationalists in other countries get the idea that the surest way to extract concessions from the United States was to attack an American embassy and burn a few American-owned automobiles. Still, Johnson understood the legitimacy of some of Panama's grievances, and of course did not want to exacerbate the Washington government's relations with the rest of Latin America. Accordingly, after a suitable display of toughness, he agreed that the United States would consider revising the treaty of 1903, whereupon, in the spring of 1964, diplomatic relations between the governments in Panama City and Washington were restored. Next, several months later, the two governments negotiated a treaty that gave Panama a larger financial return from operation of the Panama Canal as well as an increased role in its management, and provided for the gradual integration of Zonians (North Americans who lived in the Canal Zone) into Panamanian life.

## VIETNAM

However nettlesome the goings-on in Panama, events that were unfolding in Vietnam commanded far more of Lyndon Johnson's attention during his first year in the White House. The reasons why that was the case are not hard to discern. The situation in Vietnam, in the perspective of the government in Washington, moved from bad to worse in the months after Johnson repeated the presidential oath on that somber day in Dallas.

While Johnson was wrapping his large hands around the levers of power in Washington, in late 1963 and early 1964, the Vietcong continued to prowl the countryside of South Vietnam, extorting taxes from peasants and murdering village chieftains, while the successors of the late President Diem labored without success to put together a workable administration in Saigon. As for leaders in Washington, they remained persuaded that the "vital" interests of the United States required that South Vietnam be kept free of communist domination. They also continued to hope that, without any notable enlargement of involvement by the United States, the communists might be thwarted in their ambition to take control of South Vietnam. Still, they understood that the noncommunists of South Vietnam stood no chance of winning their struggle against the tightly organized and disciplined communists unless they achieved political stability. Political stability, unfortunately, continued to elude the government in Saigon. Indeed, a coup in February 1964 catapulted Gen. Nguyen Khanh, a man of dubious character, not to mention dubious commitment to the principles of democracy, to the leadership of that government.

How did ordinary Americans view the conflict in Vietnam in 1963–1964? Most who were past 30 years of age, persuaded as they had been over the preceding decade and a half of the necessity of containing the power and influence of the "international communist conspiracy" in every corner of the world, believed instinctively that South Vietnam's fall to the communists would be a calamity. That calamity would be tragically compounded, they reckoned further, if a communist triumph in Vietnam, in accord with the predictions of such respected leaders as Eisenhower and Kennedy, should open the way for a communist sweep across all of southeast Asia. Given such assumptions and views, most Americans had no quarrel with the president's assertion in early 1964: "The United States, at the request of the Republic of South Vietnam and in accord with our obligations under the Southeast Asia Treaty Organization, is helping South Vietnam defend its freedom with military advisers, ammunition and matériel. It is not engaged in war and does not intend to be."

Then, on August 2, 1964, the Washington government announced that North Vietnamese torpedo boats had attacked the U.S. destroyer *Maddox* while it was operating in international waters off the coast of North Vietnam. An attack had indeed taken place—when the North Vietnamese apparently concluded that the *Maddox* was operating in support of South Vietnamese gunboats that had bombarded a nearby North Vietnamese island the evening before. Two days later, the Washington government announced a second attack in the Gulf of Tonkin, this time on the *Maddox* and the destroyer *C. Turner Joy*. Whether a second attack had, in fact, taken place was uncertain; reports of the alleged attack rested on sonar and radar contacts that were admittedly unreliable in adverse weather conditions such as had prevailed in the Gulf of Tonkin on the night of August 3–4, 1964, and on visual sightings of torpedoes in near-total darkness. Whatever the truth, President Johnson sent U.S. bombing planes on retaliatory raids against North Vietnamese torpedo boats and their bases, charged in a national television address that North Vietnam had committed aggression against the United States, and asked Congress to approve a resolution endorsing the retaliatory raids and authorizing him to do whatever he might consider necessary to counter communist aggression in Southeast Asia until such time as he, the president, decided that the resolution was no longer necessary or Congress repealed it.

What became known as the Gulf of Tonkin Resolution was introduced in Congress without delay, and in the House of Representatives, after only 40 minutes of discussion, won approval by a vote of 414–0. In the Senate, where it was managed by J. William Fulbright of Arkansas, the chairman of the Foreign Relations Committee who would subsequently become one of the sharpest critics of the administration's policies in Southeast Asia, the discussion was more prolonged. For more than nine hours, Senators George S. McGovern, Democrat of South Dakota, Jacob K. Javits, Republican of New York, John Sherman Cooper, Republican of Kentucky, Albert Gore, Democrat of Tennessee, and Frank Church, Democrat of Idaho, expressed concern lest the United States become more deeply embroiled in the seemingly interminable conflict in Southeast Asia. Conceding that they intended to vote for the resolution, the foregoing senators wanted it understood that, so far as they were concerned, the resolution, if approved, would in no sense constitute a blank check by which the president might arbitrarily escalate America's involvement in the hostilities in Vietnam. Wayne Morse, a Republican-turned-Democrat of Oregon, and Ernest Gruening, Democrat of Alaska, took a more resolute stand. Contending that the resolution transferred the war-making power from Congress to the president, Morse argued that it was unconstitutional. To no avail, for the resolution secured the Senate's consent by a vote of 98–2. Morse and Gruening were the only dissenters.

## ELECTION OF 1964

Nineteen hundred and sixty-four was a presidential election year, of course, and the incident in the Gulf of Tonkin took place as the electoral campaign was gathering momentum. Full of vigor and heavily financed, Sen. Barry M. Goldwater of Arizona, an uncompromising conservative, had secured a lock on the Republican presidential nomination by June of 1964, and when delegates to the Republican national convention assembled in San Francisco's Cow Palace a few weeks later his supporters were in undisputed control of the instruments of decision. The outcome was a party platform that called for re-

July 16, 1964: Barry Goldwater and William Miller, candidates for president and vice president, share their moment of triumph after accepting nomination by the Republican national convention.

duced federal spending, a balanced federal budget, and a foreign policy resting on "a dynamic strategy aimed at victory." When moderates urged that the platform repudiate so-called extremist groups, including the John Birch Society, they were booed and hissed by conservatives. Next, on the first ballot, the convention nominated Goldwater for president and after that Rep. William Miller, an undistinguished conservative of New York, for vice president. The raucous convention moved to its climax when Goldwater delivered his acceptance speech. Declining to hold out the proverbial olive branch to moderates, the senator, his chin jutting forward, spoke in phrases that were uncompromising in their conservatism—and prompted millions of moderates and liberals of both major parties to wince (or erupt) when, in an apparent endorsement of the John Birch Society, he declared, "Extremism in the defense of liberty is no vice" and "Moderation in the pursuit of justice is no virtue."

Compared with the contest for leadership—indeed, it was said, the soul—of the Republican Party, goings-on among Democrats seemed downright tedious. There was, of course, no serious challenge to the nomination of President Johnson for a full term in the White House, and, frankly, the attention of Democrats in the weeks before delegates to the party's national convention gathered in Atlantic City in August of 1964 centered on the second place on the presidential ticket. To build interest in the convention, which he was orchestrating down to the most minute details, Johnson kept the country guessing as to the identity of the man whom he would ask the convention to select as his running mate. At length, as the convention opened, he ended the suspense by announcing that his choice for the vice presidency was Sen. Hubert H. Humphrey of Minnesota. After approving a transparently liberal platform designed to achieve what the president designated as a "Great Society," delegates to the convention nominated Johnson and Humphrey by acclamation.

The subsequent Goldwater-Johnson campaign was generally dull and uninspiring. Goldwater slashed away at Johnson by invoking the longtime conservative argument that Democrats had shackled the country with big government and the charge, a relic of the heyday of Joe McCarthy, that Democrats were inclined to softness when dealing with the issue of communism. For his part, Johnson spoke in generalities in support of his Great Society program, and intimated that Goldwater was an irresponsible hip shooter who was apt to manuever the United States into some dangerous confrontation with the communists, perhaps in Southeast Asia.

At length, the campaign ground to an end, and when votes were tabulated on Election Day evening, November 3, there were no surprises: As expected, Johnson and Humphrey won overwhelmingly—secured 61 percent of the popular votes, a slightly higher percentage than Roosevelt and Garner in the historic Democratic landslide of 1936. Goldwater and Miller carried only Goldwater's home state of Arizona and five states of the onetime Confederacy: Alabama, Georgia, Louisiana, Mississippi, and South Carolina. They were crushed in the Electoral College by a margin of 52–486. The Democrats also gained 39 seats in the House of Representatives and 2 in the Senate, one of which would be occupied by Robert F. Kennedy, now of New York.

## MEDICARE

Ebullient and confident, Lyndon Johnson now set about to build his cherished Great Society. The outcome was what Eric Goldman has designated "the Great Drive." The Great Drive reached high tide in the period January–November 1965 when the thirty-sixth president prevailed on Congress to approve a program of domestic reform rivaling that of the One Hundred Days of 1933 when Franklin Roosevelt inaugurated the New Deal.

Johnson set the Great Drive in motion on the evening of January 4, 1965, when, in the chamber of the House of Representatives, he delivered his annual State of the Union message, and in sweeping terms indicated what he wanted the new Eighty-ninth Congress to do. Given in his Texas drawl and its points underscored by clenched fists and pursed-lipped pauses, the speech was repeatedly interrupted by applause and cheers, particularly by representatives and senators of liberal persuasion who, as a consequence of the gains their faction had registered in the Johnson-Humphrey electoral landslide the previous November, had cracked, if not permanently broken, the power of the oft-mentioned conservative coalition of Republicans and southern Democrats, and now, by a slender margin, held the upper hand in the national legislature.

Three days after delivering the State of the Union address, on January 7,

1965, Johnson sent a message to Congress entitled "Advancing the Nation's Health," the centerpiece of which was an appeal for a measure to provide medical assistance to the elderly under the Social Security system. Why did he lead off his legislative program of 1965 with the so-called Medicare proposal? Because he reckoned that the idea of medical assistance for older Americans under Social Security, after years of acrimonious debate, had at last achieved such support among the citizenry that it was apt to pass through Congress with minimal difficulty—unless it became tangled in debate over other legislation. To prevent it from becoming so entangled, he made Medicare a first order of business.

Whatever the increase in popular support for Medicare, the American Medical Association (AMA), still committed to the proposition that medical assistance to the elderly under Social Security would constitute a giant leap toward socialized medicine in the United States, once again deployed in opposition. Most importantly, it opened its treasury to finance a lobbying campaign against legislation embodying the Medicare idea that Cecil R. King, Democrat of California, had introduced in the House of Representatives and Clinton P. Anderson, Democrat of New Mexico, in the Senate. But times were changing. No less awed by the healing powers of medical practitioners than in the past, great numbers of Americans—overlooking the fact that the AMA, by insisting on high standards of medical training and practice and zealously doing battle against medical quackery, was in no small measure responsible for the high quality of the country's medical services—had come to view the AMA as an elitist and reactionary organization that was insensitive to the financial problems and self-esteem of elderly Americans and their families.

Notwithstanding the opposition of the AMA, the King-Anderson Bill, after several months of debate, secured the consent of Congress. The legislation provided limited coverage for hospital, posthospital, and nursing home care for most Americans who were 65 and older. That coverage was to be financed by increases in Social Security taxes. For elderly citizens who elected to make a monthly supplementary payment of $3, the measure provided partial coverage for the services of physicians and surgeons. In addition to Medicare, the King-Anderson legislation established Medicaid, a public-assistance program using federal, state, and local funds to underwrite medical and dental care for low-income persons.

To sign the King-Anderson measure, President Johnson boarded Air Force One and flew to Independence, Missouri, the home of former-President Truman, who in the 1940s had appealed for a national health insurance program. Largely because of the opposition of the AMA, Truman's proposal had come to nothing, a failure that the thirty-third president had always considered one of the most disappointing of his tenure in the White House. By now a tottering old man of 81, Truman made his way to a microphone and thanked Johnson for honoring him by arranging to sign the King-Anderson Act in the Harry S. Truman Library, then made a short speech in which he said that no elderly citizen should "ever be abandoned to the indignity of charity." After Truman sat down, President Johnson approached the microphone and summed up the sentiment of all proponents of Medicare: "No longer will illness crush and destroy the savings that have been so carefully put away. . . . No longer will young families see their own incomes, and their hopes, eaten away simply because they are carrying out their deep moral obligations to their parents, and to their uncles, and to their aunts."

# EDUCATION

President Johnson meanwhile had asked Congress to appropriate $1.5 billion to assist the country's elementary and secondary schools. That the schools needed assistance was transparent. Because of the baby boom of the previous two decades, classrooms were bursting at the seams. School buildings and equipment in many locales were antiquated. Teachers were generally underpaid. And, unfortunately, local governments were finding it increasingly difficult to raise the requisite revenues to meet educational problems.

Federal aid to elementary and secondary schools was not a new idea, and indeed the National Defense Education Act of 1958 had provided a measure of assistance to elementary and secondary schools. But large numbers of Americans over the past fifteen or so years quailed at the prospect of a broad and inclusive program of "federal aid to education." Political conservatives had argued that federal aid would lead to federal interference in local school affairs, for example, in matters of curriculum and textbook selection. Such interference, in their view, would be anathema. Southern segregationists had calculated that federal aid would provide the federal government with an instrument for coercing southern school districts to accept racial integration. Many Roman Catholics had made it clear that they would stand foursquare against any federal legislation to assist the schools that did not include assistance to church-operated "parochial" schools. But millions of Protestants, Jews, and nonreligionists, contending that public assistance to church-operated schools would violate the stricture in the Bill of Rights of the Constitution that "Congress shall make no law respecting an established religion," were equally emphatic in their opposition to any proposal that included provisions for federal aid to parochial schools. The outcome? Proposals for large-scale federal aid to the country's elementary and secondary schools had come to nothing.

But Lyndon Johnson reckoned that circumstances had changed. Because, as mentioned, the election of 1964 had sent the conservative coalition of Republicans and southern Democrats into eclipse, he suspected that his administration's aid-to-education bill could survive attacks by conservatives and segregationists. He also suspected that it contained just the right mixture of compromise to assure the support of Catholics without alienating most Protestants and Jews. Taking advantage of a Supreme Court ruling of 1947 that public funds might be used to benefit students in parochial schools but not the schools themselves, the bill, in a word, provided that school boards should use some of their federal funds to help students in parochial and other private schools, for example, by financing "shared-time" programs in which students

April 11, 1965: President Johnson hands a pen to his first-grade teacher after signing the Elementary and Secondary Education Act.

of parochial and public schools would come together in the same classrooms for instruction in certain subjects and for the purchase of textbooks and library materials.

Still, many Protestants, particularly those of fundamentalist persuasion, continued to recoil at the prospect of any federal assistance whatever to Catholic education. Some liberals, moreover, argued that the legislation was not sufficiently weighted in favor of poorer states, which were in more desperate need of federal assistance than more affluent ones. Accordingly, passage of the measure appeared in doubt. Whereupon President Johnson, using both gentle persuasion and old-fashioned political arm-twisting, went to work on the denizens of Capitol Hill. The outcome? Administration lieutenants in Congress maneuvered the aid-to-education bill through the House with only minor amendments and virtually dragooned the Senate into accepting the House version without even changing a comma. A few days later, in mid-April 1965, the president drove to the remains of the one-room building in Blanco County, Texas, where he had first attended school, and sitting on a bench beside 72-year-old Kate Deadrich Loney, his first teacher (whom he addressed as "Miss Katie"), signed the Elementary and Secondary Education Act.

# VOTING RIGHTS

The King-Anderson and elementary and secondary education measures were of huge importance. Indeed, they were what commentators sometimes refer to as landmark pieces of legislation. And Lyndon Johnson had every reason to take enormous satisfaction in his part in securing their passage. But a measure to enfranchise millions of black Americans, one of genuinely historic dimension, would stand forth as the premier achievement of the thirty-sixth president and Congress during the time of the Great Drive.

When Johnson, in the weeks following his destruction of the presidential dreams of Senator Goldwater, fashioned his legislative plans for 1965, he had no intention of asking the new Congress for additional legislation to move black Americans further along the road to civil equality. According to his calculus, Congress the previous summer had enacted the most far-ranging civil rights measure in the history of the republic, and prudence required that the country be allowed some time to digest that measure before being presented with a new one. But then, in December 1964, the Reverend Martin Luther King, Jr., traveled to Oslo in Norway where he received a Nobel Peace Prize ("for the furtherance of brotherhood among men"), and after his return to America, in the first days of January 1965, announced that he would undertake a campaign to get black southerners on voting rolls.

There was ample reason for undertaking such a campaign. Despite the Civil Rights Acts of 1957 and 1960 (whose main provisions centered on voting), the Twenty-fourth Amendment to the Constitution (ratified in 1964, it stated that the right of citizens to vote in federal elections should not be denied or abridged because of failure to pay a poll tax or other tax), and Title I of the Civil Rights Act of 1964 (it prohibited discriminatory standards and procedures and restricted use of literacy tests in determining the voting qualifications of individuals), only 2 million of the South's 5 million black adults, by the beginning of 1965, were registered to exercise the most basic right of citizens in a democratic republic. Why did so many blacks remain unregistered? Reasons included widespread apathy on their part and ignorance of registration procedures, fear of economic reprisals and even physical harm if they tried to register, and assorted ruses, for example, tests requiring blacks seeking to register to enumerate the two rights available to a citizen after indictment by a grand jury, by which local election officials, behind a facade of legality, routinely rendered blacks ineligible to vote.

The extent to which some white southerners would go to discourage blacks from voting had received chilling manifestation in June of 1964 when two young white men, Andrew Goodman and Michael Schwerner, both of New York City, and a young black man, James Chaney of Meridian, Mississippi, disappeared while toiling in Mississippi in connection with the Freedom Summer project. Sponsored by four civil rights organizations and the National Council of Churches, the project aimed to encourage blacks of the deep South, few of whom had ever exercised the franchise, to do what was necessary to have their names affixed to voter registration rolls. The youths, all three of them college students, vanished after being arrested on a minor traffic charge in the town of Philadelphia, Mississippi. When their burned-out station wagon was found at the edge of Bogue Chitto Swamp, President Johnson dispatched several hundred sailors and FBI agents to search for the missing youths. While the sailors and FBI agents and assorted volunteers splashed about in snake-infested swamps in search of the bodies of the three young men—for it was generally assumed that Goodman, Schwerner, and Chaney had fallen victim of a lynch mob—they were jeered by local white youths, one of whom hooted, "We throw two or three niggers in [the swamp] every year, to feed the fish." After six weeks the bullet-riddled bodies of the missing Freedom Summer workers were found buried in a levee. Their killers were never brought to justice.

As for strategy in the voter-registration campaign, King determined to concentrate his efforts in a single city in the deep South—one in which the systematic disfranchisement of black citizens was transparent. If he could break white resistance in such a city, blacks across the entire South might be emboldened to challenge the barriers that kept them out of voting booths. Of equal import, his activity, certain as it was to attract legions of reporters, photographers, and television camera crews, would draw national attention to the fact that, despite the civil rights legislation of recent years, blacks still were being denied the right to vote. Given the commitment of a preponderance of Americans to the principle that the right to the ballot was among the most sacred right of citizens in a democratic republic, he felt confident that the outcome would be enormous pressure by enraged whites, particularly in the North and West, that barriers to black voting be eliminated forthwith.

For his target city, King selected Selma, Alabama, located on a bluff overlooking the Alabama River. As in uncounted other cities of comparable size across the region, Selma's 14,000 white citizens lived in middle-income comfort in neat frame houses along shaded streets or in graceful near-mansions, while its 15,000 blacks, surviving in the main on meager earnings from menial labor and domestic service, lived in all-black and generally run-down neighborhoods. Who ruled Selma? Obviously, the whites. Why were they in control? Because they comprised 97 percent of the registered voters.

King wasted no time in getting the Selma campaign in gear—and whites of the city wasted no time in giving the equal rights leader reams of national publicity by greeting him with jeers and catcalls and even bodily assault (two blows to the head and several kicks aimed at the groin) when he arrived at a local hotel. Next, he set up a command post in the Brown Chapel, and day after day dispatched battalions of local black citizens to the Dallas County Courthouse to seek admission to the voting rolls. At the courthouse, the marchers each day encountered Sheriff James G. "Jim" Clark, Jr., a husky, tough-talking lawman who, surrounded by deputies, would order them to disperse. Chanting, singing, and praying, the marchers would disobey Clark's order, whereupon the deputies would lead scores of them to jail—sometimes after assaulting them with billy clubs and bullwhips. Then, inevitably perhaps, a succession of incidents produced a greater outpouring of national indignation than King could have hoped for.

To further publicize the voter-registration campaign, King announced a march across fifty miles of hostile countryside from Selma to the state capitol in Montgomery, and on Sunday, March 7, 1965, some five hundred blacks moved out along U.S. route 80. After proceeding barely 300 yards, the marchers encountered a hundred of Sheriff Clark's deputies, 15 of them mounted on horseback, and 50 state troopers. When the marchers ignored an order to turn back, the helmeted deputies and troopers, swinging billy clubs and lobbing tear-gas cannisters, surged forward. Television cameras caught the action, of course, and within hours tens of millions of Americans were viewing pictures of Clark's mounted deputies charging Cossack-like through clouds of tear gas and trampling and beating defenseless marchers, gasping and groaning and screaming, to the ground. To express outrage, and also solidarity with the blacks of Selma, thousands of whites and blacks marched through the streets of Chicago, Detroit, Los Angeles, and Washington in the days that followed.

Some 1,000 blacks and about 450 whites made a second attempt to march to Montgomery on March 9, only to turn back on King's order when the civil rights leader was served with a restraining order signed by a federal district judge. Then, that same evening, yet another in a long list of tragedies that accompanied the quest of black Americans for civil equality came to pass. While walking along a street in Selma, three white clergymen who had traveled down from the North to support the voter-registration campaign came under attack by white hoodlums. Two days later, one of the clergymen, the Reverend James J. Reeb, a Unitarian minister of Boston, died of multiple skull fractures. Reeb's death heightened the national sense of indignation over what appeared to be the rampant racism of the whites of Selma, and inspired additional idealists and clergymen and nuns to make the pilgrimage to the embattled Alabama city.

At length, on March 17, Judge Frank M. Johnson, Jr., a white Alabamian, decreed that, in view of the enormous wrongs the marchers were protesting, a march from Selma to Montgomery should be permitted, and directed Gov. George Wallace not to interfere. Next, President Johnson, to guarantee the safety of the marchers, federalized the Alabama National Guard and ordered it deployed along the route of the march. So on Sunday, March 21, the marchers, bedrolls strapped to their backs, moved out of Selma. Three days later, weary but exuberant, they tramped into Montgomery where, that evening, they were entertained by more than two dozen entertainers and artists, including the singer Harry Belafonte, the comedian and dancer Sammy Davis, Jr., and the conductor Leonard Bernstein. The next day, a mass of humanity, in a holiday spirit, converged on the state capitol—the same building in which the Confederate States of America had been proclaimed in 1861 and on whose steps Jefferson Davis had taken the oath as president of the Confederacy. Finally, there came the grand climax, an oration by Dr. King. But darkness brought still another tragedy. That night, assassins drove their car alongside one in which Mrs. Viola Gregg Luizzo of Detroit, a white mother of five children, was transporting marchers back to Selma, aimed a gun at Mrs. Luizzo, and fired.

In the national capital of Washington, meanwhile, Lyndon Johnson had decided that the time was opportune to secure passage of a sweeping measure that once and for all would rid the American republic of the scandal of the calculated and cynical disfranchisement of several million of its citizens. And so, on the evening of March 15, 1965, the president went before a joint session of Congress (and a national television audience) to appeal for the enactment of legislation to protect all citizens in their right to vote. Given with great emotion and manifest conviction, the speech was the most eloquent of Johnson's long career. Declared the president, "Every American citizen must have an equal right to vote. There is no reason which can excuse the denial of that right. There is no duty which weighs more heavily on us than to ensure that right." Asserting that the effort by black Americans to secure for themselves the full blessings of American life must be the cause of all Americans, he went on: "It is not just Negroes, but all of us, who must overcome the crippling legacy of bigotry and injustice." Then, slowly, emphatically, dramatically, there rolled from his tongue the next words, borrowed from the anthem of the black revolution: "And we *shall* overcome."

The legislation proposed by Johnson set out a formula by which the federal government, on its own initiative, could move into an area and put the names of black citizens on voting rolls. In accord with the formula, the government could take such action in all counties of the republic where, on November 1, 1964, literacy tests or similar restrictions had been in effect and where fewer than half of the voting-age citizens had been registered and actually voted in the presidential election of 1964. All of which meant that the federal government would have the authority to register voters in all counties of Alabama, Georgia, Louisiana, Mississippi, South Carolina, and Virginia, and 34 counties of North Carolina.

In the Senate, the voting rights bill went to the Judiciary Committee, whose chairman, James O. Eastland of Mississippi, was a master practitioner of the tactics of delay. But Majority Leader Mike Mansfield of Montana and Minority Leader Everett Dirksen of Illinois engineered passage of a resolution instructing the Judiciary Committee to report the legislation after 15 days. The measure finally reached the floor on April 9, and after failing to weaken it with amendments, a bevy of southern senators deployed for yet another filibuster. At length, after 24 days, Johnson, Mansfield, and Dirksen decided that the southerners had talked long enough, whereupon a petition for cloture was introduced. (The grandiloquent Dirksen expressed regret that "I must cut off the voices of my distinguished colleagues, but with some measure of assurance that in the long veil of history, over the transient concerns of this fleeting day, they will find me not too far wrong.") On the afternoon of the vote on the cloture resolution, May 25, every one of the Senate's one hundred members was present in the Senate chamber, and by a vote of 70–30 terminated the filibuster. After the invocation of cloture, the vote to approve the voting rights legislation was anticlimactic.

Because of the stalling tactics of Rep. Howard W. Smith of Virginia, chairman of the Rules Committee, the voting rights measure moved even more slowly through the House. But at length, the lower chamber gave the legislation its overwhelming consent. Next, a select committee of representatives and senators turned to the task of reconciling differences between the House and Senate versions of the bill. When wrangling among the conferees threatened to get out of hand, President Johnson stepped up the tempo of his friendly persuasion tinctured with old-fashioned arm-twisting. His enterprise yielded the desired results, the House-Senate conference completed its work, and on August 6, 1965, in the ornate Presidential Room of the Capitol, Johnson affixed his signature to the historic Voting Rights Act.

## OTHER ACHIEVEMENTS

If manifestly the high points of the Great Drive, the measures establishing Medicare and Medicaid, providing federal aid to schools, and guaranteeing the right of black citizens to vote were by no means the only legislative achievements of President Johnson and the liberal-oriented Congress as they strove to build a Great Society. There was also legislation to continue and expand the war on poverty. One antipoverty measure authorized $1.1 billion, mostly for the construction of roads and highways and to stimulate industry, in the economically depressed Appalachia region. Another expanded the Economic Opportunity Act of the previous year, extended the legislation through 1968, and appropriated $1.8 billion, most of which was to be spent on job retraining and Youth Corps camps.

There was legislation to combat pollution of the natural environment, including an act authorizing the secretary of health, education, and welfare to establish standards of emission of air pollutants from new gasoline- and diesel-powered vehicles and prohibiting the sale of vehicles that did not meet those standards. The Water Quality Act established a Federal Water Pollution Control Administration, increased funds for sewage treatment grants to states, and gave states until mid-1967 to establish pollution standards for interstate waters. There was a law authorizing $350 million to support research and treatment of heart disease, cancer, stroke, and related diseases; requiring that cigarette package and cartons, after mid-1966, carry warnings that cigarette smoking might be hazardous to health; authorizing funds for mental health centers and for the care of retarded children; and providing stronger controls over the distribution of barbiturates and amphetamines.

The litany of legislative achievements in 1965 indeed seems almost endless: an omnibus bill providing $2.3 billion over a three-year period for federal guarantees of private loans to college students, federal scholarships of up to $1,000 a year for needy college students, and federal grants-in-aid for building and equipping college facilities; a new immigration statute abolishing the 41-year-old national origins quota system, setting new limits on immigration, and establishing priorities for immigrants who were close relatives of U.S. citizens or were artists, scientists, professional people, skilled or unskilled people who were needed to meet labor shortages in America, and refugees from communism or national disaster; legislation establishing an eleventh cabinet department, namely, the Department of Housing and Urban Development; a highway beautification act providing for restrictions on billboards and requiring the screening of junkyards along interstate and primary road systems; the High Speed Ground Transportation Act to investigate the possibility of a concerted national attack on mass transit problems; housing legislation that included a provision for rent supplements to low-income families; the Older Americans Act setting up the Administration on Aging; a measure reducing excise taxes by $4.7 billion; the Public Works and Economic Development Act consolidating and encouraging regional development programs; an act establishing a National Foundation on the Arts and Humanities.

Still, Lyndon Johnson was not a contented man. For notwithstanding his legislative achievements, few Americans appeared to feel genuine affection for the thirty-sixth president. On the contrary, tens of millions of citizens considered him a vain and overbearing politician of the wheeler-dealer genre. They continued to doubt the sincerity of his commitment to social and economic reform, suspected that he was an inveterate dissembler, ridiculed his Texas drawl and down-home manners. That he was failing to strike a chord with his compatriots was for the president a source of puzzlement as well as distress. Eric Goldman has quoted him as saying, "I'm giving them boom times and more good legislation than anybody else did, and what do they do—attack and sneer! Could FDR do better? Could anybody do better? What *do* they want?"

## DEFENSE, THE SOVIET UNION, AND NATO

While striving to build a Great Society, Lyndon Johnson, like his immediate predecessors in the White House, felt compelled to give careful and sustained attention to defense and foreign affairs. The reasons for his compulsion are manifest. Despite an apparent thawing of relations between the superpowers in the aftermath of the Cuban missile crisis of 1962, no serious observer of events had consigned the Cold War to the dustbin of history. Nor had any serious observer who had the best interests of the United States in mind intimated that the time had come for the North American colossus to dramatically reduce the commitments and responsibilities it had assumed across the face of the planet over the past two decades, dramatically downsize its military-naval establishment, and renounce the use of nuclear weapons except in retaliation to a nuclear attack by the Soviet Union.

When Johnson became president in 1963, the military policy of the Washington government continued to rest on the strategy of flexible response. It also continued to rest on the strategy of counterforce. Was the counterforce–city-withholding strategy apt to achieve its purpose of deterring the Soviets from undertaking an adventure that might result in a nuclear showdown with the United States? As the Cuban missile crisis of 1962 had indicated, it almost certainly would—so long as the United States retained such superiority in nuclear weapons that it could send part of its nuclear force against the Soviet Union's liquid-fueled missiles (which required lengthy preparation for launch) and keep in reserve an array of missiles and bombers with which it could rain death and destruction down on Soviet cities in a second strike in the event the first strike failed to persuade the Soviets to give up the said adventure.

But then, in the mid-1960s, the Soviets, bent on achieving parity or perhaps superiority vis-à-vis the Americans in nuclear striking power, undertook a rapid buildup of their strategic offensive forces. While the ICBM force of the United States remained constant—1,054 launchers—that of the Soviet Union enlarged from about 200 launchers in 1964 to 1,527 by 1972. The Soviets also deployed large numbers of new medium- and intermediate-range ballistic missiles, many of them targeted on Western Europe, which meant that in a nuclear showdown, a large number of Soviet missiles would doubtless survive a counterforce strike by the United States. After the counterforce strike, in a word, the Kremlin would retain the capacity to launch a nuclear strike of its own that would devastate American and European centers of population and industry.

Recognizing that the Soviet buildup of nuclear forces was undercutting the rationale on which the counterforce–city-withholding strategy of the United States rested, Secretary of Defense McNamara announced in early 1965 that the Washington government would henceforth rely on a strategy of "assured destruction" to deter a Soviet attack on the United States or its European allies; that is, in the event of a nuclear attack on the United States or the countries of NATO, or a conventional attack against the latter countries, the United States would make no attempt to control its response or limit damage to the Soviet Union. Rather, it would set about to destroy the Soviet Union as a viable twentieth-century nation. That the Soviets were likewise committed to a strategy of assured destruction in the event of a nuclear confrontation with the United States was transparent—which meant that the combined nuclear strategy of the superpowers was one of mutually assured destruction—or MAD.

The foregoing buildup of Soviet nuclear forces was set in motion by Nikita Khrushchev, the premier who had found it necessary to retreat in the face of American nuclear superiority at the time of the Cuban missile crisis. But Khrushchev lost favor among his colleagues in the hierarchy of the Soviet Communist party in the aftermath of the missile crisis, largely because they perceived him to be erratic and unmanageable, and in October 1964 the colleagues removed him from power. Leadership of the Soviet Union thereupon passed to 58-year-old Leonid I. Brezhnev, who became first secretary (later general secretary) of the Communist party, and 60-year-old Aleksei N. Kosygin, who became premier. More dynamic than Kosygin, Brezhnev within a few years emerged as the dominant figure in the Kremlin. As for relations between the Soviet Union and the United States, they remained unusually tranquil during the years of the Johnson presidency, notwithstanding Soviet support of the North Vietnamese and Vietcong in their quest to take control of South Vietnam. Beset by massive industrial and agricultural inefficiency at home and escalating tension in their government's relations with its erstwhile ally the

People's Republic of China, Soviet leaders sought to avoid friction with the United States. Indeed, some observers surmised during those years that the Cold War was at last receding into history.

In no small measure because the Cold War seemed to be giving way to what increasingly was referred to in the communications media as *détente*, the United States throughout the years of the Johnson presidency found itself at almost continual odds with its partners in NATO. Trying to cope with pressing economic problems, leaders in London hinted that they might order the withdrawal of segments of the British armed force that was deployed on the European Continent. Officials in Bonn announced that the Federal Republic of Germany would not reduce the European defense costs of the United States by purchasing additional military hardware in the United States. And leaders in various NATO capitals grumbled that in nearly all matters of consequence relating to NATO, their governments were subordinate to that in Washington. In particular did they resent the fact that the United States alone would decide whether nuclear weapons would be used in a crisis involving NATO. At the very least, the Europeans wanted the power to veto the use of such weapons in an essentially European crisis.

Easily the most nettlesome of the NATO powers from the perspective of the United States was France, led since the latter 1950s by President Charles de Gaulle. Obsessed, so Americans thought, with restoring the lost grandeur of France, de Gaulle determined to break clear of what he described as American hegemony in Europe and establish France as a "third force" between the United States and the Soviet Union. To those purposes, in 1966, he withdrew French forces from NATO's integrated military command (but did not take France out of NATO) and announced that he expected NATO's military headquarters and all foreign forces (most of them American) to be out of France by April of 1967. Accordingly, the NATO military headquarters were removed to Casteau in southern Belgium, the headquarters of the U.S. European Command, to Stuttgart in West Germany. Although de Gaulle had said nothing about NATO's political headquarters, housed in a multimillion-dollar building at the edge of Paris, the other members of the alliance decided to move it as well—to Brussels. Meanwhile, de Gaulle infuriated leaders in Washington by expressing doubt that the United States, to paraphrase the late President Kennedy, would risk its cities to save those of Europe, that is, would invite nuclear retaliation against its own territory by launching nuclear warheads on the Soviet Union in response to an invasion of Western Europe by the Soviets or their satellites.

## DOMINICAN REPUBLIC

While addressing problems relating to NATO and urging Congress to assist him in building a Great Society, in 1965, President Johnson responded to an outbreak of civil hostilities in the Dominican Republic. Occupying the eastern two-thirds of Christopher Columbus's favorite island of Hispaniola, the Dominican Republic had long attracted the interest of the United States, in large measure because of its strategic location in the Caribbean. Indeed, the administration of Pres. Ulysses S. Grant, in 1870, worked out a treaty providing for the annexation of the Dominican Republic by the United States. Fortunately, the treaty failed to win consent of the U.S. Senate. Then, in 1905, President Theodore Roosevelt, in an exercise of "big stick" diplomacy, took over the customs houses in the Dominican Republic, and 12 years later, in 1917, Pres. Woodrow Wilson dispatched U.S. Marines to bring order to the strife-torn country. The marines enforced a U.S. occupation of the Dominican Republic that did not end until 1922.

Departure of the marines scarcely signaled an era of peace and prosperity for Dominicans. On the contrary, strife and poverty remained the norm in their ill-starred republic. Then, in 1930, Rafael Leonidas Trujillo took control of the government in Santo Domingo, and over the next three decades established himself as one of the most corrupt and repressive dictators in the history of tyranny. But on the evening of May 20, 1961, a band of disgruntled army officers ambushed and gunned down Trujillo while he was riding through the countryside in an automobile. The following year, in the first democratic election in the Dominican Republic since 1924, voters elected Dr. Juan Bosch, a scholarly and charismatic idealist who had spent the previous 24 years in exile, to be president of the republic. Upon taking the presidential oath, Bosch inaugurated a bold program of social reform—one that infuriated well-to-do business people, planters, and military chieftains, who before long were charging that Bosch, if not a communist himself, was at least a dupe of communists. The outcome was predictable: In September 1963 a military junta removed Bosch and sent him packing once more into exile.

The response in Washington? Expressing outrage over the action by the junta, the Kennedy administration broke diplomatic relations with the Dominican Republic. Two months later, however, President Kennedy was in his grave, and in early 1964 President Johnson, explaining that it was necessary that the United States reinforce the junta in Santo Domingo to enable it to counter "Castro guerrillas" who allegedly were operating in the Dominican Republic, renewed diplomatic relations. But in April of 1965 a group of civilians and youthful army officers seized an army barracks and from a small radio station proclaimed what, in truth, had not taken place, to wit, that the military regime had been overthrown. The proclamation was a signal for tens of thousands of deliriously happy Dominicans to parade through the streets of the capital and for Bosch, in San Juan in Puerto Rico at the time, to pack his bags and prepare for a triumphal return to his homeland.

Officials in the U.S. embassy in Santo Domingo did not share the exuberance of ordinary Dominicans, the more so when the rhetoric beamed forth by rebel-controlled radio and television stations reminded them of that of the Castro rebels in Cuba in 1958–1959. Notwithstanding their pledges to bring liberty and democracy to Cuba, the Castro rebels had turned the Ever-Faithful Isle into a communist dictatorship and an outpost of Soviet power. Officials in the embassy wondered whether a new communist revolution, like that in

Cuba feeding on legitimate grievances, might not be in the making in the Dominican Republic.

Despite an absence of compelling evidence, embassy officials soon decided that the uprising was indeed communist-inspired and probably communist-led. In urgent messages to Washington, Ambassador W. Tapley Bennett, Jr., asserted that the rebellion in the Dominican Republic was of the Castro genre, and in one missive stated, "While leftist propaganda will fuzz this up as a fight between the military and the people, the issue is really between those who want a Castro-type solution and those who oppose it." As for President Johnson, he saw no reason to doubt the accuracy of reports emanating from the embassy in Santo Domingo, and was reported to have said privately, "We don't propose to sit here in our rocking chair with our hands folded and let the communists set up any government in the Western Hemisphere."

A short time later, Johnson received garbled and grossly exaggerated reports from Santo Domingo that the embassy itself was under rebel attack, and during a phone conversation with Bennett got the impression that the ambassador and his secretary were cowering under a desk while bullets whizzed about the room. Accordingly, on April 28, he ordered a contingent of six hundred marines from the helicopter carrier *Boxer*, already standing by a few miles offshore, to move into Santo Domingo and offer protection to several thousand North Americans and other foreigners. Although, as he explained in a TV address, he had informed the council of the Organization of American States, his action provoked grumbling throughout Latin America. In the view of many Latin Americans, Johnson had violated the cardinal principle on which the inter-American system and the OAS presumably rested, namely, that no American state had a right to intervene unilaterally in the affairs of another.

Had the marines confined their efforts to the rescue of foreign nationals, the criticism of Johnson's action would likely have abated immediately. But when Bennett reported that the tide in the civil conflict was running in favor of the rebels, Johnson issued orders that sent additional marines and also Army paratroops to the Dominican Republic. His object was not restoration of the authority of the junta, for Johnson, whatever his critics thought, felt no affinity for the military regime. Rather he hoped that the U.S. troops would terminate the rebellion, impose a cease-fire, and open the way for negotiations that would result in general elections and a return of the Dominican Republic to constitutional government.

And so it came to pass. Armed with automatic weapons as well as the usual small weapons, the marines and paratroops quickly occupied strategic points in Santo Domingo, subdued rebels who were bent on resisting, and persuaded the rebel leadership that the rebellion could achieve nothing futher. As a result, on May 1, one week after the outbreak of the civil conflict, the rebels and the junta agreed to a cease-fire. Several months later, the rebels and the junta agreed that Héctor García-Godoy, one of the most respected men in the Dominican Republic, would form a provisional government.

Surveying the outcome of the Dominican intervention, President Johnson seemed highly pleased, notwithstanding the fact that the intervention had claimed the lives of 28 U.S. fighting men. In his estimate, he had stopped a sanguinary civil war, prevented the appearance of a new Castrolike regime in the Caribbean, and made possible the return of democracy to the Dominican Republic. Believing the Dominican uprising had never been communist-inspired and if successful would not have opened the way for communist control of the country, most journalists, foreign diplomats, and other observers took a different view. In their judgment, the rebels themselves would have brought democratic government to the Dominican Republic without any help from the Colossus of the North. What Johnson had in fact done, they thought, was to offend Latin American sensibilities, revive memories of the Washington government's despised "big stick" policies of former times, and weaken North American prestige—to the advantage of communists—throughout Latin America.

## VIETNAM: ESCALATION

At the same time that he was presiding over the intervention in the Dominican Republic, in the spring of 1965, President Johnson was dramatically escalating the U.S. involvement in the conflict in Vietnam. Such had not been his expectation when he grappled with Barry Goldwater in the presidential contest a few months before, or so it seemed. During the electoral campaign of 1964, Johnson stated that "at the present time" he was "not about to send American boys nine or ten thousand miles away from home [to Vietnam] to do what Asian boys ought to be doing for themselves." But then, in the closing weeks of 1964, the situation in South Vietnam, from the perspective of leaders in Washington, slipped from bad to worse. Inflation was battering the South Vietnamese economy, Buddhist activists had again taken to the streets, Buddhist zealots were again torching themselves to death. Torn by intrigue and corruption, the Saigon government, administered by a flimsy coalition headed by General Khanh, was in disarray. And out in the countryside, the ARVN, demoralized by its own ineptitude, was again demonstrating that it was no match for the aggressive and elusive Vietcong. South Vietnam, indeed, appeared on the verge of falling to the communists.

What should the government in Washington do? Anxious to press ahead with his Great Society program, President Johnson felt no impulse to escalate America's involvement in the seemingly interminable conflict in Vietnam. Still, he shared the conviction of his predecessors Eisenhower and Kennedy that a communist conquest of South Vietnam would constitute a devastating defeat for "the free world." Like many of his compatriots, he also reckoned that the United States had a moral obligation to help the fledgling South Vietnamese republic, a virtual creation of the United States, to turn back the communist challenge and achieve the promise of a just and democratic society.

Then, on the evening of February 6, 1965, at Pleiku in South Vietnam's Central Highlands, Vietcong troops attacked a barracks in which American military advisers to the South Vietnamese were billeted, and also a nearby helicopter base. They killed 9 Americans and destroyed or damaged 20 aircraft. In retaliation, Johnson ordered implementation of Flaming Dart, a plan for air strikes against North Vietnam previously drafted by the Joint Chiefs of Staff. Although the North Vietnamese denied (and would continue to deny through the end of the war) any direct involvement in the conflict in South Vietnam—and although their sympathizers across the world were pressing (and would continue to press) the fiction that the insurgency in South Vietnam was nothing more than a determined uprising by disgruntled South Vietnamese—Johnson knew full well that the Vietcong were in fact the agents of Ho Chi Minh's communist regime in Hanoi. The result was raids by American aircraft on barracks and staging areas in the south of North Vietnam. When the VC, on February 10, attacked the quarters of U.S. advisers at the coastal town of Qui Nhon, the president again dispatched American bombers against North Vietnamese targets.

During the execution of Flaming Dart, National Security Adviser McGeorge Bundy, just returned from Vietnam, warned that in the absence of increased military action by the United States, a communist victory in South Vietnam was inevitable. Whereupon Johnson initiated Rolling Thunder, an aerial campaign by which the United States would gradually intensify the pressure on the Hanoi government to terminate the communist quest to take control of South Vietnam. The gradual intensification of pressure, leaders in Washington surmised, would demonstrate that the United States was behaving responsibly and with moderation—that, however determined to save South Vietnam from the clutches of communism, it was not intent on devastating North Vietnam or destroying the Hanoi regime.

On initiating the aerial campaign, Johnson also ordered the first American combat troops to Vietnam. To protect the air base near the coastal city of Da Nang, two battalions of American marines splashed ashore in early March of 1965. Two months later, an Army airborne brigade arrived to provide security for the air base at Bien Hoa, to the north of Saigon. The following month, June 1965, airborne troops conducted the first American ground offensive of the war, a brief action against an enemy sanctuary near Bien Hoa.

Accepting the argument that the interests and security of "the free world," not to mention America's responsibility to guarantee South Vietnam an opportunity to become a viable and democratic nation-state, required the containment of communist influence and power in Vietnam, a preponderance of the people of the United States appeared to acquiesce in this latest escalation of American involvement in the Vietnamese conflict. But Senators Frank Church of Idaho, Mike Mansfield of Montana, and George McGovern of South Dakota, and also the editors of the *New York Times* and other newspapers, expressed reservations about the wisdom of what the Johnson administration was doing in Southeast Asia. And a few Americans were openly hostile. Accordingly, what were described as teach-ins to protest the country's military involvement in Vietnam were conducted on several college and university campuses, and on a weekend in April more than ten thousand students assembled in Washington to demonstrate against that involvement.

In part in response to the critics and protesters, President Johnson on April 7, 1965, delivered a speech at Johns Hopkins University in Baltimore in which he announced that the United States was prepared to enter "unconditional discussions" aimed at resolving the conflict in Vietnam, and was prepared to expend a billion dollars to assist in the economic development of the Mekong River Valley. A few weeks later, in May 1965, he ordered a five-day pause in Rolling Thunder attacks while letting it be known that a reduction in military activity in South Vietnam by the North Vietnamese and Vietcong would be matched by a reduction in American aerial attacks. The Hanoi government was not impressed. It assailed the bombing pause as a "worn-out trick of deceit and threat," and asserted that a settlement of the conflict must be in accord with "the program of the National Liberation Front," that is, must clear the way for communist control of South Vietnam. Still, the president's peace initiatives of April and May of 1965 succeeded in quieting the critics and protesters in the United States—for the time being. Equally important, or so it seemed, Congress in May of 1965 responded to a presidential appeal by voting $400 million to support military operations in Vietnam, in Johnson's view a clear endorsement of what he was trying to do to save South Vietnam from the communists.

Confusion and intrigue, meanwhile, wracked the government in Saigon. A succession of coups and countercoups that climaxed in February 1965 brought the demise of General Khanh's regime and installation of a civilian administration headed by Phan Huy Quat. But then, in May 1965, a group led by Air Vice-Marshal Nguyen Cao Ky dissolved the Quat regime. A swashbuckling flier whose trademarks were a purple scarf and an ivory-handled pistol dangling from his belt, Ky became the prime minister. Gen. Nguyen Van Thieu assumed responsibility for commanding the armed forces of South Vietnam.

From the American perspective, alas, the military situation in Vietnam continued to deteriorate. Moving troops, including North Vietnamese regulars, and the paraphernalia of war from North Vietnam to South Vietnam across the demilitarized zone (DMZ) separating North and South Vietnam, and more importantly along the Ho Chi Minh Trail through southeastern Laos, the communists retained the initiative in the struggle in the South Vietnamese countryside.

What, if anything, ought the United States do to turn the tide of the war? Some of Johnson's advisers recommended that the United States intensify the pressure on North Vietnam to give up its adventure in South Vietnam by expanding the Rolling Thunder campaign. Viewing a mere intensification of pressure as inadequate, the commander of U.S. forces in Vietnam, Gen. William C. Westmoreland, and the Joint Chiefs of Staff urged the president to sanction an all-out-few-targets-barred aerial offensive against North Vietnam. To borrow the oft-quoted language of Gen. Curtis E. LeMay of the Air Force, they wanted permission, if it came to that, to bomb North Vietnam back to the Stone Age. Or so it seemed. Westmoreland and the Joint Chiefs also urged the president to dispatch an additional 179,000 U.S. combat troops to Vietnam—troops who would move aggressively out into the countryside and conduct offensive operations.

At that point, in July 1965, President Johnson made perhaps the most fateful decision of any American chief executive in the matter of the Vietnamese conflict. Rejecting the appeal by Westmoreland and the Joint Chiefs for an all-out bombing offensive, he sanctioned an expansion of Rolling Thunder, approved the immediate deployment of an additional 50,000 troops in Vietnam, and promised that he would sanction the deployment of another 50,000 before the end of the year. He also authorized Westmoreland to use U.S. troops in South Vietnam however he saw fit—that is, authorized their use in large-scale offensive operations.

In the months that followed, American troops cascaded into Vietnam. Likewise arriving in the beleaguered country were contingents from Australia, New Zealand, and the Republic of Korea (later to be joined by units from the Philippines and Thailand). On January 1, 1966, more than 184,000 American military and naval personnel were deployed in the Southeast Asian war theater. To support the escalating military effort of the United States and its handful of allies—an effort that in 1965 claimed 1,365 American lives—engineers built new ports or expanded existing port facilities at Cam Ranh Bay, Qui Nhon, Nha Trang, Vung Tau, Da Nang, and Saigon. They built warehouses and cantonments, airfields and maintenance facilities, roads and bridges.

Meanwhile, in September 1965, intelligence reports disclosed that three North Vietnamese regiments were deploying for an offensive in the Ia Drang Valley in the Central Highlands. Whereupon Westmoreland ordered the recently arrived First Cavalry Division (Airmobile) to move out against the enemy regiments. During the month-long action, the North Vietnamese used every tactic at their disposal: ambushes, night infiltrations, "hugging" (that is, staying close to American troops to forestall air and artillery strikes), human-wave assaults. To no avail. American troops killed more than 1,300 of the North Vietnamese regulars and sent the remainder scurrying to havens across the border in neutral Cambodia—whose neutrality, more or less respected by the Americans, was ignored outright by the communists. The action claimed the lives of some 300 American cavalrymen.

If the cavalrymen had met frustration in their attempt to encircle and destroy enemy regiments, the battle in the Ia Drang Valley demonstrated that American troops could perform effectively in the inhospitable environment of Vietnam. It also proved the validity of the Army's new airmobile tactics. Indeed, the Army thereupon set about to assure that helicopter companies were available in sufficient numbers to provide all infantry units with airmobile support. The helicopters ferried troops to and from battle areas, transported supplies and even artillery pieces, evacuated the wounded and dead, provided aerial command posts. They facilitated the gathering of intelligence and the guidance of artillery fire. And helicopter gunships, some of them endowed with incredible firepower, provided close air support for ground operations.

Still, it was the Rolling Thunder campaign on which leaders in Washington were pinning most of their hopes for success in Vietnam. Like air enthusiasts of the era of World War II, they dreamed of achieving "victory through air power."

Then, on January 2, 1966, the White House disclosed that no American bombing planes had operated over North Vietnam during the previous eight days. The bombing pause could become permanent, the Johnson administration announced, if the North Vietnamese would enter negotiations aimed at ending the war. Even as it announced the bombing pause, the administration was yanking at the cords of diplomacy in an effort to persuade the North Vietnamese to negotiate. But the yanking came to nothing. Denouncing the American peace overture as a trick , Ho Chi Minh's government proclaimed that there could be no settlement in Vietnam until the United States withdrew its forces from the country. Withdrawal of its forces, which would be tantamount to handing over South Vietnam to the communists, was unacceptable to the Washington government.

Thus, on January 31, 1966, after a pause of 37 days, U.S. bombing planes, operating from carriers in the South China Sea as well as from bases in South Vietnam and Thailand and on Guam, resumed the aerial campaign against North Vietnam. And whereas the Rolling Thunder strikes of 1965 (some 25,000 sorties) had concentrated on military bases, supply depots, and infiltration routes in the south of North Vietnam, those of 1966 (79,000 sorties) were increasingly aimed against the country's industrial and transportation apparatus far to the north. Although crewmen were under orders to avoid centers of population, the Defense Department estimated that during periods of intensive bombing the raids claimed the lives of as many as a thousand North Vietnamese civilians each week. Expansion of the bombing campaign, of course, resulted in increased losses of planes and airmen. During 1966, indeed, some 400 multimillion-dollar aircraft went down over North Vietnam, most of them victims of intensive ground fire. Death or imprisonment was the fate of most of their crewmen.

However expanded, Rolling Thunder failed to persuade the North Vietnamese to give up their vision of conquest in South Vietnam. Nor did it seriously impair their military effort. By deploying battalions of workers, most of them equipped with primitive tools or no tools at all, they usually were able to repair damaged facilities in a short time, while their Soviet and Chinese patrons compensated them for the reduced output of damaged or destroyed factories. The North Vietnamese, in truth, were able to turn the aerial campaign to their own advantage—by portraying Rolling Thunder as an inhuman enterprise by the American superpower to terrorize a small and defenseless and even benign country. Their consciences apparently undisturbed by the tactics of murder and terror methodically employed in South Vietnam by the North Vietnamese and Vietcong that likewise resulted in the deaths of uncounted noncombatants, legions of people in Europe, America, and elsewhere expressed shock and outrage when confronted with the foregoing portrayal. The result was unrelenting pressure on the Washington government to abandon its aerial campaign.

American soldiers and marines, meanwhile, continued to cascade into

Vietnam. U.S. military and naval personnel in South Vietnam and its environs would total 385,000 by the end of 1966, 486,000 by the end of 1967. Many of the marines dug in along the DMZ, where they waged mortar and artillery duels with equally entrenched North Vietnamese regulars. But President Johnson declined to approve a plan proposed by the Joint Chiefs of Staff to deny North Vietnam "the physical capacity to move men and supplies through the Lao corridor," that is, along the Ho Chi Minh Trail, by establishing a fortified line from the western terminus of the DMZ across southeastern Laos to the border of Thailand. What the Joint Chiefs were obviously proposing was transformation of the war in Vietnam into a conventional land war by establishing a conventional front line—or MLR (main line of resistance).

Various postwar critics of American military strategy in the war have surmised that the United States could have achieved its purpose in Vietnam— won the war—had Johnson consented to the foregoing plan. So the scenario has gone, American and possibly South Korean troops could have manned the MLR, one that, as indicated, would have reached from the South China Sea along the DMZ and across southeastern Laos to the Thai border, and left it to the ARVN to move through the South Vietnamese countryside and take the measure of North Vietnamese and VC units that had been cut off from their lifeline to North Vietnam.

Why did Johnson turn aside the JCS strategy? For a variety of reasons. He suspected that execution of the strategy would require that he summon Army and Marine Corps reserve personnel to active duty to provide the requisite manpower, and lest he set off a political firestorm at home, he adamantly refused to consider a call-up of reserves. Then Johnson apparently feared the political fallout, both domestically and internationally, of what great numbers of people across the world would view as a transparent violation of the neutrality of Laos if U.S. forces established an MLR across Laotian territory, although the Hague Convention of 1907 states, "A neutral country has the obligation not to allow its territory to be used by a belligerent. If the neutral country is unwilling or unable to prevent this, the other belligerent has the right to take appropriate counteractions." Finally, Johnson had no doubt that the North Vietnamese would respond to execution of the JCS strategy by taking control of all of Laos above the MLR, that is, most of Laos, and the president was no less committed to the containment of communism in Laos than in Vietnam.

## VIETNAM: FRUSTRATION

And so the communists, their enterprise only slightly impeded by almost continuous and sometimes massive interdictory attacks by U.S. bombing planes (including giant B-52s based on Guam), continued to funnel troops, equipment, and supplies from North Vietnam down the Ho Chi Minh Trail into South Vietnam or to base camps in eastern Cambodia. Denied the authority to close the trail by establishing an MLR across Laos or to move against the base camps in Cambodia, General Westmoreland and the Joint Chiefs decided that the best strategy available to them was to dispatch American troops on "search and destroy" operations against North Vietnamese and Vietcong units that were deployed hither and yon across South Vietnam, often in areas in which they had secured support of local populations and constructed many miles of intricate tunnels to facilitate military operations.

Through 1966 and 1967, therefore, American units, sometimes mere battalions, sometimes entire divisions, moved out into the countryside to locate and devastate the enemy. To locate the elusive communists, they sometimes relied on a variety of sophisticated electronic devices. To deny the communists the natural cover provided by Vietnam's tropical foliage, American aircraft sprayed millions of tons of chemical herbicides, one of them known as Agent Orange, over millions of acres of jungle. To keep their own casualties to a minimum, America ground forces sought to encircle enemy units, batter them with artillery and mortar fire, and call in aircraft to shower them with bombs, rockets, and napalm. The measure of success of a search and destroy operation was the number of enemy corpses that could be counted at the end of an operation, the much-discussed "body count."

When a search and destroy operation ended, the troops often returned to comfortable barracks where they enjoyed cold beverages and pizza or perhaps went off to Saigon or another nearby city to partake of more exotic diversions in the sleazy bars and brothels that had sprung up in South Vietnam's cities and towns since the arrival of the Americans. Still, the war was a grisly business for the American infantrymen or "grunts" (who, in truth, comprised only a fraction of the American personnel in Vietnam, for a preponderance of the troops functioned in supporting capacities and were in minimal danger). While in the field, the infantrymen had to contend with steaming heat, swamps, dense jungles, leeches, fire ants, booby traps, ambushes, and civilians who betrayed their movements to the North Vietnamese and VC. And despite the heavy reliance on sheer firepower to decimate the enemy, increasing numbers of soldiers and marines lost their lives in the operations: nearly 5,000 in 1966, some 9,000 in 1967.

Search and destroy operations had other dimensions. Shells and bombs inevitably fell on Vietnamese civilians, sometimes intentionally when American troops and airmen suspected that civilians were allowing their villages to serve as sanctuaries for the North Vietnamese and VC. In addition to scarring the landscape and disrupting agricultural activities over wide areas, the operations forced other civilians to flee to hastily constructed refugee camps or to the already overcrowded cities of South Vietnam. In the words of the historian George C. Herring, they "further undermined the social fabric of an already fragile nation and alienated the people from a government which had never had a firm base of popular support."

Transforming South Vietnam into a sturdy nation and rallying popular support for its anticommunist government was, of course, a cardinal object of the United States. Achievement of that object appeared formidable if not next to impossible from the onset of the American involvement in the country. In no small measure because of uncontrolled spending by U.S. personnel and the influx of American goods, the economy of South Vietnam remained in disarray. Both official and private corruption were rampant, a black market in stolen American commodities thrived, prostitution flourished. In the main because the VC murdered or kidnapped several thousand of its personnel, a Rural Development Program inaugurated in 1966 quickly faltered. The purpose of the program was to win the hearts and minds of peasants for the Saigon government by providing an array of social services. Further complicating matters during 1966 was a new outbreak of antigovernment demonstrations, accompanied as in the past by self-immolations by Buddhists, particularly in Da Nang and Hué. Troops dispatched by Premier Ky at length crushed the demonstrations.

Still, there was one promising development: Pressed by the United States, the Ky government arranged an election in which South Vietnamese voters, notwithstanding communist attempts to disrupt proceedings, elected a 117-member assembly to draft a new constitution for South Vietnam. Modeled after the constitutions of France and the United States, the resultant constitution included a Bill of Rights, prohibited communists and "neutralist sympathizers" from holding office, and permitted the president to assume what amounted to dictatorial powers in time of national emergency. Pressed by the United States, Ky reluctantly agreed that he would not seek the South Vietnamese presidency in the first election held in accord with the new constitution. Rather, he would run for vice president on a ticket headed by General Thieu. Again ignoring communist threats and bluster, a preponderance of the electorate made its way to polling places in September 1967 to choose leaders of the new government. Securing a modest 35 percent of the vote, the Thieu-Ky ticket won the presidential contest, and on October 31, 1966, Thieu and Ky repeated the presidential and vice presidential oaths, respectively.

Leaders in Hanoi, meanwhile, remained optimistic, indeed confident. They were under no illusion that North Vietnamese and VC formations might overwhelm and defeat the incredibly powerful, mobile, and sophisticated forces that the United States had deployed in Vietnam. But if those formations could simply keep up the fight—avoid being overwhelmed by U.S. forces and continue to kill Americans in considerable numbers, while the communist propaganda apparatus and the international communications media drew attention to the devastation and death that the United States was visiting upon the primitive Vietnamese nation—the communists stood an excellent chance of turning the American citizenry against U.S. involvement in the war, just as they had turned the citizenry of France against the French military effort from 1946 to 1954. At length, leaders in Hanoi calculated, the Americans would likely decide that their objectives in the war were not commensurate with the devastation and bloodshed, the expense and trauma that their achievement required, and at that point would evacuate their forces from South Vietnam and, in effect, concede the victory to the communists.

As for leaders in Washington, they, too, appeared optimistic. Perhaps the proposition that a global superpower might prove unequal to the task of asserting its will over a backward state such as North Vietnam was simply incomprehensible. Still, as 1966 unfolded, those leaders could exhibit scant evidence that U.S. air and ground operations were making meaningful headway toward an early achievement of America's goal in Vietnam, to wit, compelling the communists to give up their vision of conquering South Vietnam and bringing the war to an end. Of larger moment was evidence that increasing numbers of Americans, in accord with the calculations of the communists, were indeed becoming hostile toward the national adventure in Vietnam. Fueling that hostility were lengthening American casualty figures, graphic pictures of the agony of the Vietnamese people that appeared with painful regularity on evening television and in weekly newsmagazines, and reports by journalists of the ineptitude, corruption, and impulse to repression of South Vietnam's leaders.

The evidence of increasing hostility toward the war inside the United States was unmistakable. In early 1966, Chairman Fulbright of the Senate Foreign Relations Committee arranged for his committee to examine all aspects of America's involvement in Vietnam in televised hearings. His purpose clearly was to press the Johnson administration to deescalate that involvement and prepare the way for an early withdrawal of U.S. forces from Vietnam. A short time later, in an address at Johns Hopkins University, Fulbright asserted that the United States was "succumbing to the arrogance of power" in Vietnam and elsewhere. To Fulbright's charges, President Johnson responded that the United States was using its power in Vietnam reluctantly and with restraint, and spoke of "nervous Nellies" who "will break ranks under the strain." His comments failed to stay the rising tide of antiwar activism. Downtown thoroughfares of such cities as Chicago, New York, and San Francisco—also uncounted college and university campuses in every part of the country—provided backdrops for antiwar demonstrations. Young men at assorted rallies protested the American military involvement in Vietnam by burning draft cards, about a hundred veterans of World War II made their way to the gates of the White House in Washington to return medals. Also in Washington, in May 1966, ten thousand antiwar protesters, some of them flaunting Vietcong flags, paraded in front of the White House, shouted that Johnson, the official who was ultimately responsible for issuing the orders to bomb North Vietnam, was a murderer, then rallied around the Washington Monument.

Meanwhile, in early 1966, the United States placed the war in Vietnam on the agenda of the UN, but no member of the international organization betrayed any interest whatever in discussing it. Responding to a peace proposal by Secretary-General U Thant of the UN, in September 1966, the American ambassador Arthur J. Goldberg explained that the United States was prepared to remove its forces from South Vietnam if the North Vietnamese would do likewise. No reply was forthcoming from Hanoi.

Then, in mid-October 1966, President Johnson suspended plans to campaign for Democratic members of Congress in the impending election and flew off to the Pacific. After visiting Hawaii, American Samoa, New Zealand, and Australia (where antiwar demonstrators splattered his limousine with paint), he repaired to Manila where he conferred with representatives of America's allies in the war in Vietnam: Australia, New Zealand, the Philippines, South

Korea, South Vietnam, and Thailand. The conferees agreed that their governments (save, of course, that of South Vietnam) would remove their forces from Vietnam within six months of an agreement by North Vietnam to withdraw its forces and suspend terrorist activities in South Vietnam. From Manila, Johnson flew to Thailand, Malaysia, South Korea—and on October 26, 1966, to Cam Ranh Bay in South Vietnam. During his two-and-one-half-hour stopover at Cam Ranh Bay, the president told an assemblage of American troops that they were fighting against "a vicious and illegal aggression across this little nation's frontier." Outside an officer's club, he said to a group of U.S. servicemen, "I pray the good Lord will look over you and keep you until you can come home with that coonskin on the wall."

To nobody's surprise, leaders in Hanoi made no response to the declaration by the conferees at Manila in October 1966. But Johnson did not abandon the search for a peaceful settlement of the war. In June of 1967, he sought to enlist the support of Premier Kosygin of the Soviet Union in his campaign to bring the North Vietnamese to the conference table. Kosygin was in the United States to participate in debate at the UN over the recent Arab-Israeli war. Slip-

November 1967: Antiwar students protesting job interviews by Dow Chemical Company, a maker of napalm used in Vietnam, at the University of Wisconsin-Milwaukee.

ping off to Glassboro, New Jersey, Kosygin met privately with Johnson for two days—and the two men appeared to get along famously. Unfortunately, no formula for negotiating an end to the war in Vietnam emerged.

As the war dragged on, antiwar activists inevitably escalated their endeavors. Students on many campuses sought to disrupt the activities of recruiters for the armed forces—also the recruiting by such companies as Dow Chemical, a manufacturer of napalm used in Vietnam. They shouted and booed and stamped their feet when such emissaries as Secretary of State Dean Rusk appeared on campuses to defend the Washington government's Vietnam policy. Antiwar critics became particularly incensed when Rusk explained that a purpose of the United States in Vietnam was to protect Asia and the rest of the world from the expansion of a billion Chinese who, he observed, now had nuclear weapons. They expressed delight when the heavyweight boxing champion Muhammad Ali, claiming that he was a Muslim minister and hence a conscientious objector, refused induction into the Army, for which refusal he was convicted of draft evasion and also stripped of his heavyweight title. Some fifty thousand antiwar activists demonstrated in the vicinity of the Lincoln Memorial in Washington in October of 1967, and several thousand of them, shouting and screaming, tried to crash through lines of police and paratroops to force their way into the Pentagon.

For President Johnson, trying to cope with eruptions in urban ghettos as well as a frustrating war and seemingly incessant demonstrations against his Vietnam policy, those were trying times. The war by 1967 had nearly dissipated the impulse to reform that had produced the Great Drive of 1965. To meet the expense of escalating the war without cutting back on an array of social services provided by the federal government, many of them the fruits of his treasured Great Society program, he felt compelled to ask Congress to raise taxes. His popular approval rating in opinion polls plummeted. His secretary of defense, Robert McNamara, an architect of the escalation of the American involvement in Vietnam, became disillusioned with that involvement, and in late 1967 left the cabinet to accept appointment as president of the World Bank. Likewise disillusioned, Bill D. Moyers quit the White House staff and Ambassador Goldberg informed Johnson that he, too, wanted to leave the government. George Ball resigned as Undersecretary of State.

Still, the president determined to stay the course in Vietnam, declaring at one point, "We are not going to yield. We are not going to shimmy. We are going to wind up with a peace with honor which all Americans seek." He extracted expressions of support for his Vietnam policy from former-Presidents Truman and Eisenhower, former-Secretary of State Acheson, and retired-Ambassador Robert Murphy. He summoned General Westmoreland home from Vietnam in mid-November to report to Americans on the situation in Vietnam—in truth, to lend support to the administration's dubious contention that the United States and its allies were gaining the upper hand in the war. Loyal soldier that he was, the handsome and firm-jawed "Westy" never made a gloomy utterance, in public at any rate. He told an audience at the Pentagon, "The ranks of the Vietcong are thinning steadily" and one at the National

November 1967: U.S. airborne troops in Vietnam under rocket and automatic weapons fire by regular forces of the North Vietnamese army.

Press Club, "We have reached an important point when the end begins to come into view." And while discussing the possibility of a massive attack by the communists in Vietnam with a reporter of *Time*, he said, "I hope they try something, because we are looking for a fight." Such a fight was in the offing.

## RETROSPECT

Lyndon Johnson indeed stands as one of several tragic figures in the annals of the American presidency. The tall Texan was manifestly a man of high intelligence and unparalleled understanding of the political process. He was a man of energy and resolution and decent impulse. If capable of commanding the affection of only a few of his compatriots, he commanded the respect of great numbers of them. And during his tenure in the White House, he accomplished more than have most of the 39 other men who have presided over the executive branch of the national government. He was arguably the premier home affairs president of the twentieth century, Franklin Roosevelt excepted. In subsequent decades, to be sure, it became fashionable to dismiss Johnson's Great Society program as a well-intended debacle, largely because his heralded and costly war on poverty failed to slay the demon of poverty in the United States. But the initiatives of the Great Society administration, for example, those that produced Medicare and federal assistance to the schools and sought to protect the natural environment, transcended the war on poverty. And two pieces of legislation that Johnson prevailed on Congress to enact were of genuinely historic dimension: the Civil Rights Act of 1964 and the Voting Rights Act of 1965.

Alas, Lyndon Johnson, confident that he was acting in accord with a national policy that most Americans believed had saved much of the world from the scourge of Marxism-Leninism-Stalinism over the previous two decades, ordered the fateful escalation of U.S. involvement in the war in Southeast Asia, and took the country into the morass of Vietnam. And therein lay his tragedy. It was the tragedy of a president whose accomplishments in the realm of home affairs were such that, if unsullied by the misadventure in Vietnam, would have guaranteed his ranking as one of the premier presidents in the history of the republic, just behind Lincoln, Washington, and the second Roosevelt. Of course, if Johnson, to paraphrase his own words, had brought home the coonskin from South Vietnam, that is, presided over the defeat of the communists, say, by the end of 1967, historians might very well have placed him in the same exalted category as Lincoln, Washington, and FDR. But he did not bring home the coonskin—in the view of various of his critics, because his strategy for conducting the war was hopelessly flawed—and the adventure in Vietnam became one of the great disasters in the history of the republic, one that divided the people of the United States as has no other save the Civil War, tarnished the international reputation of the North American superpower, and dealt a heavy blow to its confidence and sense of purpose.

Still, time tends to be a healer of presidential reputations. Witness the esteem in which scholars in recent years have begun to hold Herbert Hoover, long perceived in scholarly circles as at best a mediocrity during his four troubled years in the White House. So it may be with Lyndon Johnson, who in the aforementioned Murray-Blessing poll of professors of American history in 1982 ranked a surprising tenth on the list of presidents—one place above Eisenhower, two places below Truman.

# Chapter
# 7

---

# Ferment and Achievement— and Normalcy

$C$asual students of history, and some scholars as well, have tended to view the 1950s as a placid and rather unexciting time in the history of the United States. The 1950s, in the popular view, were a time when the grandfatherly Eisenhower presided over the national destiny, the most daring happenings on college campuses were "panty raids" (in which male students, often encouraged by shrieking coeds, raided women's residence halls and sororities in quest of feminine undergarments), and the body politic was generally agreed on the inherent worth of traditional values and institutions, not to mention the national purpose—a time when nearly all Americans, oblivious to assorted problems that were pressing down about the republic and generally lacking in crusading zeal, were preoccupied by the search for abundance and comfort and pleasure.

Whether the 1950s were quite so placid and unexciting from the perspective of Americans as subsequent generations of students and scholars have tended to think is arguable. After all, the sixth decade of the twentieth century witnessed the Korean War, the carryings-on of Joe McCarthy, perfection of the Salk vaccine, the Montgomery bus boycott, the Suez crisis, the racial confrontation at Little Rock, development of the thermonuclear bomb and ICBM and nuclear submarine, launching of the first artificial satellites in outer space, further development of the digital computer, appearance of the jet airliner, and the advent of rock 'n' roll and Elvis.

Still, when compared with the tumultuous 1960s—the years of Kennedy and Johnson—the 1950s do appear rather placid and unexciting. For during the 1960s, traditional values and institutions came under unrelenting attack; millions of Americans experimented with new lifestyles. The people of the United States disagreed—often disagreeably—over the national purpose, and began to grapple as never before with a variety of national problems. The country endured domestic violence on a scale that was unprecedented in the national experience. Not since the Civil War of 1861–65, indeed, had Americans been so divided and angry with one another. It was a time that stirs the interest of present-day students no less than the "roaring" 1920s stirred history students of former years. That it will continue to stir the interest of students of history for many years to come appears beyond dispute.

## ENVIRONMENTALISM AND CONSUMERISM

As mentioned, the 1960s were a time when Americans became increasingly conscious of assorted problems that afflicted the national society. Such a problem was pollution of the natural environment, and it was during the 1960s that Americans for the first time confronted the term *ecology*, defined in *Webster's New World Dictionary* as "the complex of relations between a specific organism and its environment."

Raising the level of popular consciousness in the matter of the natural environment was the biologist Rachel Carson, whose book *Silent Spring* (1962) described an imaginary town in the heart of America whose people poisoned their environment by using the pesticide DDT. Other writers informed Americans that exhaust from motor vehicles and smoke from factories and power plants were poisoning the air that people breathed and polluting their streams, rivers, and lakes by dumping raw sewage and industrial wastes—and that one of the Great Lakes, Lake Erie, was already "dead," that is, could no longer sustain marine life. Americans learned that they were polluting their landscape with garbage and beer cans, billboards, and junked automobiles, and were preparing the way for the extinction of various species of wildlife, including the very symbol of the American republic, the majestic bald eagle, by promoting what they generally perceived to be progress without taking into account its effects on the balance of nature.

Nearly every American took a critical view of pollution of the natural environment. Never in the history of the republic, in truth, had a social cause so manifestly reached across the barriers of ideological and cultural distinction. Unfortunately, the movement to curb pollution collided head-on with the national lifestyle, not to mention the national standard of living. Automobile exhaust polluted the air, but in the interest of cleaner air few Americans were willing to drive less. If they were decimating the populations of assorted species of birds and animals, and threatening human life as well, pesticides make it possible for American farmers to produce food in such abundance that their compatriots could buy it at supermarkets at bargain prices. Offshore drilling rigs periodically spilled oil that devastated beaches; tankers delivering petroleum from the Middle East, Africa, and elsewhere (as a result of accidents and bilge pumpings) were covering the oceans with a thin film. But the United States could not function—at least could not maintain its current lifestyle and standard of living—without oil shipped in from overseas. However in conflict with the national lifestyle, the environmental protection movement realized modest success during the 1960s. Among its fruits were the passage through Congress of the Clean Air Act (1963) and Water Quality Act (1965) and establishment of the Environmental Protection Agency (1969).

While many Americans during the 1960s were crusading on behalf of protection of the environment, others were crusading on behalf of protection of consumers from products that were unsafe, too expensive, or not what advertisers claimed them to be. Such people had taken encouragement in a pronouncement by John F. Kennedy during his campaign for the presidency in 1960: "The consumer is the only man in our economy without a high-powered lobbyist. I intend to be that lobbyist." And in accord with the foregoing assertion, Kennedy in 1962 proposed a consumer program that was widely referred to as a Consumer Bill of Rights. To nobody's surprise, his efforts on behalf of consumers met stiff opposition by spokespeople of business who contended that consumer advocates were striving to undermine the system of free enterprise.

But then, in 1965, a book by an intense young man named Ralph Nader appeared. Entitled *Unsafe at Any Speed*, the book charged that executives of the General Motors Corporation had knowingly sacrificed safety in the interest of profit in producing the rear-engine Chevrolet Corvair automobile. As a consequence of Nader's charges, sales of the Corvair slumped so sharply that GM felt compelled to discontinue production of the car. Consumer protection, meanwhile, won the support of increasing numbers of Americans—and also their representatives in Congress. Most states and many cities set up consumer protection agencies, while Better Business Bureaus in all parts of the country enlarged their activities and improved procedures for handling consumer complaints and issuing warnings regarding frauds, known or suspected.

## FEMINISM

At the same time that Ralph Nader and others were advocating consumer protection, a new generation of feminists—or women's liberationists, as feminists of the 1960s came to be known—were speaking out against attitudes and con-

ventions in America's manifestly male-dominated society that were perpetu-
ating what they perceived to be the historic subjugation of the country's females. Theirs was not an entirely new crusade. Indeed, a feminist movement
had taken form in the United States in the middle of the nineteenth century,
reached an apogee when it prevailed on the national and state governments to
approve the Nineteenth (women's suffrage) Amendment to the Federal Constitution in 1919, then went into eclipse. By the time of World War II, it had
become almost irrelevant. But then, in 1963, a book entitled *The Feminine
Mystique* by Betty Friedan made its way into print. According to Friedan,
women of the United States had been the victims of a body of ideas (to wit, a
feminine mystique) which maintained that a woman could find happiness and
fulfillment only as a wife and mother. Although women's magazines offered
an image of women (in her words) as "gaily content in a world of bedroom,
kitchen, sex, babies and home," Friedan argued that the home had become
a "comfortable concentration camp" that prompted its female inhabitants to
infantile forms of thought and behavior. How might a housewife break out of
her concentration camp and develop an identity of her own? The surest way
was to find a career outside the household in one of the professions or in business. Friedan's argument found a mark with legions of American women, and
with many men as well. Her book sold more than a million copies, and by the
mid-1960s the feminist movement in America was experiencing a full-blown
revival.

Urged on by the National Organization for Women, founded in 1966, feminists pressed the campaign for "women's lib" in uncounted ways. They organized demonstrations and rallies, lobbied in the halls of Congress and state
capitols. Contending that women could never achieve total liberation until
they gained absolute control over their own bodies, they demanded repeal of
all statutes restricting the abortion of unborn babies. They demanded that
business and public agencies grant executive responsibilities to increasing
numbers of women and that colleges and universities appoint additional
women to faculties. They conducted consciousness-raising seminars in which
they urged wives to insist that husbands help with preparing meals and doing
laundry, mothers to insist that fathers assume equal responsibility for changing diapers.

And so it went. Why, feminists asked, were the hurricanes that each year
swept across the oceans adjacent to the Americas given feminine names, for
example, Hurricane Hazel and Hurricane Camille? Why was it customary to
address a woman as "Miss" or "Mrs.," in accord with her marital status? A
man, after all, whether single or married, was "Mr." Finding no satisfactory
answer, feminists insisted that a woman, whatever her marital status, should
be addressed as "Ms." They spoke out against what they perceived to be the
exploitation of feminine charm, and to reinforce their rhetoric a group of feminists picketed the Miss America pageant in Atlantic City in 1968. Millions of
women, meanwhile, set about to deemphasize their own feminine charms by
refusing to wear makeup or bras.

Feminists found encouragement in the early results of the enterprise of
their rejuvenated movement. The legislatures of seventeen states voted to

abolish or liberalize laws restricting abortions. The secretary of labor announced in 1970 that federal contracts would henceforth include clauses mandating the employment of specific quotas of women. The attorney general initiated suits under Title VII of the Civil Rights Act of 1964 to end job discrimination against women by several large corporations. Agents of the federal government scrutinized the personnel files of two thousand colleges and universities to determine whether women had been victims of discrimination in hiring and salaries. And on August 15, 1970, the House of Representatives in Washington, by a vote of 315–15, proposed the Equal Rights Amendment (ERA), dormant for 47 years, to the states for ratification. (Proposed in the House in 1923, the ERA had never come to a vote.) Candidates for elective office increasingly made it a point to speak out in favor of sexual equality. Corporations and public agencies elevated increasing numbers of women to positions of executive responsibility; colleges and universities appointed increasing numbers of women to faculties.

After nearly three centuries of toil, sweat, and tears, the American woman by the 1970s still had not reached the promised land of sexual equality. But there was an undeniable truth in the advertising pitch of the Virginia Slims brand of cigarettes (a brand that was unabashedly aimed at the feminine market): "You've come a long way, baby."

## BLACKS

Like feminists, crusaders for equal rights for black Americans, as described in preceding chapters, became increasingly assertive as the 1960s unfolded. Their enterprise was not without success. Largely as a consequence of protests, demonstrations, and civil rights legislation, blacks began to frequent lunchrooms, hotels, and places of amusement that hitherto had been closed to them. They integrated previously all-white neighborhoods, voted in record numbers, and three blacks, Richard Hatcher in Gary, Indiana, Carl B. Stokes in Cleveland, and Walter Washington in Washington, D.C., became mayors of major cities. A black man, Robert C. Weaver, served in a presidential cabinet; another, Thurgood Marshall, was elevated to the Supreme Court. Edward W. Brooke, a Republican of Massachusetts, became the first black member of the U.S. Senate since the time of Reconstruction (after the Civil War), and Shirley Chisolm, Democrat of New York, became the first black woman to serve in the national House of Representatives. The black film star Sidney Poitier became a matinee idol, such black performers as Bill Cosby, Diahann Carroll, and Lloyd Haynes starred in weekly television shows, and for the first time in the history of the medium blacks appeared regularly in TV commercials. Black studies became a staple of college and university curriculums. Black Americans meanwhile began to take new pride in their blackness, exalted their African heritage as never before—by adopting Afro hairstyles, for example—and summed up their sentiments in the phrase "black is beautiful."

Still, it was clear that black Americans were increasingly frustrated, and for good reason. Stated simply, the fabled promise of American life seemed only a little less remote for most of the 21 million black citizens of the United States at the end of the 1960s than in former times. Said Roger Wilkins of the Ford Foundation, "Racism is in every nook and cranny in this country, and each of us blacks has to deal with it every day of our lives." Black Americans, frankly, continued to comprise a national underclass. While 8 percent of the country's white families survived on incomes that were below the official poverty level, so *Time* reported in 1970, 29 percent of its black families survived on such incomes. Of 300,000 lawyers in the United States in 1970, only 3,000 were black. But half of the 479 condemned men on the death rows of the country's prisons were black. Blacks comprised only 0.2 percent of the membership of America's plumbers unions, 0.4 percent of the electrical workers, 1.6 percent of the carpenters.

Pondering their plight, some blacks began to question the nonviolent tactics advocated by the NAACP and Southern Christian Leadership Conference, and intimated that blacks should consider tactics of militancy. They did so, interestingly, at the same time that the most charismatic black militant of recent years, Malcolm X of the Black Muslims (who would be shot to death by dissident Muslims in 1965), was turning away from his antiwhite rhetoric of the past and instead preaching brotherhood between whites and blacks. Of larger relevance in the view of those who were inclined to militancy were the words of James Baldwin, who wrote in his book *The Fire Next Time* (1963), "The Negroes of this country may never be able to rise to power, but they are very well placed indeed to precipitate chaos and ring down the curtain on the American dream."

To what extent the preachments of black militants were responsible remains unclear, but during the year 1964 racial violence flared in several cities. Then, in August of 1965, the country experienced its worst racial eruption since that in Detroit in 1943. The eruption occurred in Watts, a predominantly black suburb of Los Angeles.

The eruption in Watts began on August 11, 1965, when a white motorcycle patrolman stopped a speeding car in a black neighborhood that was adjacent to Watts, and arrested the black driver for operating a vehicle while intoxicated. A crowd of perhaps three hundred blacks quickly gathered at the scene, and before long became hostile. Then, after the police had departed with the intoxicated man in tow, blacks began shouting insults and throwing rocks at passing cars. Next, angry blacks began stopping cars, dragging terrified white passengers from the vehicles, and beating and kicking them. Several cars were overturned and set afire. The following evening, perhaps eight thousand blacks assembled in Watts, and before long violence broke out anew. Inevitably, the rioters began smashing storefront windows and stealing merchandise. Then they started torching buildings, most of them owned by whites, and as the flames roared and smoke billowed skyward, some rioters shouted a phrase that thereafter would be associated with the Watts upheaval: "Burn, baby, burn!"

The following day, Friday, the breaking-in and looting, much of it now being done by women and children, spread to other parts of the ghetto. So did

August 1965: Black barber surveys the destruction of his shop during rioting in the Watts suburb of Los Angeles.

the burning. Meanwhile, troops of the California National Guard had begun to deploy in Watts, and in the face of massive sweeps by the guardsmen the rioting and looting slowly diminished. By Saturday evening, Watts was quiet, and remained so through Sunday. Monday brought scattered incidents of window-smashing and looting, but by Tuesday the reign of lawlessness had passed, the fires had burned themselves out. The riot had claimed the lives of 9 whites and 25 blacks.

Nine months later, in June 1966, a white assailant wounded James H. Meredith with a shotgun blast as Meredith, the man who had broken the barrier of segregation at the University of Mississippi, was leading a civil rights march through the Mississippi countryside. Whereupon Stokely Carmichael and Floyd McKissick of the Congress of Racial Equality announced that blacks should meet violence with violence. To the chagrin of proponents of nonviolence, Carmichael, a 24-year-old native of Trinidad who was a spellbinding orator, asserted that the time had come for the assertion of "black power." He shouted at one point, "It's time we [blacks] stand up and take over." In that same period, two youthful blacks, Huey P. Newton and Bobby Seale, organized the Black Panthers, and proclaimed that violent revolution offered the only path to economic and social equality for black people. Such proclamations sent shivers down the spines of many whites, infuriated others—and before long observers of current affairs were commenting on a "white backlash" against the movement aimed at achieving civil equality for blacks.

Meanwhile, during the summer of 1966, racial violence flared in Atlanta, Chicago, and Cleveland. Calm thereupon returned to the country's urban ghettos, but in Boston, in 1967, charges that policemen had used brutal methods when countering black women who were demonstrating against the city's welfare practices touched off three days of firebombing, looting, and stone-throwing. The following week, in Tampa, a policeman shot and killed a black youth who was fleeing after a break-in at a photo supply store. The outcome was a riot that resulted in the death of one black. Almost simultaneously, the arrest of a black man who was protesting a death sentence that had been given to another black provoked an outburst of racial violence in Cincinnati. Less than three weeks later, the stoning by black youths of automobiles driven by whites set off a wave of firebombing, looting, and window-smashing in Buffalo.

In mid-July of 1967, rumors, apparently false, that policemen had beaten a black cab driver for allegedly assaulting a police officer provided the catalyst for an eruption in Newark. Pitched battles between national guardsmen and police on the one hand and black snipers on the other resulted in the death of 24 blacks and 2 whites. Hardly had the national sense of shock over the riot in Newark subsided before the most devastating civil disturbance of the 1960s erupted in Detroit—following a raid by police on an after-hours drinking establishment. The burning and looting and shooting in Detroit went on for five days, and when it finally ended, five thousand Detroiters, most of them black, were left homeless. The riot had claimed the lives of 43 people, 34 of them black. Lesser outbursts, often provoked by roving bands of black youths, disturbed the calm in other cities during those tumultuous weeks of 1967, including Chicago, Cleveland, Milwaukee, New York, Philadelphia, Pittsburgh, Providence, Rochester, South Bend, Toledo, Washington, Waukegan, and Wichita.

While Detroit continued to smolder, President Johnson established a National Advisory Commission on Civil Disorders, and ordered it to determine why the recent civil disorders had taken place and what might be done to prevent recurrences. Under the direction of Gov. Otto Kerner of Illinois, the Kerner Commission issued its report the following year.

The report concluded that white racism was essentially responsible for the explosive mixture that had produced the disorders. White racism had resulted in pervasive discrimination in employment, education, and housing, which in turn had encouraged crime, drug addiction, dependency on welfare, and black resentment toward society in general. Catalyzing the mixture, the commission believed, were frustrated hopes aroused by the judicial and legislative triumphs of the civil rights movement in recent years, a popular climate that tended toward approval of violence as a form of protest, and the defiance of law and federal authority by local officials who were bent on resisting desegregation.

What might be done? The Kerner Commission recommended that local governments develop neighborhood action task forces, establish comprehensive grievance-response mechanisms, bring the institutions of government close to the people they served, expand opportunities for ghetto residents to participate in the formation of public policy and the implementation of programs affecting them. It urged reforms aimed at eliminating the abrasive relationship that existed between the police and ghetto communities; elimination of de facto segregation of schools and an expansion of the opportunities for education and training open to disadvantaged people of all ages; a federal program to create 2 million new jobs for disadvantaged people; reform of the welfare system; a federal system of income supplements; and a federal program aimed at providing 6 million units of decent housing over the next five years for families of low and moderate income.

## MEXICAN AMERICANS

Meanwhile, another of the country's minority groups, one that numbered about 6 million in the years of Kennedy and Johnson, was becoming increasingly assertive: the Mexican Americans or, as they had been referred to for several decades, the Chicanos. Seldom noted as such in official statistics published by the Washington government, Mexican Americans had comprised an important minority in the national population since the 1840s when Texas, California, and the sprawling area lying between the Lone Star and Golden states passed to the rule of the United States.

Through World War II, most Mexican Americans, a preponderance of whom continued to live in the great southwestern region of the republic, particularly in Texas and California, survived as poorly paid migratory farm workers who made their way, in accord with the turn of the seasons, from cotton and lettuce fields to vineyards to orange groves. But by the 1960s, as a consequence of the accelerating mechanization of agriculture, almost half of the Chicano population lived in Mexican-American neighborhoods or *barrios* in such cities as El Paso, Los Angeles, and San Antonio. Poorly educated, lacking skills, and like blacks the victims of rank discrimination by whites, or "Anglos," most Chicanos languished. Efforts by the League of United Latin American Citizens, the Mexican-American Political Association, and the Political Association of Spanish-speaking Organizations to improve the employment opportunities of Chicanos and secure the election of Chicanos to public office achieved only minimal results. So why did Chicanos remain quiescent in those years when the black ghettos were erupting? In part, it seems, because many of them, almost indistinguishable in appearance from Anglos, were able to enter the social mainstream—in part, too, because a relatively high level of family stability and a lively sense of ethnic pride tended to keep their frustrations in check. Observing that the rioting in Watts in 1965 did not spill over into nearby barrios, the historian Benjamin Muse later wrote, "Mexican Independence day [in Los Angeles] brought forth many Mexican flags, and public buildings displayed streamers congratulating citizens of Mexican origin on the glorious anniversary. No flags ever flew for Negro Americans."

But then, during the years of Kennedy and Johnson, Reies López Tijerina organized the Alianza, which asserted that great tracts of land in the Southwest presently owned by Anglos rightfully belonged to Chicanos, and several Mexican-American student organizations began to press Chicano interests. Out of one of the latter organizations, the Mexican-American Youth Organization, emerged a new political party, La Raza, which in the 1970s succeeded in electing several Chicano candidates to school boards and city councils in Texas—and also promoted *chicanismo*, that is, pride in Mexican history and culture. Of larger moment was the enterprise of César Chavez, 38, a onetime

April 10, 1968: Following a 300-mile, 35-day pilgrimage from Delano, California, to Sacramento, César Chavez, the leader of striking grape workers, waves to followers from the steps of the state capitol.

migratory farm worker who in the mid-1960s organized what became the United Farm Workers Organization (UFWO).

The first goal of Chavez, a devout Roman Catholic and proponent of nonviolence, was to improve the conditions of grape pickers, among the most poorly paid workers in America—workers who enjoyed no job security or medical or retirement benefits. In pursuit of that goal, he had support of the AFL-CIO, an array of religious spokespeople, and political liberals in all parts of the country. And in 1966, he scored an important victory: In the face of a boycott of their products arranged by Chavez's organization, the growers of wine grapes negotiated union contracts with the UFWO. The growers of table grapes proved more intractable, and when Chavez ordered a strike they were able to minimize its effects by employing thousands of illegal immigrants from Mexico. Chavez, meanwhile, felt compelled to subject himself to a fast to check militants within his organization who wanted to resort to violence. On ending the fast, after 25 days, Chavez attended an ecumenical Mass in Delano, California, which was attended by Sen. Robert F. Kennedy of New York. Kennedy lauded Chavez as "one of the heroic figures of our time." At that point, a nationwide boycott of table grapes was organized, and at length, in 1969, the boycott, which won support of the mayors of several large cities and a variety of food store chains, prompted ten major growers of table grapes in California to negotiate with the UFWO.

## RELIGION

The years of Kennedy and Johnson were a time of change in the religious climate of America. Encouraged by the preachments of Pope John XXIII, large numbers of Catholics and Protestants put aside old antagonisms, talked tolerantly and frankly about differences, and engaged in cooperative activities, including public worship, that would have been unthinkable a few years before. For the country's 40 or so million Catholics, indeed, the period was particularly notable. Buoyed by the accession of John Kennedy, a Catholic, to the presidency, Catholics discarded historic resentments resulting from an awareness that large numbers of their Protestant compatriots thought the Americanism of Catholics seriously flawed, and felt that they had at last achieved equality of citizenship with Protestants. Of equal moment, as a result of Vatican Council II, another legacy of John XXIII, Catholicism was purged of many of its medieval trappings. The ancient Latin liturgy virtually disappeared, priests, now *facing* their congregations, celebrated Mass in the vernacular, and the solemn atmosphere of Catholic churches was punctured for the first time by the sounds of guitars and what tradition-oriented Catholics deplored as "foot-stomping" music.

Still, from the perspective of institutional religionists, the change in the religious climate during the years of Kennedy and Johnson offered minimal cause for celebration. The percentage of the citizenry that was listed on membership rolls of religious congregations, it was true, declined only slightly, from 64 to 62 percent, and per capita contributions to congregations increased, from $66.76 in 1961 to $82.46 in 1969. But of larger moment, or so it seemed, was a Gallup poll in 1969 in which 74 percent of the respondents expressed the view that the influence of religion in America was in decline—compared with 14 percent who so responded in a similar poll in 1957.

Indeed, it appeared indisputable in the time of Kennedy and Johnson that institutional religion had lost much of the appeal that it had enjoyed during and after World War II. Attendance at religious services and observances declined. Books exalting traditional religious values seldom moved near the top of bestseller lists. Apparently in response to the changing tastes of audiences, filmmakers turned out fewer films offering sympathetic portrayals of traditional religious themes.

Particularly distressing from the perspective of institutional religionists was evidence that younger Americans, historically preoccupied with earthly pursuits and disinclined to accept the behavioral restrictions required by most religious institutions, found institutional religion even less attractive than had young Americans in former times. Millions of young Americans during the Kennedy and Johnson years simply concluded that religion was irrelevant. More than that, many youths, sometimes in savage language, expressed outright contempt for religion, at least in forms traditionally observed by institutional religionists in the United States. Such youths tended to the view that institutional religion in America was and always had been repressive of the human spirit and an impediment to social change. They also called attention to the failure of most religionists over past decades to speak out against transparent social evils, for example, the mistreatment of racial minorities.

Adding to the discomfort and dismay of many religionists during the time of Kennedy and Johnson were rulings by the Supreme Court that classroom prayer and Bible reading in public schools, long a practice in many locales, particularly in the southern "Bible Belt" and the Middle West, violated the federal Constitution's provisions regarding the separation of church and state. Of larger concern was dissension within the ranks of institutional religionists. Many Catholics resented the departure from traditional practice wrought by Vatican II; others resented (and increasingly ignored) their church's continuing condemnation of contraception. Catholics and Protestants alike quarreled among themselves over the question of what should be the role of churches in movements to reform society and achieve social justice. And most institutional religionists recoiled when a handful of theologians asserted that the traditional perception of God was invalid and, in any event, had no relevance in the modern world—that, to invoke an oft-repeated phrase, "God [or at least God as traditionally perceived] is dead."

## SEXUAL REVOLUTION

Concurrent with the decline of the influence of institutional religion—and, it was widely thought, in some measure a consequence of that decline—the country experienced what millions of Americans perceived to be a veritable revolution in sexual mores and practices. The term *revolution*, to be sure, may have been a misnomer. Alfred Kinsey and others, after all, had established in previous decades that sexual activity outside the bond of matrimony was far more extensive than popularly assumed. Still, in some measure perhaps because the birth control pill reduced the risk of pregnancy, the incidence of such activity appeared to explode in the 1960s, notably among adolescents and young adults. In the words of the Methodist bishop Gerald Kennedy of Los Angeles, "The atmosphere is wide open. There is more promiscuity, and it is taken as a matter of course." Apparently assuming that most young men had always been primed and ready for sexual adventure, a few commentators surmised that the foregoing explosion was in no small measure a consequence of the increased willingness of girls and young women of middle- and upper-income families, to wit, girls and young women of a genre that traditionally had tended to guard its chastity with a vengeance, to involve themselves in casual sexual relationships. However explained, there was unloosed during the 1960s a new tendency to celebrate uninhibited sexual activity. So purveyors of the new sexual freedom maintained, sex in all of its myriad forms was exhilarating, and ought to be experienced to the fullest without inhibition. The maintenance of chastity was no virtue, so the argument went, hence nobody should feel the slightest sense of guilt or shame for giving himself or herself over to the pursuit of sexual adventure and savoring the resultant delights.

How did middle-aged and older Americans respond to the new sexual mores? Many of them embraced the new mores with abandon. But millions of middle-aged and older Americans, particularly those who were parents and grandparents of sexually active young people, viewed the seemingly new impulse to promiscuity as shocking. Particularly shocking to their sensibilities was what older Americans considered the scandal of massive cohabitation. In a word, legions of unmarried couples, a large percentage of them the progeny of middle- and upper-income parents who during their own youths would never have dreamed of carrying on in such fashion, lived openly together on a scale that was without precedent.

The alleged sexual revolution, of course, transcended personal attitudes and behavior. It also included what in the view of most Americans was nothing less than an obscenity explosion, one made possible in the United States by Supreme Court rulings that found most legal sanctions against allegedly dirty books and magazines, not to mention performances generally perceived as obscene, to be in violation of the guarantee of freedom of expression as set out in the First Amendment.

Manifestations of the obscenity explosion were, well, manifest. Book publishers appeared bent on flooding bookstores with titles, including D. H. Lawrence's long-suppressed *Lady Chatterley's Lover* and Henry Miller's likewise long-suppressed *Tropic of Cancer*, which dealt explicitly (and, many Americans thought, salaciously) with sexual themes. What some people deplored as bathroom language become commonplace in books and magazines and on the stage, and, frankly, it challenged the imagination to recall that only a decade and a half before, while composing *The Naked and the Dead,* Norman Mailer had felt constrained to substitute "fug" for one of his favorite four-letter words.

The new sexual freedom (or license) also found expression in sexually explicit films, for example, the Swedish production *I am Curious (Yellow)* (about the life and endless sexual exploits of a Swedish hippie) and *I, A Woman* (centered around the multiple orgasms of a seldom-clothed actress), often shown at what were designated as "art" theaters. It found expression in stage productions, for example, *Oh! Calcutta!*, in topless bathing suits, in the so-called adult bookstores that came to dot the urban landscape, in the titles and lyrics of pop music. It found expression in the slick magazine *Playboy* (founded in 1953, nearly a decade before most Americans decided that the country was in the throes of a sexual revolution) and an array of imitators, in big-city Playboy Clubs (later described by a reporter as "purveyors of pop hedonism"), essentially elegant nightclubs where diners and revelers were served by nubile hostesses, called "bunnies," who were attired in rabbit ears, tuxedo cuffs and collar, and figure-tight black-satin suits with fluffy white tails. Meanwhile, sex made its way into nearly every living room in the republic when television producers succeeded in putting on the airwaves an unending array of shows in which apparently nude men and women simulated lovemaking (under bedcovers, of course)—an almost shocking commentary on the dimension of the sexual revolution in the view of millions of Americans who could recall the national furor in 1946 when Howard Hughes offered a similar scene in the film *The Outlaw*, starring Janes Russell (that being a time when even married couples of Hollywood films invariably slept in twin beds).

Regarding the sexual revolution, the historian Max Lerner asserted in 1967, "We're living in a Babylonian society [that is] perhaps more Babylonian than Babylon itself. It's what's called a late sensate period. The emphasis in our society today is on the senses and the release of the sensual. All the old codes have broken down."

## DRUGS

Apparently related to the sexual revolution, inasmuch as both seemed rooted in the manifest weakening of traditional standards of moral or at least acceptable behavior, was a veritable explosion during the years of Kennedy and Johnson in the use of mind-influencing drugs. The explosion came as a total surprise and, more than that, a shock to most older citizens, for a few years before, in the mid-1950s, scarcely any self-respecting Americans, save for a handful of beatniks and other bohemians, scatterings of Mexican Americans, and a comparatively few denizens of black ghettos, had given even passing thought to the use of drugs, including marijuana. Had someone deigned to offer a marijuana "joint" to the typical clean-cut and clean-shaven young American male of the mid-1950s—or to his female companion, possibly attired in sweater and skirt, bobby socks and saddle shoes—the latter, imbued with the conventional wisdom that smoking marijuana was only slightly less dangerous and decadent than injecting heroin, almost certainly would have shunned the offer, possibly with an oath. But then, in the early 1960s, young Americans by the millions—influenced, no doubt, by the beatniks and kindred social rebels who exalted the euphoria or "highs" produced by "grass," or "pot"—discovered marijuana, and before Lyndon Johnson departed the White House in 1969 the smoking of grass was as acceptable (and also as commonplace) in many circles, for example, on college and university campuses, as social drinking.

Smoking marijuana provided aficionados with peculiar sensations and delights. Many users maintained that it provided a sort of lens that heightened one's perception of color and beauty—even his or her sense of reality. For many users, the delights were less ethereal. Although it was clear from the moment young America went on what older citizens viewed as a marijuana binge that the laws prohibiting the sale and possession of the drug were virtually unenforceable, the activity of the users was manifestly illegal, hence in the words of one teenage user offered the thrill of "doing something illegal together." Various psychiatrists, indeed, suspected that the smoking of marijuana by burgeoning numbers of young people was essentially an expression of exhibitionist rebellion against adult authority. They observed that marijuana smoking by young people seemed to rattle parents and other older citizens even more than sexual escapades (perhaps because, at one time or another, many of the parents and older Americans had experienced sexual escapades of their own and, in any event, understood the allure of sexual adventure). Thus the smoking of pot offered the thrill of defying authority and partaking of forbidden pleasure.

If the smoking of marijuana by millions of youthful Americans was an expression of rebellion against the authority of senior generations, it also was an expression that often transcended exhibitionism. As explained in an essay that appeared in *Newsweek* in 1967, "Marijuana has become for some of this new generation a symbol of its discontent with basic American values, with the goals and life style of the older generation." Or in the words of the historian William L. O'Neill in his book *Coming Apart*, pot smoking by youthful Americans during the 1960s "helped further distinguish between the old world of grasping, combative, alcoholic adults and the turned-on, cooperative culture of the young." Observed O'Neill, one did not clutch one's joint as the conventional party-goer clutched his or her solitary glass of booze, but shared it with others.

The explosion in its use inevitably prompted a national debate over the effects of marijuana on users. The debate was heated, often angry. Proponents of marijuana contended that puffing grass was no more harmful to the individual or to society than consuming alcoholic beverages—indeed they argued that it was less harmful, inasmuch as grass made one gentle and pacific, whereas alcohol often made the individual surly and belligerent. Unlike heroin and other so-called hard drugs, moreover, it was not addictive, inasmuch as it produced no withdrawal symptoms when the user set about to dispense with the habit. Opponents maintained that marijuana was apt to prompt the user to experiment with such hard and inarguably dangerous drugs as heroin and the deadly compound referred to as "speed," while assorted scientists suggested that the use of marijuana might produce adverse psychological and even physiological changes in the user, for example, changes in composition of the individual's genes. But the evidence offered by opponents to reinforce their arguments seemed inconclusive, hence the use of marijuana continued to accelerate.

In truth, many users of marijuana did experiment with other drugs, notably the compound known as LSD, popularly referred to as "acid." LSD is a hallucinogenic drug that according to its users can produce "trips" which are sheer ecstasy. As was demonstrated during the Kennedy and Johnson years, unfortunately, it also is capable of producing trips that are so terrifying that they leave the user psychologically impaired. The guru of what became nothing less than a drug cult resting primarily on the use of LSD was Timothy Leary, a onetime scientific researcher at Harvard who was dismissed by the university for involving undergraduate students in his experiments with LSD. According to Leary, who during the years of Kennedy and Johnson moved about the country in long white robes preaching his gospel, one could achieve total freedom and put oneself in touch with ultimate truth only through the use of "consciousness-expanding" drugs. Thus he urged his auditors to "tune in, turn on, drop out."

## YOUTH REBELLION

That great numbers of young Americans were indeed turning on with drugs and in many instances dropping out of what young people referred to as straight society prompted middle-aged and older Americans—often with a mixture of wonder and bewilderment and cold fury—to conclude that the country was in the throes of a full-dress rebellion by millions of its own youths. The impulse to rebellion, of course, had historically touched the spirits of young Americans, in the 1920s, for example. But never in the country's past had the rebelliousness of young citizens so disturbed the national tranquility. Never had it seemed so pervasive. Never had it caused such anguish among the senior generations.

What accounted for the youth rebellion of the years of Kennedy and Johnson and their successor in the White House, Richard Nixon—a rebellion that transcended sex and drugs and included a large-scale rejection or at least questioning of the entire gamut of traditional values and institutions? Answers to that question varied.

Many older Americans suspected that the young people of the present generation had been pampered and ultimately spoiled as a consequence of the rampant prosperity that had prevailed in the United States since World War II, to wit, that the youthful rebels had not been tempered by hard work or the uncertainties and insecurities of economic depression and global war. Accordingly, they lacked a proper appreciation of traditional American values that emphasized discipline, industry, and patriotism. Others surmised that the spoiling of the country's young had resulted from a social climate contaminated by the subversive gospel of permissiveness advanced in recent years by Dr. Spock and other child psychologists. More virulent were the explanations offered by two members of the administration of President Nixon. Branding the young rebels as "effete snobs," Vice Pres. Spiro T. Agnew charged that the youth rebellion sprang from youthful arrogance, while Attorney General John N. Mitchell contended that it rested on the monumental ignorance of young people about the realities of life as well as their unmitigated naïveté.

Apologists of what critics referred to variously as the Now Generation and Me Generation tended to the view that many and perhaps most of the young rebels were not simply arrogant and spoiled hedonists and mindless disturbers of the national tranquility. Rather, they perceived the youthful rebels—or at least many of them—as perceptive and acutely sensitive young men and women who were earnestly trying to expand their consciousness and who understood that there were goals to be achieved in life that were of more intrinsic value than the acquisition of jobs or positions providing inflated incomes, outsized automobiles, and acceptance by the social elite. Many of the young rebels, their apologists thought, were on the mark when they argued that there was no legitimate excuse for the persistence of widespread poverty in affluent America, the more so when the country could afford to spend billions of dollars to put men on a worthless planet in outer space, and when they deplored what they perceived to be the hypocrisy permeating American society—for example, the pretention that the United States, once a citadel of the abominable institution of slavery and since the abolition of slavery in the 1860s a citadel of racial abuse and injustice, was and always had been the world's grand exalted champion of freedom, democracy, and justice. Apologists tended to view the rebels as people who revered the beauty and grandeur of nature and felt a deep and abiding commitment to protection of the natural environment.

Whatever the sources of their attitudes and behavior, legions of young Americans of the period, many of them bright and promising students of prestigious colleges and universities, did indeed appear to be in open rebellion against the values and institutions of "straight" society. Some of them became hippies, whose views and lifestyles were akin to those of the beatniks of the 1950s. Hippies rejected formal government as oppressive and the monogamous family as outmoded, and settled into such hippie communities as those in the Haight-Ashbury section of San Francisco and New York's Lower East Side. The hippie phenomenon was relatively short-lived, a victim of the wanton abuse of drugs by its aficionados and adverse publicity resulting from the involvement of hippies in assorted acts of violence, most notably the ritual murder in 1969 of the pregnant actress Sharon Tate and four of her friends in the Bel-Air district of Los Angeles by the "family" of the hippie guru Charles Manson. However short-lived—and however few its active adherents—the hippie movement visibly influenced millions of rebellious young Americans who did not themselves become hippies.

Likewise influencing youthful rebels during the 1960s, particularly those who were college and university students, was the Students for a Democratic Society (SDS), an organization that found inspiration in a provocative volume by the sociologist C. Wright Mills entitled *The Power Elite*, published in 1956. It was in 1962 that Tom Hayden, a student at the University of Michigan, assumed responsibility for composing what turned out to be the enabling document of the SDS, the Port Huron Statement pledging the organization to the establishment of what was described as a New Left in American higher education. Prodded and guided by the New Left, colleges and universities were to become agents of radical change in American society.

Although a fair number of college and university students and other New Leftists in the course of the 1960s professed empathy with the principles spelled out in the Port Huron Statement, it was clear from the outset that the statement's essentially revolutionary agenda stood no chance of achieving realization, however distraught and frustrated the people of the United States often appeared to be during those tumultuous years. And had Lyndon Johnson refrained from dramatically escalating America's involvement in the war in Vietnam, the SDS would have made no notable imprint at all on the national consciousness. Alas, the president, beginning in 1965, did dramatically escalate that involvement, and the SDS, its membership numbering only a few thousand, became an engine of organization and leadership in the burgeoning

April 1967: Hippies of San Francisco turn out on a warm spring day to parade the streets of the Haight-Ashbury District.

antiwar movement. And while rallying Americans against the war, it sought to propagate the gospel of the New Left. Large numbers of its auditors listened respectfully, indeed sympathetically, but few accepted conversion. By 1970, the SDS, rent by factionalism, had disintegrated.

Likewise giving expression to the spirit of rebellion that animated millions of young Americans during the 1960s were the Free Speech Movement (FSM), the Weathermen, and the Youth International Party. Scorned by its critics as "the Filthy Speech Movement" (because of its apparent preoccupation with obscene language), the FSM took form during disturbances involving radical students and authorities at the University of California at Berkeley in 1964—disturbances that continued intermittently into 1965 and beyond. (By stirring the passions of millions of nonradical voters, those organizations were instrumental in the election of the conservative Ronald Reagan to the governorship of California in 1965.) Under the leadership of Mark Rudd, a student of Columbia University, the Weathermen—their name borrowed from a Bob Dylan lyric, "You don't need a weatherman to know which way the wind blows"—sought to apply the principles of the revolutionaries Ché Guevara and Mao Zedong in an effort to radicalize dissatisfied young workers, motorcycle outlaws, so-called street kids, and other youths who had hitherto expressed no interest in radical politics. The Weathermen and their "New Red Army" generated considerable publicity when they confronted "the pig power structure" via a succession of provocative and indeed violent stunts, but failed to recruit many disaffected youths and quickly faded from the public consciousness.

Equally short-lived was the Youth International Party, better known as the Yippies, a faction of the SDS founded in 1967 by the veteran radicals Abbie Hoffman and Jerry Rubin. According to Hoffman, the Yippies were onetime hippies who, concluding that Flower Power was dead, decided to join the SDS and convert the latter organization, guided as it was by angry and hot-blooded activists, to a more lenient and joyful approach to revolution. In addition to an end to war, the Yippie platform urged elimination of pay toilets, legalization of all psychedelic drugs, free food, and a heart transplant for President Johnson. Explained the irrepressible Rubin, "The Youth International Party begins with the premise that politics should be a party. It's dancing, it's guerrilla theater."

The Yippies indulged in some guerrilla theater in August of 1967 when some of them invaded the New York Stock Exchange, and from the galleries showered startled brokers on the floor below with one-dollar bills. Supposedly they were showing contempt for money. A few months later, another band of Yippies, to protest air pollution by utility companies and express disdain for corporations, forced their way into the Manhattan offices of Consolidated Edison, the utilities behemoth of the Northeast, and presented black chrysanthemums to secretaries, hurled soot at company executives, and detonated smoke bombs. Next, in March of 1968, a horde of Yippies, decked out in capes, gowns, feathers, and beads, poured into Manhattan's Grand Central Station, crowded with commuters and long-distance travelers. The Yippies tossed hot cross buns and firecrackers, floated balloons, snake-danced through the concourse of the venerable rail terminal, unfurled a huge banner emblazoned with a "Y."

August 1969: A segment of the tens of thousands of people who gathered for the Wood-stock Festival in upstate New York.

While fellow Yippies hooted and cheered, several members of the horde climbed atop the station's information booth, ripped off the hands of the large clock above the booth, scribbled graffiti, and passed lighted marijuana joints to one another.

In sum, the youthful rebels of the 1960s expressed their rebellion in seemingly countless way. Scorning the clean-cut styles of grooming and dress that long had prevailed among young Americans, they grew beards and long hair, wore outlandish costumes and "granny" eyeglasses. They smoked grass, tripped out on LSD, made a fetish of obscene language, flouted the sexual conventions of their elders, experimented in communal living, occupied buildings on college and university campuses, resisted the military draft, scorned institutional religion, voiced contempt for guns and bullets and military chieftains. They held mammoth festivals, most notably the one at Woodstock in New York in 1969, during which they "grooved" to rock music, got stoned on marijuana and LSD, took off their clothes, fornicated with abandon. Large numbers of them lashed out against the alleged materialism and greed of "the establishment," renounced hot war and cold war, lamented the mistreatment of blacks and Chicanos and Indians, demanded that prosperous countries share their wealth with the poor countries of the Third World, called for the overthrow of "exploitive capitalism," professed solidarity with the working class—although, in truth, most were of bourgeois origins, felt nothing but contempt for what, in fact, were the ambitions and values of America's proletariat, and were roundly despised by most of those proletarians whom they were bent on rescuing from capitalist oppressors. Many were virulently anti-American, flaunted Vietcong flags, defiled the Stars and Stripes, hailed Ho Chi Minh as an emancipator, branded the president of the United States as a war criminal, plastered the walls of their pads with pictures of Lenin and Mao, Ché and Fidel, and expressed contempt for America's constitutional processes.

## POPULATION AND THE ECONOMY

The carryings-on of young rebels aside, the life of the republic went on during the 1960s, one rather humdrum day at a time. The years of Kennedy and Johnson, indeed, were a time of impressive population growth and economic prosperity. The national population advanced from 179.3 million in 1960 to 203.2 million in 1970, an increase of 13.5 percent. Experiencing the largest population increase during the period were the Pacific states (including Alaska and Hawaii): from 21.2 million to 26.5 million with California registering the largest increase, from 15.7 million to nearly 20 million, an increase of 27 percent. But it was Florida that experienced the largest growth in population in terms of percentage, from 4.9 million to 6.7 million, an increase of 37.1 percent. Meanwhile, the movement of population from the countryside to the cities continued. The urban population—an urban area being one that had at least one city or town of 2,500 people—increased from 125.2 million (69.9 percent of the total population) in 1960 to 149.3 million (73.5 percent of the total) in 1970. The rural population, conversely, declined from 54.0 million in 1960 to 53.8 million in 1970.

The years of Kennedy and Johnson, notwithstanding occasional recessions, were a time of unprecedented economic expansion and prosperity in the United States. The gross national product (GNP) in constant (1958) dollars was $487.7 billion in 1960, $720.0 billion in 1970. Translated to per capita terms, the figures for the GNP were $2,699 in 1960, $3,516 in 1970. Per capita disposable personal income in constant (1958) dollars was $1,883 in 1960, $2,595 in 1970. Personal consumption expenditures for goods and services per capita in constant (1958) dollars totaled $1,749 in 1960, $2,324 in 1970. The index of manufacturing output went from 66 in 1960 to 111 in 1969. The value of new construction increased from $54.6 billion in 1960 to $93.9 billion in 1969. The total value of farm output advanced from $39.2 billion in 1960 to $46.4 billion in 1969, although the country's farm population declined from 15.6 million in 1960 to 10.3 million in 1970. Automobile registrations increased from 61.6 million in 1960 to 89.2 million in 1979. Unemployment, meanwhile, declined steadily, from 6.7 percent of the labor force in the recession year of 1960 to 3.9 percent in 1969. And from 1960 to 1965, consumer prices remained fairly stable, advancing less than 2 percent per year during that period. They advanced almost 3 percent in 1966 and 1967, more than 4 percent in 1968, and more than 5 percent in 1969.

## CONGLOMERATES AND THE MILITARY-INDUSTRIAL COMPLEX

It was during the rampant prosperity of the 1960s that Americans became increasingly conscious of the emergence of a relatively new corporate phenomenon, namely, the conglomerate. A conglomerate resulted from a merger of several corporations. Corporate mergers, of course, were nothing new. But historically, corporate mergers had been of either the horizontal genre, in which companies producing the same or similar products or services were brought together, or the vertical, in which a corporation merged with its suppliers and distributors. In a conglomerate merger, several corporate entities (or companies) whose product lines or services were totally different were brought together.

Usually formed when one company acquired several other companies, the conglomerate had a variety of attractions. Because the goods and services produced by its components were essentially unrelated, the federal government seemed unlikely to institute antitrust proceedings against a conglomerate. Horizontal and vertical mergers, inasmuch as they often appeared to threaten the viability of smaller companies, long had attracted the critical attention of the Justice Department, committed as it was to enforcement of the antitrust laws. Endowed with larger financial resources than competitors, the conglomerate could presumably outbid and outspend competitors and also absorb greater losses. It could afford to advertise more intensively, defend its legal rights more effectively, hire the most enterprising and resourceful executives and technicians. Its components could share a common pool of accountants and financial planners, market analysts and labor experts, lawyers and purchasing agents. It could realize myriad tax advantages.

Notwithstanding widespread and often vehement criticism that conglomerates (or supercorporations) represented a dangerous concentration of corporate power, and also assailed because of their unorthodox financing techniques and accounting procedures, new conglomerates took form, among them Gulf + Western, International Telephone & Telegraph (ITT) and Ling-Temco-Vought (LTV). Reaching full flower in the 1960s and early 1970s, conglomerates, for better or for worse, appeared to have become a permanent part of the corporate landscape. In the view of their defenders, they encouraged efficient business operations and reflected the creative energy and iconoclasm of the times.

Making a larger imprint on the national consciousness during the 1960s than the phenomenon of corporate conglomerates was that of the military-industrial complex, to wit, the armed forces of the United States and the vast network of corporations that strove to supply them with everything from fighter planes and submarines and tanks to canned food and blankets and garbage cans—also the research facilities of an array of corporations and laboratories, colleges and universities—which were collectively responsible for building and maintaining the enormous military-naval establishment of the North American superpower. By the latter 1960s, as reported in *Newsweek* in June 1969, the military-industrial complex (or MIC) had become "an $80-billion-a year juggernaut consuming a tenth of the nation's giant-sized gross national product."

The MIC, which in truth had existed in America from the birth of the republic in the 1770s, did indeed appear to have become a juggernaut by the later 1960s. The four largest defense contractors in 1969 were the Lockheed Aircraft Corporation (contracts totaling $2.0 billion), the General Electric Company (contracts totaling $1.6 billion), the General Dynamics Corporation (contracts totaling $1.2 billion), and the McDonnell Douglas Corporation (contracts totaling $1.0 billion). Among the colleges and universities receiving the largest sums from the Department of Defense in fulfillment of research and development contracts were the Massachusetts Institute of Technology, the University of Michigan, and Stanford University. According to the aforementioned report prepared by *Newsweek*, the armed forces in 1969 would expend $7 billion for the purchase of aircraft, nearly $3 billion for ammunition, nearly $1 billion for ships, more than $20 million for furniture, and $1.5 million for musical instruments. "Thus dispensed," the report continued, "the money flows into every state in the Union and at least 363 of the nation's 435 Congressional districts." Proclaimed Sen. Gaylord Nelson, Democrat of Wisconsin, "The whole economy is infiltrated. We are a warfare state."

If the sheer size of the military-industrial complex—and the fact that more than two thousand retired military and naval officers of high rank were in the employ of corporate contractors of the MIC, mainly, it appeared, for lobbying and public relations purposes—stirred the concerns of many Americans, the soaring costs and technical problems connected with a succession of defense projects during the 1960s dismayed and infuriated millions of citizens and most of their representatives in Congress. Among the most publicized cases were those of the TFX—eventually the F-111—a swing-wing fighter aircraft, built by General Dynamics, and the C-5A "Galaxy" supertransport plane, built by Lockheed. Regarding the F-111, charges circulated that civilians in the government had applied improper influence on the Department of Defense to award the contract for its design and production to General Dynamics. Thereafter, the F-111 was beset by a variety of problems, including malfunctioning electronic equipment. It also was the victim of a succession of unexplained crashes. More infuriating in the view of Congress, or so it seemed, were the huge cost overruns in the matter of the F-111. The Department of Defense (or Pentagon) awarded the contract to build the F-111 to General Dynamics on the basis of estimates that each plane would cost $3.4 million. In the end, each of the 550 F-111s cost the government (and ultimately the country's taxpayers) $13.1 million. Regarding the C-5A, it was disclosed in 1969 that the 120 C-5As for which the Pentagon had contracted were going to cost $2 billion more than the estimated $3.4 billion on which the contract had been awarded. Pressed by an angry Congress, the Pentagon reluctantly reduced the order for

C-5As to 81 planes. At that, the cost of the fleet of global-range transports to the country's taxpayers would exceed $3 billion.

Still, in regard to cost overruns on weapons and support systems for the armed forces, appearances did not always square with realities. In some measure, such overruns were a result of the enormous technological complexity of the systems themselves. "As technologies grow more complicated," it was explained in one report, "the engineering problems can mount to a point where all the computer work in the world will not really produce an accurate estimate." In the fabrication of incredibly sophisticated weapons systems that the government considered essential to defend the country's interests and guarantee its security, in truth, basic research, engineering development, and preparations for production often proceeded simultaneously. In the words of an executive of one aerospace corporation, "The industry is the only one that contracts to invent something." Notwithstanding cost overruns, moreover, the margin of profit realized by corporate defense contractors often was minimal. A study of the profits of the largest defense contractors in 1969 by the Logistics Management Institute disclosed that the profit on each dollar of defense sales presently was running at about 4.2 cents, as opposed to an average of 8.7 cents on sales by manufacturing industries in the United States as a whole.

## TRAVELING FROM HERE TO THERE

Weapons systems were not the only undertakings of the federal government to generate whopping cost overruns during the 1960s. Of particular note was the 42,500-mile interstate highway system, the estimated cost of which was approximately $40 billion when sanctioned by Congress and President Eisenhower in 1956. Revised estimates made public in 1970 indicated that the system (expanded in that same year by 1,500 miles) would ultimately cost more than $70 billion. But virtually no taxpayers appeared to mind. On the contrary, millions of taxpayers viewed the interstate highway system as a blessing almost beyond compare, particularly when they whizzed along those magnificent four- and six-lane limited access freeways in their favorite conveyances, namely, automobiles, and marveled at the swiftness with which they could cover vast distances, not to mention the comparative ease and safety of traveling along the interstates, as compared with former times when they had made similar trips over narrow and often winding and steeply graded two-lane highways that always seemed clogged with slow-moving vehicles and almost inevitably compelled the motorist to thread his or her way through the congested downtown areas of cities and towns. More than 30,000 miles of the interstate highway system were in place by 1970, and when completed the system would link more than 90 percent of the cities of the republic claiming populations of 50,000 or more, as well as thousands of smaller cities and towns. Transparently stupendous in dimension, the social and economic consequences of construction of the interstates have yet to be measured by social scientists.

Making travel by car—and also bus—faster and safer, the interstate highway system signaled the long-predicted demise of the traditional intercity passenger train, that is, the intercity passenger train owned and operated by a private carrier. The railroads of the United States recorded a total of 21.2 million passenger-train miles in 1960, 10.7 million in 1970. That the end of the traditional passenger train was at hand became manifest on December 3, 1967, when the most celebrated train in the history of American railroading, the New York Central System's Twentieth Century Limited, made its final run between New York and Chicago. All save a handful of intercity passenger trains followed the fabled Century into oblivion on April 30, 1971, and on the next day a corporation of the federal government, the National Railroad Passenger Corporation, began operating a skeletal passenger train service (skeletal, that is, except in the Boston-New York-Washington "corridor") under the name of AMTRAK.

At the same time that Americans were deserting passenger trains by the millions, they were crowding aboard the sleek planes of the country's airlines in ever-increasing numbers. The domestic air carriers of the United States recorded a total of 34 billion passenger-miles in 1960, 119 billion in 1970. Occasional crashes of airliners—and also the intermittent highjacking (or "skyjacking") of a big plane, as in August of 1961, when a onetime convict and his 16-year-old son held a gun to the head of the pilot of a Boeing 707 of Continental Airlines and ordered him to fly the craft to Cuba—deterred few travelers from taking to the airways.

Air travelers took passage aboard such splendid new aircraft as the trijet Boeing 727 and twin-jet Douglas DC-9, both put in service in the early 1960s. After 1969, American travelers bound for an overseas destination were not unlikely to find themselves streaking through the skies in one of the cavernous Boeing 747s. A wide-bodied or "jumbo" jet, the 747 could accommodate an incredible 360 to 490 passengers (depending on the configuration of its interior). And before long it would be possible for overseas travelers to make their way from the United States to Europe in three hours instead of five, for in 1969 the Anglo-French Concorde, a supersonic airliner, made its first successful test flight.

Although a jet airliner offered the fastest means of moving about the country, the private automobile nonetheless remained the principal conveyance of Americans who traveled from city to city, the more so as the interstate highways opened to traffic. In 1960, private automobiles carried an estimated 90.1 percent of the intercity passenger traffic (706 billion passenger-miles), in 1970 an estimated 86.6 percent (more than a trillion passenger-miles).

For the domestic manufacturers of automobiles, the enduring passion that scores of millions of Americans continued to feel for the automobile spelled continuing prosperity. During the years 1962–65 in particular, the industry led the entire national economy to new peaks of prosperity. Meanwhile sales of imported cars continued to climb—from 499,000 in 1960 to 1.2 million in 1970. Far and away, the most popular import was the Volkswagen, built in West Germany. As for Japanese cars, the first Toyota had been sold in the United States in 1958, but sales remained modest, and in 1970 auto buyers in the United States purchased only 381,000 cars of Japanese manufacture.

# COMPUTERS AND PHOTOCOPIERS

Through the 1960s, the computer industry, increasingly concentrating on "minicomputers," which compared with the first generation of computers were small and flexible, expanded at a rate of about 10 percent per year, and indeed ranked as the fastest-growing major industry in the world during the decade. The value of its output totaled $5.67 billion in 1970. The premier manufacturer of computers and computer equipment was IBM, whose sales during the latter 1960s represented 70 percent of the total for the industry. Its dramatic growth notwithstanding, the computer industry was highly competitive, and not all computer companies found prosperity. After five years of failure to achieve profitability with its computer operations, for example, the electronics giant RCA in 1971 exited the computer business.

Spurring the impressive growth of the computer industry during the 1960s was an almost mind-boggling expansion in the application of computers. Beginning in 1962, computers were employed to set type for newspapers. Then, in 1966, they provided the basis for an electronic type-composition system—one that completely bypassed mechanical typesetting. Railroads put computers to work to improve accounting and payroll operations, provide shippers with up-to-date information on the movement of cargoes, and provide management with copious data on which to base cost, rate, and marketing decisions. By feeding data into what one writer described as whirring electronic wizards at its National Computing Center in Martinsburg, West Virginia, the Internal Revenue Service could determine whether taxpayers had reported all of their incomes and whether deductions claimed by taxpayers seemed reasonable. Assorted libraries came to rely on computers to produce catalog cards, book catalogs, and reading lists. The Post Office Department in 1968 spent $33.5 million to install a computer system at Paramus, New Jersey, that would enable managers to adjust work crews to the flow of mail in 14 eastern cities. The department calculated that in terms of man-hours saved the system would pay for itself within three years. By resolving within a few minutes perhaps a million equations that in former times would have occupied dedicated scientists for several years, computers became indispensable to research chemists. High-speed computation also dramatically enhanced the productivity of—and, equally important perhaps, opened new vistas to—anthropologists, astronomers, biologists, economists, geographers, political scientists, social and economic historians, and sociologists.

At the same time that some men and women were designing and building more powerful and more sophisticated computers, others were perfecting the process and improving the machinery used in electrostatic copying—or xerography (a term that derives from two Greek words, *xeros,* which means dry, and *graphia,* meaning writing). In xerography, invented in 1938 by the American physicist Chester F. Carlson, a drum, belt, or plate coated with light-sensitive material is charged with static electricity. Light is then reflected from the item being copied through a lens, whereupon a positively charged image corresponding to the dark areas of the original copy forms on the light-sensitive surface. At that point, the remainder of the surface loses its charge of static electricity. Next, negatively charged powdered ink, or toner, is dusted onto the surface and adheres to the image. The inked image is thereupon transferred to positively charged paper and heated for an instant. When the heat melts the toner, the result is a permanent copy.

Development of the process of xerography by the Haloid Company of Stamford, Connecticut, did not result in a satisfactory electrostatic copying machine until 1959. Two years later, in 1961, the Haloid Company became the Xerox Corporation. Before long, Xerox and other manufacturers were turning out electrostatic copying machines by the tens of thousands, and the results were far-reaching. Research scholars could photocopy documents and other materials (for example, the pages of books and journals) instead of taking copious notes by hand or with typewriters. Classroom teachers could distribute photocopies of selected passages from novels and books of poems to students, not to mention copies of maps and graphs, for their perusal. More notable perhaps, office secretaries could photocopy letters, memoranda, reports, and other materials that in the past could be reproduced only with typewriter and carbon paper (or mimeograph or duplicating machines that required a specially prepared—usually stenciled—original that turned out copies of modest quality). Xerography, indeed, produced a veritable revolution in the modus operandi of the offices of businesses, government agencies, hospitals, libraries, schools, and other enterprises in the United States and across much of the world. By the late 1960s, a half-million electrostatic copiers were turning out 10 billion copies per year.

## MEDICINE, HEALTH, AND THE GREEN REVOLUTION

Meanwhile, impressive developments and happenings were taking place in the field of medical science that directly touched the lives of great numbers of Americans. Among those developments was the perfection of vaccines to prevent measles and rubella (German measles). To be sure, antibiotic drugs had taken the measure of secondary bacterial infections, notably pneumonia, which before 1945 had taken the lives of thousands of measles victims annually. Unfortunately, complications resulting from measles continued to claim the lives of several hundred Americans each year. On occasion, the measles virus also caused measles encephalitis, an inflammation of the brain that sometimes resulted in mental retardation. Then, in 1963, largely as a consequence of the enterprise of John F. Enders and Thomas C. Peebles, a measles vaccine became available. The outcome? The number of measles cases reported annually in the United States before 1963 had totaled about 4 million; the number reported in 1968 came to 220,000. As for rubella, it produced a veritable array of congenital malformations in fetuses when contracted by expectant mothers during the early months of pregnancy. But in 1966, Paul D. Parkman and Harry M. Myer, Jr., reported the development of a rubella vaccine, and by the mid-1970s rubella appeared to have become a disease of the past in the United States.

Nearly every branch of medical science registered important advances during the 1960s. Researchers developed enzymes that reduced inflammation and blood clots—also new penicillins that were capable of attacking germs that had become resistant to older penicillins. Corneal transplants in which the clouded or scarred window of the eye in front of the pupil and iris was replaced with clean and healthy tissues obtained from the cornea of someone who had died within the preceding five hours, became a common surgical procedure. Other researchers experimented with the use of the laser in eye surgery. The physician William M. Chardack and engineer Watson Greatbatch developed a transistorized, self-contained internal pacemaker to prevent heart failure and regulate the beat of the heart.

Improvements in treatment techniques dramatically increased the remission rate for children who had fallen victim of acute leukemia. In former times, more than half of all children stricken with acute leukemia had routinely died within four months, 95 percent within a year. Now, as a consequence of the new treatment techniques, 90 percent of such children were surviving for one year, 60 percent for as many as five years. Researchers in 1964 and 1965 perfected an intrauterine contraceptive device (IUD): a tiny loop, usually made of plastic, that was inserted in a woman's uterus and, most researchers thought, prevented conception by altering tubal motility (although some researchers suspected that the device triggered very early abortions of fertilized eggs). Unlike oral contraceptives, which on occasion caused high blood pressure and blood clots, the IUD had no apparent side effects that prompted concern. Moreover, the device was always in place, whereas the pill required a daily regimen that could generate confusion and mistakes, particularly among poorly educated women.

Increasingly effective drugs to combat rheumatoid arthritis and related inflammatory diseases were developed during the 1960s. Researchers discovered that disoldium cromoglycatem, a drug that inhibits the release of various mediators of the anaphylactic (or allergic) response, provided victims of asthma with a defense against attacks. Other researchers found new methods for prolonging the lives of victims of inoperable cancer, and also new methods for relieving the pain suffered by cancer victims. Nearly every hospital of any size set up an intensive care unit during the 1960s. In such a unit, a patient could be resuscitated and given artificial assistance in cases of cardiac, circulatory, kidney, or respiratory failure. Indeed, the accelerating demand by hospitals for electrical life-support and monitoring devices fostered a new paramedical industry, generally referred to as bioelectronics.

Although they resulted in the saving of greater numbers of lives, intensive care units generated less interest among Americans at large than organ transplants. Like the astronaut who rode a minuscule vehicle into the dark reaches of outer space, the surgical team that removed an organ from the body of one human being and implanted it in another was maneuvering on a frontier of science that hitherto had been explored only by the imaginations of science fiction writers. Its activity, in a word, contained the stuff of high drama. Requiring the most difficult surgical procedure was transplantation of the liver.

Unfortunately, the results of liver transplants, first executed in the latter 1960s, were not encouraging. Far more successful were kidney transplants, particularly if the donor was a sibling of the recipient of the transplanted kidney. First performed in the 1950s, the transplantation of kidneys became more frequent during the 1960s when researchers developed improved methods to suppress the body's immune reaction to transplanted tissues.

The transplantation of a heart from the body of one human being—after the person had been pronounced dead—to the body of another (who, because of the extent of disease to his or her own heart, had almost no life expectancy) generated even greater excitement among Americans. Never in history, indeed, had an achievement of medical science so captivated the popular imagination and so commanded the attention of the communications media. The heart transplantation procedure rested on a variety of discoveries and developments in recent decades, most notably the development in the early 1950s by the surgeon John H. Gibbons, Jr., and his associates at the Jefferson Medical College in Philadelphia (with engineering and financial support by the IBM corporation) of the pump-oxygenator, or heart-lung machine. Taking over the functions of the heart and lungs during surgery, the heart-lung machine, its performance greatly improved by other researchers in the latter 1950s and the 1960s, permitted the surgical team that was performing an open-heart operation to stop the heart for an extended period and work in a dry field with good visibility.

Heart surgeons began serious consideration of heart (or cardiac) transplantation in the early 1960s. Then, in Cape Town in South Africa in December of 1967, 44-year-old Chistiaan N. Barnard and a team of 30 surgeons, anesthesiologists, nurses, and technicians performed the first cardiac transplant that was considered technically successful. Barnard and his team implanted the heart of a 24-year-old woman who had died in an automobile crash in the body of a 55-year-old businessman, Louis Washkansky, a victim of diabetes whose fibrotic heart had nearly given out. A few days later, Washkansky was sitting up, taking solid food, and engaging in animated conversation. But then he came down with pneumonia and died. He had survived for 18 days following the surgery. A short time later, in January 1968, Barnard and his associates implanted a "new" heart in Philip Blaiberg, a 58-year-old dentist. After overcoming complications that appeared to have been a result of tissue rejection reactions, Blaiberg resumed a normal routine, which, he told reporters, included sexual relations with his wife.

During 1968, surgeons in Britain, Canada, Czechoslovakia, India, Israel, South America, and the United States performed more than a hundred heart transplants. The most active surgeon in the field in the United States was Denton Cooley of Houston, who in one 5-day period replaced three diseased hearts. Unfortunately, heart transplants in the 1960s proved more spectacular than successful, for only a fraction of those individuals who received "new" hearts survived for as long as one year. And when Philip Blaiberg died in August of 1970, 19 months after his surgery, so one writer commented, "The enthusiasm for cardiac transplantation appeared to die with him." After 1970, in truth, the operation was rarely performed. As with kidney transplantation, surgical teams performing heart transplants found it hard to counter the impulse of the body's immunization system to reject alien tissue. But at length, in the early 1980s, researchers perfected improved drugs to counter tissue rejection, whereupon heart surgeons accelerated their activity in the field of heart transplantation—and with demonstrably improved results.

Less publicized than heart transplants, another surgical procedure perfected in the latter 1960s was of far greater importance: the coronary bypass. The aim of the bypass procedure was to counter coronary artery disease, which clogs the arteries that course over the surface of the heart and supply blood to the heart muscle itself. The procedure usually involves removal of the saphenous vein from the leg of the patient and use of sections of the vein to make one or more bypasses around the obstructed arteries—that is, inserting one end of the graft into the aorta and the other into a coronary artery beyond the point of obstruction.

The pioneer in the field of coronary bypassing was René G. Favaloro. A native of Argentina who had spent more than a decade as a rural practitioner, Favaloro arrived in the United States in 1962, and at length became chief resident at the Cleveland Clinic. His special interest was thoracic and cardiovascular surgery. Then, in May of 1967, the 44-year-old Argentinian operated on a woman who had endured angina pectoris during the past three years, a result, he determined, of a complete occlusion of a coronary artery. After removing a segment of the saphenous vein from the woman's leg, he sewed one end of the vein into the aorta and the other into the coronary artery beyond the point of obstruction. By thus bypassing the point of obstruction, the vein reestablished the flow of blood in the artery. The medical historians James Bordley III and A. McGehee Harvey reported that the patient recovered and suffered no further attacks of angina pectoris. Over the next four years, before Favalora returned to Argentina, he and his associates at the Cleveland Clinic performed coronary bypass operations on 2,200 patients. The operative mortality rate was only 3 percent. Surgeons performed the operation on hundreds of thousands of individuals during the 1970s and 1980s, and the result was the prolongation of uncounted lives.

Likewise preoccupied with prolonging life were medical researchers who during the 1960s brought forth overwhelming evidence, mainly statistical, that cigarette smoking constituted a hazard to the health of smokers. Most striking were the statistics regarding lung cancer. A preponderance of the recent victims of lung cancer, the incidence of which had increased dramatically in recent decades (at the same time that the per capita consumption of cigarettes was also increasing dramatically), were shown to have been moderate to heavy smokers of cigarettes—as were most victims of emphysema, a disease marked by the swelling and atrophying of tissues in the lungs and resultant impairment of breathing. The upshot of the research was a concerted attack on cigarette smoking that received powerful reinforcement in 1964 when an advisory committee to the surgeon general of the United States issued a report entitled "Smoking and Health" that was nothing less than an indictment of cigarettes.

The attack on cigarettes featured magazine and television announcements designed to dissuade Americans, particularly younger ones, from taking up cigarette smoking, or, if they were already "hooked" on cigarettes, to "join the unhooked generation" by "kicking" the cigarette habit. A special target of the antismoking campaign was television commercials promoting cigarettes that almost invariably portrayed smoking as a diversion of beautiful, active, and sophisticated young people. The antismoking campaign struck a popular chord, and in 1966 Congress passed legislation requiring that packs of cigarettes sold in the United States henceforth include the warning "Caution: Cigarette smoking may be hazardous to your health." Then, in 1970, the Federal Communications Commission decreed that after January 1, 1971, radio and TV stations in the United States would be prohibited from broadcasting commercials promoting cigarettes. The FCC acted despite the laments of radio and TV broadcasters (who stood to lose more than $200 million a year in advertising revenue as a result of that action) and the interminable complaint of the cigarette industry that science had failed to prove a link between the smoking of cigarettes and disease.

The results of the campaign against cigarette smoking were transparent. Believing (or at least hoping) that filters prevented most of the toxic substances in cigarettes from passing into their bodies, great numbers of smokers turned to filter-tipped cigarettes. Millions of others reduced their consumption of cigarettes—and other millions gave up the cigarette habit altogether. Of larger moment perhaps, uncounted potential smokers declined to take up the habit. In 1968, accordingly, for the first time since the antismoking campaign got under way, the consumption of cigarettes in the United States declined.

Men and women meanwhile, were exploring the depths of the world's oceans and isolating the human gene, but arguably the most important achievement by individuals who toiled on the frontiers of science and technology during the 1960s was brought to fruition by teams of plant pathologists who developed hybrid strains of corn, rice, and wheat that, when properly irrigated and adequately treated with chemical fertilizers and pesticides, would result in dramatically increased yields. The outcome was the "Green Revolution." Of incalculable importance to the poverty-ridden and malnourished countries of the Third World, the Green Revolution held out the hope that, provided birthrates could be controlled, the incidence of hunger and famine across the globe might be substantially reduced.

The premier personage of the Green Revolution was Norman E. Bourlaug, the shy and retiring head of the International Maize and Wheat Center near Mexico City. Born on a farm near Cresco, Iowa, in 1914, the son of Norwegian immigrants, Borlaug received a Ph.D. in plant pathology from the University of Minnesota in 1941, studied the effects of new chemicals on plants and plant diseases as an employee of the E.I. du Pont de Nemours & Company in Delaware for three years, then, in 1944, set off for Mexico as part of a small team of agricultural scientists assembled by the Rockefeller Foundation (at the request of the Mexican Ministry of Agriculture) whose purpose was to export the U.S. agricultural revolution to Mexico. Borlaug's most notable achievement was the development of high-yield, highly adaptable dwarf wheats. Using hybrid seeds developed by Borlaug, India increased its output of wheat from 12 million tons in 1965 to 21 million tons in 1970. In recognition of his accomplishments, the Nobel Committee in 1970 awarded Borlaug the Nobel Peace Prize, the first agricultural scientist to be so honored.

## ARCHITECTURE, ART, THEATER, LITERATURE

The enterprise of the architects of any period of history in one way or another touches the consciousness of most of their contemporaries, and that of succeeding generations as well. It was at the turn of the 1960s that architects developed the split-level and bilevel design that guided the construction of hundreds of thousands of middle- and upper-income residences in new subdivisions that took form on the fringes of cities and towns across the length and breadth of the republic. Regarding the large and more permanent structures that imprint the minds of most people upon mention of the word architecture, what was described as a sculptural trend was apparent during the early years of the 1960s in two projects designed by Eero Saarinen. One was the terminal of Dulles International Airport outside Washington, a structure whose two parallel rows of 65-foot concrete stanchions supports the swung roof canopy after the fashion of a hammock. The other was the TWA terminal at Idlewild (later Kennedy) International Airport in New York, its external shape, it was often said, akin to a giant bird graced with huge concrete wings. Buildings designed during the latter 1960s tended to be large of scale (even when modest in actual dimension) and aggressively sculptured in form.

Still, the conservative school of Ludwig Mies van der Rohe retained much of its former vitality, particularly during the middle 1960s. A major achievement of the Mies school was the Chicago Circle campus of the University of Illinois, designed by Walter Netsch. Grouped by building type—administrative, auditorium, classroom laboratory—the individual buildings, one of them a helical building for the School of Arts and Architecture, were clustered about what was described as a two-level circulation. More in vogue, particularly in the latter 1960s, was what some critics deplored as "playboy" architecture, the premier example of which was the 55-story pyramidical skyscraper topped by a 240-foot spire that was built for the Transamerica Corporation in San Francisco.

Architectural criticism during the 1960s transcended design. Critics lamented construction of the New York Port Authority's World Trade Center—two identical towers of 110 stories designed by Minoru Yamasaki—on the grounds that the giant building would further strain Manhattan's already overly taxed transportation facilities by bringing an additional 130,000 workers and visitors into the area on a typical weekday. Other critics deplored the razing of Pennsylvania Station in New York, a magnificent example of the Victorian architecture of the second half of the nineteenth century, to make way for construction of the new Madison Square Garden.

While architects were at work, other citizens were investing their talents and energies in an array of artistic enterprises. Unfortunately, those who sought to express themselves via painting achieved minimal success in the 1960s. That works executed in the "pop" style, that is, the hyperrealistic commentaries on the visual monstrosities of the modern environment, for example, Andy Warhol's portrayal of Campbell's soup cans, attracted more attention than other types of painting testified to the low estate of painting in the United States during those years. If most serious critics thought poorly of paintings of the pop school, they tended to be no more generous in their appraisal of those executed by painters of the "new realism" school, which attracted wide attention at the end of the decade. The work of the new realists, critics complained, simply aped photography. Some painters, in truth, became sculptors, in some measure no doubt because art critics of the 1960s tended to be more lavish in their acclaim of the largely abstract enterprise of sculptors than that of painters.

The 1960s were a time of achievement in the field of classical music. Supported by generous grants by the Ford Foundation, city after city across the United States organized symphony orchestras, and indeed there was a shortage of established conductors to lead them. Doubtless the best-known classical musician of the time was Leonard Bernstein, conductor of the New York Philharmonic, the only conductor in the country's history whose name was widely recognized among the vast throng of Americans who knew little and cared less about classical music. Another of the premier personages in the field during the 1960s was Beverly Sills, the Brooklyn-born coloratura soprano of the New York City Opera whose virtuoso performances stirred audiences and won the acclaim of critics in America and across the world.

A succession of memorable musical events marked the period, one of them a performance by the renowned cellist Pablo Casals before President and Mrs. Kennedy and a gathering of musicians and composers, critics and government dignitaries at the White House in 1961. Casals had performed once before at the White House, in 1904, when Theodore Roosevelt was its occupant. But the most glittering musical event of the 1960s came to pass on the evening of September 16, 1966, when the doors of the new Metropolitan Opera House in New York formally opened with the premiere of Samuel Barber's *Antony and Cleopatra*. Heading the audience of 3,800 people were President and Mrs. Johnson and many of the elite of society and the arts. As for the building, an architectural masterpiece by Wallace K. Harrison, its interior marked by an upward circling double staircase, glistening chandeliers, and colorful murals, it stands majestically on the horizon of New York City's Lincoln Center.

The field of dance in America gained immeasurably in prestige and popular acceptance during the 1960s. The number of dance performances in the United States increased by about 200 percent in the course of the decade, and, in the view of critics, there was a corresponding improvement in the technical skills of American dancers. Ballet companies, including the Ballet of Los Angeles,

New York City Ballet, and Robert Joffrey Ballet, offered productions that won the praise of critics. At least as highly regarded were the efforts of companies performing modern dance, generally acknowledged to be America's unique contribution to dance in the twentieth century. As she had been since the 1940s, the inestimable Martha Graham remained the premier figure in the field of modern dance during the 1960s. Although near the end of her career as an active performer, Graham stirred audiences in 1969 by dancing the role of Hecuba, the queen of Troy, in *Cortège of Eagles.*

From the perspective of the thirty or so theaters that lined Broadway in New York City, the 1960s were considerably less than a golden era. For the most part, only musical productions seemed capable of attracting audiences that resulted in satisfactory returns for theaters—and scarcely a handful of new musicals (as opposed to the revival of musicals of former decades) achieved large box-office success. One of the more successful musicals of the period was *Camelot* (1961), the King Arthur comedy by Alan Jay Lerner and Frederick Loewe whose strength resided in pleasant music, a few interesting lyrics, and an effective cast headed by Julie Andrews. Another was *Hello Dolly!* (1964). Adapted from Thornton Wilder's philosophical farce *The Matchmaker, Hello Dolly!,* in the words of one critic, provided a lavish vehicle for the comedienne Carol Channing.

Among nonmusical productions, many of the best that Broadway offered through the 1960s were imported from Great Britain, a consequence of a renaissance in British theater. Such a production was the biographical dramatization of the life of Sir Thomas More, *A Man for All Seasons,* which opened on Broadway in 1962 with a largely British cast. As for plays by American authors, a few won critical acclaim (but not always box-office success), among them Tad Mosel's Pultzer Prize-winning *All the Way Home* and Dore Schray's *Advise and Consent,* both of which opened during the season of 1960–1961. Of larger moment was Edward Albee's *Who's Afraid of Virginia Woolf?* (1963), starring Uta Hagen and Arthur Hill, a searing study of marital discord whose savagery and acrid language offended many people.

By the latter 1960s, theatrical productions were mirroring new currents of thought and behavior that were moving about the country. Such a production was the rock musical *Hair* that originally opened off-Broadway in 1967. In its off-Broadway version, *Hair* was a spirited and good-natured hippie folk musical. But then it was rewritten, recast, and restaged by Tom O'Horgan, an exponent of the "new theater," the principal innovations of which were audience confrontation and sexual explicitness. In its new incarnation, it opened on Broadway in the spring of 1968. Offering the first nude scene in the history of Broadway (men and women briefly deployed about a dimly lit stage), the revised *Hair* was a lurid and militant antiestablishment polemic. In the course of the production, which was without plot, performers moved through the aisles and in raucous language sought to offend and rattle the audience.

*Hair* seemed to set off what one writer referred to as a nudity fad. In *Sweet Eros,* which opened off-Broadway in 1968, an actress performed nude during the entire length of a one-act play. In *Ché!,* a political parable that opened off-

Broadway in March 1969, naked performers simulated sex acts to represent what the playwright (Lennox Raphael) perceived to be the relationship between the United States and Latin America. A climax of sorts was achieved (again off-Broadway) in June 1969 with the opening of *Oh! Calcutta!* Billed as "elegant erotica," *Oh! Calcutta!* was preoccupied almost exclusively with sex and performed largely in the nude. Generally accorded poor reviews by critics, it was a box-office smash.

During those years of the 1960s when the country was experiencing the high tide of the civil rights crusade, the youth rebellion, and the commitment of U.S. forces in the war in Vietnam, book publishers brought out thousands of new titles; tens of millions of Americans bought and read books. There were all kinds of books: commentaries on world and domestic affairs and problems, histories, and an incredible assortment of "how to" books and book aimed at aficionados of every conceivable type of hobby and sporting activity.

There were, of course, works of fiction. Like the decade and a half following World War II, American writers of fiction produced many books that were competently crafted and provocative but few, if any, that seemed apt to be viewed as classics by future generations. Considering that social ferment and an impulse to rebellion were widely thought to have made the years after the Great War of 1914–1918 perhaps the most illustrious in the history of American fiction, one might have expected the ferment that pervaded American society during the 1960s to yield similar results. Unfortunately, it did not. Perhaps historians of literature have tended to exaggerate the importance of ferment and rebellion when searching for the sources of literary achievement. That the passing (by his own hand) of Ernest Hemingway in 1961 and of William Faulkner in 1962 made much difference so far as concerned the record of literary achievement during the 1960s is doubtful, for both men had apparently long since lost the touch that had made them literary giants of previous generations.

Among the most highly regarded writers of fiction in the United States during the 1960s were Saul Bellow, Truman Capote, John O'Hara, Philip Roth, and John Updike. Among the more notable novels were Peter Beagle's *The Last Unicorn* (1968), Bellow's *Herzog* (1964), Richard Bradford's *Red Sky at Morning* (1968), Capote's "non-fiction novel" *In Cold Blood* (1966), Arthur Hailey's *Airport* (1968), Joseph Heller's bitterly satiric story of World War II, *Catch-22* (1961), Richard McKenna's *The Sand Pebbles* (1963), Edwin O'Connor's *All in the Family* (1966), O'Hara's *The Lockwood Concern* (1965), Katherine Anne Porter's best-selling *Ship of Fools* (1962), Charles Portis's *True Grit* (1968), Chaim Potok's *The Chosen* (1967), Philip Roth's raunchy but (so many people thought) hilarious *Portnoy's Complaint* (1969), William Styron's *The Confessions of Nat Turner* (1967), and Updike's *Of the Farm* (1965).

## POPULAR CULTURE

The reading of what were generally perceived to be quality novels (and also mysteries, romances, westerns, and tales of horror and incredible science, most of them of dubious literary merit that publishers cranked out by the millions) was a source of diversion for uncounted Americans during the 1960s. Another source of diversion was hunting and fishing. Some 23.3 million Americans bought fishing licenses in 1960, 31.1 million in 1970. Americans (and foreign visitors as well) flocked to the country's magnificent national parks: 26.6 million in 1960, 45.9 million in 1970. They drank beer: 24.02 gallons per capita in 1960, 28.55 in 1970. They also paused increasingly for nourishment and refreshment at the franchised outlets of McDonald's.

It was in 1954 that Ray A. Kroc, the owner of a small company that distributed milk shake mixers, observed that a small restaurant in San Bernadino, California, that sold only hamburgers, french fries, and milk shakes was doing a remarkable business. The restaurant's owners were two brothers, Mac and Dick McDonald. Kroc thereupon concluded an agreement with the McDonald brothers, under the term of which he would open a chain of drive-in restaurants modeled on their format. He opened the first McDonald's unit at Des Plaines, Illinois, a suburb of Chicago, on April 15, 1955. There were 228 McDonald's restaurants by 1960 (selling hamburgers at 15 cents apiece), 1,592 by 1970, each of them marked by twin "golden arches."

Male Americans found diversion in the 1960s by pondering the increasingly revealed figures of females. The years of Kennedy and Johnson were the period of the miniskirt, a fashion that sent hemlines several inches above the knee and shocked people of an earlier generation who could recall an era in which a self-respecting (and respectable) female publicly bared no part of her anatomy between the neck and ankles.

Males and females both found diversion in popular music and motion pictures. In popular music, one might label the Kennedy and Johnson years as the era of the Beatles, for it was in 1964 that four long-haired young men who had emerged from the grimy streets of Liverpool in England traveled to the United States and stirred the emotions of young Americans with rhythms and sounds that seemed to capture the many moods of the Now Generation. Following the Beatles across the Atlantic was another British group, the Rolling Stones, whose sounds and styles tended to be less inhibited than those of the Beatles. Other performers who captivated audiences were Bob Dylan, a sensitive young singer whose music often combined protest and nostalga, Joan Baez, a folk artist who sang of love and nonviolence, the "soul singers" Aretha Franklin and Jimi Hendrix, and the tough-talking and impassioned Janis Joplin. Then there was Johnny Cash, a craggy country singer whose ballads about convicts and railroad men and a boy named Sue appealed to Americans of all ages, colors, and regions.

As for motion pictures, many Americans, reading of the financial difficulties of old-line Hollywood studios, calculating the numbers of people who each evening sat before television sets rather than going to the movies, and noting that the annual output of motion pictures was a fraction of what it had been a decade or two before, were inclined to the view that the movies were a dying industry. Such was not the case, for the movies continued to have millions of devotees, particularly among younger Americans, who in the 1960s jammed movies houses to experience such films as *Romeo and Juliet*, one of the most tender films of the period; *The Sterile Cuckoo*, a story of young love in which

September 16, 1964: In their final appearance of a tour of the United States before returning to England, the Beatles perform at a charity show in New York City.

Liza Minelli gave a memorable performance; *Guess Who's Coming to Dinner?*, a searching story of interracial romance starring Katharine Hepburn, Spencer Tracy, and Sidney Poitier; *The Graduate,* a portrait of a confused adolescent starring Dustin Hoffman; *Dr. Strangelove,* a caustic antiwar comedy starring Peter Sellers; and *Bonnie and Clyde,* a blend of gore and humor based on the escapades of the infamous Barrow gang of the 1930s. The years of Kennedy and Johnson also were a time when Hollywood released several superb musical films, some of them adapted from stage productions, including *My Fair Lady,* starring Rex Harrison and Audrey Hepburn; *The Sound of Music* and *Mary Poppins,* starring Julie Andrews; and *Funny Girl* and *Hello Dolly!,* starring Barbra Streisand. The Walt Disney studios turned out a succession of delightful films for younger audiences, and for those Americans whose tastes drew them to "shoot-'em-up" westerns in which men were men—and minded their manners in front of women—the year 1969 produced the film *True Grit,* for his performance in which the veteran film hero John Wayne received an Academy Award.

Although most Americans went to the movies only intermittently or not at all during the 1960s, millions of them spent many hours each week in front of television sets. They watched "The Ed Sullivan Show," a variety show that had been introduced in the pristine days of television (in the late 1940s), such seemingly interminable series as "Lassie" and "Gunsmoke," "The Dick Van Dyke Show" (a situation comedy), "Ben Casey" (about a no-nonsense medical doctor), and "The Defenders" (about lawyers), game shows, such daytime soap operas as "The Young and the Restless" and "As the World Turns," evening news programs, and news documentaries. The period witnessed the advent of movies made exclusively for television, the National Geographic Society's superb programs exploring nature, and such irreverent and racy programs as "Laugh-In" and "The Smothers Brothers Comedy Hour" attracted millions of viewers each week. At the close of the 1960s, there appeared a program entitled "Sesame Street" that sought to provide young children with entertainment combined with instruction in letters and numbers. Seldom in the history of the medium had a program received such critical acclaim. The years of Kennedy and Johnson also witnessed many technical improvements in television production, the introduction of intercontinental programming via space satellites, and the virtual end of black-and-white transmission (except for old movies and old TV serials.)

No less than television—and in part because of it—spectator sports enjoyed another memorable era. The sport that experienced the most spectacular growth in popularity was professional football. So great was the enthusiasm for pro football that a new league, the American Football League, survived in spite of the scorn of the 40-year-old-National Football League, and in 1969 its champion, the New York Jets, guided by quarterback Joe Namath, defeated the Baltimore Colts of the NFL in the third annual Super Bowl. Meanwhile, major league baseball, long considered the national pastime, was under incessant criticism for being "too slow," and except during the World Series was a distant second to professional football as a TV attraction. Still, major league baseball drew record crowds, located franchises in such cities as Atlanta and Houston, Kansas City and Minneapolis-St. Paul, and produced some of the premier moments in sports during the period: in 1961, when Roger Maris of the Yankees broke the record of the legendary Babe Ruth by hitting 61 home runs in a single season, and in 1969, when the New York Mets, renowned since their formation in 1962 for bumbling futility, confounded the sports world by winning the National League championship and then overcoming the Baltimore Orioles in the World Series.

Elsewhere in sports, professional basketball was dominated by such superlative players as Bill Russell of the Boston Celtics and Wilt Chamberlain of the Philadelphia Seventy-Sixers. Thanks to television and such stellar performers as Arnold Palmer and Jack Nicklaus, professional golf achieved new levels of popularity. Thoroughbred racing continued to have a huge following, and each year on the first Saturday in May, at 4:30 P.M., the national attention, via radio and TV, appeared to fix on the Kentucky Derby. Featuring such celebrated drivers as A. J. Foyt, Jr., and Mario Andretti, open-cockpit motor racing won millions of new adherents among Americans who responded to the roar or turbo-charged internal-combustion engines—and indeed no one-day sporting event in the world attracted as many spectators (more than 300,000) as the annual 500-mile auto race at Indianapolis. Motor sports aficionados also warmed to the derring-do of such stock-car drivers as Fireball Roberts (who died as a result of burns sustained in a crash) and the incomparable Richard Petty.

The central figure in boxing during the years of Kennedy and Johnson was Cassius Clay, who after joining the Black Muslim sect changed his name to Muhammad Ali. One of the quickest and most agile boxers in the history of the sport—one who claimed to "float like a butterfly and sting like a bee"—Ali won the heavyweight title from Charles "Sonny" Liston in 1964, handily defeated all challengers, and then was stripped from his title when, on the grounds, that he was a conscientious objector, he refused to be drafted into the armed forces. The best tennis players of the period were the Australians Rod Laver and John Newcombe. The stellar American performer was bespectacled Billie Jean King. The Toronto Maple Leafs finally broke the dominance of the Montreal Canadiens in professional hockey, but the Detroit Red Wings boasted hockey's outstanding player of the period, the talented Gordy Howe. Intercollegiate sports also enjoyed rampant prosperity and had a variety of superlative performers, for example, Namath and O. J. Simpson in football and John Havlicek and Lew Alcindor (later Kareem Abdul Jabbar) in basketball. One superteam, the Bruins of the University of California at Los Angeles, under the guidance of Coach John Wooden, totally dominated college basketball in the latter 1960s. Meanwhile, as television broadened its coverage, American sports enthusiasts became increasingly interested in the Olympic games.

In the winter games at Innsbruck in 1964, athletes representing the United States managed just 6 medals (only 1 of them gold), those representing the Soviet Union 25. But at the summer games in Tokyo, athletes from the United States, overshadowed by the Soviets in recent Olympiads, made an impressive comeback. Although the Soviets won more medals all told, 96–90, the Americans won the larger number of those that were gold, 36–30. Among the memorable performances by Americans was that by the sprinter Robert Hayes, who equaled the world record in the 100-meter dash. Only one American won a gold medal at the Winter Olympics at Grenoble in France in 1968. But that American was 19-year-old Peggy Fleming, a soft-spoken and petite brunette, sometimes described as an ice ballerina, almost universally considered the most graceful skater ever to beautify an arena. At the summer games in Mexico City, U.S. athletes once again were dominant, winning 107 medals (45 of them gold) to 91 (29 of them gold) for Soviet athletes. Of special note was the performance of the U.S. swimming team. Led by Charles Hickox, the winner of 2 gold medals, and Debbie Meyers, the winner of 3, American swimmers won 23 of the 33 gold medals awarded in the sport.

Alas, the games of 1968 are best remembered for the action of Tommie Smith and John Carlos of the U.S. track and field team. After finishing first and third, respectively, in the 200-meter dash, Smith and Carlos, both of them black, wore black gloves on their right hands when they mounted the platform

February 1968: The world champion of women's figure skating, Peggy Fleming, works out at Grenoble, France, during the Winter Olympics.

during the victory ceremony. When the band played "The Star-Spangled Banner," the two athletes raised clenched fists above their heads in black power salutes. Millions of their compatriots back in the United States felt embarrassment tinctured with outrage. (Their annoyance was assuaged when the black American boxer George Foreman, after winning the heavyweight championship, paraded about the ring waving a small Stars and Stripes.)

Finally, one ought to take note of one of the greatest sports performers in America during the 1960s, a young man who received comparatively little publicity: Jim Ryun, the human running machine from the plains of Kansas. Shortly after completing his freshman year at Kansas University, in July of 1966, the 19-year-old Ryun lowered the world record for the mile run to 3 minutes, 51.3 seconds. Only 12 years before, in 1954, Roger Bannister of Great Britain had shattered the myth that no human could run a mile in less than 4 minutes by running one in 3:59.5. Had Bannister been on the track with Ryun at Berkeley, California, in July of 1966 and achieved a time identical to that during his historic performance of 1954, he would have finished 60 yards behind the Kansas flyer.

## RETROSPECT

In Webster's *New World Dictionary*, the word *ferment*, part of this chapter's title, is defined as "a state of excitement or agitation." Although no period of the recorded experience of humankind in any part of the world has been without excitement and agitation, it does seem fair to say that the years in which John Kennedy and Lyndon Johnson presided over the national destiny generated an unusual measure of excitement and agitation in the United States. Certainly, the historians and other writers who have commented on the society of the North American superpower during the 1960s have tended to emphasize the ferment, disruption, and tumult that marked those years. Consider Gerald Howard's volume entitled *The Sixties: Our Most Explosive Decade* and William L. O'Neill's "informal" history of the decade, *Coming Apart*, Arthur M. Schlesinger, Jr.'s *Violence: America in the Sixties* and Milton Viorst's *Fire in the Streets: America in the 1960's*. It seems fair to say, moreover, that if one were to conduct a survey among present-day Americans who were 20 years of age or older during the 1960s, a substantial majority would agree that ferment was, indeed, central to the life of the United States during that historical season. Few of those surveyed would be apt to find it difficult to enumerate examples of the agitation and tumult that marked the decade.

Still, most Americans during the 1960s did not participate in civil rights demonstrations or ghetto riots, burn draft cards or flaunt Vietcong flags, call policemen pigs or express contempt for the traditional values and folkways of the national society, trip out on LSD or live in hippie communes. However dismayed and often exercised by the carryings-on of protesters and social rebels—and however their own attitudes and behavior might be influenced by various of the attitudes and modes of behavior adopted by protesters and rebels—all save a comparative handful of Americans in the 1960s managed their lives in about the same way as they had during the 1950s. For most Americans, then, life tended to be humdrum and routine. Day in and day out, year in and year out, whether in the crowded confines of the Bronx or in the scrubby valleys of Appalachia, the luxuriant prairies of middle Illinois or the thriving coastal areas of California, a preponderance of Americans toiled and studied, reaped and sowed, dreamed and despaired, loved and hated, laughed and cried, sang and danced, worshipped and mourned—more or less after the fashion of those hundreds of millions of other Americans who over the previous two centuries had taken passage on the national voyage across the expanse of time. Families, jobs, careers, housing, food, drink, clothing, cars, health, movies, TV, sports, and vacations, continued to be at the center of the concerns and interests of most Americans.

Indeed, if the ferment of the 1960s has tended to command the attention of historians and others who have written and spoken about the seventh decade of the twentieth century (and are the aspects of life in the 1960s that made the most enduring imprint on the minds and spirits of Americans who experienced it), it is nonetheless arguable that trends and happenings that had little if anything to do with disruption and agitation were, in the long view of history, of equal and perhaps larger moment. Most notably, future generations of historical scholars may very well look back on the 1960s and conclude that the achievements of men and women of science and technology—advances recorded in humankind's interminable war against disease and infection, the Green Revolution, further development of the digital computer, perfection of the electrostatic copying machine, not to mention the continuing exploration of outer space and the beginning of the revolution in global communications— were at least as important as was all of the agitation and disruption and tumult that exhilarated millions of Americans during the 1960s and dismayed and exasperated, distressed and infuriated many millions of others.

# Chapter
# 8

---

# Anguish and Triumph

*H*owever discouraged by the refusal of the communists to give up their dream of conquest in Vietnam and the anger and dissension, discord and turmoil that had afflicted the national society in recent years, Lyndon Johnson at the dawn of 1968 found satisfaction in assorted happenings and developments in 1966 and 1967, and, accordingly, felt confident that he would secure election to another term in the White House the following November. With consent of the Senate, he had placed a black man on the Supreme Court. At his behest, Congress had approved legislation establishing the Department of Transportation, passed the Truth-in-Packaging Act, Highway Safety Act, Model Cities Act, and a new GI Bill of Rights for men and women who had served in the armed forces since 1955. Various happenings in foreign affairs had likewise brought satisfaction to the president. Johnson's personal emissary Cyrus

Vance had mediated the latest round in the ancient feud between Greeks and Turks on the island of Cyprus. A coup in the West African state of Ghana had toppled Kwame Nkrumah, a leftist dictator renowned for his shrill anti-Americanism. A military junta led by General Soeharto had thwarted a coup, widely believed to have been masterminded in Beijing, that sought to bring the Indonesian archipelago under communist control. Making use of the hot line linking Washington and Moscow, Johnson and leaders of the Soviet Union had avoided a confrontation during the Six-Day War of 1967, in which Israel drove the forces of Egypt out of the Sinai Peninsula, those of Jordan out of the Old City of Jerusalem and the West Bank (that is, the area between Israel and the Jordan River), and those of Syria out of the Golan Heights on Israel's northeast frontier.

## PUEBLO AND TET

But then, on January 23, 1968, Johnson and his compatriots endured a new shock: Four North Korean gunboats seized a lightly armed intelligence vessel, the USS *Pueblo*, in the Sea of Japan off the coast of North Korea. Commanded by Lt. Comdr. Lloyd C. Bucher, the *Pueblo* surrendered without a fight. On reaching port, the North Koreans locked Bucher and 81 other officers and men of the *Pueblo* in prison, where in the months that followed the Americans were beaten and subjected to cruelties intended to persuade them to sign confessions that they had been guilty of espionage. Several of the U.S. seamen signed. As for Johnson, he determined to avoid a precipitous response to the *Pueblo* outrage lest he provoke the North Koreans to execute Bucher and his men or touch off a new war in East Asia which, because of its involvement in Vietnam, the United States would be ill-prepared to fight. Fortunately, after months of vexing negotiations, in December of 1968, the North Koreans released the captives—also a coffin containing the remains of the one American seaman who had died during the *Pueblo*'s confrontation with the North Korean gunboats eleven months before.

One week after learning of the seizure of the *Pueblo*, the people of the United States absorbed yet another shock: On January 30–31, 1968, the North Vietnamese and Vietcong unleashed a monstrous assault against the cities of South Vietnam while the South Vietnamese people were celebrating the *Tet* holiday. Communist leaders calculated that the offensive would touch off a popular uprising against the Saigon government, whereupon the Americans would agree forthwith to establishment of a communist-dominated coalition regime for South Vietnam—and, of course, to withdrawal of U.S. forces from the country.

The so-called *Tet* offensive was an incredible performance. During the early weeks of January, the communists smuggled tons of munitions and supplies into South Vietnam's cities, and carefully hid them away, for example, in coffins in cemeteries and in rented buildings. Then, in the last days of January, under cover of a cease-fire in observance of *Tet* that they, the Saigon gov-

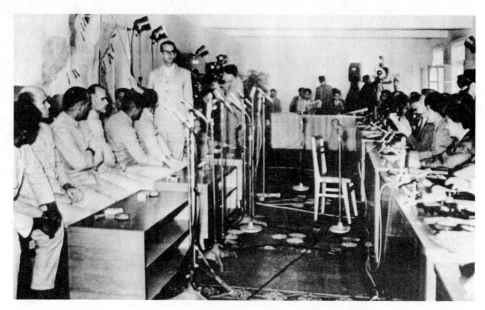

September 12, 1968: Crewmen of the USS *Pueblo* face foreign reporters in a press conference arranged by their North Korean captors.

ernment, and the U.S. command had agreed to, the communists slipped thousands of guerrillas and additional arms and ammunition (much of it moved over the border from Cambodia) into Saigon and 26 provincial capitals. At the same time, North Vietnamese and VC units moved into position on the outskirts of the cities, and set up rocket launchers and mortar tubes. Then, on January 30 and 31, the communists let fly their *Tet* offensive. What transpired was mind-boggling.

While rockets and mortar shells crashed into downtown areas, squads of guerrillas, armed with small weapons and satchel charges of high explosives, roamed city streets, seeking out and killing public officials, blowing up strategic installations, and in general touching off mass confusion and terror. In Saigon, a squad of VC blasted a hole in the wall surrounding the U.S. embassy, rushed through the opening and took up positions in the embassy buildings, then held out for more than six hours against American troops who were brought in to reinforce the three marines who had been assigned to guard the embassy. At the same time, the communists sought to stir the South Vietnamese people to revolt against the Saigon government.

Through the first days of February of 1968, the communists continued to pound urban areas up and down South Vietnam. They also dispatched terror squads into the countryside to disrupt the Saigon government's rural pacification program. Still, U.S. and South Vietnamese forces responded quickly to the communist offensive, and after a week or so, in one city after another, turned the tide of battle. Unfortunately, the results were often devastating for South

Vietnamese civilians and their property, for communist soldiers had entrenched themselves in office buildings, houses, and other structures that afforded protection, and prompted their enemies to blast them out with tanks and cannons, airplanes and helicopter gunships.

In terms of its stated objective, the *Tet* offensive was a colossal failure, for it did not touch off a popular uprising against the Saigon government. Moreover, counterattacking American and South Vietnamese forces decimated North Vietnamese and VC regiments. But the offensive resulted in a tremendous psychological victory for the communists—in the United States. That the communists could unleash such an offensive at all appeared to make a mockery of assertions by General Westmoreland and others that the United States and its allies were taking the measure of the enemy in Vietnam. Of comparable moment, the violence visited upon the South Vietnamese people by American forces fighting to expel the communists from South Vietnam's cities, graphically witnessed via television, benumbed millions of Americans. Accordingly, uncounted people in the United States who hitherto had acquiesced in their country's involvement in the war became disillusioned, while the arguments, not to mention the spirits, of antiwar activists received fresh reinforcement. The outcome was a dramatic subversion of the national willingness to see the war through to the expulsion of the communists from South Vietnam.

The *Tet* offensive also impacted electoral politics in the United States, for on March 12, 1968, while the South Vietnamese continued to sift through the rubble of their battered cities, Democratic voters in New Hampshire sent a political shock wave across the republic by giving President Johnson only 49.9 percent of the vote in the Granite State's primary election. Sen. Eugene J. McCarthy of Minnesota, an articulate and scholarly opponent of the U.S. involvement in the war in Vietnam, received an astonishing 42.2 percent. Notwithstanding the advantages of incumbency, the president suddenly seemed politically vulnerable. And four days after the balloting in New Hampshire, Sen. Robert F. Kennedy, like McCarthy a "dove" on the issue of the war, announced that he, too, was a candidate for the Democratic nomination for president.

Meanwhile, Johnson was weighing a request by General Westmoreland that he authorize deployment of an additional 206,000 U.S. troops in Vietnam. Responding to the recommendation of the recently appointed secretary of defense, Clark Clifford, hitherto a "hawk" in the matter of the war, he authorized deployment of only 13,000 troops in Vietnam, which raised the number of U.S. military-naval personnel in the Vietnam war theater to 536,000. Inaugurating what subsequently would be known as Vietnamization of the war, Johnson also began to press the Saigon government to enlarge the combat role of the ARVN.

Then, on March 31, from the Oval Office in the White House, Johnson made a televised report to the nation. Proclaiming that he was taking the first step to deescalate the war, he announced a halt to the bombing of most of North Vietnam, and urged the communists to respond by agreeing to peace

March 30, 1968: President Johnson pores over the televised speech, to be delivered the next day, in which he will tell his compatriots that he will not seek another term as president.

negotiations. That announcement surprised nobody, inasmuch as news corre-spondents had been speculating for days that the president was about to make a new effort to lure the North Vietnamese to the negotiating table by virtually terminating the bombing of their country. But the millions of his compatriots who were viewing and listening to the report were puzzled when Johnson went on, "With American sons in the fields far away, with America's future under challenge right here at home, and with our hopes and the world's hopes for peace in the balance every day, I do not believe that I should devote an hour or a day of my time to any personal partisan causes or to any duties other than the awesome duties of this office—the presidency of your country." And most were thunderstruck when he concluded, "Accordingly, I shall not seek, and I will not accept, the nomination of my party for another term as your president."

## DAYS OF THE ASSASSIN—AGAIN

On April 3, 1968, the government in Hanoi signaled its willingness to open negotiations with the United States to determine whether it might be possible to arrange peace negotiations. The people of the United States were universally delighted. But then, the following day, they were confronted with a new tragedy, not in Vietnam, but in Memphis, Tennessee: Martin Luther King, Jr., fell victim of a bullet fired by a white ex-convict, James Earl Ray. In Memphis to organize nonviolent demonstrations on behalf of the city's striking garbage workers, most of whom were black, King was standing on the outdoor balcony adjoining his room on the second floor of the Lorraine Motel when the sharp crack of a rifle, fired from a window of a bathroom in a dingy brick hotel across

April 3, 1968: Flanked by the Rev. Jesse Jackson, the Rev. Martin Luther King, Jr., stands on the balcony of the Lorraine Motel in Memphis where he will fall to an assassin's bullet approximately twenty-four hours later.

the street from the Lorraine, shattered the twilight calm. The apostle of nonviolence never knew what hit him.

When the news of King's murder flashed from Memphis, the black ghettos of America's cities began to rumble, then erupted. Hardest hit were Chicago and Washington, where blacks roamed through business districts smashing windows, looting everything from baby shoes to color television sets, putting buildings to the torch. At length, the pillaging and burning passed, the earthly remains of Dr. King were laid to rest, and President Johnson signed the Civil Rights Act of 1968, rushed to a vote in the aftermath of King's assassination, a measure that prohibited discrimination on account of race in the sale or rental of an estimated 80 percent of the country's housing.

In the weeks that followed, the attention of Americans turned increasingly to the contests for the Republican and Democratic presidential nominations. Although challenged by Gov. Nelson A. Rockefeller of New York, former-Vice President Richard Nixon was the clear front-runner in the Republican contest. As for the Democrats, Vice Pres. Hubert H. Humphrey had announced his candidacy following President Johnson's dramatic announcement of March 31, but was clearly generating less enthusiasm among Democrats than Eugene McCarthy and Bobby Kennedy. Indeed, when returns disclosed that Kennedy had scored an impressive victory in the Democratic primary election in California on June 4, 1968, it appeared that the brother of the late president stood an excellent chance of capturing the Democratic nomination when delegates to the party's national convention gathered in Chicago two months hence. But then the Kennedy campaign ended. Shortly after issuing a victory statement in a ballroom of the Ambassador Hotel in Los Angeles in the first minutes of June 5, Kennedy suffered fatal wounds from pistol shots fired by a Jordanian immigrant, Sirhan Bishara Sirhan, while walking through a crowded serving pantry adjacent to the ballroom on his way to a press conference.

## CHOOSING A PRESIDENT

At length, the process of nominating presidential candidates moved to a climax. In early August of 1968, Republican delegates assembled in national convention in Miami Beach, and duly nominated Richard Nixon for president. At Nixon's behest, they nominated Spiro T. Agnew, the little-known governor of Maryland, for vice president. Democrats convened in Chicago three weeks later, and the outcome was an unmitigated political disaster.

On the eve of the Democratic convention, some ten thousand youthful antiwar activists who espoused the candidacy of Eugene McCarthy made their way to Chicago. The youthful influx naturally jangled the nerves of Chicago's authorities, and lest demonstrations by the young people get out of hand the city's police made careful preparations to control any riotous activities. The outcome perhaps was inevitable: In a succession of confrontations over three days, the youths, some of them flaunting Vietcong flags, taunted and heckled the police—"pigs," in the youthful lexicon—and also tossed rocks and bottles;

the police, their heads protected by helmets, responded by lobbing tear-gas cannisters at the youths and bashing youthful heads with billy clubs. Observing the confrontations via television, millions of Americans looked on with a mixture of horror and disbelief.

Inside the International Amphitheatre, meanwhile, delegates to the Democratic convention were caught up in the most tumultuous political conclave in anybody's memory, one marked by interminable shouting, name-calling, and gavel-pounding. The central issue was Vietnam. Antiwar delegates, all of them supporters of McCarthy's quest for the presidential nomination, insisted that the party's platform pledge unconditional cessation of all bombing of North Vietnam and the early withdrawal of all U.S. forces from Vietnam. Supporters of Vice President Humphrey were willing to commit the party to a total bombing halt—provided such a halt would not increase the risk to American troops deployed in the vicinity of the DMZ. And they were willing to support a pledge of deescalation of U.S. involvement in the war—as the South Vietnamese proved themselves capable of taking over responsibility for their own defense. By a margin of three to two, the proposals of the Humphrey faction in the matter of Vietnam won the convention's endorsement.

The rest was anticlimactic. When McCarthy's supporters were vanquished in the platform struggle, the nomination of Humphrey was assured, and delegates duly ratified the inevitable on the first ballot. Humphrey thereupon designated Sen. Edmund S. Muskie of Maine to be his vice presidential running mate.

There was another candidate of consequence in the presidential contest in 1968: Gov. George C. Wallace of Alabama, the founder and undisputed chieftain of the American Independent Party. A bantam-rooster-like politician, Wallace for several years had delighted audiences with folksy harangues against federal bureaucrats, "pointy-headed" intellectuals, and the Supreme Court, that is, those of his compatriots who favored racial integration and initiatives by the national government to guarantee equal opportunity in education and the workplace for all Americans. He also professed to be a champion of "law and order," a claim that found a mark among millions of Americans who felt outrage as a result of recent ghetto riots and campus disorders. Wallace, of course, had no chance of winning the White House, but by carrying most of the states of the onetime Confederacy on Election Day, he stood a chance of preventing either Humphrey or Nixon from mustering a majority of votes in the Electoral College, in which event the election would pass to the House of Representatives. To secure his endorsement in the balloting in the House, Humphrey or Nixon might be willing to make concessions to his points of view.

Meanwhile, Nixon, operating with a bulging campaign fund and taking care to say as little as possible that might offend any large segment of the electorate, and Humphrey, who never had enough money and was continually heckled by antiwar protesters, commanded the attention of most voters. Who was the front-runner? In the early stages of the campaign, opinion polls indicated that Nixon was the leader by a wide margin. To close in on Nixon, Humphrey determined to win over antiwar Democrats who had thus far declined to support his candidacy. Thus, at the end of September, he announced that if he were president he would unconditionally terminate all bombing of North Vietnam. Whereupon many antiwar Democrats fell in behind the vice president.

Then, in the latter half of October, the Humphrey campaign caught fire, in no small measure because legions of Wallace's erstwhile supporters rallied to Humphrey's candidacy. Next, on October 31, five days before the election, President Johnson announced that in return for pledges by the North Vietnamese that they would stop violating the DMZ, make no new attacks on South Vietnam's cities, and begin serious peace negotiations in Paris, he was ordering a total halt to the bombing of North Vietnam. The presidential announcement provided the Humphrey campaign with a new burst of energy, and by Election Day opinion pollsters were reporting that the contest between Nixon and Humphrey was too close to call.

Finally, on November 5, 1968, the voters made their choices, and the tabulation of ballots disclosed that Nixon had edged Humphrey in the popular balloting, 31,770,237 to 31,270,533. In the Electoral College, the outcome was not so close, and the Wallace strategy was undone when Nixon won a clear majority of electoral votes, 321 to 191 for Humphrey to 46 for Wallace (who carried Alabama, Arkansas, Georgia, Louisiana, and Mississippi). But Nixon's triumph was not total, for the Democrats would control both the House and Senate when the new Congress assembled in January of 1969.

## THE THIRTY-SEVENTH PRESIDENT

Born in 1913 in the farming community of Yorba Linda in southern California, Richard Nixon grew up in middle-income comfort. Otherwise, young Dick Nixon was a serious boy who dutifully attended Quaker religious services, played the piano, and graduated from high school with honors. At Whittier College, where he enrolled in 1930, he was an outstanding student and champion debater—also a bench warmer on the football team. After Whittier, Nixon enrolled in the Duke University Law School in North Carolina and again compiled an enviable academic record. After graduating from law school, he returned to Whittier to undertake the practice of law, and a short time later met and married Thelma "Pat" Ryan. Although a Quaker and hence eligible for deferment from military service as a conscientious objector, he accepted a commission in the Navy after the United States entered World War II, and at length found himself involved in transportation activities on assorted islands of the southwest Pacific.

Nixon was back in the United States working on the termination of naval contracts when the war ended in August of 1945. Then, before his discharge from the Navy, an ad hoc committee of Republicans of the Twelfth Congressional District of California invited him to run for the district's seat in Congress in 1946. Nixon accepted the invitation, and after what he later described as a "rock 'em, sock 'em" campaign against the liberal Democratic incumbent Jerry Voorhis—a stooge of communists, according to Nixon—he won a clear-cut victory when voters marked ballots on Election Day. On taking his seat in the Eightieth Congress in early 1947, he received appointment to the House Un-American Activities Committee, whose overarching purpose in those years was to expose communist subversion in the United States. He shortly won renown when, with minimal reinforcement by other members of the HUAC, he produced incontrovertible evidence that Alger Hiss, a onetime official of the State Department, had passed secret documents to Soviet spies during the 1930s.

In 1950, Nixon ran for the Senate, and in another rock 'em, sock 'em campaign defeated the liberal Democrat Helen Gahagan Douglas—also a stooge of communists, according to the Republican candidate. Two years later, in 1952, he was elected to the vice presidency on the Republican ticket headed by General Eisenhower, and in 1960 narrowly lost the presidential election to John F. Kennedy. Returning to California after Kennedy's inauguration, he crafted a book entitled *Six Crises* that recounted critical points of his career. Then, in 1962, he suffered a stunning defeat when he ran for governor of California— and on the morning after the election told reporters, whom he thought had treated him unfairly over the years, that they would not have Nixon to kick around anymore, because, he said, "Gentlemen, this is my last press conference." A few months later, he and his family moved to New York where he became a partner in a prestigious Wall Street law firm.

Nixon, it turned out, was no political corpse, and within a year of the move to New York was about to begin one of the most remarkable comebacks in the annals of American politics. The comeback got under way at the Republican national convention of 1964 when he presented the GOP's presidential nominee, Barry Goldwater, to cheering delegates. He labored mightily on behalf of the Goldwater campaign in the months that followed. He labored mightily again on behalf of Republican candidates for Congress two years later, in 1966, and when the GOP picked up 47 seats in the House and 3 in the Senate he could claim a share of the credit. In 1967, he had made up his mind to reach out once more for the White House.

When assorted presidential aspirants began campaigning in earnest, in late 1967, Nixon appeared to be the first choice for the GOP nomination of only a fraction of Republicans. But for a variety of reasons, not the least of which were feelings of gratitude for his many services to the party over the years, he clearly was the second choice of great numbers of the Republican faithful. So when such aspirants as Governors Nelson Rockefeller of New York and George Romney of Michigan failed to stir the enthusiasm of voters, Nixon emerged as the principal contender for the nomination, and on the first roll call at the Republican national convention in 1968 received a clear majority of votes. The climax of the incredible comeback from the political scrap heap took place on November 5, 1968, when the electorate accorded Nixon his razor-thin triumph over Hubert Humphrey.

Ten weeks later, on January 20, 1969, in the traditional ceremony at the

Capitol, Nixon repeated the presidential oath. After delivering a low-key and thoughtful inaugural address, he joined his wife in a limousine to lead the inaugural parade down Pennsylvania Avenue to the White House. Because of reports that trouble was brewing along the avenue, Secret Service agents attached a sunroof (or "bubble top") over the limousine to protect the new president and his lady. For the first several blocks, the crowds lining the avenue were friendly, but in the vicinity of Thirteenth Street the presidential party encountered a concentration of youthful rebels and antiwar protesters. The resultant scene was the ugliest in 180 years of presidential inaugurations.

When the Marine Band came into view, a protester threw a firecracker into the street. A joint armed forces color guard was the target of a smoke bomb. When the presidential limousine and those conveyances carrying the cabinet designates appeared, the protesters threw more smoke bombs, clods of dirt, pennies—also sticks, pebbles, a table fork and spoon, a beer can. Secret service agents at full trot all around the president's car batted away most of the missiles, and when a softball-size sphere of tinfoil arched toward the limousine the driver stepped on the accelerator. Infuriated that he and his wife were veritable captives inside their limousine, Nixon—when the car reached Fifteenth Street, where crowds were again friendly—ordered the driver to stop and Secret Service agents to remove the sunroof. The thirty-seventh president and Mrs. Nixon thereupon stood in full view of spectators until they reached the enclosed reviewing stand in front of the White House.

Like Lyndon Johnson, Richard Nixon appeared to be an unusually complicated man. Indeed, no American personage of modern times has generated so much analysis of his or her character-personality than he. One scholar decided that Nixon had an active-negative character marked by a powerful attachment to achievement that was translated into a determination to exercise power over others, a determination that was pursued with intense dedication and was justified idealistically. A psychiatrist thought him a compulsive-obsessive personality, that is, one whose exaggerated feelings of anxiety made him overly inhibited and overly conscientious as well as compulsive. Another considered him a passive-aggressive personality, and as a result was indirect and devious, ambivalent and secretive. A writer of speeches for Nixon, Raymond Price, has disclosed that individuals who worked with Nixon over the years often referred to his light side and dark side. The light side was considerate, sentimental, generous of spirit, kind. The dark side was angry, vindictive, illtempered, mean-spirited. (A third side, neither light nor dark but according to Price necessary to statecraft, was coldly calculating, devious, craftily manipulative.)

Professional and amateur analyses aside, Nixon was a man of intelligence—not brilliant perhaps, but manifestly intelligent. The journalist and chronicler of presidential elections Theodore H. White observed, "The Nixon mind is neat, disciplined, severely sequential, compulsively orderly." If an acute mind was an asset of Nixon when he ran for president in 1968, drive and energy were others. To invoke a tired expression, Nixon was a confirmed workoholic. Like Lyndon Johnson, he had no hobbies. Save for spectator sports, usually savored via television and the daily papers, he had few outside interests. Like Johnson, he was a politician through and through. As Henry A. Kissinger has written, Nixon could be very decisive—had a rare talent for looking straight on at hard and sometimes dangerous problems and making hard and sometimes dangerous decisions. He was an introspective man who, in the words of his longtime friend and aide Herbert Klein, was deeply embroiled in his own ego and pride. Individuals who worked with him have attested that he was a basically shy man who tended to shrink from familiarity or contact with others. They also observed that he was hounded by a sense of insecurity and feelings of inadequacy. It clearly bothered him, for example, that he was generally perceived to be lacking in charisma.

As has often been remarked, Nixon tended to take an extraordinarily ungenerous view of opponents and critics. He was inclined to look upon them as enemies rather than as mere opponents and critics. Those enemies, he sometimes appeared to think, were besieging him. At times, his siege mentality, as students of his psyche have observed, seemed to border on paranoia—on occasion seemed to cross the border. Or as a historian once wrote of Henry Ford, Nixon was a man who was haunted by assorted goblins. Foremost among Nixon's enemies (or goblins) were scions of the so-called liberal establishment of the northeastern region of the republic, many of them heirs of wealth and privilege, socially prominent, cosmopolitan, sophisticated, graduates of exclusive preparatory schools and Ivy League colleges and universities. Other enemies were the communications media, dominated, he was persuaded, by northeastern establishmentarians, and youthful rebels, many of them the privileged offspring of the former, who blamed the United States and its system for most of the ills of the world, burned draft cards, flaunted Vietcong flags, and were "running down" America and giving aid and comfort to "her" enemies. (Nixon always referred to America as *her* or *she*.)

In retrospect, one may surmise that Nixon's penchant for hating and impugning motives, combined with an abiding reluctance to concede error or shortcomings, added up to a tragic flaw in the character of this man of manifest intelligence, knowledge, and ability. Like the flaws that burdened the heroes of Greek and Elizabethan tragedies, that flaw would ultimately prove the ruination of Richard Nixon.

## TO THE MOON—AND BEYOND

In the lexicon of young Americans of the 1960s, Richard Nixon was a square, that is, he was animated by a kind of old-time, flag-waving patriotic fervor that tended to be quite unfashionable among nonsquares. From Nixon's perspective, accordingly, the supreme moment of his first year in the White House, apart, of course, from his own inauguration as president, was doubtless that of July 20, 1969, when from the surface of the moon the astronaut Neil

July 20, 1969: Astronaut Edwin E. Aldrin, Jr., walking on the lunar surface during the historic mission of Apollo II. The lunar module is reflected in Aldrin's visor.

A. Armstrong, huddled inside a tiny spacecraft alongside fellow astronaut Edwin E. Aldrin, Jr., reported matter-of-factly, "Houston, Tranquility base here. The Eagle has landed."

The splashdown in the Atlantic in May 1963 of the astronaut L. Gordon Cooper in the spacecraft *Faith* 7 marked the end of America's first man-in-space program, Project Mercury. Whereupon the country's space scientists and engineers and technicians turned to Project Gemini and, later, Project Apollo:

the development of the hardware, techniques, and procedures that would climax with a voyage to the surface of the moon. At length, in July of 1969, the climactic moment arrived. The outcome was the most memorable event of the space age, the flight of *Apollo 11.*

The blast-off from Cape Kennedy (formerly and subsequently Cape Canaveral) on July 16 went flawlessly. Three days later, *Apollo 11,* comprising the command module "Columbia" and lunar module "Eagle," moved into orbit around the moon. The following day, July 20, Armstrong and Aldrin crawled from Columbia to Eagle, and a short time later the lunar module was cut loose from the command module. While Columbia, piloted by the astronaut Michael Collins, continued to orbit the moon, Eagle began its gradual descent toward the lunar surface. Some two hours and fifteen minutes later, the little spacecraft was hovering a few feet above the moon's waterless Sea of Tranquility, and to avoid craters and assure an upright landing Armstrong, a 38-year-old native of Ohio, was manually maneuvering the vehicle. Finally, at 4:27 P.M., Eagle's landing pods settled gently in the dust of the Sea of Tranquility.

Several hours later, as millions of earthlings watched via TV, Armstrong stepped out of Eagle, slowly descended a ladder, and appeared almost to float from the bottom rung to the lunar surface. Said the first man to set foot on the moon, "That's one small step for a man, one giant leap for mankind." Twenty minutes later, Aldrin joined Armstrong on the lunar surface, and for the next two hours the astronauts gathered samples of moon soil and rocks and set up scientific experiments. The two men thereupon returned to Eagle, sealed the hatch, and shortly after noon the next day, July 21, Armstrong ignited Eagle's engines, and amid a swirl of dust the spacecraft (because of the minimal pull of the moon's gravity) appeared to pop off from the lunar surface. After some three hours of maneuvering, Eagle docked with Columbia, Armstrong and Aldrin rejoined Collins in Columbia, and Eagle was cast adrift. A short time later, Columbia was streaking across the heavens, destination: earth.

Meanwhile, as *Apollo 11* was speeding triumphantly back toward earth, Americans were pondering another event that was to leave a large imprint on the life of their country: Two days after *Apollo 11* had blasted off for its flight to the moon, on the evening of July 18, 1969, Sen. Edward M. "Ted" Kennedy, the 38-year-old brother of John F. and Robert F. Kennedy, accidentally drove his automobile off a bridge on tiny Chappaquiddick Island, some twelve miles from the southeastern shore of Cape Cod. The car plunged into the water of Nantucket Sound. Kennedy managed to extricate himself from the sunken vehicle and make his way to the surface, but his pretty companion, 28-year-old Mary Jo Kopechne, drowned. The senator did not report the accident until the following day.

Millions of Americans doubted Kennedy's explanation of the events of July 18–19 on Chappaquiddick Island, and millions more believed that his behavior before and after the tragedy had been irresponsible. The result was a devastating blow to the presidential ambitions that the senator almost certainly entertained. Kennedy recognized as much. Although nearly every pundit had considered it a foregone conclusion before Chappaquiddick that he would be the

Democratic party's nominee for president in 1972 or 1976, Kennedy removed himself from the competition before serious campaigning for the Democratic presidential nomination in each of those years got under way. Apparently hoping that after 11 years the Chappaquiddick affair had been laid to rest, he made a determined run for his party's presidential nomination in 1980. To his dismay, he found that millions of Americans had not forgotten that awful night in July of 1969, for as Kennedy's friendly biographer James MacGregor Burns had written a few years before, Chappaquiddick was a tragedy that would not die.

Two days after the funeral of Mary Jo Kopechne, *Apollo 11* parachuted down in the Pacific. On hand to greet the returning astronauts when a helicopter delivered them to the flight deck of the carrier USS *Hornet* was President Nixon. The astronauts wisely made no response when the president exulted, "This is the greatest week in the history of the world since the creation." The return of *Apollo 11*, of course, did not signal the end of the moon program—far from it. Five additional Apollo voyages to the moon followed over the next several years. But the latter voyages seemed anticlimactic, and only the troubled voyage of *Apollo 13* captured popular attention on a grand scale.

If the launching of men and hardware into space tended to become routine from the perspective of most Americans, those launchings nonetheless continued to consume billions of dollars—and to result in achievements that were at once impressive and of great scientific and technological import. In 1970, NASA launched *ITOS 1*, a weather satellite, in near-polar orbit; *Nimbus 4*, an extraordinarily sophisticated research-and-development satellite; and another communications satellite for the Communications Satellite Corporation. In 1971, it launched *OSO 7*, the seventh in a series of Orbiting Solar Observatories, its purpose to report data on a variety of solar phenomena, particularly solar flares. Of larger interest was the voyage of *Mariner 9*, a 2,272-pound vehicle that was equipped with two TV cameras for photographing Mars and its two moons—also instruments for acquiring data on both the atmosphere and surface of Mars and for measuring the planet's gravitational field. Launched at the end of May of 1971, *Mariner 9*, after a flight of 248 million miles, went into an elliptical orbit around Mars in mid-November 1971. From a low point of 863 miles, the TV cameras of *Mariner 9* sent back amazingly clear pictures of the "Red Planet." In 1972, NASA launched *Pioneer 10*, a 550-pound spacecraft that soared across the heavens at a speed of 72,000 miles an hour. Laden with instruments, *Pioneer 10*, in December 1973, traveled to within 80,000 miles of Jupiter, took pictures of the planet's orange- and blue-striped Jovian cloud cover, measured the intensities of its magnetic field, and took its temperature.

The United States undertook a new chapter in space exploration in May 1973 when it launched *Skylab*, a 118-foot by 80-foot space station in which astronauts were to live and work for extended periods. After *Skylab* achieved orbit at an altitude of approximately 270 miles, an Apollo spacecraft carrying three astronauts was rocketed into space, and after docking their craft with *Skylab* the astronauts made their way into the space station. Over the next 28 days, the three men conducted an array of scientific experiments and took thousands of photographs of the earth and the sun. In November 1973, NASA launched *Mariner 10* on a voyage to the planet Mercury by way of Venus. The 1,160-pound spacecraft obtained closeup pictures of the Venusian clouds in early February 1974 when it flew by Venus en route to Mercury. Six weeks later, in March of 1974, *Mariner 10* passed within 460 miles of Mercury. The spacecraft's cameras revealed the terrain of the latter planet to be incredibly rough, while its radiometer recorded temperatures ranging from 370°F to −300°F.

The year 1975 brought a historic rendezvous in space between a Soyuz spacecraft manned by three Soviet cosmonauts and an Apollo spacecraft manned by three U.S. astronauts. Millions of earthlings watched via television when, after the docking of the Soyuz and Apollo, a hatch opened between the two vehicles and the Soviet and American spacemen shook hands and exchanged national flags. In June of 1976, the U.S. spacecraft *Viking 1*, after a ten-month voyage across interplanetary space, went into orbit around Mars, and on July 20, 1976, the spacecraft's lander descended successfully to the surface of the planet. Cameras produced pictures of remarkable detail showing a desertlike landscape of reddish tint that was littered with shaped and structural rocks. An experiment to test for the evidence of life on Mars found a surprising quantity of oxygen in the soil—also traces of carbon dioxide. But a test for evidence of complex organic molecules proved negative, hence scientists concluded that life almost certainly did not exist on the fabled Red Planet.

Of comparable interest, in September 1976, NASA unveiled Orbitor 101, christened *Enterprise*, the space shuttle that had been in the making for several years. Carrying a crew of seven, the shuttle would be a reusable vehicle, that is, would be propelled into space by a giant rocket, orbit the earth after the fashion of a conventional spacecraft, then return to earth and make an airplanelike landing. It would move people, instruments, and a large variety of satellites in and out of earth orbit at a substantially lower cost than hitherto possible. The first manned orbital flight by a space shuttle (Orbitor 102) was scheduled for the spring of 1979.

## NIXON AND HOME AFFAIRS

If Richard Nixon was a pragmatic man who clung to no immutable theory or philosophy about the way society functioned and what the role of government ought to be, his instincts tended to be to the right of center, that is, conservative. And his agenda in the area of home affairs when he repeated the presidential oath in January 1969 was in rhythm with that of most political conservatives in the United States during the latter 1960s. He determined to move against crime and rioting, civil disobedience and unlawful demonstrations. He intended to restore a conservative balance to the Supreme Court by appointing conservative justices to fill vacancies as they occurred. He determined to overhaul the federal welfare system, viewed by conservatives and liberals alike to be in drastic need of overhaul. He wanted to achieve what would be described as a "New Federalism"—in the words of his onetime speech writer and aide William Safire, he wanted "to reverse the flow of power, which had been steadily (and for a long time properly) moving from the states and localities to the Federal Government in Washington." Finally, he sought to halt the rise in the cost of living. Consumer prices had increased 2.9 percent in 1967 and 4.2 percent in 1968, compared with an annual average of 1.3 percent from 1960 to 1965. In the view of Nixon and many other Americans, those numbers were cause for concern, even alarm.

What might the new administration do to meet the problem of inflation? Well, it could engineer a reduction in federal spending. But as matters turned out, the main burden of controlling inflation fell to the Federal Reserve Board, an agency that according to the law was supposed to function independently of the executive branch. The "Fed" responded by implementing a policy of tight money: It raised the rediscount rate (the rate of interest on money borrowed from the Federal Reserve by member banks) and mandated an increase in the volume of cash that banks were required to keep in reserve. By discouraging borrowing, tight money, it was hoped, would put a brake on economic activity. Reduced economic activity would result in reduced inflation. Alas, inflation continued at about the same rate after the imposition of tight money.

Then, in 1970, the national economy slipped into its first bona fide recession since 1960–1961. The recession dragged on into the summer of 1971. But contrary to conventional economic theory, the economic slowdown failed to stay the tide of inflation. Equally distressing were figures disclosing that the country's balance of international trade was heading toward its first annual deficit since 1893, and that as a consequence the deficit in its international payments for 1971 was approaching $20 billion—a deficit that threatened to exhaust the national gold reserve if the Washington government continued to balance international accounts by shipping gold.

In such circumstances, President Nixon felt compelled to act. To counter inflation, he announced a 90-day wage-price freeze. Largely to afford American manufacturers a measure of protection, he imposed a 10 percent surcharge on imports. To stimulate exports, and also to stop the drain of the country's gold reserve, he suspended the Washington government's longtime commitment to balance international accounts by exchanging gold for dollars at a rate of $35 an ounce. In a word, the dollar would now "float" in value in relation to the currencies of other countries. It would no longer be artificially pegged by gold, a circumstance that was certain to result in its devaluation. Devaluation would presumably stimulate the U.S. economy and eliminate its deficits in international trade and international payments by encouraging exports.

For whatever reasons, the national economy rebounded from the dreary recession, and in 1972 achieved a level of performance that was almost without precedent. Measured in constant dollars, the GNP surged forward by 6.5 percent. The rate of inflation fell from 6 percent in 1971 to 3.5 percent in 1972. Personal income and private profits soared, stock prices boomed to their highest level ever. Unemployment underwent a modest decline. By 1973, the country was recording a surplus in its balance of international trade, and also a surplus (barely) in its balance of international payments.

Meanwhile, President Nixon affixed his signature to an array of domestic measures passed by the Democratic-controlled Congress: emergency unemployment legislation; a federal loan of $250 million to save the Lockheed Aircraft Corporation from bankruptcy; legislation making the Post Office Department a government-owned corporation and establishing AMTRAK, a government-owned corporation to operate intercity passenger trains; legislation defining safety and health standards for virtually every type of occupation and establishing the Occupational Safety and Health Administration (OSHA); measures appropriating funds for research into cancer and sickle-cell anemia and prevention of drug abuse; legislation granting limited home rule to the District of Columbia. With Nixon's blessing, Congress submitted to the states a constitutional amendment—when ratified in 1971, the Twenty-sixth Amendment—lowering the voting age in all elections to 18. Nixon established (by executive order) the Environmental Protection Agency, then encouraged Congress to pass a variety of environmental protection measures. But the premier legislative achievement of the Nixon presidency was enactment of Public Law 92-512, the State and Local Assistance Act of 1972. Public Law 92-512 appropriated $30.2 billion in federal tax money for a five-year revenue-sharing program under which state and local governments were to receive funds that they might expend almost without stipulations.

Nixon took great satisfaction in the revenue-sharing measure. But a more compelling goal than revenue-sharing, he believed, was reform of the federal welfare system. In the president's view, the existing welfare system was a veritable monster that was driving states and municipalities (which shared welfare costs with the federal government) to the edge of financial calamity while failing to meet the elementary needs of the poor. What might be done? Nixon recommended the dismantling of the centerpiece of the existing welfare system, the Aid to Families with Dependent Children (AFDC) program, a legacy of Franklin Roosevelt's New Deal of the 1930s that by the end of the 1960s provided benefits for upward of 6 million people. (Welfare assistance to the blind, the disabled, and the elderly would remain unchanged.) To replace AFDC, he asked Congress in 1969 to consent to what he termed a Family Assistance Program (FAP) that would guarantee a minimum annual income of $1,600 to each family of four in the country. In a word, if a family of four was headed by a female or an unemployed father, the federal government would pay that family $1,600 a year—on one condition: If children were of school age, the head or heads of the household would be required to register for job training or employment.

To Nixon's annoyance and disappointment, legislation to inaugurate the FAP failed on Capitol Hill. Still, Congress passed and the president signed a measure authorizing a new category of welfare assistance (Supplemental Security Income), and voted substantial increases in funding for food stamps, Medicaid, Medicare, public housing, Social Security, and other forms of welfare. Appropriations for the Food Stamp program, for example, enabled the program to accommodate 13.5 million participants in 1974, the year Nixon exited the White House, compared with 2.4 million in 1968, the last year of the Johnson presidency.

A man who had never been anywhere near the front rank of those Americans who sought to purge the country of discrimination, abuse, and segregation on account of race, President Nixon took a cautious approach on the question of civil rights. He ordered departments and agencies to act affirmatively to end discrimination in all areas of federal employment. At his behest, those same departments and agencies scrutinized federal contractors to make certain they were complying with equal employment clauses of contracts. The Justice Department moved against discrimination in housing. And in 1969, the Nixon administration unveiled the "Philadelphia Plan" requiring every contractor bidding on a federal construction project to pledge a "good-faith" effort to hire a fair percentage of minority employees for the project. But Nixon proposed amendments that were clearly intended to weaken the historic Voting Rights Act of 1965. Unlike his predecessor Lyndon Johnson, he declined to use the threat of withholding federal funds (distributed in accord with the Elementary and Secondary Education Act of 1965) to achieve school desegregation. During his first year in the White House, indeed, his administration twice asked the Supreme Court to sanction further delays in the desegregation of the schools of the South. Both requests were denied, and by the time Nixon left the presidency in 1974, de jure (legally imposed) segregation of schools, largely because of the Supreme Court's insistence that dual public schools systems be eliminated forthwith, had ceased to be an issue.

If de jure segregation of schools gradually faded as an issue, de facto segregation did not. De facto segregation resulted from the fact that in urban areas school district boundaries almost invariably coincided with neighborhood boundaries, and neighborhoods, in the North and West as well as the South, tended to be all black or all white.

Was de facto segregation discriminatory? Did it—or, more to the point, did pronounced racial imbalances in schools—tend to present an impediment to the educational progress and social development of minority children? Answering both questions in the affirmative, many civil rights activists argued that de facto segregation of public schools must be eliminated by the massive busing of children from predominantly black neighborhoods to schools in predominantly white neighborhoods and vice versa. In a decision in 1971, the Supreme Court agreed that busing might indeed be necessary to break up all-black public schools that had survived in spite of the high court's desegregation ruling of 1954. But when federal judges ordered the busing of schoolchildren in an array of cities, great numbers of whites, many of them parents of children who were to be bused, erupted—and in Pontiac, Michigan, torched ten school buses. Meanwhile, President Nixon, who had spoken out against busing during the electoral campaign of 1968, ordered the Departments of HEW and Justice to restrict busing plans to "the minimum required by law." Some months later, in 1972, he urged a temporary moratorium on busing, and Congress passed a measure prohibiting new busing for the purpose of achieving racial balance. (Large numbers of children nonetheless continued to be bused in the interest of racially balanced public schools.)

Of more immediate concern to Nixon than the issue of civil rights during his first months in the White House was the matter of nominating a new chief justice of the United States, for 77-year-old Earl Warren, who had presided over the Supreme Court since 1953, had announced his intention to retire before Nixon's election to the presidency. Nixon, who had long deplored the liberal proclivities of Warren and "the Warren Court," was delighted. To succeed Warren, Nixon nominated 61-year-old Warren E. Burger of Minnesota, a man of distinguished mien, conservative outlook, and, so it was widely reported, modest intellect. Whatever his qualifications, Burger won quick confirmation by the Senate, and in June of 1969 was sworn in as the fifteenth chief justice. Meanwhile, Justice Abe Fortas, another liberal, had resigned from the Supreme Court, and to succeed him Nixon nominated Judge Clement F. Haynsworth, Jr., a conservative of South Carolina—in no small measure because Haynsworth was a southerner, and Nixon believed the South had been underrepresented on the high court for many years. To Nixon's dismay, liberals erupted, in part because Haynsworth had not been a fervent supporter of civil rights for racial minorities. When the Haynsworth nomination failed in the Senate, Nixon nominated Judge G. Harrold Carswell, a conservative of Florida—and liberals again erupted. Liberals accused Carswell of racial bias, a charge that appeared to have some substance, and also accused him of having compiled a poor judicial record, a charge that could scarcely be confuted. Like Haynsworth, accordingly, Carswell failed to win confirmation by the Senate.

At that point, Nixon nominated Judge Harry A. Blackmun of Minnesota, a conservative of impeccable credentials who secured confirmation without difficulty. The president nominated two additional conservatives to fill vacancies on the Supreme Court in 1971: Lewis F. Powell, Jr., of Virginia, and William H. Rehnquist of Arizona. Liberals were not pleased, for Powell and Rehnquist would assure conservative dominance of the high court, probably for many years to come. But like Blackmun, Powell and Rehnquist were thought by a substantial majority of senators to be eminently qualified to be associate justices, so liberals were unable to prevent their confirmation.

## NIXON AND THE YOUNG REBELS

At the same time that President Nixon was striving to fill vacancies on the Supreme Court with men who stood foursquare for "law and order," legions of students across the country were continuing the disruptive activities that had become commonplace on college and university campuses in recent years. On an array of campuses in the spring of 1969, irate students shouted obscenities and hurled smoke bombs during rallies protesting what they styled the immoral and imperialist involvement by the United States in the war in Vietnam. More serious, they disrupted classes and trashed administrative offices, seized buildings and set fires. At Cornell and at Voorhees College (in South

Carolina), militant black students protesting alleged racial discrimination occupied campus buildings, brandished guns, and threatened to shoot anybody
who tried to evict them.

Responding to such goings-on, President Nixon, in a fiery oration in April
1969, lashed out at the student dissidents. He declared that the time had come
for boards of trustees, campus administrators, and faculties to exhibit some
backbone in dealing with campus rebels. A preponderance of the citizenry
agreed. The upshot was enactment of a flurry of laws by state legislatures to
counter campus disruption. Still, the disruptions continued, an ugly climax
coming to pass at the end of May of 1969 when police and national guardsmen
clashed with three thousand students on the Berkeley campus of the University of California. A few months later, in the autumn of 1969, a courtroom in
Chicago became a center of radical pyrotechnics when several militant radicals went on trial for allegedly conspiring to foment a riot during the Democratic national convention of 1968. The defendants continually interrupted
proceedings by shouting epithets at the judge—called him a pig and a fascist—
and when five of "the Chicago Seven," in February 1970, were found guilty of
having crossed state lines to provoke violence, youthful radicals in several
cities stormed through downtown areas, breaking windows and hurling bottles, paint, and rocks.

The trial of the Chicago Seven and resultant rioting when verdicts were
handed down provided grim counterpoint to another disruptive phenomenon
of recent origin in the United States: radical terrorism. The goal of the country's radical terrorists? The destruction of traditional American institutions
and values. Although radical terrorists, who numbered only a few thousand,
stood no chance whatever of achieving their goal, they nonetheless generated
a great deal of anger and a measure of concern among the citizenry at large.

The depredations of the radical terrorists reached a crescendo in 1970. In
February of that year, a bomb exploded in a police station in San Francisco,
killing one man and injuring nine others. Later that month, radical students
in Santa Barbara attacked a shopping center, burned a branch of the Bank of
America, and destroyed a police car. A few weeks thereafter, a group of radicals
set off explosions in the New York offices of three large corporations. In June
of 1970, a bomb rocked police headquarters in New York City; in August, a
postdoctoral student died when a bomb gutted the building that housed the
University of Wisconsin's physics department and the Army's Mathematics
Research Center; in October, bombs reportedly planted by the Weathermen
exploded on the campus of the University of Washington in Seattle and in two
towns in northern California. On the first day of March of 1971, the Weathermen set off a bomb in the Senate wing of the U.S. Capitol in Washington that
caused extensive damage but resulted in no injuries.

Infuriated by the violent activities of radical terrorists, President Nixon in
the summer of 1970 weighed the merits of a plan fashioned by a young conservative member of the White House staff, Tom Charles Huston, to counter radical terrorists. Subsequently denounced by civil libertarians as sanctioning Ge-
stapo-like tactics, the "Huston Plan" provided that the country's intelligence

agencies and the FBI would resort to covert mail-openings, break-ins, and increased electronic surveillance, and rely on an array of informants to gather information about terrorists and their enterprise. As for Nixon, he approved the Huston Plan in modified form, then, he later insisted, withdrew his approval. Still, the FBI, with or without presidential approval, moved in on radicals, particularly the Weathermen, by tapping phones, opening mail, and breaking into and searching apartments without warrants or authority granted by any court.

The effectiveness of the government's campaign against the radical terrorists is hard to measure. Indeed, the full extent of the campaign may never be known. In any event, the incidence of terrorist activity in the United States declined dramatically after 1971, and by the mid-1970s was little more than a haunting memory.

## IN THE WORLD ARENA

Fueling the activities of campus protesters and radical terrorists, of course, was the war in Vietnam. And the great overbearing purpose of President Nixon from the day he took up residence in the White House was to bring that war to an early end on terms that he considered honorable. Still, in the matter of foreign affairs, he was by no means totally preoccupied with Vietnam. He determined to improve relations between the United States and its allies in NATO that had been marked by apathy, discord, and mistrust for at least a decade. To that purpose, he made an eight-day trip to Western Europe during his first weeks in the presidential office, during which he conferred with presidents and prime ministers, NATO officials, and Pope Paul VI. Nixon announced that the United States would never resort to biological (or germ) warfare, and would use chemical weapons only if an enemy used them first. He signed the instrument of ratification of the Treaty on the Non-Proliferation of Nuclear Weapons, negotiated by the Johnson administration to prevent the spread of nuclear weapons to countries that did not already have them. He put his signature to an agreement whereby the United States would return control of Okinawa to Japan in 1972. Overcoming vigorous opposition by critics who thought the installation of antiballistic missiles would constitute a new acceleration of the nuclear arms race and others who suspected ABMs would prove ineffectual during an attack by Soviet ICBMs, he prevailed on Congress to approve the Safeguard ABM system—ostensibly to protect the national command center in Washington and 12 other strategic locations around the country, in truth to provide U.S. negotiators with bargaining counters (or "chips") during anticipated strategic arms limitation (SALT) talks with the Soviets. (As matters turned out, the Safeguard system was never put in place.)

At the same time that he was seeking congressional sanction of Safeguard, in the spring of 1969, Nixon was confronted with what had the potential of becoming a full-blown international crisis: North Korean MiG fighter planes blasted a four-engine EC-121 aircraft of the U.S. Navy from the sky as it monitored North Korean radio traffic and radar activity over the Sea of Japan. All 31 members of the crew perished when the big plane crashed into the sea. Although Nixon had denounced Lyndon Johnson's failure to make a forceful response when the North Koreans seized the *Pueblo* 14 months before, he declined to order a retaliatory attack against North Korea. No less than Johnson in early 1968, he determined to avoid any action that risked touching off a new war in Korea while the United States remained preoccupied with the war in Vietnam.

## VIETNAM

The overarching concern of the thirty-seventh president when he moved into the White House in January 1969, as mentioned, was the war in Vietnam. Nixon desperately wanted to arrange an end to the bloody and divisive conflict, inasmuch as termination of the war appeared essential if the new administration was to move forward with assorted plans for establishing a new balance between federal and state authority at home and building what Nixon liked to refer to as a structure of peace in the world at large. How did he hope to bring the war to an early termination? Manifestly, by negotiated settlement. Unfortunately, it soon became clear that diplomacy was unlikely to yield such a settlement, at least anytime soon: The opening session of armistice negotiations involving representatives of the governments in Hanoi, Saigon, and Washington—also representatives of the Vietcong—that got under way in Paris a few days after Nixon repeated the presidential oath quickly deadlocked. The reasons for the deadlock were transparent. The North Vietnamese and VC were bent on achieving a settlement that would deliver South Vietnam to communist rule; the Saigon regime and the Americans were equally bent on achieving a settlement that would keep South Vietnam free of the communist scourge.

While the diplomatists wrangled, the fighting and dying in Vietnam went on, and American fighting men continued to fall at a rate that appalled their compatriots back home. (A total of 9,414 U.S. military and naval personnel would lose their lives in Southeast Asia in 1969, a one-year figure exceeded only by that of 14,589 in 1968.) Americans back in the United States were particularly appalled (and exercised) in May of 1969 when they learned of the abandonment of Hill 937 in the A Shau Valley—"Hamburger Hill"—eight days after GIs had taken the hill following a brutal and bloody battle.

Nixon, meanwhile, had determined to do something about the "sanctuaries" in Cambodia, that is, the base camps and assembly points that the communists had established in the sparsely populated eastern region of the Khmer kingdom, just over the border from South Vietnam. His determination is not hard to understand. In the sanctuaries, the communists continuously stockpiled equipment and supplies trundled down from North Vietnam over the Ho Chi Minh Trail—also equipment and supplies unloaded from Soviet-bloc vessels at the Cambodian port of Sihanoukville on the Gulf of Thailand and moved overland to the sanctuaries. And from the sanctuaries, North Vietnamese and VC troops routinely slipped over the border to disrupt life in South Vietnam and kill American and ARVN soldiers, only to flee back over the border into Cambodia when countered by American or ARVN forces. Instructed to respect Cambodia's official neutrality vis-à-vis the war in Vietnam, U.S. and ARVN troops normally broke off pursuit on reaching the border.

What Nixon opted to do was to order U.S. aircraft, mostly giant B-52s, to pulverize the sanctuaries. In no small measure because Prince Norodom Sihanouk of Cambodia, who according to Nixon secretly requested that the sanctuaries be put under attack, would feel compelled to demand its termination if it were publicly acknowledged, the bombing of the sanctuaries was kept secret. Because of leaks from within the Washington government itself, however, the secret was poorly kept. The leaks naturally stirred the wrath of the president, and without obtaining court-approved warrants but securing consent of Attorney General John N. Mitchell he directed the FBI to tap the phones of 13 White House and State Department officials and 5 news correspondents in an effort to identify the leakers. As for the bombing, it caused minimal disruption of communist operations in the sanctuaries.

Meanwhile, antiwar Democrats were demanding that the president effect an early and total withdrawal of American forces from South Vietnam and thereby, for all practical purposes, abandon the country to the North Vietnamese and Vietcong. Believing that a precipitous abandonment of the South Vietnamese republic would besmirch the honor of the United States and give pause to other allies who might fear abandonment by the North American superpower in time of crisis, Nixon turned aside such demands. Still, the pressure on him to set about to terminate involvement by U.S. armed forces in Vietnam was well-nigh overbearing. Lest he trigger an eruption of antiwar protests and rioting compared with which previous protests and demonstrations would doubtless pale, he could scarcely bring the war to a dramatic and violent conclusion by unleashing the full fury of American military-naval power against North Vietnam. So he opted, almost inevitably perhaps, for the policy of "Vietnamization" of the war.

The idea of Vietnamization was to initiate a gradual withdrawal of American forces from Vietnam while building up the ARVN and helping the government in Saigon (in an oft-repeated phrase) "to win the hearts and minds of the people of South Vietnam." U.S. forces, in a word, would continue for an indeterminate period to provide a shield, albeit a steadily diminishing one, for the Republic of Vietnam. Leaders in Washington hoped (or professed to hope) that by the time the last American forces departed Vietnam, the ARVN would have achieved sufficient strength and aggressiveness that it would be able to fend off the North Vietnamese and VC, and the Saigon government would have gained the unwavering allegiance of most of South Vietnam's citizenry. In the unfortunate event that the situation unraveled after the final withdrawal of American forces and the communists gained control of South Vietnam, the people of the United States could take comfort in the knowledge that their government had dealt honorably with its erstwhile ally, and had done everything that might reasonably have been expected to save South Vietnam from the clutches of the communists. That the United States had declined to make a precipitous withdrawal of forces from South Vietnam would likewise offer a measure of reassurance to the country's allies and friends in East Asia, Europe, and the Middle East.

Leaders of the Saigon government inevitably took a negative view of Vietnamization. But they were in no position to speak out against the policy, and at a meeting on the island of Midway on June 8, 1969, Presidents Thieu and Nixon announced that some 25,000 U.S. troops would begin to leave Vietnam in 30 days. In what Nixon would later concede was a diplomatic exaggeration, Thieu told reporters that it was he who had proposed that the withdrawal of American forces be initiated. A jubilant Nixon explained (another exaggeration) that the troops could be withdrawn because of progress in the training and equipping of the South Vietnamese army. Still gamely trying to feign satisfaction with the policy of Vietnamization, Thieu told reporters, "We will do our best from now on to alleviate the burden of the United States people."

Six weeks after the meeting with Thieu on Midway, Nixon was back in the Pacific, first to greet the astronauts of *Apollo 11* on their return from the moon, then to undertake a whirlwind trip around the world in an obvious attempt to make diplomatic and political capital out of the spectacular voyage of American spacemen to the lunar surface. After welcoming Armstrong, Aldrin, and Collins back to earth, he flew westward, and in a conversation with newspeople during a stopover on Guam enunciated what quickly became known as the Nixon Doctrine. The crux of the latter doctrine was that the United States would henceforth assume a lower profile in Asia—and, for that matter, throughout the world. Except where treaty obligations required, the Washington government would feel no compulsion to act in defense of noncommunist regimes that appeared threatened by communist neighbors. Equally important, it would not feel compelled to shore up every noncommunist regime that was under attack by communist insurgents. However unsettling to some of America's friends, particularly in Asia, the doctrine struck a chord with Nixon's compatriots, sick and tired as most of them were of the burden they had assumed over the past two decades, to wit, the burden of trying to preserve every part of the noncommunist world from international communism.

From Guam, Nixon flew to Manila, where he conferred with Pres. Ferdinand E. Marcos, thence to Djakarta in Indonesia and Bangkok in Thailand. From Bangkok, he flew to Saigon, where he conferred briefly with Thieu, then visited a U.S. military installation to the north of Saigon. He asked a soldier from Texas whether he thought the Dallas Cowboys could defeat the Green Bay Packers during the impending football season and a soldier from Chicago whether he had seen the Cubs play during the current baseball campaign. Turning to a black soldier from North Carolina, he asked, "Do they ever get any black-eyed peas and collard greens out here?" His black loafers caked with red clay, the president, after about five and a half hours, was again airborne. He said of the South Vietnamese, "They are going to make it." Saigon, he asserted, was not going to become Ho Chi Minh City.

Indochina During the Vietnam War

Nixon's next stop was New Delhi in India, and after that Lahore in Pakistan. From Lahore, he flew to Bucharest in Romania, where he was greeted by Pres. Nicolae Ceauşescu, a slightly built communist chieftain who commanded a tightly ordered and manifestly repressive police state but who had managed to assert a measure of independence from the Soviet Union. Not since Franklin Roosevelt, at the Yalta Conference in 1945, had a president of the United States set foot in a Soviet-bloc country. An estimated quarter-million Romanians lined the thoroughfares—and their exuberance appeared bound-less. People flung bouquets of roses, waved Romanian and U.S. flags, shouted "Urrah Neek-son!" On three occasions, Nixon jumped from the car, which because of the people pressing about it had slowed to a crawl, and plunged into the crowd to shake hands and exchange greetings with his admirers.

Nixon and his administration, meanwhile, had continued to tug vigor-ously at the cords of diplomacy in an effort to terminate the war in Vietnam. Before leaving Washington for the Pacific, on July 15, 1969, the president ad-dressed a personal letter to Ho Chi Minh urging that the North Vietnamese cooperate with the United States to achieve a negotiated settlement of the conflict. Then, after the presidential stopover in Romania—while Nixon was making his way back to the United States—the president's national security adviser Henry Kissinger flew to Paris to meet secretly with Xuan Thuy, North Vietnam's plenipotentiary at the stalemated peace negotiations. The two men agreed only that their respective governments should be free to contact each other and that the two of them ought to meet again. A few weeks later, Ho replied to Nixon's letter of July 15. As Nixon later conceded, the reply was a cold rebuff. Ho's rebuff aside, Nixon announced on September 16 that an addi-tional 40,600 U.S. troops would leave Vietnam by December 15.

Meanwhile, on September 3, Ho died, apparently of a heart attack. He was 79 years old. Might the passing of Ho result in a weakening of communist intransigence in Vietnam? It was soon manifest that it would not. Possibly reinforcing the intransigence of leaders in Hanoi were antiwar demonstrations on "Moratorium Day" in mid-October by perhaps a million Americans in cities and on college campuses across the United States. The demonstrations were largely peaceful, the oratory muted. A different mood prevailed one month later, in mid-November, when more than 200,000 antiwar protesters rallied in Washington under the aegis of the New Mobilization Committee to End the War in Vietnam, its activities guided by avowed political leftists. Many demonstrators displayed Vietcong flags, others, banners extolling the Cuban revolutionary Ché Guevara. When demonstrators hurled bottles and rocks at the Justice Department, police showered them with choking gas. Demonstrators thereupon divided into street gangs and moved through the capital's commercial area, smashing plate-glass windows as they went.

As for President Nixon, he declared in the autumn of 1969 that antiwar demonstrators would exercise no influence on decisions in the matter of the war—that, in his words, national policy would not be made in the streets. He appealed to Americans to support the policy of Vietnamization. In particular, he sought support for his Vietnam policy by "the great silent majority" of the citizenry. The response of the Silent Majority, as the term would come to ap-pear in the print media, gladdened the presidential heart. Letters and telegrams endorsing Nixon's approach to the war cascaded into the White House; 77 percent of the respondents to a Gallup telephone poll indicated approval of what the president was trying to do in Vietnam.

While the Silent Majority continued to rally around Nixon, in mid-No-vember 1969, the popular conscience endured a horrendous jolt: Via a succes-sion of news stories, the people of the United States learned that American soldiers, nearly all of them seemingly clean-cut and patriotic young men, had wantonly gunned down several hundred Vietnamese civilians at a hamlet known as My Lai 4, situated along the northeastern coast of South Vietnam, in March 1968. Stories of atrocities emanating from Vietnam, of course, were nothing new. Only the previous March (1968), an ARVN soldier had tripped over a wire on a sand flat near the old imperial city of Hué—a wire that was attached to a pair of skeletal hands. Subsequent digging disclosed the bodies of nearly three thousand Vietnamese civilians whom the North Vietnamese and VC had shot, beaten to death, and buried alive during their three-week occupation of Hué at the time of the *Tet* offensive of 1968. But the people of the United States were shocked to learn that American soldiers no less than communist were capable of atrocious and barbaric conduct that might have prompted the warriors of Genghis Khan to blush.

However sickened by disclosures that GIs in Vietnam had committed unspeakable atrocities, a majority of the people of the United States continued to support Nixon's policy of gradual disengagement of American forces from Southeast Asia. That American casualties in the battle zone were diminishing doubtless enhanced the appeal of the policy. (A total of 4,221 U.S. servicemen would die in Southeast Asia in 1970, fewer than half as many as in 1969, largely because American units now tended to be drawn in closer to air bases, cities, and seaports, their positions along the Cambodian and Laotian borders and the DMZ taken over by the ARVN.) Support for the Nixon policy increased in April 1970 when the president announced that an additional 150,000 U.S. servicemen would leave Vietnam over the next year.

Meanwhile, the Accelerated Pacification Program, instituted in 1969 for the purpose of extending the Saigon government's control over the South Vietnamese countryside, appeared to be making headway. At the same time, the CIA pressed ahead with the enterprise of infiltrating the "infrastructure" (or political structure) of the Vietcong with Vietnamese agents who were loyal to the Saigon government, which agents were under orders to arrange for the arrest or slaying of VC organizers, propagandists, tax collectors, and the like. Undertaken in 1967, the enterprise was designated the Phoenix Program. According to statistics released by the U.S. mission in Saigon in 1969, the program had resulted in the "neutralization" over the past year of 19,534 members of the VC infrastructure—6,187 of them killed. On learning of the undertaking, antiwar activists in the United States assailed the Phoenix Program as a blatantly immoral exercise in mass murder. Most news correspondents in Vietnam thought the program, whatever its morality, largely ineffective. But after the war, various communist commanders conceded that the program had presented serious problems for the VC.

## CAMBODIA, PENTAGON PAPERS

In part because of the activities of the provocateurs of the Phoenix Program, but in larger measure because of the effectiveness of conventional ground and air operations by South Vietnamese and U.S. forces, communist military operations by the spring of 1970 had lost much of their steam. Accordingly, those sanctuaries in Cambodia, only moderately damaged by President Nixon's "secret bombing" campaign, had become increasingly important in the calculations of the North Vietnamese and VC. Deployed in the sanctuaries, the communists could undertake strike-and-run operations in South Vietnam whenever an opportunity appeared, and otherwise bide their time until the Americans completed their troop withdrawal program and more or less left the South Vietnamese to fend for themselves. Then, in the closing days of April of 1970, President Nixon ordered American troops to cross the border into the territory of the Khmer kingdom, and the result was a convulsion—in the United States.

Several weeks before, an anticommunist cabal headed by General Lon Nol had deposed Prince Sihanouk, Cambodia's head of state, while Sihanouk was undergoing medical treatment in France. The new regime thereupon terminated the movement of equipment and supplies from the port of Sihanoukville to the communist sanctuaries in eastern Cambodia. At that point the North Vietnamese and Vietcong, supported by Cambodian communists of the Khmer Rouge, began to move out of the sanctuaries into Cambodia. The outcome was several bloody clashes in which the tough and skillful Vietnamese easily routed the ragtag troops of Lon Nol.

Carefully monitoring events in Cambodia, President Nixon calculated that those events provided him with a heaven-sent excuse to render a blow to the communist sanctuaries in Cambodia that would prove far more devastating than raids by B-52 bombers. Rendering a blow to the sanctuaries was no trifling matter, for it was clear that the presence of North Vietnamese and VC bases in Cambodia constituted a grave threat to the Washington government's objective of keeping South Vietnam free of the communist grip after withdrawal of U.S. forces from Vietnam. Accordingly, on the evening of April 20, 1970, Nixon told his compatriots in a televised address that U.S. and South Vietnamese army units had moved into Cambodia for the purpose of destroying the sanctuaries. Those units would not proceed to the interior of the Khmer kingdom, he emphasized, and would withdraw on completing their mission.

Unimpressed by news pictures of captured supplies and reports that U.S. and South Vietnamese troops were meeting almost no resistance and hence suffering few casualties, uncounted millions of Americans were outraged. In their estimate, the Cambodian incursion constituted a dangerous and perhaps fateful expansion of the war in Southeast Asia. And, inevitably, the antiwar movement, dormant in recent months, sprang to life anew. As in the past, much of the antiwar activism was centered on the country's college and university campuses. The upshot, alas, was a tragedy that benumbed all Americans, whatever their view of the war in Vietnam: During a raucous confrontation with student protesters on the campus of Kent State University in Ohio, national guardsmen shot and killed four students. The tragedy, of course, heightened the rage of opponents of the Cambodian incursion and prompted a new wave of angry demonstrations. To take some of the steam out of the protests, a beleaguered Richard Nixon issued a pledge that U.S. troops would be out of Cambodia by June 1, 1970. (Several months later, in January 1971, Congress approved the Cooper-Church amendment prohibiting the use of funds appropriated by Congress for "the introduction of United States ground combat troops into Cambodia, or to provide United States advisors [to Cambodia].")

In the aftermath of the Cambodian incursion, the number of U.S. military-naval personnel deployed in Southeast Asia continued to dwindle—to 234,000 by the end of 1970, 156,000 at the end of 1971, 24,700 at the end of 1972. As American troop strength declined and the ARVN assumed larger combat responsibilities, American casualties inevitably diminished. During 1971, U.S. servicemen died in Vietnam at a rate of 26 per week (a total of 1,831), during 1972 at a rate of about 6 per week (a total of approximately 300). Still, the war in Southeast Asia remained near the center of the national consciousness, and the citizenry responded with apprehension in early 1971 when Nixon sanctioned U.S. aerial and artillery support for what proved to be a futile movement into southern Laos by 19,000 ARVN troops for the purpose of putting a crimp in the Ho Chi Minh Trail.

Causing a much greater stir in the United States than the ARVN's foray into Laos was publication by the *New York Times* on June 13, 1971, of the first installment of "the Pentagon Papers," a 7,000-page study of the U.S. involvement in Southeast Asia from World War II through 1968. Commissioned by President Johnson's first secretary of defense, Robert S. McNamara, the study abounded with documents that remained officially classified and disclosed that the appearances of America's policy and behavior in the matter of Southeast Asia had not always squared with the reality. Its purveyor turned out to be Daniel Ellsberg, a onetime defense researcher in the Pentagon. Ellsberg later explained that he passed the study to newspapers because he had become disillusioned with what the United States was doing in Southeast Asia.

Although the Pentagon study did not bear on his management of the war in Southeast Asia, President Nixon was furious that Ellsberg had leaked classified documents to the news media. At the same time, Nixon became increasingly exercised about the leakage of top secret information within his own administration, and in July 1971 his assistant John Ehrlichman assigned Egil "Bud" Krogh, a youthful member of the White House staff, to take charge of an antileak project. Among those recruited for the project were E. Howard Hunt, a former operative of the CIA, and G. Gordon Liddy, a former FBI agent. Because their job was to repair leaks, Krogh and his men eventually became known as the Plumbers.

Seven weeks later, in the middle of the night of September 3, 1971, the Plumbers set about to obtain documents that would discredit Daniel Ellsberg. Apparently under the direction of Charles W. "Chuck" Colson of the White House staff, Hunt and Liddy, assisted by three Cubans, broke into the office of Ellsberg's psychiatrist, Dr. Lewis Fielding, in Beverly Hills, California. They found no file with Ellsberg's name on it. Did Nixon know of the plan to break into Fielding's office? He later wrote that he was not certain. He also wrote that in retrospect the break-in seemed wrong and excessive. But, he went on, he did not think it as wrong or excessive as what Ellsberg had done.

## CHINA, DÉTENTE

At the same time of the national furor over publication of the Pentagon Papers, in June and July of 1971, the Nixon administration was engaged in delicate negotiations with leaders of the People's Republic of China, a sworn enemy of the United States over the past two decades (although in the years 1954–1968 representatives of the Beijing and Washington governments had engaged in 134 unpublicized and largely unproductive conversations in Geneva and Warsaw). The purpose of the negotiations was transparent: to prepare the way for an eventual normalization of relations between the North American superpower and the world's most populous nation-state. Encouraging the administration in its dealings with "Red China" was the steadily escalating hostility that had marked the Beijing government's relations with its longtime ally, the Soviet Union, for more than a decade. Indeed, beginning in early 1969, Chinese and Soviet troops had clashed intermittently at various points along the meandering frontier separating the territory of the communist giants. The clashes had been brief but bloody.

As for Nixon, he had hinted before his election to the presidency that he thought the time had come for the United States to establish normal diplomatic relations with the government of mainland China. Then, late in 1970, Mao Zedong told the writer Edgar Snow that Nixon would be welcome should he wish to visit the People's Republic. Several months later, in April of 1971, an American table tennis team that was competing in Japan received a surprise invitation to play several exhibition matches in China. The White House approved acceptance of the invitation, and in a matter of days astonished people across the world were pondering photographs of Premier Chou En-lai of the People's Republic entertaining the American Ping-Pong players. Next, in a digression during a speech in Washington, President Nixon remarked that he hoped someday to visit China. A fortnight later, the Beijing government indicated that it was prepared to receive a special envoy whom the president might dispatch to the Chinese capital—or the president himself. The White House thereupon arranged for Henry Kissinger to make a secret trip to Beijing to work out details of a presidential visit to the People's Republic. The Kissinger undertaking met success, and on July 15, 1971, Nixon made a televised announcement that he would travel to China sometime in 1972. All save a handful of Americans were thunderstruck.

If Nixon's announcement won wide approval among his startled compatriots, it nonetheless caused a stir in the diplomatic community. Arrangements for an official invitation to the president to visit China had been worked out in utmost secrecy, and the Washington government's allies wondered whether the affair might signal a new "go-it-alone" style of diplomacy by the United States. Downright distressed by the announcement, of course, were the Chinese on Taiwan, who feared that the United States was about to abandon them in the interest of a rapprochement with the government of mainland China. To reassure the latter Chinese, the Washington government advised leaders in Taipei that it would neither withdraw recognition of their government nor renounce its mutual security commitment to Taiwan.

Likewise upset by Nixon's announcement of July 15, 1971, were leaders in the Kremlin. The Soviets clearly suspected that the United States was trying to exploit the ever-widening rift between the premier communist powers, and might even be preparing the groundwork for a Sino-American alliance directed against the Soviet Union.

As already noted, relations between the United States and the Soviet Union underwent steady improvement in the aftermath of the Cuban missile crisis of 1962. In that climate of improved relations, people in the United States and elsewhere began to wonder whether the two superpowers might at last find it possible to work out an agreement to limit the production and deployment of strategic nuclear weapons. Intertwined with talk of strategic arms limitation was speculation that the superpowers might achieve *détente*, defined in Webster's as "an easing or relaxation of strained relations and political tensions between nations."

Sensing that the time might be opportune for working out a strategic arms limitation treaty, President Johnson in 1967 and 1968 prodded the Soviets to enter negotiations aimed at achieving such a treaty. And at length, in July 1968, the Soviets responded favorably to his prodding. But then, in the following month, they sent forces of the Warsaw Pact rumbling into Prague to extinguish an experiment in communist liberalism recently undertaken by the Czech government. Whereupon the Johnson administration made it clear that it would not enter strategic arms limitation (SALT) talks so long as Warsaw Pact forces remained in Czechoslovakia. Still, Johnson determined that the invasion of Czechoslovakia would not disrupt the pursuit of détente or result in an indefinite postponement of SALT negotiations.

No less than Lyndon Johnson, Richard Nixon was committed to arms limitation and détente, and in June 1969 he authorized Secretary of State William B. Rogers to inform the Soviets that the United States was now prepared to undertake SALT negotiations. Accordingly, the first round of SALT negotiations got under way in Helsinki in Finland in November 1969. Negotiators were unfailingly serious and businesslike, and on suspension of the first round of talks in December 1969 they agreed that their enterprise would resume in Vienna the following spring. The negotiations in Vienna quickly deadlocked, largely because the Soviets sought an agreement that would limit only defensive ABM systems, while the Americans insisted that it limit offensive weapons, for example, ICBMs, as well. But at length, the Soviets dropped their objection to including limitations on offensive weapons in a SALT treaty.

Then, on July 15, 1971, Nixon announced his intention to visit China in 1972. The announcement, as mentioned, upset the Soviets. But it also appeared to quicken the pace of détente, for a few weeks later, in August of 1971, the Soviets reached a new agreement with Britain, France, and the United

States by which they agreed that the movement of people and commodities via the land routes linking West Germany and West Berlin would be "unimpeded," and eased restrictions on West Berliners who wished to travel and trade in East Germany. During that same month, moreover, on August 10, the Soviets invited Nixon to visit the Soviet Union in May or June of 1972, and on October 12 the president announced acceptance of that invitation.

Meanwhile, President Nixon's impending visit to China was having repercussions at the UN. The reasons for those repercussions are not hard to discern. Lest they antagonize the United States, a coalition of allies and other countries that for one reason or another felt beholden to the North American superpower, had for many years supported the Washington government's dubious contention that the Nationalist regime on Taiwan remained the legitimate government of China and thus was entitled to represent the old Middle Kingdom in the world organization. Most had done so grudgingly. But now the United States itself was moving toward rapprochement with the People's Republic of China, hence its allies and friends no longer feared that supporting a resolution to seat a delegation at the UN representing the Beijing government and expel the one representing the government in Taipei might invite reprisals by the United States. As a result, it was clear by the autumn of 1971 that the General Assembly of the world organization was about to vote to seat a Beijing delegation. Confident that its action would not jeopardize its emerging relationship with the People's Republic, the United States sought support for a proposal to seat a Beijing delegation while retaining a seat for the delegation from Taipei, a solution that proved no less unacceptable to leaders in Taipei than those in Beijing. Pressed by George H. W. Bush, the U.S. ambassador at the UN, the proposal stirred no enthusiasm at all, and on October 25, 1971, the General Assembly voted to expel the Taipei delegation and seat one representing the government in Beijing.

At the same time that delegates from Beijing were taking seats in the UN, the Washington government was striving to cope with a bitter conflict on the Indian subcontinent that had large importance in terms of the interests of the United States. The conflict came to a head in 1971 when the armed forces of West Pakistan (present-day Pakistan) set about to suppress a burgeoning movement whose object was total autonomy for East Pakistan (present-day Bangladesh). Delighted that its longtime enemy Pakistan was on the verge of breaking apart, India, which in August 1971 had signed a treaty of friendship and cooperation with the Soviet Union, projected itself into the civil conflict in early December of 1971 by sending forces smashing into East Pakistan to counter the West Pakistanis. A fortnight later, the Indians captured Dacca, the capital of East Pakistan, the West Pakistanis and Indians agreed to a cease-fire terminating the 15-day war, and East Pakistan became the independent nation-state of Bangladesh.

During the war on the Indian subcontinent in December 1971, the Washington government "titled" in favor of West Pakistan. The tilt resulted in diplomatic pressure on India to refrain from a full-dress attack on the territory of West Pakistan. At least two considerations accounted for the tilt. While India over the past decade or so had tended to align itself with the Soviet Union and frequently pilloried the United States, Pakistan (its political center in West Pakistan) had been a stalwart ally of the United States, and a link in the barrier that the Washington government sought to erect against Soviet expansion in Central and South Asia. The United States, in a word, felt indebted to the general government of Pakistan, its capital now in Islamabad in West Pakistan. The latter government, moreover, was closely aligned with that in Beijing, presently hostile to both India and the Soviet Union, and had taken an important part in arranging President Nixon's impending trip to China. Anything less than a tilt in favor of West Pakistan during its confrontation with India, American leaders suspected, might jeopardize the latter trip.

## HISTORIC JOURNEYS

On the morning of February 17, 1972, President and Mrs. Nixon and a battalion of aides and other officials set off for Beijing. After several stopovers en route, the presidential jet touched down at an airport outside the capital of mainland China. Standing at the foot of a ramp that reached to the cabin of the big Boeing 707, hatless in the winter cold, was Premier Chou En-lai, and when Nixon emerged from the cabin and began to descend the ramp the 72-year-old Chou began to clap. In accord with Chinese custom, Nixon, smiling broadly, returned the gesture. When the president reached the runway, the two men, both wearing overcoats, shook hands and exchanged pleasantries. Noting that no throng of ordinary citizens was on hand to wave and cheer, some observers thought the arrival lonely. The formalities at the airport over, Nixon and Chou entered a curtained limousine for the ride into the city. Scarcely any people were to be seen along the roadside. Inside Beijing, the streets were also almost vacant of people.

Later that same day, Nixon was ushered to the residence of Chairman Mao, an unimposing house in the historic Imperial City. When the president entered his cluttered study, Mao, old and fat and obviously in failing health, rose from an overstuffed chair, and with a smile extended his hand. The chairman was animated and full of good humor during the one-hour conversation that followed. As for Nixon, he returned Mao's humor and was unfailingly polite.

The next day, the people of China learned for the first time that the president of the United States was in their midst when the *People's Daily* bannered the meeting of Mao and Nixon. Official restraint thereupon gave way to warmth and cordiality, and friendly crowds gathered when President and Mrs. Nixon toured the Ming Tombs, the Forbidden City, and the Great Wall. Nixon and Chou, meanwhile, passed 15 hours in a ranging discussion of issues and ideas, and in Shanghai, at the end of the president's one-week visit, issued the "Shanghai Communiqué." Acknowledging their differences regarding Vietnam and Korea, the communiqué announced that the Washington and Beijing governments accepted the principle of peaceful coexistence, renounced the use

February 22, 1972: An aging Mao Zedong greets President Nixon at Mao's residence in Beijing during Nixon's historic trip to China.

of force to settle disputes, and agreed that neither country would try to dominate the Pacific area. Nixon acknowledged that Taiwan was a part of China, and intimated that the United States would withdraw its military contingent from that island. Finally, the two leaders agreed that there should be "people-to-people" exchanges involving Americans and Chinese, increased trade between their countries, and periodic consultations between their governments.

On returning from what nearly all of his compatriots were acclaiming as a triumphant pilgrimage to the ancient and mysterious Middle Kingdom, President Nixon began to prepare for his impending journey to the Soviet Union, a venture in personal diplomacy that he expected would be no less a triumph than that in China. His mood was almost euphoric. But then his euphoria was shattered: In the spring of 1972, the communists unleashed a new and ferocious battlefield offensive in Vietnam.

The war in Vietnam had appeared to be winding down in the closing months of 1971. But, in fact, the North Vietnamese at that time were preparing for combat on a scale they had not undertaken since the departure of the French nearly two decades before. Their movements largely hidden under the jungle canopy, they dispatched an array of vehicles, including tanks, down the

Ho Chi Minh Trail to the sanctuaries in Laos and Cambodia. They deployed guns, tanks, and battle-ready troops in their own territory just to the north of the DMZ. Then, in the last days of March of 1972, they let fly a massive artillery barrage against South Vietnamese strongpoints in the vicinity of the DMZ. Next, in the first days of April, they sent hundreds of Soviet tanks and more than 120,000 troops crashing across the DMZ into Quang Tri province. From sanctuaries in southeastern Laos and Cambodia, they subsequently launched large-scale attacks against ARVN forces deployed to the northeast of Saigon and in the Central Highlands.

Surveying the events that were unfolding in Vietnam, President Nixon seethed. What might he do? Only 95,000 GIs, most of them service troops, remained in Vietnam, and an order dispatching fresh American combat troops to reinforce the outmanned and outgunned ARVN divisions was out of the question. But he could and did order fighter-bombers and B-52 stratofortresses of the U.S. Air Force and carrier-based fighter-bombers of the Navy to sortie in support of the beleaguered South Vietnamese. He ordered warships of the Navy that were deployed in the South China Sea to turn their guns against onrushing North Vietnamese divisions in the vicinity of the DMZ and blast military targets in coastal areas to the north of the DMZ. He also ordered American bombing planes to strike supply dumps and other military targets to the north of the DMZ (thus terminating the moratorium on air raids over North Vietnam imposed by President Johnson in November 1968).

Other events of large import transpired during those tumultuous weeks in the spring of 1972. Declining to withdraw their invitation to Nixon to visit the Soviet Union, notwithstanding his vigorous response to the latest communist offensive in Vietnam, leaders in the Kremlin received Henry Kissinger cordially when he arrived in Moscow to discuss an agenda for the presidential visit. Doubtless to take some of the steam out of protests by antiwar activists who had again taken to the streets of America's cities as a consequence of his resumption of the bombing campaign against North Vietnam, Nixon announced that another 20,000 U.S. troops would depart Vietnam over the next two months. At the same time, Kissinger met secretly in Paris with Le Duc Tho, the special adviser to the North Vietnamese delegation at the stalemated peace negotiations. In a concession that would severely compromise South Vietnam's chances of surviving as a noncommunist state, he indicated that the Washington government would no longer insist on a withdrawal of North Vietnamese forces from South Vietnam, Laos, and Cambodia in the aftermath of a cease-fire in Vietnam. Only U.S. forces would be required to withdraw. But he continued to insist that a post-cease-fire government in South Vietnam must be determined by free elections in which all parties, including communists, might participate. To such a condition the North Vietnamese would not consent. They continued to insist on a settlement that would compel the immediate overthrow of the Thieu regime in Saigon and imposition of a coalition government rigged to assure communist domination of South Vietnam.

Then, on May 8, President Nixon went before television cameras and announced that the United States would bomb all railway supply routes reaching down from China across North Vietnam—and had planted mines in six North Vietnamese ports, including Haiphong. His purpose was obvious: to prevent war equipment and supplies dispatched by China and Soviet-bloc countries from reaching North Vietnam and sustaining communist military operations in Cambodia, Laos, and South Vietnam. Nixon's compatriots were again thunderstruck, particularly by news of the mining of North Vietnam's harbors. What would happen if a Soviet cargo vessel was disemboweled by one of the mines while delivering implements of war to North Vietnam? Might such a happening touch off a full-blown crisis involving the superpowers? In the face of such questions, antiwar activists across the republic accelerated their demonstrations.

Inasmuch as the mines that the United States had planted in North Vietnam's harbors were clearly intended to stop—and in fact did stop—the movement of Soviet and Soviet-bloc ships in and out of the harbors, most Americans, including Nixon and Kissinger, suspected that the president's bold and dramatic action would prompt the Soviets to cancel Nixon's invitation to visit the Soviet Union. But leaders in the Kremlin were no less committed to détente between the superpowers than those in Washington, whatever the situation in Vietnam. They also were bent on preventing the Americans and Chinese from entering any sort of alliance. Accordingly, the invitation remained in place, and on May 20, 1972, the president and his lady, accompanied by the usual entourage of aides and advisers, boarded Air Force One and took to the air, destination: Moscow. The trip was a rousing triumph.

In the course of his visit, during which General Secretary Leonid Brezhnev and other Soviet leaders exuded charm and high humor, Nixon attended a gala performance of *Swan Lake* at the Bolshoi Theater, flew to Leningrad where he made an emotion-packed visit to the Piskaryev Cemetery, the final resting place of thousands of Soviet citizens who perished during the German siege of the city in the years 1941–1944, and made a television address to the Soviet nation in which he spoke of the dangers of the arms race and emphasized his own country's yearning for peace. But the high point of the Moscow summit came to pass on the evening of May 26 when Nixon and Brezhnev made their way down a red-carpeted stairway, seated themselves at a table beneath the giant gilt chandelier of the Kremlin's St. Vladimir Hall, and signed documents that were spread out before them in blue-and-red-leather folders. The documents spelled out the provisions of a treaty that would become known as SALT I.

SALT I had two parts. The first part limited each signatory to two ABM sites, at neither of which could the signatory deploy more than a hundred antiballistic missiles. Because such a modest force of ABMs could not begin to protect either the Soviet Union or the United States against a full-dress missile attack by the other, that part of the treaty gave permanence to the conception of deterrence to nuclear war by mutually assured destruction, for in effect each signatory agreed to leave its population and military-industrial apparatus exposed to attack by the other's strategic missiles. The second part of SALT I provided that neither superpower would undertake construction of additional land-based ICBMs after July 1, 1972. Modern submarines and submarine-launched ballistic missiles would be limited to those at sea or under construction on the day the treaty was signed. The limitations spelled out in the second part of the treaty were to expire in five years unless reconfirmed or extended before 1977.

Nixon and the Soviets confirmed other agreements during the Moscow summit of May 1972. They consented to establishment of a joint commission to encourage trade between their two countries and also a commission to expand cooperation in science and technology. They achieved accord in matters relating to environmental pollution, medicine, and public health, and they agreed that their countries should undertake a joint orbital mission in outer space. (The latter agreement came to fruition in 1975 when Apollo and Solyuz spaceships achieved a docking several hundred miles above the earth.)

In Vietnam, meanwhile, the great communist offensive of the spring of 1972 had ground to a halt, largely as a result of the battering administered to communist armored and infantry divisions by U.S. air and naval power. In the words of Stanley Karnow, the communists "had not crushed the United States and its South Vietnamese allies in a showdown battle, as they had beaten the French force at Dienbienphu [in 1954]."

## RETROSPECT

The 53 months from the dawn of 1968 through May of 1972 were indeed a time when the emotions of the people of the United States, after the fashion of a roller coaster, gyrated from valleys of anguish to peaks of triumph. Americans experienced genuine anguish when North Koreans seized the *Pueblo* and shot down the EC-141, when assassins gunned down Martin Luther King, Jr., and Robert Kennedy, when urban ghettos erupted in the aftermath of King's murder and police and antiwar protesters collided at the time of the Democratic national convention in Chicago, when the North Vietnamese and Vietcong uncorked their *Tet* offensive and the communications media reported the My Lai atrocity, when national guardsmen shot down four young people at Kent State University. They felt supremely triumphant—more than that, unabashedly exhilarated—when U.S. astronauts set foot on the surface of the moon and returned safely to earth, arguably the premier technological achievement in the history of the world to the present day, an achievement that appeared to prove that America's time-honored ingenuity and "can-do" spirit were alive and well. Most citizens of the North American superpower felt a sense of triumph or at least profound satisfaction when President Nixon made his historic journey to the People's Republic of China and when he affixed his signature to the SALT I treaty in the capital of the Soviet Union. Alas, the moments of anguish were more numerous than those of triumph.

The commanding personage of the period, in the perspective of Americans at any rate, was of course Richard Nixon, a man who experienced a political resurrection in 1968 and moved into the White House in January 1969. From the time of his inauguration through May of 1972, the thirty-seventh president proved himself to be a man of insight and skill who could keep his emotions in check and act prudently, as in the affair of the EC-141, but could also look challenges squarely in the face and make hard decisions, as in the spring of 1972 when, at the risk of provoking the Kremlin to cancel his invitation to visit the Soviet Union—and, worse, at the risk of provoking a dangerous confrontation with the Kremlin should an American mine destroy a Soviet ship—he unleashed American air and naval power to stay the tide of a communist military offensive in South Vietnam and ordered the mining of the harbors of North Vietnam.

Nixon's most pressing challenges obviously emanated from the war in Southeast Asia. Notwithstanding his remark many years later that on entering the White House he should have subjected the North Vietnamese to the unmitigated fury of American military-naval power if they refused to give up their campaign of conquest in South Vietnam, he understood full well when he affixed his hands to the levers of presidential power that, because of the climate of opinion in the United States, such a response to North Vietnamese intransigence was out of the question. So he opted for Vietnamization of the war, which appears to have been a genuine and honorable attempt to extricate the United States from the bitter conflict while providing its longtime client South Vietnam with a reasonable chance to keep itself free of communist totalitarianism. And he did everything in his power to make Vietnamization succeed—by trying to neutralize the communist sanctuaries in Cambodia and Laos and then, in the spring of 1972, as mentioned, by ordering U.S. air and naval forces to move to South Vietnam's rescue when the North Vietnamese and Vietcong let fly what they hoped would be a showdown offensive.

Scarcely any American is apt to quarrel with the proposition that Nixon's "opening" to China was a monumental achievement, one that only an American political leader such as he, that is, a Republican Cold Warrior who could never be accused (as Democratic presidents had been accused) of being "soft on communism," could have brought off. His attempt to achieve détente vis-à-vis the Soviet Union represented a serious effort to move the Cold War to a final termination. And the SALT I treaty that he and Brezhnev signed in Moscow represented a first step toward fulfillment of the dream of every American president since World War II, to wit, the dream of nuclear disarmament or at least a reduction in the stocks of nuclear arms.

In home affairs, Nixon wrestled, apparently with a modicum of success, with a truculent economy, prevailed on Congress to accept what many Americans thought was historic legislation aimed at returning a measure of federal authority back to the states, offered a plan for welfare reform that many observers thought sensible, and did more to encourage protection of the natural environment than any American president to his time. Unfortunately, he displayed scant interest in encouraging the crusade on behalf of civil rights for racial minorities. He displayed even less interest in the crusade for women's liberation.

What was worse, Nixon gave vent to the darker elements of his character-personality when he ordered what appears in retrospect to have been the illegal tapping of phones, encouraged the FBI in its transparently illegal campaign of harassment against political radicals and war protesters, and probably sanctioned the break-in at the office of Daniel Ellsberg's psychiatrist. Indeed, as Nixon was winging home in triumph from the historic summit meeting in Moscow, individuals connected with his administration and his campaign for re-election to a second four-year term in the White House, doubtless encouraged by Nixon's "us-against-them" syndrome, one that adjudged as acceptable almost any tactic aimed at thwarting the president's "enemies," were about to undertake a bizarre and transparently criminal political espionage operation that would result in the ruination of Richard Nixon and his presidency.

# Chapter
# 9

---

# Tragedy and
# Transformation

$W$hile President Nixon was recording diplomatic triumphs in Beijing and Moscow and acting to contain the latest battlefield offensive by the communists in Vietnam, during the first months of 1972, other Americans were concentrating on the impending presidential election. Inasmuch as it was a foregone conclusion that the Republicans would renominate Nixon and Agnew for president and vice president, respectively, the attention of the communications media tended to fix on the Democrats.

At the dawn of 1972, Sen. Edmund S. Muskie of Maine was widely assumed to be the front-runner among Democratic aspirants to the White House. But when the Muskie campaign faltered and the senator withdrew from the competition, the Democratic field was left to Hubert Humphrey, the party's standard-bearer of 1968, Sen. George S. McGovern of South Dakota, and Gov.

George C. Wallace of Alabama. Then, on the afternoon of May 15, 1972, a gunman reduced the field to two. In the parking lot of a shopping center in Laurel, Maryland, 21-year-old Arthur H. Bremer, an unemployed misfit, pushed a pistol between spectators who were striving to shake hands with Wallace, squeezed the trigger five times, and sent the governor crumpling to the asphalt. Paralyzed below the waist, Wallace would never walk again.

## McGOVERN VS. NIXON

By the time of Wallace's exit from the campaign, Senator McGovern, an ultra-liberal who had fashioned a highly efficient campaign organization, had emerged as the odds-on favorite to win the Democratic presidential nomination. The South Dakotan's message had struck a chord with blacks, campus intellectuals, Chicanos, feminists, and homosexuals, not to mention legions of long-haired youths who despised the war in Vietnam and dreamed of engineering a peaceful revolution of American society. And when delegates to the Democratic national convention assembled in Miami Beach, supporters of McGovern were in firm control of the party machinery. Accordingly, the delegates approved a platform representing McGovern's ultraliberal views, and on the first ballot nominated the senator for president. At McGovern's behest, they nominated Sen. Thomas F. Eagleton of Missouri to be his vice presidential running mate.

Then, within days of the convention, the McGovern campaign suffered a devastating blow: It was disclosed that Eagleton had previously been hospitalized for psychiatric treatment, and in the course of the treatment had undergone shock therapy. When great numbers of Americans made manifest their dismay that a man burdened with a history of mental depression might become president, McGovern prevailed on Eagleton to forfeit his nomination, then designated R. Sargent Shriver, the brother-in-law of the late President Kennedy, to be his running mate. Although Shriver appeared the equal of Eagleton in ability and appeal, the episode nonetheless was a staggering embarrassment for McGovern and the Democrats.

Nixon and the Republicans, meanwhile, had been more fortunate, for they had managed to escape embarrassing disclosures with little apparent damage. Charges circulated in early 1972 that, in return for a gift of $400,000 to assist the Republican Party in meeting expenses at its forthcoming national convention in San Diego, the Nixon administration had prevailed on the Justice Department to withdraw an antitrust action against the ITT Corporation, a giant conglomerate. Although no hard evidence appeared to support the charges, Republican leaders decided to shift the party's national convention from San Diego to Miami Beach.

Of what would prove to be of infinitely larger moment, police on the evening of June 17, 1972, arrested five men during a break-in of the headquarters of the Democratic National Committee (DNC) in the Watergate, a fashionable apartment, hotel, and office complex on the banks of the Potomac in Washington. Wearing rubber globes and equipped with the tools of electronic espionage, the five men were in the act of installing electronic listening devices in the offices of the DNC, including that of Lawrence F. O'Brien, the chairman. One of the men was James McCord, a former security officer of the CIA who presently was security coordinator of the Republican National Committee and the Nixon re-election committee. The others were anti-Castro émigrés from Cuba who resided in Miami. Five days later, President Nixon, having returned to the capital after a vacation at Key Biscayne in Florida, addressed the break-in at the Watergate in a public statement: "This kind of activity . . . has no place in our electoral process or in our government process. And . . . the White House has no involvement whatever in this particular incident." At length, in the latter half of August of 1972, delegates assembled for the Republican national convention in Miami Beach, cheered a rousing attack on the Democrats by Gov. Ronald Reagan of California, and duly renominated Nixon and Agnew.

In the perspective of Republicans, only one gray cloud was visible on the horizon when their convention adjourned: Watergate. Persuaded that there was more to the incident than met the eye, the editors of the *Washington Post* had pressed the Watergate story, and published the names of White House aides alleged to have been associated with the men indicted as a result of the break-in. But on August 29, during a news conference, the president announced, "[W]ithin our own staff, under my direction, counsel to the president, Mr. [John W.] Dean [III], has conducted a complete investigation of all leads which might involve any present member of the White House staff or anybody in the government. I can say categorically that his investigation indicates that no one in the White House staff, no one in this administration, presently employed, was involved in this very bizarre incident."

A preponderance of Americans took the president at his word, hence declined to respond to efforts by Senator McGovern to make the Watergate affair a campaign issue. Accordingly, the McGovern campaign, its ultraliberal theme repugnant even to millions of citizens who in previous elections had tended to vote Democratic, continued to sputter, and on November 7, the electorate presented the Nixon-Agnew ticket with the landslide victory that everybody had anticipated: 47.1 million votes (60.7 percent) to 29.1 million (37.5 percent) for McGovern and Shriver. Winning all electoral votes save those of Massachusetts and the District of Columbia, Nixon and Agnew triumphed in the Electoral College by a margin of 570–17. To their chagrin, however, the Republicans failed to win control of the House of Representatives and actually lost strength in the Senate.

## "PEACE WITH HONOR"

During the political campaign of 1972, the Nixon administration continued to search for an armistice agreement that would enable the United States to exit the war in Vietnam on terms perceived by most Americans to be honorable. Then, in early October of 1972, Le Duc Tho of North Vietnam advised Henry Kissinger that the communists no longer insisted on the overthrow of the

October 1972: Le Duc Tho of North Vietnam and Henry Kissinger of the United States after reaching tentative agreement on the terms of an armistice in Vietnam.

Thieu government and installation of a coalition regime in Saigon as a condition of such an agreement. He thus removed what long had stood as the most formidable obstacle to an armistice. That obstacle put to rest, the broad outline of an agreement quickly emerged, and Kissinger on October 26 announced, prematurely, as matters turned out, that "peace is at hand" in Vietnam. In accord with the agreement, U.S. forces would depart Vietnam, the North Vietnamese would not enlarge their forces in South Vietnam, the North Vietnamese and the Vietcong would leave the territory of Cambodia and Laos, and the assorted factions in the country, including the communists, would settle the question of the political structure of South Vietnam in the aftermath of an armistice.

But then, on November 1, President Thieu in Saigon issued a public statement in which he denounced the agreement as a surrender document. Pressed by President Nixon to announce approval of the armistice agreement, Thieu demanded that it be amended to provide for the withdrawal of all North Vietnamese troops and military equipment from South Vietnam. In a communication dated November 14, 1972, Nixon told Thieu that what he was seeking was unrealistic, then pledged, "You have my absolute assurance that if Hanoi fails to abide by the terms of this agreement it is my intention to take swift and severe retaliatory action."

A few days later, Kissinger was on his way back to Paris to resume negotiations with Le Duc Tho for the purpose of resolving assorted "technical" questions pertaining to the execution of an armistice agreement. The negotiations quickly stalled when Tho raised one frivolous issue after another. Aware that sentiment was building in the U.S. Congress for passage of a resolution demanding the immediate withdrawal of all remaining American troops in Vietnam and termination of American military and economic assistance to the Saigon government, the North Vietnamese apparently had decided that it might not be a bad idea to allow the draft armistice agreement of October 8 to twist slowly in the wind. In addition to weakening the bargaining position of the United States in the armistice negotiations, the passage of such a congressional resolution might break the morale of the Saigon government, in which event South Vietnam would become easy pickings for the determined and disciplined communists.

Frustrated and piqued, Nixon on November 22 instructed Kissinger to warn the North Vietnamese that the United States would take whatever action it deemed necessary to protect its interests—and to inform representatives of the Saigon government that Congress was apt to terminate all military and economic assistance to South Vietnam if an armistice agreement was not reached. As for the North Vietnamese, they continued to stonewall, and following an unproductive session with Tho on December 13, Kissinger broke off the discussions and returned to Washington.

Four days later, on December 17, in accord with an order issued by President Nixon, the Navy began to reseed Haiphong harbor with mines and the Air Force unleashed its B-52 stratofortresses against strategic targets in the area of Hanoi and Haiphong. Save for a six-hour pause in observance of Christmas Day, the so-called Christmas bombing campaign, during which the North Vietnamese shot down 26 U.S. aircraft, 15 of them B-52s, continued until December 30. The purpose of such a fearsome display of military-naval power was transparent: to compel the Hanoi government to quit its haggling and accept the draft armistice agreement of October 8.

Contrary to news reports bannered across the world, U.S. aircraft did not engage in terror-bombing of populated areas of North Vietnam during the Christmas bombing campaign. The bombers sought out such strategic targets as air-defense installations and electric power stations, and the accuracy of the bombing was almost surgical. As the historian Guenter Lewy later wrote, the death toll reported by the Hanoi government in the aftermath of the Christmas bombing—between 1,300 and 1,500—was surely not indicative of terror-bombing. Part of the death toll, moreover, was attributable to the North Vietnamese themselves, who, Lewy wrote, "launched about 1,000 SAMs [surface-to-air missiles], many of which impacted in the cities of Hanoi and Haiphong and took their toll on their own people." In a commentary published shortly after the Christmas bombing, the editors of the London *Economist* observed that the resultant number of deaths during the bombing, as reported by the Hanoi government, "is smaller than the number of civilians killed by the North Vietnamese in their artillery bombardment of [the South Vietnamese town of] An Loc in April [of 1972] or the toll of [South Vietnamese] refugees ambushed when trying to escape from Quang Tri at the beginning of May [of 1972]."

How did the people of the United States respond to the Christmas bombing? Despite the fact that a preponderance of Americans seemed wearily resigned to the Nixon administration's attempt to bludgeon the North Vietnamese to accept an armistice agreement satisfactory to the United States, no small number of citizens were outraged by what the news columnist James Reston described as the president's "war by tantrum." Senate Majority Leader Mike Mansfield considered the bombing "a Stone Age tactic," and Sen. Edward Kennedy declared, "This should outrage the conscience of all Americans."

Meanwhile, criticism rolled in from beyond the borders of the United States. France's largest weekly, *L'Express*, described the B-52 bombing plane as a "nearly blind monster," and proclaimed, "Mr. Nixon is no longer, and will never be again, a respectable man. That is, if he ever was one." The editors of the liberal Hamburg weekly *Die Zeit* declared, "Even allies must call this [bombing campaign] a crime against humanity. . . . The American credibility has been shattered." The governments of Belgium, Denmark, Finland, and the Netherlands assailed the Christmas bombing. Premier Olof Palme of Sweden, his memory apparently purged of any recollection that his country had suckled the Nazi war mechanism during World War II, condemned the bombing as a crime against humanity that on a moral scale compared to Nazi atrocities at the death camp at Treblinka.

Whatever the criticism, Nixon refused to order a halt to the bombing of Hanoi and Haiphong—until the Hanoi government in the last days of December 1972 signaled its wish to resolve the remaining issues that stood in the way of an armistice agreement. Events thereupon moved quickly. On January 2, 1973, "technical" negotiations between the combatants resumed. On that same day, the Democratic caucus in the House of Representatives voted 154–75 in favor of a cutoff of all funds for military operations in Indochina, contingent only upon the willingness of the communists to permit a safe withdrawal of remaining U.S. forces and the release of all American POWs. On January 8, Kissinger met with Tho in Paris, and over the next few days resolved remaining problems relating to an armistice agreement, most of them almost trivial.

One question remained: Would the South Vietnamese acquiesce in the agreement that Kissinger and Tho had worked out? In no mood to meet obstruction in Saigon, Nixon advised President Thieu that the United States would continue to provide military equipment and supplies to South Vietnam, and would "respond with full force" if North Vietnam violated the cease-fire agreement. He also made it clear that if Thieu refused to endorse the armistice agreement the United States would sign it anyhow—and would cut off further assistance to the Saigon government. Having no viable option, Thieu indicated on January 21, the day after Nixon had repeated the presidential oath for the second time, that he would not oppose the agreement. Remarked the South Vietnamese president, "I have done all that I can for my country." (The following day, January 22, death claimed Lyndon Johnson, a casualty, many Americans thought, of the dreary war that apparently was about to pass into history.)

Representatives of the combatants in Vietnam affixed signatures to the Agreement on Ending the War and Restoring Peace to Vietnam in a ceremony in the ballroom of the Majestic Hotel in Paris on January 27, 1973. The agreement provided for an immediate cease-fire across Vietnam, the withdrawal from the country of remaining U.S. troops (about 27,000), and the release of POWs throughout Indochina. The North Vietnamese were prohibited from infiltrating troops and the paraphernalia of war into South Vietnam (but could replace men and equipment on a one-for-one basis). An international supervisory commission was to police the cease-fire and regulate the passage into South Vietnam of replacement personnel and equipment through designated checkpoints. North Vietnam and the VC were to withdraw their forces from Cambodia and Laos, and refrain from using the territory of the latter countries for military action against South Vietnam. The assorted factions of the country were to determine the political future of South Vietnam.

That evening, in Washington, President Nixon appeared on television to announce the achievement of "peace with honor" in Southeast Asia. Claiming that the agreement signed earlier in the day had the full support of President Thieu, he said, "The people of South Vietnam have been guaranteed the right to determine their own future without outside interference." A few hours before, Secretary of Defense Melvin Laird had announced termination of the military draft in the United States, while in the waters off the coast of Vietnam naval crews awaited signals to remove the mines that their comrades had seeded in North Vietnam's harbors. Next, a few days later, America's POWs, their emotion-packed arrivals at Clark Air Force Base in the Philippines monitored by millions of their compatriots via television, began to return from captivity in North Vietnam.

Had the United States achieved "peace with honor" in Vietnam? More to the point, did South Vietnam stand a reasonable chance of surviving as a noncommunist republic, or was the armistice agreement nothing more than a fig leaf to permit the United States to exit the conflict in Indochina before the communists resumed the war and overwhelmed South Vietnam's noncommunists? Certainly, nobody reckoned that leaders in Hanoi had given up their dream to destroy the Saigon regime and to assert their authority over South Vietnam—to turn all of Vietnam into a communist and totalitarian nation-state. Still, Henry Kissinger has written that he was persuaded that South Vietnam had a chance to stay clear of the clutches of North Vietnam: "We believed that Saigon was strong enough to deal with guerrilla war and low-level violations [of the armistice agreement]. The implicit threat of our retaliation would be likely to deter massive violations."

Whatever the thoughts of Kissinger, Nixon, and other leaders of the United States, the ultimate fate of South Vietnam was not much on the minds of Americans at the end of January of 1973. So far as most citizens were concerned, the war in Vietnam belonged to a past that they wished to forget. It was a war in which 47,318 Americans had died as a result of enemy action, 10,449 of accidents and disease. In a word, approximately 1 of every 50 American servicemen deployed in Vietnam from 1959 to 1973 had lost his life. America's sacrifices, of course, paled before those of the Vietnamese. What some writers referred to as the Second Indochina War (the First Indochina War having been that from 1946 to 1954 involving the French and noncommunist Vietnamese on the one hand and the Vietminh on the other) had resulted in the death of 184,000 military and naval personnel who wore the uniforms of the Saigon government and an estimated 927,000 of those who served North Vietnam and the Vietcong. Nobody this side of heaven knew for certain how many civilians had perished as a result of the war.

## AFTER VIETNAM

America's agony in Southeast Asia had passed, or so Americans thought in early 1973. But what of the future? Might a president, acting without the advice and consent of the people's representatives in Congress, succumb to the temptation to project the country into "another Vietnam"? Congress determined that it would not. Accordingly, in the autumn of 1973, it passed—over President Nixon's veto—the War Powers Act. The War Powers Act provided that when the president committed the country to hostilities abroad or ordered a substantial increase in the number of U.S. combat troops deployed in foreign countries, he must report the circumstances and scope of his action to Congress within 48 hours. He must terminate the commitment to hostilities or withdraw the troops he had deployed after 60 days unless he received sanction by Congress to do otherwise, although he might continue the commitment or deployment for another 30 days if the safety of American forces appeared to require it. The measure provided that Congress might order termination of a presidential commitment of the country to hostilities or deployment of troops abroad at any time by passing a concurrent resolution (a type of resolution not subject to a presidential veto). More ominous in the perspective of America's friends in Indochina were initiatives by Congress that prohibited U.S. forces to engage in combat activities in, over, or off the shores of Cambodia, Laos, and Vietnam, and the use of funds appropriated by Congress to finance paramilitary operations in Indochina.

Meanwhile, other facets of foreign relations commanded the attention of President Nixon. Although refusal by the United States to sever ties with the Chinese Nationalist regime on Taiwan remained an impediment, the president continued his effort to normalize relations between the United States and the People's Republic of China, and to that end, in the spring of 1973, the Washington government opened a liaison mission in Beijing and the Beijing government a similar mission in Washington. Of equal moment, Nixon continued to press the policy of achieving détente vis-à-vis the Soviet Union. In accord with that policy, General Secretary Leonid Brezhnev was invited to visit the United States and engage in summit conversations with President Nixon. Brezhnev accepted the invitation, and in June 1973 arrived from Moscow for an eight-day sojourn in the territory of the North American superpower. In addition to conferring with Nixon in Washington and at camp David in Maryland, he met with members of Congress, spoke to a group of American businesspeople, and addressed the people of the United States via television. He and Nixon signed accords intended to achieve scientific cooperation in the peaceful uses of atomic energy, reduce the risk of nuclear confrontation and avoid nuclear war, and establish basic principles for negotiating new strategic arms limitation agreements.

However frequent his smiles during the Brezhnev visit, Nixon, to borrow a time-worn phrase, had not gone soft on communism. That became apparent less than three months after Brezhnev's return to the Soviet Union, in September 1973, when he took unalloyed satisfaction in the violent overthrow of one of Brezhnev's comrades, Salvador Allende Gossens, the 65-year-old president of Chile.

Securing 36.3 percent of the votes, Allende, a onetime medical doctor and avowed Marxist who professed to believe the United States responsible for most of the ills of the world, had finished first in the popular balloting in a three-man contest for the Chilean presidency in September 1970. Inasmuch as no candidate had received a majority of popular votes, the election passed to the chilean Congress. Whereupon Nixon, persuaded that Allende would turn Chile into a Cuba-like bastion of communism and a base for the encouragement of Marxist revolutions throughout Latin America, urged the Congress in Santiago to reject Allende's candidacy. To no avail: The congress elected Allende. At that point, Nixon instructed the CIA to explore the possibility of arranging a coup d'état aimed at preventing Allende's inauguration. The exploratory operation came to nothing. Accordingly, Allende, committed (so he told a French Marxist) to the establishment of "total, scientific Marxism" in Chile, took the presidential oath.

That leaders in Washington took a jaundiced view of the Allende regime was no secret. But did the Nixon administration, as was widely asserted after Allende's overthrow in 1973, try to "destabilize" that regime? Henry Kissinger has written, "Contrary to anti-American propaganda around the world and revisionist history in the United States, our government had nothing to do with planning . . . [Allende's] overthrow and no involvement with the plotters" who eventually brought down Chile's Marxist president. The extent of U.S. involvement in the internal affairs of Chile during Allende's presidency, according to Kissinger, was the transfer of comparatively modest sums of money to support opposition political parties in Chile and also segments of the Chilean news media that were threatened with shutdown.

Whatever the behavior of the United States vis-à-vis his regime, Allende began to accumulate troubles almost from the moment he repeated the presidential oath. Millions of Chileans were dismayed by the Marxist orientation of the policies and initiatives of his regime. Equally serious, inflation was soon galloping out of control, and by the summer of 1973 the economy was a shambles. The upshot was a succession of crippling strikes that further ravaged the economy, while massive street protests of food shortages and spiraling prices by housewives of Chile's middle-income families, not to mention escalating violence involving ideologues of the political left and right, had polarized the population and brought the country to the edge of civil war. As for the government in Washington, Kissinger has written that during those weeks of chaos in Chile, he directed Ambassador Nathaniel Davis in Santiago to keep the U.S. embassy clear of the developing crisis.

At length, in the early morning of September 11, 1973, the commander in chief of the Chilean armed forces and national police demanded Allende's immediate resignation. When Allende refused to resign, aircraft of the Chilean air force bombed the presidential palace, and at mid-day army troops stormed the smoldering building and, so they later reported, found Allende dead, slumped on a velvet-covered sofa, shot once in the mouth. Many people across the world suspected that the troops had murdered the president, but Allende's wife conceded that he had indeed shot himself to death—with a submachine gun given him as a present by Fidel Castro.

Less than a month after the fall of Allende, in early October of 1973, a happening of arguably much greater import jarred the world: Yet another—the fourth—Arab-Israeli war erupted in the Middle East. Like the previous wars, that of October 1973 inflamed anew the passions of Arabs and Israelis in their interminable struggle for dominance of a minuscule patch of Middle Eastern desert that Arabs and Israelis alike perceived to be sacred. It also triggered events that at once startled and dismayed the people of the United States, and prompted them to confront for the first time the fact that they had become dangerously dependent on foreign sources of energy.

If the region tended to pass from the consciousness of most Americans in the years following the U.S. military intervention in Lebanon in 1958, the Middle East nonetheless continued to seeth with anger and frustration, hatred and resentment. It seethed in no small measure because Arab peoples from the Persian Gulf to the Mediterranean and across northern Africa remained steadfast in their refusal to reconcile themselves to the existence of Israel as a Jewish nation-state in the former Arab domain of Palestine. Permeating the region, accordingly, was persistent tension that was intermittently punctuated by terrorist attacks and other acts of violence, many of them the enterprise of various guerrilla groups that, after its formation in 1964, operated under the aegis of the Palestine Liberation Organization (PLO), an umbrella organization that was dedicated to Israel's destruction and the restoration of Palestine.

At length, beginning in late 1966, a succession of military actions and diplomatic maneuvers moved the Middle Eastern antagonists toward a new crisis, and in early June of 1967 the Israelis, certain that an Arab attack was imminent, unleashed their air force and army against Jordan, Syria, and the United Arab Republic (Egypt). As in the past, the Israelis prevailed against their enemies on every front, and on June 10, 1967, what would become known as the Six-Day War ended when Israel, Jordan, Syria, and the UAR, responding to a resolution by the UN, agreed to a cease-fire.

Arabs of course, continued to seethe. The Six-Day War had marked their third humiliation at the hands of the Israelis. The Israelis, moreover, had driven Egyptian forces from the Gaza Strip and Sinai Peninsula, Jordanian forces from the West Bank of the Jordan, and Syrian forces from the Golan Heights, and also had seized control of the Old City of Jerusalem. The Suez Canal was closed. Still, the Soviets had replaced the arms the Arabs had lost in the war, and the Arab dream of exterminating Israel burned as fervently as ever. Particularly animated by that dream were the assorted factions of the PLO, which in 1969 fell under control of its largest member, al-Fatah, whose leader Yasir Arafat became chairman of the PLO's executive committee. The PLO thereupon accelerated its campaign of terror against the Israelis and their supporters. A principal purpose of PLO terrorism was to draw world attention to the unhappy plight of the Palestinian people, which plight they believed to be the fruit of Zionism. The campaign reached a horrendous climax in the summer of 1972 when Palestinian terrorists murdered two and kidnapped nine members of the Israeli team during the Olympic games in Munich. All nine of the kidnapped athletes subsequently died in a shootout between the terrorists and West German police.

At length, in early 1973, the Arabs and Israelis began to edge toward yet another full-dress war, and on October 6, 1973, while large numbers of Israelis were in synagogues observing Yom Kippur, the Day of Atonement, Egyptian forces crossed the Suez Canal and attacked Israeli positions in the Sinai; those of Syria smashed at the Golan Heights. In the first days of the so-called Yom Kippur War, the Egyptians and Syrians made impressive gains, but within a week Israeli forces had turned the tide of the battle, and a week after that were advancing toward the Syrian capital of Damascus and the Egyptian capital of Cairo.

Carefully monitoring the latest armed conflict in the Middle East were leaders in Washington and Moscow. Indeed, the fourth Arab-Israeli war in 25 years appeared to threaten policies aimed at achieving détente that the superpowers had been nurturing in recent years. Ignoring American efforts to moderate the level of outside assistance to the combatants, the Soviets in the first week of the war undertook a large-scale airlift of equipment and supplies to Syria and Egypt, in response to which action President Nixon ordered C-130 cargo transports of the U.S. Air Force to make a comparable airlift of equipment and supplies to Israel. Nixon also ordered delivery to Israel of ten Phantom jet-fighter planes.

At that point, responding to an invitation by Leonid Brezhnev, Henry Kissinger (now the secretary of state as well as national security adviser) flew to Moscow, and with Brezhnev worked out a resolution to achieve a cease-fire in the Middle East that was promptly adopted by the Security Council of the UN and, on October 24, 1973, accepted by the combatants. But when the United States turned aside a request by Pres. Anwar el-Sadat of Egypt that both superpowers send troops to help stabilize the cease-fire, the government in Moscow dispatched a bristling note to Washington in which it threatened to respond to Sadat's request whether the United States did so or not. Nixon thereupon placed U.S. military-naval forces around the world on alert. The danger of a Soviet-American confrontation deriving from the crisis in the Middle East passed when the Security Council of the world organization authorized a UN force of seven thousand troops to police the cease-fire.

Although the Yom Kippur War had left a legacy of unresolved questions that would plague the world for years to come, a quietude of sorts now settled over the Middle East. Unresolved questions regarding the Middle East notwithstanding, the Washington government could take satisfaction in the realization that its policy of striving to achieve détente remained intact and that its friend Israel had survived yet another military challenge. Still, an ominous event had transpired in the course of the Yom Kippur War—one that gave pause to Americans of perceptive mind: On October 17, 1973, 11 Arab states agreed to reduce the production and export of crude oil and to embargo the sale of oil to several nations, including the United States, that were deemed to be friendly to Israel.

## A TIME OF TRANSFORMATION

Scholars of history are fond of identifying watersheds in the experience of nations, that is, points at which a nation, normally for economic, political, or social reasons, appears to complete a transition from one era or epoch in its national experience to another. Historians, for example, have viewed 1890, the year in which (according to the U.S. Bureau of the Census) the western frontier finally passed into memory, as a watershed in the experience of the United States. Another watershed in the American experience, historians have surmised, was 1920, the year in which (again according to the U.S. Bureau of the Census) the country's population finally became predominantly urban. Another was 1945, the year in which the United States brought forth the atomic bomb and emerged as a global superpower. Still another watershed in the experience of the United States, or so historians might very well conclude in the years to come, was 1973–1974.

In the latter years, as mentioned, Congress set about to constrict the authority of what the historian Arthur M. Schlesinger, Jr., has described as "the imperial presidency" to project the country into conflicts beyond its own frontiers. Meanwhile, the growth of the national population, which had helped fuel the country's economic boom in the decades following World War II, was slowing perceptibly. Reaching 210.4 million in 1973, the population of the North American superpower increased by 0.7 percent during that year, the lowest percentage ever recorded. Responsibility for the decline of the country's population was to be found in the declining birthrate, which in the United States in 1973 was 14.9 births per thousand people (compared with 24.1 in 1950), the lowest figure ever recorded.

Generating manifestly greater concern in the United States in the early 1970s was the increased competition that American manufacturers, for more than a half century the undisputed giants of most of the world's manufacturing industries, were encountering from abroad, particularly Western Europe and Japan. Whereas the United States had produced 46.6 percent of the world's steel in 1950, it produced only 19.6 percent in 1973. Whereas it had accounted for half of the world's output of motor vehicles as recently as 1965, it accounted for less than a third in 1973. And not only were foreign manufacturers making serious inroads in overseas markets long dominated by Americans; they were now doing likewise in the United States itself, for nearly a century an almost exclusive preserve of American producers. Cascading into the United States were ever-increasing volumes of clothing, shoes, clocks, watches, and electronics equipment. Whereas the United States had imported 1.0 million short tons of steel in 1950, it imported 15.2 million in 1973. Whereas it had imported a mere 26,000 new cars from Japan in 1965, it imported 625,000 in 1973.

More urgent in 1973, or so it seemed, was what millions of Americans would come to refer to as an energy crisis. It was a crisis whose economic implications for the United States appeared to be at once frightening and incalculable. More than that, it was one that appeared to have grave implications for the strategic calculations of the North American superpower with respect to its interests around the globe as well as the security of the national homeland.

The evolution of the United States from a third-rate economic backwater in the middle of the nineteenth century to a pulsating economic colossus by the middle of the twentieth had rested on a variety of circumstances, one of which was an abundance of energy resources within the national domain, notably coal, oil, and natural gas. So abundant were their energy resources that Americans gave scarcely any thought at all to the obvious fact that those resources were not inexhaustible. Accordingly, they expended—or squandered—energy in a manner that, in retrospect, was outrageously irresponsible. By the 1970s, in truth, Americans, comprising 6 percent of the world's people, were consuming more than 30 percent of its output of energy.

In the early years of what historians refer to as America's industrial revolution, its principal energy source was coal. But in the 1920s and 1930s, largely as a result of the transportation revolution prompted by massive acceptance of the automobile and motor truck, the balance began to shift, and by 1950 coal accounted for 38.1 percent of the country's energy consumption, oil 39.8 percent, and natural gas 18.1 percent. In subsequent years, as steam locomotives gave way to diesel-electrics, electric-generating plants and factories turned increasingly to oil for power, and millions of homeowners and proprietors of businesses replaced dirty coal-fired furnaces with those fired by oil and natural gas, the balance continued to shift. By 1973, coal represented 17.8 percent of the country's energy consumption, oil 46.7 percent, natural gas 30.2 percent, hydropower about 4 percent, and nuclear power 1 percent.

Regarding oil, the United States from the second decade of the twentieth century both imported and exported crude petroleum—in 1938 imported 26.4 million barrels while exporting 77.2 million. Meanwhile, as oil fields were opened in many areas of the country, particularly in California, Louisiana, Oklahoma, and Texas, the domestic production of crude steadily increased, from 1.2 billion barrels in 1939 to 2.5 billion in 1960 to 3.5 billion in 1970. The United States indeed continued to produce more crude than any other nation-state, followed by the Soviet Union and Saudi Arabia. Still, domestic production could not keep pace with the country's burgeoning demand for oil, so imports of crude increased dramatically: from 178 million barrels in 1950 to 372 million in 1960 to 483 million in 1970 to 811 million in 1972 to 1.2 billion in 1973. (The country was likewise importing increasing quantities of natural gas: from 10.9 billion cubic feet in 1955 to 820.8 billion in 1970 to more than a trillion in 1973.) Notwithstanding the development of new oil fields in recent years in the Gulf of Mexico and on Alaska's North Slope, the United States by 1973 was importing more than a third of its domestic requirements of petroleum energy.

However startling the foregoing numbers may appear in retrospect, only an occasional voice was raised to express concern that the country might be edging toward an energy crisis. Realizing record profits from the country's pulsating economy, oil companies through the 1960s and into the 1970s actively encouraged Americans to increase their consumption of energy. Likewise realizing record profits, automobile manufacturers continued to concentrate on the production of cars that would come to be called gas-guzzlers (for the return on the sale of a big car was substantially greater than that on the sale of a small car)—and ordinary citizens, seemingly infatuated with large automobiles, continued to buy them (in no small measure because gasoline in the United States was incredibly cheap—ranged in price through the 1960s and into the 1970s between 28 and 35 cents per gallon, only a dime or so more than during the time of the Great Depression). Environmentalists, meanwhile, labored to block construction of nuclear power plants intended to augment or replace coal- and oil-fired facilities. And what of the country's political leaders? Down to the 1970s, few of them betrayed even passing awareness that its voracious appetite for energy and increasing dependence on imported oil might one day imperil the economic well-being, not to mention the security, of the United States—seldom made even a passing suggestion that the national interest might require a national policy aimed at conserving and developing new sources of energy.

## ENERGY CRUNCH

At length, in the spring of 1971, President Nixon sent a 5,000-word energy message to Congress. Asserting that "we cannot take our energy supply for granted any longer," he asked Congress to appropriate $3 billion over the next decade to develop new sources of "clean" energy from fossil and nuclear fuels. In response to the presidential request, Congress in 1972 appropriated $285 million for construction of a liquid metal fast breeder reactor (LMFBR), for demonstration purposes, along the Clinch River in eastern Tennessee. (Fueled by uranium isotopes, conventional thermal fission reactors result in wastage of 99 percent of the uranium that is mined for the production of energy; breeder reactors, by contrast, use nearly all of the uranium ore that is so mined. Indeed, a properly designed breeder reactor actually produces more nuclear fuel—plutonium—than it consumes, hence the name "breeder." Unfortunately, breeder reactors promised to be far more costly than conventional thermal fission reactors, and the waste materials that they produced were far more toxic.) Otherwise, Congress made minimal response to Nixon's energy message of 1971.

Then, in January 1973, the United States confronted a bona fide energy shortage when domestic and foreign suppliers could not keep pace with the country's burgeoning appetite for petroleum products. Homeowners in Des Moines found themselves without heating oil, factories in Illinois and West Virginia had to suspend operations, numerous flights from John F. Kennedy International Airport in New York had to be canceled, barges laden with grain on the Ohio and Mississippi Rivers were stranded. It was a jarring experience, and many Americans for the first time began to face up to the hard reality that, in the matter of energy, times were changing. Remarked Secretary of Commerce Peter G. Peterson: "Popeye [the United States] is running out of cheap spinach."[1] In the estimate of Adm. Hyman G. Rickover, "The energy crunch is the most serious problem that has faced the United States, including the Civil War."[2]

A few months later, on April 18, 1973, President Nixon sent a new message to Congress on the subject of energy—one that opened with the words, "At home and abroad, America is in a time of transition." He sought a variety of initiatives intended to increase the country's energy supplies, among them construction of a pipeline from the North Slope of Alaska to the forty-ninth state's south coast. He also asked Congress to sanction a new federal agency, to be designated the Department of Energy and Natural Resources.

Then, on October 16, 1973, during the Yom Kippur War, 6 Arab states unilaterally raised the posted price of oil by 70 percent, from $3.01 a barrel to $5.12. On October 20, 11 Arab states announced an embargo on the sale of oil to the United States and all countries deemed friendly to Israel. Inasmuch as

---

[1] *Newsweek*, Jan. 22, 1973, p. 52.

[2] *The American People's Encyclopedia Year Book*, 1974, p. 40.

January 1973: Gasoline ration lines in Connecticut during the first of several gasoline shortages in the 1970s.

the United States received the bulk of its imported oil from Canada, Nigeria, Venezuela, and such non-Arab countries as Indonesia and Iran, its economic life was not devastated. Still, it was estimated that the embargo would deprive the United States, whose daily consumption of oil was 17 million barrels, of 3 million barrels of crude each day. Of larger moment perhaps were the embargo's psychological consequences: The action by the 11 Arab states demonstrated the North American superpower's vulnerability to energy blackmail.

As the effect of the Arab embargo began to be felt across the United States, President Nixon, on November 7, 1973, outlined initiatives and policies for dealing with the national energy shortage in a television address. While issuing a new appeal for action by Congress, he asked his compatriots to unite behind a program aimed at achieving energy independence. The response of the compatriots was decidedly negative. The plain truth was that a substantial number of Americans suspected (or claimed to suspect) that the energy shortage was a giant hoax fabricated by the oil companies in the interest of profits, and had been embraced by Nixon as a means of diverting attention from the scandal that had closed about his presidency in the aftermath of new revelations relative to the Watergate break-in the year before. In the face of such popular negativism, Congress responded cautiously to Nixon's appeal that it act. It authorized construction of a 789-mile pipeline across Alaska and established a speed limit of 55 miles per hour on the country's highways. But it was unable to agree on omnibus energy legislation.

Meanwhile, on December 22–23, representatives of the Organization of Petroleum Exporting Countries (OPEC) meeting in Kuwait raised the price of crude petroleum produced by those countries from $5.12 a barrel to $11.65, an increase of 387 percent from the price of $3.01 that had prevailed before October 20. Not since World War II had the international community endured an economic shock of comparable dimension. Particularly devasted were the poor countries of the Third World. Because of the need to divert a sharply increased percentage of their meager resources to pay for oil, a circumstance that made it difficult for them to obtain the requisite financing in the world's money markets, most of them had to curtail plans for industrial development. Equally serious, the increase in oil prices resulted in dramatic increases in the prices of chemical fertilizers derived from petroleum, heavy applications of which were essential to the production of the high-yield hybrid grains that such countries had to produce if they were to feed their burgeoning populations.

What was happening to the poor peoples of the Third World was of small concern to most Americans. Until it was lifted by all countries save Libya and Syria on March 18, 1974, the Arab oil embargo caused nettlesome shortages of diesel fuel, gasoline, and heating oil in various parts of the United States. Among the consequences were lines of cars reaching for many city blocks from gasoline stations as motorists waited for two hours and more to have their tanks filled—and also a violent strike by independent truckers who were frustrated by the shortage of diesel fuel.

Of equal moment in the view of most Americans was the new round of inflation that apparently was touched off by the increase in the price of OPEC oil. The price of nearly everything that Americans consumed, from clothing to food to hardware, seemed linked with the prices of diesel fuel and gasoline. Priced in the area of 30 cents a gallon only a few years before, gasoline now edged toward 60 cents. Whatever the explanation, the consumer price index advanced by 11.0 percent in 1974, compared with 6.2 percent in 1973 and 3.3 percent in 1972. Inflation was not the extent of the country's economic woes. The percentage of the labor force that was unemployed, which had declined from 5.6 percent in 1972 to 4.9 percent in 1973, moved back to 5.6 percent in 1974. Sales of new passenger cars plummeted from 11.4 million units in 1973 to 8.8 million in 1974. Before the year 1974 ended, indeed, some analysts suspected that the country might be drifting into its most severe economic recession since the time of the Great Depression of the 1930s.

Unbeknownst to most Americans, meanwhile, "petrodollars" (dollars earned from the export of petroleum) that were cascading into the sparsely populated and arid states of the Middle East were increasingly finding their way back to the United States in the form of investments. In the mid-1970s, for example, Arab interests invested $150 million in a casino-resort complex in Las Vegas, $200 million in an apartment complex in St. Louis, $50 million in a real estate investment company in Louisville, tens of millions in a downtown hotel and shopping complex in Atlanta. In the years ahead, Arabs—and also Iranians—would use petrodollars to purchase office buildings and hotels and vast tracts of choice farmland in the United States. Other millions of petrodollars, most of them emanating from Saudi Arabia, found their way to Arab states that had little or no oil, notably Egypt, Jordan, and Syria, in the form of grants and loans—also to the Palestine Liberation Organization. Still other millions were disposed of in France, the United States, and elsewhere, particularly by Iran, Iraq, and Saudi Arabia, to purchase ground-to-air missiles, jet fighter planes, and other military hardware.

## THE REEMERGENCE OF WATERGATE

What many Americans increasingly perceived to be a bona fide energy crisis was nowhere near the center of President Nixon's attention in 1973 and 1974. At the center of Nixon's attention was the survival of his presidency.

During the autumn of 1972, the *Washington Post* published a succession of reports by the investigative reporters Carl Bernstein and Robert "Bob" Woodward spelling out their conviction that, contrary to official denials, the Nixon re-election committee and also members of the inner circle of the White House—and perhaps President Nixon himself—had been party to the events that culminated in the break-in of the offices of the DNC in the Watergate in June of 1972. Providing much of the information for those reports was an individual code-named "Deep Throat" by the reporters, his identity a closely guarded secret to the present day, who held a sensitive position in the Executive Office. Unfortunately, Bernstein and Woodward could offer no ironclad proof of malfeasance by Nixon and his people.

Then in January 1973, the very month that Nixon repeated the presidential oath for the second time, the trial of the seven men who had been charged in the Watergate break-in got under way. Five of the defendants promptly admitted their guilt; a jury subsequently returned guilty verdicts in the cases of the remaining two. But the judge in the proceedings, John J. Sirica, a 70-year-old son of Italian immigrants, remained troubled, and announced his suspicion that the trial had not produced all of the facts pertinent to the case. To produce the missing relevant information, he urged a congressional inquiry. Responding to Sirica's urging, the Senate on February 7, 1973, established a seven-member Senate Select Committee on Presidential Campaign Activities to investigate alleged irregularities in the presidential election campaign of 1972. Chosen to chair the committee was 76-year-old Sam J. Ervin, Jr., a bushy-browed, Bible-quoting Democrat of North Carolina. Next, on March 23, 1973, at the time he sentenced all of the Watergate Seven save James McCord to prison terms, Sirica read a letter that he had received from McCord. In the letter, McCord asserted that persons other than the Watergate Seven had been involved in the break-in at the Watergate, that pressure had been applied on the seven to remain silent about the involvement of those persons, and that perjury had been committed during legal proceedings involving the seven.

The pace of events now quickened. A federal grand jury began to listen to the testimony of witnesses and to examine evidence regarding the Watergate case. Then, during a press conference on April 17, 1973, President Nixon announced that he had inaugurated "intensive new inquires" into the Watergate affair—also that there had been "major new developments in the case." Two days later, the *Washington Post* reported that Jeb Stuart Magruder, former deputy director of the Committee for the Re-election of the President and presently an official in the Department of Commerce, had told federal prosecutors that former-Attorney General John N. Mitchell, the director of the Nixon re-election campaign, and John W. Dean III, the White House counsel, had approved and helped plan the Watergate break-in and later arranged to buy the silence of the Watergate Seven. On the same day, Dean issued a statement that he would not become a scapegoat in the Watergate case. Other disclosures followed. According to newspaper reports, L. Patrick Gray, the acting director of the FBI, had destroyed incriminating documents relating to the Watergate affair at the direction of Dean and presidential assistant John D. Ehrlichman. On April 29, the *Washington Post* reported that H. R. "Bob" Haldeman, the

July 10, 1973: Suit jacket open, settled back in his chair, the former attorney general and onetime confidant of President Nixon, John N. Mitchell, testifies before the Senate Watergate Committee.

White House chief of staff, and Ehrlichman had directed Dean to make certain that the Watergate break-in would never be linked to the White House. Whereupon Nixon fired John Dean and during an emotion-packed weekend at Camp David, extracted letters of resignation from Haldeman and Ehrlichman, hitherto his most trusted aides.

Nixon now took his case to the country—in a television address on April 30, 1973. He denied any foreknowledge of the Watergate break-in, as well as any part in attempts to cover up involvement by members of the White House staff in the Watergate affair. Intoned the president, "I want the American people . . . to know beyond the shadow of a doubt that during my term as president, justice will be pursued fairly, fully, and impartially, no matter who is involved. This office is a sacred trust and I am determined to be worthy of that trust. . . ."

On May 18, 1973, Attorney General-designate Elliot L. Richardson, responding to a resolution by the Senate, appointed a special prosecutor to take charge of all aspects of the Watergate case: 61-year-old Archibald Cox, a law professor at Harvard. Four days later, President Nixon issued a 4,000-word statement in which he acknowledged for the first time that there had been "wide-ranging efforts to limit the [Watergate] investigation . . . [and] to conceal the possible involvement of members of the administration and the campaign committee" in the Watergate affair. Those efforts, he insisted, had been undertaken without his advice and consent.

Startling disclosures, meanwhile, had emanated from Los Angeles, where Daniel Ellsberg and Anthony J. Russo, Jr., had been undergoing trial on charges of conspiracy, espionage, and theft in connection with publication of the Pentagon Papers. On April 27, 1973, the presiding judge revealed that two of the Watergate conspirators, E. Howard Hunt, Jr., and G. Gordan Liddy, had broken into the office of Ellsberg's psychiatrist in September of 1971. It was disclosed in subsequent days that the White House had authorized illegal wiretaps on the phones of government officials and news correspondents to determine the sources of leaks of national security information. The foregoing disclosures prompted Judge W. Matthew Byrne to dismiss the charges against Ellsberg and Russo.

Back in Washington, the seven-member Senate Select Committee, often referred to as the Ervin Committee, was preparing for public hearings on the matter of the Watergate break-in and related questions, and at length, on May 17, 1973, in the ornate Senate Caucus Room on Capitol Hill, Senator Ervin banged his gavel and called the committee to order. Millions of Americans looked on via television. Over the next 12 weeks, until August 7, the committee interrogated 33 witnesses.

The Watergate burglar James McCord testified that John J. Caulfield, a former presidential staff assistant, had urged him "to remain silent, take executive clemency [to be granted in due time by President Nixon] by going off to prison quietly, and I was told that while there I would receive financial assistance and later rehabilitation and a job." Following McCord to the witness chair, Caulfield admitted that he had offered executive clemency to McCord in exchange for the latter's silence, but denied telling McCord that the offer had come from Nixon. Jeb Stuart Magruder, a boyishly handsome man of 38, testified that John Mitchell, the onetime attorney general in the Nixon administration who had overseen Nixon's re-election campaign, had approved plans to bug the headquarters of the DNC during a campaign strategy meeting in Florida in March of 1972. Taciturn and terse, Mitchell denied that he had been party to plans to bug the DNC. Testy and combative, John Ehrlichman, 48, denied all charges of illegal conduct—also denied that Nixon had offered executive clemency to the Watergate Seven in exchange for their silence. Like Ehrlichman, 46-year-old Bob Haldeman denied illegal conduct.

Inarguably, the stellar witness of the Senate Watergate hearings was 34-year-old John Dean. Poised, articulate, and believable, Dean told the senators that the Watergate affair "was an inevitable outgrowth of a climate of excessive concern over leaks, an insatiable appetite for political intelligence, all coupled with a do-it-yourself White House staff, regardless of the law." He did not accuse the president of having been party to the plan to break into the headquarters of the DNC at the Watergate. But he contradicted Nixon's assertion of August 29, 1972, that Dean had made a thorough investigation of the Watergate incident and found no White House involvement. Rather, according to the former counsel to the president, he (Dean) had been involved in preventing any disclosure of—that is, in covering up—White House involvement, and, so he told the Ervin Committee, Nixon on September 15, 1972, complimented his enterprise. According to Dean, in a word, the president had been guilty of the crime of obstructing justice, and hence had lied to his compatriots when he proclaimed in his television address of April 30, 1973, that in the summer and autumn of 1972 he had striven to discern the truth of the Watergate affair and concluded that no member of his administration had been involved.

If Dean's testimony were true, of course, Nixon's assertion in the speech of April 30, 1973, that he had not become aware of the involvement of members of his administration in the Watergate affair until March of 1973 had likewise been a bald-faced lie. Another bald-faced lie (assuming the accuracy of Dean's testimony) was the president's assertion in the address of April 30 that on becoming aware of the involvement of members of his administration he had "determined that we should get to the bottom of the matter, and that the truth should be fully brought out—no matter who was involved."

Dean testified that on March 13, 1973, at a meeting in the White House, he had told the president that the Watergate Seven were demanding money in exchange for their silence. Nixon allegedly asked how much their silence would cost. About a million dollars, Dean estimated. Whereupon, according to Dean, the president "told me that was no problem, and he also looked over at Haldeman and repeated the same statement." Dean told the senators that on March 21, 1973, he told Nixon "that there was a cancer growing on the presidency" and if it were not removed "the president himself would be killed by it."

Dean also provided the committee with a copy of a confidential memorandum that he had prepared on "dealing with our political enemies" and a copy of one by Charles "Chuck" Colson, a special counsel in the White House, listing the names of 20 persons—businesspeople, congressional liberals, labor leaders, news correspondents, and others (including the film actor Paul Newman)—who were to be given priority in that "dealing." According to Dean, "available federal machinery" was to be used against the enemies of the Nixon administration: audits by the IRS, denial of federal grants, prosecution, and litigation.

However credible his testimony, Dean had been unable to provide much supporting evidence for his charge that Nixon and his principal assistants had committed the crime of obstructing justice to cover up White House involvement in the Watergate break-in. And in the absence of supporting evidence, the Nixon presidency appeared apt to survive the Watergate scandal, whatever the tarnish to its popular image. But then, because one of his former colleagues, Gordon Strachan, had mentioned him in passing during an interview with the committee staff, the Ervin Committee summoned Alexander P. Butterfield, administrator of the Federal Aviation Agency and a onetime White House aide, for closed-door questioning.

During the questioning of Butterfield, one of the committee's minority (Republican) lawyers—in what was subsequently described as a "just fishing" question—asked the witness whether there was any substance to John Dean's suspicion, expressed during the latter's appearance before the committee, that one of his last conversations with President Nixon might have been taped. Looking pained, Butterfield replied, "I really hoped you guys wouldn't ask that." Whereupon he explained that in 1970 the president had authorized the installation in the Oval Office, and also in his office in the Executive Office Building, of listening devices that were plugged into tape recorders. The purpose of the tape recording system? Its purpose was to provide posterity with a verbatim transcript of presidential conversations—an historical source that would be of incalculable value to scholars of the future. According to Butterfield, the presence of Nixon in either of his offices would trigger the listening devices, or "bugs." The bugs, he said, would pick up any sound or conversation, including the lowest tones. Reported *Newsweek* a short time later, "The committee, scenting blood, worked Butterfield instantly into its schedule—and kept the secret until he himself reluctantly sprung [sic] it on America" (in testimony given under the glare of television lights on the afternoon of July 16, 1973).

The disclosure that presidential conversations relating to Watergate—those described by Dean, as well as undisclosed conversations that Nixon must have had with Ehrlichman, Haldeman, Mitchell, and others—were on tapes presently in Nixon's possession was stupefying. Almost certainly etched into the tapes was an answer to the celebrated question previously posed by Sen. Howard H. Baker, Jr., Republican of Tennessee, a member of the Ervin Committee: "What did the president know and when did he know it?" Or as set out in a report in *Newsweek*, Butterfield's testimony "on its face suggested that Mr. Nixon had been sitting on a whole trove of hard evidence of his guilt or innocence in the scandals." As for the president, hospitalized with a digestive disorder on the day Butterfield offered his testimony, he was sorely tempted to order destruction of the tapes. Vice President Agnew recommended that they be destroyed. But, Nixon later recalled in his memoirs, Gen. Alexander M. Haig, Jr., Haldeman's successor as chief of the White House staff, "made the telling point that, apart from the legal problems it might create, destruction of the tapes would forever seal an impression of guilt in the public mind."

## THE FALL OF AGNEW

While Nixon weighed his options in the new light of Butterfield's startling disclosure, both Special Prosecutor Cox and the Senate Select Committee set about to gain access to the tapes. But before the issue of the tapes could be resolved, a new scandal rocked the Nixon administration: The news media disclosed that Vice President Agnew faced charges of bribery, conspiracy, and income tax evasion, most of them stemming from activities during the 1960s when he was county executive of Baltimore and governor of Maryland. Although Agnew promptly denounced the charges as "damned lies," he appeared several weeks later, on October 10, 1973, in the federal district court in Baltimore where he announced his decision to resign the vice presidency (and on that same day did, in fact, resign) and entered a plea of nolo contendere (the equivalent of a guilty plea without an actual admission of guilt) to the charge of having failed to report $29,000 of income in 1967.

Who would become president if Nixon should die or resign before a new vice president could be nominated and confirmed in accord with the provisions of the Twenty-fifth Amendment to the Constitution? The answer: the 5-foot-4-inch speaker of the House of Representatives, 65-year-old Carl L. Albert, Democrat of Oklahoma. A man of minimal achievement since his arrival in Washington as a member of Congress in 1947—and also reputed to be an alcoholic—Albert made it abundantly clear that he had no ambition whatever to accede to the presidency.

As for Nixon, he had already weighed the question of a successor to Agnew, and in a glittering and, indeed, festive ceremony in the East Room of the White House on the evening of October 12, 1973, only two days after Agnew's resignation, presented his nominee for vice president: Rep. Gerald R. Ford, Jr., the leader of the Republicans in the lower house of Congress. In the weeks that followed, the 60-year-old Ford was scrutinized as no public official in the country's history had ever been. More than three hundred agents of the FBI investigated his correspondence, finances, and friendships. Committees of the House of Representatives and the Senate interrogated him for many hours. He told his interlocutors that he had no prior knowledge of allegedly illegal activities undertaken by the Nixon campaign committee in 1972, believed Nixon innocent of wrongdoing in the Watergate affair, thought Nixon ought to prove his innocence by disclosing documents "and so forth." Although Democrats on Capitol Hill tended to take a low view of Ford's conservative record in Congress in matters of civil rights and social welfare, and also considered him to be a man of modest intellect and insufficient administrative experience, most members of Congress respected him as a man of candor and integrity. Accordingly, in late November-early December of 1973, Ford won confirmation by a vote of 92–3 in the Senate and 387–35 in the House. That Ford's confirmation brought much comfort to Richard Nixon is doubtful, for by the closing months of 1973 the noose of Watergate was squeezing ever tighter around the Nixon presidency.

## NIXON AT BAY

Contending that their release would contravene the constitutional doctrine of separation of powers and the principle of executive privilege, President Nixon on July 23, 1973, formally refused Senator Ervin's request that he turn over White House tapes to the Senate Select Committee. Three days later, he defied subpoenas obtained by the committee and by Special Prosecutor Cox demanding tapes and assorted documents. At length, on October 19, Nixon proposed that he turn over a printed summary of the subpoenaed tapes to Judge Sirica and the Ervin Committee. Charged with listening to the tapes to verify the summary would be the elderly Sen. John C. Stennis, Democrat of Mississippi. Nixon also ordered Special Prosecutor Cox to terminate efforts to obtain the tapes and other materials related to Watergate. When Cox announced that he would not abide by the order, Nixon directed Attorney General Richardson to dismiss the special prosecutor. Asserting that he felt obliged to defend Cox's freedom of action, Richardson refused, and then resigned. The president's chief of staff Alexander Haig thereupon directed that Deputy Attorney General William D. Ruckelshaus fire Cox. Like Richardson, Ruckelshaus refused, then resigned. Next in the line of authority was Solicitor General Robert H. Bork. Bork dismissed Cox.

Nixon had misjudged the temper of his compatriots. What was widely referred to as the "Saturday Night Massacre" (of Richardson, Ruckelshaus, and Cox) touched off a tumultuous response—and Nixon' approval rating in popular opinion polls, which had stood at 68 percent in late January of 1973, at the time of the Vietnam armistice agreement, plummeted to 27 percent. Whereupon, on October 23, the president promised that he would turn over the tapes subpoenaed the previous July to Judge Sirica. He also appointed a new special prosecutor, Leon Jaworski, a Texas lawyer and former president of the American Bar Association who the president clearly thought would be less aggressive than Cox had been in pressing the Watergate case. But then a new disclosure rocked the republic. The White House announced that two of the nine subpoenaed tapes did not exist. Next, it was revealed that an 18-minute segment of the tapes was blank, apparently as a result of an accidental or deliberate erasure.

The travail of the president in the summer and autumn of 1973 had other dimensions. Most importantly, it was disclosed (in documents released by the White House) that Nixon had paid only $792.81 in federal taxes in 1970 and

$878.03 in 1971 on income totaling more than $400,000 during the two years. Large numbers of Americans whose earnings were a fraction of Nixon's but who had paid thousands of dollars more in taxes in 1970–1971 were incensed. At a press conference on November 17, 1973, the president explained that his minuscule tax liability in 1970–1971 had been perfectly legal, and was the consequence of deductions claimed when he donated his vice presidential papers (allegedly worth more than a half-million dollars) to the National Archives. Declared Nixon, "I made my mistakes, but in all my years of public life, I have never profited, never profited from public service. I have earned every cent. Well, I'm not a crook. I have earned everything I have got."

Leaving aside the question of whether he was a crook, Senator Weicker of the Senate Select Committee suspected that the president was, in fact, not entitled to all that he recently had netted in income (or "earned"). According to the senator, it appeared probable that the deed transferring Nixon's vice presidential papers had been executed after July 25, 1969, the date of repeal of the law permitting such deductions—although the president's tax attorney had affixed his notary seal on the deed certifying that a presidential lawyer had prepared the deed on March 27, 1969. Delivery of the deed to the National Archives had not taken place until April 10, 1970.

Still, it was the Watergate affair that threatened to unmake the Nixon presidency, and in the aftermath of the Saturday Night Massacre increasing numbers of Americans demanded that Nixon resign his office or be removed via the constitutional process of impeachment. Indeed, the feeling that the Nixon presidency was doomed was becoming pervasive. When, on December 6, 1973, Gerald Ford repeated the vice presidential oath in a ceremony in the chamber of the House of Representatives while Nixon stood uneasily to his rear, many observers suspected that they were witnessing a preview of a not-too-distant presidential inauguration. Following a short address by Ford—one in which he told his auditors, "I am a Ford, not a Lincoln"—one senator reportedly asked another, "How did you like President Ford's first speech?" The second senator may not have considered the question entirely facetious, for over the previous six weeks the House Judiciary Committee had begun to weigh the possibility of recommending the impeachment of Nixon.

The Nixon presidency remained afloat as 1973 passed into history, and in his State of the Union address of January 30, 1974, Nixon declared, "One year of Watergate is enough." But to his chagrin, Leon Jaworski had not proved a lethargic special prosecutor, and in early March of 1974 a federal grand jury indicted John Ehrlichman, H. R. Haldeman, John Mitchell, and other former officials of the Nixon administration and Nixon re-election committee for conspiring to obstruct justice in the matter of the Watergate break-in. It was subsequently disclosed that the grand jury had secretly named the president an unindicted coconspirator in the case. Because the Constitution protected him against any legal action save impeachment so long as he occupied the presidency, the grand jury was prevented from returning an indictment against Nixon.

Meanwhile, the House Judiciary Committee had begun to gather evidence to support any recommendation that it might elect to make to the House of Representatives that the president be impeached. The committee was proceeding cautiously, inasmuch as its mild-mannered chairman, Peter W. Rodino, Jr., Democrat of New Jersey, was bent on avoiding any appearance that his committee, 21 of whose 38 members were Democrats, was animated by partisanship. Still, headway was slow, for the White House, continuing to invoke the principle of executive privilege, refused to relinquish tapes and documents. At length, on April 11, 1974, the committee voted to subpoena the materials it sought, and when Republican leaders on Capitol Hill told him that defiance of the subpoena would hasten his impeachment, the president, in a nationally televised address on April 29, 1974, announced that he would release to the committee edited transcripts of 46 presidential conversations and make public more than 1,200 pages of transcripts. Conceding that the transcripts would cause him embarrassment, Nixon expressed confidence that the material he was releasing would establish his innocence in the matter of Watergate.

The president had miscalculated. Reproduced in newspapers, newsmagazines, and at least four paperbound books, the edited transcripts persuaded millions of Americans that Nixon and his confederates had indeed labored to cover up White House involvement in the Watergate outrage. Transcripts of the now-renowned conversations between John Dean and the president in March of 1973, for example, appeared more consistent with the testimony that Dean had given before the Ervin Committee than with the explanation offered by Nixon in his television address of April 30, 1973. The transcripts clearly established that in the aftermath of his conversations with Dean in March 1973 the president, contrary to the assurances given in his speech of April 30, had made no serious effort to expose the perpetrators of the break-in. Uncounted millions of citizens likewise recoiled when they confronted the incredibly coarse language of the presidential conversations—often denoted in the transcripts by the phrase "expletive deleted." Hitherto a stalwart supporter of the president, Sen. Hugh Scott, Republican of Pennsylvania, described the impression conveyed by the transcripts as "disgusting, shabby, immoral." Assorted newspapers, which like Scott had given unflagging support to Nixon, among them the *Chicago Tribune* and *Omaha World-Herald*, appealed to the president to resign.

Meanwhile, on May 20, 1974, Judge Sirica ordered Nixon to turn over the tapes of 64 conversations that Special Prosecutor Jaworski had subpoenaed the previous month. White House lawyers announced that they would appeal Sirica's order, whereupon Jaworski asked the Supreme Court to bypass the court of appeals and hear the case itself. The high court acceded to Jaworski's request.

With the obvious intent of somehow resuscitating his gasping presidency, Nixon on June 10, 1974, boarded Air Force One and took off for the Middle East. During a stopover in Salzburg, his left leg became swollen and inflamed. The president was suffering from phlebitis, a potentially lethal inflammation of a vein, but he determined to continue the trip. Despite the pain in his leg, he was exhilarated on being greeted in Egypt by perhaps the largest and most demonstrative crowd ever to welcome an American president during a trip abroad. From Egypt, he flew to Saudi Arabia, Syria, Israel, and Jordan. Six days after his return from the Middle East, on June 25, 1974, Nixon was off again, this time to the Soviet Union. Contrary to his hope, this latest venture in summitry with the Soviets, conducted in Moscow and at Leonid Brezhnev's villa on the Black Sea (near Yalta) in the Crimea, failed to produce a new SALT treaty, and resulted in only a few agreements of minimal import.

## THE FALL OF NIXON

There was, of course, no escape from the Watergate trauma, and five days after Nixon's return from the Soviet Union, on July 8, 1974, Special Prosecutor Jaworski and James D. St. Clair, a prominent and articulate attorney from Boston who was now representing the president in the Watergate case, presented arguments to the Supreme Court in the matter of the White House tapes. At length, on July 24, the high court ruled by a vote of 8–0 that the president must turn over the tapes to the special prosecutor. Would Nixon obey the Supreme Court? Fully aware that defiance of the high court in this instance would guarantee his impeachment and subsequent conviction and removal from office, he announced that he would.

On the same day that the Supreme Court directed the president to release the tapes, the House Judiciary Committee, under the glare of television lights, began formal debate on the question of whether Nixon should be impeached— in effect, indicted by the House of Representatives, after which the Senate, acting as a jury, would determine whether he was to be removed from office. Chairman Rodino and the other members of the committee were manifestly conscious of the awesome responsibility that had befallen them, and the 35 hours of debate that unfolded over the next 6 days, if tense and occasionally sharp, was generally devoid of histrionics. The result? By margins of 27–11, 18–10, and 21–17, the committee voted to send three articles of impeachment to the floor of the House. Article I charged that president with having obstructed justice by trying to cover up involvement by his campaign committee in the Watergate break-in. Article II accused him of abuse of power by misusing and interfering with government agencies, especially the CIA, FBI, IRS, and Secret Service. Article III charged him with impeding the impeachment process by defying the Judiciary Committee's subpoenas.

Nobody doubted that the House, accepting the Judiciary Committee's articles, would vote to impeach the president. Still, Nixon's removal from office would require a two-thirds vote by the Senate, and as July of 1974 turned to August the president's dwindling corps of supporters reckoned that he might yet survive. On what did they rest their hope? Thus far, there had been no disclosure of a "smoking gun," that is, a piece of documentary evidence that demonstrated beyond the proverbial shadow of a doubt that the president had been party to the Watergate cover-up. In the absence of such evidence, they thought, more than a third of the members of the Senate might vote to acquit.

Alas, there existed a smoking gun. Tapes that Nixon had turned over to

Judge Sirica in response to the order by the Supreme Court contained evidence contradicting the president's repeated assertion that he had known nothing of a Watergate cover-up until so informed by John Dean on March 21, 1973. The tapes disclosed that in conversations with H. R. Haldeman on June 23, 1972, six days after the Watergate break-in, Nixon had approved a scheme for thwarting the FBI's investigation of the case.

On August 5, 1974, the president released transcripts of the damaging tapes, admitted that he had withheld knowledge of those tapes from his attorneys and supporters on the Judiciary Committee, and conceded that his impeachment was a foregone conclusion. But he asserted that what he had done did not justify his removal from office. Scarcely anybody agreed. The ten Republicans members of the Judiciary Committee who had voted against all articles of impeachment unceremoniously reversed their positions. Clinging to the hope that he might somehow escape conviction by the Senate, notwithstanding the smoking gun tape, Nixon nonetheless resisted pressure by White House aides, notably Alexander Haig, that he resign. It mattered not. During a tense meeting in the Executive Office Building on the afternoon of August 7, 1974, a delegation of congressional leaders that included Senators Barry Goldwater and Hugh Scott, longtime Republican stalwarts, told the president that he could count on no more than 12 or 18 votes for acquittal if the case went to trial in the Senate.

The curtain was about to close. After asking his longtime personal secretary Rose Mary Woods to notify his family that he had decided to resign, the president walked to the solarium in the residential area of the White House where his wife Pat, daughters Tricia and Julie, sons-in-law Edward Cox and David Eisenhower, and Rose Mary Woods were waiting. After tearful embraces and a few verbal exchanges, Nixon and Tricia went down to the Rose Garden for a photograph. Back upstairs in the residence, the president and his family lined up and linked arms, and while forcing broad smiles posed for a final family portrait in the White House. Moments later, the photographer captured the president in an emotion-rocking embrace with Julie. After a dinner for which none of the family had much appetite, Nixon retired to work on the resignation speech that he planned to deliver on the evening of the following day. Summoned by the president, Henry Kissinger arrived at the White House around 9 P.M. During much of the more-than-two-hour conversation in the Lincoln Room that followed, the president, manifestly devastated but in iron control of his emotions, reminisced about his successes in foreign affairs, pondered the art and meaning of politics, speculated about his probable place in history. Near midnight, as Kissinger was taking his leave, the president invited the national security adviser and secretary of state to kneel with him in prayer.

At 11 A.M. the next morning, August 8, 1974, the president met with Vice President Ford in the Oval Office. He informed Ford of his decision to resign. That evening, while seated at the same desk in the Oval Office, Nixon peered into television cameras and announced his resignation. "To leave office before my term is completed is opposed to every instinct in my body," he told his compatriots. But, he said, he had elected to resign in order to serve "the interests of America." The resignation would be effective at noon the following day. Regarding the crimes that he was alleged to have committed in connection with Watergate, he admitted nothing.

The next morning, August 9, 1974, Nixon signed a statement that read, "I hearby resign the Office of President of the United States." The statement would be delivered to the secretary of state at 11:35 A.M.—on the 2,027th day of the Nixon presidency. Shortly after 9:30 A.M., the president and his family made their way to the East Room of the White House, where Nixon made a rambling and sentimental farewell speech to his cabinet and several hundred members of the White House staff. From the East Room, the president and Mrs. Nixon, accompanied by Vice President and Mrs. Ford, walked down a red carpet on the south lawn of the White House to the helicopter Army One. The time was a few minutes before 10 o'clock. A cordon of airmen, marines, seamen, and soldiers presented arms. After an exchange of handshakes, embraces, and kisses mingled with tears, the Nixons boarded the helicopter. Pausing at the top of the ramp, the president raised his hands in his familiar double V-for-victory salute. On the grass below, his daughter Julie flashed a thumbs-up sign. A few moments later, its engines roaring and rotors washing those standing in the grass with a gust of wind, Army One lifted off from the lawn and moved off in the direction of the Jefferson Memorial. Hardly had the craft become airborne before uniformed White House guards began rolling up the red carpet.

At Andrews Air Force Base, the Nixons boarded Air Force One for the flight to California, and at noon, as the huge white-and-blue aircraft streaked over Jefferson City, Missouri, Richard Nixon, age 61, ceased to be the president of the United States.

## PRESIDENT FORD

While Nixon was flying westward into apparent oblivion, at midday on August 9, 1974, Gerald Ford and his wife Betty walked to the East Room of the White House, where Chief Justice Burger administered the oath of office to the thirty-eighth president of the republic. Smiling and waving as the room reverberated to an eruption of cheering and clapping, Ford thereupon stepped to the same podium at which his predecessor had offered maudlin farewell remarks less than three hours before and delivered a short inaugural statement—in truth, a brief homily, not a rousing address. Intoned the new chief executive: "My fellow Americans, our long national nightmare is over."

Born in Omaha in 1913, Gerald Ford had entered the world as Leslie King, Jr. But a short time after his birth, his mother divorced Leslie King, Sr., and with her infant son returned to her hometown of Grand Rapids, Michigan. At length, the mother of the future president married Gerald Rudolph Ford, a paint manufacturer and civic leader, and when Ford adopted his new wife's son, Leslie King, Jr., became Gerald R. Ford, Jr. As he matured, the principal interest of Gerald Ford, Jr., a strapping and square-jawed youth, was athletic competition, and in 1931 and 1932 he was the center on the University of Michigan's undefeated national championship football teams. Turning aside offers to play professional football, he entered the Yale University Law School. He received his law degree in 1941, joined the Navy in 1942, took part in carrier operations in the Pacific from 1943 to 1945. On receiving his discharge in early 1946, he returned to Grand Rapids to practice law.

Ford married Elizabeth "Betty" Bloomer in 1948 while he was conducting what would prove to be a successful campaign for a seat in the national House of Representatives. He took his seat in the House in early 1949, and soon established himself as a conscientious and hard-working congressman. On domestic issues, he tended to align himself with the conservative wing of the Republican Party; in foreign affairs, he advocated toughness in America's dealings with the Soviet Union and the "international communist conspiracy." Repeatedly reelected, he had by 1960 become a fixture on Capitol Hill, and his Republican colleagues in the House in 1965 elected him their leader. In the latter capacity he participated with the Republican leader in the Senate, Everett M. Dirksen, in weekly press conferences that were nationally televised. The "Ev and Jerry Show," as the press conferences were popularly referred to, gave Ford national visibility and reinforced his position in the hierarchy of the GOP. At length, in 1973, he became vice president, and on the resignation of Nixon acceded to the presidency.

When Ford moved into the White House, of course, the vice presidential office was again vacant, and in accord with the Twenty-fifth Amendment he nominated the 66-year-old former governor of New York, Nelson A. Rockefeller, to fill the vacancy—choosing "Rocky" over 49-year-old George Herbert Walker Bush, at that time the chairman of the Republican National Committee. To Ford's dismay, the confirmation of Rockefeller did not proceed smoothly, but after more than three months, on December 19, 1974, Congress confirmed the nominee.

Meanwhile, on September 8, 1974, the new president, who basked in popular favor during his first weeks in the White House, sat down before television cameras and told his compatriots that he had granted former-President Nixon an absolute pardon for all federal crimes that he had committed or might have committed or taken part in during the time he was president of the United States. Ford professed to believe the time had come to shut and seal the book on the matter of the alleged crimes of the former president. Months and perhaps years would pass, he said, before litigation involving Nixon could be completed, during which time passions would remain aroused, opinions polarized, and the credibility of the country's institutions challenged. As he later wrote in his autobiography, "The hate had to be drained and the healing begun."

Tens of millions of Ford's compatriots thought otherwise—were outraged that the former president, as a result of the pardon, would not be required to stand trial and perhaps serve time in jail for his alleged crimes. Ford's recently appointed press secretary Jerald terHorst quit the Ford administration. Angry letters and telegrams poured into the White House. The president's popular approval rating in opinion polls plummeted. Great numbers of citizens expressed the suspicion that the pardon was, in fact, the result of a deal struck between Nixon and Ford before Nixon's resignation: Nixon would pass the presidency to Ford; in return Ford would pardon Nixon. Had Nixon openly admitted his guilt and expressed genuine contrition for his alleged crimes, so many Americans indicated, the pardon might have been warranted. But he had done nothing more than accept the pardon. Such citizens seemed little impressed when legal experts observed that acceptance of a pardon was in itself an acknowledgment of guilt.

Had Nixon and Ford struck a bargain before Nixon's resignation? To meet that question, Ford took an action that was unprecedented in the annals of the presidency: On October 17, 1974, he made his way to Capitol Hill and testified under oath before a subcommittee of the House Judiciary Committee that his pardon of the former president had been the result of no preresignation arrangement.

If infuriated that Nixon had escaped the ignominy of standing trial and if convicted serving a term in jail, millions of Americans found a measure of satisfaction in the knowledge that other members of the discredited administration of the former president who had taken part in the Watergate outrage and related criminal activities would not be (or had not been) so fortunate. By January of 1975, in truth, a veritable covey of men who had served Nixon in assorted capacities had been convicted for participation in the Watergate break-in, the Watergate cover-up, the break-in of the office of Daniel Ellsberg's psychiatrist, and the perpetration of illegal acts of political sabotage (or "dirty tricks"), among them John Dean, Dwight L. Chapin, Charles Colson, John Ehrlichman, H. R. Haldeman, Egil Krogh, Frederick C. LaRue, Jeb Stuart Magruder, Robert C. Mardian, John Mitchell, Donald H. Segretti—and, of course, G. Gordon Liddy, Howard Hunt, and James McCord. Former-Attorney General Richard Kleindienst had pleaded guilty to one count of refusing to testify fully to the Senate Judiciary Committee, and Edward L. Morgan, a former White House lawyer, to participating in a conspiracy to fabricate a fraudulent income tax deduction of $576,000 for Nixon in connection with Nixon's gift of vice presidential papers to the National Archives. Most of those convicted had served or would serve time in minimal security federal prisons.

## THE CONTINUING TRAVAIL OF GERALD FORD

Of larger moment than the fate of former White House lawbreakers, at least in the perspective of President Ford, was the faltering national economy. Of the assorted economic problems that were bedeviling the United States in the autumn of 1974, so the president thought, the most urgent was that of inflation, which had nettled the country for several years but had become exacerbated in recent months as a result of the dramatic increase in the price of imported oil engineered by OPEC. In his first major address to his compatriots, shortly after taking the presidency, Ford had proclaimed inflation to be public enemy number one.

August 28, 1974: President Ford responds to questions during his first nationally tele-vised news conference after moving into the White House.

Fiscal restraint by the federal government and jawboning, that is, appeals to business and labor to hold the line on prices and wages, were the principal instruments in the struggle against inflation. Results, unfortunately, were dis-appointing, and in 1975 the country slipped into its most severe economic downturn since the Great Depression of the 1930s. The production of durable goods, including automobiles, plummeted, while unemployment at one point had overtaken almost 9 percent of the country's toilers. Alas, the recession failed to contain the monster of inflation. On the contrary, the monster gal-loped on, and in 1975 the consumer price index advanced by 9.1 percent.

The faltering economy was not the only domestic problem to command the attention of President Ford in 1974 and 1975. The chief executive took note of the angry reactions of white citizens, notably in Boston and Louisville, when federal judges ordered the busing of children from their own neighbor-hoods to achieve racial balances in public schools. No friend of busing, Ford clearly felt empathy with the angry whites. He also took note when the gov-ernment of New York City edged toward bankruptcy, and at one point indi-cated that he would veto any congressional enactment intended to save the country's largest city from default. But at length, in late 1975, he signed legis-lation that provided more than $2 billion in federal loan guarantees to rescue the city's finances.

More pressing was the problem of energy. As had his predecessor, President Ford urged Americans to conserve energy and appealed to Congress for energy legislation. After many months, in December 1975, Congress passed the Energy Policy and Conservation Act, a central provision of which mandated a phased decontrol of domestic oil prices over a 40-month period. Higher oil prices resulting from decontrol would supposedly result in reduced consumption of oil—also increased exploration for new sources of oil in the United States. Rejecting the counsel of various of his advisers, Ford, who had appealed for immediate decontrol of oil prices, reluctantly signed the measure.

Of comparable concern to President Ford, inasmuch as they reinforced the suspicion and cynicism that great numbers of Americans had come to feel in recent years regarding the national government and its leaders, were disclosures that the CIA, FBI, IRS, and other federal agencies had abused their authority and, more than that, violated the law. Particularly shocking were disclosures relating to the CIA and FBI.

As discerned by an eight-member investigative commission appointed by Ford in January 1975 and headed by Vice President Rockefeller, the CIA had spied on political dissenters, opened the mail of private citizens, and planted informers inside domestic protest groups. It had assembled dossiers on some ten thousand U.S. citizens, and tried to arrange the assassination of such foreign leaders as Fidel Castro of Cuba and Patrice Lumumba of the Congo. A report issued in 1976 by the Senate Select Intelligence Committee chaired by Frank Church, Democrat of Idaho, confirmed the findings of the Rockefeller Commission. As for the FBI, investigators discovered that its agents had conducted at least 238 illegal house and office break-ins over a 26-year period against what its longtime director J. Edgar Hoover had viewed as domestic subversive targets and had infiltrated civil rights groups and the women's liberation movement as well as antiwar organizations. It had conducted an operation of harassment and wiretapping against the Reverend Martin Luther King, Jr., arranged to have political dissidents fired or transferred from jobs, sent anonymous letters to disrupt marriages, and assembled files on 500,000 citizens. To prevent disclosure of its illegal activities, it had hidden or destroyed files. In response to the foregoing disclosures, George Bush, director of the CIA, and Clarence Kelley, director of the FBI, issued orders aimed at containing any impulses to illegality and impropriety that might be lingering within their organizations.

## MILITARY POLICY

Meanwhile, Ford found it necessary to wrestle with complicated problems relating to military policy. Why military policy commanded his attention is not hard to discern. The continuing buildup of its arsenal of nuclear weapons by the Soviet Union, not to mention rapid (indeed mind-boggling) developments in weapons technology, were rendering obsolete the equations on which America's military policy had rested over the past decade or so.

In the aftermath of the disengagement of U.S. military-naval forces from

Vietnam, the prevailing mood of the citizenry was inhospitable to large expenditures for the armed forces. Responding to that mood, the administrations of Nixon and Ford acquiesced in substantial reductions in expenditures for the country's conventional (non-nuclear) armed forces. But to guarantee the continuing credibility of the assured destruction strategy of the United States (adopted in 1965), both administrations pressed for development of a powerful and potentially mobile new ICBM, designated the MX, to replace the increasingly vulnerable silo-based Minutemen missiles that were the centerpiece of the country's land-based nuclear deterrent—also for development of the Trident submarine (to be armed with larger and longer-range missiles) and the B-1 bombing plane (a strategic bomber capable of supersonic speeds). In the view of the Nixon and Ford administrations, the Soviets, as a result of a frenetic program of building nuclear weapons systems of various types and the application of multiple warhead technology, had achieved parity and perhaps superiority vis-à-vis the United States in nuclear striking power. In the present circumstances, they reasoned, the Soviets might be tempted to launch a preemptive first strike against the United States with their array of missiles and bombers. But the temptation would subside considerably if leaders in the Kremlin understood that a sufficient number of MXs, Tridents, and B-1s would survive a preemptive first strike to enable the United States to retaliate with a devastating strike of its own.

Whatever its rationale, the program to build up the country's nuclear arsenal generated a fierce opposition. Opponents of the MX, Trident, and B-1 cited the incredible expense of the three weapons systems. In the event the Soviets unleashed a preemptive first strike against the United States at any time in the foreseeable future, they contended, the United States would be quite capable of making a retaliatory strike with existing weapons systems—Minutemen ICBMs that survived the Soviet assault, submarine-launched ballistic missiles, and B-52 aircraft armed with thermonuclear bombs—that would render unacceptable damage to the Soviet Union. Hence the balance of nuclear terror and its resultant capacity to deter a nuclear exchange between the superpowers, they were confident, remained intact.

What the opponents of the MX, Trident, and B-1 were saying, of course, was that the United States retained the capability of deterring a surprise nuclear strike by the Soviet Union against its own territory. That may very well have been true. But what of extended deterrence, that is, the capacity of the North American superpower to deter Soviet attacks in other areas deemed critical to its ideals and interests, notably in Western Europe? While building their intercontinental nuclear forces to a point where they had achieved parity in such forces with the United States, the Soviets had also perfected and were deploying, particularly in Europe, a formidable arsenal of highly accurate, mobile, and largely invulnerable IRBMs (the SS-20s), a new medium-range bombing plane (the Backfire), and a new generation of short-range theater weapons armed with nuclear warheads.

As a consequence of the foregoing buildup, the Soviets had tilted the balance of nuclear forces deployed in Europe in their favor, and rendered America's aforementioned doctrine of flexible response obsolete, inasmuch as flexible response (an adjunct of the counterforce and assured destruction strategies formulated in the 1960s) provided that the United States, bringing to bear its superiority in tactical (or short-range theater) nuclear weapons deployed in Europe, would compel the Soviets to give up any aggressive operation they might undertake against America's NATO allies. It now appeared that the Washington government's only viable options in the event of Soviet aggression in Europe, to wit, an invasion of a NATO country or a limited attack against selected military targets, was (1) to unleash its ICBMs (based in its own territory—in Arkansas, Kansas, Nebraska, and elsewhere) against the Soviet Union, in which event the Soviets would doubtless unleash their own ICBMs against the United States, or (2) make no armed response at all. Calculating that no American president would risk destruction of his country's cities, the Soviets might be tempted to gamble that the United States would choose the latter option—do nothing—in response to a Soviet invasion of a NATO country or some other act of aggression. So reckoned strategists in Washington.

To meet the foregoing dilemma and rescue extended deterrence, Secretary of Defense James D. Schlesinger, in March of 1974 (as the Nixon administration was moving toward collapse), announced the doctrine of "essential equivalence," the cardinal article of which called for the employment of "limited nuclear options." The first Single Integrated Operation Plan prepared in accord with the doctrine was formally approved by the National Security Council in December of 1975, during the presidency of Gerald Ford.

Reminiscent of the controlled response or counterforce doctrine of the early 1960s, the doctrine of essential equivalence provided that in the event of Soviet aggression in Europe or elsewhere (for example, in the Middle East) the United States would respond by launching nuclear weapons against selected Soviet targets. The purpose of such limited and selective strikes—which would be gradually escalated if the aggression continued—would be to persuade the Soviets to terminate the aggression by changing their perceptions regarding the possibility of achieving victory. If the Soviets failed to change their perceptions and instead continued the aggression, the assured destruction capability of the United States would remain in reserve to enforce rationality.

Refined in 1980 when Pres. Jimmy Carter's secretary of defense Harold Brown announced the "countervailing strategy" by which the United States would strive to develop counterpolitical options in coping with the Soviet Union, for example, by exploiting the Soviet Union's vulnerability to attack by China, the doctrine of essential equivalence would remain the nuclear doctrine of the United States into the 1980s. It was a doctrine that raised nightmarish questions. Would not the Soviets likely respond to selected and limited attacks on their territory by making selected and limited attacks on the territory of the United States? And if the superpowers started making selected and limited attacks on each other's territory, was it not likely that Armageddon, that is, a nuclear holocaust resulting from an unlimited unleashing by the superpowers of missiles and bombers, would become almost unavoidable? Recognizing that a selected and limited attack was apt to result in Armageddon, would a president in Washington actually order such an attack in the event of, say, a Soviet invasion of Iran? Was the doctrine of essential equivalence thus not a sham?

## DEFEAT IN INDOCHINA

Of more immediate concern to President Ford than essential equivalence and limited nuclear options was the situation in Southeast Asia. In the perspective of the Washington government, that situation had worsened in the aftermath of Ford's accession to the presidency in August 1974. By the spring of 1975, it had become desperate.

In the months following the armistice of January 1973, President Thieu of South Vietnam ordered the launching of military operations aimed at seizing areas occupied by the North Vietnamese and Vietcong in the Mekong delta and along the Cambodian border. The operations were initially successful. For their part, the North Vietnamese, in the months after the armistice dispatched fresh troops and new military hardware to South Vietnam. More important, the communists undertook a massive improvement and expansion of their logistical support system. Through jungles and across mountains, their labor battalions constructed an all-weather highway from Quang Tri Province, just below the DMZ, down through Laos and Cambodia to the Mekong delta (to the southwest of Saigon). They also put down oil pipelines, most notably from Quang Tri to the town of Loc Ninh, their main headquarters, 75 miles to the northwest of Saigon. They turned the Ho Chi Minh Trail, hitherto a labyrinth of trails and paths, into a modern highway, complete with machine shops, oil tanks, rest stops, and service areas. Then, in the autumn of 1973, North Vietnamese and VC infantry units, suckled as always by the Soviet Union and its satellites and the People's Republic of China, began assaulting ARVN outposts, small airfields, and storage facilities, and by the spring of 1974 had recaptured areas in the Mekong delta taken by the ARVN the year before.

Meanwhile, chaos was overtaking the South Vietnamese economy. Unemployment became rampant; inflation began to run out of control. Whereupon assorted factions, some of them doubtless encouraged by the communists, accelerated their verbal assaults on President Thieu and his government. Thieu responded by accelerated repression of dissidents. At the same time, South Vietnam's American patrons were becoming increasingly parsimonious. From $2.3 billion in 1973, Congress slashed U.S. economic and military assistance to South Vietnam to $700 million in 1974. To make matters worse, the morale of the ARVN was disintegrating, in part because soaring prices and the embezzlement of payrolls by commanding officers were making it impossible for ordinary soldiers to support their families. The knowledge that corruption was, in fact, pervasive in the ARVN—that quartermaster units, for example, were wont to demand payment of bribes before they would deliver rice and ammunition and gasoline and spare parts to combat units in the field—further eroded the morale of troops. Eroding morale inevitably prompted large-scale desertions.

Fully conscious that the balance of strength in the third incarnation of the seemingly interminable Indochina war had shifted decidedly and perhaps decisively in their favor, leaders in Hanoi in December 1974, four months after Gerald Ford had taken over the White House in Washington, sanctioned a military offensive in Phuoc Long Province, some 60 miles to the north of Saigon. The principal objective of the offensive was the provincial capital of Phuoc Binh, and to achieve it the North Vietnamese dispatched eight thousand troops from their sanctuaries in Cambodia over the border into Phuoc Long Province. The victory was quickly achieved. After pulverizing Phuoc Binh with artillery shells and rockets (an attack that made casualties of uncounted civilians, but prompted no protests by Americans, Asians, Europeans, and others who had lashed out against the Christmas bombing campaign of the United States in December 1972), the communist force easily overcame the outmanned and outgunned ARVN garrison, and on January 6, 1975, the triumphant communists raised the Vietcong banner over Phuoc Binh. The response in the United States? The communist victory stirred scarcely a ripple of interest, much less concern.

What followed was anticlimactic. Operating as usual from base camps in Cambodia, the communists launched a new offensive in the Central Highlands—and quickly put the ARVN to rout. Moving across the DMZ, other communist forces moved toward Hué, and on March 25, 1975, captured the old imperial city. In neighboring Cambodia, meanwhile, the communist Khmer Rouge began to close in on General Lon Nol's regime in Phnom Penh. Recognizing the inevitable, Lon Nol fled the country on April 1. A fortnight later, after communist artillery fire had closed the Pochentong Airport, Marine helicopters lifted off the decks of U.S. carriers that had been steaming for several weeks in the Gulf of Thailand, flew to Phnom Penh, and evacuated 276 Americans, other foreign nationals, and Cambodians, among them Ambassador John Gunther Dean of the United States, under whose arms as he strode to a helicopter, rolled in a plastic bag, was the Stars and Stripes that had flown over his embassy. Khmer Rouge troops occupied Phnom Penh on April 17.

Two weeks before, in the first days of April, the North Vietnamese and Vietcong, had opened their Ho Chi Minh campaign, the objective of which was the capture of Saigon and final victory in the war in Vietnam. The communists utterly routed the ARVN, and on April 21, Nguyen Van Thieu resigned the South Vietnamese presidency and flew off to Taiwan. Two days later, on April 23, speaking at Tulane University in New Orleans, President Ford consigned the war in Vietnam to history. "Today, Americans can regain the sense of pride that existed before Vietnam. But it cannot be achieved by refighting a war that is finished. . . . Those events [that produced the collapse of the Saigon government], tragic as they are, portend neither the end of the world nor of America's leadership in the world."

As Ford spoke, U.S. officials in Saigon were making plans to evacuate about a thousand Americans and nearly six thousand Vietnamese who had been employed by assorted American agencies. Because the communists were shelling the Saigon airport, it became impossible to evacuate the Americans and Vietnamese by plane after the fashion of the evacuation of several thousand Americans and Vietnamese, many of the latter of whom were children, during recent weeks. Thus, on April 29, 70 Marine Corps helicopters, moving back and forth between several points in Saigon and U.S. carriers in the South China Sea, executed the final evacuation.

The scene was one of chaos, particularly at the U.S. embassy, where marines used rifle butts and tear gas to hold back hundreds of shouting and screaming Vietnamese, many of whom had scaled a 10-foot wall, who begged to be evacuated. At length, the marines retreated to the embassy building. Reported a correspondent of *Time*, "Floor by floor, the Marines withdrew toward the roof of the embassy with looters right behind them. Abandoned offices were transformed into junkyards of smashed typewriters and ransacked file cabinets."[3] Finally, shortly before 5 A.M., Ambassador Graham Martin notified Secretary of State Kissinger that he was destroying communications equipment and closing the embassy. Whereupon the ambassador, accompanied by his wife and clutching the folded Stars and Stripes that had flown above his embassy, climbed to the chancery roof and boarded a helicopter. A few minutes later, the helicopter pilot radioed, "Lady Ace Zero Nine, Code Two is aboard." Lady Ace 09 was the chopper; Code Two was the ambassador. In the sea below, hundreds of Vietnamese were moving out in boats. They hoped to be picked up and taken to America.

As Martin was leaving, at dawn on April 30, 1975, communist troops began to make their way into the almost deserted streets of Saigon. Shortly before 11 o'clock, North Vietnamese tanks rumbled into the courtyard of the presidential palace, whereupon a soldier emerged from a tank, sprinted up a stairway, and unfurled a red, yellow, and blue Vietcong flag from a balcony. Awaiting the communists at the palace was Gen. Duong Van Minh—the well-known "Big Minh" on whom Americans at one point had placed great hope—the successor to Thieu who was accompanied by members of an improvised cabinet. As reported by Stanley Karnow in his book on the war, Minh, dressed in a business suit, said to the ranking North Vietnamese officer, "I have been waiting since early this morning to transfer power to you." Responded the officer, "There is no question of your transferring power. Your power has crumbled. You cannot give up what you do not have."

## RETROSPECT

What a difference 30 years can make! Thirty years to the day before the communist soldier unfurled the Vietcong banner from the presidential palace in Saigon, on April 30, 1945, the tyrant Adolf Hitler, a veritable personification

---

[3]*Time*, May 12, 1975, p. 11.

of evil in the perception of most Americans, shot himself to death in his bunker in Berlin. Hitler took his life as troops of the United States and its allies were closing in on his "Thousand-Year Reich," and within a week Americans would give themselves over to a delirious celebration of "VE Day." In the Far Pacific, meanwhile, the armed forces of the United States and its allies were closing in on another empire that Americans perceived to be a symbol of evil, and in less than three months the people of the United States would be celebrating "VJ Day." Those months of April to August 1945 were a time when the American spirit reached high tide, when the people of the United States were buoyed by a sense of national purpose and triumph. And in those heady days of spring and summer 1945, as noted earlier, there were few Americans (or so it appeared) who entertained the slightest doubt that their continental republic was indeed the gem of the ocean—that what the magazine publisher Henry Luce had defined as "the American Century" had certainly arrived.

It seems fair to say that on April 30, 1975, no American anywhere felt buoyed by a sense of national purpose and triumph. Nor is it probable that any American was toasting the American Century, for the unfurling of the VC flag marked a bitter defeat for the United States. As a North Vietnamese military commander later told Col. Harry G. Summers, Jr., of the U.S. Army, the fact that the communists never defeated the Americans on the battlefield was irrelevant; the United States was the loser in a war. Defeat in war had hitherto appeared unthinkable in the minds of most Americans. After all, gems of the ocean—great nation-states that enjoy the special favor of Providence—are supposed to be invincible. At the onset of the country's belligerency in World War II, in the aftermath of the devastation of U.S. military-naval forces in Hawaii and the Philippines, while the legions of the dictator Hitler were deployed only a few leagues from Moscow, scarcely any American doubted the words of their president: "We will gain the inevitable triumph." For those millions of Americans who had continued to cling to time-honored perceptions (or illusions) regarding the special virtue and invincibility of the United States, the defeat in Vietnam struck hard at the spirit. Save for a comparative handful who had cheered every success of the communists in Southeast Asia (so-called Vietcong rooters), few of those citizens who had deplored U.S. involvement in the war in Vietnam saw in their country's defeat any cause for celebration.

Alas, what the historian-diplomat Chester L. Cooper had previously identified as America's "lost crusade" in Vietnam was not the only source of the frustration and disillusion that gnawed at the national spirit during the historical season from 1973 to 1975. The disgrace and collapse of a presidency—the revelations of deceit and contempt for the law, not to mention the banality of everyday goings-on in the White House—stripped away much of the aura of majesty that in the popular mind had enveloped the presidential office (as did public exposure during that same period of the extramarital liaisons of a dashing young chief executive in the years 1961 to 1963 within the hallowed walls of the executive mansion itself). Americans, of course, or most of them, were not fools; they had always understood that their presidents, like all people, were subject to human weakness and shortcomings. But few of them had ever dreamed that a presidential administration could sink to the depths of depravity that the Watergate affair—particularly the White House tapes—disclosed the Nixon presidency to have sunk. For those millions of Americans for whom the White House had been a veritable national icon, the disgrace of a president and destruction of a presidency were acutely demoralizing.

Finally, there was the revelation in the years 1973 to 1975 of the economic vincibility of the United States. On the day that Hitler shot himself to death in 1945, the United States had been an economic powerhouse compared with which the economies of other nations appeared puny and almost irrelevant. Although the Soviets had killed more of the enemy than had Americans in the crusade against the Axis aggressors, the industrial might of the United States had been the critical factor in the equation that had brought the Axis to ruin. Or so believed nearly every American. That the economies of other nation-states, particularly those that lay in rubble in the spring and summer of 1945, might one day achieve such proficiency that the output of their manufacturing industries could challenge the supremacy of the manufacturing industries of the North American superpower, even within its own borders, was unthinkable. That the United States, the world's premier producer of energy in 1945, might one day run short of energy and thus become dependent on energy (in the form of oil and natural gas) shipped in from beyond its borders—and thus become vulnerable to economic blackmail or worse—crossed the minds of few Americans. But, on that day in 1975 when communist tanks rolled through the streets of Saigon, the economy of the United States appeared tired and creaky, wracked by inflation and unemployment and declining productivity, its manufacturers hard-pressed to compete with those of other industrial powers (and some nonpowers) in its home market, not to mention the global market. It was an economy that was manifestly vulnerable to blackmail (or worse)—one that no longer appeared in almost total command of its own destiny. The people of the United States were painfully aware of what had happened, the more so when they waited in line to buy gasoline that cost double what it had a few years before and observed the ever-increasing numbers of Toyotas and Datsuns zipping along their streets and highways. Small wonder that a sort of malaise appeared to have settled over the American republic.

# Chapter
## 10

# In the Time
# of Malaise

Yet another scene in the drama of America's humiliation in Southeast Asia, one that went almost unnoticed by the people of the United States, was playing during those traumatic weeks of the spring of 1975 when communists completed their conquests in Cambodia and South Vietnam—in Laos, ruled since early 1973 by a coalition government presided over by noncommunists and representatives of the communist Pathet Lao. Doubtless stirred by what was taking place in Cambodia and Vietnam, the Pathet Lao expelled noncommunists from the government, at which point U.S. officials quietly closed all American installations and departed the country. Several months later, in December 1975, the communist leadership in Vientiane announced that the ancient Kingdom of a Million Elephants had become the Democratic People's Republic of Laos.

Generating larger headlines were dramatic events that transpired in the Gulf of Thailand in May of 1975—events that most Americans interpreted to have resulted in a glorious victory for the United States. Those events began to unfold twelve days after North Vietnamese tanks rumbled into Saigon, on May 12, 1975, when Cambodian gunboats stopped the American merchant-man *Mayaguez* as it passed 65 miles to the southwest of the port of Kompong Som. After stopping and then boarding the *Mayaquez,* the Cambodians spirited the ship's captain and 38 crewmen to the nearby islet of Kas Tang and thence to the Cambodian mainland. En route from Hong Kong to Thailand, the *Mayaguez* was laden with a cargo of commercial goods and supplies for U.S. servicemen and embassy personnel in Thailand. When, after two days, diplomacy failed to secure release of the *Mayaguez* and its crew, President Ford ordered the U.S. Air Force, Marine Corps, and Navy into action in the Gulf of Thailand.

Inasmuch as the Cambodians had abandoned the ship, retrieval of the *Mayaguez,* which was riding at anchor near Kas Tang, was easily accomplished. The attempt to rescue the crew of the *Mayaguez* proved more harried. On the mistaken assumption that the crew was still on Kas Tang, 205 marines were ferried to the islet by helicopter. Coming under intensive fire from the ground, three choppers were shot down. One of the three crash-landed on a beach, a second crash-landed in the surf about a hundred feet offshore, but the third went down farther out to sea, carrying 13 of the 26 men aboard to their deaths. As for the marines who managed to form on Kas Tang, they met fierce resistance. Then, when intelligence data established that the crew of the *Mayaguez* was not on the islet, the marines were instructed to terminate the attack.

At length, on May 15, the Cambodians put the captain and crew of the *Mayaguez* aboard a Thai fishing boat, which in turn delivered them to a U.S. guided-missile destroyer—at the same time that U.S. A-6 Intruders and A-7 Corsairs of the USS *Coral Sea* were blasting Ream Airfield near Phnom Penh. Less than an hour later, U.S. fighter-bombers destroyed an oil depot near Kompong Som. Several hours after that, under the cover of darkness, helicopters retrieved the marines on Kas Tang, and delivered them to Utapao in Thailand.

President Ford was immensely pleased by the outcome of the *Mayaguez* affair. So, apparently, were most of his compatriots. Observed the editors of the *Atlanta Journal,* "There seems to be a feeling of joy that at last we have won one." Only a smattering of citizens appeared to be in rhythm with assorted critics, most of them Democratic liberals, who contended that Ford should have made a more vigorous and prolonged effort to obtain the release of the *Mayaguez* and its crew by diplomatic means. As the critics noted, to obtain release of the crew of the *Mayaguez*—and to demonstrate the will and resolve of the United States in the immediate aftermath of the debacle in Vietnam—41 U.S. servicemen sacrificed their lives. Eighteen men died as a result of enemy action, 13 of them, as mentioned, in a helicopter downed by Cambodian gunfire. Twenty-three others perished in a helicopter crash in Thailand before they could be committed to the combat in the Gulf of Thailand.

## ELSEWHERE IN THE OUTER WORLD

Meanwhile, other questions and problems in the area of foreign relations had crowded in about President Ford, one of them the longtime conflict between Greeks and Turks on the island of Cyprus. Inasmuch as it threatened a rupture in the North Atlantic alliance (for both Greece and Turkey were members of NATO), the conflict was a matter of no small concern in the view of the chief executive in Washington. Unfortunately, Ford's efforts, and more importantly those of the UN, to negotiate a just settlement of the Cypriot conflict achieved little.

More fraught with peril, or so it seemed, was the interminable confrontation involving Israel and its Arab neighbors. The sources of the latter confrontation were transparent: Israel continued to occupy Arab lands seized during the Six-Day War of 1967, the Arab states continued to dispute Israel's right to exist as an independent nation-state. What might be done? As a first step in a process that it hoped would result in termination of the confrontation, the Ford administration determined to achieve an accord resolving differences between Israel and Egypt. To that purpose, Secretary of State Kissinger, in early 1975, resumed his much-heralded shuttle diplomacy, flying back and forth between Jerusalem and Cairo, pressing Israeli and Egyptian leaders to reach an accommodation.

Kissinger's proposals found a mark with Anwar el-Sadat, the Egyptian president who had earned the esteem of Americans when, after taking the reins of power in Cairo on the death of Gamal Abdul Nasser in 1970, he expelled a corps of Soviet advisers and technicians whom Nasser had brought to Egypt, and at the same time set about to improve his government's long-strained relations with the United States. But the Israelis rejected all appeals that they make meaningful concessions in the interest of peace. Whereupon Ford let it be known that the United States was reassessing its Middle Eastern policy— a policy that had resulted in billions of dollars of military and economic assistance to Israel over the years, not to mention unflagging diplomatic support.

Ford's signal jolted the Israelis, who at length, in September 1975, dispatched emissaries to Geneva where they and representatives of the Cairo government signed an agreement patterned after proposals set out in recent months by the United States. The agreement provided that Israel would make a modest withdrawal of its forces in the Sinai and give up the Abud Rudeis oil fields on the Gulf of Suez, seized during the Six-Day War and presently providing about 60 percent of Israel's petroleum requirements. Egypt agreed to allow Israeli cargoes to move through the Suez Canal and to renounce war as an instrument of policy vis-à-vis Israel. The United States agreed to provide about $2.3 billion of economic and military assistance to Israel, about $800 million to Egypt. Several weeks later, Sadat traveled to the United States, where he was greeted warmly by President Ford and invited to address a joint session of Congress.

The month after Sadat's visit to the United States, at the end of November of 1975, President Ford flew to Beijing where he conferred with 81-year-old

Mao Zedong and other officials of the People's Republic of China. The conversations were amicable, but because of Ford's refusal to consider a termination of U.S. diplomatic relations with the Chinese Nationalist regime on Taiwan his hope that he and leaders in Beijing might find a formula that would result in the establishment of normal diplomatic relations between their governments came to nothing.

Meanwhile, Ford sought to shore up the North Atlantic alliance, troubled in recent years by increasing European resentment of American domination of the alliance and European doubt that an American president would, in fact, risk a nuclear confrontation with the Soviets in the event of Soviet or Soviet-orchestrated aggression against a NATO ally. To that purpose, in June of 1975, Ford flew to Brussels where he addressed a meeting of the NATO council. He urged improvement in the process of political consultation between member states, signaled his hope that Spain would be admitted to the alliance (notwithstanding the objections of Denmark, the Netherlands, and Norway), and, most important perhaps, sought to reassure the allies regarding the strength and reliability of the United States. The Europeans seemed only mildly impressed.

While striving to shore up the NATO alliance, President Ford sought to continue the policy of achieving détente vis-à-vis the Soviet Union. His task appeared formidable, for détente had fallen on hard times since Ford's accession to the presidency in the summer of 1974. It had so fallen for a variety of reasons. Americans believed the Soviets intransigent in the SALT II negotiations. They also resented the Kremlin's support of Israel's enemies during the Yom Kippur War. For their part, the Soviets resented the contention of political conservatives in the United States that the Soviet Union remained an expansionist and aggressive power that could never be trusted. They also resented the insistence of America's political liberals that the Kremlin relax its repression of political dissent in its empire and accelerate the issuance of exit visas to Jewish citizens who yearned to leave the Soviet Union. Putting additional strain on détente was the enthusiastic reception accorded the dissident Russian novelist Aleksandr I. Solzhenitsyn when he arrived in the United States in 1975.

Whatever the strains and annoyances, neither the government in Washington nor that in Moscow was inclined to give up on détente. Most importantly, the two governments determined to keep alive the hope of achieving a permanent SALT agreement. Thus President Ford responded affirmatively to an invitation by the Soviets that he meet with General Secretary Brezhnev to resolve differences in the matter of SALT. And in November of 1974, during his fourth month in the White House, the American chief executive set out for the Siberian port of Vladivostok. En route, he stopped in Tokyo and Seoul to confer with leaders of Japan and South Korea.

On the second day of the two-day summit meeting at the small resort town of Okeanskaya near Vladivostok, Ford and Brezhnev signed the Vladivostok Declaration, an agreement in principle which they hoped would result, during 1975, in a ten-year SALT II treaty that would supersede SALT I, the treaty signed by Nixon and Brezhnev in 1972 that was scheduled to expire in June 1977. The new treaty, according to the declaration, would limit each superpower to 2,400 strategic delivery vehicles, that is, ICBMs, SLBMs, and intercontinental bombing planes. A total of 1,320 of each side's ICBMs could be armed with multiple warheads (that is, could be "MIRVed"). President Ford was ecstatic. Unfortunately, his ecstacy soon turned to disappointment, for negotiations in Geneva aimed at translating the Vladivostok Declaration into a SALT II treaty quickly became deadlocked.

At the same time that the SALT negotiations in Geneva were making no substantial progress—the identical fate that had befallen the Mutual Balanced Forces Reduction negotiations in Vienna (1973–1975) aimed at achieving a reduction of NATO and Warsaw Pact forces in Middle Europe—President Ford prepared to attend the climactic session of the Conference on Security and Cooperation in Europe. The climactic session was to take place in Helsinki in the last days of July and the first day of August of 1975.

The Soviets had sought such a conference since 1954, in the main to secure formal recognition by the United States and its NATO allies of territorial changes brought about during World War II, for example, annexation by the Soviet Union of the Baltic states of Estonia, Latvia, and Lithuania, and annexation by Poland of large areas of prewar Germany. At length, in May 1972, in the interest of détente—also in the hope that in exchange for recognition of the postwar boundaries (which seemed permanent in any event) the Soviets might pledge noninterference in the internal affairs of other countries, including the communist states of Eastern Europe, and accept a relaxation of their strictures against dissent within the Soviet Union—the United States consented to such a conference. Formally opened in July 1973, the conference would complete its work in July and August of 1975. At the final session, General Secretary Brezhnev, President Ford, and other leaders would put their hands to "the Helsinki accords."

Reckoning that the only meaningful result of the Helsinki accords would be recognition by the West of the permanency of existing borders in Eastern Europe, many Americans were aghast that their government was prepared to sign the documents, and that the president himself would do the signing. "Jerry, don't go [to Helsinki]," implored the editors of the *Wall Street Journal.* Acquiescence in the handiwork of the conference, in the view of the editors of the *New York Times,* would be misguided and empty. Of the president's determination to attend the last session of the conference and sign the accords, former-Governor Ronald Reagan of California said, "I am against it, and I think all Americans should be against it." Americans of Estonian, Latvian, and Lithuanian extraction conducted a protest vigil in front of the White House.

Ignoring the critics, Ford and Secretary Kissinger flew off to Helsinki in late July of 1975. Then, after three days of largely conciliatory oratory by Brezhnev, Ford, and other spokespeople of the 35 governments that were represented at the conference, the delegates, on August 1, signed the conference's Final Act by which the participating states reaffirmed their commitment to peaceful relations, agreed that European boundaries could be changed only by peaceful means, pledged noninterference in each other's internal affairs, and pledged respect for human rights and fundamental freedoms, including the freedom of conscience, religion, and thought. Other articles of the Final Act committed the participants to cooperation in education, environmental protection, science and technology, tourism, and trade and industrial development.

If President Ford found satisfaction in the Helsinki Conference and its Final Act, many of his compatriots did not. Such Americans deplored the Final Act's recognition of the inviolability of territorial changes wrought by the Red Army during World War II. They also had not the slightest doubt that the Soviets would give scant heed to pledges to respect the freedom of conscience, religion, and thought. Events would prove the critics correct. When Poles, in the latter 1970s and early 1980s, set about to move their country away from Soviet-style communism, the Kremlin made it abundantly clear that it would tolerate no such deviation. Regarding freedom of conscience and thought, Soviet leaders moved against those of its citizens who dared to speak out in opposition to the practices and principles of the Soviet regime, sending some to slave labor camps, placing others under house arrest, confining still others to psychiatric hospitals. Most notably, they banished Andrei D. Sakharov, a physicist who became a veritable symbol of dissent in the Soviet Union and was awarded a Nobel Peace Prize in 1975, to the city of Gorky where he was virtually cut off from communication with foreigners and other Soviet dissidents. By August 1, 1985, at the time Secretary of State George Shultz and other dignitaries assembled in Helsinki to observe the tenth anniversary of acceptance of the Final Act, Sakharov and other Soviet dissidents were all but forgotten.

## BICENTENNIAL

One month after his return from Helsinki, on September 4, 1975, President Ford was in Sacramento to confer with Gov. Edmund G. "Jerry" Brown and address the California legislature. While shaking hands with friendly citizens, he found himself looking into the barrel of a .45 caliber pistol. But before the would-be presidential assassin, Lynette "Squeaky" Fromme, a 26-year-old disciple of the imprisoned mass killer Charles Manson, could squeeze the trigger of the pistol, a secret service agent wrestled her to the ground. Fromme was subsequently convicted of attempting to murder the president, and sentenced to life imprisonment. Eighteen days later, on September 22, 1975, Ford was again in California, this time in San Francisco, and as he was making his way from the St. Francis Hotel to an armored limousine a plump and emotionally disturbed 45-year-old woman, Sara Jane Moore, aimed a .38 caliber pistol in the direction of the president and squeezed the trigger. The slug was off target by about 4 feet, perhaps because a bystander deflected Moore's aim by striking her arm. Like Fromme, Moore was subsequently sentenced to life imprisonment.

Attempts to assassinate the president certainly were not in keeping with a grand national celebration that by September 1975 was in full swing: observance of the two hundredth anniversary of the founding of the United States.

July 4, 1976: "Old Glory" frames the United States Capitol, the Washington Monument, and the Lincoln Memorial during the Grand Finale of the bicentennial celebration in Washington.

The celebration had got under way on April 19, 1975—at the time that North Vietnamese and Vietcong infantrymen and tankers were closing in on Saigon—when 150,000 Americans, including President Ford, attended a reenactment of the Battles of Lexington and Concord in which in April 1775, according to the poet Ralph Waldo Emerson, "embattled farmers . . . fired the shot heard round the world." The subsequent observance of the bicentennial took uncounted forms. The American Freedom Train, powered by a succession of steam locomotives, rolled across the landscape, attracting huge crowds when it paused at cities and towns. Inside its display cars were some seven hundred artifacts that included historical documents, American inventions, a gallery of American paintings and sculpture, and assorted memorabilia that mirrored the country's development and progress over the past two hundred years. The players of several major league baseball teams wore nineteenth-century-style caps.

The celebration touched every strata of the national society. Millions of Americans viewed David Brinkley's three-part bicentennial television essay entitled "Life, Liberty, and the Pursuit of Happiness." The U.S. Postal Service issued special stamps to commemorate the country's two hundredth birthday. Art galleries and museums offered innumerable bicentennial exhibitions, publishers brought out an array of books for readers of all ages celebrating the

American heritage, merchants stocked shelves with an incredible array of bi-centennial novelties. Great numbers of men grew beards, men and women went about in pioneer-style clothing, boys and girls shot basketballs through red, white, and blue nets, street departments painted fireplugs red, white, and blue.

The bicentennial observance, of course, reached its climax on July 4, 1976. The celebrating on that day began at 4:33 A.M. atop Mars Hill Mountain in Maine, where sunlight first touches the United States, when national guards-men hoisted a bicentennial flag and fired a 50-gun salute. During the hours that followed, Americans did precisely what President Ford had urged them to do, to wit, "Break out the flag, strike up the band, light up the sky." In Balti-more, 30,000 people witnessed a reenactment of the bombardment of Fort McHenry in 1814, during which Francis Scott Key had penned the lyrics of "The Star-Spangled Banner." In Chicago, 1,776 immigrants were sworn in as citizens. That evening, in Boston, 400,000 people jammed the banks of the Charles River to hear the Boston Pops orchestra, conducted by an exuberant and coatless Arthur Fiedler (82 years of age) perform Tchaikovsky's "1812 Overture" and a stirring rendition of "The Stars and Stripes Forever" to the accompaniment of booming howitzers, pealing church bells, and nonstop fire-works. In Philadelphia, a million people witnessed a reenactment of the sign-ing of the Declaration of Independence and, at 2 P.M., the striking of the Liberty Bell—with a rubber mallet.

In New York, an estimated 6 million people lined both sides of the Hudson when, shortly after noon, hundreds of sailing vessels, including 16 of the world's most splendid "tall ships," began a triumphant passage up the river. Reported *Newsweek*, "As they passed the reviewing ship, the USS *Forrestal*, they raised sail; in one spectacular salute to America, the sailors of the Italian tall ship *Amerigo Vespucci* climbed the rigging, then doffed their hats and held them aloft." At 1:50 P.M., a helicopter settled on the flight deck of the *Forres-tal*, and to the strains of "Hail to the Chief" President Ford stepped out. Promptly at 2 o'clock, as the Liberty Bell was being sounded in Philadelphia and bells were pealing across the entire nation, the president rang the *Forres-tal's* bicentennial bell 13 times in honor of the 13 colonies that on July 4, 1776, by their own declaration, became states of a new republic. That evening, as millions of people who had gathered about the New York harbor looked on in awe and tens of millions of others watched via television, an extravaganza of fireworks burst over the Statue of Liberty.

## ELECTION OF 1976

Few Americans needed to be reminded that the year of the bicentennial, 1976, was also one in which the country's voters would designate one of their com-patriots to preside over the national destiny during the next four years. As the months of 1976 unfolded, indeed a preponderance of citizens doubtless gave considerably greater thought to the impending presidential election than to the celebration of their superpowerful republic's 200th birthday. Only on the climactic day of July 4, it seems fair to say, was the bicentennial at the absolute center of national attention.

Large numbers of Americans by July 4, 1976, had embraced the presidential candidacy of James Earl Carter, Jr., the former governor of Georgia who preferred to be addressed as "Jimmy," a man of manifest intelligence, energy, and ambition. Unknown to all save a fraction of the national electorate 12 months before, Carter had won a succession of Democratic primary elections, and on the climactic day of the bicentennial observance was assured of his party's presidential nomination. Carter's premier asset in his quest for the presidency? His lack of experience in national politics and almost nonexistent connection with the national political establishment. Why would the lack of political experience and connections at the national level be an asset? Because in that historical season, one in which Americans continued to recoil in disgust when they pondered the Watergate scandal, the pardon of Nixon, and what they perceived to have been the web of lies and deceptions relating to the war in Vietnam, the political establishment in Washington stood in unusually low repute.

Carter had other assets. While an officer in the Navy, he had served with Adm. Hyman Rickover in the prestigious nuclear submarine program. A peanut farmer, he had been a highly successful agribusinessman. A onetime proponent of racial segregation, he had changed his views about race and managed to win the respect of Georgia's blacks without alienating its whites. A bornagain Southern Baptist, he appeared to be a man of impeccable integrity. His steel-blue eyes indicating that he was a man of great intensity (which he assuredly was), he could also flash a ready smile and display a fine sense of humor.

Assembling in Madison Square Garden in New York City in mid-July 1976, delegates to the Democratic national convention duly nominated Carter, widely perceived to be moderately liberal in political orientation, on the first roll call, then, at Carter's behest, nominated Sen. Walter F. Mondale, an unflinching liberal of Minnesota, for the vice presidency.

Gerald Ford, meanwhile, had pressed ahead with a campaign for the Republican presidential nomination. It was not an easy campaign. Ford had presided over the executive branch of the national government during the country's most severe economic decline since the Great Depression, legions of his compatriots remained incensed because of his pardon of Nixon, and Republican conservatives remained resentful because of his nomination of Nelson Rockefeller, a longtime nemesis of conservatives, for the vice presidency. Determined to exploit Ford's obvious vulnerability and seize the nomination for himself was Ronald Reagan, the former governor of California and a zealous conservative. Tracing most of the ills of the country to what he perceived to be the crushing weight of central authority in the federal system, Reagan proposed a massive transfer of authority and resources from the federal government to the states. Such a transfer, he argued, would result in a balanced federal budget and reduction of the national debt.

Although Reagan won Republican primary elections in California, Indiana, and several southern states, Ford was the victor in Florida, Illinois, Massachusetts, Michigan, New York, Pennsylvania, and Wisconsin, and when, in August of 1976, GOP delegates assembled in Kansas City, it was evident that in delegate commitments the president had an edge of approximately 110 over the former governor of California. Accordingly, Ford secured the nomination on the first roll call. At his behest, delegates thereupon nominated Sen. Robert Dole of Kansas, a disabled veteran of World War II and a hard-hitting campaigner, to be his vice presidential running mate. Republicans of the stalwart conservative genre held Dole in high esteem.

When serious campaigning got under way in early September of 1976, the president trailed Carter in the opinion polls by a seemingly insurmountable 30 points. Before long, however, the Ford campaign began to gather momentum, in no small measure as a result of the president's contention that Carter's pledge to balance the federal budget did not square with his appeal for new federal initiatives on behalf of the unemployed. Then, during a televised so-called debate between the two candidates, the president committed what stands to the present day as the most embarrassing gaffe in the annals of face-to-face confrontations between presidential candidates when, inexplicably, he insisted that Eastern Europe was free of Soviet domination. Great numbers of Americans concluded that perhaps Lyndon Johnson had been on the mark when he surmised that Ford had played football for too long without a helmet.

Ford's gaffe aside, most commentators thought the election "too close to call" when voters began streaming to polling places on November 2, 1976. And the outcome indeed was close. When votes were tabulated, Carter was credited with 40.8 million popular votes, Ford 39.1 million. By carrying all of the so-called border states save Oklahoma and all ten of the states of the one-time Confederacy save Virginia—in addition to Hawaii, Massachusetts, Minnesota, New York, Ohio, Pennsylvania, and Rhode Island—the Georgian defeated the president in the electoral college, 297–241. As a result of the election, the Democrats, as usual, would retain control of both houses of Congress.

## PRESIDENT CARTER

On January 20, 1977, on a platform that stood atop the east steps of the Capitol, Jimmy Carter repeated the presidential oath, offered a moving tribute to his predecessor in the presidential office "for all he has done to heal our land," and in his inaugural address appealed to Americans to "learn together and laugh together—confident that in the end we will triumph together." Then, forsaking his open limousine, he strode down Pennsylvania Avenue, hand in hand with his wife Rosalynn, to begin his term in the White House.

Born in the small town of Plains in southwestern Georgia in 1924, Jimmy Carter had grown up in middle-income comfort. His father was a successful merchant-farmer and devout Baptist, his mother a registered nurse and social

January 20, 1977: After repeating the presidential oath, Jimmy Carter, hand-in-hand with his wife Rosalynn, walks down Pennsylvania Avenue from the Capitol to the White House.

activist. At age 19, he entered the U.S. Naval Academy at Annapolis, graduated in 1946 with distinction, and in 1951 joined the Navy's fledgling atomic submarine program. But on the death of his father in 1953, he left the Navy to take over direction of the Carter family's assorted enterprises in southwestern Georgia. Under his guidance, the enterprises prospered and expanded.

Increasingly interested in politics, Carter in 1962 won election to the Georgia legislature, went down to what for him was a spirit-cracking defeat when he ran for governor of Georgia in 1966, and a short time later, as a consequence of what he later described as a profound religious experience, became a born-again Christian. He ran again for governor in 1970, and, following a campaign in which he purposefully appeared to be friendly with Lester Maddox, the incumbent governor of Georgia, and Gov. George Wallace of Alabama, both of them militant segregationists, emerged victorious. But then, in his inaugural address in January 1971, he stunned his white auditors by repudiating racial discrimination. His pronouncement may not have come as a total surprise to many black Georgians, for during the recent gubernatorial campaign, at the same time that he was making his oblique appeal to the racist impulses of many of the state's white voters (by appearing to be friendly with Maddox and Wallace), Carter had promised blacks that he would be more sensitive to their interests and concerns than Maddox and previous governors of Georgia had been. In any event, to the delight of blacks and chagrin of segregationists, he ordered that a portrait of Martin Luther King, Jr., be hung in the state capitol, and brought several blacks into the state government. His enterprise caught the attention of the national communications media, and in a cover story in May 1971, *Time* portrayed him as the exemplar of a new breed of southern governor, moderately liberal in the matter of social issues, nonracist, and fiscally conservative.

The Georgia constitution prevented Carter from running for a second term as governor, and in December 1974, as he prepared to leave the gubernatorial office, he announced that he was running for president. Few people took the announcement seriously. But the Carter candidacy eventually found a mark with tens of millions of Americans who were weary of what some commentators described as "the old politics," and as a result, on January 20, 1977, the 5-foot-9-inch Georgian, wearing gloves and a black overcoat but no hat, waving and flashing his sunburst smile, strode down Pennsylvania Avenue to the White House.

## ENERGY

The thirty-ninth president executed his first official act of large moment during his second day in the White House when, in accord with a campaign pledge, he issued an executive order granting full and unconditional pardon to nearly all young men who had resisted the military draft during the time of the war in Vietnam. More importantly perhaps, he set about in those pristine days of his presidency to find a solution to what he was certain was a national energy crisis. A fortnight after taking office, to persuade his compatriots of the seriousness of the energy situation, Carter delivered from the White House (via television) what was literally a fireside chat, for, wearing a cardigan sweater, he was seated by an open fireplace in which a brisk fire crackled and popped. The main point of the speech was that the energy problem was genuine, and that Americans must conserve energy and develop energy resources within their own country. One month later, he asked Congress to authorize a new cabinet-level department, the Department of Energy. When Congress acceded to his request, he appointed James R. Schlesinger to be the first secretary of energy. Next, on April 18, 1977, he delivered a televised address to the nation on energy in which he described the effort to meet the energy problem as the "moral equivalent of war."

Two evenings later, Carter made his way to the Capitol, and in a speech before a joint session of Congress presented an array of proposals for energy legislation. The response to his proposals was less than enthusiastic. Continuing to view the energy crisis as a monstrous hoax perpetrated by the oil companies to bring about increases in prices (and, of course, profits), large numbers of Americans did not consider energy legislation urgent. Arguing that deregulation of their industries and a reduction in taxes on their products would resolve the energy shortage, the oil and natural gas industries assailed the president's proposals that taxes on oil and natural gas be increased. Automobile manufacturers denounced the proposal for a new tax on gas-guzzler cars. Environmentalists deplored those proposals intended to encourage the use of air-polluting coal. Accordingly, other than the measure establishing the Department of Energy, the only energy legislation of note to pass through Congress in 1977 was an act authorizing $150 million for continued work on the controversial Clinch River Breeder Reactor in eastern Tennessee. As for Carter, he believed that previous estimates of an impending shortage of uranium ore had been grossly exaggerated (and thus conventional nuclear plants would face no shortage of fuel in the foreseeable future). He also feared that plutonium-fueled breeder reactors, if put in service throughout the world, were apt to result in the proliferation of nuclear weapons, inasmuch as plutonium produced to fuel the reactors could be diverted to the manufacture of nuclear bombs. He therefore vetoed the latter legislation.

For a variety of reasons, the world found itself awash in crude oil in 1978, but a majority of the members of Congress agreed that the oil glut would prove transitory. The upshot was passage through the national legislature in the autumn of 1978 of the Energy Tax Act. Although it did not include the tax on domestically produced crude oil that had been a centerpiece of the energy program proposed by President Carter in April 1977, the legislation provided penalties to be paid by manufacturers on gas-guzzling automobiles, reformed utility rate-making, encouraged the use of coal, encouraged solar power developments and gasohol production, provided tax credits for home insulation, and provided for the carefully phased decontrol of natural gas prices.

The energy legislation of 1978 had scarcely received the signature of President Carter before the petroleum surplus or glut of previous months began to evaporate, and by the spring of 1979 the United States again was enduring a serious shortage of petroleum products, the most tangible evidence of which was the reappearance of long lines of automobiles in the streets· adjacent to gasoline stations across the country. The principal cause of the shortage was the cessation of oil exports by Iran as a result of a political revolution in that country. Not only did Americans have less oil to consume; they had to pay more for that which they did consume. Largely because of the removal of Iranian oil from the market, prices of crude increased dramatically—to as much as $40 a barrel on the so-called spot market in Rotterdam. As a consequence, the United States, which continued to import about half of the oil it consumed, paid nearly $60 billion for imported oil in 1979, compared with $40 billion in 1978.

At length, in April 1980, Congress responded to new appeals emanating from the White House by passing legislation providing for the decontrol of domestically produced crude and subjecting the producers of oil to what was referred to as a windfall profits tax that would divert to the federal treasury a substantial percentage of the increased revenues resulting from decontrol. Two months later, it consented to legislation providing that much of the foregoing revenue would be expended to support the enterprise of a new federal corporation, the Synthetic Fuels Corporation. The corporation was to achieve the rapid development of a synthetic fuels industry that by 1992 would produce 2 million barrels of crude equivalent per day. Concentrating on the production of synfuels from coal, oil shale, and tar sands, the corporation was authorized to expend $92 billion over the next 12 years.

At the same time that Congress was enacting new energy legislation, in 1980, the world again found itself awash in oil, in part because of a return to production in Iran and a global economic recession that resulted in reduced demand for petroleum products. Because of the oil glut, American motorists did not have to endure the annoyance of waiting in lines at gasoline stations during 1980. Still, the United States imported 7 million barrels of crude petroleum per day through that year, most of it from Nigeria and Saudi Arabia, and because of increased prices—from $22.00 a barrel in 1979 to $33.50 in 1980, an increase attributable to a dramatic increase in the price of crude mandated by OPEC—the country expended some $80 billion on imported oil in 1980, compared with about $60 billion the year before. Because the increased price of imported oil pushed up the pump price of gasoline to approximately $1.30 a gallon (almost four times the price in 1970), Americans drove less and were increasingly inclined to buy small fuel-efficient automobiles. The consequence was a modest decline in gasoline consumption in the United States.

## THE ECONOMY

The realization by Americans that the days of cheap energy, one of the bases of the phenomenal growth of their national economy over the past century, now belonged to history made a profound contribution to the sense of malaise that appeared to hang over the country during the middle and latter 1970s. Making an even more powerful contribution to that sense were continuing economic troubles, some of them attributable in part to problems relating to energy.

When Jimmy Carter moved into the White House in early 1977, the national economy was recovering from the Great Recession of 1975–1976. Fueled by a willingness of millions of Americans to assume ever-heavier burdens of debt and dip into their savings to buy automobiles, houses, and countless other commodities, the recovery continued as the months unfolded. Unfortunately, after the fashion of a raging disease, as one writer expressed it, inflation continued to ravage the national economy. The consumer price index advanced from 6.5 percent in 1977 to 7.7 percent in 1978, and it was duly noted that what had cost $1 only 11 years before, in 1967, now cost $2. What prompted the inflation that was wracking the country? Economists cited spending by the federal government that had contributed to budget deficits of $44.9 billion in 1977 and $48.8 billion in 1978, save for the deficit of $66.4 billion during the Great Recession of 1976, the largest peacetime deficits in history. They also cited the impulse of a large percentage of the population to borrow heavily and deplete savings to maintain affluent living standards—also the accelerating cost of energy.

To counter inflation, President Carter imposed voluntary wage-price standards, and pledged to curtail federal spending and reduce federal budget deficits. Of larger import, the Federal Reserve Board (or "Fed"), an independent agency of the federal government endowed with the authority to exercise enormous influence over the volume and cost of credit in the United States, sought to "cool" the economy by raising the rediscount rate, that is, the rate at which the Federal Reserve system lends to member banks, to 9.5 percent, the highest rate in history to that time. As a consequence, member banks increased interest charges to customers—to businesses, farmers, and ordinary people who wanted to buy appliances, automobiles, houses, or whatever. The Fed also shaved $3 billion from the funds that banks were authorized to lend.

Nothing seemed to work. Continuing to negotiate loans, using credit cards ("plastic money") with no visible restraint, and in many cases depleting savings almost to the vanishing point, Americans continued to spend almost frenetically. At the same time, oil prices continued to move up. Despite the president's pledge to hold the line on spending by the national government, federal expenditures increased (although the budget deficit declined to $27.7 billion in 1979). The outcome? The cost-of-living index advanced a staggering 11.3 percent in 1979. The year 1980 brought no improvement. On the contrary, the condition of the economy worsened. The gross national product experienced its steepest quarterly decline ever from April to June of 1980, and by the summer of that year it appeared that the country was in the grip of a new recession. Notwithstanding the recession, alas, the monster of inflation remained untamed. Thus the consumer price index advanced a staggering (again) 13.5 percent in 1980, and instead of $30 billion as predicted by the president at the start of the year, the federal budgetary deficit for 1980 soared to $59.6 billion.

Reinforcing the sense of dismay and frustration that great numbers of Americans felt when pondering the national economy during the middle and latter 1970s (and into the 1980s) was the continuing influx of automobiles, cameras, clothing, motorcycles, shoes, steel, stereo equipment, television sets, and other commodities from overseas. During 1979 and 1980, for example, when domestic sales of automobiles manufactured in the United States declined precipitously, sales in the country of cars manufactured overseas, particularly in Japan, increased. Even as they bought Datsuns and Toyotas made in Japan, shoes made in Italy, and apparel made in Singapore and South Korea, Taiwan and Yugoslavia, many American consumers deplored the apparent inability of domestic manufacturers to produce cars and slippers and sport jackets of comparable quality for sale at comparable prices.

Adding to the dismay of large numbers of Americans was the increasing tendency of American manufacturers to purchase commodities of foreign manufacture for sale under their own brand names—for example, the Dodge Colt automobile, built by the Mitsubishi Corporation of Japan. Of greater moment was the accelerating practice of American corporations of setting up manufacturing operations abroad—not for the production of commodities for sale in foreign areas (as historically had been the raison d'être of the "offshore" operations of American manufacturers), but rather for the production of commodities, notably semiconductor devices and clothing and shoes, to be sold back in the United States. Why did corporations move manufacturing operations offshore? The reason was transparent: to take advantage of the willingness of workers in developing countries of the Third World, particularly in East Asia and Latin America, to toil for minuscule wages.

Still, the condition or state of manufacturing industries in the United States in the middle and latter 1970s was not quite as bleak as it appeared to many Americans. For as the "smokestack industries" declined and American transnational (or multinational) corporations expanded offshore manufacturing operations, such industries as aerospace and electronics, increasingly referred to as high-technology (or high-tech) industries, were experiencing impressive growth within the borders of the North American superpower. Indeed, it was often asserted in the latter 1970s and early 1980s that the United States was in the midst of a new industrial revolution—was exiting the century-old era in which manufacturing industries of the smokestack genre, particularly steel and automobiles, had dominated the industrial life of the country and entering one of dominance by high-tech industries.

Although an array of high-tech manufacturers had set up operations in the northern Frostbelt, for example, in the vicinity of Boston, a preponderance of the country's high-tech manufacturing facilities were located in the Sunbelt, that is, in that rim of states reaching from the Carolinas, Georgia, and Florida along the Atlantic Coast across the continent through Oklahoma and Texas to California and the Pacific Northwest. The decisions to locate high-tech industries in the Sunbelt were easily explained. Particularly for aerospace manufacturers, climate was a consideration, inasmuch as the testing of their sleek and incredibly sophisticated flying machines required mild temperatures and clear skies. An abundant supply of skilled and productive workers, as was available particularly in the states of the Pacific Coast, was another. A veritable mecca of high technology by the latter 1970s was what had become known as Silicon Valley—actually the Santa Clara Valley—just to the south of San Francisco. An array of corporations and ingenious electronics engineers had made Silicon Valley a thriving center of innovation and enterprise.

High-tech industries were not the only industries that were inclined to sink roots in the Sunbelt during the 1970s and early 1980s. Attracted by a variety of considerations, including low (and in the case of Texas nonexistent) corporate income taxes and laws that restricted the activities of labor unions (and thus resulted in lower labor costs), corporations and entrepreneurs increasingly elected to locate new operations in the Sunbelt (and also in the Rocky Mountain states of the West). If, contrary to a widely held assumption, relatively few corporations actually moved manufacturing operations from the Frostbelt of the Northeast and Middle West to the Sunbelt, growth in capital spending was two and a half times greater in the South and Far West from 1971 to 1980 than in the Northeast and Middle West.

New opportunities in the Sunbelt, combined with the shutdown of steel mills (because of the inability of American steelmakers to meet foreign competition in both the domestic and overseas markets) and factories (largely as a result of decisions by apparel manufacturers to move operations offshore) in the Northeast and Middle West prompted a substantial migration of people from the Frostbelt to the comparatively flourishing Sunbelt, a phenomenon often referred to as the Sunbelt surge. In paragraphs reminiscent of John Steinbeck's famous description of the westward migration of displaced farmers from Arkansas and Oklahoma in the 1930s, an essay that appeared in the *New York Times* in February 1977 described the scene along Interstate 95 in Virginia: "All day through the lonely night, the moving vans push southward, 14-wheeled boxcars of the highway, changing the demographic face of America. . . . They return toward the North in a few days, riding high and empty, racing to shoehorn another household into the rig in Providence or Pittsburgh for transplanting to the nation's fastest growing region, the Sunbelt. . . ."

Statistics were less graphic but no less insightful. In the period from 1970 to 1985, the population of the Northeast increased from 49.0 million to 49.8 million, that of the Middle West from 56.6 million to 59.2 million. In that same period, the population of the South increased from 62.8 million to 81.8 million, that of the Far West from 34.8 million to 47.8 million. The population of the Empire State of New York *declined* from 18.2 million in 1970 to 17.7 million in 1985, while that of Florida surged from 6.8 million in 1970 to 11.3 million in 1985, that of Texas from 11.2 million to 16.4 million, that of California from 20.0 million to 26.3 million. As a result of population shifts, as recorded in the federal census of 1980, the states of the Northeast and Middle West lost 15 seats in the national House of Representatives to the states of the South and Far West.

Although expanding economic opportunities were resulting in the impressive and even phenomenal growth of such Sunbelt cities as Atlanta and Houston, Phoenix and San Diego, economic stagnation appeared to have overcome many cities of the Frostbelt. What were the northeastern and midwestern cities to do? Appointed by President Carter in 1977, the President's Commission for a National Agenda for the Eighties reported in January 1981 that contemporary trends in the country had rendered the traditional city of the country's longtime industrial heartland, that is, the city in the Northeast and Middle West, largely obsolete. Since cities were first and foremost economic entities, the report explained, the cities of the Frostbelt had no choice than to adjust to the new economic realities. Since efforts to reindustrialize would be self-defeating, it went on, the cities of the Northeast and Middle West should concentrate on service functions. And since service functions increasingly required employees of considerable educational achievement, the federal government ought to support the "historical role of migration as the dominant means of linking people to opportunity." The latter proposal, conjuring visions as it did of hordes of poor people from the slums of Detroit, New York, and Philadelphia descending on the Sunbelt, prompted an angry response in the Sunbelt. Branding the proposal ridiculous, the mayor of Jacksonville fumed, "The report seems to be saying, 'Let's pack them up in buses and ship them down to the Sunbelt like refugees.'"

## IMMIGRANTS

Exacerbating the country's economic problems, so many Americans suspected during the years of national malaise, were hundreds of thousands of immigrants who were flooding into the United States each year from Latin America, most of them from Mexico. (By 1980, it was estimated that between 5 and 12 million Mexicans were living illegally in the United States.) So the argument went, the illegals put new burdens on hospitals, law enforcement agencies, and schools. They often became public charges. And who picked up the tab? Gringo taxpayers. More than that, the troubled economy of the United States was presently unable to provide employment for all of its own people who wanted work. An illegal alien who had a job, it was widely contended, was therefore depriving a U.S. citizen of his or her livelihood.

What might be done about the illegals? The answer appeared to be not much. Trying to round up several million illegal aliens for shipment back to Mexico and elsewhere would require police-state tactics that would be totally repugnant to most Americans, and laws fashioned to punish employers who hired illegals would likely rebound against legitimate U.S. citizens of Latin American origin, that is, employers would be fearful of hiring people who claimed to be Chicanos lest they, in fact, be illegals. Further inhibiting strong action to deport illegals was oil. Geological explorations in recent years had disclosed that some of the world's most extensive petroleum deposits were locked beneath the soil and seabed of Mexico. The petroleum-thirsty United States hoped to become a principal consumer of Mexican oil and natural gas.

But if the Washington government offended Mexican sensibilities by treating Mexican illegals with a heavy hand, the business of striking bargains for the large-scale purchase of Mexican oil and gas might become painfully complicated.

The arrival of great numbers of Latinos and the resultant swelling of the country's Spanish-speaking population raised other questions. Of special concern, should instruction in the public schools in areas, for example, east Los Angeles, where Hispanic populations were concentrated be offered in Spanish as well as English? Proponents of bilingual education argued that instruction in English retarded the achievement of Spanish-speaking children, an outcome that was apt to handicap most of them for the rest of their lives. Opponents argued that bilingual education would prove frightfully expensive. They argued further that Spanish-speaking children would eventually be compelled to compete in a predominantly English-speaking society, and hence it was essential that they master English by confronting the language head-on in the schools, just as had millions of immigrant children in former times.

Meanwhile, other questions pertaining to immigration commanded the attention of Americans. What, for example, was the United States to do regarding the so-called boat people of Indochina?

The saga of the boat people began in 1978 when the communist leaders of

December 1978: More than 2,300 Vietnamese ''boat people'' aboard the refugee ship *Tung An*, anchored in Manila Bay, prepare to return to sea after authorities refuse to allow them to go ashore in the Philippines.

Vietnam determined to uproot Vietnam's ethnic Chinese, that is, Vietnamese citizens of Chinese origin. In the view of the Hanoi government, the ethnic Chinese were interlopers whose loyalty to Vietnam would forever be suspect. What were the options open to the ethnic Chinese? They could repair to "economic zones" in Vietnam where they would live apart from the bulk of the Vietnamese population, or they could leave the country. Perhaps a quarter-million ethnic Chinese fled northward to China in the years after 1975; thousands of others elected to leave Vietnam by boat. In the aftermath of a brief but bloody war between China and Vietnam in early 1979, the exodus of Vietnam's ethnic Chinese became a veritable flood. Joining the exodus were substantial numbers of ethnic Vietnamese who sought to escape the rigidities of rule by the communists.

By the summer of 1979, uncounted boats and tiny ships were bobbing about in the South China Sea and Gulf of Thailand. Some were without means of locomotion. Most were jammed beyond capacity with their human cargoes. Few were adequately provisioned with food or fresh water. The outcome was another of the human tragedies of modern times. Pirates, mainly from Thailand, swooped down on some of the boats, looting and raping. Dilapidated and overloaded, many boats slipped beneath the rolling sea, taking terrified passengers to watery graves. In all, an estimated 50 percent of the more than half-million ethnic Chinese and Vietnamese who set out in boats in 1978–1979 perished at sea.

At length, the world took note of the plight of Indochina's boat people, and the upshot was a massive rescue operation, much of it carried out by the U.S. Navy. On rescue, the boat people were resettled in noncommunist countries across the world, a majority of them in the United States. Indeed, from April 1975, when Cambodia and South Vietnam fell under communist rule, through September 1979, more than 385,000 Indochinese refugees were resettled. More than 260,000, or 68 percent, found refuge in the United States. Nor was that the end of it. In the autumn of 1979, the United States agreed to accept an additional 168,000 Indochinese, many of them Cambodians as well as Vietnamese, who were languishing in refugee camps in Thailand and elsewhere in Southeast Asia. Although many Americans felt less than enthusiastic about this new wave of immigration from East Asia, the Indochinese immigrants (like migrants from South Korea and elsewhere in the Great East who settled in the United States in the 1960s and 1970s) seemed consumed by the work ethic so admired by most citizens of the North American colossus. And most were manifestly determined to accommodate themselves to life in the United States, learn English, and prove themselves worthy Americans.

By the spring of 1980, most of the people of the United States had allowed the tragedy of the boat people to slip to the recesses of their minds. Then, almost overnight, U.S. shores were the object of yet another unexpected wave of migration. This time, the immigrants were arriving from Fidel Castro's bastion of communism, Cuba.

During the 15 years after Castro's accession to power in Havana, some 800,000 Cubans migrated from the Ever-Faithful Isle to the United States.

Most of them settled in Florida, particularly in the area around Miami. Then, in April of 1980, as the conditions of life in Cuba went from bad to worse, six Cubans drove a bus past Cuban guards stationed outside the Peruvian embassy in Havana. They crashed the bus through the embassy gates and asked the startled Peruvians for political asylum. At that point, Castro inexplicably removed the guards from outside the embassy, whereupon ten thousand additional Cubans poured through the gates, squatted on the embassy grounds (and on rooftops and in trees), and also requested asylum. For Castro, the spectacle of thousands of his people jammed inside the embassy and clamoring to get out of Cuba was an enormous embarrassment. Still, the dictator had little room for maneuver. So he announced that the would-be émigrés, labeled "bums" and "parasites" by Cuban authorities, would be granted exit visas.

Events now took another dramatic turn. Several Cuban Americans set out from Florida in small boats, destination: the port of Mariel on the northwest coast of Cuba. Their purpose? They hoped the Castro regime would allow them to evacuate squatters from the Peruvian embassy—and, more importantly, evacuate some of their own relatives. Castro allowed them to do both. The return of the refugee-laden boats electrified the Cuban-American community in Florida. Apparently Castro was willing to grant exit visas to any Cubans who wanted to leave the country, not just the squatters in the Peruvian embassy.

What happened next boggled the mind. At great personal expense, Cuban Americans organized a massive sealift to deliver relatives and other dissidents from Cuba. Soon hundreds of boats of all sizes and shapes, jammed with deliriously happy Cubans on the northward voyage, were churning back and forth across the Straits of Florida, scarcely pausing when the seas became heavy. In all, during a period of thirty or so days, they delivered more than 115,000 new immigrants to the shores of the United States. Wondering when this business of taking in refugees might end, many North Americans were dismayed. Clearly, the United States could not accommodate all of the poor and oppressed people of the entire world. Sharing the popular dismay was the government in Washington. But at length, President Carter let it be known that the country would honor its heritage as a haven for the oppressed and make room for the Cuban refugees—and also several thousand Haitians who, fleeing the poverty and oppression of their Caribbean homeland, recently had made their way in tiny boats to Florida.

## INITIATIVES IN FOREIGN AFFAIRS

On assuming the presidency in 1977, Jimmy Carter determined that the advancement of basic human rights would be a centerpiece of his administration's foreign policy. Accordingly, he informed the UN that the United States accepted its Genocide Convention and the Treaty for the Elimination of All Forms of Racial Discrimination. In June 1977, he signed the Inter-American Convention on Human Rights. And in October 1977, he made his way to UN headquarters in New York, and while Secretary General Kurt Waldheim looked on approvingly, signed two international covenants that had been drafted in 1966. The International Covenant on Civil and Political Rights emphasized the integrity of individual persons and the right of the individual to receive equal treatment under the law, participate in public affairs, and be guaranteed what Americans often refer to as First Amendment freedoms. The International Covenant on Economic, Social, and Cultural Rights dealt with the individual's entitlement to high standards of health care, family rights, social security, working conditions, and a good deal more.

The Carter administration, meanwhile, sprinkled policy statements with references to human dignity and fundamental freedoms, set about to deny economic and military assistance to governments that in the American perspective were guilty of the "gross violation" of the rights of their peoples, and spoke out in support of such Soviet dissidents as Andrei Sakharov. It protested the apartheid or racial separation policies of the Republic of South Africa, and threatened diplomatic action if South Africa continued to deny basic human rights to its nonwhite majority.

As assorted critics (and no doubt Carter himself) anticipated, the human rights initiatives produced complications. Most importantly, they put a new strain on U.S. relations with the Soviet Union, for statements emanating from the White House in support of Sakharov and other Soviet dissidents infuriated leaders in the Kremlin, who viewed the statements as unwarranted and intolerable interference in the internal affairs of their empire. After a year or so, in truth, the human rights policy of the Carter administration had lost a good deal of its momentum.

Carter, meanwhile, sought to bring about a dramatic reduction of arms sales by the industrial powers to countries of the Third World. His enterprise came to little. He also tried to achieve a rapprochement between the Washington government and Fidel Castro's communist regime in Havana. Although the two governments agreed to set up a "diplomatic interest" section in each other's capital, Cuba's continuing military involvement in the civil war in Angola and, in 1978, Castro's decision to send Cuban troops to support the Marxist government of Ethiopia in its war against Somalia for control of the Ogaden desert in the horn of East Africa—also new questions about the Soviet Union's military presence in Cuba—returned the Washington government to a stance of out-and-out hostility vis-à-vis the Castro regime.

Carter, likewise, sought to improve the Washington government's relations with its counterpart in Mexico City—relations that had been strained in recent years as a result of disputes over trade, friction deriving from the campaign of the United States to curb the illegal migration of Mexicans to its territory, and Mexico's failure to curtail the movement of marijuana and other narcotics from Mexico to the United States. To that purpose, the president made a state visit to Mexico in February 1979. The visit proved diplomatically difficult. During a luncheon, the Mexican president López Portillo virtually tongue-lashed his guest from north of the border, and when Carter tried to relieve tension by making a joke about "Montezuma's Revenge" he merely irritated his hosts. Later in the year, however, representatives of the two governments signed an agreement in which Mexico agreed to sell 300 million cubic feet of natural gas to U.S. companies.

More important—and assuredly more satisfying to President Carter—were the so-called Panama Canal treaties. Signed in 1977, the two treaties conceivably headed off a nasty confrontation between the North American superpower and the small Central American republic of Panama. Such a confrontation, had it ever come to pass, might well have resulted in disruption of the Panama Canal, an interocean waterway of large strategic importance to the United States.

From the outset of his presidency, Carter made clear his conviction that, in view of the continuing ill temper of Panamanians in the matter of the Panama Canal and the vulnerability of the canal (because of its lock system) to sabotage, the time had come to arrange for the transfer of ownership of the canal to Panama. That conviction greatly exercised those of his compatriots who were militantly conservative. As the former governor of California, Ronald Reagan, expressed it, "When it comes to the canal, we built it, we paid for it, it's ours, and we should tell . . . [the Panamanians] that we are going to keep it." Laments by militant conservatives notwithstanding, the Carter administration pressed ahead with negotiations (begun during the presidency of Lyndon Johnson) aimed at resolving differences with Panama regarding the canal.

At length, on September 7, 1977—at the White House, in the presence of former-President Ford, former-Secretaries of State Rogers and Kissinger, and Lady Bird Johnson—President Carter and Panama's "Supreme Leader," Gen. Omar Torrijos, signed two treaties. The first provided that Panama would take full control of the canal at noon on December 31, 1999. In the meantime, Panama would receive an annuity of $10 million (up from $2.3 million) and as much as $10 million annually from canal tolls if revenues warranted. Panamanians would assume increasing responsibility for operating and defending the canal. Panama would receive more than half of the land of the Canal Zone immediately, and gain jurisdiction over the Zone in three years. The second treaty provided for the permanent neutralization of the Panama Canal, that is, the isthmian waterway would always be open to the vessels of all nations. Thanks in no small measure to the enterprise of the Republican leader in the Senate, Howard Baker of Tennessee, the upper chamber of the U.S. Congress subsequently consented to both treaties.

President Carter also found satisfaction in other developments in foreign affairs. His administration steadfastly supported British efforts to bring genuine majority rule to strife-torn Rhodesia in southern Africa, an overwhelmingly black country that long had been ruled by a tiny white minority. The British determined to bring all of the country's competing (or, more accurately, warring) factions into the political process, and the outcome, in the spring of 1980, was the birth of the Republic of Zimbabwe. The first government to open an embassy in the capital of the new republic was that of the United States.

More satisfying from the perspective of the thirty-ninth president was the establishment, on the first day of 1979, of full diplomatic relations between the United States and the People's Republic of China, the culmination of President Nixon's trip to the fabled Middle Kingdom in 1972. (Before signing the treaty, the United States severed diplomatic relations and terminated its mutual defense treaty with Taiwan, but in April of 1979 President Carter signed legislation establishing unofficial relations with the regime in Taipei and granting it limited security assurances.) The new relationship with the Beijing government received reinforcement in early 1979 when the diminutive vice premier of China, Deng Xiaoping made a nine-day tour of the United States and signed agreements providing for cultural and technological exchanges between his country and the North American superpower. The new Sino-American relationship suffered no cracks when, barely ten days after Deng's return home, tens of thousands of Chinese troops poured across China's 500-mile frontier with Vietnam at 26 points. After a fortnight of intense combat, Chinese infantry had advanced as much as 25 miles.

Prompting China's military incursion into Vietnam were recent events in Cambodia. Those events began to unfold in 1975 when the communist regime of the shadowy Pol Pot, on achieving absolute political control of Cambodia, set about to restructure Cambodian society and make the country economically self-reliant. In the words of one writer, Cambodia (officially the Khmer Republic from 1972 through 1975, Democratic Kampuchea since early 1976) came to resemble a huge prison work camp as the regime herded people by the hundreds of thousands from cities and towns to the countryside to build dikes and irrigation canals and to cultivate rice. Disease, executions, overwork, and starvation resulted in the deaths of an estimated 500,000 to 2 million people.

Then, in December 1978, the communist government in Hanoi sent 12 divisions of battle-tested troops crashing into Cambodia—to achieve its longtime ambition of asserting control over all of Indochina, it appeared, rather than to terminate the massacre of Cambodians by their own communist government. Within two weeks, the Vietnamese had driven Pol Pot from Phnom Penh into the jungles of western Cambodia (where, in 1988, his and other Cambodian factions were continuing the struggle against the Vietnamese) and installed a puppet Cambodian regime. Inasmuch as the Pol Pot regime had aligned itself with China in the latter's ongoing quarrel with the Soviet Union, while the Vietnamese had aligned with the Soviets, the Beijing government viewed Vietnam's conquest of Cambodia as a setback for China. The upshot was China's military incursion into Vietnam of early 1979, the purpose of which was to punish the Vietnamese. It was an incursion that the Vietnamese met vigorously and with surprising effect.

As for leaders of the United States, they felt nothing save contempt for both of the principals in the conflict in Cambodia, that is, for the regime of Pol Pot and that in Hanoi. But China's attack stirred their concern, for they feared that the Chinese incursion in Vietnam might prompt a retaliatory attack on China by Vietnam's ally, the Soviet Union—an attack that conceivably could get out of hand and escalate into a global war. Leaders in Washington, therefore, urged restraint on the Chinese. As events turned out, the Soviet

Union made no military move against China, and the Chinese confined themselves to a 17-day punitive exercise in Vietnam, one that claimed the lives of several thousand Vietnamese. It was an exercise that failed to persuade the Vietnamese to give up their adventure in Cambodia. So the miniwar in Cambodia continued. Caught in the middle were the long-suffering people of the ancient Khmer nation.

In the year and a half following China's military action against Vietnam, ties between China and the United States appeared to become stronger. The two countries signed a major trade agreement, and the United States indicated a willingness to supply nonlethal equipment that would strengthen the Chinese military. Meanwhile, neither the Chinese nor the Soviets hinted that they might smooth over differences and achieve a rapprochement. Of particular moment, the Chinese announced that they would not renew the 30-year Sino-Soviet mutual security pact of 1950.

## CAMP DAVID ACCORDS

Inarguably a happening of great historic import, the establishment of full-dress diplomatic relations between the governments in Washington and Beijing warmed the heart of President Carter. But the outcome of his administration's enterprise aimed at resolving the thirty-year Arab-Israeli conflict in the Middle East caused feelings of undisguised elation to animate the spirit of the thirty-ninth chief executive, at least in 1978 and 1979.

The political climate in the Middle East remained as volatile as ever when Jimmy Carter entered the White House in 1977. Then, in a surprise move in October 1977, the United States and Soviet Union announced a joint initiative aimed at resolving the Arab-Israeli conflict. Suspecting that the superpowers were preparing the way for establishment of a Palestinian state in the West Bank and Gaza Strip, the response in Israel was decidedly negative. But a few weeks later, in November 1977, Pres. Anwar el-Sadat of Egypt, hitherto an implacable foe of Israel, astonished people across the entire world (and infuriated Arab leaders from Iraq to West Africa) when he accepted an invitation by the Israeli prime minister Menachem Begin to visit Israel and address the Israeli parliament. The citizenry of Israel greeted Sadat with unparalleled enthusiasm—and Egyptians, mired in poverty and weary of war, extended a similarly warm welcome when Begin a short time later visited Egypt.

For several months, it appeared that the Begin-Sadat initiative would come to nothing. Then, in September 1978, on the invitation of President Carter, the Egyptian president and Israeli prime minister traveled to the longtime retreat of U.S. chief executives at Camp David in Maryland. Carter determined to break the deadlock and bring Egyptian and Israeli leaders to some sort of agreement. Achievement of that goal did not come easily, and the atmosphere at Camp David fairly crackled during the 11 days of the negotiations. But at length, the persistence of the American president resulted in an agreement described by the negotiators as a framework for peace.

September 17, 1978: Presidents Sadat and Carter and Prime Minister Begin clasp hands after signing the Camp David Accords in the White House.

Popularly referred to as the Camp David accords, that framework included two documents: "A Framework for the Conclusion of a Peace Treaty Between Egypt and Israel" and "A Framework for Peace in the Middle East." By terms of the first of the two documents, Israel would return the Sinai to Egypt, but Egypt would deploy no military forces in that desert peninsula. The governments in Jerusalem and Cairo would sign a peace treaty within three months, and at some point establish normal diplomatic relations. The second document dealt with the West Bank and Gaza, as noted, Arab territories occupied by Israel since the Six-Day War of 1967. Its central article provided that negotiations between Egypt, Israel, Jordan, and representatives of the Palestinians would take place over a five-year period to determine the future of the West Bank and Gaza.

On Sunday evening, September 17, 1978, after 13 days at Camp David, Begin, Carter, and Sadat made their way to Washington, and in the East Room of the White House signed the documents (or accords). A few weeks later, Egyptian and Israeli negotiators assembled in Washington to draft a treaty of peace. The negotiations quickly bogged down, but the Washington government continued to press both the Egyptians and Israelis to reach a settlement. At length, American persistence was rewarded, and on March 26, 1979, a bright and sunny spring day in Washington, Begin and Sadat sat down at a table on the lawn of the White House and signed an Israeli-Egyptian treaty of peace. Looking on, President Carter beamed.

Unfortunately, the American president's attempts to secure support for the treaty by other Arab governments came to nothing. Non-Egyptian Arabs denounced Sadat for striking a separate peace settlement with Israel and thereby, in their view, abandoning the Palestinian people. Most Arab states broke diplomatic relations with Egypt, the Arab League suspended Egypt from membership and removed its headquarters from Cairo to Tunis, and the Conference of Islamic States likewise suspended Egypt. Arab denunciations of Egypt aside, Egyptian and Israeli negotiators now turned to the hard task of working out an agreement guaranteeing Palestinian autonomy in the West Bank and Gaza in accord with the second of the Camp David documents. During the months that followed, progress was almost nil. Meanwhile, the Israelis infuriated Arabs by continuing to establish settlements of Israeli nationals in the West Bank, and Prime Minister Begin, who insisted on referring to the West Bank by its biblical names of Judea and Samaria, declared that Israel would never dismantle Jewish settlements in the area. Begin likewise insisted that Israel would never consent to an independent Palestinian state on its borders.

By the summer of 1980, the "Camp David process" had broken down, and in the view of America's allies in Europe was beyond repair. Hence the West Europeans organized their own initiative to bring peace to the Middle East, central to which was a determination to include the PLO in negotiations. Continuing to rest his hopes for a Middle Eastern settlement on the Camp David process, President Carter deplored the West European initiative, and also shared the Israeli contention that the PLO, committed as it appeared to be to terrorism, must have no part in negotiations.

## SALT II

While campaigning for re-election in 1980, President Carter cited the Camp David accords as a premier achievement of his years in the White House. A second major achievement, he reckoned, was negotiation of the SALT II treaty with the Soviet Union. He may have been right. But at the time of the electoral campaign of 1980, SALT II remained unratified by the U.S. Senate, and relations between the United States and the Soviet Union had reached their lowest point since the Cuban missile crisis of 1962.

Relations between the superpowers had begun to cool in the aftermath of the fall of South Vietnam to the communists in 1975. To the annoyance of the United States, the Soviets stepped up efforts to expand their influence in the Middle East. They meddled in civil wars in Angola and the horn of Africa. And when American leaders warned that continuation of the process aimed at achieving détente depended on Soviet behavior regarding other matters, the Soviets reiterated their oft-stated rejection of the principle of "linkage" between détente and other aspects of world affairs. Meanwhile, the Kremlin undertook a frenetic buildup of conventional or (largely) non-nuclear armed forces. The Soviets had hitherto maintained a huge army that had limited operational capability beyond the frontiers of the Soviet empire. But in recent years, they had dramatically enlarged their naval forces, and now had a substantial fleet of surface vessels and submarines that was particularly active in the Indian Ocean. Through the Indian Ocean, of course, moved armadas of tankers transporting precious cargoes of oil to America, Japan, and Western Europe. The Soviets also had developed the capacity to airlift ground troops and their equipment thousands of miles from bases inside the Soviet homeland.

U.S. and Soviet negotiators nonetheless pressed on with the task of hammering out a second Strategic Arms Limitation Treaty: SALT II. The issues to be resolved were hopelessly technical. But after many months, a SALT II treaty emerged, and in June 1979 President Carter and General Secretary Brezhnev came together in the Hofburg Palace in Vienna, embraced, and signed the document. Put very simply, SALT II, to be effective through 1985, established limits on strategic weapons launchers, that is, bombing planes and missiles. It imposed limits on the modernization of ICBMs, and established rules for verifying the terms of the treaty. Following the ceremony of signature, the SALT II treaty passed to the U.S. Senate, which in accord with the Constitution would approve or reject the handiwork of President Carter and his administration.

The treaty met a barrage of criticism, most of it unleashed by political conservatives, who argued that the Soviet buildup of nuclear weapons over the past decade had already undermined strategic stability—had already upset the delicate balance of terror. The buildup having emphasized highly accurate ICBMs, the Soviets now were in a position (and, critics believed, would so remain under SALT II) to make a surprise attack with part of their ICBM force that would devastate intercontinental ballistic missile bases in the United States while sparing the country's centers of population. In the event of such an attack, critics of arms control continued, the Washington government would likely be paralyzed by the knowledge that a retaliatory attack by U.S. SLBMs and intercontinental bombing planes against the Soviet Union would result in an attack against American cities by ICBMs remaining in Soviet silos after the surprise first strike. The victory would thus belong to the Soviets. In truth, the critics recognized, the Soviets were not apt to launch a preemptory first strike against the ICBM bases of the United States. But that was beside the point. The point was that the threat of such an attack, as the reporter Pat Towell pointed out in *Congressional Quarterly* in June 1979, would cast a large political shadow: "Soviet decision-makers would be emboldened to take risks in pursuit of their global ambitions; U.S. policy-makers would be more hesitant to challenge them, and other nations would see the prudent course as accommodation to the Soviet Union."

As noted, critics of SALT II believed the treaty would allow what they insisted was the existing imbalance in nuclear weapons in favor of the Soviets to continue. It would permit the Soviets to retain 326 very large SS18 ICBMs, each of them capable of carrying 10 large and very accurate warheads. The SS18s alone, critics maintained, could destroy all of America's ICBMs in a surprise attack—leaving more than a thousand Soviet ICBMs remaining to deter the Washington government from ordering a retaliatory strike with SLBMs and manned bombing planes. Moreover, the Soviet fleet of Backfire bombers, capable of striking the United States if refueled en route or if dispatched on a one-way suicide mission, was exempted from SALT II's numerical ceilings. "Hard-liners" argued further that the Soviets were inveterate cheaters, hence were certain to violate the terms of the treaty, the procedures for verifying compliance with which, critics maintained, were hopelessly inadequate.

Senators who supported the treaty without reservation, most of them political liberals, argued that the alternative to SALT II was continuation of the scandalously expensive competition between the superpowers to achieve supremacy in nuclear weapons. It was a competition, they suspected, that if not terminated might one day result in the obliteration of humanity. Even if SALT II allowed the Soviets an edge in strategic weaponry—a point that supporters of the treaty were reluctant to concede—the United States would retain the capacity to survive a surprise nuclear attack by the Soviets and still wreak unacceptable destruction on the Soviet homeland, particularly when the country's fleet of two hundred MX missiles, its construction recently approved by President Carter, was deployed.

Then, in August 1979, U.S. intelligence agents disclosed the presence of a Soviet army brigade in Cuba. The result was a firestorm of controversy. What were the Soviets up to? Were they embarking on some new adventure in the Western Hemisphere? President Carter proclaimed that the brigade's presence in Cuba was unacceptable, then changed his mind, perhaps persuaded by the Soviet explanation that the brigade's mission was merely to advise and train the Cubans. Still, the affair weakened the chances that the Senate would approve the SALT II treaty.

The Carter administration, meanwhile, soldiered on in its effort to secure the Senate's consent to SALT II. To appease critics of the treaty, it agreed to modest increases in military spending to strengthen the country's conventional forces. It also pressed ahead with plans to deploy the MX missile in a manner designed to guarantee that a fair number of the MXs would survive a preemptive attack by the Soviets. The 200 missiles would be deployed in 4,600 blast-resistant and interconnected shelters in Nevada and Utah. Because they would be moved randomly from shelter to shelter on no fixed schedule, the Soviets would never know their precise location at any given time. Unfortunately, the estimated cost of such an elaborate deployment of the MXs was staggering: $33 billion (and largely because of its cost, the plan to so deploy the MXs was eventually given up).

But then, in November 1979, Iranian militants seized the U.S. embassy in Teheran and made 66 Americans their hostages. Manifestly delighted by America's discomfort, the Soviets expressed sympathy with the Iranians—and offered no help whatever in securing release of the captive Americans. The consequences for SALT II? The chances of early approval of the treaty by the

Senate further diminished. They became almost nonexistent seven weeks after seizure of the embassy in Teheran, in late December of 1979, when the Soviets dispatched upward of 100,000 troops, spearheaded by planes and tanks and supported by artillery and helicopters and other paraphernalia of modern conventional warfare, over their southern frontier into Afghanistan, a primitive country of rugged mountains and widely scattered villages, the homeland of 21 million people, most of them committed Muslims.

## AFGHANISTAN

From the perspective of the government in Washington, Afghanistan during the decades after World War II constituted a nonaligned buffer between the Soviet Union and areas of U.S. interest to the south and west of Afghanistan, notably Iran and Pakistan. Then, in the spring of 1978, radical leftists of the Afghan army overthrew the civilian government in Kabul, and a few days later the leader of a pro-Soviet faction of the radical leftists, Nur Mohammed Taraki, emerged as president and prime minister of Afghanistan. In December 1978, the new government signed a treaty of friendship with the Soviet Union. Meanwhile, tribal groups across Afghanistan, recently caught up anew in a spirit of Islamic fundamentalism and thus outraged by the antireligious impulses of the new Marxist government, undertook an armed resistance against the Taraki regime, and by the turn of 1979 Taraki's writ ran scarcely beyond the capital of Kabul. Next, in September 1979, President Taraki was mortally wounded in a confused shootout that had the appearance of a palace coup. With the blessing of the Kremlin, he was succeeded by Hafizullah Amin, who, notwithstanding the presence of a corps of Soviet advisers, proved no more able to curb the rebellion in the countryside than had his predecessor.

By early December of 1979, Soviet forces were deploying along the Afghan border, and a fortnight later elite Soviet paratroops crossed the border into Afghanistan. Then, on December 25, Soviet troops began to pour into the country. According to the Kremlin, they were marching in response to a request by President Amin who, according to the Soviets, had massive popular support. But within a few days, Amin was dead, murdered apparently by or with the connivance of his Soviet patrons, who thereupon returned Babrak Karmal, a former deputy prime minister, from exile and installed him as head of the government.

Most Afghans clearly despised Karmal's Soviet-sponsored regime. They manifested their sentiments when they treated the Soviet invaders with sullen contempt and subjected them to continuing harassment—to which the Soviets responded with bombs and bullets and shells. Poorly armed and forced to resort to guerrilla tactics in countering their country's tormentors, Afghan rebels refused to knuckle under to Soviet power. Massive defections from the regular Afghan army provided them with reinforcements.

The response of people across North America to the Soviet aggression in Afghanistan was one of outrage. Still, leaders in Washington perceived the aggression to be considerably more than outrageous. In their perception, it constituted a threat to "vital" interests of the United States; to wit, they feared that the invasion might be the initial move of a Soviet thrust in the direction of the oil-rich Persian Gulf. In his State of the Union address of January 23, 1980, accordingly, President Carter issued what came to be known as the Carter Doctrine: "Any attempt by any outside force to gain control of the Persian Gulf region will be regarded as an assault on the vital interests of the United States of America and such an assault will be repelled by any means necessary including military force." He thereupon asked the Senate to delay consideration of the SALT II treaty (although he announced that the United States would take no action contrary to the terms of the treaty so long as the Soviets did likewise). He imposed an embargo on grain shipments to the Soviet Union (a heavy blow to American farmers who in recent years had realized handsome returns from grain sales to the Soviets). He ordered a stop to shipments of electronic and engineering equipment to the USSR, and called for an international boycott of the Olympic games to be held in Moscow the following summer. To Carter's dismay, most other governments in the world, including those of America's NATO allies, took the view that the United States was overreacting to what the Soviets were doing in Afghanistan, hence rendered precious little support to the president's initiatives aimed at punishing Soviet aggression in South Asia—save for a boycott of the Moscow Olympiad by 50 nations.

The tepid response of most of the outer world to their aggression aside, the Soviets found no easy solution to the problem of coping with the Afghan rebels. And so the war dragged on—year after dreary year. By 1985, the combat had actually intensified, and both the Soviets, relying largely on elite commando and paratroop units, and the Afghan *mujahidin* (or guerrillas), provided with weapons, ammunition, and other supplies by the United States and probably China (by way of Pakistan), suffered perhaps the heaviest casualties of the six-year war.

The Soviets, meanwhile, accelerated the campaign begun at the time they undertook their invasion to "Sovietize" Afghanistan via internal espionage, police terror, propaganda, and assertion of control over schools and youth organizations. They took new steps to control the dissemination of information from Afghanistan to the outer world—threatened severe punishment to newspeople of the West who entered Afghanistan illegally. And the Kremlin warned Pres. Mohammad Zia ul-Haq of Pakistan that it viewed assistance to the Afghan rebels as an unfriendly act. It issued the latter warning in the belief (one that rested on fact) that America's CIA was maintaining rebel bases and operating guerrilla training camps in Pakistani territory.

Because of Soviet censorship, alas, there was minimal coverage of the war by the communications media, hence, contrary to what had happened during the U.S. military-naval involvement in Vietnam, people across the world seldom gave even passing thought to what was going on in Afghanistan. West Europeans and others who had routinely denounced the U.S. military-naval campaign in Vietnam seldom expressed outrage over the Soviet rape of the ancient Afghan nation. No trials of Soviet "war criminals" were staged in Stockholm. In the Soviet Union, needless to say, there were no demonstrations of protest against the Red Army's enterprise in Afghanistan—no public burnings of the Soviet flag or waving of banners of the Afghan rebels or pilloring of leaders in the Kremlin who had authored the Afghan invasion. Still, a report prepared by the UN Human Rights Commission and released in 1985 accused the Soviet Union of relying on terror generated by atrocities and genocide to subdue the Afghan rebels. Also in 1985, Amnesty International, a private organization concerned primarily with human rights violations across the world, compared global indifference to the massacre of Afghans by the Soviets to international indifference to the slaughter of European Jews by Germans during World War II.

## CRISIS IN IRAN

While responding to the Soviet invasion of Afghanistan, President Carter and his administration had to grapple with the aforementioned seizure in late 1979 of 66 Americans by revolutionary militants in Iran. Arguably much less important in terms of the strategic interests of the United States than the Soviet thrust into Afghanistan, the so-called hostage crisis in Iran held the emotions of millions of Americans in its grip for more than a year. Save for those of the hostages and their families, the emotions of no American felt the pain of that grip in greater measure than the occupant of the White House.

After his restoration to the Peacock Throne as a result of the enterprise of the CIA in 1953, Shah Mohammad Reza Pahlavi of Iran became a veritable autocrat, albeit one with at least a few ideals. He used his country's burgeoning oil revenues to build factories, hospitals, and schools, brought about land reform and erected low-rent housing, removed centuries-old restrictions on the activities and dress of women. He also remained steadfastly anticommunist and staunchly pro-American. Generously supported by the United States, he built up his military forces until Iran became the foremost military power in the area. American leaders were delighted. They viewed Iran as a bulwark against expansion of the influence and power of the Soviet empire in the Middle East.

Social revolutions, of course, beget dissatisfaction, and the shah's revolution in Iran was no exception. Most importantly, his ambitious programs failed to meet the expectations of most of Iran's people. Unemployment and underemployment and attendant poverty remained pervasive in the country. Then, in the middle 1970s, inflation began to rage ahead at an annual rate of 40 to 50 percent. Meanwhile, large landowners of former years whose lands had been expropriated in the interest of the shah's land reform program continued to seethe—and dream of retriving lost estates. Many fundamentalist Muslims in overwhelmingly Muslim Iran deplored the Westernization of Iranian society over the past two decades, that is, the movement away from traditional modes of behavior spelled out in the Koran. Such people believed that in their frenetic

November 6, 1979: Iranian militants shake their fists and display anti-American banners near the U.S. embassy in Teheran, seized by militants two days before.

quest for the comforts and pleasures of Euro-American society, Iranians were abandoning their heritage and Iran was losing its soul.

Dissatisfaction had still other roots. The shah lived much too lavishly for the tastes of many Iranians—appeared bent on keeping too much of the national largesse for himself and his family. In 1971, he squandered $100 million to stage an extravagant and pompous celebration commemorating the 2,500th anniversary of the Peacock Throne. Many Iranians thought such a display of opulence in what remained an essentially poor country outrageous, and their sense of outrage did not diminish when the outer world seemed singularly unimpressed by the shah's spectacular production. Equally serious, the shah declined to match social reform with political reform. Put simply, his people yearned to have greater input in government. But the shah, determined to play the part of the benevolent autocrat, clung to his royal prerogatives.

Dissatisfaction inevitably begot dissidence, the shah's response to which was at once misguided and deplorable. To counter dissent, the monarch relied increasingly on censorship and intimidation. He also gave free reign to his dreaded secret police, known by the acronym SAVAK, whose methods included torture and even murder. The people of the United States, of course, did not condone torture and murder, not to mention intimidation, to keep dissidents in line. But, Americans tended to reason, cruelty and violence were imbedded in the tradition of the Middle East. Besides, the shah appeared to be an unwavering friend of the United States (although it was the shah who in 1973 prodded the OPEC countries to dramatically increase the price of oil at the time of the Yom Kippur War).

Then, in the summer of 1978, the shah's position began to crumble when his police opened fire on religious dissenters in the Holy city of Quom, whereupon rioting spread across the country. What did the rioters want? Increasingly, they demanded the overthrow of the shah. By January 1979, the disorders in Iran were raging out of control. Clearly, the shah was finished, and in the latter part of the month the dispirited monarch flew to exile in Egypt. A short time later, he made his way to Morocco, then to the Bahamas, and after that to Mexico. He hoped that he might settle in the United States, but the government in Washington made it known that he was not welcome.

The shah's departure opened the way for the return to Iran, on February 1, 1979, of Ayatollah Ruhollah Khomeini, a 79-year-old Islamic cleric whom the shah had sent into exile in 1963 after Khomeini publicly denounced the monarch. Settling in France, the ayatollah in recent years had become a veritable symbol of defiance to the shah's rule. Thousands of screaming, hysterical Iranians greeted the grim-faced ayatollah when he arrived at the Teheran airport, and he immediately became the fountain of political authority in the turbulent country. In uncompromising language, he denounced the shah and all of his works. He assailed the United States as the instrument of Satan and the ravisher of Iran, reiterated his determination to rid Iran of the corruption and evil that he thought decadent and materialistic Americans and Europeans had brought to Iran, and announced his determination to return Iran to the purity of its Islamic heritage.

The return of the ayatollah notwithstanding, chaos continued to reign in Iran. Oil output—and with it oil revenues—fell by 80 percent; the general economy virtually collapsed. Only the revolutionary tribunals seemed to function efficiently, and between February and October 1979 they meted out death sentences to more than six hundred persons, most of them charged with crimes committed in service of the shah. Then, in the autumn of 1979, the exiled shah asked for permission to enter the United States for treatment of the lymphatic cancer that had afflicted him for several years and for removal of his diseased gall bladder. President Carter granted the request—an act of mercy to a perilously ill man, he later explained. Learning of the shah's arrival in New York, tens of thousands of Iranians, on November 1, 1979, marched to the U.S. embassy in Teheran. They shouted epithets, among them "Death to Carter" and "Death to Americans," and displayed banners reading "Give us the shah." On that same day, Khomeini contributed to the din by delivering a fiery anti-American speech.

Apparently goaded by the events of November 1, some four thousand youthful Iranian militants, on November 4, undertook their own march on the U.S. embassy. They reiterated demands that the former monarch be returned to Iran in order that the death sentence to which Khomeini's revolutionary tribunals had sentenced him in absentia could be executed. They also demanded the return to Iran of all of his fortune. Dispatched to the scene at the behest of the U.S. chargé d'affaires, Iranian security forces made no move to disperse the demonstrators. At length, several hundred of the youths, after forcing their way into the embassy compound, seized control of the embassy buildings and made hostages of the 66 diplomatic and military personnel inside. (A short time later, they released 13 of the hostages—blacks and women. Eight months after that, they released a hostage who was suffering from multiple sclerosis.) As for Khomeini, he gave the action of the youthful militants ("students," in his lexicon) his blessing, and warned that any military action by the United States against Iran would result in death for the hostages.

The people of the North American superpower, of course, were thunderstruck—and infuriated. They seethed when they viewed television news pictures of carefully orchestrated Iranian militants demonstrating about the embassy in Teheran, day after day, shouting anti-American slogans, desecrating the Stars and Stripes. They also seethed when thousands of youthful Iranians who had been allowed to enter the United States to study staged similar anti-American demonstrations in cities and on campuses in scattered parts of the country.

President Carter shared the outrage of his compatriots. But what was he to do? Well, he might dispatch bombing planes to blast Iran's oil fields and military installations. Many Americans thought he should do precisely that, despite the probability that such drastic action would result in the summary execution of the hostages. As for the president and his advisers, they gave careful thought to what they described as the military option. But they were restrained by the realization that a bombing strike would doubtless provoke an eruption of superheated anti-Americanism across the entire Muslim world, from Morocco to Indonesia. Such an eruption might compel Libya, Saudi Arabia, and other Muslim states to curtail shipments of oil supplies to the United States. The avoidance of any action that might provoke the Muslim or Islamic world became even more compelling in the aftermath of the Soviet invasion of Afghanistan at the end of December of 1979, eight weeks after seizure of the hostages in Teheran. As Carter's national security adviser Zbigniew Brzezinski later explained in his memoir *Power and Principle*, the administration in Washington felt compelled to do nothing in the matter of Iran that might split Islamic opposition to the Soviet aggression in Afghanistan.

Rejecting the bombing option, Carter did what he could. He froze Iranian assets in the United States, which meant that Iran would not be able to withdraw upward of $8 billion it had on deposit in American banks. He stopped the importation of Iranian oil in the United States, stopped the shipment to Iran of American goods (food and medical supplies excepted), dispatched a powerful naval force to the Arabian Sea. He prevailed on the UN to condemn the attack on the embassy in Teheran and demand immediate release of the hostages. Unfortunately, nothing worked, in no small measure, Americans believed, because of the refusal of other governments, including those most staunchly allied to that in Washington, to do anything more than protest the outrageous behavior of the Islamic revolutionaries in Iran.

The crisis, meanwhile, dragged on. When after a few weeks of treatment in New York the shah, appearing wan and depressed, was flown out of the United States—to Panama, because Mexican authorities refused to allow him to return to Mexico—the Iranians yielded not an inch. (The Panamanians had no more interest in providing a sanctuary for the shah than the Mexicans, and in March 1980 the dying former monarch gratefully accepted an invitation by President Sadat that he settle in Egypt.)

Diplomacy having yielded no hint of success, President Carter on April 11, 1980, sanctioned a daring attempt to rescue the hostages. Vigorously opposing such a maneuver was Secretary of State Cyrus Vance, who later recalled in his memoir *Hard Choices*, "In addition to risking the lives of the hostages, I believed military action could jeopardize our interests in the Persian Gulf and perhaps lead Iran to turn to the Soviets." Because of his opposition, Vance submitted his resignation, effective at the conclusion of the rescue operation, whatever its outcome.

Code-named Operation Blue Light, the rescue plan called for eight large RH-53 Sea Stallion helicopters to sortie from the carrier USS *Nimitz* in the Gulf of Oman and put down near Posht-e Bādām, a remote spot in the Iranian desert some 300 miles southeast of Teheran. At the same time, six 4-engine C-130 Hercules transports, flying less than 500 feet above the desert to avoid radar detection, would ferry an elite force of about 90 specially trained commandos from an airfield in Egypt to Posht-e Bādām. In the middle of the night, the helicopters would deliver the troops to a secret hideaway not far from Teheran. At dawn, the troops would make their way to the embassy compound, presumably in buses assembled by American agents inside Iran. After overwhelming the surprised Iranian guards, they would rescue the hostages. Whereupon the helicopters would appear at the embassy, take commandos and hostages aboard, and move out for Posht-e Bādām. At Posht-e Bādām, everybody, including helicopter crews, would board the C-130s. The helicopters would be destroyed, the C-130s would take off, and in a few hours everybody would arrive safely in Egypt.

It was a daring plan. Only it did not work out. Put in motion on April 24, 1980 (Washington time), the rescue operation turned into a fiasco. Two of the helicopters experienced mechanical difficulties in flight and were forced to return to the *Nimitz* before reaching Posht-e Bādām. A third broke down at the rendezvous site. Because of the helicopter problems, President Carter, on the advice of officers at the site, ordered the operation scrubbed. At that point, fiasco turned into tragedy. During the evacuation movement, a helicopter crashed into a parked C-130 that was loaded with ammunition. Both chopper and plane burst into flames. Five airmen and three marines perished in the resultant inferno. After blowing up the helicopters, the remaining Americans withdrew in C-130s, destination: Egypt. They left behind the charred remains of their fallen comrades, and a few days later Iranian authorities, as reported in *Time*, tore open the plastic bags that contained the corpses of the five American servicemen who had perished at Posht-e Bādām, poked them with knives, and held up body parts to be filmed by television crews.

President Carter shook off his own disappointment and frustration. He also rejected charges that by authorizing such a risky venture he had behaved with inexcusable irresponsibility. He now adopted a low profile in dealing with the crisis, an approach that some critics thought he should have assumed at the outset. According to his critics, Carter's frenetic efforts to secure release of the hostages had merely called world attention to the plight of the captive Americans and enhanced their propaganda value to the Iranian militants. Alas, even the low profile and reliance on quiet diplomacy seemed ineffectual. Nor did the death of the shah in July 1980 soften the stance of the Iranians. What was apt to happen? The popular wisdom was that the Iranians might accept some formula for releasing the hostages—after the American presidential election in November 1980.

## RETROSPECT

The inability of the Carter administration to secure release of the captive Americans in Teheran at once dismayed and depressed the people of the United States. Indeed, the frustrating and humiliating hostage crisis of 1979–1980 was merely the latest of a succession of happenings and developments in the years of the Ford and Carter presidencies that had prompted Americans, save perhaps during fleeting moments in 1976 when they were caught up in the excitement and pageantry of the bicentennial celebration, to feel dispirited about the state or condition of their republic: betrayal of the public trust by President Nixon and numerous of his associates; the abject failure of the long, costly, and trauma-filled effort by the United States to save South Vietnam, Cambodia, and Laos from the scourge of communism; the energy crisis; rampant inflation and escalating interest rates; the highest rate of unemployment in the national homeland in more than three decades; the inability of various of the country's "basic" manufacturing industries to meet foreign competition and the resultant decline of those industries; soaring deficits in the federal budget; a nagging suspicion that the Soviet Union had equaled and perhaps surpassed the United States in nuclear striking power; the low esteem in which the United States appeared to be held by allies and foes alike; angry controversies regarding abortions, drugs, and the civil rights of blacks, homosexuals, and women. To describe the collective mood of Americans in those years, media commentators intermittently invoked the term *malaise*, that is, a sense of ill-being or depression. It was a term that became fixed in the national consciousness in the summer of 1979 when Jimmy Carter, appearing grim-faced and rather forlorn, peered into television cameras and lamented the malaise that had settled over the superpowerful republic.

As for Presidents Ford and Carter, they coped as best they could with various of the phenomena that had produced the national sense of ill-being. But as even the most successful presidents in the American experience have learned, the power of the presidential office to meet problems confronting the republic is limited. There was little, for example, that either president might do to prevent the OPEC cartel from pushing up the price of oil. Even with respect to problems that fall within the capability of the presidential office to address, a president can be severely circumscribed by popular opinion, the petulance of Congress, and the competing interests of assorted constituencies. Indeed, in the absence of a consensus that includes a large segment of the general public, a majority of the members of Congress, and most of those competing constituencies, coherent and effective responses to the problems afflicting or confronting the United States are seldom forthcoming.

The problems that were most responsible for the national sense of malaise during the years of Ford and Carter, it seems fair to say, were those relating to the troubled economy. And, arguably, the problems that were at the heart of the country's economic troubles in those years were (1) the accelerating dependence of the United States on foreign oil, the price of which skyrocketed between 1973 and 1980, and (2) the diminishing or at best static productivity of important components of America's manufacturing industries. Soaring outlays for imported energy fueled inflation—and pushed up interest rates and complicated the task of balancing the federal budget. Declining productivity made it difficult for American manufacturers to compete, both in the domestic and world markets, with those of Japan, Germany, and various areas of the Third World. Particularly in the matter of energy, both Ford and Carter (as had Nixon before them) recommended multifaceted initiatives to make the United States less dependent on imported oil. And while Congress wrote some of their recommendations into law, no national consensus regarding energy emerged—and when in the early 1980s the OPEC cartel came unglued and the price of imported oil plummeted, Americans, seemingly accepting the assumption of a new president that somehow the energy problem had disappeared, continued their frenetic importation of petroleum.

The foregoing is not to say that the Ford and Carter presidencies were without achievement—far from it. To his enduring credit, Gerald Ford restored the popular faith in the essential integrity of the presidential office in the aftermath of the scandals of the Nixon administration. He continued the effort to improve America's relations with the Soviet Union and China, strove manfully to find solutions to the intractable problems of the Middle East. As for Carter, he made a noble effort to further the cause of human rights in the world, prevailed on Egypt and Israel to make peace, oversaw negotiation of honorable treaties intended to resolve long-standing differences with Panama, sanctioned the establishment of full-dress diplomatic relations between the United States and the People's Republic of China. And, not to be overlooked, the president from Georgia, a descendant of onetime Confederates, was uncompromising in his espousal of equal opportunity, equal justice, and equal dignity for all Americans.

The 846 professors of U.S. history who responded to the aforementioned presidential performance poll conducted in 1982 by Robert K. Murray and Tim H. Blessing ranked Gerald Ford twenty-fourth and Jimmy Carter twenty-fifth among the presidents—placed both men near the bottom of the "average" category (behind such undistinguished occupants of the White House as Martin Van Buren, Rutherford B. Hayes, and Chester A. Arthur). One wonders in 1989 whether historians of the years to come will be equally as negative in their assessments of the two chief executives who presided over the national destiny during the country's time of malaise.

# Chapter
# 11

# *A More Mellow Society*

*I*n the perspective of great numbers of citizens of the United States, particularly those who felt a deep and abiding commitment to traditional institutions and values and modes of behavior, the years from the middle 1960s through the early 1970s comprised a nightmarish interlude in the national experience, a time of seemingly incessant upset, tumult, and trauma. Many Americans, indeed, wondered whether the republic (to borrow the title of William L. O'Neill's provocative book about America's society during the 1960s) was coming apart. Rocking the consciousness of tradition-oriented citizens during the years from 1964 to 1973 were an array of happenings and developments: seemingly interminable outbursts of civil turbulence and violence, notably in urban ghettos and on college and university campuses; the enthusiastic response of legions of their compatriots, most of them under 30, to the superheated rhetoric of would-be revolutionaries who mocked traditional notions of fidelity to flag and country, proclaimed the decadence of America's political institutions and economic system, and appealed for establishment of a new political and social order; the discarding by other legions of Americans, often to the accompaniment of displays of defiance and celebration, of conventional mores and modes of behavior regarding the nuclear family, religion, extramarital sex, and the use of mind-expanding and intoxicating drugs.

But then, in the early 1970s, the era of rampant tumult and trauma appeared to pass, and a relative calm settled over the republic. Campuses became quiet, black ghettos took on the appearance of stilled volcanoes, purveyors of revolutionary rhetoric and proponents of the so-called counterculture found themselves with few auditors. What had happened? Perhaps the psychic impulses that during the years 1964 to 1973 had produced campus unrest, ghetto eruptions, and the response by uncounted citizens to revolutionary appeals and the lure of the counterculture simply ran out of steam (or energy), particularly when the country's disastrous war in Indochina receded into history and the national economy became troubled. To be sure, the makers and shakers of much of the turmoil and trauma of the years 1964–1973 had no intention of giving up what they perceived to have been the gains they had realized over the past decade, for example, in matters of sexual mores and the use of drugs, but most of them (militant feminists a notable exception perhaps) seemed prepared to reach an accommodation of sorts with traditional society. Many of them became "yuppies" (young, upwardly mobile professionals) who wore three-piece suits (at least male yuppies did), drove flashy sports cars, and pursued with undisguised relish the affluent lifestyle so admired by tradition-oriented citizens.

Thus, to invoke a term that had made its way into the national vocabulary by way of the drug culture during the 1960s, the national society became more *mellow*. Or perhaps, as the journalist Frederick Lewis Allen had written many years before in his memoir of the 1920s, the riotous party of the 1960s and early 1970s was over; the authors of the turmoil and trauma of preceding years decided that the time had come to sober up (more or less).

## FADS, CRAZES, AND OTHER PHENOMENA

As they had in all eras in the American experience, assorted fads and crazes animated life in the United States during the years of relative mellowness. Such a fad (or was it a craze?) was streaking, a phenomenon that amused most Americans (but outraged a few) during the spring of 1974. Streaking occurred when a male or female, usually a youthful one, dashed across a college campus, along an urban thoroughfare, or through a public building in the buff. Another fad of the middle 1970s was citizens' band radios (or CBs), usually installed in trucks and cars, which enabled truck drivers and other motorists to converse with one another, invoking an array of clever terms and phrases as they whizzed over the country's highways. Still another craze of the period was electronic video games featuring gaudy colors, flashing lights, and assorted gongs and shrieks that combined with ever-changing numbers to mesmerize a new generation of citizens in much the same manner as pinball machines had mesmerized previous ones.

It was during the years of relative mellowness that increasing numbers of Americans discovered what were imperfectly described as martial arts, that is, various forms of ritualistic and stylized unarmed combat between individuals that were vaguely akin to ancient combative systems of East Asia. And it was during those same years that Americans by the millions discovered disco, defined in *Webster's New World Dictionary* as (1) "a nightclub or other public place for dancing to recorded music" and (2) "a kind of popular dance music with elements of soul music, a strong Latin American beat, and simple and repetitious lyrics, usually accompanied by pulsating lights." Definitions aside, every city in America of any dimension during the middle and latter 1970s had its array of discos to which patrons, mostly youthful, flocked to listen to the disco sound and dance the bus stop, hustle, and rope and the roach trailing behind.

Americans, meanwhile, took to household pets as never before. The national pet population in 1974 included an estimated 100 million dogs and cats, 350 million fish, and 22 million birds. Large numbers of Americans owned snakes, many of them venomous, and ten thousand citizens owned big cats, including lions and leopards. Pet owners in the United States in the mid-1970s spent $2.5 billion annually on commercially prepared pet food, more than six times as much as Americans spent on baby food, more than enough, it was said, to feed one-third of the world's population that was undernourished.

During the years of relative mellowness, Americans flocked to an array of "theme parks" that dotted the national landscape—more than 70 million people per year to the 24 largest theme parks, a third of that total to Disneyland in Anaheim, California, and Walt Disney World in Orlando, Florida. The 1970s also witnessed what in some quarters was described as the "back-to-the-'50s" phenomenon, that is, an exaltation of the lifestyles of a decade that many social critics perceived to have been one of the most bland and banal in the annals of the republic. Criticism of the 1950s notwithstanding, enthusiasts of back-to-the-'50s twirled hula hoops, a sort of cultural symbol of the decade. Fashion shops, boutiques, and department stores featured clothing in styles that had been popular in the decade of Eisenhower (and also Joe McCarthy, the Korean War, and the crisis at Little Rock). The comparatively innocent rock 'n' roll rhythms of the 1950s experienced a revival, the motion pictures *American Graffiti* and *Grease* were box-office smashes, and hubcaps from Edsel automobiles became collectors' items.

The phenomena that captured the fancy of the people of the United States during the 1970s and 1980s were nothing if not varied. Caught up in what sometimes was termed "dietmania," great numbers of citizens bought diet books by the millions, lavished huge sums of money on appetite suppressants and diet foods, joined Weight Watchers, sweetened their coffee with artificial sweeteners, consumed enormous quantities of diet soft drinks. Closely related to dietmania was the so-called fitness boom that became a passion of millions of health-conscious Americans. Legions of citizens joined health clubs where they lifted weights and performed aerobic exercise routines, swam, and played racquetball. They jogged and rode bicycles (and as a result the sale of bicycles soared).

Several million Americans, meanwhile, fell in with "the consciousness movement," an amorphous and diffuse movement whose babas, gurus, lamas, and psychotherapists sought to combine the disciplines of Eastern religions (especially Buddhism) and the methods of Western psychotherapy. The goal of the babas and others was to raise the level of awareness (or consciousness) of their disciples by guiding them into intimate contact with themselves, with nature, and (most importantly) with the fundamental forces of the cosmos.

Other millions of Americans sought release by gambling, assuredly not a new phenomenon in the United States, but one that experienced a veritable explosion in the 1970s and 1980s (by one estimate, grew by 57 percent between 1983 and 1988), in no small measure, many people thought, because of the enormous interest in televised sports, particularly professional football. In fact, casino gambling (which handled bets totalling $126 billion in 1988, well over half of the money bet legally in the United States during the latter year) was both the largest and fastest-growing component of the country's burgeoning gambling industry. How much money were Americans wagering, legally and illegally (in card rooms and on bingo, as well as at casinos and on horse and dog races and other sporting events, not to mention on slot machines and lotteries), by the latter 1980s? Nobody could say for sure. But the figure probably topped $225 billion. Of the dollars turned over illegally, half were handled by organized criminals—the mob.

Because comparatively few of the awesome returns deriving from gambling were making their way into state treasuries, state after state modified strictures against gambling during the years of relative mellowness. Most dramatically, the voters of New Jersey in 1976 approved a resolution to legalize casino gambling in Atlantic City. And, inevitably perhaps, state after state organized lotteries. Studies disclosing that lotteries yielded less revenue than would result if lottery-sponsoring states raised state income taxes one-quarter of 1 percent could not easily overcome news pictures of people of all colors, creeds, and socioeconomic classes standing in long lines all across the state of New York in August 1985 to buy tickets for a $41-million jackpot, or of reports of people cascading into Pennsylvania from other states in April 1989 to buy tickets for a jackpot totaling $115.5 million. (In 1964, New Hampshire was the only state in the republic that operated a lottery. By 1990, 32 states, as well as the District of Columbia, would be in the lottery business.) As for buyers of lottery tickets, most appeared to be undaunted by the fact that the odds against winning a large jackpot were mind-boggling: in the popular "pick-six" games (in which the bettor chooses and arranges six numbers), 1 in 12.9 million!

In those same years, Americans discovered the microwave oven and the "TV dinner." Still, they flocked to restaurants, delicatessens, and fast-food outlets in record numbers. Accounting for the swelling of the eating-out phenomenon were a variety of factors, among them the affluence of much of the citizenry and the increasing number of gainfully employed wives who often felt little inclination to prepare meals after expending long hours in the workplace. Whatever the explanation, the U.S. Department of Agriculture estimated in 1983 that 41 cents of every dollar spent on food by Americans ended up in the cash registers of restaurants (compared with 33 cents in 1970). A source of satisfaction to restaurateurs and the makers of ketchup and mustard, that statistic was bad news for the country's $150-billion supermarket industry.

## BOOZE, DRUGS, EROTOMANIA

Millions of Americans gave up cigarette smoking during the years of relative mellowness, or declined to take up the cigarette habit. In 1970, 36.7 percent of the national population smoked cigarettes, in 1985, 29.8. But in those same years the people of the United States increased their consumption of alcoholic beverages, from 22.4 gallons per capita in 1970 to 29.1 gallons in 1984. Why were Americans drinking more? In part perhaps because of what was widely perceived to be the increasing secularization of American society, that is, religious restraints that in former times had dissuaded many Protestant Americans from partaking of strong drink were becoming increasingly ineffectual. A more likely explanation was the saturation of the airwaves with television commercials, particularly during telecasts of sporting events, extolling the various pleasures to be derived from drinking beer.

During the 1980s, many citizens became increasingly concerned about the extent and consequences of alcohol use in the United States. Such citizens felt dismay when confronted with figures indicating that 92 percent of the country's college and university students partook of alcohol during the year 1985. Other statistics disclosed that teenage alcoholism had become a serious problem, that tens of thousands of high school students were alcoholics. Meanwhile, the National Highway Traffic Safety Administration reported that of the approximately 43,000 Americans who lost their lives in traffic accidents in 1985, more than half died in accidents in which at least one driver had been drinking. Still other statistics indicated that more than 12 million Americans (about 10 percent of those who drank) were "problem drinkers," that is, abusers of alcohol, an appalling circumstance in the view of millions of citizens.

A more menacing problem in the view of most Americans during the 1970s and 1980s was to be found in what appeared to be the exploding use of mind-affecting drugs other than alcohol. In the electoral campaign of 1988, indeed, assorted orators proclaimed drugs to be the most serious crisis facing the United States.

In the early 1970s, most "straight" Americans began to take a more tolerant view of marijuana, the drug that had been a veritable symbol of the youth revolt of the 1960s, and by 1974 the federal government and 44 of the states had made the possession of small amounts of marijuana a misdemeanor rather than a felony. As for the use of marijuana, it remained extensive, and a survey disclosed that in 1985 approximately 42 percent of the country's college and university students had used "pot," or "grass." Generating far more concern than marijuana in the early 1970s was a surge in heroin addiction in the United States. From an estimated sixty thousand in the mid-1960s, the number of American heroin addicts had enlarged to perhaps a half million by the early 1970s. From where did the heroin shot into the veins of American addicts come? At the start of the 1970s, most of it came from Turkey by way of secret laboratories in the south of France and on the French island of Corsica. Other sources were Afghanistan, Pakistan, and Thailand. By the latter 1970s, much of the heroin being injected by junkies in New York and elsewhere in the United States was being produced in Mexico, and at that time, according to one report, heroin accounted for 6 percent of Mexico's gross national product.

By the early 1980s, America's communications media were devoting scant attention to heroin addiction and trafficking. Rather, they had become preoccupied with the exploding use of and traffic in cocaine, a white powder extracted from the dried leaves of coca plants that are indigenous to Bolivia, Colombia, Ecuador, and Peru in South America, and until the middle 1980s was usually taken intravenously or sniffed. Cocaine was refined in clandestine laboratories in Argentina, Bolivia, Brazil, Colombia, Ecuador, Mexico, Nicaragua, Peru, and Venezuela, then smuggled into the United States by an array of routes and methods. Providing fresh impetus to what was widely described as the cocaine epidemic was the introduction in the mid-1980s of crack, a solid form of cocaine that the user smokes. Purified, concentrated, and highly addictive, crack was relatively inexpensive (cost as little as $10 a dose), hence found a ready market in low-income areas of such cities as Los Angeles and Miami, New York and Washington. But cocaine use was not restricted to citizens of low income. It was estimated in 1986 that upward of 24 million Americans of all socioeconomic classes had experimented with cocaine, and that 30 percent of all college and university students, ignoring appeals by leaders of government, famous athletes, and other celebrities that they "say no to drugs," had used cocaine by their senior year.

Meanwhile, there was no decline in the United States of what some observers defined as erotomania, that is, a preoccupation or even obsession with sexual gratification. The evidence of erotomania abounded. Millions of Americans purchased and presumably pored over how-to sex manuals—studied various positions for intercourse, and sought to learn the precise location of the body's "erogenous zones." Women and men attended masturbation workshops. Dr. Ruth Westheimer, a German-born orphan of the Holocaust who in the 1980s presided over radio and television programs devoted to sex therapy and spoke matter-of-factly about orgasms and premature ejaculations, became a sort of sex guru to legions of Americans. Shere Hite's survey of the sexual experiences of three thousand women entitled *The Hite Report* (1976) was a bestseller.

The manifestations of erotomania during the 1970s and 1980s were nothing if not pervasive. Sex shops and adult bookstores featuring peep shows, pornographic materials, and sex-gratification implements did a flourishing business, as did massage parlors, where "masseurs" massaged and also masturbated customers. Millions of men relished the monthly issues of *Hustler*, *Penthouse*, *Playboy*, and *Screw*, slickly produced "girlie" magazines. Beginning in 1973, moviegoers flocked to theaters to view the explicitly erotic film *Last Tango in Paris*, starring Marlon Brando. In that same year, *Deep Throat*, celebrated by aficionados of smut for its showing of eleven separate acts of oral sex, became the most profitable film in the annals of the porno-film industry. Other aficionados ogled such films as *Children Love*, in which preadolescent boys and girls engaged in sexual intercourse, and *Young Lolitas or Youthful Lust*, in which girls between the ages of 6 and 11 were shown having oral sex with both male and female adults. Still others bought tickets to experience films extolling sadomasochism (or S-M), that is, sexual pleasure derived from dominating and inflicting pain on a partner—or from being dominated and made to suffer pain. With the advent of the videocassette recorder in the 1980s, uncounted Americans regularly satisfied erotic impulses by viewing pornographic films in the privacy of their own households.

Erotomania, particularly its more sleazy manifestations, outraged great numbers of citizens, and the upshot in the latter 1970s was a spirited attack on the sleaze trade by angry citizens from New York to California. Such citizens picketed X-rated movie houses and massage parlors, and sometimes harassed their customers. They pressed city governments to adopt zoning ordinances intended to disperse the establishments trading in sleaze. The effect of the nationwide attack on the porno trade? It may have prompted a few or even many purveyors of sleaze to give up the dissemination of pornography of the S-M and child genres. Otherwise, its consequences appeared minimal.

## MOVIES, TV, SPORTS

As in former decades, great numbers of Americans during the 1970s and 1980s savored motion pictures other than those of the pornographic genre—in theaters and, via television, in the comfort of their own homes. Film enthusiasts certainly had an impressive array of films of every variety to savor.

Early in the 1970s, moviegoers made *The Godfather*, a film derived from Mario Puzo's novel about a Mafia family that starred Marlon Brando, one of the greatest box-office successes in the history of motion pictures. Films whose principal players were black found large audiences, among them *Super Fly*, a comedy about a cocaine pusher in Harlem that stirred a storm of protest but was a box-office smash. Film patrons who found fascination in the occult flocked to *The Exorcist* and *The Omen*. Nostalgia enthusiasts delighted in *Superman* (*I* and *II*), films in which Superman (Christopher Reeve) performed precisely as he had in comic books since the mid-1930s, and in *Raiders of the Lost Ark*, a melodrama that recalled the Saturday afternoon serials of a bygone era.

Several films that attracted huge audiences chronicled catastrophic disasters, among them *The Towering Inferno* and *The Poseiden Adventure*. Woody Allen directed a succession of comedies that secured his reputation as the outstanding film comedian of the contemporary era. The fantasy of a killer shark that terrorizes a town in New England, *Jaws* was a box-office sensation in the mid-1970s. Meryl Streep emerged as perhaps the premier American actress of the period as a result of her performances in such films as *Kramer vs. Kramer* and *Out of Africa*. Bringing together Henry Fonda and Katharine Hepburn for the first time in their long careers, *On Golden Pond* was a poignant film that considered the problem of aging and tensions between the young and the elderly. John Wayne died in 1979, but even before his passing a new superhero had captivated film audiences in the United States and indeed across the world: Sylvester Stallone, who like Wayne exuded raw courage (grit?) and resourcefulness. In the four incarnations of *Rocky*, Stallone portrayed an untutored and unyielding prize-fighter; in two incarnations of *Rambo* he was a veritable one-man army who in an interminable orgy of gunfire and explosions visits death and destruction on enemies of the United States.

Still, the 1970s and 1980s are apt to be best remembered as the time when science-fiction films reached full flower. Renowned for visual and sound effects (called special effects) that boggled the senses, the sci-fi flicks had enormous appeal. Among the best films of the sci-fi genre were Steven Spielberg's *Close Encounters of the Third Kind*, about unidentified flying objects (UFOs) landing on earth, and Spielberg's *E.T.—The Extra-Terrestrial*, a heartwarming story about a creature from outer space who is stranded on earth and befriended by earth children. But the premier sci-fi film of the period was George Lucas's *Star Wars*, a fairy tale about the rebellion against the evil Galactic Empire that has banished freedom from the galaxy. According to a report that appeared in *Time* in 1977, *Star Wars* was "a riveting tale of suspense and adventure, ornamented with some of the most ingenious special effects ever contrived for film." The report continued, "It has no message, no sex and only the merest dollop of bloodshed here and there. It's aimed at kids—the kid in everybody."

Whatever the pleasures to be derived from viewing motion pictures, Americans expended far more time during the 1970s and 1980s lounging in front of television sets. And it was in the years of relative mellowness that communications satellites, soaring in stationary orbit high above the national landscape, became the principal instruments of transmission for the country's television networks. Although scarcely aware of the change to satellite transmission, ordinary television viewers were certainly conscious of the arrival in their communities of cable television (CATV) companies. CATV, frankly, revolutionized television in the United States. Viewers had hitherto been more or less limited to whatever programs ABC, CBS, and NBC, and perhaps a local independent station cared to offer. But CATV carried network and non-network programs from a variety of sources, and by the 1980s provided the viewer with the offerings of 30 channels and more. The TV revolution, to be sure, transcended CATV. Of special moment was the advent of the videocassette recorder (VCR) introduced in the middle 1970s, an electronic marvel that further widened the viewing options of the TV watcher. Sluggish for several years, sales of VCRs exploded in the 1980s.

When Americans turn their thoughts to television, of course, they tend to think of programming—more often than not, programming by the big-three commercial networks. In truth, the types and quality of network programs remained essentially unchanged from the previous decade or so. Still, there were a few program innovations in network television during the 1970s and 1980s, the most notable of which was the miniseries. Essentially a movie that was much too long for presentation in a single evening, the miniseries was broadcast over a succession of evenings. The most widely acclaimed of the miniseries was "Roots," the saga of a black American family from its roots in Africa through the years of slavery to the modern era. An estimated 80 million people, the largest audience ever to experience a single TV event to that time, viewed all or part of the concluding episode. Other miniseries of note included "Holocaust," a gripping drama based on the destruction of European Jews during World War II, and "Shōgun," a drama set in feudal Japan that starred Richard Chamberlain.

Who was the premier TV performer during the years of relative mellowness? Arguably, it was Bill Cosby, the main attraction and principal architect of "The Cosby Show," the top-rated television program for three consecutive seasons in the middle 1980s. According to a report that appeared in *Time* in 1987, no other television star since the days of Lucille Ball and Milton Berle in the 1950s had so dominated the medium. That assertion was hard to confute. An estimated 63 million viewers watched "The Cosby Show" each Thursday evening during the viewing season of 1986–1987, an audience surpassed in the annals of television only by "Bonanza" in 1964–1965.

In no small measure because so many sporting events were televised, spectator sports stirred the enthusiasm of ever-enlarging numbers of Americans during the 1970s and 1980s. Intercollegiate football remained a premier attraction, although, to the consternation of football enthusiasts, all proposals to organize a tournament by which the outstanding teams would actually compete on the field for the right to be proclaimed the national champion came to naught. Intercollegiate basketball became increasingly popular, and unlike football had a tournament to determine the national champion. Indeed, the NCAA (National Collegiate Athletic Association) basketball tournament that took place each March became a crown jewel of spectator sports in the United States. An odor of scandal that came to pervade intercollegiate sports during the 1970s and 1980s—the routine admission to colleges and universities of student-athletes who had almost no chance of succeeding academically, under-the-table payments to "amateur" student-athletes, the use of drugs by student-athletes—did little to quell popular enthusiasm for intercollegiate sports.

Disclosures that many professional athletes were users and even traffickers in drugs, particularly cocaine, tarnished the popular image of professional sports. And some sports enthusiasts took a critical view of the skyrocketing salaries commanded by professional athletes in the 1970s and 1980s. Salaries skyrocketed in part because associations or unions of athletes succeeded in compelling owners of sports franchises to grant performers larger shares of revenues, swollen in recent years by television, in part because of the leverage in salary negotiations accorded to players when the courts eliminated the hoary "reserve clause" in the contract of the professional athlete involved in a team sport—a clause that bound the athlete to the franchise with which he originally signed until the franchise traded or sold his contract to another franchise or released him.

Still, professional sports of all types—automobile racing, baseball, basketball, boxing, football, golf, hockey, tennis, thoroughbred racing—generated popular enthusiasm on an unprecedented scale (thanks in no small measure to television). Thoroughbred racing produced, arguably, the greatest racehorse in history, Secretariat, who won the Belmont Stakes in 1973 by an incredible 31 lengths. And baseball produced two genuinely historic moments: in 1974, when Henry Aaron of the Atlanta Braves broke the most hallowed record in baseball, to wit, the immortal Babe Ruth's career record of 714 home runs, and in 1985 when Pete Rose of the Cincinnati Reds overcame a record that most baseball fans had thought inviolable, namely, Ty Cobb's career record of 4,191 base hits.

Whatever the charms of intercollegiate and professional sports, no small number of Americans believed the ultimate sporting events transpired every four years: the Olympic Games. At the Winter Olympiad of 1972 at Sapporo, Japan, Barbara Ann Cochran of the United States won a gold medal in women's alpine skiing; Dianne Holum and Anne Henning won gold medals in speed skating. At the Summer Olympiad in Munich, the swimmer Mark Spitz won an incredible seven gold medals—although Soviet athletes won many more gold medals than Americans. American athletes, one of them the youthful speed skater Dorothy Hamill, won three gold medals during the Winter Olympiad at Innsbruck in Austria in 1976. At the Summer Olympiad in Montreal in 1976, Ray Leonard, Leon Spinks, and Michael Spinks won gold medals in boxing, Bruce Jenner a gold in the decathlon. At the Winter Olympiad of 1980, at Lake Placid, New York, the speed skater Eric Heiden claimed five gold medals; "the Boys of Winter," the youthful and spirited U.S. hockey team, after upsetting the vaunted Soviet team in the semifinal match, claimed one. In retaliation for the Soviet invasion of Afghanistan, as previously mentioned, the United States did not compete in the Summer Olympiad in Moscow in 1980. At the Winter Olympiad of 1984, at Sarajevo in Yugoslavia, Bill Johnson became the first American male to win a gold medal in alpine skiing. At the Summer Olympiad of 1984 in Los Angeles, athletes of the Soviet Union and most of the satellite and client states of the Soviet Union, in retaliation for the American boycott of the summer games in Moscow in 1980, were absent. As a result, athletes representing the United States won an unprecedented 83 gold medals. Among the premier performers representing the United States were Carl Lewis, who won gold medals in the 100-meter and 200-meter dashes, the long jump, and the 400-meter relay; Joan Benoit, winner of the first ever Olympic women's marathon; sixteen-year-old Mary Lou Retton, the

April 8, 1974: Forty-year-old Hank Aaron of the Atlanta Braves breaks the record of the legendary Babe Ruth for career home runs by smashing his 715th "round-tripper."

winner of 5 medals in gymnastics; and the men's basketball team, coached by Bob Knight of Indiana (arguably the finest amateur basketball team ever to take to the hardwood). Figure skater Brian Boitano won a gold medal in what for Americans was an almost disastrous Winter Olympiad in Calgary in Canada in 1988, but performers representing the United States won 36 gold medals at the Summer Olympiad in Seoul in 1988. Three of those belonged to Florence Griffith Joyner, the incomparable "Flo-Jo," arguably the premier woman sprinter in the history of sport.

## NEWSPAPERS, MAGAZINES, BOOKS

As had been the case for several generations, millions of Americans during the 1970s and 1980s at least scanned a newspaper nearly every day. The paper enjoying the largest daily circulation by the mid-1980s was the *Wall Street*

*Journal* (circulation approximately 2 million), followed by the *The New York Daily News* (circulation 1.4 million). Ranking third in circulation (1.1 million) was *USA Today*, a national daily launched in 1982. Still, financial problems plagued the newspaper publishing industry through the period, and the names of an array of famous newspapers passed into history, among them the *Philadelphia Bulletin*, *Minneapolis Star*, and *St. Louis Globe-Democrat*.

Although newspaper publishing seemed beset by problems, magazine publishing flourished. Among the more successful magazines during the period were those aimed at women readers: *Cosmopolitan*, *Good Housekeeping*, *Family Circle*, *Ladies' Home Journal*, *McCall's*, *Ms.*, *Woman's Day*. The three weekly newsmagazines, *Newsweek*, *Time*, and *U.S. News & World Report*, continued to be devoured by millions of Americans. Citizens who wanted to keep abreast of goings-on in the world of business pored over the pages of *Business Week*. Millions of television enthusiasts subscribed to *TV Guide* and *TV-Cable Week*. Emulating *Saturday Evening Post*, the weekly photojournalism magazines of former times, *Life* and *Look*, reappeared as monthlies. *Life* survived; *Look* did not. The male-oriented sex magazines *Hustler*, *Penthouse*, and *Playboy* were savored each month by millions of readers (or viewers). Published weekly, *Sports Illustrated* secured its ranking as the country's leading sports magazine. *Car and Driver* and *Motor Trend* continued to appeal to automotive enthusiasts, *Trains* to devotees of the high iron. Readers of a more intellectual bent read *Atlantic Monthly*, *Commentary*, *Commonweal*, *Harper's*, *New Republic*, *The New Yorker*, *Saturday Review*, and a splendid new magazine that appeared in the period, *The Wilson Quarterly*.

The number of magazine titles that competed for the attention of Americans in an era in which, it was widely assumed, the citizenry was preoccupied with television almost boggled the mind. An array of new scholarly journals appeared, until, by the 1980s, their number ran into the thousands. But the magazines that registered the most impressive successes during the 1970s and 1980s were of the special-interest genre, for example, *American Photographer*, *Gentlemen's Quarterly*, *Money*, *National Geographic*, *Skateboard World*, and assorted magazines focusing on airplanes, antiques, art, automobile racing, baby care, bicycling, camping, cooking, computers, crafts, dressmaking, fashions, finance, fishing, guns, hobbies, hunting, model building, physical fitness, sailing. The special-interest magazines that sparked the most interest were, it seemed, science magazines: *Discovery*, *Omni*, *Psychology Today*, *Scientific American*, *Smithsonian*.

The distractions of television notwithstanding, Americans spent billions of dollars on books each year during the 1970s and 1980s: $9.7 billion in 1982 (to buy 1.1 billion softbound and 566 million hardbound books). In addition to Bibles, dictionaries, and school textbooks, they bought books on astrology, auto repair, birds, computer programming, do-it-yourself household repair, gardening, investment guidance, religion, physical fitness, psychology, solutions to the Rubik's Cube puzzle, sexual performance, sports and games, travel. They bought mysteries and thrillers, romances and Westerns, most of them in paperback, by the millions. They made bestsellers of Lee Iacocca's *Iacocca* and Chuck Yeager's *Yeager*.

A fair number of Americans tackled the works of Aleksandr I. Solzhenitsyn: *August 1914* (1972) and *The Gulag Archipelago, 1918–1956* (3 volumes, 1974–1979). Aficionados of fiction read the works of Saul Bellow, John Cheever, E. L. Doctorow, John Gardner, Joseph Heller, John Irving, Norman Mailer, Bernard Malamud, Philip Roth, John Updike, Gore Vidal, and Kurt Vonnegut, Jr., all of whom produced novels that won critical acclaim. But not one author of the period appeared apt to be viewed by succeeding generations as the equal of such literary giants of former times as Faulkner, Fitzgerald, and Hemingway. The best novelist of the period may have been Bellow, and his best novel may have been *Humboldt's Gift* (1975), an exuberant piece that dealt with the problems bedeviling the author in America.

By no means were all novels of merit that were published in the United States during the 1970s and 1980s written by men. Among the women novelists who achieved critical acclaim were Ann Beattie (*Chilly Scenes of Winter* and *Love Always: A Novel*), Joan Didion (*Democracy: A Novel* and *Play It as It Lays: A Novel*), Annie Dillard (*Tickets for a Prayer Wheel* and *Pilgrim at Tinker Creek*), Toni Morrison (*The Bluest Eye: A Novel* and *Song of Solomon*), and Anne Tyler, (*Celestial Navigation* and *The Accidental Tourist*). Meanwhile, Joyce Carol Oates, one of the country's most prolific writers, continued to turn out quality short stories and poems, as well as novels—also commentaries on literature and the craft of writing. Clearly captivated by the feminist movement, several women authors composed sharp, witty works in which women were presented as victims of men, of cultural conditioning, and of their own neuroses. Works of the foregoing genre included Cynthia Buchanan's *Maiden* and Alix Kate Shulman's *Memoirs of an Ex-Prom Queen*, both published in 1972. Generating much comment (and eventually the basis of a motion picture) was Alice Walker's *The Color Purple* (1982), a powerful and exquisitely written work treating violence and rape within a black family in the rural South during the early years of the twentieth century, and the emergence of strength through friendship.

Writers of fiction, of course, comprised only a fraction of the country's literati. Those men and women of letters who concentrated on nonfiction turned out an impressive array of provocative books in the 1970s and 1980s.

The Watergate scandal resulted in a spate of books, the most widely acclaimed of which was *All the President's Men* (1974), by Carl Bernstein and Robert Woodward. Studs Terkel compiled the oral recollections of Americans in *Working People* (1974) and *The Good War* (1984). Recalling the experience of the United States during World War II, the latter volume took on a special poignancy in light of the country's recent nightmare in Vietnam. An array of books focused on aspects of the Vietnam experience, the most comprehensive of which was Stanley Karnow's *Vietnam: A History* (1983). David Halberstam analyzed the influence of television and news media magnates in *The Powers That Be* (1979), Daniel Bell defended humane liberalism and traditional capitalism in *The Cultural Contradictions of Capitalism* (1976), and Tom Wolfe analyzed American astronauts in *The Right Stuff* (1979).

Arthur M. Schlesinger, Jr., explored the expansion of presidential power in *The Imperial Presidency* (1973); Dumas Malone completed his monumental

multivolume biography of Thomas Jefferson. Robert Fogel and Stanley Enger-
man stirred the historical profession when they argued in *Time on the Cross:
The Economics of American Negro Slavery* (1974) that slavery provided a more
efficient labor system than historians hitherto had suspected. In *Stilwell and
the American Experience in China* (1970), Barbara Tuchman brought fresh insight to a question that long had tormented Americans, to wit, the policy of
the Washington government regarding China before the Maoist victory in the
historic Middle Kingdom. Once and for all, it would seem, Allen Weinstein
established the guilt of Alger Hiss in *Perjury: The Hiss-Chambers Case* (1978).
Archibald Cox surmised that the judiciary power was approaching the limits
of its utility for strategic innovation in *The Role of the Supreme Court in
American Government* (1976). John Kenneth Galbraith argued that poverty
was self-perpetuating in *The Nature of Mass Poverty* (1979), hence the only
realistic choice for Americans was an "accommodation to the culture of poverty." In *The Second Stage* (1981), Betty Friedan intimated that a new "feminine mystique" had imposed a new set of constraints that were compelling
many women to deny themselves the satisfactions to be derived from homemaking and rearing children. Jonathan Schell considered the perils of nuclear
war in *The Fate of the Earth* (1982), Elie Wiesel explored the condition and
circumstances of contemporary Jews in *A Jew Today* (1978), Christopher Lasch
commented on what he perceived to be the trivialization of emotions, the extensive employment of the confessional mode in contemporary literature, and
the devaluation of the national past in *The Culture of Narcissism* (1979). In
*Heroes of Their Own Lives: The Politics and History of Family Violence: Bos-
ton, 1880–1960* (1988), Linda Gordon explored what one might describe as a
dirty little secret of family life in America. Alas, the phenomenon of family
violence was far from "little"; it was, in fact, pervasive.

## ARCHITECTURE, ART, THEATER, MUSIC

A fair number of Americans during the 1970s and 1980s were interested in the
enterprise of architects, and of the structures that achieved completion during
those years the one that drew the most comment was the John F. Kennedy
Center for the Performing Arts, built along the Potomac in Washington. One
critic described the Kennedy Center, opened in 1971, as "a cross between a
concrete candy box and a marble sarcophagus in which the art of architecture
is buried," but a few critics praised its "magnificence" and "timeliness." Other
buildings that drew attention were the Hyatt Regency Hotel in San Francisco,
the Sears Tower in Chicago (which displaced the twin-towered World Trade
Center in New York as the tallest building in the world), the Kimball Art Museum in Fort Worth, and the Trump Tower in New York. The most renowned
of America's architects during the period was, arguably, the personable Chinese-American I. M. Pei, who designed the East Building of the National Gallery of Art in Washington and the John F. Kennedy Library in Boston. (Pei told
an interviewer in the 1980s that his crowning architectural achievement had

been to persuade the Communist leaders in Beijing *not* to commission the construction of a high-rise building in the vicinity of the legendary Forbidden City.)

As for trends in architectural design, the international style (or modernism), marked in the words of one commentator by buildings that had the appearance of squared-off boxes, prevailed into the 1980s, particularly in the design of commercial buildings, hospitals, housing projects, libraries, and administrative, classroom, and residential buildings on college and university campuses. But by the mid-1980s, the more decorative postmodern style was gaining adherents. Wrote Charles K. Hoyt of *Architectural Record* in 1984, "Corporations today are no longer satisfied with the often boxy, ungainly and forbidding buildings of yesterday and are seeking a more memorable urban presence."

Although nearly every metropolitan center in the United States during the 1970s and 1980s had its art museum (or museums), the work executed by the country's painters, it seems fair to say, imprinted the consciousness of Americans at large in lesser measure than did that executed by architects. To invoke the language of the time, the work of architects had higher visibility—indeed could scarcely be avoided. Still, painters labored on. At least during the early 1970s, they labored in what one commentator described as an atmosphere of relaxed eclecticism, that is, one in which they felt free to paint in accord with any of several styles in the knowledge that they had a fair opportunity to achieve critical recognition and commercial success. Among those styles was the "new realism" that had generated wide interest during the 1960s. Scorned in some quarters as essentially illustrative (or "photographic"), paintings by new realists were more apt to find a mark with people who were artistically unsophisticated than were avant-garde pieces created by, say, the "lyrical abstractionists." As for the sculpture executed during the 1970s and 1980s, it was predominantly abstract. Some of the pieces, for example, Gordon Allen's exquisite "Windy Day," could scarcely fail to appeal to the sense of beauty of any viewer. But many other pieces, particularly those abstract creations, many of them commissioned by the federal government that were to be found outdoors in most of the country's large cities, appeared to many observers, artistically sophisticated and unsophisticated alike, to be plain, junk.

It seems probable that the number of Americans who were capable of conversing intelligently about the theater exceeded the number who could converse on painting and sculpture. Be that as it may, the 1970s and 1980s scarcely constituted a golden era for theater in America. During much of the period, an unmistakable malaise hung over Broadway, the grand center of theater in the United States. Part of the malaise was attributable to economic problems resulting from ever-increasing production costs and the reluctance of many theatergoers of former times to pay from $35 to $50 for a ticket to a Broadway production, the more so when they pondered the increasing crime rate in the area of the fabled Great White Way. Adding to the malaise was the inability of large commercial theaters of Broadway to generate many productions that were artistically distinguished. Even musical comedy, the one distinctly

American contribution to the theatrical arts, tended to languish during the years of relative mellowness. Only *Chorus Line,* portraying the hopes and dreams of dancers who back up the stars, drew favorable comparison with the blockbuster musical comedies of former times. Still, a succession of finely crafted and entertaining plays and musicals composed by America's playwrights and tunesmiths played to large audiences on Broadway and elsewhere across the country. Of particular note were the plays of Neil Simon and Sam Shepard.

In financial terms the most successful playwright in history, Simon turned out one hit play after another in the 1970s and 1980s, most notably his autobiographical trilogy, "Brighton Beach," "Biloxi Blues," and "Broadway Bound." His best plays were light and funny, tended to abound with Jewish humor, much of it tinged with irony, and provided a steady stream of wisecracks and a minimum of raunchiness. Alas, critics regularly took Simon to task because his plays lacked intellectual depth, hence wrote him off as a clever craftsman rather than a serious artist. As for Shepard, a chiseled-featured westerner who also become a movie star, he, too, fashioned a family trilogy: "Curse of the Starving Class," "Buried Chief" (for which he won a Pulitzer Prize in 1979), and "True West." A report that appeared in *Newsweek* in 1985 commented, "As a playwright Shepard has overturned theatrical conventions and created a new kind of drama filled with violence, lyricism and an intensely American compound of comic and tragic power."

Although Martha Graham remained "the grande dame of modern dance," the dominant personality in dance during the 1970s and 1980s was the ballet dancer Mikhail Baryshnikov, a native of the Soviet Union who (at age 26) defected to the United States in 1974. Baryshnikov arrived at a time when dance and particularly ballet was flourishing in North America as never before. (The total audience for dance in the United States advanced from approximately 1 million in 1965 to some 15 million in 1975.) Considered the greatest male dancer in the world, he was best known for his soaring leaps. Indeed, it was written that he was capable of achieving almost godlike levitation.

The theater and dance touched the consciousness of a mere fraction of the national population in any given year, but music in some form or another touched the consciousness of scores of millions of Americans every day. Given the omnipresence of radios, TV sets, and stereos in the United States, in truth, the sounds of music were almost inescapable.

Seemingly interminable financial difficulties notwithstanding, symphonic orchestras in Boston, Chicago, Cleveland, Dallas, New York, San Francisco, Washington, and elsewhere played to large audiences during the 1970s and 1980s. Financial problems also plagued opera, but in 1983 many of the great names in opera gathered to celebrate the Metropolitan Opera's one hundredth anniversary, and connoisseurs experienced adventurous and ambitiously produced opera in such cities as Kansas City, Minneapolis, San Francisco, Santa Fe, and Seattle. Meanwhile, jazz underwent such far-ranging renovation that, according to one observer, its founding parents would scarcely recognize it at all. Still, jazz betrayed no sign of passing into oblivion; indeed, as the 1980s unfolded, it displayed a new vitality with the appearance of several young performers of rare talent, among them the brilliant trumpeter Wynton Marsalis.

Long dismissed by many Americans as an unrefined form of music performed in the main by semiliterate southern "hillbillies," country music soared in popularity during the 1970s and 1980s. In the view of the casual observer, country music probably appeared to undergo little change from former times, and it was true that the lyrics of country ballads, as they had for decades, often conveyed a message of despair, hope, loss, and death by offering sentiment-dripping yarns about convicts, drunkenness, trains, trucks, and unfaithful women. Observed a report that appeared in *Time* in 1974, "The ideal country song might be about a guy who finally gets out of prison, hops a truck home, finds that his wife is slippin' around, gets drunk, and staggers to his doom in front of a high-balling freight." But like jazz, country music had, in fact, undergone extensive renovation in recent decades, largely with respect to its sound. One aspect of that renovation resulted from the influence of rock 'n' roll—an influence that dismayed many tradition-oriented devotees of country music.

During the mid-1980s, a new generation of listeners discovered the sweet sounds of soul, and the result was the reissuance of rhythm-and-blues recordings of the 1950s and 1960s. Meanwhile, new issues of recordings cut in the 1940s and 1950s by the likes of Frank Sinatra and Sarah Vaughan were snapped up by individuals who appreciated what one writer described in 1986 as "a great native [American] art form." Still, the musical form that had been dominant in the United States through the 1960s remained so during the 1970s and 1980s: rock 'n' roll.

For a year or so in the middle 1970s, "punk rock" (or "new wave") commanded the rock music scene. Originating in Britain, punk rock imparted a sense of cynicism, outrage, and raw and untamed energy. The decline of punk rock signaled the ascent of disco, an ascent that was fueled by the hit film *Saturday Night Fever*. By the early 1980s, the disco sound had gone into eclipse, and a new music based on electronic technology and utilizing synthesizers and computers (electro-pop, it was sometimes called) came into vogue. In truth, rock tended to be defined by its assorted performers, the most durable of whom were the Rolling Stones, after the Beatles the premier rock group of the 1960s. By the 1980s, long after the Beatles had disbanded, the Stones played to overflow audiences during tours in the United States.

If the Stones were the most durable, arguably the most exciting rock performers of the period were Michael Jackson and Bruce Springsteen. Released in 1982, Jackson's album *Thriller* sold more than 45 million copies worldwide, making it by all odds the greatest financial success in recording history. Jackson's "Victory Tour" in 1984 grossed an incredible $90 million. A report in *Newsweek* in 1985 proclaimed that Springsteen, whose anthem was "Born in the U.S.A.," had become a kind of American archetype: "He is rock and roll's Gary Cooper—a simple man who expresses strong beliefs with passion and unquestioned sincerity. He is rock and roll's Jimmy Cagney as well—street-wise and fiery, a galvanic mixture of body and soul." In a single day in 1985, Ticketron in New York sold 236,000 tickets to Springsteen concerts.

It was during the years of relative mellowness that millions of Americans discovered the Walkman, tiny headphones tethered to a diminutive battery-powered radio and cassette player, which enabled the listener to absorb music (or anything else that might be recorded on a cassette) while walking, jogging, poring over books in a library, or traveling in a bus. Then there was the music video (often called MTV), which appeared at the end of the 1970s. Filmed versions of popular songs, music videos began as a promotional device in the marketing of rock recordings, but at length took on a life of their own. Of larger moment in the view of connoisseurs of musical sounds was the introduction in 1983 of the CD, the compact audio-disc player, developed by N. V. Philips of the Netherlands and Sony of Japan. Using a laser beam to read music encoded on a small silvery disc spinning at high speed, the CD delivers sound that aficionados have described as having dynamic range and startling purity.

Requiring mention in any account of the musical events of the years of relative mellowness was the enterprise of "U.S.A. for Africa," a group comprising 45 of the world's best-known musical performers. The group produced a video recording entitled "We Are the World" whose sales in the early 1980s generated millions of dollars for the relief of starving people in Africa. The video gave birth to Live Aid, a mammoth benefit rock concert featuring more than 60 of rock 'n' roll's premier performers that was broadcast from JFK Stadium in Philadelphia and Wembley Stadium in London on July 13, 1985. Beamed by satellite across the world, Live Aid was the largest live-television event in history—reaching an estimated 1.6 billion people—and raised more than $17 million for the victims of famine in Africa. A few weeks later, in September 1985, Willie Nelson, John Cougar Mellencamp, and Neil Young organized the Farm Aid concert to raise money for financially distressed farmers in the United States.

Finally, one must note the passing of six giants in the field of musical performance: Louis Armstrong (1971), Duke Ellington (1974), Elvis Presley (1977), Bing Crosby (1977), John Lennon (1980), and Count Basie (1984).

## CARS, PLANES, COMPUTERS

Americans continued their proverbial love affair with the motor car during the 1970s and 1980s. As the national population increased, and as growing numbers of families came to own more than one car, automobile registrations in the United States advanced from 89.2 million in 1970 to 135.7 million in 1986 (compared with 40.4 million in 1950). Persuaded that imported cars provided greater value for the dollar than those built in the United States, legions of Americans bought cars built in Europe and (especially) Japan. Hence sales of imported cars in the United States went from 1.2 million in 1977 to 3.2 million in 1986. Meanwhile, small high-performance sports cars became more commonplace—as did the antithesis of the sports car, the cavernous van. By the early 1980s, nearly all new cars, save large luxury models, had front-wheel drive and were powered by four- or six-cylinder engines. More sophisticated suspension and steering systems and the application of radial tires improved the handling characteristics of automobiles, and when the price of gasoline skyrocketed after 1973, automotive engineers figured out ways to make cars more fuel efficient. As for styling, cars went from the rounded look of the Chevrolet Nova and Ford Maverick to the boxy look of the Ford Granada and Chrysler Corporation K-cars to the "jelly bean" shape of the Ford Taurus.

Thanks in no small measure to the interstate highway network, private automobiles continued to be the principal means by which Americans traveled from city to city. But the automobile's percentage of the total passenger-miles recorded by the various modes of intercity transport slipped from 86.8 in 1970 to 83.2 in 1983. The percentage of the total passenger-miles recorded by the domestic airlines, conversely, advanced from 10.0 in 1970 (up from 4.3 in 1960) to 14.5 in 1983. Viewed in terms of passenger-miles, the performance of the domestic airlines appears even more impressive. The airlines recorded 119 billion passenger-miles in 1970 (up from 34 billion in 1960), 320 billion in 1986. Still, most commercial airlines, because of intense competition (encouraged after the latter 1970s by deregulation of the industry), found themselves in financial trouble at one point or another during the period. One of the country's oldest airlines, Pan American, the first airline to carry the Stars and Stripes to the far corners of the earth, edged toward bankruptcy. Another of America's oldest air carriers, Eastern, and also Braniff International, an innovative airline whose planes were painted in bright and varying colors, went "belly up."

Although a jet airliner zooming down a runway and slowly disappearing in the distant blue yonder made a more stirring impression on the emotions, that encased conglomeration of integrated circuits and transistors that emitted a dull hum and an occasional squeaky beep (usually when the operator depressed the wrong key)—the ubiquitous computer—was the author of what the columnist Robert J. Samuelson in 1985 described as "one of the immense stories of our era," namely, "the computerization of America." Random statistics offer insight into the dimension of what has often been referred to as the computer revolution. The number of computer and data-processing establishments in the United States increased from 6,016 in 1972 to approximately 26,100 in 1985. Colleges and universities in the United States awarded 2,388 degrees in computer and information science in 1971, 38,878 in 1985. Total outlays for computers went from $21.6 billion in 1982 to $45.4 billion in 1986.

Assuming that the country indeed experienced a computer revolution in the 1970s and 1980s, the microcomputer was the agent of that revolution. More to the point perhaps, the microcomputer, by dramatically enhancing the ability of ever-increasing numbers of individuals—in the armed forces, business, community service, education, government, medicine, and science, not to mention (by 1985) the occupants of 15 million households—to make intricate calculations, store, sort through, and rapidly retrieve incredible quantities of information, fashion and test statistical models, and process words, was the agent of what was nothing less than an information revolution. Critical to development of the microcomputer was perfection in the early 1970s of the microprocessor, designed by Ted Hoff, a young engineer of Intel Corporation. As explained in a report that appeared in *Time* in 1983, "With the microprocessor, a single chip could be programmed to do any number of tasks, from running a watch to steering a spacecraft. It could also serve as the soul of a new machine: the personal computer."

The first personal computers went on the market in the mid-1970s. And before long, assorted firms in California's Silicon Valley were gearing up to produce personal computers, one of them a shoestring outfit founded by Steven Wozniak, a computer wizard, and Steven Jobs, a youthful entrepreneur in his early twenties, who christened their new company Apple. Sales were slow in the beginning, and in 1979 the manufacturers of personal computers in the United States shipped only 246,000 units. But then sales took off, and in 1984 American manufacturers shipped 5 million "PCs."

The uses of personal computers, the calculating power of almost any one of which exceeded that of the 30-ton ENIAC of 1947, boggled the mind. Corporations and institutions relied on small computers to manage payrolls and keep track of inventories, maintain records and dispatch bills. Executives as well as secretaries used computers equipped with word processing programs to compose letters, prepare reports, and draft memoranda. Newspaper reporters used word processors to prepare copy. Manufacturers used banks of PCs to control sensors and mechanical arms of robotic devices. Physicians connected PCs in their offices with the AMA/NET that provided information on more than fifteen hundred drugs and to Medline, a compendium of medical articles that had been published in the United States. Salespeople used personal computers to file names and telephone numbers of potential customers and pull up accounts when calling on customers in selected zip code areas. Working at home on weekends, enterprising executives used PCs to analyze and work through alternative proposals. To secure precise information on legal precedents, lawyers connected PCs with Westlaw, a legal database in St. Paul. To secure weather information and learn the latest prices of grain and hogs on the Chicago commodities exchange, agribusinesspeople connected their computers with the Illinois farm bureau's AgriVisor service.

Only a computer aficionado, or "hacker," meanwhile, could keep abreast of the improvements, innovations, and technological breakthroughs in the realm of computer hardware and software. Of particular moment was introduction in the mid-1980s of the small battery-powered "minicomputer" (sometimes referred to as "laptop"), a portable machine that a businessperson might use while flying from city to city or a scholar might carry to a research library. Then there was the "supercomputer," an incredible machine that could crunch numbers almost immeasurably faster than existing computers. The fastest of the fast in the realm of supercomputers was the Cray-2, developed by Cray Research. Capable of doing 1.2 billion arithmetic operations per second, the Cray-2 was more than 40,000 times faster than any personal computer currently on the market. Referring to supercomputers, Robert Brothers, the associate director of computations at Lawrence Livermore National Laboratory, observed in 1985, "What took a year in 1952 we can now do in a second." All things considered, it seemed entirely appropriate when the editors of *Time,* instead of designating a "Man of the Year," as they had done each year for several decades, designated the computer the "Machine of the Year" in 1982.

## SCIENCE AND MEDICINE

While many men and women in the 1970s and 1980s were occupied with ever more powerful and sophisticated computers, others were toiling on the frontiers of science. An assortment of paleoanthropologists sought to unravel the mysteries of the origins of humankind. Astrophysicists concentrated on deep space—pondered mysterious nonobjects that they identified as "black holes"—in quest of answers to the puzzle of the universe. Perceived as bottomless pits in deep space in which atomic particles, stars, and even giant suns disappear without a trace, that is, are literally crushed out of existence, black holes prompted astrophysicists to surmise that in perhaps 50 billion years the galaxies will crush together to form the ultimate black hole, at which point the universe will cease to exist.

Of more immediate moment, physicists and chemists by the latter 1980s were frenetically searching for a compound that would enable them to fabricate room-temperature "superconductors." Discovered in 1911, superconductors, wondrous devices that conduct electricity without resistance, functioned only at minus 459°F, hence had no practical utility. But room-temperature superconductors promised a revolution in technology: electrical transmission lines that lose no power, supercompact supercomputers, ultraefficient energy-storage devices, high-speed trains that float on magnetic fields. By 1988, more than 30 U.S. corporations and corporations elsewhere in the world were expending $300 million annually on superconductor research, and as a consequence the threshold temperature for superconductivity had been raised to −243°F.

Of comparable (and, arguably, of greater) import was the work of genetic engineers who learned to duplicate and manipulate the process whereby DNA molecules, by unraveling and replicating, transmit inherited traits throughout the organism—of simple bacteria, not humans. DNA (deoxyribonucleic acid) is the chainlike molecule from which genes are made, that is, the chemical packets, found in every cell, which carry inherited characteristics, a substance that has been described as the master molecule of life. As Robert Wetzel surmised in an article that appeared in *American Scientist* in 1980, gene splicing, as the process of unraveling and replicating DNA molecules came to be called, might enable scientists to leap biological barriers to the cross-breeding of different species of plants and animals to produce combinations of characteristics that would result in increased crop yields and improved livestock. By the latter

1980s, indeed, Americans were becoming increasingly aware of the enterprise of genetic engineers and other "bioengineers" who toiled in the field of bio-technology (defined in *Webster's New World Dictionary* as "the use of the data and techniques of engineering and technology for the study and solution of problems concerning living organisms"). Most bioengineers in the United States are the employees of more than 400 companies that are presently apply-ing the techniques of biotechnology to develop and produce genetically altered bacteria (to increase the production and improve the techniques of processing food; enhance the mining of pure copper; rejuvenate presumably depleted oil fields; transform the waste products of cheese into compounds used by brewer-ies), hybrid plants and animals, and vaccines to counter disease-causing vi-ruses (notably the AIDS virus). Among the achievements of bioengineers to date has been a hybrid strain of potato whose leaves repel the destructive Colo-rado potato beetle. Via the controversial transplantation of human growth-hor-mone genes into pig embryos, bioengineers have produced larger and more valuable animals. Other scientists, meanwhile, successfully cloned frogs; that is, using the body cells of a single frog, they asexually generated offspring, each of which had a genetic makeup identical to its single parent.

At the same time that many Americans were becoming acquainted with the technique of cloning, in July 1978, in the United Kingdom a baby girl, Louise Brown, entered the world. The birth of baby Louise was an historic event, for she had been conceived outside the womb of her mother—was a product of in vitro (literally, "in glass") fertilization (IVF); that is, an egg surgi-cally extracted from a women is fertilized by sperm in a laboratory. In the popular lexicon, Louise Brown was a test tube baby. At length, in December 1981, in Norfolk, Elizabeth Carr became the first IVF baby to be born in the United States. Although many Americans entertained serious misgivings in the matter of IVF, it soon became clear that test tube conception was a phe-nomenon that would not disappear.

Test tube conception captured newspaper headlines across the world, but several million Americans, most of them senior citizens, took larger interest in the perfection in the latter 1970s of the intraocular implant procedure for persons suffering from cataracts. A tiny plastic lens that an ophthalmologist implants in the eye upon removing the clouded natural lens, the intraocular implant often restores almost normal vision to the patient.

Facilitating the procedure for implanting artificial lenses in the human eye were instruments that were the products of modern high technology. That comes as no surprise, for as most everyone knows, high technology and ad-vances in surgical procedures and medical diagnosis and treatment went hand in hand during the 1970s and 1980s. Electronic fetal monitors warned physi-cians that they must act to prevent brain damage caused when a baby's oxygen was diminished during labor and birth. The brilliantly colored beams of high-energy light of the laser became a standard operating room tool for cutting and closing blood vessels, and in 1986 doctors explored two new uses for lasers: to pulverize kidney stones and to replace stitches in various types of surgery. Ophthalmologists used lasers to repair torn or detached retinas. Of equal moment was computerized axial tomography or (as it was popular referred to) CAT scanning. Initiated in Britain in the early 1970s and hailed as one of the greatest advances in medical diagnosis ever developed, inasmuch as it often made possible precise diagnoses in cases in which conventional X rays or radioactive scans provided unclear pictures of abnormalities, CAT scanning is especially valued in diagnosing cancer, the second-ranking killer of Americans.

During the 1970s and 1980s, researchers, physicians, and surgeons pressed ahead in the never-ending battle against the many varieties of cancer. Radiotherapy, or the use of X rays, to destroy cancers that were difficult to reach by surgery, became more effective as a consequence of the adoption of neutron therapy (whereby a cyclotron or atom-smasher projects neutrons at a cancer with pinpoint accuracy). Chemotherapy (whereby the patient is injected with chemical drugs) underwent improvement. Researchers and physicians, meanwhile, supported the campaign against use of tobacco and exposure to asbestos. Still, the annual rate of death as a result of malignancies in the United States continued to inch upward: from 162.8 per 100,000 people in 1970 to 193.3 in 1985. In such circumstances, it is not surprising that in the latter 1970s legions of cancer victims, prompted by hope born of desperation, would pin their hopes on laetrile, a worthless drug that recently had been compounded in Mexico.

Cancer, of course, ranked only second as a killer of Americans during the 1970s and 1980s. As they had been for many decades, diseases of the heart were the number one killer of Americans. Heart diseases were responsible for 38.1 percent of the deaths in the United States in 1981, malignancies 21.3 percent. But while, as noted, the rate of deaths per hundred thousand Americans from malignancies inched upward during the 1970s and 1980s, that from heart diseases inched downward—from 362.0 in 1970 to 323.0 in 1985. Accounting for the decline in the death rate from diseases of the heart were a variety of developments and happenings, among them the success of an array of drugs, particularly beta-blockers, in controlling blood pressure, the establishment of emergency cardiac units in increasing numbers of hospitals, the increasing ability of surgeons to repair defective hearts, and the kicking of the cigarette habit by growing numbers of Americans.

No less than the heart surgeons Michael E. DeBakey (the celebrated "Texas tornado"), Christiaan Barnard, and their associates in the 1960s, the men and women who toiled to counter diseases of the heart continued during the 1970s and 1980s to comprise a veritable scientific and surgical elite. Among their achievements was the perfection of new drugs to suppress the tendency of the body's immune system to reject foreign tissue. The latter achievement resulted, in the 1980s, in a dramatic revival of the previously discussed procedure of transplanting the human heart from the body of a deceased donor to that of a patient whose own heart was diseased beyond repair, a procedure that had been almost dormant since the early 1970s. Surgeons and bioengineers, meanwhile, worked to perfect a mechanical heart fashioned from plastic and tethered by hoses to an air compressor that might serve as a replacement for a heart that was damaged beyond repair. A surgical team headed by the cardiovascular surgeon William C. DeVries of the University of Utah Medical Center, in December 1982, implanted such a heart, the JARVIK-7, perfected by the bioengineer Robert K. Jarvik, in the chest of Barney Clark, a retired dentist of Seattle who was near death. Clark survived for 112 days. In November 1984, at the Humana Heart Institute in Louisville, a team headed by DeVries replaced the diseased heart of 52-year-old William Schroeder of Jasper, Indiana, with a modified version of the JARVIK-7. After making slow but steady progress, Schroeder suffered a succession of strokes that left him speechless and debilitated until his death in August 1986.

Certainly of more immediate import than the implantation of artificial hearts was the implantation of scores of thousands of atomic-powered heart pacemaker units for regulating the heartbeat and also the perfection of a new technique for depressing obstructions in diseased coronary arteries. Introduced in the early 1980s, the latter technique involved the threading of a balloon-tipped catheter by way of an artery into the diseased heart vessel and inflating the balloon in an effort to stretch the constriction. Still, the development of the pacemaker and perfection of the balloon technique attracted a fraction of the attention that the public and the news media accorded to the implantation of artificial hearts in humans, not to mention the implantation in 1984 of the heart of a baboon in the tiny chest of an infant girl who became known to the world as Baby Fae (and who died on the twenty-first day after the operation).

The remarkable achievements of medical science notwithstanding, large numbers of Americans continued to seek the manipulative therapy of chiropractors, particularly for treatment of lumbago and other pain in the back, arthritis, hay fever, and high blood pressure. They did so in the face of the contention of nearly every medical doctor that chiropractors were "quacks" who, in the words of the American Medical Association, rigidly adhered to "an irrational, unscientific approach to disease causation." Many Americans who had no medical insurance patronized chiropractors because the fees of chiropractors tended to be markedly lower than those of medical doctors. Moved by the claims of chiropractors that they had achieved notable success in treating an array of disorders, other citizens sought chriropractic therapy after medical doctors had failed to cure their maladies. In any event, the number of chiropractic offices and clinics in the United States increased from fewer than nine thousand in 1980 to nearly seventeen thousand in 1986.

## HEALTH CARE AND DISEASE

During the 1970s and 1980s, Americans wrestled with the soaring cost of health care—a result (particularly in the latter 1970s and early 1980s) of the inflation that afflicted the national economy, the expense of the high-tech equipment and paraphernalia that enabled hospitals to provide patients with increasingly sophisticated and effective care and treatment, and the inflated expense of malpractice insurance premiums that resulted from the rising incidence of malpractice claims filed against physicians. They also pondered troublesome ethical and moral questions relating to the care of the sick and infirm. Was it murder, for example, if a friend or relative responded to the request of a terminally ill person by taking the life of that person? Equally disturbing in the view of large numbers of Americans was the question of whether a hopelessly ill or injured or deformed person who could make no decisions for herself or himself—as in the cases of Karen Ann Quinlan of Denville, New Jersey (in the mid-1970s), and "Baby Doe" of Bloomington, Indiana (in 1982)—should be allowed to die, a question that came to the fore with increasing frequency in an era when high-tech life support systems had the capacity of sustaining life indefinitely.

At the same time that they were wrestling with the spiraling cost of health care and ethical and moral questions brought to their attention by the cases of Karen Ann Quinlan and Baby Doe, Americans were confronting a variety of diseases that few of them had ever heard of. Such a disease was genital herpes (or Herpes II), a debilitating, painful, and recurring malady that is usually acquired as a result of sexual intercourse with an infected person. Female victims of genital herpes, in addition to enduring the debilitating and painful consequences of the disease, are five to seven times more likely than other women to develop cervical cancer. The chances are 50-50 that a pregnant woman with an active case of genital herpes will pass the disease to her baby during delivery. And if victims touch herpes sores and rub their eyes, they may develop herpes keratitis, a serious eye infection. Thousands of Americans lost their sight annually during the 1970s and 1980s as a result of the latter disease.

Another malady that increasingly caught the attention of Americans during the 1970s and 1980s was Alzheimer's Disease, a devastating and incurable disease that results in senile dementia, that is, the progressive loss of intellectual functions, mostly among the elderly. More dramatic if far less momentous than the ravages of Alzheimer's was the mysterious fever that in the summer of 1976 struck more than 180 Pennsylvanians who recently had attended an American Legion convention in Philadelphia. Twenty-nine of the victims died. At length, after several months of frenetic investigation, the Centers for Disease Control in Atlanta discovered the bacillus bacterium that was responsible for "Legionnaires' Disease." Researchers decided that Legionnaires' Disease, whose victims responded to treatment with the antibiotic erythromycin, was not a new phenomenon. Indeed the Centers for Disease Control concluded that the Legionnaires' bacterium was probably responsible for 1.5 percent of the cases of unexplained pneumonia in the United States, hence may have been responsible for as many as six thousand deaths in the country each year.

Medical scientists had scarcely resolved the mystery of Legionnaires' Disease before they were confronted with a more baffling—and more deadly—malady: AIDS, the acronym for acquired immune deficiency syndrome. The disease is apparently caused by a single retrovirus that devastates the body's immune system. His or her immune system devastated, the victim of AIDS stands defenseless against a variety of illnesses, the most common of which is pneumonia. AIDS is incurable, and 40 percent of its victims, usually ravaged and wasted by one infection after another, die within one year, 80 percent within two years.

A preponderance of the victims of AIDS, which apparently originated in Central Africa, were male homosexuals to whom the deadly virus had been transmitted in the semen of sex partners during anal or oral intercourse. Other victims were intravenous drug users who contracted the disease when they injected themselves with "dirty" needles that AIDS carriers had used. Before perfection of a simple laboratory test to determine whether blood was AIDS-contaminated, an undisclosed number of people fell victim to the disease when they received hospital transfusions of blood that AIDS carriers had donated. Also, a smattering of infants contracted the disease while in the wombs of AIDS-carrying mothers, apparently when blood from the mothers leaked into the blood supplies of the babies by way of the placentas.

On learning of the existence of AIDS, millions of Americans perceived it as essentially a disease of homosexuals. Accordingly, homosexuals often became pariahs who were turned out of apartments by landlords and shunned by employers. No small number of religious zealots believed the disease a form of punishment directed against homosexuals by an angry deity or by "nature." Meanwhile gays, and heterosexuals as well, who came down with the disease were sometimes treated after the fashion of lepers of biblical times. Notwithstanding assurance by medical scientists that there was little to suggest that one could contract AIDS except as a result of intimate contact with the blood or semen of victims, nurses and paramedics often refused to touch AIDS patients, some dentists declined to fill the teeth of people known to have AIDS, and a few morticians refused to embalm the corpses of people who had died of the disease.

Meanwhile, the surgeon general of the United States urged schools and parents to undertake sex education programs to inform children about how AIDS can and cannot be spread, the city administration of New York inaugurated an advertising campaign urging sexually active people to use condoms, and large numbers of Americans (in 1987) demanded a nationwide program of mandatory blood testing to identify the estimated 1.5 million citizens who were unwitting carriers of the AIDS virus. What was desperately needed, of course, was a vaccine that would prove effective against the disease. Otherwise, upward of 200,000 Americans appeared apt to fall victim to the dreaded disease by 1991. To accelerate the search for an AIDS vaccine and do what it might to protect the infected, the federal government in 1987 had committed itself to support the campaign against AIDS during the following year to the amount of $500 million.

## RELIGION

Religious impulses continued to animate millions of Americans during the 1970s and 1980s. As in the 1960s, a fair number of Americans, most of them youthful, were attracted to esoteric forms of Buddhism that emphasized prayer and meditation. Particularly in the early 1970s, the "Jesus Movement," which emphasized the person of Jesus, captivated an indeterminate number of Americans. Apparently linked with the Jesus Movement was an increase in the invocation of religious themes in popular entertainment. The rock opera *Jesus Christ Superstar* played to overflow crowds in both theaters and churches in the early 1970s. Notwithstanding criticism by conservative religionists, the Broadway musical *Godspell*, derived from the Gospel according to Matthew, found a similarly enthusiastic audience.

Meanwhile, the country was experiencing what was often described as a charismatic revival that was marked by such traditional practices of Pentecostal congregations as "baptism in the spirit," faith healing, and speaking in tongues—a revival that made its way into "mainline" churches, among them the Episcopal, Lutheran, Presbyterian, and Roman Catholic. The spiritual impulses of other Americans found outlets in what were commonly referred to as religious cults. Such cults often required that members surrender all that they owned to the community, extend unquestioning obedience to the leaders of the cult, sever all contact with families. The world learned more than it cared to know about cults in 1978 when, at Jonestown in Guyana (on the north coast of South America), more than nine hundred cultists, all or most of them North Americans, took their own lives (or, in the case of infants, were murdered by their parents) on the order of the cult leader Jim Jones.

The 1970s and 1980s were a memorable time for the Jews, Roman Catholics, and Muslims of the United States. As for Jewish Americans, they became caught up in a veritable renaissance that marked the passage of world Jewry across the two decades. Reflecting that upsurge was the enlarging popularity of Judaic studies, religious discussion groups, and kosher kitchens on college and university campuses, not to mention a tendency of Jewish novelists to construct their works around Jewish themes. Still, Jewish leaders, citing the low birth and high abortion rates among Jews of child-producing age and the continuing tendency of large numbers of Jewish Americans to marry "outside the culture," periodically warned of the ultimate "extinction" of Jewry in the United States.

Catholic Americans celebrated the visits in 1979 and again in 1987 of Pope John Paul II to the United States, and took pride in the world acclaim accorded Mother Teresa of Calcutta, the diminutive Albanian nun who was awarded a Nobel Peace Prize for her work among the impoverished. Still, Catholicism appeared to have lost a measure of its former vitality (except perhaps in the ever-increasing numbers of predominantly Hispanic parishes). The percentage of Catholics who attended Sunday Mass declined sharply, a large percentage of youthful Catholics felt little or no commitment to the Catholic faith, and millions of Catholics deplored the Vatican's continued condemnation of contraception and refusal to allow priests to marry or permit women to become priests. Meanwhile, the Catholic community in the United States fell victim of a severe shortage of priests, as fewer young men opted for the priestly (and celibate) life and tens of thousands of priests left the priesthood, usually to take wives.

Muslim Americans numbered more than 2 million by the 1980s, many of them members of the families of physicians and other professional people who had made their way to the United States from Islamic areas or countries in the decades following World War II. The Muslim Americans with whom other Americans were most familiar, of course, were the Black Muslims, best known for their denunciation of white people as devils. On the death in 1975 of the founder of the Black Muslim movement, Elijah Muhammad, the movement divided. Most Black Muslims joined the American Muslim Mission, headed by Elijah's son Warith Muhammad, who set about to purge his followers of black racism and move them toward Islamic orthodoxy. Others fell in behind Louis Farrakhan, the outspoken leader of the Nation of Islam who became a center of controversy when he denounced the Jewish people and the state of Israel.

However arresting the activities of charismatics and the tragedy at Jonestown, the Jewish renaissance and the enlarging visibility of Muslims in the United States, the religious phenomenon that made the largest imprint on Americans during the 1970s and 1980s was the dramatic resurgence of fundamentalist Protestantism. A catalyst for that resurgence was television. By 1980, fundamentalists and nonmainstream Protestants who styled themselves as evangelicals (but who, in the perspective of outsiders, scarcely differed from fundamentalists) were reaching an estimated 14 million Americans each week via television—and scores of millions via radio. The principal source of support for "the electronic church"? Contributions sent by listeners. In 1986, the organization of the Reverend Jim Bakker took in nearly $130 million; and the organizations of the Reverend Jerry Falwell and the Reverend Pat Robertson, more than $100 million each. It was estimated in 1987 that the total receipts of the country's gospel broadcasters approached $2 billion annually.

Apart from appeals for funds (a central part of nearly every broadcast by radio and TV evangelists), the message that most fundamentalist preachers sent out over the airwaves during the 1970s and 1980s was militant and judgmental, stressed biblical literalism, insisted that no non-Christian could achieve eternal salvation. Scorning ecumenism, the fundamentalist message took a particularly hostile view of Roman Catholicism, and intimated that few, if any, Catholics were apt to pass through the portals of heaven. Fundamentalists were also inclined to anti-Semitism, and the Reverend Bailey Smith shocked nonfundamentalists when he proclaimed, "God Almighty does not hear the prayer of a Jew." More importantly, their message offered unambiguous answers to social and religious questions, hence conveyed an image of certainty and strength.

The fundamentalist surge disturbed great numbers of Americans, the more so when Jerry Falwell in 1979, appealing for "a coalition of God-fearing moral Americans" to "reverse the politicization of immorality in our society," organized the Moral Majority, Incorporated, a conservative lobbying organization that in 1980 sought to rally fundamentalists behind the presidential candidacy of Ronald Reagan. But in 1987, fundamentalism endured what Falwell conceded was "a broadside" when Jim Bakker was disclosed to have had a one-day sexual encounter with a church secretary—and to secure the secretary's silence had arranged for the payment of $115,000 in cash and establishment of a trust fund of $150,000, presumably from funds contributed by members of his radio and TV audience. Next, in 1988, the Reverend Jimmy Swaggart, whose ministry the year before had taken in an estimated $140 million, was established to have had liaisons with one and perhaps a succession of prostitutes.

Accompanying the fundamentalist surge during the 1970s and 1980s was a precipitous decline in the membership of the mainstream Protestant churches. From the mid-1960s to the mid-1980s, the latter churches lost 4.7 million members. Once the largest Protestant denomination in the United States, the United Methodist Church experienced a membership decline of 2 million during the two decades after 1965, from approximately 11 million to 9 million. The membership of northern Presbyterian churches declined by a third from 1965 to 1985, that of the Disciples of Christ by 40 percent. Among the mainstream Protestant groups, only the Southern Baptist Convention (which in theology and general outlook tended to be closer to the fundamentalists than to other mainstream denominations) continued to expand its membership—and indeed became the largest Protestant denomination (some 13 million members by the early 1980s) in the United States.

## CITIES AND POVERTY

Although televangelists appeared to be wallowing in money during the 1970s and 1980s, the governments of most of the country's cities manifestly were not. Particularly in the 1970s, governments of city after city across the republic, among them Cleveland, Detroit, Philadelphia, St. Louis, and San Francisco, found themselves strapped for the revenues that were required to maintain essential services. Only the intervention of Pres. Jimmy Carter, who in 1978 prevailed on a reluctant Congress to pass the New York City Loan Guarantee Act, saved the country's largest metropolis from tumbling into bankruptcy.

Carter turned over the White House to Ronald Reagan in 1981, and the new president soon made clear his dearth of enthusiasm for the transfer of federal funds to cities. From 1980 through 1985, accordingly, federal funding for cities declined from $69 billion to $17 billion. Then, in 1986, at Reagan's instigation, Congress passed the Tax Reform Act which, among other things, terminated the $4.2 billion-a-year general revenue-sharing program that President Nixon had prevailed on Congress to accept in 1972—a program that in recent years had been the source of 6 percent of the revenue of the country's larger cities.

More disturbing than the financial woes of urban governments, or so millions of Americans reckoned, were the ever-increasing number of homeless or "street" people who waged a pitiful day-to-day struggle to survive in nearly every city of any size in the United States in the 1970s and 1980s. So numerous had the street people become in recent years, in all candor, that the affluent citizen strolling the sidewalks of New York or Philadelphia, San Francisco or Washington could scarcely avoid the sight of forlorn and often disoriented (and sometimes intoxicated) people wandering aimlessly (sometimes pushing shopping carts laden with all of their earthly possessions) or more often sitting vacantly or sprawled on sidewalks. Who were the street people? Some studies indicated that many of them were drug abusers and members of ethnic minorities, and that between 30 and 40 percent were mental patients who had been discharged from hospitals in accord with deinstitutionalization programs. As for the precise number of homeless Americans, the federal government's Department of Housing and Urban Development in the early 1980s placed the number at between 250,000 and 350,000.

Whatever their number, the street people comprised only a fraction of the poverty-ridden population of the United States during the 1970s and 1980s. According to the U.S. Bureau of the Census, some 35.3 million Americans were living in poverty in 1983. That figure came to 15.2 percent of the national population (compared with 12.1 percent in 1969 and 11.7 percent in 1979). That so many citizens continued to be mired in poverty in what most of the populace perceived to be the richest and "best" country in the world was, in the view of some Americans a national scandal.

Any discussion of poverty, of course, almost inevitably found its way to the federal government's programs aimed at countering poverty in the United States, many of them part of the legacy of Lyndon Johnson's attempt to build a Great Society in the 1960s. Millions of Americans, particularly those who were political conservatives, became persuaded well before the passing of the 1970s that those programs had become bloated and in any event were largely ineffectual, hence constituted a colossal waste of the hard-earned funds of the country's overly burdened taxpayers.

In truth, only a fraction of the funds disbursed by the federal government each year under the heading of "social welfare expenditures" were intended to deal specifically with the problem of poverty. Of the $302.8 billion of federal funds expended for social welfare in 1980, $191.1 billion went for "social insurance" (notably Social Security benefits), $21.2 billion for veterans programs, and $12.8 billion for health and medical programs that were only marginally related to programs of assistance to Americans who were poor. Still, increasing numbers of middle- and upper-income citizens concluded that federal outlays for food stamps ($9.0 billion in 1980), Medicaid ($14.5 billion), vocational rehabilitation ($1.0 billion), child nutrition ($4.2 billion), and other poverty programs—outlays that totaled approximately $64 billion—were exorbitant. And in 1980, voters elected a president who shared that conclusion.

## CRIME AND PUNISHMENT

For reasons that are readily understandable, criminal activity was never far from the consciousness of virtually every American during the 1970s and 1980s. In each year between 1974 and 1986, between 10 and 14 million crimes were reported in the United States: as many as 1.4 million violent crimes (aggravated assault, forcible rape, murder, robbery), as many as 12 million property crimes (burglary, larceny, and motor vehicle theft). But official statistics did not begin to disclose the actual extent of crime, for uncounted criminal acts committed every day simply went unreported. What caught the attention of the citizenry at large, of course, were crimes that found their way onto the front pages of newspapers and into the evening news programs of television networks: the bizarre escapades in the mid-1970s of Patricia Campbell "Patty" Hearst, the newspaper heiress who joined the tiny revolutionary Symbionese Liberation Army that had kidnapped her, then participated in a bank robbery and shoot-out with police in California; the grisly activities in 1977 of "Son of Sam," David Berkowitz, a pudgy and mild-mannered postal employee in New York who shot to death seven young persons and wounded several others with a .44-caliber revolver; the depravations of Wayne B. Williams, an aspiring talent scout in Atlanta who over a period of 22 months in 1980–1981 dispatched 24 victims, most of them youthful black males.

Meanwhile, organized crime continued to flourish. Occasionally the mobsters made headlines, as in 1975 when hit men of the mob apparently rubbed out James R. "Jimmy" Hoffa, the notorious former president of the International Brotherhood of Teamsters. More chilling perhaps, an orgy of looting and burning that was reminiscent of the ghetto explosions of the 1960s rocked New York City on the hot, muggy night of July 13–14, 1977, when a thunderstorm knocked out high-voltage power lines and plunged most of the sprawling metropolis into darkness. Then there was "Koreagate," the illegal acceptance by several members of Congress in the latter 1970s of cash gifts offered by South Korean lobbyists. Equally distressing was the Abscam scandal that captured national attention in 1980. Abscam involved seven members of Congress and several state and local officials in New Jersey and Pennsylvania who accepted bribes from agents of the FBI who posed as Arab sheiks.

However disgusted by the Koreagate and Abscam scandals, many Americans felt ambivalent in 1984 when they weighed the case of Bernhard Hugo Goetz. An electronics engineer who had been severely beaten by muggers four years before, Goetz shot and wounded four black teenagers aboard a subway train in New York City. One of Goetz's bullets left its young victim paralyzed from the waist down. A white man, Goetz suspected that the teenagers, two of whom were, in fact, carrying sharpened screwdrivers, were about to attack him. No ambivalence at all animated Americans in 1986–1987 when a succession of investment bankers and traders on Wall Street were disclosed to have used inside information to turn profits running into the tens of millions of dollars. Insider trading was a crime. Most notorious of the insider trading criminals was Ivan F. Boesky, the dapper "king of the arbitrageurs" who realized uncounted millions by exploiting knowledge not available to the investing public concerning proposed corporate takeovers. When pondering Boesky and his ilk, most Americans felt nothing save contempt.

Intertwined with the question of crime, of course, was that of the punishment of criminals. The latter question came to the fore from time to time

September 1971: A policeman and a guard collect baseball bats and other weapons from an exercise yard in the state prison at Attica, New York, where rioting prisoners had set up a stronghold and held thirty-eight hostages for five days.

during the 1970s and 1980s when violence erupted at a prison, as in September 1971, when 1,200 inmates, most of them blacks and Puerto Ricans, at the Attica maximum security facility in upstate New York, seized 39 guards and other prison employees as hostages and entrenched themselves in a segment of the prison. When order was restored at Attica—after state troopers had rushed that part of the prison held by the rebels—11 guards and other civilian employees and 32 inmates lay dead. The riots at Attica and other prisons notwithstanding, the question in the realm of criminal punishment that most often touched the popular consciousness during the time of relative mellowness, particularly in the 1970s, was that of the effectiveness as a crime inhibitor and, more than that, the morality of putting criminals to death. In the front rank of those citizens who opposed the death penalty, on the grounds that it was at once ineffectual as a crime inhibitor and immoral, were political liberals. The principal defenders of the death penalty were political conservatives.

At length, in 1972, the question of the death penalty made its way to the Supreme Court, and the result prompted many liberals to rejoice. Observing that states had been considerably more inclined over the years to execute black prisoners who had been convicted of capital crimes than whites, the high court ruled in the case of *Furman* v. *Georgia* that most of the state statutes sanctioning capital punishment, because of their capricious and discriminatory application, were in violation of the federal Constitution. Whereupon some 35 states, urged on by conservatives, enacted new statutes providing for the death penalty for at least some crimes, notably murder, and by the summer of 1976 a total of 611 inmates of prisons across the country were under sentences of death. Still, because of constitutional uncertainty, authorities were hesitant about carrying out those sentences. Then, in 1976, the Supreme Court ruled in the case of *Gregg* v. *Georgia* that capital punishment did not violate the prohibition of "cruel and unusual punishments" spelled out in the Eighth Amendment of the Constitution. According to the justices, capital punishment was "an expression of society's moral outrage at particularly offensive conduct"—an expression that "may be unappealing to many, but is essential in an ordered society that asks its citizens to rely on legal processes rather than self-help to vindicate their wrongs."

The first convicted felon to be executed after the Supreme Court's decision in the *Gregg* case was Gary Mark Gilmore, who had slaughtered gasoline station attendants in Utah during two armed robberies. While opponents of capital punishment demonstrated outside the Utah State Prison, Gilmore was dispatched by firing squad on January 17, 1977. Still, only five convicted felons (four whites and one black) were put to death in the five years after the execution of Gilmore. Then the pace of executions began to quicken. Five prisoners were executed in 1983, 21 in 1984, more than 40 in 1985—many of them by lethal injection while strapped to hospital gurneys. So routine had executions become by the mid-1980s that they tended to attract minimal attention.

## EDUCATION

Of far greater moment than the question of the death penalty were assorted questions relating to education, including that of how to meet financial problems that began to weigh heavily on the national educational establishment at all levels in the early 1970s. Financial problems were in some measure a consequence of rampant inflation, which pushed up the cost of operating schools and colleges and universities—also (insofar as public education was concerned) a consequence of what was widely described as a revolt of taxpayers, that is, a reaction against seemingly ever-higher taxes, which swept much of the republic during the 1970s. Still, the educational issue that most stirred popular passions, at least through the 1970s, was the busing of children in the interest of achieving racial balance in public schools, in the main in cities, in the North and West as well as the South, where neighborhood schools tended to be all-black or all-white because the neighborhoods themselves tended to be all-black or all-white.

Busing would supposedly result in better schooling for culturally disadvantaged black children, while at the same time heightening the racial sensitivity of white youths and furthering the cause of racial justice in the United States. Whatever its rationale, busing exacerbated feelings regarding race, for example, those deriving from the perception of legions of whites that black children tended to be more inclined to violence and more sexually promiscuous than white children. Still, white opponents of busing usually insisted that the inconvenience of busing children for long distances rather than racial considerations was at the root of their opposition to busing. To which contention the National Association for the Advancement of Colored People, in 1975—during the same year that upward of ten thousand antibusing protesters in Louisville threw rocks, built bonfires and stalled traffic on a main highway for hours, damaged 37 school buses and burned 2—issued an angry report entitled "It's Not the Distance, It's the Niggers."

Although a preponderance of the citizenry had never taken an exalted view of busing in the interest of achieving balance between the races in the schools, it was clear by the turn of the 1980s that the tide of political and legal opinion was running decidedly against busing. And in 1986, the Supreme Court, by declining to review cases in which black parents and civil rights leaders sought the continuation of busing in Norfolk and Oklahoma City, sent an unmistakable signal that a school district might terminate a busing program once its schools were integrated, whatever the racial balances of individual schools. In truth, by the time the Supreme Court conveyed the foregoing signal, equal rights activists had largely given up on the busing of children as an instrument to advance the cause of equal opportunity in the public schools.

Busing may have passed into eclipse as an issue in American education in the 1980s, but other issues relating to the country's schools remained. Such an issue was "school prayer," that is, the offering of prayers and reading of the Bible in the public schools, a longtime practice in many parts of the republic that the Supreme Court in the early 1960s had proclaimed to be in violation of the constitutional principle of separation of church and state. Critics, the most vehement among them Protestants of the fundamentalist persuasion, denounced the action by the high court as a hacking away at practices and values that in their perspective had made the United States a veritable promised land. Notwithstanding support by the administration of Pres. Ronald Reagan, proposals to amend the federal Constitution to permit "voluntary prayers" in the schools failed to secure ratification. The Supreme Court, meanwhile, nullified a law in Alabama setting aside daily moments of silence in the state's public schools—an improper attempt "to return prayer to the public schools," in the view of the high court. Compounding the frustration of fundamentalist Protestants in that same period was a ruling by a federal district judge in 1982 that nullified laws of Arkansas and Louisiana requiring schools to devote equal time to the teaching of "creation science" (the account of the creation of the universe as set out in the Bible's book of Genesis) and "evolutionary theory."

Of greater urgency during the 1970s and 1980s than controversies over busing, school prayer, and the teaching of creationism was a running controversy that centered on the quality of formal education in the United States. Fueling the controversy were declining national scores on scholastic aptitude tests (SATs) taken annually by high school seniors across the length and breadth of the republic, and also statistics disclosing that as many as 15 percent of high school graduates were "functionally illiterate," that is, lacked the reading skills that were required for proper functioning in a complex society.

What or who was to blame for the manifest shortcomings of American education? Attention increasingly focused on teachers. In the view of various researchers, many teachers were not requiring that students meet high standards of achievement. More unsettling perhaps were estimates that as many as 20 percent of the country's elementary and secondary teachers had themselves failed to master basic skills in arithmetic, reading, and writing, and that a higher percentage lacked competency in the subject areas in which they were teaching. The foregoing estimates prompted demands that teachers be subjected to minimal competency examinations. Over the objections of most teachers, 37 states had mandated minimum competency examinations by the early 1980s—exams that critics castigated as being ridiculously easy.

Then, in 1983, a spate of reports spelling out what were purported to be the grave deficiencies of the country's elementary and secondary schools caught the attention of millions of Americans and generated new appeals for reform of public education in the United States. Stirring the most extensive comment, not to mention concern, was a report issued by the National Commission on Excellence in Education, an 18-member panel that had been appointed by Secretary of Education T. H. Bell. Entitled "A Nation at Risk," the report asserted, "If an unfriendly foreign power had attempted to impose on America the mediocre educational performance that exists today, we might well have viewed it as an act of war." The commission urged that requirements for graduation from high school be strengthened; schools, colleges, and universities adopt higher expectations of academic performance and student conduct; students be required to devote significantly increased time to "basic" courses, for example, English and math; and steps be taken to improve the preparation of teachers and make teaching a more rewarded and respected profession.

Although the indictment set out in "A Nation at Risk" was drawn in the main against elementary and secondary schools, critics were soon zeroing in on higher education as well. Such a critic was Charles E. Finn, Jr., of Vanderbilt University, who argued, in an essay entitled "Trying Higher Education: An Eight Count Indictment" that appeared in *Change* in 1984, that the moral and intellectual state of American colleges and universities was scandalous. Equally devastating was the critique offered by Allan Bloom, a philosophy professor at the University of Chicago, in a book entitled *The Closing of the American Mind*, published in 1987. Charging that American universities had abandoned their historic principles and purpose, Bloom wrote, "These great universities which can split the atom, find cures for the most terrible diseases, conduct surveys of whole populations and produce massive dictionaries of lost languages—cannot generate a modest program of general education for undergraduate students." According to Bloom, the country's institutions of higher education had replaced liberal arts core studies with "a democracy of disciplines" that offered "no distinctive visage." As the 1980s drew to a close, alas, there was little evidence that critiques such as those offered in "A Nation at Risk" and in the writings of Finn and Bloom had signaled any serious effort to engineer drastic renovation of education in a republic whose educational establishment at all levels cried out for renovation.

## BLACKS AND INDIANS

Life had never been easy for African Americans and Indian Americans in the world's oldest survivng democracy. The victims of interminable abuse and discrimination by the white majority of the citizenry, uncounted millions of blacks and Indians over the past two centuries had felt frustration tinctured by outrage. Sadly, blacks and Indians during the 1970s and 1980s saw minimal reason to revise perceptions of the conditions of their existence in the self-proclaimed citadel of justice and equal opportunity.

Most black Americans felt frustrated (and many felt outraged) when they pondered the angry response of whites to the attempt to mitigate the educational disadvantages that had impeded the intellectual growth and blighted the socioeconomic opportunities of several generations of black children via the school busing initiative. Compounding their dismay was the ruling by the Supreme Court in 1978 in the case of Allan P. Bakke, a white veteran of the war in Vietnam whose application for admission to the medical school of the University of California at Davis was twice rejected. Aware that the university had a policy of reserving 16 out of every 100 openings in the medical school for minority students, and learning that his scores on tests required for admission to the medical school were higher than those of most minority students who had been granted admission, he believed himself a victim of reverse discrimination. To the dismay of blacks, who feared that the decision threatened the entire structure of affirmative action programs inaugurated in recent years to assure the entry of blacks in assorted professions, the high court struck down the university's admissions system and ordered Bakke admitted to its medical school (but ruled that affirmative action programs might legally continue, provided they did not rest on rigid quotas).

Racial tension and even violence found myriad expression in the United States during the 1970s and 1980s. Recalling the racial confrontation at Central High School in Little Rock in 1957, tensions boiled over in 1974 when buses delivered black youths for enrollment in South Boston High School. A ghetto eruption reminiscent of those in the 1960s came to pass in Liberty City, Florida, in 1980 when an all-white jury acquitted a white policeman of all charges in the fatal beating of a black businessman. Large numbers of whites in 1978 vigorously opposed the Humphrey-Hawkins Full Employment Bill, a central purpose of which was to provide jobs for legions of blacks who were out of work. Nearly a decade later, millions of the country's whites irritated blacks by responding negatively when Congress mandated that the third Monday in January be set aside to honor the memory of the Reverend Martin Luther King, Jr.

However much blacks resented the attitudes of uncounted white compatriots regarding the Humphrey-Hawkins legislation and the national holiday honoring Dr. King, that resentment was nothing compared with the anger tinctured with frustration they felt over the poverty that continued to enchain millions of black citizens. Poverty indeed remained one of the great overbearing problems weighing down on the lives of black people in the self-proclaimed citadel of democracy and opportunity. Wrote the sociologist William Julius Wilson in the *Wilson Quarterly* in 1984, "While rising rates of crime, drug addiction, out-of-wedlock births, female-headed families, and welfare dependency have afflicted American society generally in recent years, the increases have been most dramatic among what has become a large and seemingly permanent black underclass inhabiting the cores of the nation's major cities." In an essay that appeared in *Time* in 1987, Walter Shapiro made similar observations, noting that 4 million black Americans remained trapped in inner-city ghettos, that a third of the country's blacks remained mired in poverty, that

February 1978: Leaders of Indian Americans prepare to consecrate the start of a 3,000-mile trek by Indians from California to Washington to discuss legislation pertaining to Indians by smoking a peace pipe on Alcatraz Island in San Francisco Bay.

the jobless rate for black teenagers stood at 40 percent, that 60 percent of all black babies were born out of wedlock.

Compounding the miseries of the black underclass in the urban ghettos, particularly in the 1980s, were the depredations of roving gangs that peddled drugs and violence. In Los Angeles alone, a total of 187 gang-related homicides took place in 1986. Of Los Angeles, Jon D. Hull wrote in a report in *Time* in 1987, "Drive-by shootings are more common than smog alerts, and the burgeoning trade in crack cocaine has turned gangs from stray hoods into multi-million-dollar enterprises equipped with Uzis and AK-47 assault rifles."

No less frustrated during the 1970s and 1980s than millions of black Americans were thousands of original or Indian Americans. That frustration was easily explained. Unemployment and underemployment on many Indian reservations (the dwelling place of 68 percent of the country's Indians, described by one writer as open-air slums) exceeded 50 percent. Large numbers of Indian families, accordingly, were stuck in poverty. Alcoholism among Indian Americans was rampant. Many Indians chafed under the system of tribal administration imposed on them by the government in Washington. Frustration, of course, prompted restiveness, and that restiveness caught national—indeed international—attention in 1973, in what was widely referred to as the Second Battle of Wounded Knee.

Wounded Knee II was a bizarre affair. It began when some three hundred militant members of the American Indian Movement (AIM) occupied the sleepy hamlet of Wounded Knee, South Dakota (on the Pine Ridge Indian Reservation). The ostensible purpose of the occupation was to force revision of the constitution of the Oglala Sioux, adopted in accord with the Indian Reorganization Act of 1934, that provided for an elected tribal government. The revisions sought by the AIM would restore the autocratic powers of the Oglala Sioux chiefs—revisions of a sort that were strongly opposed by many and perhaps most Indians. Determined to maintain the system of administration by elected tribal organizations, the government in Washington turned aside the demands of the AIM. The upshot was what amounted to a siege of Wounded Knee by federal lawmen who intermittently fired rifles in the direction of the hamlet. Indians returned the fire. Two Indians died in the sporadic combat, several Indians and lawmen suffered wounds. Indians vandalized Wounded Knee. At length, on May 5, 1973, both sides agreed to end the confrontation.

Whatever the purpose and eventual outcome of the AIM's occupation of Wounded Knee in 1973, the confrontation stirred the consciousness of many Indians, and raised the level of consciousness of many non-Indians regarding the plight of the descendents of the original Americans. In response, Congress in the mid-1970s made clear its commitment to a policy of self-determination for Indians for the purpose of preserving distinct and independent tribal communities. Although scattered Indian tribes achieved incredible prosperity during the 1970s when coal and oil were discovered on reservations, most Indian communities needed a good deal more than self-determination. They also needed economic stimulation and additional jobs, improved health care and better schools, all of which required extensive subsidization by the federal government. Through the years that Gerald Ford and Jimmy Carter presided over the national destiny, the Washington government was reasonably responsive to the latter needs. But the fiscal policies of the administration of Pres. Ronald Reagan resulted in a sharp reduction of federal subsidies to Indians during the 1980s. Wrote one observer (Stephen Cornell) in 1986, "With no economic base to draw on, most [tribes] have found themselves powerless in the face of rising unemployment, deteriorating health care, and a falling standard of living."

## FEMINISM AND ABORTION

At the same time that Indian activists were pressing the federal government to act to improve the conditions of life of original Americans, feminists were campaigning for approval of the Equal Rights Amendment (ERA). Their enterprise came to grief. The reasons are not hard to discern. Large numbers of citizens simply reckoned that a victory by feminists in the matter of the ERA would reinforce feminists in their campaigns on other issues that bore on what many tradition-oriented Americans perceived to be traditional family values, for example, the campaign in support of abortion. At length, in 1982, the deadline that Congress had mandated for ratification of the ERA expired, and when reintroduced in the House of Representatives in 1983 the ERA was rejected. Feminists likewise met frustration in their effort to eliminate the widespread disparity between men and women in wages and salaries (the disparity, of course, almost invariably favoring men) when men and women were performing the same work and accepting identical responsibilities. (In 1983, the median weekly earnings of full-time wage and salary workers in the United States who were male was $378, of those who were female, $252; in 1986, $419 for males, $290 for females.)

Still, women in the United States registered substantial advances in their quest for equality of opportunity and treatment with men during the 1970s and 1980s. The number of females in the national work force continued to increase: from 17.7 million in 1950 to 31.2 million in 1970 to 52.9 million in 1987. The number of gainfully employed women in the United States who were functioning in managerial or professional capacities increased from 5.0 million in 1970 to 11.1 million in 1987.

Statistics aside, women found themselves holding jobs and pursing careers in the 1970s and 1980s that few, if any, women had held or pursued in former times. They worked on assembly lines in auto plants, toiled in coal mines and steel mills, drove 18-wheeled tractor-trailer rigs. The first women cadets entered the U.S. Military Academy at West Point in 1976. Women of the U.S. Air Force piloted AWACS early-warning aircraft and cargo planes. Army women piloted helicopters and won airborne wings by jumping out of airplanes. Women served aboard ships of the U.S. Coast Guard in all capacities. Women were ordained as priests in the Episcopal Church; Sally Priesand became reform Judaism's first female rabbi. Women became thoroughbred racing jockeys; Janet Guthrie became the first woman driver to compete in the India-

August 1977: Hazel Hunkins Hallinan, a onetime "suffragette" who had campaigned for the right of women to vote more than a half-century before, fans herself after marching down Pennsylvania Avenue in Washington with thousands of supporters of the Equal Rights Amendment.

napolis 500-mile auto race (and finished a respectable ninth in the 500-mile classic of 1978). The number of women mayors increased from 566 in 1975 to 1,680 in 1981. Sally K. Ride became the first American woman astronaut—propelled into space aboard the space shuttle *Challenger* in 1983. Appointed by President Reagan in 1981, Sandra Day O'Connor became the first woman justice of the Supreme Court. Geraldine Ferraro became the first woman to win a place on the presidential ticket of a major party. She was the Democratic nominee for vice president in 1984.

An issue that plagued Geraldine Ferraro during the electoral campaign of 1984 was one that had become a veritable preoccupation of militant feminists of the United States: abortion, the induced expulsion of a human embryo or fetus from the womb before it is sufficiently developed to survive. It was an issue that had been a source of stormy and unrelenting controversy in the country for more than a decade. (During the electoral campaign of 1984, opponents of abortion demonstrated against and heckled Ferraro, a Roman Catholic who personally opposed abortion but believed a woman should have the right to choose for herself whether she would give birth.)

James C. Mohr has explained in his book *Abortion in America: The Origins and Evolution of National Policy, 1800–1900* (1978) that a centuries-old attitude of English common law governed the legal status of abortion in the pristine years of the American republic. That attitude rested on the assumption that neither a woman nor anybody else could be certain that she was pregnant until she experienced fetal movement or "quickening," hence nobody could say for sure that any medicine administered or procedure performed, say, for the purpose of restoring menstrual flow after one or more missed periods (on the assumption that something unnatural might be obstructing a woman's normal cycle), would result in the abortion of an embryo or fetus. Ostensibly for the removal of obstructions, then, many American women during the closing decades of the eighteenth century and the early decades of the nineteenth, often consulting home medical guides on drugs, potions, and techniques that were believed effective in removing "unnatural blockages," doubtless acted to terminate unwanted pregnancies.

At length, in the 1820s, the legislatures of five states approved legislation making abortion at any time during pregnancy a crime; five others made it a crime only after quickening. As matters turned out, anti-abortion laws proved unenforceable, and in the 1840s the United States experienced what appeared to be a dramatic increase in the incidence of abortion, largely because substantial numbers of women, most of them white, married, Protestant, native-born women of middle- and upper-income groups, wanted to postpone childbearing or wanted no more children than they already had. Meanwhile, an amorphous movement to outlaw abortion, fueled in part by widespread concern over a decline in the national birth rate, was gathering momentum. The legislatures of state after state, accordingly, enacted new antiabortion statutes or strengthened existing ones. Then, in the second half of the nineteenth century, the national medical establishment mounted what James Mohr has described as a physicians' crusade against abortion. Morally opposed to the extermination of life in the making, a preponderance of America's physicians of the time viewed abortion as an outrage, except when performed for a therapeutic purpose, that is, to save the life of the expectant mother. The crusade of the physicians found a mark with legislators of those states that had not yet outlawed abortion, and by the turn of the twentieth century abortion, save for the purpose of sparing the life of the mother, was a crime across the length and breadth of the republic. Few citizens ever spoke out in opposition to the anti-abortion statutes.

Through the first six decades of the twentieth century, there were no notable changes in public attitudes, and hence no important changes in the law, regarding abortion. Except for the purpose of saving the life of the mother, abortion was almost universally condemned in the United States. Condemnation, of course, did not prevent uncounted women over those decades from arranging for the illegal termination of unwanted pregnancies. Meanwhile, during the years following World War II, strictures on abortion began to be relaxed in other parts of the world, for example, in Japan and Sweden. Then, in the 1960s, a movement to remove restrictions on abortion began to take form in the United States, and in 1967 the National Organization of Women (NOW), adopting the view that a woman could never achieve the personal freedom to which she was manifestly entitled until she was guaranteed absolute control over her own body, to wit, until she gained the legal right to terminate unwanted pregnancies for whatever reason, mounted a nationwide campaign of agitation and publicity on behalf of abortion reform. Feminists dismissed the contention of their adversaries, the most resolute of whom in the 1960s and early 1970s were spokespeople of the Roman Catholic Church, that a human embryo or fetus is not simply an inchoate mass of cells and tissues (and hence aborting an unborn baby is of no larger moment than removing an infected appendix) but rather a pulsating, living human being who has an unqualified right to life.

Responding to the feminist campaign, more than a dozen state legislatures from 1969 to 1972 relaxed abortion statutes; those of Hawaii and New York virtually erased strictures regarding abortion entirely. Accordingly, the number of legal abortions performed in the United States went from an estimated 8,000 in 1966 to 587,000 in 1972. Then, on January 22, 1973, the Supreme Court issued a ruling in the case of *Roe* v. *Wade* that brought jubilation to militant feminists and other proponents of abortion, dismay to millions of Americans who believed that human embryos and fetuses were human beings and thus endowed with the same right to life with which all humans are endowed, however inconvenient or even traumatic their presence inside the womb might be to their mothers. *Roe* v. *Wade* virtually eliminated restrictions on abortion in the United States, and the result was a further increase in the number of legal abortions performed annually in the country—to 1.0 million in 1976 to 1.5 million in 1981. The ratio of legal abortions per thousand live births went from 184 in 1972 to 429 in 1981.

Alas, the decision of the Supreme Court in *Roe* v. *Wade* did not put to rest the controversy over abortion, arguably the most emotion-packed and divisive controversy to rock the republic in more than a century. Champions of what they perceived to be the right to life of unborn children were bent on overturning or circumventing the *Roe* decision; proponents of abortion were equally determined that the *Roe* decision would not be upset or circumvented. But right-to-lifers and proponents of abortion (or advocates of "choice" regarding the question of whether to terminate a pregnancy) organized demonstrations and rallies. Antiabortionists lobbied to prohibit federal funding for any agency providing information regarding abortion and related services, and urged adoption of a constitutional amendment that would prohibit abortions except in cases in which the mother's life was in danger or where conception had occurred as a result of incest or rape. They distributed "The Silent Scream," a sonogram videotape of an abortion in which a fetus appears to be waging a vain struggle for life as a surgical instrument tears at its limbs and torso. More militant right-to-life champions, many of them fundamentalist Protestants (who in the aftermath of the *Roe* decision had become as active as their longtime adversaries, the Catholics, in protesting abortion), picketed and sometimes vandalized abortion clinics and harassed employees and patients as they entered and left clinics.

What might be the eventual outcome of the great abortion controversy was hard to say. It was a controversy in which there appeared to be no middle ground. As observed in a report in *Newsweek* in 1985, "A system [that is, the American political system] built on interest-group bargaining is well-suited to producing compromise, but abortion is one of the rare issues that inherently does not admit compromise. Just as a woman cannot be a little bit pregnant, neither can her fetus be a little bit aborted. And if one side adopts the relativist view that human life is achieved by degrees over nine months of gestation, while the other takes the absolutist position that life begins at conception, it is nearly impossible to imagine the meeting point that would satisfy both."

## HOMOSEXUALS

At the same time that the abortion controversy appeared to tear at the social fabric of the United States, during the 1970s and 1980s, militant homosexuals were crusading on behalf of "gay rights." Theirs was a crusade that outraged the sensibilities of millions of Americans who clung to what often were referred to as traditional family values only slightly less than the crusade on behalf of abortion on demand.

Viewed from time immemorial as a sin against God and nature, sodomy ("abnormal" sexual intercourse) was defined as a crime in all of England's colonies in North America in the seventeenth and eighteenth centuries and eventually by all of the states of the United States. At that, few homosexuals, a preponderance of whom sought to live out their years in the proverbial closet, that is, sought to keep their homosexuality a secret, were ever brought to trial. Then, after World War II, the American Civil Liberties Union, the American Law Institute, and a few religious groups urged decriminalization of all sexual activities between consenting adults. Such appeals found little response among the public at large. Meanwhile, scattered organizations of homosexuals had taken form. Their ostensible purpose was to help members to live well-oriented and socially productive lives. And like similar organizations in preceding decades, they sought to attract as little public attention as possible. Then, in the mid-1950s, the homosexual movement went public when it began to publish such magazines as *Ladder* (edited by lesbians), *Mattachine Review*, and *One Magazine*.

How many Americans were homosexual? No one can say for certain, but in their famous study of the sexual behavior of the human male, published in 1948, Alfred Kinsey and his associates estimated that 17 percent of the country's males—an astonishing 12.7 million—were essentially homosexual. In their study of sexual behavior in the human female, published in 1953, Kinsey and his colleagues concluded that the percentage of the country's females who were lesbians was only marginally less.

Whatever their numbers, homosexuals or "gays," as they increasingly referred to themselves, became more and more restive during the 1960s. They doubtless found inspiration in the crusade on behalf of civil equality for black Americans, not to mention that for women's liberation. And they obviously sensed that the current climate of rebellion against traditional customs and mores offered them a rare opportunity to press for what came to be termed "gay rights" or "gay liberation," that is, the decriminalization of all sexual activity by consenting adults and recognition by the population at large that homosexuals were not perverts or queers and, on the contrary, were apt to be honorable citizens who merited the respect of all members of the national society. What they sought ultimately was recognition by their heterosexual compatriots that homosexual behavior and lifestyles were neither deviant nor immoral, that they were normal and morally acceptable alternatives to heterosexual behavior and lifestyles.

Caught up in the gay liberation movement, uncounted men and women of homosexual (and also bisexual) impulse emerged during the 1970s and 1980s, that is, discontinued the charade that they were heterosexuals, and openly acknowledged their sexual preferences. Homosexuals (and bisexuals as well) who hitherto had seldom, if ever, engaged in homosexual activity became sexually active. Many became promiscuous. So-called gay bars where homosexuals gathered to socialize and arrange sexual liaisons came to dot the urban landscape. Gay bathhouses where men often had casual and fleeting sexual relationships appeared in the larger cities. Homosexuals strolled on urban streets hand in hand, on occasion pausing to embrace and kiss. Large numbers of homosexual couples openly cohabitated. Some went through marriage ceremonies.

Meanwhile, the governments of more than 40 cities across the republic passed ordinances prohibiting discrimination in employment and housing based on the sexual preferences of individuals. Twenty-six states removed all felony strictures pertaining to sexual acts between consenting adults. The voters of California in 1978 rejected a ballot proposition requiring the dismissal of any public school employee who was an avowed homosexual or advocated a homosexual lifestyle.

Still, the opposition to gay liberation proved formidable. Great numbers of heterosexual (or "straight") Americans, including many of those who favored decriminalization of homosexual activity between consenting adults, rejected the contention of gay activists that homosexual lifestyles were as natural and as morally defensible as heterosexual lifestyles. Such Americans deplored the manifest increase in gay promiscuity. Observing that many psychologists suspected that homosexuality was a conditioned trait, that is, was not congenital, they were particularly fearful that gay adults might attract or even lure impressionable children to experiment with homosexual practices or give vent to repressed gay tendencies. Hence they were inclined to insist that homosexuals be denied employment as elementary and secondary school teachers. That determination to keep gays out of classrooms was at the heart of an impassioned campaign against gay liberation in Dade County, Florida, in 1977—one that was led by Anita Bryant, a mother of four children and onetime Miss America runner-up, a born-again Baptist and well-known singer and television personality.

Notwithstanding their brave rhetoric, gays must have felt increasingly iso-
lated as the 1970s and 1980s unfolded. Twenty-four states, most of them in
the South and West, refused to repeal sodomy statutes; the Supreme Court
ruled that states do not violate constitutionally protected rights to privacy by
outlawing homosexual conduct involving consenting adults. Of greater moment, Americans in the early 1980s learned of the dreaded disease AIDS, and
that 90 percent of the victims of AIDS were male homosexuals. Inevitably
perhaps, the AIDS epidemic reinforced the antigay hostility of great numbers
of heterosexual Americans. Not only were gays the practitioners of what many
heterosexuals viewed as a perverted and disgusting lifestyle, male gays were
the principal carriers of a deadly disease that threatened to become a veritable
plague. Because AIDS was looked upon as essentially a disease of homosexuals, moreover, the government in Washington, reflecting the perspective of the
great heterosexual majority of the national population, was slow to extend
full-dress support to a scientific campaign to conquer the AIDS virus—or so it
appeared to millions of homosexuals.

## THE NATURAL ENVIRONMENT

As previously noted, environmentalism became a cause célèbre of great numbers of Americans during the tumultuous 1960s. The cause appeared to lose
little if any of its appeal during the 1970s and 1980s. During the latter decades,
indeed, Americans found themselves confronted with a succession of serious
and even frightening (and, arguably, cosmic) questions relating to the natural
environment.

Their natural surroundings, of course, were never far from the consciousness of the people of the United States during the 1970s and 1980s. In addition
to the usual succession of tornados and hurricanes, floods and forest fires, mud
slides and earthquakes (minor ones, fortunately) that caught their attention
during the eighth and ninth decades of the twentieth century, Americans pondered the worst blizzards in memory that swept the midwestern region of their
republic in 1978, the volcanic eruption of Mount St. Helens in southwestern
Washington in 1980, and the most severe drought in more than a half century
that in 1988 devastated the country's agricultural heartland from the Southeast across the Middle West to the High Plains. They also pondered the presence in the national homeland of myriad environmental hazards that threatened the health and, more than that, the lives of people. Most frightening of
all, they considered the possibility that they and the rest of humankind were
rendering such damage to the natural environment that life on earth as it presently exists stands in grave jeopardy.

Raising the level of consciousness of Americans in the matter of the natural environment during this period were a succession of environmental disasters and minidisasters. For example, in 1978 it was disclosed that chemical
wastes oozing from metal drums buried in the 1930s had poisoned the sur-

May 1980: Victims of the environmental catastrophe at Love Canal near Niagara Falls in western New York.

roundings and damaged the health of residents of Love Canal, a comfortable neighborhood situated only 8 miles from the roaring splendor of Niagara Falls in western New York.

Of larger concern was acid rain, that is, rainfall laced with sulfur dioxide and nitrogen oxide emitted by automobiles and electric power plants, steel mills, and other facilities that burn coal. Americans learned in 1978 that acid rain was killing entire populations of fish in lakes in upstate New York. Before long, fish were also reported to be dying of the consequences of acid rain in Wisconsin and in Ontario and elsewhere in Canada—and in the 1980s in Colorado. A killer of trees as well as fish, acid rain also was causing extensive damage to forests, particularly in Canada. As for leaders in Washington, Pres. Jimmy Carter in the latter part of his presidency pledged that the United States would attack the problem on its side of the Canadian-U.S. border. But the administration of Pres. Ronald Reagan in the 1980s, arguing that it needed more information than was presently available regarding the origins and consequences of acid rain, turned aside appeals by the government in Ottawa that the United States redeem Carter's pledge; it only agreed to support research into emissions-control technology.

Generating a great deal more sound and fury than concern over acid rain during the 1970s and 1980s were the often impassioned arguments of environmentalists regarding the horror that might result in the event of an accident at a nuclear power plant. The arguments were not new. Indeed, environmentalists had sought for many years to stir public concern in the matter of nuclear power. They had repeatedly raised the specter of a hydrogen explosion in the reactor of a nuclear generating plant or a meltdown of a reactor core following failure of vital cooling systems. Either calamity presumably would result in the release of lethal radioactivity over a wide area, and the resultant death toll, it was thought, would be catastrophic. Environmentalists also called attention to the problem of disposing radioactive waste materials from nuclear power plants. Such materials would remain lethal for thousands of years. Was there, they asked, any moral justification in leaving such a monstrous bequest to future generations? The laments and warnings of environmentalists had minimal effect. Maintenance of America's economy and lifestyle required mind-boggling outputs of electricity, and a piece of nuclear material the size of a baseball could generate as much electricity as a trainload of coal—and emitted no pollutants into the atmosphere. The outcome during the 1970s was the construction of one nuclear power facility after another, and in 1978 70 operating reactors generated 12.5 percent of the country's total output of electric power.

Then, in the early hours of March 28, 1979, the most frightening accident in the history of the nuclear power industry to that time came to pass: a reactor at Three Mile Island in the Susquehanna River near Harrisburg, Pennsylvania, malfunctioned, its core nearly melted down, and small quantities of radioactive gases were released into the atmosphere. It was an accident that sent shock waves across the country, and touched off a wave of protest demonstrations against nuclear power that were reminiscent of demonstrations against involvement by the United States in the war in Vietnam a few years before. Still, nobody had died or, so far as anyone knew, suffered damage to health as a consequence of the accident at Three Mile Island. In view of the country's ever-increasing appetite for electricity, therefore, it appeared unlikely that nuclear power facilities would be dismantled or the construction of new ones prevented. By the end of 1985, indeed, 95 nuclear power plants were generating 15.5 percent of the country's output of electricity. When a far more serious nuclear accident than that at Three Mile Island, at Chernobyl in the Soviet Union in 1986, resulted in only 31 deaths rather than the thousands—perhaps tens of thousands—that opponents of nuclear power had long contended would be the result of a nuclear accident of such dimension, various of the arguments against nuclear power appeared to lose a good deal of their force.

As the 1980s moved to their close, Americans confronted other environmental problems. They absorbed reports that tides bearing hospital wastes such as hypodermic needles and vials of blood had washed onto beaches at Staten Island and elsewhere and that the "black mayonnaise" at the bottom of Boston harbor contained human sewage and high concentrations of toxic chemicals. They learned that radioactive wastes were poisoning the air and water near facilities in Ohio, South Carolina, and elsewhere that produced components for nuclear weapons. Even more chilling were reports that chlorofluorocarbons (CFCs) emitted by air conditioners, refrigerators, and plastic foam (as used in fast-food containers) were depleting the thin ozone layer in the lower stratosphere (about 15 miles above the earth) that shields the earth from dangerous levels of ultraviolet (UV) radiation. Scientists feared that higher levels of UV would induce mutations in organisms that sustain the food chain in the world's oceans and devastate farm crops, prompt an increase in the incidence of skin cancer among humans and (more frightening) weaken the immune systems of humans. Of the threat presented by destruction of the ozone layer, David Doniger of the Natural Resources Defense Council said in 1988; "It is no exaggeration to say that the health and safety of millions of people around the world are at stake."

## RETROSPECT

The distinguished French historian Pierre Goubert, who has made a point in his writings of emphasizing the assorted activities and struggles of ordinary Frenchmen, has taken the view that the struggles and diversions of ordinary people over the eons of the human experience have been as important as the activities of kings and generals and philosophers. His point is indisputable. But when he writes, for example, of the ordinary people of medieval France, Goubert is writing of a comparative handful of people, most of them peasants, who passed their lives in a fairly uncomplicated preindustrial society. In the early Middle Ages, he observes in *The Course of French History*, France, save for scattered urban islets, was an immense forest, at once dense and frightening, and most ordinary French people were preoccupied with the tasks of clearing little tracts to cultivate a few crops and scouring the forest for berries, nuts, and the meat of wild animals to grace the tables of their unheated hovels. Generalizations about the lives of ordinary people, and nonordinary people as well, come easily when dealing with such a primitive society.

The student of history confronts a far more formidable challenge when striving to offer a portrait of the workaday routine—also the joys and sorrows, hopes and fears, strengths and shortcomings, triumphs and failures—of both ordinary and nonordinary people in a modern industrial society, huge and pulsating and hopelessly diverse, such as that of the United States (or France) in the second half of the twentieth century. Americans are farmers, factory workers, shopkeepers, miners, clerks, computer programmers, students, merchants, pilots, architects, sanitation workers, doctors, lawyers, truck drivers, fire fighters, chemists, therapists, lawyers, criminals, engineers, electricians, police people, teachers, secretaries, accountants, artists, bakers, butchers, bankers, musicians, janitors, carpenters, salespeople, technicians, mechanics, plumbers, bulldozer operators, and practitioners of uncounted other occupations besides. A comparative handful of them are unemployed and homeless. In their leisure hours—and most of them enjoy many leisure hours in the course of a typical week—Americans scan newspapers, watch TV, cruise shopping malls, take in movies and sporting events, concerts and stage plays, listen to recorded music, read books and magazines, work out at health clubs, space out on drugs, seek sexual excitement, participate in religious services, fish and hunt, visit museums and theme parks, visit relatives and friends, play bridge, play poker, buy lottery tickets and bet on horses, travel about their magnificent continental republic, patronize night spots, socialize and consume spirits at local bars or at the Elks Club or American Legion. Although not impossible to formulate, generalizations about the activities and lifestyles of Americans, day in and day out, do not come easily.

The foregoing aside, the 1970s and 1980s were a time when the society of the United States, as noted in the present chapter, was somewhat less agitated—somewhat more mellow—than during the tumultuous 1960s. Still, one must exercise caution or at least discretion when pressing the mellowness theme, for the 1970s and 1980s, if less turbulent than the 1960s, were nonetheless a time when the people of the United States confronted issues and problems, some of them new, some carried over from the 1960s, that generated genuine upset and division among the citizenry: the abortion of living human embryos and fetuses; the country's increasing dependence on foreign sources of energy; the decline of America's manufacturing industries in the face of foreign competition and decisions by multinational corporations to move manufacturing operations offshore; the persistent imbalance in the country's foreign trade; hitherto unimaginable deficits in the federal budget; the "buying of America" by foreign investors; the flood tide of illegal immigration from Latin America and elswhere; homosexuality and gay rights; the continuing quest of women for full equality with men; continued weakening of the traditional nuclear family; day care for the children of gainfully employed parents; the delivery of adequate health care to all citizens, an estimated 37 million of whom were not covered by health insurance in 1988; care of the country's elderly and terminally ill; the manifest shortcomings of the national education establishment; the explosion of the culture of hard drugs and the country's inability to contain, much less make inroads on, the traffic in drugs; how to cope with widespread poverty in the midst of unparalleled abundance; how to cope with crime and criminals; pornography, particularly when it involved children; child molestation and the increasing incidence of rape; the AIDS epidemic; the persistence of racial tension and hostility, not to mention rampant discrimination on account of race, in a republic supposedly committed to absolute equality before the law and equality of opportunity; the sad plight of large numbers of Indian Americans; how to stop the poisoning and devastation of the natural environment.

Although the foregoing litany of some of the more obvious sources of upset and division that nettled Americans during the 1970s and 1980s appears almost interminable, the people of the United States obviously (and inevitably) made their way through the two decades. And it seems fair to say that a majority of them found life, day in and day out, to be reasonably satisfying, particularly during those leisure hours when they could relax in front of the TV and scan all of the channels that were now available to them, go to a movie or a concert or a ball game, go fishing, or drink beer and swap tall tales at the local Moose lodge. Most of them had steady and adequate incomes and plenty to eat, lived in comfortable surroundings, owned or had access to at least one automobile, owned or had access to modern laundry facilities. Most could afford to dine out from time to time (often several times a week) and buy alcoholic and nonalcoholic beverages and snacks galore—also could afford to restock their wardrobes periodically, buy gifts for loved ones at holiday time, and take at least one vacation in the course of a year. Indeed, Americans during the 1970s and 1980s, urged on by advertisers and the dispensers of credit, seemed taken up in what many observers perceived to be a veritable orgy of consumption.

Citizens of the North American superpower could also contemplate achievements by American people of letters and artists, scientists and engineers during the 1970s and 1980s. The achievements of the country's literati and artists may not have been of historic dimension, but they were noteworthy nonetheless. Achievements by scientists and engineers, particularly those who toiled in the vineyards of medicine and digital computers and telecommunications were of genuinely historic dimension. Abiding upset and tension notwithstanding, the 1970s and 1980s were, in the perspective of a majority of the people of the United States, doubtless a fairly propitious time to be alive.

# Chapter
# *12*

# *Conservatism Triumphant*

*T*he terms customarily invoked to denote the political philosophies and principles that have animated a preponderance of Americans from the founding of their republic in the closing decades of the eighteenth century to the present era have been *conservatism* and *liberalism*. According to *Webster's Third New International Dictionary* (1976), conservatism is "the disposition in politics to preserve what is established—a political philosophy based on a strong sense of tradition and social stability, stressing the importance of established institutions (as religion, property, the family, and class structure), and preferring gradual development with preservation of the best elements of the past to abrupt change." Liberalism, according to the same dictionary, is "a political philosophy based on belief in progress, the essential goodness of man, and the autonomy of the individual and standing for tolerance and freedom for the individual from arbitrary authority."

Of the two philosophies (or ideologies), conservatism tended to command the politics of the United States during the first two decades after World War II, notwithstanding victories in presidential elections by the liberals Harry Truman in 1948 and John Kennedy in 1960. But in 1964, conservatism appeared to pass into eclipse when Barry Goldwater, a conservative of the uncompromising genre, went down to crushing defeat when he challenged Lyndon Johnson for the presidency. Conservatism's demise proved transitory. By the time of the next presidential campaign, it had undergone an impressive revival, and when ballots were tabulated on election night in November 1968 two essentially conservative candidates, Richard Nixon and George Wallace, had won 56.9 percent of the popular vote.

Still, the collective voice of the conservative majority of the citizenry was surprisingly muted at the onset of the Nixon presidency in 1969. Only on the issue of busing children to achieve racial balance in public schools did conservatives seem particularly outspoken as the 1960s drew to a close. Then, in the early 1970s, conservatives, a great preponderance of them white, most of them prosperous or even wealthy, or members of middle- or upper-income families, began to express their conservative convictions with increasing vehemence.

Never in the front rank of the movement aimed at achieving civil equality for ethnic and racial minorities (or for women), conservatives accelerated their opposition to "forced busing." They spoke out against affirmative action programs by which minorities, particularly blacks, were guaranteed equal opportunity in the quest for employment and schooling—and often were guaranteed what conservatives thought was more than equal opportunity, that is, were assured that a fixed percentage or quota of available jobs or places in professional schools, even though nonminority applicants for jobs and places might present superior credentials. Conservatives, of course, rejoiced when the Supreme Court sustained the aforementioned challenge by Allan Bakke to the policy of the medical school of the University of California at Davis whereby 16 percent of the openings were reserved for minority students.

Conservatives delighted in the failure of the Equal Rights Amendment to achieve ratification and the inability of liberals to secure some measure of gun control in the United States. They applauded the enactment by assorted municipalities of strictures against the employment of homosexuals and the restoration of capital punishment. Millions of them deplored the Supreme Court's decision in the case of *Roe* v. *Wade* and the resultant elimination of restrictions on abortion—also decisions by the high court forbidding prayer in public schools and, in the view of conservatives, enlarging the rights of criminals and impeding the work of enforcers of the law. Almost to a person, they believed that the country's welfare system was bloated and riddled with corruption, that tax liabilities were outrageous, that the federal bureaucracy was a citadel of waste and inefficiency. They deplored what they believed was the widespread erosion of traditional family values and the love of flag that had animated a preponderance of the citizenry from the founding of the republic. They stood forth as inveterate defenders of free enterprise, and legions of them took a negative view of labor unions. Nearly every true-blue conservative believed that leaders in the Kremlin were the personification of evil, and insisted that the United States must maintain a fearsome arsenal of nuclear and conventional weapons to stay the impulse to aggression and conquest of those evil men in the Kremlin and their clients.

Who emerged as the country's most eloquent and uncompromising champion of conservatism in the 1970s? Easy question. Ronald Wilson Reagan.

## A CONSERVATIVE'S ROAD TO THE WHITE HOUSE

Born in an apartment above a general store in Tampico, Illinois, in 1911, Ronald Reagan grew up in middle-income comfort in Dixon, Illinois, graduated from Eureka College, a small liberal arts college in central Illinois, and became a sports announcer for a radio station in Davenport, Iowa. Then, in 1937, while covering the spring training activities of the Chicago Cubs on Catalina Island off the coast of southern California, he took a screen test and signed a contract offered by the Warner Brothers studio. As a film actor, he received a measure of recognition in 1940 when he portrayed the legendary football player George Gipp in the film *Knute Rockne—All American*, and again in 1941 when he played a small-town playboy whose legs are needlessly amputated in *King's Row*. He married the film actress Jane Wyman in 1940, and entered the armed forces in the spring of 1942. Living at home, he spent most of the next three years making training films for the Army Air Forces in Hollywood.

Reagan's film career went into decline in the years after World War II, his marriage to Wyman ended in divorce in 1949, and in 1952 he married the fledgling film actress Nancy Davis. In the same year that he married Davis, Reagan, to that point a political liberal as well as a Democrat, became the host of television's "General Electric Theater," traveled about the country giving talks in behalf of the General Electric Company, and in the process became an ardent conservative, and also a Republican. Via television, he delivered an impassioned speech in support of Barry Goldwater near the end of the presidential campaign of 1964, and a short time later determined to seek the governorship of California. Elected governor of the Golden State in 1966 and reelected in 1970, Reagan reinforced his credentials as an ardent conservative during his eight years (from 1967 to 1975) in the governor's mansion in Sacramento. He came within an eyelash of wresting the Republican nomination for president from the incumbent chief executive Gerald Ford in 1976, and when Ford went down to defeat the following autumn, he set his sights on the next presidential canvass, although in 1980 he would turn 69, an age traditionally thought to be much too advanced for a presidential aspirant. A handsome man of sunny disposition, one whose skill in delivering prepared remarks rivaled that of Franklin Roosevelt, he felt confident that his age would prove no barrier, and that in the era of television campaigning his looks and skills in communication would strike a chord with voters, most of whom he suspected were in rhythm with his lantern-jawed conservatism, and would propel him into the White House.

Reagan's assessment proved to be squarely on the mark. After a shaky start—his rival for the Republican nomination, George Bush, emerged the winner in the party caucuses in Iowa in January 1980—he swept to victory after victory in Republican presidential primary elections, and was duly nominated when delegates to the GOP national convention assembled in Detroit in July 1980. After failing to persuade former-President Gerald Ford to join him on the ticket, Reagan, in an obvious attempt to appeal to moderate Republicans who might be wary of the ultraconservatism that he appeared to represent (and which had been written into the party's platform for 1980), selected Bush to be his vice presidential running mate.

As for Democrats, few of them felt much enthusiasm for the incumbent president, Jimmy Carter, widely perceived to have been an ineffectual chief executive. Many of them, indeed, favored the candidacy of Sen. Edward M. "Ted" Kennedy. But a rash of newspaper stories reminded voters that a young woman passenger in Kennedy's car had died at Chappaquiddick Island in 1969 under circumstances that in the view of many Americans raised serious questions about Kennedy's character. Accordingly, Carter won most of the primary election contests during the first months of 1980, and he and the incumbent vice president Walter F. Mondale were renominated at the Democratic national convention the following August.

Reagan-Bush and Carter-Mondale, as matters turned out, were not the only presidential tickets that were attracting the attention of America's voters in the late summer and early autumn of 1980. Rep. John M. Anderson, a liberal Republican of Illinois, was seeking the presidency as an independent candidate. His vice presidential running mate was a former governor of Wisconsin, Patrick J. Lucey, a Democrat. An attractive candidate and compelling orator, Anderson sought the support of both anti-Reagan Republicans and anti-Carter Democrats. But well before Election Day it was clear that the Anderson-Lucey ticket would have no bearing on the outcome of the contest between Reagan and Carter.

The Anderson-Lucey candidacy aside, the prospects of President Carter appeared bleak when the electoral campaign moved into high gear in the late summer of 1980. Largely because of rampant inflation, unprecedented interest rates, and the president's inability to resolve the seemingly interminable hostage crisis that had resulted from seizure by Iranian militants of the U.S. embassy in Teheran, not to mention widespread dissatisfaction resulting from his effort to punish the Soviet Union for its invasion of Afghanistan by imposing a partial embargo on grain shipments to the USSR and withdrawing U.S. participation from the Moscow Olympiad, Carter's approval rating in opinion polls had recently plummeted to 21 percent, the lowest figure accorded an incumbent chief executive in the history of polling. But then, in late September of 1980, the Carter campaign began to gather momentum as the president called attention to several bellicose statements made by Reagan and set about to rally blacks, Jews, members of labor unions, and other Americans who had traditionally voted Democratic to his standard.

Ronald Reagan, meanwhile, proved a formidable candidate, notwithstanding occasional gaffes. (He issued a ridiculous statement that "Air pollution has been substantially controlled.") He often made jest of his age, almost always found easy rapport with audiences. His appeal for a New Federalism—essentially a transfer of a fair measure of governmental authority and responsibility, particularly in the matter of social welfare, from the federal government to the states—found a mark with millions of voters. He was adjudged by most observers to have been the winner in a nationally televised "debate" with Carter near the end of the campaign. Exuding warmth and good humor, he remarked in the latter debate that the so-called misery index, representing the combined rates of unemployment and inflation, had increased sharply during Carter's years in the White House, then asked his compatriots, "Are you better off than you were four years ago?" When the aggressive Carter made a point that Reagan appeared to think misstated the latter's actual position, Reagan smiled, tilted his head, and with his melifluous voice intoned, "There you go again."

As the campaign moved to its climax, most pundits were predicting that the balloting between Carter and Reagan would be close. Perhaps pundits had spent too much time trying to analyze the influence on the campaign of "the New Christian Right," that is, adherents of evangelical and fundamentalist Protestant denominations and groups that, urged on by the Reverend Jerry Falwell, had rallied behind the candidacy of Ronald Reagan. In any event, the pundits proved embarrassingly mistaken, for when voters made their way to polling places on November 4, 1980, they accorded Reagan-Bush an overwhelming victory—in popular votes, 51 percent to 41 percent for Carter-Mondale, to 7 percent for Anderson-Lucey, to 1 percent for other tickets. The margin for the GOP ticket in the Electoral College was 489–49. As for Congress, Republicans captured a dozen seats in the Senate hitherto held by Democrats, which meant that when the new Congress convened they would have a majority in the upper chamber for the first time since 1954, and gained 33 seats in the House of Representatives (not enough to give them control of the lower chamber).

## A CONSERVATIVE IN THE WHITE HOUSE

On a platform constructed (for the first time) above the huge steps on the west side of the Capitol, Ronald Reagan repeated the presidential oath on January 20, 1981, then delivered an inaugural address in which he reiterated the familiar conservative theme that big government (or, as he pronounced it, "govment") was largely responsible for the country's current difficulties, particularly in the realm of the economy, and made clear his determination to sharply reduce the role of the federal government in the life of the republic. In their book *The Reagan Record* (1984), John L. Palmer and Isabel V. Sawhill wrote that there had not been such a redirection of public purpose since Franklin Roosevelt's accession to the presidency in 1933.

In the same hour that Reagan repeated the presidential oath, 6,000 miles to the east of Washington, 52 American hostages, near the end of their 444th day of captivity, were shoved past a gauntlet of cursing and kicking Iranian

militants at the Teheran airport and ushered aboard a Boeing 727 of Air Al-
gérie. Within moments, the big aircraft was streaking into the night, the destination of its passengers: the United States. Seventeen days later, the new president, who on moving into the White House had replaced the portrait of Harry
Truman that had hung in the Cabinet room with one of Calvin Coolidge, celebrated his seventieth birthday. Fifty-one days after that, his presidency came
perilously close to termination.

After addressing a convention of the AFL-CIO in the early afternoon of
March 30, 1981, Reagan emerged from the VIP entrance of the Washington
Hilton Hotel. Smiling, the president raised his right arm to wave to onlookers
as he walked to a waiting limousine. At that moment, John Warnock Hinckley, Jr., standing behind a rope barricade about 25 feet from the chief executive,
whipped out a .22 caliber pistol, pointed it in Reagan's direction, and in an
instant fired six shots. Secret Service agent Jerry Parr shoved Reagan into the
limousine and slammed him to the floor. But one of Hinckley's bullets had
ricocheted off the armor of the limousine, pierced Reagan just below the left
arm, traveled down his side, bounced off a rib, punctured a lung, and come to
rest within 3 inches of his heart. Other slugs had caught the presidential press
secretary James Brady (in the forehead, leaving him permanently disabled), a policeman, Thomas Delahanty, and Secret Service agent Timothy
McCarthy.

As the presidential limousine sped away, Reagan began to have trouble
breathing. Whereupon Parr grabbed a radio and advised his headquarters, "Going to George Washington University Hospital. Notify hospital Rawhide
[Reagan's code name] en route." At the hospital, Reagan walked toward the
emergency room, then nearly fainted, and was carried the last steps into the
room. Two hours after surgeons had removed the bullet, the president was
awake and in good spirits. "I forgot to duck," he chided. Notwithstanding his
advanced age, Reagan's recovery was rapid, and in a short time he was back in
the Oval Office. As for Hinckley, a drifter and loner, a jury found him not
guilty by reason of insanity on 13 counts of shooting President Reagan, James
Brady, Thomas Delahanty, and Timothy McCarthy. But he was to be confined
to a mental hospital until such time as authorities might declare him competent.

A fortnight after the attempt on his life, in mid-April 1981, Reagan issued
a statement welcoming the return to earth of the two astronauts who had piloted the space shuttle *Columbia* on its successful maiden flight. A fortnight
after that, to the satisfaction of his fellow conservatives (and to the delight and
relief of great numbers of American farmers) he lifted the partial embargo on
grain shipments from the United States to the Soviet Union that President
Carter had imposed 15 months before following the Soviet invasion of Afghanistan. Next, in July 1981, he warmed the hearts of many (but not all) conservatives (and also the hearts of many feminists) when he nominated the moderately conservative Sandra Day O'Connor, a 51-year-old judge of the Arizona
Court of Appeals and the mother of three sons, to be an associate justice of the
Supreme Court. Quickly confirmed by the Senate, by a vote of 99–0, O'Connor

March 30, 1981: President Reagan grimaces and is shoved into a limousine after being struck by a bullet fired by John W. Hinckley, Jr., outside the Washington Hilton Hotel.

September 24, 1981: Judge Sandra Day O'Connor and Chief Justice Warren Burger before O'Connor's investiture as the first woman associate justice of the Supreme Court.

became the 102nd justice of the the country's highest tribunal, the first of her gender.

Meanwhile, Reagan pondered the condition of the national economy, in truth the great overbearing preoccupation of the fortieth president during the months following John Hinckley's attempt on his life. That condition was anything but robust. Most notably, consumer prices were bounding upward at an annual rate of 14 percent, the prime lending rate was fluctuating around 20 percent, nearly 8 million Americans who wanted jobs were jobless, mortgage rates of 18 percent had overwhelmed the housing market, and imported cars were devastating the country's automobile manufacturers. As for Reagan's perception of what ailed the economy and what was required to restore the economy to health, it was akin to that of Rep. Jack Kemp of New York, Sen. William V. Roth of Delaware, and other proponents of "supply-side" economics. Supply-siders insisted that the federal government, by dramatically reducing taxes and paring down the regulation of business, must provide greater incentives to the suppliers of goods and services, that is, entrepreneurs, investors, and workers. Expansion of the supply side of the economic equation (rather than the demand side) would create its own demand—and energize the economy. In addition to reducing taxes, paring down government regulation of business, and providing incentives to the suppliers of goods and services, Reagan determined to bring about a sharp reduction in federal spending, in the main, he indicated during the electoral campaign in the autumn of 1980, by eliminating waste and "fat" that, in his view, pervaded the federal bureaucracy. The outcome of an attack on waste and fat by a Reagan administration? According to the GOP standard-bearer, the outcome would be a surplus in the federal budget of $23 billion in 1983. (While campaigning for the Republican presidential nomination several months before, George Bush had dismissed Reagan's economic perceptions as "voodoo economics.")

Six weeks after entering the White House, on February 18, 1981, the fortieth chief executive reiterated his views regarding the economy in an address to a joint session of Congress. In accord with those views, he asked the national legislature to reduce federal spending by $41.4 billion during the next fiscal year, in part by reducing funding for such "entitlements" as food stamps and school breakfasts and lunches. (While urging drastic reductions in outlays for entitlements, he urged sharp increases in appropriations for national defense.) But the centerpiece of the new president's "Program for Economic Recovery" was to be a dramatic reduction in taxes.

Turning aside arguments by David A. Stockman, the administration's youthful director of the Office of Management and Budget, that the tax cuts and increased spending for defense that Reagan had proposed would result in a huge deficit in the federal budget, the president prevailed on Congress to approve the substance of his economic recovery program. And by mid-summer of 1981, Congress had lopped $35.2 billion from the budget that Jimmy Carter had presented for fiscal 1982. Then, in mid-August of 1981, Reagan signed legislation that provided the most generous tax reduction in the country's history: an estimated $749 billion through the year 1986. With congressional sanction, meanwhile, the administration, in what appeared to be nothing less than a concerted assault on the social service (or welfare) state inaugurated by Franklin Roosevelt's New Deal administration in the 1930s and enlarged in accord with Lyndon Johnson's Great Society program of the 1960s, tightened eligibility requirements for recipients of Medicaid and Aid to Families with Dependent Children, food stamps and student loans.

How did the economy respond to the initiatives of the new Republican administration? The initial response was distressing. Inasmuch as the Federal Reserve Board, guided by its unflappable chairman Paul A. Volcker, stayed with the policy of high interest rates (to curb inflation), loan rates on new cars reached a wrenching 18 percent, and as a result, during the autumn of 1981, newly manufactured domestic automobiles sold at an annual rate of only 5.3 million. (In 1980, the country's auto dealers had sold 6.5 million new cars of American manufacture, in 1978, 9.3 million.) By November of 1981, the national unemployment rate had moved up to 8.4 percent. And on December 3, Dun & Bradstreet reported that 15,983 businesses had failed during the current year, compared with 11,050 during the same period of 1980. By the dawn of 1982, indeed, the country was in the grip of a full-dress economic recession. The output of the country's manufacturing industries declined sharply, the construction industry endured new reverses, 24,908 commercial and industrial enterprises failed in the period from January to December 1982. In constant (1982) dollars, the GNP in 1982 grew at a rate of *minus* 2.5 percent. By December of 1982, 10.8 percent of the national work force was unemployed.

But then, in 1983, the national economy experienced a strong recovery, and in the view of large numbers of Americans, including the president, that recovery vindicated the conservative economic philosophy that had come to be popularly referred to as Reaganomics. In constant (1982) dollars, the GNP advanced during 1983 by a respectable 3.6 percent, while unemployment declined to 8.2 percent. The prime interest rate fell to 10.8 percent, and, thanks in no small measure to Volcker's persistence in keeping interest rates at a high level during 1981–1982, the consumer price index advanced by only 3.2 percent (compared with 13.5 percent in 1980, the last year of the Carter presidency).

Still, business failures continued at an appalling rate in 1983: 31,334 for the year. Of larger moment in the view of many observers, the country's international trade deficit leaped upward in 1983. What the country paid for imported commodities in 1983 exceeded what it received for its exports by $57.5 billion, up from $31.8 billion in 1982. Responsible in the main for the soaring trade deficit was the country's continuing thirst for foreign oil, its insatiable appetite for an array of foreign manufactured commodities ranging from automobiles and electronic equipment to cameras and clothing and shoes—also to a continuing increase in the value of the dollar in international money markets (largely because foreigners were frenetically buying dollars for investment in the United States). A more highly valued dollar, of course, pushed up the prices of U.S. exports in terms of foreign currencies.

Even more distressing in the perspective of millions of Americans than the trade deficit was the deficit in the federal budget: a staggering $207.8 billion in 1983 (compared with $73.8 billion in 1980, the last year of Jimmy Carter's presidency). Interest charges on the national debt, which by the end of the year stood at an incredible $1.3 trillion, soared to $89.8 billion (compared with $52.5 billion in 1980). But were budgetary deficits a genuine problem? Assorted supply-side enthusiasts contended that they were not—insisted that, in time, federal revenues generated by an economy energized by application of supply-side theories would cause the budget to move into balance.

Whatever nine-digit deficits in the federal budget and a ten-digit national debt might portend, the economic surge of 1983 continued through 1984. In the words of the business news analyst John Cunliff, "Gross national product soared, personal income rose, employment reached record highs, inflation was held in check, interest rates fell, and consumer and business confidence were at levels that seemed unlikely or even impossible just two years before." Still, the country's international trade deficit spiraled to an incredible $107.9 billion, nearly double the record trade deficit of 1983. Down from 1983, the deficit in the federal budget nonetheless stood at $185.3 billion, a staggering figure in the estimate of many Americans. Meanwhile, the national debt advanced to $1.5 trillion.

## GALLOPING CONSERVATISM

The conservative renaissance in public policy at the federal level of government in the United States during the early 1980s assuredly received its most dramatic expression in President Reagan's program for regenerating the national economy. But it also received manifestation in other actions and initiatives undertaken by the fortieth president (various of them, to be sure, bearing in one way or another on his program to restore the North American colossus to economic health).

Reagan determined to relax the federal effort to protect the natural environment. He appointed a former legislator of Colorado, Anne Gorsuch Burford, who had opposed air quality and toxic waste regulations, to head the Environmental Protection Agency (EPA). With Burford's acquiescence, the EPA's budget was thereupon drastically reduced. Under her guidance, the EPA supported revisions of the Clean Air Act that critics thought would severely weaken the existing clean air statute, and urged extensive revision in existing regulations governing the disposal of hazardous wastes which, in the view of critics, would result in reduced protection at existing disposal sites. Under Burford, the EPA also reduced enforcement actions to about one-eighth of what they had been during the presidency of Jimmy Carter. To head the Department of Interior, meanwhile, Reagan appointed an ultraconservative westerner whom he described as his "soul mate," namely, James G. Watt, a man whose preoccupation appeared to be to open lands and resources that were the preserve of the federal government, that is, the preserve of all Americans, to private development and exploitation.

Sharing the conviction of many conservatives that energy decisions should be made in the private sector rather than by the government, Reagan sought to eliminate the Department of Energy. Failing that, he engineered large reductions in the department's budget. Encountering no serious opposition, inasmuch as a world oil glut had pushed down the price of crude oil and prompted at least a temporary abundance in supplies of petroleum, he also arranged a drastic reduction in the budget for the Synthetic Fuels Corporation that Congress had sanctioned in 1980 at the behest of President Carter. He prevailed on Congress to reduce federal assistance to the country's elementary and secondary schools, tried unsuccessfully to dismantle the Department of Education. He spoke out in favor of a constitutional amendment that would clear the way for public schools to set aside time for prayer, and his administration sought to bar federal courts from jurisdiction in legal cases involving prayer in public schools. The Reagan administration sought to lift a 12-year ban on tax relief for educational institutions, notably Bob Jones University in South Carolina, which in the judgment of the IRS practiced racial discrimination. Even the attempt on his life did not prompt Reagan to reverse his opposition to legislation that would regulate the private traffic in firearms in the United States.

To the delight of most conservatives, President Reagan in 1981 blacklisted from all government employment 11,500 striking members of the Professional Airline Traffic Controllers Organization (the controllers were federal employees)—the most devastating defeat for organized labor since the New Deal administration of Franklin Roosevelt in the 1930s had set about to encourage labor unions. To the consternation of feminists, he stood foursquare against the ERA. An outspoken opponent of abortion, he endorsed a resolution offered in the Senate in 1982 by Jesse Helms, Republican of North Carolina, contending that the Supreme Court had erred in 1973 in its decision in *Roe* v. *Wade*. His administration asked the Supreme Court in 1985 to overturn its decision in the *Roe* case. Meanwhile, he endorsed restrictions on criteria that allowed impoverished women to pay for abortions with Medicaid funds.

A man who had opposed the Civil Rights Act of 1964 and the Voting Rights Act of 1965 and supported a ballot proposition in 1964 that invalidated California's fair housing law, Reagan, while insisting that he was totally devoid of racial bigotry, made it clear when he entered the White House that he had no intention of enlarging the function of the federal government in the realm of civil rights and equal opportunity for racial minorities. During the first three years of his presidency, total outlays (when adjusted for inflation) for the enforcement of civil rights and equal opportunity by the federal government declined 9 percent. The budget of the Equal Employment Opportunity Commission (EEOC) was reduced by 10 percent, that of the Office of Federal Contract Compliance Programs (OFCCP) 24 percent. Employment discrimination cases brought by the EEOC and the Department of Justice declined by 50 percent between 1980 and 1983; the number of complaints filed by the OFCCP against federal contractors declined from 53 in fiscal 1980 to 5 in fiscal 1983. Through the first three years of the Reagan administration, the Civil Rights Division of the Justice Department, whose staff was reduced by 13 percent in that period, filed only one school desegregation suit. It filed only 6 fair-housing suits during its first 30 months, compared with 48 during the administration of Jimmy Carter over a comparable period. Like nearly all political conservatives, Reagan took the view that affirmative action was nothing less than reverse discrimination.

On taking the presidency, Reagan warmed the hearts of many conservatives when he set about to reduce the growth in federal outlays for Medicaid, the program by which state and federal funds are disbursed to assist citizens of low income or no income at all in meeting medical and hospital expenses. Federal outlays for Medicaid had increased from $2.7 billion in 1970 to $14.0 billion in 1980 (from $13 per capita to $62 in 1980). To the dismay of conservatives, the president's attempt to trim federal outlays for Medicaid met minimal success. Accordingly, those outlays reached $26.7 billion in 1987 ($110 per capita), total annual payments (from state and federal funds) to Medicaid beneficiaries soared from $23.3 billion in 1980 to $40.8 billion in 1986. As for Medicare, the national health program by which federal (mostly Social Security) funds are disbursed to assist elderly and poverty-ridden Americans in meeting medical and hospital expenses, Reagan, like many conservatives, had never felt much affection for it. But Medicare claimed a huge constituency, namely, tens of millions of senior citizens who would assuredly recoil against the man in the White House should he make a determined effort to slash Medicare benefits. So Reagan proceeded cautiously in the matter of Medicare. He prevailed on Congress to approve marginal increases in the cost-sharing that Medicare requires of its beneficiaries. Otherwise, he left the program alone. Accordingly, outlays for Medicare, which had advanced from $6.2 billion in 1970 to $32.0 billion in 1980, soared to $71.6 billion in 1987 (from $31 per capita in 1970 to $142 in 1980 to $294 in 1987).

Doubtless aware that 30 million retired, widowed, and disabled citizens depended on Social Security—also that millions of youthful and middle-aged citizens expected to receive Social Security benefits when they reached retirement age—Reagan, a longtime critic of the actuarial soundness of Social Security, pledged during the political campaign of 1980 that if elected he would protect the long-term integrity of the Social Security system and maintain benefits for those already receiving them. Still, outlays for Social Security seemed to be spiraling out of control when he entered the White House in 1981—outlays that were placing heavy strain on the federal budget and apparently threatening the viability of the Social Security system. Largely responsible for the spiral were outlays for OASDI: Old Age, Survivors, and Disability Insurance. In 1970, 26.2 million beneficiaries of OASDI had received $31.8 billion in benefit payments. In 1980, 35.5 million beneficiaries received $120.4 billion. Accordingly, in the spring of 1981, Reagan asked Congress to pass legislation that would gradually reduce benefits for existing recipients of OASDI by 23 percent and the benefits of all individuals who henceforth chose to retire at age 62 by 40 percent. The response on Capitol Hill? The Republican-controlled Senate rejected Reagan's proposals by a vote of 96–0, and then came within a single vote of adopting a resolution censuring the president for a "breach of faith" with the millions of gainfully employed Americans who were approaching retirement.

Still, it was clear that something needed to be done about Social Security, and in December 1981 the president appointed a bipartisan National Commission on Social Security Reform. The commission at length offered recommendations that resulted, in 1983, in adoption of Public Law 98-21. PL 98-21 provided for an acceleration of increases in Social Security payroll taxes that already had been scheduled, higher Social Security taxes for the self-employed, a six-month delay in payment of cost-of-living allowances (COLAs) to beneficiaries, and a raising of the retirement age from 65 to 66 by the year 2009 and to 67 by 2027.

An enactment of historic dimension, PL 98–21 put Social Security on a sound actuarial footing—literally rescued the system from fiscal calamity. But to the dismay of such conservatives as David Stockman, it imposed no effective restraints on OASDI benefit payments. Hence those payments, which had totaled $31.8 billion in 1970 and $120.4 billion in 1980, advanced from $167.0 billion in 1983 (the year in which PL 98–21 was adopted) to $196.6 billion in 1986. Outlays for Social Security and Medicare totaled $268.8 billion in 1986, or 27.4 percent of the federal budget. If hemorrhaging deficits in the federal budget were to be brought under control without dramatically increasing taxes, an alternative that was anathema to all conservatives and many liberals as well, or so Stockman and others believed, outlays for Social Security and Medicare must be curtailed.

Whatever the consequences for the federal budget, President Reagan believed it essential that the United States set about to strengthen its armed forces, both nuclear and conventional. From the onset of the Cold War, of course, the Soviets had enjoyed decided superiority vis-à-vis the United States and its allies in conventional land forces. But now they were challenging American superiority on the high seas, and also were developing the capability of projecting their conventional power across the globe. Worse, Reagan suspected, the Soviet Union had probably surpassed the United States in nuclear striking capacity. In such circumstances, the ability of the United States to protect its interests throughout the world and guard its own security had been seriously compromised. Nearly every one of his conservative compatriots, and not a few liberals, shared his assessment. In any event, the revised federal budget drawn up shortly after Reagan's entry in the White House in early 1981 provided for an increase in military-naval spending by $28 billion, the largest increase in such spending in peacetime in the history of the republic. What the president and his secretary of defense, Caspar W. Weinberger, had in mind, in truth, were outlays for the armed forces totaling a mind-boggling $1.46 trillion over the next five years.

The misgivings of many of its members notwithstanding, Congress went along with Reagan, and outlays for national defense in current dollars went from $157.5 billion in 1981 to $265.8 billion in 1986, in constant (1982) dollars from $171.4 billion to $232.0 billion. The result was a substantial strengthening of the national military-naval establishment: more missiles, planes, ships, tanks, aircraft, sealifts. In the contentious and dangerous world of the 1980s, that result was of critical importance, or so thought Ronald Reagan and millions of his compatriots.

# THE EVIL EMPIRE

The political scientist Robert A. Pastor, in an essay that appeared in Kenneth A. Oye et al. (eds.), *Eagle Resurgent?: The Reagan Era in American Foreign Policy* (1987), has written, "Ronald Reagan [on becoming president] offered a vision of the world that was uncluttered with complexities that had distracted previous presidents. All one needed to know was that the United States was engaged in a global struggle against Soviet communism." Pastor's assessment is hard to confute. During his campaign for the White House in the autumn of 1980, Reagan made clear his commitment to the proposition that the passage of time had in no way invalidated the essential verities of the Cold War, to wit, that America and its allies and friends (to paraphrase Pastor) were locked in a death struggle with a ruthless and expansionist Soviet empire. Accordingly, he made little effort to disguise his contempt for the policy of recent administrations in Washington, Republican as well as Democratic, that sought to achieve détente in America's relations with the Soviet empire, and intimated that under his leadership the United States would enter a period of confrontation vis-à-vis the Soviet Union. He proclaimed that if it was to prevail in the interminable struggle with the rival superpower, the United States must build new muscle in its military-naval establishment. He gave voice to what in time would be known as the Reagan Doctrine, to wit, that the United States ought to stand prepared to assist anticommunist resistance movements anywhere in the world. He made clear his determination to restore the much maligned CIA to its former place of eminence in the foreign policy apparatus. The CIA, in a word, would again be an important instrument for covertly achieving the objectives of the United States in international affairs. Reagan's views underwent no perceptible change during his first four years in the White House, and in March 1983 he made one of the most widely quoted utterances of his presidency when, in remarks to a convention of Christian evangelicals in Orlando, Florida, he portrayed the Soviet Union as "an evil empire," and declared that Soviet leaders were "the focus of evil in the modern world."

How did President Reagan intend to deal with the evil empire? Certainly, he intended to deal with it from a position of strength, hence his determination to build up the striking power of the United States. As part of that buildup, the White House announced in 1981 that the United States would assemble enhanced radiation weapons—or, as they were popularly referred to, neutron bombs, that is, nuclear warheads capable of being installed on howitzer shells or Lance battlefield missiles that released great volumes of energy in the form of radiation, very little energy in the form of blast and heat. Presumably, neutron bombs could be used with devastating effect to kill the crews of enemy tanks in the event of a Soviet invasion of Western Europe, and thus offset the overwhelming advantage of the Soviets and their satellites in armored forces. In truth, neutron bombs had been a subject of sometimes heated discussion for several years. And a proposal by President Carter in 1977 that NATO's forces in Western Europe deploy neutron bombs had generated vigorous opposition, both in Western Europe and America. Whereupon, in 1978, Carter let it be known that the United States would merely stockpile components of neutron bombs—in its own territory. Then, in the summer of 1981, the Reagan administration announced that the United States would assemble neutron bombs. Although stockpiled in the United States, the bombs could be dispatched to Europe in a matter of hours should a Soviet or satellite attack appear imminent.

More important, Reagan in the autumn of 1981 announced initiatives intended to close the country's much-discussed "window of vulnerability" to a surprise or preemptive attack on its strategic nuclear forces by the more accurate and powerful ICBMs that the Soviets had deployed in recent years. Analysts in the Pentagon reckoned that the Soviets, by unleashing their missiles in a sneak attack (by way of the North Pole), might destroy up to 90 percent of the land-based ICBM force of the United States (deployed in hardened subterranean "silos" in Arizona, Arkansas, Colorado, Kansas, Missouri, Montana, Nebraska, North Dakota, South Dakota, and Wyoming). During such an attack, it was also reckoned, the Soviets would be able to hold a fair number of ICBMs in reserve—a sufficient number to discourage a retaliatory attack by SLBMs of the U.S. Navy and the U.S. Air Force's aging fleet of B-52 intercontinental bombing planes.

To close the alleged window of vulnerability, President Reagan announced plans to build and deploy a hundred MX "Peacekeeper" ICBMs. Whereas a Minuteman III could carry three 170-kiloton warheads for a distance of 7,000 miles, an MX could carry ten 350-kiloton warheads for a distance of 8,000 miles. The president also announced his administration's intention to build one hundred swept-wing B-1 intercontinental bombers; proceed with research aimed at producing a "Stealth" bomber capable of defying detection by radar; place longer range and more accurate D-5 missiles on the new Trident submarines; improve radar capabilities against enemy bombers by augmenting continental air defenses with AWACS (airborne warning and control system) aircraft; and deploy up to five additional squadrons of F-15 jet interceptors.

Criticism of the new weapons systems sought by the president was impassioned. Critics argued that the systems would prove frightfully expensive and that the MX, given its destructive power and accuracy, would undercut "strategic stability," according to President Carter's national security adviser Zbigniew Brzezinski "the holy grail to defense planners," that is, the dubious assurance that either superpower could absorb a preemptive attack by the other and still respond with an absolutely devastating attack of its own. In a word, the presence of MXs in the American arsenal might tempt the Soviets, during a confrontation with the United States, to fire their missiles first lest they lose them in a preemptive strike by the rival superpower. However vehement and impassioned the critics, Congress responded favorably to the president's appeal for funding for the new weapons systems, including the MX.

Reagan, meanwhile, pressed ahead with plans formulated before he became president to deploy 108 nuclear-tipped Pershing 2 intermediate-range ballistic missiles (IRBMs) and 464 Tomahawk cruise missiles in the territory of the NATO allies in Europe, a deployment proposed by Chancellor Helmut Schmidt of West Germany in 1977 in response to deployment by the Soviets of more than two hundred SS-20 IRBMs, each armed with three nuclear warheads, in Eastern Europe. He pressed ahead after the Soviets categorically rejected his "zero-option" proposal of November 1981 whereby NATO would forgo its plan to deploy Pershing 2 and Tomahawk missiles provided the Soviets would dismantle all of the SS-20s as well as the aging SS-4 and SS-5 missiles that they had deployed in Eastern Europe. The presence of hundreds of Soviet IRBMs in Eastern Europe notwithstanding, Reagan's plan to deploy Pershings and Tomahawks in the territory of his government's European allies touched off a firestorm of criticism in Europe and, at length, in 1983, massive and impassioned protest demonstrations in Amsterdam, Bonn, Brussels, Dublin, Hamburg, Helsinki, London, Madrid, Paris, Rome, Stockholm, Stuttgart, and also in dozens of cities and towns across Canada and the United States.

However impassioned, the demonstrations and protests failed to force a reversal of the decision to deploy the Pershings and Tomahawks. The leaders of West European governments, among them Prime Minister Margaret Thatcher of Great Britain and Chancellor Helmut Kohl of West Germany, agreed with former-Secretary of State Henry Kissinger that failure to deploy the "Euromissiles" would constitute "the first step toward a Soviet veto over any kind of deployment [of weapons systems by NATO] and the first step toward some kind of [West European] neutralism." Accordingly, the deployment of the Pershing 2s and Tomahawks proceeded almost without incident.

Meanwhile, large numbers of Americans were rallying to support of a movement demanding that both the Soviet Union and the United States adopt an immediate, mutual, and verifiable "freeze" on the testing, manufacture, and deployment of nuclear weapons, a freeze that would be followed by systematic reductions in the number of nuclear weapons maintained by the rival superpowers. Giving impetus to the nuclear freeze movement was Jonathan Schell's powerful book *The Fate of the Earth*, published in 1982. Not only would a full-dress nuclear exchange between the superpowers devastate the populations and totally disrupt the economies of the Soviet Union and the United States; according to Schell, it would result in partial destruction of the layer of ozone that surrounds the entire earth in the stratosphere and protects the earth from excessive ultraviolet radiation. The outcome of even partial destruction of the ozone layer? An environmental disaster that would put every human being on earth at risk.

Providing additional impetus to the nuclear freeze movement was a demonstration in June 1982 by an estimated 700,000 freeze proponents who assembled in Central Park in New York City for what *Time* described as a festive day of speeches by antinuclear activists and pop music by antinuclear performers. Less than a year later, in the spring of 1983, the Roman Catholic bishops of the United States issued a 140-page pastoral letter appealing for "immediate bilateral agreements to halt the testing, production, and deployment of new nuclear weapons," and proclaiming, "Under no circumstances may nuclear weapons or other instruments of mass slaughter be used for the purpose of destroying population centers or other predominantly civilian targets." The following autumn, a conference of scientists in Washington posited a bone-chilling "nuclear winter" in the aftermath of a nuclear exchange by the super-powers: frigid temperatures and death by freezing or starvation of all humans in the Northern Hemisphere who survived the nuclear blasts and radioactive fallout, the result of a massive cloud of dust and smoke that would envelop the hemisphere.

However chilling the prospect of a nuclear winter, the climactic moment of the nuclear freeze movement in the United States in the early 1980s came to pass on November 20, 1983, when an estimated 100 million Americans watched the television movie "The Day After," a dramatization of a full-dress nuclear exchange of ICBMs by the superpowers that Harry F. Waters described in *Newsweek* as "The most visually horrific—and politically explosive—two hours of drama ever to ignite the home screen." But contrary to the expecta-tions of proponents of a freeze on the manufacture and deployment of nuclear weapons, "The Day After" prompted no perceptible change in the opinions of the people of the United States in the matter of a freeze. Indeed, in the follow-ing year, 1984, during which Americans concentrated on yet another presiden-tial election, the movement for a freeze appeared to pass from the conscious-ness of all save a veritable handful of the people of the United States.

All questions relating to nuclear weapons, of course, were bound up in the larger question of relations between the Soviet Union and the United States. During the first four years of the Reagan presidency, to nobody's surprise, rela-tions between the United States and "the evil empire" underwent no notable improvement, although, in the view of some commentators, Reagan was more uncompromising in attitude and rhetoric regarding his government's relations with its counterpart in Moscow than in policy and behavior. After all, he aban-doned President Carter's attempt to punish the Soviets for their aggression in Afghanistan by embargoing the shipment of American grain to the Soviet Union. And when the Solidarity trade union in Poland, in the early 1980s, pressed its campaign against the communist regime in Warsaw, little more than a puppet of the Kremlin, he resisted pressure by various of his compatri-ots that he push the Warsaw government to bankruptcy by forcing a default on its American loans. Still, Reagan accelerated his opposition to transactions that would hasten industrial development in the Soviet empire or increase the flow of "hard" currency (especially North American, West European, and Japanese) to the Soviet Union and its satellites. Most importantly, he hotly opposed cooperation by West Europeans in construction of the Yamal pipeline that would deliver natural gas from Siberia to Western Europe and hard cur-rency to Moscow. He also continued his predecessor's program of providing sustenance to those Afghan patriots who were resisting the Soviet invasion of their forbidding homeland.

Overseeing the program of assistance to Afghanistan after Reagan's acces-sion to the presidency, as Bob Woodward has explained in his book *Veil: The Secret Wars of the CIA, 1981–1987* (1987), was the director of the CIA, Wil-liam J. Casey, a crusty and freewheeling lawyer-businessman who had served in the Office of Strategic Services, the CIA's predecessor, during World War II. In the main, the latter program involved the shipment of arms to Islamabad in Pakistan. From Pakistan, presided over by Pres. Mohammed Zia-ul Haq, a military strongman who was a stout ally of the United States, the arms were funneled across the historic Khyber Pass and other rugged mountain passes into Afghanistan.

Reagan and Casey, not to mention millions of their compatriots, took undisguised satisfaction in the results of U.S. endeavors regarding Afghanistan, inasmuch as the Soviets, after the fashion of the Americans in Vietnam more than a decade before, were unable to crush Afghanistan's *mujahidin* (freedom fighters)—and on two occasions in 1982 the mujahidin ambushed Soviet columns, killed scores of Soviet soldiers, then melted away into the mountainous countryside. Still, the campaign to rid Afghanistan of its Soviet conquerors weighed heavily on the Afghan people. To intimidate Afghans, the Soviets blew up villages, burned crops, slaughtered livestock, planted deadly antipersonnel mines in grain fields and pastures. Then, in 1983, they unleashed their air force in a full-dress effort to destroy the civilian base of support for the mujahidin. Eliciting almost no protests from the same people who had denounced aerial warfare by the United States during the war in Vietnam, the Soviets carpet bombed villages and towns. And in a detailed report submitted to the U.S. Congress and the UN in 1983, Secretary of State George Shultz presented laboratory evidence that the Soviets were resorting to chemical warfare—using poison gas—in Afghanistan.

The Soviets further escalated the level of violence in Afghanistan in 1984. Continuing their carpet-bombing tactics, they also unleashed ground attacks against villages and towns. Supported by tanks, artillery, and aircraft, they sought to drive the rebels from strategic valleys. They shelled and bombed targets across the border in Pakistan in an effort to interdict the movement of arms and supplies from Pakistan to the mujahidin and to intimidate the Pakistanis. To little avail. The Afghan rebels became even more determined to resist the Soviet aggressors.

## ARMS CONTROL AND SDI

Whatever the outrages perpetrated by the Soviets in Afghanistan, President Reagan felt compelled to commit his administration to negotiations aimed at producing new arms control agreements with the Kremlin. Accordingly, he allowed so-called intermediate-range nuclear forces (INF) talks, their purpose to produce a treaty reducing intermediate-range nuclear forces, to get under way in Geneva in November 1981. Of larger concern than intermediate-range weapons, of course, were strategic weapons, that is, the long-range ICBMs and SLBMs that the superpowers had targeted on one another.

Persuaded that the SALT II treaty signed by President Carter and General Secretary Brezhnev in 1979 was weighted in favor of the Soviets, Reagan turned aside appeals that he revive that dormant treaty. But at length, in November 1981, he announced that the United States "proposes to open negotiations on strategic arms as soon as possible next year." Six months later, in May 1982, in an address at his alma mater Eureka College, he invited the Soviet Union to join the United States in START (Strategic Arms Reduction Talks), presumably different from SALT in that the emphasis would be on reduction of strategic nuclear arms rather than limitation. The Soviets accepted the presidential invitation, and within a few weeks representatives of the governments in Moscow and Washington had convened in Geneva to undertake negotiations.

Progress in both the INF and START negotiations was agonizingly slow, and in December 1983, in response to deployment by the United States of intermediate-range Pershing 2 and Tomahawk missiles in Western Europe, the Soviets walked out of the INF negotiations. Similarly, when in the same month the fifth round of START negotiations adjourned, they declined to agree to a date for a sixth round. Meanwhile, President Reagan turned aside appeals by arms control advocates that the Washington government strive to negotiate a treaty with the Kremlin proscribing antisatellite (ASAT) weapons systems, that is, systems capable of destroying satellites as they orbited the earth. Arms control advocates believed that reconnaissance by orbiting satellites provided each superpower with essential intelligence information on the military-naval activities of the other, and in so doing reduced uncertainties and misunderstandings about what the other was up to. The prospect that the satellites of either superpower might be destroyed would thus tend to destabilize the superpower relationship and make for uncertainties and misunderstandings that conceivably could have disastrous consequences.

Of greater moment than ASAT weapons, or so it appeared, was SDI, the Strategic Defense Initiative, or "Star Wars," as SDI would soon be popularly referred to. It was in a televised address on March 23, 1983, that President Reagan challenged the country's scientists and engineers to develop SDI, a high-tech and indeed futuristic defensive system that would enable the United States, probably with laser weapons, to zap Soviet ICBMs in flight should the demented masters of "the evil empire" ever have the temerity to send their ICBMs streaking over the top of the world, destination: the missile bases and population centers of the North American citadel of liberty and democracy. Although Reagan was vague in his speech regarding the structure of the strategic defense system he had in mind, the structure and basic technologies of the SDI system that the United States might one day deploy, perhaps in the middle or late 1990s, quickly became public knowledge. Presumably, the system would provide a "layered" defense that would attack Soviet ICBMs at various stages in the course of their flight, destroying a larger number at each stage.

Technologies and strategies aside, the response to the presidential challenge to scientists and engineers to develop SDI came under instant attack. Rep. Theodore S. Weiss, Democrat of New York, caught the sentiment of many critics when he declared, "Never in my wildest dreams could I ever imagine our president taking to the national airwaves to promote a strategy of futuristic 'Star Wars' schemes as Mr. Reagan did last night. . . . Clearly Mr.

Reagan seeks to elevate the current nuclear madness to a new dimension." Critics charged that SDI would prove frightfully expensive and, worse, ineffectual against Soviet ICBMs. Meanwhile, according to critics, the very effort to develop a system for the purpose of defending the United States against nuclear devastation would upset "strategic stability" between the superpowers, to wit, the balance of terror that would presumably prevent either the Soviet Union or the United States from unleashing its ICBMs against the other.

The critics made no perceptible impression on the president. He persisted in his conviction that the United States needed a Star Wars defense because the Soviet Union was a barbarous and treacherous superpower—an evil empire—that in its quest to achieve world supremacy might be tempted to take advantage of what he was certain was its clear superiority in nuclear striking power and at some opportune moment unleash its ICBMs in a preemptive attack on its North American rival. He also professed to believe that the Kremlin, no less than his own administration, intended to develop and deploy a strategic defense or Star Wars system—indeed, had already undertaken development of such a system.

Five and a half months after he inaugurated the great Star Wars debate, on September 1, 1983, Reagan's contention that the Soviet Union was an evil empire received dramatic reinforcement when a Soviet SU-15 fighter plane shot down a Korean Air Lines 747—Flight 007—at the southern tip of the Soviet island of Sakhalin (off the coast of Siberia). On plunging into the Sea of Japan, the huge aircraft took all 269 of its passengers and crew to their deaths. Sixty-one of the victims were Americans, one of them a member of Congress, another a renowned biophysicist. Several months later, in the spring of 1984, Congress authorized $1.4 billion for SDI research.

## EAST AND SOUTH ASIA

KAL Flight 007 went down in the Far East, a vast and teeming area of incalculable import in the economic and strategic calculations of the United States. It was an area of diverse nation-states, which some observers believed was fated to be at the center of America's concerns and interests in world affairs in the decades to come.

The foregoing belief appeared to rest on a firm foundation. A nation-state with which the North American superpower over the past decade had sought to improve political relations and expand trade and cultural exchanges, the People's Republic of China, was the homeland of a quarter of the people of the earth. In ruins at the end of World War II, Japan had become an economic powerhouse whose national output of goods and services (gross national product) trailed only the outputs of the United States and the Soviet Union and whose foreign trade trailed only that of the United States and the Federal Republic of Germany (and did not trail that of West Germany by much). The economies of the Republic of Korea, Taiwan, Hong Kong, Malaysia, and Singapore were thriving—like that of Japan, in no small measure, because of exports of manufactured commodities to North America. (Indeed, Japan and the lesser free enterprise countries of "the Pacific rim" were the source of nearly 40 percent of the imports of the United States in 1983.) Japan, South Korea, and the Philippine Republic were bound to the United States by mutual security treaties. A couple of time zones to the west of Singapore lay India, the world's most populous democracy, a nation-state wracked by poverty and internal discord, one whose relations with the world's second most populous democracy, the United States, had long been strained. To the north of India lay Pakistan, an implacable enemy of India, a friend of the People's Republic of China, and for many years a bulwark of the U.S. policy of containing Soviet power in south-central Asia.

Relations between the United States and the People's Republic of China (PRC) tended to be querulous during Ronald Reagan's first three years in the White House, in no small measure because of the determination of Reagan, a longtime champion of the Chinese Nationalists on Taiwan, to bolster the armed forces of the government in Taipei. But because of their mutual hostility to the Soviet Union, leaders in Beijing and Washington did not permit querulousness to get out of hand. Then, in 1984, relations between China and the United States took a turn for the better. Premier Zhao Ziyang of the PRC traveled to the United States in January 1984, and during his visit signed an agreement to encourage cooperation between China and the United States in industry and technology, and another renewing scientific and technical exchanges. A few months later, in the spring of 1984, President Reagan returned Zhao's visit. He spent six days in the PRC and signed a treaty on corporate income taxes, a pact renewing cultural exchanges, and a nuclear cooperation accord. Exulted the Chinese press, the president's visit "broke ground for an enduring and steady growth in Sino-U.S. relations."

Of no less importance than China in the diplomatic calculations of the United States was Japan. Why that was the case is no mystery. Although its population was a mere 12 percent of that of mainland China and its land area only 4 percent, Japan was one of the world's premier economic powers. (The gross national product of Japan totaled $1.2 trillion in 1984, that of mainland China, $310.5 billion.)

When Ronald Reagan became president in January 1981, at least two problems appeared to cloud the longtime relationship between Japan and the United States: (1) the fact that Japan was making a minuscule contribution to its own national defense; that is, as it had since the end of World War II, Japan was resting secure behind the military-naval shield maintained in the Far East by the United States (and paid for by American taxpayers); and (2) the huge imbalance of trade between the United States and Japan, an imbalance in favor of Japan. Those and other problems came under discussion when Prime Minister Zenko Suzuki conferred with Reagan during a two-day summit meeting in Washington in May 1981. As for defense, the Tokyo government subsequently increased outlays for the Japanese armed forces. Still, as officials in Washington observed, Japan continued to expend less than 1 percent of its GNP for defense.

Of larger moment than Japan's unwillingness to assume what Americans calculated to be a fair share of the burden of its own defense, or so officials in Washington reckoned, was the aforementioned imbalance of trade between Japan and the United States. Totaling $9.9 billion in 1980, that imbalance came to $15.8 billion in 1981. Accounting for a lion's share of Japan's trade surplus vis-à-vis the United States were automobiles. Imports of Japanese cars in the United States, which had totaled 381,000 in 1970, totaled 1.9 million in 1980.

Whatever its much-publicized commitment to the principle of free and un-restricted trade, the Reagan administration in its first months pressed the Japanese to reduce the shipment of automobiles to the United States, and warned that if they failed to do so Congress was apt to impose import barriers against Japanese cars. Heeding the warning, the Tokyo government in May 1981 announced that exports of automobiles to the United States would be cut back (and, as a result, imports of Japanese cars in the United States declined from 1.9 million in 1981 to 1.8 million in 1982, then increased to 2.1 million in 1983 and soared to 3.4 million in 1985). During the following year, 1982, officials in Washington pressed the Tokyo government to reduce barriers to the importation of agricultural commodities and thus clear the way for shipment to Japan of increased quantities of the output of U.S. farmers. President Reagan continued the pressure during a state visit to Japan in November 1983. Turning aside angry protests by Japanese farm organizations, the Tokyo government in the spring of 1984 agreed to a considerable expansion of Japan's import quota on high-grade beef from the United States and to an increase in the importation of citrus fruit products. Nothing seemed to work. Hence the imbalance in trade between Japan and the United States moved to $19.2 billion in 1983, then rocketed to $33.5 billion in 1984 and $56.3 billion in 1987.

Strained during the latter 1970s—in part because of resentment when President Carter pressed the Seoul government to purge itself of its impulse to repression—relations between the United States and the Republic of Korea underwent immediate improvement when Ronald Reagan became president. Indeed, the first head of state (as opposed to head of government) welcomed to the United States by the new Reagan administration in early 1981 was Pres. Chun Doo Hwan of South Korea. Relations between the Seoul and Washington governments became even warmer in 1983 when Reagan traveled to Korea, conferred with Chun, and inspected a U.S. Army outpost along the DMZ. Meanwhile, South Korea's exports to the United States, which had totaled $1.4 billion in 1975, soared to $7.4 billion in 1980 and $16.9 billion in 1987.

Korea was an Asian country whose soil had been stained by the blood of tens of thousands of U.S. fighting men. Vietnam was another. Like such sister clients of the Soviet Union as Cuba and North Korea, Vietnam was a seedy citadel of inefficiency and repression when Ronald Reagan moved into the White House in 1981. However seedy and inefficient, it continued to deploy an estimated 200,000 troops in Cambodia (or, as the ancient Khmer kingdom was now officially known, Kampuchea), and its troops continued to pursue Cambodian resistance groups, the most prominent of which was the Khmer

December 1984: The city of Bhopal in India some eleven days after methyl isocynate gas that leaked from a plant jointly owned by Union Carbide and Indian investors killed 3,000 persons.

Rouge commanded by the infamous Pol Pot. As for the government in Washington, it felt pulled by the Reagan Doctrine to assist insurgents who were countering the Vietnamese and their puppets in Cambodia, and at length, in 1982, Reagan authorized the CIA to dispense $5 million of "nonlethal" assistance to Cambodian resistance groups that were anticommunist (that is, groups other than the Khmer Rouge).

Meanwhile, assorted Americans pressed their government to open a dialogue with its counterpart in Hanoi aimed at discerning the truth of rumors that an undisclosed number of U.S. servicemen taken captive during the late war remained prisoners in Vietnam. Other Americans urged the Washington government to prevail on the Vietnamese to locate and return the bodily remains of several thousand U.S. military-naval personnel, many of them fliers, who presumably had been killed during the war but continued to be listed as MIA (missing in action). Responding to such pressure, the Reagan administration sanctioned low-level negotiations with Vietnam that in 1983 resulted in the return of the remains of eight U.S. servicemen who had died during the war. Two years later, in 1985, U.S. officials flew to Hanoi to secure an accounting of the American MIAs. The Vietnamese indicated that they would provide information regarding MIAs if the Americans would pledge improved relations between the Hanoi and Washington governments. Asserting that the question of MIAs was not negotiable, the Washington government advised leaders in Hanoi that Vietnam's withdrawal from Cambodia was a prerequisite of improved relations between Vietnam and the United States.

One of the few countries other than the Soviet Union and its clients that was extending a hand of friendship to Vietnam at the turn of the 1980s was India, the homeland of 700 million people of diverse and often hostile ethnic and religious groups, and also a land of massive illiteracy and excruciating poverty. Long strained, relations between India and the United States took a turn for the better in 1982 when Prime Minister Indira Gandhi made a state visit to the United States. Unfortunately, Gandhi was near the end of her tenure as leader of India, and on the morning of October 31, 1984, members of her own special security force shot the 66-year-old prime minister to death as she emerged from her residence. (Barely one month later, on December 3, 1984, Indians pondered yet another tragedy: Perhaps 2,000 people died and 150,000 suffered injuries in the city of Bhopal in Central India when toxic gas leaked from a storage tank at a pesticide plant jointly owned by Union Carbide, a U.S. corporation, and Indian investors.)

As for relations between the New Delhi and Washington governments, they remained lukewarm at best. The new prime minister, Rajiv Gandhi, son of Indira Gandhi, made a five-day state visit to the United States in June 1985, conferred with President Reagan, and appeared to make a favorable impression during an address to a joint session of Congress. But Indians continued to take a jaundiced view of arms sales by the United States to Pakistan, and in April 1986 Gandhi roundly denounced the North American superpower in the aftermath of a punitive raid on Libya by U.S. military and naval aircraft.

## IN AFRICA AND THE MIDDLE EAST

The great overbearing problem in Africa when Ronald Reagan entered the White House in 1981 was the inability of much of Africa to provide adequate nourishment for its people. The problem worsened during the years that followed, and as a consequence the people in the United States confronted grisly pictures on television screens and in newsmagazines of veritable herds of starving Africans, many of them crowded into ramshackle refugee camps in Eritrea, Ethiopia, Somalia, and Sudan, their bodies emaciated, bellies swollen, facial expressions vacant. A compassionate man, President Reagan doubtless shared the dismay of his compatriots regarding the famine in Africa. Still, his overarching concern in the matter of that vast continent of 61 nation-states appeared to be the influence of the Soviet Union. Accordingly, he authorized the CIA, in accord with the Reagan Doctrine, to assist resistance groups that were giving battle to the Marxist government of Ethiopia, a client of the Soviet Union, its armed forces presently reinforced by perhaps thirteen thousand troops of Fidel Castro's Cuba. He tried unsuccessfully to prevail on Congress to repeal the so-called Clark Amendment of 1976 prohibiting the Washington government from assisting anti-Marxist guerrillas in Angola, the onetime Portuguese colony presently ruled by a Marxist regime that was aligned with the Soviet Union and bolstered by several thousand Cuban troops.

Of larger import than Ethiopia and Angola in the perspective of leaders in Washington was the Republic of South Africa. Although the object of only one percent of the foreign direct investment of the United States, South Africa provided the North American superpower with such "strategic" metals as chromium, cobalt, manganese, platinum, and vanadium. It also commanded the Cape of Good Hope, and hence the sea lane linking the Indian Ocean with the South Atlantic.

As every knowledgeable American knew in 1981, the year Reagan moved into the White House, South Africa was a country in which a white minority of the population, most of it of Dutch and British descent, maintained absolute control of the general government in Pretoria and enforced with an iron fist the country's abominable system of apartheid, that is, uncompromising discrimination and segregation on the basis of race. Most Americans also knew that seemingly interminable rioting had wracked South Africa since the middle 1970s—ever since an outburst by angry blacks in Soweto, a sprawling ghetto on the fringe of Johannesburg, triggered riots across the length and breadth of the republic.

Precisely what Ronald Reagan thought about South Africa may be open to dispute. Still, it was clear that he was not in agreement with the ideas of Jimmy Carter regarding the country. Unlike Carter, he had no apparent interest in pressing South Africa to get out of Namibia, the onetime colony of German Southwest Africa that South Africa had occupied illegally since the 1960s (when the UN withdrew the mandate to administer Namibia that the League of Nations had assigned to South Africa in the 1920s). Nor did he have any intention of badgering white South Africans after the fashion of Carter regarding apartheid and minority rule, hence had no inclination to fall in with demands by his liberal compatriots that the United States impose an economic boycott against South Africa pending revolutionary modification of the country's socioeconomic system. Rather, he took manifest satisfaction in the militant anticommunism of South Africa's white rulers, the Pretoria government's unflinching support of anti-Marxist rebels in Angola, and the unflagging commitment of South Africa's whites to entrepreneurial capitalism.

Whatever his perceptions, Reagan, after becoming president, gave no heed to those of his compatriots who wanted the United States to take a hard line aimed at coercing the government in Pretoria to abolish the system of apartheid and eliminate obstacles to full participation by blacks in South Africa's political process. At his behest, indeed, the U.S. delegation at the UN was instrumental in turning back efforts to secure international support for mandatory economic sanctions against South Africa pending the dismantling of apartheid and elimination of rule by the republic's white minority. The U.S. delegation likewise opposed initiatives at the UN intended to prevail on South Africa to grant independence to Namibia.

Commanding far more of the attention of the Reagan administration than sub-Saharan Africa was the area reaching from Algeria and Libya across northern Africa to the Arabian Sea and beyond: (very broadly speaking) the Middle East. Devoting large attention to the Middle East marked no new departure by the Washington government. Various its countries blessed with extensive deposits of oil, its politics wracked by seemingly incessant turbulence, the Middle East had been near the center of the concerns of American leaders for the better part of a decade.

Defining Ronald Reagan's view of the Middle East was his conviction that the Soviet Union had evil designs on the oil-rich area (or region), which designs presented a clear and immediate danger to the interests of the United States and its allies and friends. Persuaded that the setbacks endured by the United States in the Middle East in recent years, particularly in regard to Iran, were a consequence of what he perceived to have been his predecessor's lack of toughness and will, Reagan determined to flex American muscles if necessary to protect the interests of the United States in the region. He reckoned further that, because of its financial power and strategic importance, the region of the Persian Gulf was that part of the Middle East in which the interests of the United States were most critical. Thus the fortieth president, turning aside objections by Israel, prevailed on Congress in 1981 to sanction the sale of AWACS intelligence and surveillance aircraft and other military hardware to Saudi Arabia, the linchpin of his strategy for protecting U.S. interests in the region of the gulf. Largely to enable the United States to project its power in the latter region on a moment's notice, he ordered a buildup of the Rapid Deployment Force inaugurated during the presidency of Jimmy Carter.

Meanwhile, another threat to American interests and purposes in the Persian Gulf had taken form: full-dress war between Iran and Iraq. The populations of both Iran and Iraq were overwhelmingly Muslim in religious faith, but only Iraq was Arab. Both countries were important producers of oil. As for the Reagan administration, it began in 1982 to provide minimal covert assistance to Iraq, notwithstanding Iraq's ties with the Soviet Union—when it appeared that the forces of Iran might overwhelm those of Iraq. Its reasons for doing so were scarcely complicated. A grand victory over Iraq by the Ayatollah Khomeini's Islamic republic might give tremendous impetus to Islamic fundamentalism throughout the Muslim world, and the Washington government considered Islamic fundamentalism to be only slightly less dangerous in terms of American interests in the Middle East than Soviet communism.

As for the war, it remained stalemated for year after dreary year, and still remained stalemated at the dawn of 1988. Periodically, the Iranians would mount an offensive in which they would throw youthful Iranians, promised eternal happiness in an afterlife if they became martyrs for the cause of Islamic fundamentalism, against entrenched Iraqi defenders. Occasionally, the Iraqis would launch an aerial strike against Teheran or other targets in Iran. But neither side appeared capable of bringing the other to final defeat, and neither was willing to consider a peace settlement that might be acceptable to the other.

Another source of trouble for the United States in the Middle East when Ronald Reagan became president was Col. Muammar el-Qaddafi, the charismatic and unpredictable leader of oil-rich but sparsely populated Libya since

1969, in the view of many Americans a dangerous radical, a fanatic, and a troublemaker. Anti-Western in orientation and on friendly terms with the Soviet Union, Qaddafi in 1981 was providing support to rebels in pro-Western Oman and Somalia and to the Marxist Sandinista regime in Nicaragua. He also was a fervent Arab nationalist who was dedicated to the destruction of Israel.

As for the Reagan administration, it accused Qaddafi's government of directing a campaign to assassinate Libyan dissidents who had fled the country, and in the spring of 1981 ordered the expulsion of Libyan representatives from Washington. Following a clash between Libyan and American fighter planes in August 1981 during U.S. naval maneuvers in the Gulf of Sidra (off the coast of Libya), which clash claimed two of the Libyan aircraft, President Reagan urged U.S. oil firms to terminate operations in Libya. Next, in December 1981, when intelligence reports indicated that Qaddafi had dispatched Libyan "hit men" to assassinate President Reagan, the chief executive in Washington appealed to the two thousand U.S. citizens who were living in Libya, most of them employees of oil companies, to leave the country at once. And in March 1982, Reagan imposed embargos on the importation of Libyan oil in the United States and on the exportation of American technology to Libya. Following charges by the government in Cairo, in early 1983, that Libyan planes had violated Egyptian air space, the United States dispatched several AWACS planes to Egypt and deployed warships, including the super-carrier USS *Nimitz*, in waters off the Libyan coast. Undaunted, the Libyan strongman in the summer of 1983 dispatched up to four thousand Libyan troops and units of the Libyan air force to assist leftist rebels who were striving to overthrow the central government in neighboring Chad. In that same year, 1983, he also signed a treaty of cooperation and friendship with the Soviet Union.

Of larger import than the carryings-on of Colonel Qaddafi, or so the administration of Ronald Reagan surmised from 1981 to 1984, was the interminable conflict involving Arabs and the Israelis. It was a conflict that gave no indication of abating when Reagan moved into the White House in January 1981.

The peace worked out between Egypt and Israel in the latter 1970s was holding—and would continue to hold after Muslim extremists leaped from an army truck while passing in review during a military parade in Cairo in October 1981 and gunned down Pres. Anwar el-Sadat, on whose initiative peace between Egypt and Israel had come to fruition. Of special moment, the Israelis had completed their withdrawal from the the Sinai peninsula in conformity with the Camp David accords of 1978. Return to Egypt of the Sinai, occupied by the Israelis since 1967, had been one of the two principal objectives of the Camp David agreement. But the Israelis clearly had no intention of pressing ahead toward early fulfillment of the second principal objective of the latter agreement, to wit, negotiations between Egypt, Israel, Jordan, and representatives of the Palestinians to determine the final political status of the West Bank and Gaza. (The dwelling places of perhaps 1.4 million Palestinian Arabs, the West Bank and Gaza had likewise been under Israeli military occupation since 1967.) Indeed, the government in Jerusalem of Prime Minister Menachem Begin, contrary to what American leaders believed was a commitment made by Begin at Camp David, continued to encourage the establishment of settlements of militant Zionists in the West Bank, an area that Begin believed was part of the patrimony promised the Jewish people by God in biblical times. Meanwhile, it became increasingly evident that Begin, also contrary to what leaders of the United States believed he had pledged at Camp David, likewise had no intention of eventually arranging for the extension of "full autonomy" to the Palestinians in the West Bank and Gaza. Rather, eventual annexation of the West Bank and Gaza appeared to be the goal of Begin and militant Zionists. Other Israelis, particularly those who were liberal in political orientation, quailed at the thought that annexation by Israel of the West Bank and Gaza would result in the addition of 1.4 million Palestinians to the Israeli population. Only by wantonly denying political rights to the Palestinians after the fashion of the white-dominated government of South Africa would Israel, should it annex the West Bank and Gaza, find it possible to preserve its distinctive Jewish character. Or so thought Israeli liberals.

As for Ronald Reagan, he took a tolerant view of the policies and initiatives of the Begin government during his first two years in the White House—acquiescing in a daring raid by the Israeli air force on a nuclear reactor in Iraq in June 1981 and the dismissal of Arab mayors on the West Bank in May 1982. Still, as he explained in an address in September 1982, Reagan favored a freeze on Israeli settlements in the West Bank and, while opposing establishment of an independent Palestinian state, gave no support to annexation of the West Bank and Gaza by Israel. His solution to the problem of the West Bank and Gaza? An arrangement whereby the Palestinians would govern themselves under the general supervision of King Hussein's Jordan.

Meanwhile, events transpiring in Lebanon were commanding the attention of Reagan and his advisers. Space limitations prevent a detailed discussion of the tragedy of Lebanon. Suffice it to say that when Reagan became president in 1981 the tragedy was continuing to unfold. Exacerbated by the presence of tens of thousands of Palestinian refugees and several thousand Syrian troops who were deployed in Lebanon, the civil strife involving assorted factions of Muslims and Christians that had devastated Lebanon since the mid-1970s betrayed no sign of letting up. Adding to the tumult was intermittent aerial combat over Lebanon involving Syrian and Israeli warplanes, and also sporadic commando and air raids by Israelis against Palestinian guerrilla strongholds in southern Lebanon.

Then, in June 1982, the Israelis dispatched three columns of tanks and infantry over the Lebanese frontier, ostensibly to destroy the PLO as a political force in Lebanon. Within a fortnight, Israeli forces had reached Beruit, whereupon they put the capital under siege. A cease-fire worked out by the UN in August 1982 and the arrival of a multinational peacekeeping force (MNF) that included U.S. Marines failed to bring an end to the agony of Lebanon. A bomb planted at the headquarters of the Christian Phalangist Party in Beruit in mid-September 1982 killed the country's newly elected president. Two days later,

Christian Phalangist militiamen, "entrusted" by the Israelis with the mission of clearing two thousand PLO guerrillas from Palestinian refugee camps, massacred hundreds of Palestinian children, men, and women.

The situation remained volatile in the months that followed, and in April 1983 a "car bomb" (an automobile laden with high explosives) demolished the U.S. embassy in Beruit and killed more than 60 people. The following summer, artillery shells fired by militia units of the Druze faction killed two U.S. Marines of the MNF who were deployed near the international airport to the west of Beruit. In retaliation—also in support of a drive by government and Phalangist forces to secure control of positions around Beruit recently evacuated by the Israelis—U.S. warships lying offshore and artillery batteries of the Marine Corps pounded Druze positions in the nearby hills. At length, on September 26, 1983, the disputants in the interminable conflict in Lebanon consented to what according to some calculations was their 179th cease-fire agreement since 1976.

Five weeks later, the tragedy of Lebanon struck the emotions of the people of the United States as it never had before. At approximately 6:20 A.M. on October 23, 1983, a yellow Mercedes truck laden with explosives roared past sentries at the entrance to the Marine compound near Beruit's international airport. The driver steered the vehicle straight toward a massive four-story reinforced concrete structure that served as the Marine headquarters and also a barracks. Inside the building more than 300 Marine and Navy personnel were still asleep. The truck crashed into the building. There followed a horrendous explosion that blew the truck and its terrorist occupants to smithereens and turned the barracks into a smoking rubble. Within moments, 241 of the marines lay dead or dying, the worst slaughter of U.S. military personnel since the war in Vietnam. Several weeks later, the interminable conflict again drew the blood of Americans when Syrian artillerists in the hills beyond Beruit zeroed in on U.S. positions near the international airport. The resultant shelling claimed the lives of eight additional U.S. Marines, and during retaliatory air strikes two U.S. fighter-bombers fell victim of Syrian antiaircraft fire.

At length, in February 1984, President Reagan, the American military involvement in Lebanon under increasing criticism by his compatriots, announced plans to redeploy the 1,400 marines of the MNF from the Beruit international airport to ships of the U.S. fleet that were anchored off the shore of Lebanon. For a time after the redeployment of the marines, the superdreadnought USS *New Jersey* hurled heavy ordnance at Druze and Syrian artillery batteries that were shelling east Beruit. But at length, the U.S. flotilla weighed anchor and sailed away, thus terminating the North American superpower's tormented military-naval involvement in Lebanon.

During 1985, the Israelis withdrew the last of their forces from Lebanon, but the Syrians enlarged their influence in the country, and Lebanon became a base from which international terrorists launched attacks hither and yon in Europe and the Middle East and detained foreigners as hostages, usually for the purpose of securing release of Islamic terrorists who had been jailed in various countries. The Lebanese economy, of course, was a shambles. Still, the sectarian factions agreed in 1985 to terminate the ten-year civil war, hence some Lebanese glimpsed a ray of hope that better times might lie ahead.

## IN THE AMERICAS

A global power since the 1940s, the United States had been a hemispheric power for well over a century. Even across those decades when it was pursuing a foreign policy often described as isolationist, the government in Washington repeatedly involved itself in the political affairs of a variety of nation-states in the Western Hemisphere. Its policy of isolation (or nonentanglement or national reserve), in a word, applied to the political affairs (and squabbles and armed conflicts) of the Old World, not the New. The foregoing aside, at the dawn of the 1980s, goings-on in the Americas were never far from the consciousness of the makers and shakers of policy in the State Department and White House in Washington.

Canada and the United States long had been one another's principal trading partners, and the two democratic nation-states shared the longest unfortified international frontier in the world. Still, for a variety of reasons, most of them relating to Canadian trade policy and NATO, relations between Canada and the United States had tended to be nettlesome, if not acerbic, during the 1970s, a decade in which the articulate and suave Pierre Elliott Trudeau, a political liberal, presided over the government in Ottawa. Although Ronald Reagan's first venture outside the United States after his entry in the White House was a two-day state visit to Ottawa in March 1981, relations between Canada and the United States remained troubled during the first years of the Reagan presidency. The governments of the two countries were at odds over a wide assortment of questions: defense, disarmament policy, energy, environmental pollution, fisheries, Latin America, trade.

Then, in 1984, M. Brian Mulroney, a political conservative who shared President Reagan's commitment to unharnessed free enterprise, became Canada's prime minister, and in March 1985 he and Reagan, both men of Irish extraction, held a two-day "shamrock summit" in Quebec that appeared to produce a warming of Canadian-U.S. relations—and, more important, an agreement to begin discussions that historians of the future might rank as the most important negotiations in the annals of the relationship between Canada and the United States, to wit, negotiations aimed at bringing forth a treaty removing all barriers to trade between the two countries. The latter negotiations came to fruition in the autumn of 1987, and on January 2, 1988, Prime Minister Mulroney and President Reagan, in separate ceremonies in Canada and the United States, signed a 250-page treaty which, if consented to by the Senate in Washington and implemented (via the passage of enabling legislation) by the Parliament in Ottawa, would lift all tariffs on trade between the world's two premier trading partners (a total volume of $113.5 billion in 1986—compared with $108.7 billion between Japan and the United States).

As for the U.S. Senate, it quickly ratified the free trade treaty. But in Canada, a vociferous opposition to the handiwork of Reagan and Mulroney took form, whereupon, on the first day of October 1988, the Canadian prime minister called a general election that he knew full well would be for all practical purposes a referendum on free trade with the United States. Effectively countering opposition claims that free trade with Canada's superpowerful neighbor to the south would undermine Canadian sovereignty, threaten regional development and social programs in Canada, and function to Canada's economic disadvantage, Mulroney's Conservative party won a decisive victory when voters trooped to polling places on November 21, 1988. It was a victory that assured the survival of the free trade treaty with the United States.

If Ronald Reagan hoped to improve relations between the United States and Canada when he moved into the White House, he was downright determined to improve relations between the United States and its neighbors to the south, Cuba excepted. Indeed, the first foreign head of government received by the fortieth president was Prime Minister Edward P. G. Seaga of Jamaica, whose conservative Jamaica Labour party had won a landslide victory over the leftist People's National party in the autumn of 1980, only a few days before Reagan's destruction of Jimmy Carter at the polls in the United States. Of larger moment were conversations involving Reagan and Pres. José López Portillo of Mexico, first in Washington in June 1981, then in Mexico City the following October. Amicable relations between Mexico and the United States were essential for a variety of reasons, not the least of them the fact that Mexico was the third-ranking trading partner of the United States (behind Canada and Japan), the United States the first-ranking trading partner of Mexico.

The Reagan-López Portillo talks went well, and in 1982 the United States moved to the aid of Mexico when the government in Mexico City edged toward default on interest payments on its huge foreign debt. Still, relations between Mexico and the United States tended to be labored during the years of the Reagan presidency. López Portillo and his successor Miguel de la Madrid Hurtado repeatedly criticized the Central American policy of the United States, and the de la Madrid government objected vigorously in 1984 when the Congress in Washington considered legislation that threatened to return to their poverty-ridden homeland thousands of Mexicans who had migrated illegally to the United States. For its part, the Reagan administration complained that the Mexicans were doing little to prevent the production of narcotics in Mexico and their export to the United States—indeed charged that relatives of President de la Madrid were involved in the narcotics traffic.

Stemming what appeared to many North Americans to be a torrential flow of drugs, most importantly cocaine, into the United States from Central and South America and the Caribbean was an abiding purpose of the Washington government's policy vis-à-vis its neighbors to the south during the 1980s. But the overarching concern of the Reagan administration when it cast its gaze across the Western Hemisphere was the scourge of communism. In the perception of the so-called Reaganauts, the scourge had spread in recent years, most notably to Nicaragua, and the danger that it would consume other countries, particularly in Central America and the Caribbean, was real and present. However aware that poverty and social inequities were the root causes of political unrest in the countries to the south of the United States, President Reagan and his lieutenants had no doubt that the Soviet Union and its client Cuba were providing encouragement, not to mention guidance and military hardware, to insurrectionists in the countries of the central and southern regions of the hemisphere. Reagan and his cohorts, animated by an almost theological zeal, determined to stand up to the challenge of the Soviets and Cubans and bring the spread of communism in the Americas to a proverbial screeching halt. More than that, in accord with the Reagan Doctrine, they determined to engineer a rollback of communism in the Americas and elsewhere in the world whenever the chances of doing so appeared promising.

In the interest of solidarity among the governments of the hemisphere in the face of the communist threat, the Reagan administration, unlike that of Jimmy Carter, also determined to withhold public expressions of concern regarding human rights violations by noncommunist governments in Latin America. Thus, when police in Argentina in February 1981 arrested three of the country's most prominent human rights activists, the new administration in Washington registered no protest. A short time later, indeed, Reagan received his first state visitor from Latin America, Gen. Roberto Viola, the president-elect of the repressive (indeed murderous) military regime in Buenos Aires. In subsequent months, the administration approved the sale of military equipment to Guatemala and expressed support of development loans to Argentina, Chile, Paraguay, and Uruguay, in all of which countries human rights violations had been rampant. During a visit to Chile in August 1981, the U.S. ambassador to the UN, Jeane J. Kirkpatrick, refused to meet with the country's premier human rights activist Jaime Castillo.

The result of Reagan's new policy toward the undemocratic and repressive noncommunist regimes of Latin America was an immediate warming of U.S. relations with those regimes. Improved relations with those regimes were important, or so reckoned officials in Washington. Of more immediate concern was the situation in Central America, particularly in El Salvador and Nicaragua, where it appeared to many North Americans in the early 1980s that Sovietism and Castroism were on the march.

Nestled along the Pacific coast of Central America, El Salvador was the homeland of 5 million people, several thousand of them employed in the "offshore" factories of such North American corporations as Maidenform and Texas Instruments. It long had been a poverty-ridden country in which much of the work force was unemployed and 2 percent of the population owned 60 percent of the land. Following takeover of the government in San Salvador by a military junta in 1978, El Salvador had fallen victim of a veritable reign of intimidation and violence perpetrated by both the right-wing junta and left-wing insurgents. The agony of El Salvador captured headlines across the world in March 1980 when a gunman, identified as a professional hit man in the hire of ultraconservatives, murdered Archbishop Arnulfo Romero y Galdámez, an eloquent champion of El Salvador's impoverished farmers and workers who regularly protested the depredations of the junta, while the archbishop was celebrating Mass in the cathedral in San Salvador.

The level of violence escalated in the months that followed, as leftist guerrillas and rightist "death squads" prowled urban streets and rural byways, meting out torture and death to individuals deemed hostile to their respective purposes. Among the victims were four churchwomen, three of them nuns, who were citizens of the United States, apparently halted and gunned down by rightists as they drove through the countryside. Eleven days after discovery of the bodies of the four North American women, in December 1980, the reigning junta, in a desperate attempt to restore a measure of stability to the country, elevated the centrist José Napoleon Duarte to the presidency of the Salvadoran republic. An opponent of ultraconservatism as well as Marxism, Duarte favored large-scale redistribution of land, tax reform, and industrial development.

One month after Duarte became president of El Salvador, in January 1981, Ronald Reagan became president of the United States. Persuaded that El Salvador's leftists were, in fact, communists who shared the perceptions and purposes of communists in the Soviet Union and Cuba, Reagan suspected that El Salvador stood in danger of falling under the heel of communism. To counter that danger, he ordered an increase in the number of U.S. military advisers in El Salvador (from 20 to 50). Meanwhile, CIA Director William Casey advised Reagan that the Soviet Union and its East European satellites had shipped arms (including U.S. M-16 rifles captured by the North Vietnamese during the war in Vietnam) and medical supplies to El Salvador's leftist guerrillas by way of Cuba and Nicaragua. As Bob Woodward wrote a few years later in his book *Veil*, "It was a near-perfect case, painting a paper picture of Communist global conspiracy. . . . The hands of the Soviet Union, Cuba, North Vietnam, Eastern Europe and Nicaragua were all involved in directing a supply route aimed at El Salvador. The case was almost as tight as a drum."

## NICARAGUA

The final link in the conduit by which Salvadoran Marxists received munitions and supplies from the Soviet Union and its satellites was of course Nicaragua. Occupying five times the land area of El Salvador but inhabited by one-fourth as many people, Nicaragua itself had been a center of revolutionary turmoil in recent years.

Commanding the government in Managua after 1937 was the dictator Anastasio Somoza García, a right-wing strongman who, to the delight of the Washington government, outlawed Nicaragua's Communist party in the pristine years of the Cold War and assisted the CIA in the overthrow of the leftist Arbenz regime in Guatemala in 1954. In response to Somosa's foursquare anticommunism, the United States established military missions in Nicaragua and provided Somoza's regime with military hardware and economic aid.

Somoza died in 1956 at a U.S. military hospital in the Panama Canal Zone—flown there on the order of President Eisenhower after a Nicaraguan poet and print shop worker had pumped four .38 caliber slugs into Somoza's 220-pound body. Inheriting the Somoza dynasty were the sons of the late dictator, Luis Somoza DeBayle and Anastasio Somoza Debayle. Following the death of Luis as a result of a heart attack in 1967, Anastasio (a graduate of the U.S. Military Academy at West Point in 1946) assumed absolute control of the Managua government. Although the brothers Somoza Debayle proved no less animated by an impulse to tyranny than their late father had been, the Washington government through the 1960s and into the 1970s continued its military and economic assistance to the regime in Managua.

Meanwhile, in 1961, three youthful Nicaraguans, all of them admirers of Fidel Castro, formed the Sandinista National Liberation Front, and before long a minuscule band of Sandinista guerrillas was operating in the mountains near the Honduran border. The goal of the Sandinistas, some of whom were avowed Marxist-Leninists, was overthrow of the Somoza regime and establishment of a socialist government in Nicaragua. It was a goal that found a mark with Nicaragua's peasants, most of whom did not own the land on which they toiled. Still, the Sandinistas made slow headway—until 1972 when an earthquake devastated Managua. Blatant profiteering by Somoza and his cronies in connection with the reconstruction effort alienated large segments of the country's middle- and upper-income groups, and the upshot was new support or at least sympathy for the Sandinistas and other dissident groups. Accordingly, when Jimmy Carter took the presidential oath in Washington, in 1977, the Somoza regime found itself confronted by accelerating insurrection.

The new Carter administration promptly made the Somoza regime a target of its human rights initiative, and to reinforce its pressure on the regime to improve its performance in the area of human rights substantially reduced the Washington government's military and economic assistance to Nicaragua. Contrary to Somoza's charges, the Carter administration did not favor the Sandinistas. Rather, it sought replacement of Somoza's regime by a government presided over by political moderates. Whatever their purposes, the policies of the Carter administration had the effect of reducing the effectiveness of Somoza's armed forces. Meanwhile, the Cuban regime of Fidel Castro, which hitherto had provided scant support to the Sandinistas, dramatically accelerated the shipment of arms to the revolutionaries in Nicaragua. At length, the tide of the struggle turned in favor of the Sandinistas, and in July 1979 Somosa announced his resignation and flew off to Miami. The Sandinistas seized the reins of power in Managua within 24 hours. (Fourteen months later, assassins terminated the 54-year-old Somoza as he rode in his Mercedes along a residential street in Asunción in Paraguay. The ex-dictator left an estate estimated to be in excess of $300 million.)

As for the government in Washington, fully aware of the Marxist orientation of the Sandinistas, it hoped for the best in Nicaragua, and the White House in 1980 prevailed on Congress to vote a credit of $75 million to the new government in Managua. Recalled Jimmy Carter in his memoirs, "We were trying to maintain our ties with Nicaragua, to keep it from turning to Cuba and the Soviet Union." Of comparable moment, Carter also signed a top-secret "finding" authorizing the CIA to encourage the political opposition in Nicaragua—to work against one-party rule in the country and strive to fashion democratic alternatives to groups and individuals suspected of close ties with the Soviet Union and Cuba. By the time Ronald Reagan became president, it was known in Washington that perhaps five hundred Cubans had become entrenched in the communications, intelligence, and military organizations of Nicaragua, and that in addition to the Cubans, agents of the Soviet Union and its European satellites, North Korea, and the PLO were active in the new citadel of Marxism in Central America. Of equal concern to the government in Washington, Nicaragua, as mentioned, had by 1981 become a conduit for the covert shipment of implements of war from the Soviet Union and its satellites to leftist guerrillas in El Salvador. Then, in the spring of 1981, the Sandinistas, apparently in the hope of receiving continued financial aid from the United States, stopped the movement of munitions and supplies to El Salvador's insurgents by way of Nicaragua. Their new restraint availed them nothing, for the Washington government in those same weeks announced the suspension of financial assistance to Nicaragua—arguably a grievous mistake, inasmuch as by suspending financial assistance the United States forfeited its most effective instrument of influence in Nicaragua.

Meanwhile, civil conflict marked by assassination, kidnappings, and sabotage, not to mention murderous shoot-outs between guerrillas and soldiers, kept Nicaragua's neighbor El Salvador in turmoil. Still, 90 percent of the eligible voters of El Salvador trooped to polling places in March 1982 to elect members to a constituent assembly, and the following year the electorate returned José Napoleon Duarte to the presidency. Duarte promptly moved against right-wing "death squads" and in general tried with modest success to eliminate human rights abuses. He also issued a surprise invitation to leaders of the left wing of Salvadoran politics, who presumably represented the interests of the insurgents, to meet with him. The left-wing leaders accepted the invitation, and during an all-day session in a village church in October 1984 discussed an array of issues with Duarte. Although nothing substantive resulted, the meeting encouraged many Salvadorans to hope that a negotiated end to the civil war might not be beyond reach.

The interminable tragedy of El Salvador never ceased to engage the concern of the Reagan administration. Still, as Reagan's first term in the White House unfolded, the Sandinista regime in Nicaragua, presided over by Daniel Ortega Saavedra, was increasingly the focus of the fortieth president and his closest advisers when they weighed the situation in Central America, a situation that in their view was fraught with danger for the strategic interests and indeed the very security of the United States.

Trying to cope with a domestic economy that was a shambles, at odds with the hierarchy of the Roman Catholic Church in Nicaragua—also with the press and labor unions—the Sandinista regime in mid-summer 1981 resumed shipment of munitions and supplies to the guerrillas in El Salvador. In response, in December 1981, President Reagan signed a top-secret finding authorizing political and paramilitary operations aimed at curtailing support by the Sandinistas to the assorted rebel groups in Central America, the substance of which quickly became public knowledge. By spring of 1982, however, interdiction of arms shipments to El Salvador had ceased to be Reagan's principal objective regarding Nicaragua. Clearly, his principal purpose was overthrow of the Sandinista regime. How was overthrow of the Sandinistas to be accomplished? By a "contra" military force made up of anti-Sandinista Nicaraguans that already had taken form, its buildup to be managed by the CIA. It was a force whose members President Reagan would persist in referring to as "freedom fighters," notwithstanding the presence in the contra ranks of many onetime thugs of the infamous Somoza regime. Assisting rebels in a campaign to overthrow a government with which the United States continued to maintain diplomatic relations was, of course, an enterprise that Reagan was reluctant to admit openly. Hence the president and his administration stood by the transparent fiction that the United States was supporting the contras for no other purpose than to interdict shipments of arms from Cuba to El Salvador by way of Nicaragua.

Large numbers of the president's compatriots took a skeptical or even jaundiced view of what his administration was about in Central America, and in December 1982 both houses of Congress passed—and the president signed—the first of several versions of the so-called Boland Amendment prohibiting the CIA and Defense Department from furnishing military equipment, support, or training to anyone "for the purpose of overthrowing the Government of Nicaragua." In the summer of 1983, the House of Representatives voted down an administration request for $80 million to support covert operations in Central America, but then, in December 1983, Congress voted $24 million (rather than the $50 million requested by the administration) to continue covert activities in the region.

Meanwhile, the Reagan administration had sanctioned a succession of operations that were nothing less than acts of war by the United States against Nicaragua. Just before dawn on October 11, 1983, gun-toting speedboats piloted by CIA-trained operatives, raided fuel storage tanks at Nicaragua's port of Cortino. Three days later, the speedboats struck Puerto Sandino. Next, operatives in the hire of the CIA blew up an oil pipeline in the interior of Nicaragua. Then, in early 1984, speedboats and helicopters operating under the control of the CIA planted mines in three Nicaraguan harbors. When Congress almost by accident learned of the mining of the three harbors, most of its members were outraged, and by a vote of 84–12 the Senate adopted a resolution condemning the mining and proclaiming that no federal funds should be expended for "planning, directing, or supporting the mining of the ports or territorial waters of Nicaragua."

As Director Casey of the CIA anticipated, the furor over disclosure of the mining of Nicaraguan harbors quickly dissipated. But the problem of providing the contras with funds remained, and by the thrid month of 1984 funds hitherto voted by Congress had nearly expired. Whereupon the CIA turned to Saudi

Arabia. The outcome, in May 1984, was a secret deal whereby President Reagan, in possible violation of the aforementioned Boland amendment, authorized shipment of 400 Stinger antiaircraft missiles to Saudi Arabia in return for a pledge by the Rhyad government that it would funnel $8 million to the contras. The CIA also extracted a few million dollars for aid to the contras from Israel. Wealthy conservatives in the United States provided additional financial assistance to the contras.

## THE FALKLAND ISLANDS AND GRENADA

Momentarily distracting leaders in Washington from Central America and other areas of concern across the world, in the spring of 1982, was the brief but bitter war between Argentina and Great Britain over control of the Falkland Islands in the South Atlantic, a windswept collection of sparsely populated islands and islets that the British long had occupied and the Argentinians long had claimed. The Falkland Islands War of 1982 broke out when the military junta in Buenos Aires, anticipating that the British would not rally to the defense of a distant island territory that had little economic or strategic importance, ordered an invasion of the islands. As President Reagan had warned the junta, the British responded with unmitigated fury to the invasion. As for the government in Washington, it made no secret of its support for its longtime ally Great Britain in the struggle, but made a frenetic effort to prevail on leaders in both London and Buenos Aires to accept a cease-fire and mediation of the conflict. That effort, as well as a parallel one by the UN, came to nothing. Then, on June 14, 1982, the war ground to a halt when the British expeditionary force compelled the surrender of the last Argentinian garrison in the Falklands. The minuscule war had claimed the lives of 255 Britons and 748 Argentinians.

Citizens of the North American superpower took much interest in the mini-war in the Falkland Islands. Then, in the following year, 1983, they again focused on a mini-war for control of a small piece of insular real estate in the Western Hemisphere: on Grenada in the Eastern Caribbean.

Approximately 21 miles long and (at its widest point) 12 miles across, Grenada, a longtime British colony, became an independent nation-state in 1972. The first prime minister of the new nation-state proved a tyrant, and in 1979, Maurice Bishop, a youthful and charismatic Marxist, and his followers overthrew the tyrant and seized control of the general government. To the annoyance of the United States, Bishop's regime established close ties with Cuba and the Soviet Union, and the prime minister periodically unleashed rhetorical broadsides against the United States. Annoyance became serious concern in 1980 when Bishop's government, a beneficiary of financial and technical assistance extended by Cuba, set about to build, at Point Salines, an airport that was to have a 9,000-foot runway. Leaders in Washington suspected that the airport would provide a new base for MiG fighter aircraft of Fidel Castro's air force and a refueling station for aircraft ferrying munitions and other equipment and supplies from the Soviet Union and Eastern Europe to the Sandinista regime in Nicaragua.

While construction of the airport proceeded, from 1981 to 1983, Bishop found himself increasingly at odds with Grenadian Marxists whose views were more radical than his own. At length, in October 1983, soldiers of the Grenadian army who were loyal to the radicals gunned down Bishop and perhaps a hundred of his supporters. Whereupon the radical general Hudson Austin proclaimed that a "Revolutionary Military Council" would rule the island. At that point, leaders of the six nations of the Organization of Eastern Caribbean

October 25, 1983: A U.S. Marine helicopter hovers over the landing zone during Operation Urgent Fury on Grenada.

States (OECS) (Antigua, Dominica, Montserrat, St. Lucia, St. Kitts-Nevis, and St. Vincent), fearing that the bloody takeover of Grenada by leftist radicals might embolden Castro-admiring revolutionaries within their own borders, appealed to the United States to provide the requisite military muscle to counter the radical leftists in Grenada.

The appeal by the OECS—endorsed by the leaders of Barbados and Jamaica—found a mark with Ronald Reagan, and on the evening of October 23, 1983, the president signed an order that set in motion Operation Urgent Fury, an invasion of Grenada by armed forces of the United States. In addition to restoring democracy and order to the island, so he subsequently explained, the United States was also acting out of concern for the safety of upward of a thousand North Americans who were marooned in strife-torn Grenada, many of them students at St. George's Medical College.

As for the invasion, it got under way on October 25, and involved Navy commandos, airborne Rangers and paratroops of the Army, and U.S. Marines. The sharpest combat involved the Rangers, who met stiff resistance by units of the Grenadian army and an undisclosed number of Cuban construction workers and military advisers when they parachuted onto the airfield at Port Salines. But within an hour or so, the Rangers and troops of the 82nd Airborne Division who had arrived aboard C-130 troop carriers, supported by A-6 Intruders and A-7 Corsairs launched by the carrier USS *Independence* and Cobra helicopter gunships, secured the airfield, and for all practical purposes terminated the battle for Grenada.

Operation Urgent Fury claimed the lives of 18 U.S. servicemen, 59 soldiers of the Grenadian Army, 71 Cubans, and 160 Grenadian civilians. It was an operation that appeared to warm the hearts of most of President Reagan's compatriots. People in most other areas of the world, including the countries of the NATO allies of the United States, took a decidedly different view, and by a vote of 108–9 (with 27 abstentions) the General Assembly of the UN "deeply deplored" the invasion and described it as a "flagrant violation of international law." Still, it soon became clear that the Soviet Union and Cuba had indeed been turning Grenada into a bastion of support for their adventures in the Caribbean and Central America. U.S. troops uncovered large caches of weapons, ammunition, and other supplies that were far beyond the requirements of the tiny Grenadian army—also documents disclosing arrangements whereby Cuba, North Korea, and the Soviet Union would deliver additional weapons. Of equal import, at least in the view of many people in the United States, a preponderance of the citizenry of Grenada clearly welcomed the action by the United States against the Marxists who had taken control of their little island and were striving to make it an outpost of Soviet-Cuban power. Indeed, most Grenadians appeared to view the North Americans as liberators. Grenadians nonetheless made it clear that they did not want their liberators to remain indefinitely. Accordingly, they were manifestly pleased when on December 15, 1983, the last U.S. troops—save for three hundred advisory personnel—departed their island.

# RETROSPECT

Arguably, Ronald Reagan was the least cerebral of the ten men who have occupied the Oval Office in Washington since World War II. He was (like most of his predecessors, in all candor) poorly read. He was not given to hard, logical thinking. His friends and admirers could only wince when in public remarks he confused events that had transpired in the illusory world of Hollywood films with reality. In the words of David Stockman, "Reagan's body of knowledge is primarily impressionistic; he registers anecdotes rather than concepts." Reagan was, moreover, a president who, unlike such predecessors as Lyndon Johnson, Richard Nixon, and Jimmy Carter, tended to disengage himself from the details of administration. He often appeared disinterested if not bemused by fine points of argument relating to high policy. On occasion, he appeared to doze off when ranking members of the administration debated those fine points.

Still, Reagan, whatever his intellectual deficiencies and administrative detachment, had a clear vision of the direction in which he wanted to move the republic and a grim determination to bring that vision to fruition. The vision, of course, was unabashedly conservative. The fortieth president was bent on reversing the half-century trend whereby the national government assumed ever-increasing responsibility for guaranteeing the economic security and general welfare of the people of the United States and attacked what Americans of liberal orientation believed were transparent abuses that weighed down on the national society. Most importantly, he wanted to slash federal taxes, reduce federal spending, pare down federal regulation of business—removing what he perceived to be federally imposed shackles that were thwarting the entrepreneurial spirit which he believed had been responsible for making the United States the world's premier economic power. He also was bent on restoring the armed forces of the United States to their onetime position of supremacy vis-à-vis those of its rival superpower, the Soviet Union, and countering the expansionism of the Soviets and their clients as the United States had done in the two decades before the misadventure in Vietnam drained its people of the will to contain the expansionist impulses of "the evil empire."

Because of his grim determination—and because, for all of his deficiencies, intellectual and otherwise, he was able to retain the confidence and support (and more than that, the abiding affection) of a fair majority of his compatriots—Reagan succeeded during the years from 1981 to 1984 in moving the country in accord with his vision. Of post–World War II presidents, only Lyndon Johnson in 1964–1965 had comparable success in converting vision to reality. Reagan brought about cutbacks in the funding of federal programs that fell in the category of public welfare and eliminated others. He engineered a reduction in federal taxes of historic proportions, managed at least a marginal reduction in the annual rate of increase in federal spending. He arranged the removal of assorted restraints on entrepreneurial enterprise and presided over a dramatic buildup of the country's armed forces. He challenged the Soviets and their clients at a variety of points across the world. Contrary to the popular wisdom, he was not a revolutionary; there came to pass no such event as a "Reagan Revolution." The structure of the social service (or guarantor or welfare) state that had taken form in the republic from 1933 to 1938 by the initiative of Franklin Roosevelt and his New Deal administration was not dismantled. The national clock was not turned back to 1932. Still, the creeping expansion of the social service state was brought to a halt. More than that, the social service state was pared down—not a great deal, in truth, but pared down nonetheless.

Reagan, then, proved himself to be a strong president, one who made important strides toward realigning the relationship between the federal government and the citizenry in accord with his conservative vision. Alas, the question remains: How well did the policies and initiatives of the fortieth president serve the republic and its people during the years 1981–1984?

Apparently responding to the fiscal policies of the Reagan administration—also the monetary policies of the Federal Reserve Board—the national economy, after enduring a bitter recession in 1982, moved into a lengthy period of growth and stability that resulted in prosperity for a preponderance of Americans, one that had not yet run its course at the dawn of 1989. The country's armed forces became demonstrably stronger, and Americans perceived that enhanced military-naval power had prompted the outer world to accord the United States, often viewed with disdain by foes and friends alike in the years before 1981 (or so most Americans believed), renewed respect. The United States was instrumental in thwarting Soviet imperialism in Afghanistan. It prevented Grenada from becoming a new outpost for Sovietism and Castroism in the Caribbean. Meanwhile, for whatever reasons, most Americans came to take a more optimistic view of the condition and prospects of their republic than they had entertained on that cold day in January of 1981 when Ronald Reagan repeated the presidential oath. Gone was the malaise that had appeared to hang over the republic during the presidencies of Gerald Ford and Jimmy Carter.

There was, alas, another side to the Reagan record. Deficits in the federal budget raged out of control. (Only people who believed in the tooth fairy swallowed the president's inane contention that blame for the deficits rested exclusively with his Democratic adversaries.) The outstanding gross debt of the federal government skyrocketed. Deficits in the country's international trade balance likewise raged out of control. And, indeed, unbeknownst to most Americans at the time, the United States, which for six decades had been the world's premier creditor nation vis-à-vis the outer world was about to become a debtor nation—and in 1986 would become the premier debtor nation in the world. Meanwhile, the number of Americans living in poverty increased, from a scandalous 29.3 million in 1980 to an even more scandalous 33.7 million in Reagan's fourth year in the White House. As was often remarked, rich Americans became richer during the years of Ronald Reagan, poor Americans poorer. The administration in Washington clearly had little interest in advancing the cause of civil rights for racial and ethnic minorities or the cause of environmental protection. Drugs cascaded into the country in ever-increasing volumes. For all of the administration's emphasis on law and order, urban streets were no less dangerous to law-abiding citizens than formerly. In foreign affairs, the United States found itself at loggerheads with the rival superpower; arms control negotiations appeared to go nowhere. The country's involvement in the interminable conflict in Lebanon proved disastrous; its tacit support of the racist regime in South Africa, not to mention repressive regimes in Latin America, was scandalous. Its policy in Central America was of dubious wisdom, some of its initiatives regarding the area of dubious legality.

What individual Americans thought of Reagan's first years in the White House probably depended in the main on their economic circumstances and skin color, and also their perception of the threat posed to "the free world" by "the evil empire" and its clients. What Americans collectively thought of the Reagan stewardship would soon become apparent, for in November 1984 millions of them would make their way to polling places to pass judgment on the performance of the pink-cheeked man of sunny disposition who had presided over the national destiny since January 20, 1981.

# Chapter
# *13*

# *In the Second Term of Reagan*

Although Ronald Reagan would be nearly 78 years old by the time he completed a second term in the White House on January 20, 1989, scarcely any Republican at the dawn of 1984 gave even passing thought to the proposition that the Grand Old Party might be advised to choose a different (and of course younger) nominee for president when delegates to its national convention assembled in Dallas the following summer. The reason was transparent. Four years in the Oval Office had in no way diminished Reagan's hold on the affections of a preponderance of his compatriots. Indeed, opinion polls in January 1984 disclosed that 57 percent of the citizenry approved of Reagan's presidential performance and only 32 percent disapproved, numbers that were impressive by any standard of measure. Democrats might grouse that Reagan was a "Teflon president," that after the fashion of cookware treated with the synthetic substance polymer (Teflon), the blame for policy failures of his administration did not stick to him. But the plain truth was that as 1983 gave way to 1984 a clear majority of Americans remained mesmerized by the onetime film actor who had presided over the national destiny since January 20, 1981. No less than in 1980, millions of citizens continued to view Reagan as a kind, friendly, and honorable man whose persona they found totally captivating. They also perceived him to be a wise and effective leader who during the preceding three years had regenerated the national economy and restored the prestige and power of the United States in the world arena. In the view of Republicans, then, Reagan, a remarkable physical specimen for a man who had reached his mid-seventies, was a sure bet to win re-election in 1984.

It is almost axiomatic, of course, that neither of the major political parties in the United States is apt to deny its presidential nomination to a sure winner, provided the sure winner is willing to be a candidate. Well, Ronald Reagan was clearly willing, indeed anxious, to be a candidate for re-election in 1984. Accordingly, delegates to the Republican national convention, in August 1984, enthusiastically and unanimously renominated President Reagan, and Vice President George Bush as well.

Reagan's soaring popularity notwithstanding, a covey of Democrats at the onset of 1984 was seeking the opportunity to try to unseat the incumbent president in the impending electoral contest, among them former-Vice President Walter F. Mondale of Minnesota and Sen. Gary Hart of Colorado—also the charismatic civil rights activist and Baptist minister, the Reverend Jesse L. Jackson of Illinois, the first black American to organize a full-dress presidential campaign. Although nobody, himself included, reckoned that he stood any chance at all to win his party's nomination for president, Jackson hoped to rally to his candidacy what he referred to as a "rainbow coalition" of diverse ethnic and racial groups that would enable him to make an imprint on the platform to be adopted at the Democratic national convention in July 1984 and exercise a measure of influence on the subsequent campaign against the Republicans. Clearly, the front-runner for the presidential nomination of the world's oldest political party at the start of 1984 was "Fritz" Mondale. And at length, on June 5, Mondale secured the requisite delegate commitments to assure his nomination. A short time later, he announced that he would ask delegates to the party's national convention to nominate Congresswoman Geraldine A. Ferraro of New York for the vice presidency. That announcement was genuinely historic, for never before had either of the major American political parties placed a woman on a presidential ticket.

Delegates to the Democratic convention in San Francisco in July 1984, their spirits lifted by a stirring keynote address by Gov. Mario M. Cuomo of New York, duly nominated Mondale and Ferraro. Then, in his speech accepting the nomination, Mondale, committed as he was to bringing the federal budget into balance, intoned, "Let's tell the truth. Mr. Reagan will raise taxes, and so will I. He won't tell you. I just did." The latter statement scarcely ignited the country's voters, most of whom regarded the prospect of paying higher taxes as sheer anathema. In any event, the outcome of the subsequent Reagan-Mondale campaign was apparent long before Election Day. The Republicans conducted what *Newsweek* could describe as "the richest, slickest,

August 1984: The Democratic nominee for vice president, Geraldine Ferraro, waves to supporters during a noon rally in downtown St. Louis.

smartest campaign in recent memory." Reagan struck a chord with millions of Americans when he challenged voters with the rhetorical question, "Are you better off now than you were four years ago?" And when votes were tabulated on the evening of November 6, the ticket of Reagan-Bush had buried that of Mondale-Ferraro by 54.4 million popular votes (58.8 percent of the total) to 37.5 million. Reagan-Bush won the electoral votes of 49 states, Mondale-Ferraro those of only 1 state, Minnesota, and the District of Columbia. The outcome in the Electoral College was 525–13, the most one-sided count in the antiquated "college" since Franklin Roosevelt overwhelmed Alfred M. Landon in 1936. Still, as the pundits expressed it, Reagan's coattails proved short, hence the Democrats retained firm control of the House of Representatives and reduced the Republican majority in the Senate by two seats.

## THE ECONOMY AND THE BUDGET

Ronald Reagan repeated the presidential oath for the second time on January 20, 1985, and to his immense satisfaction the national economy continued its impressive performance in the months and years that followed—indeed, generally exceeded the expectations of most economists. Encouraged by healthy profits, corporate leaders accelerated investment in new equipment, plants, products, and services. The appetites of domestic consumers for the goods and services generated by the country's myriad producers of goods and services seemed insatiable. Caught up LBOs the prevailing mood of optimism, inevitably perhaps, were investors and speculators in corporate stocks, whose frenetic buying pushed stock market quotations to record heights. The frenzied buying of stocks did not diminish in 1986–1987 in the face of disclosures that prominent brokers had reaped illegal profits of monstrous dimension via "insider trading," that is, taking advantage of information regarding the activities and true conditions of corporations that was not available to ordinary traders in securities.

Still, no small number of economists expressed concern about the state of the U.S. economy and also about assorted goings-on and phenomena that were influencing the economic life of the country. Many economists were disturbed by figures disclosing that corporations and individuals were borrowing with unprecedented abandon. According to a report issued by the Morgan Guaranty Trust Company of New York in 1985, "Credit use has virtually exploded. Credit growth no longer is moving in close step with economic growth, as it did for decades."

Economists also fretted about the spate of "leveraged buyouts" (LBOs) of corporations in recent years. In an LBO, another corporation or entrepreneur or group of entrepreneurs, financing activities with "junk bonds" (high-yield, extra-risky securities often issued by little-known firms with low credit ratings), would acquire a majority share of a target company by offering shareholders above-market prices for their stock. LBOs caught the attention of the citizenry at large in the late autumn of 1988 when so-called buyout barons waged a titanic struggle for control of the giant tobacco-and-food conglomerate RJR Nabisco. The winner of the latter struggle, the buyout firm of Kohlberg Kravis Roberts, paid shareholders $109 per share (a total of $25 billion) for stock that two months before had traded for $56 a share. Critics lamented that LBOs tended to result in the diversion of capital from research and development, and also in the gutting of large corporations, inasmuch as the new owners of a corporate conglomerate acquired by leveraged buyout often found it necessary to sell off profitable divisions of the corporation to raise the funds required to meet interest payments on the gargantuan loans transacted to execute the LBO. Critics also complained that the country's taxpayers were, in fact, underwriting LBOs in the amount of billions of dollars, inasmuch as interest payments on those gargantuan loans were deductible as business expenses. And what, critics asked, would be the fate of corporations weighted down with huge debts resulting from LBOs in the event of a sharp economic recession? What would be the consequences for the economy at large during a recession if an array of such corporations faltered?

Of larger concern in the estimate of many economists and certainly millions of citizens who knew next to nothing about the principles and theories of economics were annual deficits in the country's balance of trade with the rest of the world, annual deficits in the federal budget, and the ever-enlarging public (or national) debt. From $8.3 billion in 1976, the deficit in the annual balance of international trade soared to $152.7 in 1986. From $73.8 billion in 1980, the annual deficit in the federal budget reached $220.7 billion in 1986. From $907.7 billion at the end of 1980, the public debt of the United States soared to $2.1 trillion by the end of 1986. Totaling $74.9 billion in 1980 (12.7 percent of total federal outlays), interest payments on the public debt totaled $179.8 billion in 1985 (18.9 percent of total federal outlays).

As Ronald Reagan's second term in the White House unfolded, Americans became increasingly aware of some of the consequences of trade and budgetary deficits. Most startling perhaps, the North American superpower in 1985, largely as a result of of its craving for foreign commodities (for example, oil from Africa, Latin America, and the Middle East and cars from Japan) and the need to borrow from abroad to finance interest payments on the huge deficits in the federal budget (as already mentioned), joined the ranks of an array of struggling Third World countries by becoming a debtor nation. In a word, U.S. assets in foreign countries (including credits and other long-term assets held by the U.S. government, the direct investments of U.S. corporations and individual Americans, and claims against foreigners held by U.S. banks) were now less than foreign assets in the United States (for example, U.S. government securities held by foreigners, the direct investments of foreign corporations, governments, and individuals, and claims by foreigners against corporations and individuals in the United States). Writing a short time later in their book *Buying into America: How Foreign Money Is Changing the Face of Our Nation* (1988), Martin and Susan Tolchin asserted, "The magnitude of the debt [of Americans and their national government to foreigners] is rapidly approaching the $1 trillion mark. If allowed to continue, it will soon far exceed that of Latin America and eventually all of the developing countries [combined]."

In an effort to cope with the problem of deficits in the federal budget, Congress in December 1985 passed the Gramm-Rudman-Hollings Act, a controversial measure mandating that the deficit for 1987 not exceed $144 billion and that it thereupon be steadily reduced until the budget achieved balance in 1991. In accord with the legislation, the Office of Management and Budget and the Congressional Budget Office on August 20 of each year were to jointly forecast whether the federal budget would meet the Gramm-Rudman-Hollings target for the coming fiscal year. If the joint forecast determined that the budget would not meet the target, the General Accounting Office would compile a list of across-the-board reductions (save for Social Security, several antipoverty programs, and most veterans benefits), evenly divided between domestic and military-naval programs, that were deemed necessary to bring the budget into compliance with the target. To avoid the automatic across-the-board reductions, Congress would have until September 30 to write new legislation—which might include a tax increase—to bring the budget into compliance with the Gramm-Rudman-Hollings target.

Annoyed that the Gramm-Rudman-Hollings buzz saw would not exempt outlays for the armed forces, President Reagan signed the legislation with undisguised reluctance—in the privacy of his office rather than in a gala public ceremony. Then, a few weeks later, he released his budget for fiscal 1987. The budget anticipated a deficit of $143.6 billion, just under the maximum of $144 billion permitted by the Gramm-Rudman-Hollings deficit reduction schedule for the fiscal year. (As matters turned out, the deficit for fiscal 1987 totaled $148 billion, compared with $220.7 billion for fiscal 1986.)

While pondering the nagging problem of deficits in the federal budget, millions of middle- and lower-income Americans became increasingly persuaded that because of an array of shelters and "loopholes" the federal tax code functioned to the unfair advantage of a comparatively small number of upper-income taxpayers. A majority of the members of Congress agreed, and in the autumn of 1986 the national legislature passed and the president signed the Tax Reform Act. Although "revenue neutral," that is, not intended to bring about a net increase in federal tax revenues, the tax reform legislation—in addition to repealing an array of tax preferences—modified tax burdens for different categories of taxpayers. Most importantly, the tax liabilities of individual taxpayers would be reduced by approximately $120 billion over the next five years; those of corporate taxpayers would be raised by a corresponding amount.

When Reagan signed the Tax Reform Act, on October 22, 1987, his compatriots were pondering what appeared to most of them to have been a happening of more immediate and conceivably of far greater moment, to wit, they were striving to sort out the causes and probable consequences of a frightening shock that the financial community had absorbed three days before. It was a shock the likes of which the financial community had not absorbed in 58 years, since those memorable days of October 1929.

The proverbial bull that had commanded the stock market in recent years drove the Dow Jones average of 30 leading industrial stocks to a record 2,722 on August 25, 1987. There followed, over the next several weeks, a gradual slide in stock prices. Then, suddenly, on October 14, the Dow plunged 95 points. It lost 57 points on October 15 and 108 on Friday, October 16. The weekend brought no reprieve, and when brokers and money managers in New York went to work on Monday morning, October 19, they found themselves deluged by orders of panic-gripped owners of securities to sell said securities. In a scene reminiscent of the Great Crash of October 1929, pandemonium broke out on the floor of the New York Stock Exchange (NYSE), a crowd of anxious and curious onlookers gathered along Wall Street outside the citadel of finance, and by the time the closing bell rang inside the NYSE, at 4 o'clock in the afternoon, the Dow had lost an incredible 508 points—had plummeted 22.6 percent to close the day at 1,738.

What had caused the great stock market crash of October 1987? In the view of many Americans, the crash was an inexorable consequence of what such citizens perceived to have been an orgy of greed that had captivated their compatriots who bought and sold corporate securities. More sophisticated observers of the stock market were inclined to attach considerable blame for the crash of 1987 to "program trading," a complicated phenomenon in one form

October 28, 1987: Traders scramble to keep pace with the plunging stock market at the New York Stock Exchange.

of which a decline in stock prices in New York prompted computers to instruct money managers to compensate for the decline by selling stock-index futures (that is, contracts to deliver packages of stock at fixed prices at future dates) in the futures market in Chicago, which in turn pushed stock prices down further and prompted computers to instruct money managers to sell more futures—according to a report in *Newsweek*, a vicious cycle.

Whatever the causes of the stock market debacle of 1987, nearly every analyst, or so it seemed, began his or her prescription on what must be done to prevent the great crash of 1987 from becoming the harbinger of a great recession or even depression in 1988–1989 (as the Great Crash of 1929 had signaled the Great Depression of the 1930s) by demanding that the legislative and executive branches of the national government organize a new attack on the federal budgetary deficit. Accordingly, in late December 1987, Congress and the president approved legislation providing for reductions in federal outlays and a modest increase in taxes that, it was hoped, would result in a deficit of $115 billion in 1988 rather than the anticipated $148 billion.

Contrary to the fears of many economists—and to the relief of nearly every American—the stock market crash of 1987 did not signal a depression or even a recession in 1988. The economy of the United States continued to function at something approximating full throttle through the latter year, and the Dow hovered between 1,900 and 2,200 (an indication that investors remained confident in the essential strength of the American economy). Meanwhile, the deficit in the country's international trade balance began to diminish, a result, it was widely assumed, of a gradual decline in the value of the dollar against other currencies—a decline engineered from 1986 through 1988 by the Reagan administration (and managed by Secretary of the Treasury James A. Baker III) that caused the dollar to lose 40 percent of its value against the Japanese yen and the German mark. A devalued dollar, of course, encouraged exports and discouraged imports (by making commodities produced in the United States less expensive in foreign markets and commodities produced abroad more expensive in the United States). Indeed, the citizenry had reason to take satisfaction in reports in early 1988 that, largely as a result of the dollar's slide, manufacturing in the United States was experiencing a renaissance. Reported *Time* in March 1988, "Marching proudly under the MADE IN THE U.S.A. banner, [manufacturing] companies are boosting their exports and winning back sales [hitherto] lost to imports."

Still, millions of Americans fretted about the state of their national economy. Great numbers of them, for example, were dismayed that U.S. corporations were continuing to move manufacturing operations offshore—that the owner of a new Ford automobile might be driving an "American" car that had been assembled in Mexico, the owner of a Pontiac, a car assembled in South Korea. Those same Americans found it unsettling to ponder reports disclosing that by the mid-1980s foreign investors had come to own 16 percent of the total bank assets in the United States, and that foreign governments and corporations had acquired a fast-food chain (Hardee's), a firearms manufacturer (Smith & Wesson), food companies (for example, Carnation and Pillsbury), land (much of it choice acreage in the midwestern farm belt), newspapers (including the *Washington Times*), a major newspaper wire service (UPI), publishing houses (among them Doubleday & Company and Viking Press), supermarket chains (most notably, A&P), skyscrapers (some of them by a Canadian corporation that reportedly owned 8 percent of all of the office space in Manhattan).

Americans found it disconcerting that foreign investors, in the words of Martin and Susan Tolchin, had become "the lions of Wall Street" as a consequence of their acquisition of partial ownership of an array of investment houses in the United States, among them Wertheim & Company, Smith Barney Harris, and Goldman Sachs & Company, that 4 of the country's 10 major producers of chemicals were foreign-owned, that Japanese investors were the proprietors of 17 sales and distribution and 13 manufacturing companies in the state of Tennessee alone. Many Americans found it upsetting that political action committees organized by scores of foreign-owned companies operating in the United States (among them Nissan Motor Company and Royal Dutch Shell) had contributed at least a million dollars to the campaigns of candidates for Congress (most of them Republicans) in 1984.

Notwithstanding reports of a renaissance in American manufacturing, millions of Americans remained disturbed by figures disclosing that from 1970 to 1987 foreign competitors had steadily enlarged their shares of the American market for manufactured commodities—that the share of the home market commanded by U.S. automakers had fallen from 85 percent to 69 percent, the share commanded by domestic manufacturers of machine tools from 90 percent to 50 percent, that commanded by domestic manufacturers of textiles and clothing from more than 75 percent to 45 percent. From 1977 to 1987, domestic manufacturers of consumer electronics had seen their share of the home market decline from 50 percent to 15 percent. As reported in *Time* in May 1988, not a single U.S. manufacturer was turning out such new electronics products as camcorders and videocassette recorders. Equally disconcerting, the giant General Motors Corporation, whose share of new car sales in the United States had plummeted from 45.0 percent in 1984 to 37.5 percent in 1987, disclosed in the spring of 1988 that it would reduce productive capacity, a retreat that would make it difficult for GM to recover its lost share of the domestic car market. Observed Barbara Rudolph in *Time*, "That strategy by GM—America's leading industrial company—will bolster its profitability but do nothing to help the U.S. close the trade deficit."

Ought the government in Washington act to restrict the importation of commodities in the interest of protecting domestic manufacturers from foreign competition in the domestic market and reducing those whopping deficits in the country's international balance of trade? Many Americans thought the time had come to erect new barriers against imports, and indeed the sentiment for some sort of protectionist legislation by Congress or agreements with foreign governments negotiated by the executive branch to limit imports reached a level in 1987–1988 that was without precedent in the years since World War II. But the occupant of the White House, notwithstanding his devotion to the memory of that stern protectionist Calvin Coolidge, remained committed to the principle of almost-free trade, hence turned aside all appeals that the federal government impose severe restrictions on imports. Most professional economists appeared to endorse his stand.

Whopping trade and budgetary deficits notwithstanding, a majority of Americans remained steadfast in their devotion to Ronald Reagan as the fortieth president's second term in the White House unfolded, and felt genuine relief when in the summer of 1985 the president recovered quickly from surgery for removal of a cancerous section of his lower intestine. They appeared little moved by the incredible disclosure in 1988 in the memoir of Donald Regan, the former chief of the White House staff in the Reagan administration, that the president allowed his wife, on the basis of her consultations with an astrologer in San Francisco, to influence his schedule. Nor did the admiration of most Americans for the fortieth chief executive seem to diminish as a consequence of an unprecedented succession of disclosures that lent credence to the contention of assorted journalists that a "sleaze factor" pervaded the Reagan administration. By the summer of 1988, indeed, allegations of unethical behavior and illegal activities had tarnished the reputations of more than a hundred men and women of Reagan's official family, and his closest personal aide Michael K. Deaver and onetime press secretary Franklyn "Lyn" Nogziger had been convicted in cases stemming from charges of influence peddling. (An appellate court later overturned Nofziger's conviction.)

So far as most citizens were concerned, Reagan's obvious decency and love of country transcended his own shortcomings and deviations by members of his official family. The president never exhibited that decency and patriotism more poignantly than during a memorial service at the Johnson Space Center in Houston for the seven astronauts, one of them the ebullient schoolteacher S. Christa McAuliffe, who perished on January 28, 1986, when the space shuttle *Challenger* exploded shortly after liftoff from its launching pad at Cape Canaveral. Visibly sharing the anguish and grief of uncounted millions of Americans, he intoned on that bright and sunny afternoon in Texas, "We mourn seven heroes."

## OTHER TRIBULATIONS

In his eulogy for the fallen astronauts of *Challenger*, the president pledged, "To reach out for new goals, and even greater achievements, that is the way we shall commemorate our seven *Challenger* heroes." The brave words of the commander in chief notwithstanding, there would be no reaching out for more than two years, at least by astronauts of the space shuttle program. Shuttle flights scheduled at the time of the *Challenger* disaster were postponed indefinitely pending resolution of the problem of the defective O-ring in the booster rocket that had brought the demise of *Challenger*. Not until the autumn of 1988 did a U.S. space shuttle again streak across the heavens. Meanwhile, in early 1986, the Soviets launched their modular space station *Mir* ("Peace"), intended to be the central component of a permanently manned Soviet space complex. Over the next three years, teams of Soviet cosmonauts spent lengthy periods—two of them an incredible 366 days—aboard *Mir*, and conducted an array of scientific experiments.

Another source of tribulation for the fortieth president was what was widely referred to as the AIDS epidemic. Thought by some observers to have the potential of rivaling the horrendous plagues of medieval Europe as a scourge of humankind, the latter epidemic struck terror in the hearts of millions of Americans. And as had become their wont, great numbers of citizens looked to the national government in Washington for leadership in the grim struggle to counter the disease.

Although consenting to modest appropriations of funds to support scientific research aimed at finding a cure for AIDS, the Reagan administration remained practically mute on the subject of AIDS during the early years of national distress over the dreaded disease. Then, in the spring of 1987, after the president had issued a statement on AIDS that contained no new initiatives, Secretary of Education William J. Bennett urged mandatory testing of hospital patients and couples seeking marriage licenses, as well as prison inmates and

October 1988: Giant quilt memorializing victims of AIDS as viewed from the Washington Monument in the national capital.

would-be immigrants, to determine whether they were carriers of the AIDS antibody. Believing that mandatory testing for AIDS would constitute a violation of the individual's right to privacy, civil libertarians were incensed. Meanwhile, Bennett took a jaundiced view of the proposition that schools should encourage sexually active students to use condoms when having sexual relations.

Of larger concern than the AIDS epidemic, or so Reagan appeared to think, was the traffic in illicit drugs. Millions of his compatriots shared the president's apparent belief. Such belief rested on logic that was hard to confute. After all, the number of Americans who were known or suspected of having fallen victim of acquired immune deficiency syndrome paled before the number whose lives, it was popularly assumed, were being devastated by drugs.

At the time he moved into the White House in 1981, Ronald Reagan pledged to bring the burgeoning drug traffic under control. To redeem that pledge, he authorized increased outlays of federal funds to support a variety of antidrug initiatives, and by the mid-1980s those outlays were totaling about $1.7 billion annually. He authorized formation in 1982 of the South Florida

Task Force to impede the movement of drugs into the United States by way of southern Florida. Still, the drug traffic continued to flourish, the more so after millions of Americans, in the mid-1980s, discovered the cocaine-derived crack. Stirred by the cocaine phenomenon, Reagan in July 1986 authorized Operation Blast Furnace, in accord with which some 175 U.S. troops made their way to Bolivia, a major producer of cocaine, and in cooperation with Bolivian police set about to attack the cocaine traffic at a point of origin. The troops assisted in the destruction of 18 clandestine cocaine-producing laboratories, but by November 1986 officials in Washington adjudged Blast Furnace a failure and ordered the troops to return home.

Meanwhile, in August 1986, President Reagan announced that he intended to invoke "the full power of the presidency" to counter the traffic in illicit drugs as well as their use. He urged federal employees to accept voluntary testing to establish that they were not drug users, and to set an example he and Vice President Bush submitted urine samples for testing. Later in that same month, Attorney General Edwin Meese III unveiled Operation Alliance, its purpose to stay the transit of drugs into the United States across the country's border with Mexico. Then, in September 1986, the president and Mrs. Reagan, the latter of whom had made the drug traffic a central object of her considerable energies, delivered a joint television address on the subject of drugs, and the following day the president issued an executive order mandating drug testing of federal employees who were involved in law enforcement and other activities "requiring a high degree of trust and confidence."

In the following month, October 1986, Congress passed and Reagan signed omnibus legislation aimed at escalating the federal government's "war" on drugs. The legislation authorized $1.7 billion in new funds to strengthen the enforcement of drug laws and expand the federal effort to interdict the movement of illicit drugs into the United States, enhance the federal program of educating the citizenry about the consequences of drug use, and enlarge and improve programs to treat and rehabilitate drug addicts. It stiffened penalties for individuals convicted of violating federal drug statutes, and authorized the president to impose trade sanctions against any nation whose government declined to cooperate with efforts by the United States to counter the international drug traffic.

What were the results of the Reagan administration's war on drugs? In an incredible statement on February 18, 1988, the president declared that the war constituted "an untold American success story." The tide of the battle had turned, he said, "and we are beginning to win the crusade for a drug-free America." The authors of an essay entitled "Losing the [Drug] War?" that appeared in *Newsweek* in March 1988 responded to the presidential pronouncement with faintly disguised scorn. With good reason. According to surveys by the National Institute on Drug Abuse in 1987, 25 million Americans were regular users of marijuana, 5 million were regular users of cocaine. More than a half-million Americans were addicted to heroin. That the war against drugs was being lost was taken as axiomatic by most Americans, or so it appeared.

For in the spring of 1988, as the presidential electoral campaign heated up, opinion polls disclosed that the citizenry was inclined to identify drugs as the country's number one problem.

Meanwhile, in the autumn of 1987, President Reagan had met acute frustration when the Senate rejected his nomination of Judge Robert H. Bork of the U.S. Court of Appeals for the District of Columbia to succeed Associate Justice Lewis F. Powell of the Supreme Court. A onetime law professor at Yale, Bork was a jurist of inarguable intellectual power. He also was rigidly conservative, both in his politics and judicial perspective.

Reagan had taken abiding interest in the activities of the Supreme Court since repeating the presidential oath in January 1981. And while he found no cause for satisfaction in various of the high court's decisions—for example, its refusal to nullify the ruling in *Roe* v. *Wade* (striking down most sanctions against abortion) and a ruling that states may not require the teaching of creationism in public schools that teach biological evolution—he took a warm view of a ruling that cities and towns could use zoning laws to determine the location of theaters that show X-rated films, one that school officials and law officers were not required to have warrants in order to search students suspected of possessing drugs or weapons, and another that state laws prohibiting private homosexual conduct between consenting adults did not violate constitutionally protected rights of privacy. And he felt manifest delight when the Senate in 1986 (by a less than overwhelming vote, 65–33) confirmed his nomination of Associate Justice William H. Rehnquist, a judicial conservative, to succeed Warren E. Burger as chief justice of the United States—also when the Senate confirmed Antonin Scalia, another conservative, to be an associate justice of the Supreme Court (to fill the vacancy resulting from the retirement of Burger).

Then, in 1986, Justice Powell announced that he would retire from the court at the end of the current session, and to replace him the president nominated Bork: articulate, scholarly, and self-assured—and, as mentioned, a conservative. As millions of Americans soon learned, Bork had authored numerous treatises elaborating his conservative judicial philosophy. Various of the views set out in those treatises raised the hackles of liberals on Capitol Hill, for example, his contention that there existed no constitutional right to privacy and that the one-person-one-vote decision by the Supreme Court in 1962 (in *Baker* v. *Carr*) and the exclusionary rule (that the courts must always exclude evidence that agents of law enforcement have obtained illegally) rested on flawed reasoning. But generating the most concern among liberals (and assorted nonliberals as well) was Bork's conviction that the Supreme Court's ruling in *Roe* v. *Wade* was "an unconstitutional decision, a serious and wholly unjustified usurpation of state legislative authority." His view was no trifling matter, for if Bork won confirmation by the Senate, five of the nine justices of the Supreme Court would be critics of the decision in *Roe*. As a consequence, the high court might very well overturn the controversial abortion decision.

At length, after the Senate Judiciary Committee had completed a five-day grilling of Judge Bork, one that was witnessed via television by millions of

Americans, the Senate, by a vote of 58–42, rejected the Bork nomination. "Saddened" by the Senate rejection of Bork, the president promptly nominated 41-year-old Judge Douglas H. Ginsburg, a conservative member of the U.S. Court of Appeals for the District of Columbia, to replace Powell. Several days after his nomination, Ginsburg admitted that while a college student in the 1960s and a law professor at Harvard during the 1970s he had smoked marijuana, a source of profound embarrassment to an administration that had made the slogan "Just Say No" to drugs a centerpiece of its antidrug crusade. Nine days after his nomination, accordingly, Ginsburg withdrew his name from consideration. Reagan thereupon nominated 51-year-old Judge Anthony Kennedy of California to replace Powell. Viewed as a "pragmatic conservative" and a centrist, Kennedy won speedy confirmation by the upper chamber of the national legislature.

If the difficulty of filling Powell's seat on the Supreme Court dismayed the president during his second term in the White House, so did a succession of revelations that Americans had betrayed national secrets. Most of his compatriots shared his dismay. Drawing special media attention in 1985, "the year of the spy," were the activities of Jonathan J. Pollard and his wife and John A. Walker, Jr., and his accomplices. Pollard was a 31-year-old civilian employee of the Naval Intelligence Service and committed Zionist who, with his wife, passed secret documents to agents of Israel. On conviction, Pollard was sentenced to life in prison, his wife to five years. Far more destructive in terms of the security interests of the United States than the espionage by the Pollards was that of what came to be known as the Walker spy ring. A retired warrant officer of the Navy, John Walker had been passing secret documents to agents of the Soviet Union for more than twenty years. Assisting him in his espionage were his son Michael L. Walker, a seaman aboard the aircraft carrier USS *Nimitz*, his brother, Arthur J. Walker, a retired lieutenant commander of the Navy, and his longtime friend, Jerry A. Whitworth, a retired chief petty officer of the Navy. John and Arthur Walker received sentences of life imprisonment, Whitworth 365 years, and Michael Walker 25 years.

FBI agents in 1986 arrested a bevy of Americans, one of them an enlisted man of the Navy and two others who were enlisted personnel of the Air Force, for allegedly offering secrets to the Soviet Union in return for cash payments. Of larger import, so it was widely believed, were the activities, disclosed in 1987, of two enlisted men of the Marine Corps who, while serving as guards at the U.S. embassy in Moscow, had allegedly admitted Soviet agents to the embassy while on night watch and allowed said agents to peruse the embassy's sensitive areas, including its communications center. The sexual favors of Soviet women and cash payments were supposedly at the root of the alleged treason of the two marines. For want of corroborating evidence, charges that the two marines had allowed Soviet agents to prowl the embassy were eventually dropped, but a Marine tribunal later convicted one of the men of having passed documents and the names of U.S. agents to the Soviets, and sentenced him to 30 years in prison.

Still another source of tribulation to the president and his compatriots during the years 1985–1988 were reports of widespread waste, fraud, and abuse in the military-industrial complex. In the perspective of Reagan, the reports were especially painful, inasmuch as they reinforced Congress in its determination to reject the administration's requests for ever-larger appropriations for the armed forces (and, indeed, the pace of the fortieth president's much-discussed buildup of the armed forces declined substantially during his second term in the White House).

However painful to the president, it was disclosed in 1985 that the country's largest defense contractor, General Dynamics Corporation, in the words of the secretary of the navy, had been guilty of pervasive disregard of the public trust. Federal investigators found that General Dynamics had long padded its bills to the Department of Defense (DOD), and had even charged the DOD with such "overhead charges" as country club dues for executives, the expense of lobbying government officials, and the cost of boarding the dog of one of the company chieftains. By way of punishment, the DOD canceled $22.5 million in contracts with two General Dynamics subsidiaries and fined the company $676 million. Then, in the summer of 1988, the citizenry learned of a huge weapons-procurement scandal involving military contractors and highly placed civilian employees of the DOD. In return for handsome fees, the civilian employees had allegedly passed secret technical and contractual information to companies that were bidding for lucrative DOD contracts.

## BITBURG, SOUTHERN AFRICA

Three months after the national electorate rendered its verdict in the Mondale-Reagan contest for the presidency, in February 1985, the fortieth chief executive delivered his annual address on the State of the Union. On turning to foreign affairs, he announced, "We have resumed our historic role as a leader of the free world." Pledging that his administration would continue to seek an arms control agreement with the Soviet Union, he reiterated his commitment to development of a Strategic Defense Initiative. Without invoking the term (which was an invention of journalists), he reiterated his commitment to the Reagan Doctrine: "We must not break faith with those who are risking their lives—on every continent, from Afghanistan to Nicaragua—to defy Soviet-supported aggression and secure rights which have been ours from birth."

Reagan also asserted that Americans "must stand by our democratic allies," and in accord with that assertion, in May 1985, he made his way to Europe to commemorate the fortieth anniversary of the end of World War II and also to attend the eleventh annual economic summit conference involving six of the closest allies of the United States (Canada, France, Great Britain, Italy, Japan, and West Germany), which, along with the United States, comprised the seven major industrial countries of the noncommunist world. The trip was to be a triumphal tour for the recently reelected president of the North American superpower. It turned into a political debacle.

Before traveling to Europe, Reagan agreed to a request by Chancellor Helmut Kohl of West Germany that he visit a cemetery near the picturesque town of Bitburg in which the remains of two thousand German soldiers who had died in World War II were interred. Unbeknownst to Reagan, 49 of those soldiers had been members of the elite and infamous Waffen SS. When the news leaked that the president would be visiting a cemetery in which SS troops were buried, millions of Americans were aghast. Particularly scandalized were Jewish Americans, some of them survivors of the brutalities perpetrated by the SS, nearly all of them psychologically scarred by those brutalities. Lest he offend the West German allies, Reagan went through with the visit, then (on the same day) sought with minimal success to make amends for the offense he had given Jews by taking part in a moving ceremony at the concentration camp of Bergen-Belsen where hundreds of thousands of Jews had perished at the hands of their German tormentors during the war 1939–1945. And what of the economic summit? To Reagan's chagrin, the allies responded negatively to the president's appeal that they assist the United States in correcting its interminable imbalance in international trade.

At the time of the president's trip to Europe, in the spring of 1985, the Washington government was monitoring accelerating turbulence in that citadel of apartheid, the Republic of South Africa. It also continued tedious negotiations begun several years before aimed at securing the withdrawal of Cuban troops from Angola and terminating the 60-year occupation of Namibia by South Africa.

In the matter of the South African republic, millions of Americans believed it high time that the self-proclaimed citadel of democracy and freedom throw its weight once and for all in the balance against the despicable system of apartheid. As a consequence, the governments of 14 states and 41 cities by the end of 1985 had passed laws or resolutions restricting or prohibiting altogether the investment in South Africa of funds to provide pensions for state and urban employees. As for President Reagan, who in an incredible utterance, on August 24, 1985, declared that South Africa had "eliminated the [kind of] segregation that we once had in our own country," he was perceived by many of his compatriots as an incorrigible apologist for the white minority in the South African republic. In the perspective of domestic politics, Reagan came to understand, such a perception was intolerable, the more so since even conservative Republicans, hitherto not inclined to criticize institutionalized racism in South Africa, were increasingly speaking out in opposition to apartheid. Accordingly, the president in July 1985 recalled the U.S. ambassador in Pretoria to protest the South African government's declaration of a state of national emergency. Of larger moment, a couple of months later, he signed an executive order restricting new bank loans and prohibiting the sale of nuclear technology to South Africa. The order also prohibited the sale of computer systems to South Africa's security forces and importation in the United States of South African Krugerrands (gold coins).

Violence in South Africa became even more rampant in 1986, and in response the Congress in Washington voted to expand U.S. sanctions against South Africa. The new sanctions included a ban on public and private loans to

South Africa, a ban on investments in South Africa (except for the reinvestment of profits), and a ban on importation in the United States of an array of South African commodities, including uranium, and revoked the right of South African Airways to land its aircraft in the United States. When President Reagan vetoed the legislation, Congress overrode the presidential veto. A short time later, four of America's largest corporations, General Motors, Honeywell, IBM, and Warner Communications, announced that they would sell their South African operations. Bell & Howell, Coca-Cola, General Electric, Phillips Petroleum, Procter & Gamble, Rohm & Haas, and General Signal had previously announced plans to withdraw from South Africa.

Unfortunately, sanctions by the United States and many other countries across the world brought no apparent improvement in the situation in South Africa. Nor did withdrawal from the country of an array of foreign corporations. Acts of civil disobedience and demonstrations punctuated by violent reprisals continued through 1987–1988. At the same time, the government of Pres. Pieter W. Botha in Pretoria proclaimed new restrictions on the civil liberties of nonwhites, while a majority of the white voters of South Africa took what *Time* in May 1987 described as "a lurch to the right." In early 1988, the Pretoria government announced a new crackdown on antiapartheid organizations.

More satisfying than goings-on in South Africa in the perspective of President Reagan and many of his compatriots was the outcome of an eight-year negotiation patiently managed by Chester Crocker, the Washington government's assistant secretary of state for African affairs, in the matter of Angola and Namibia—a negotiation brought to fruition with behind-the-scenes assistance by the Soviet Union. Signed just before Christmas in 1988, the resultant agreement provided for the gradual withdrawal from Angola (where the Marxist central government for more than a decade had tried without success to take the measure of American- and South African-supported UNITA [União Nacional para Independência Total de Angola] rebels) of fifty thousand troops of Fidel Castro's Cuba. It also provided that South Africa would give up its rule of and remove its troops from Namibia, that a small UN peacekeeping force would deploy in the onetime German colony and that Namibians, by the mechanism of free elections, would determine their own political destiny.

## THE PHILIPPINES, HAITI, KOREA

Millions of Americans scarcely noticed the diplomatic success registered by the Reagan administration in the matter of Angola and Namibia. Such had not been the case when the administration assisted in the overthrow of repressive regimes in the Philippines, Haiti, and South Korea.

Trouble abounded in the Philippine republic when Ronald Reagan became president in 1981. In part because of the soaring price of petroleum, the economy of the Philippines was in disarray. And ruling the country with an iron fist was Ferdinand E. Marcos, president of the republic since 1965, a venal man who had enriched himself and a coterie of cronies while presiding over the national destiny. Adding to the country's troubles were the depredations of the New People's Army, a motley organization of Marxist insurgents that was dedicated to the overthrow, by fair means or foul, of the existing social and political order in the Philippines.

As for Marcos, whatever his impulse to tyranny and corruption, the government in Washington long had viewed him as a stalwart ally of the United States and a bulwark against communism in the Far East. Moreover, two of America's most important military-naval bastions in the western Pacific were located in the Philippines: Clark Air Force Base and the Navy's base at Subic Bay. Accordingly, President Reagan received Marcos warmly in 1982 when the Filipino strongman made his first state visit to Washington in 16 years. Then, in August 1983, military guards shot and killed Benigno S. "Ninoy" Aquino, Jr., a bright and cocky politician who strongly opposed Marcos, whereupon anti-Marcos demonstrators took to the streets of Manila. The demonstrations subsided, but unrest remained pervasive in the islands. Then, in November 1985, perhaps in response to President Reagan's expression of concern about goings-on in the Philippines, the 68-year-old Marcos, responding to a question by George Will during an appearance via satellite on ABC-TV's "This Week with David Brinkley," announced that a "snap election" would take place in the island republic. A short time later, Corazon C. Aquino, the pious and spir-

February 25, 1986: Stating that "I take power in the name of the Filipino people," Corazon Aquino repeats the presidential oath of the Philippine Republic.

ited 53-year-old widow of Ninoy Aquino, although a political neophyte, announced her candidacy for the presidency of the Philippine republic.

Fraud, intimidation, and violence marked the subsequent election in early 1986, and both Marcos and Aquino claimed victory. But massive street demonstrations in support of Aquino by all manner of Filipinos—businesspeople, farmers, housewives, laborers, nuns, priests, students—made it clear that most Filipinos sought an end to the Marcos dictatorship. Whereupon governments around the world, including that in Washington, began to withdraw recognition of the Marcos regime. Indeed, the administration of Ronald Reagan (whose vice president George Bush in 1981 had praised Marcos's "adherence to democratic principles") projected itself into the political crisis in the Philippines, urged Marcos to accept the election of Aquino, and arranged for a peaceful transition of power from dictatorship to at least the promise of democracy. Accordingly, on the morning of February 25, 1986, Corazon Aquino, wearing a bright yellow dress, placed her hand on a Bible and repeated the presidential oath. A few hours later, Marcos, his wife, and entourage made their way to Clark Air Force Base, boarded a U.S. military transport, and flew off to exile in Hawaii.

On the same day that voters in the Philippines signaled the end of a dictatorship as a consequence of Ferdinand Marcos's "snap election," February 7, 1986, what arguably was an even more brutal and repressive dictatorship passed into history. The latter dictatorship was that presided over by Jean-Claude Duvalier (the son of the late and infamous François "Papa Doc" Duvalier) in the Caribbean republic of Haiti. In the perspective of people across the face of the globe who despised dictators, February 7, 1986, assuredly was a day to celebrate.

Like his late father, "Baby Doc" Duvalier depended on thugs of the Tontons Macoute ("bogeymen") to secure his authority and enable him to sustain his luxuriant lifestyle. Then, in 1984, a spate of popular disturbances interrupted the tranquility of Haiti for the first time since the Duvalier family's accession to power in 1957. The disturbances abated when Duvalier allowed voters to adopt a new constitution that sanctioned political parties—one that also proclaimed that "Baby Doc" would be president for life and authorized him to designate his successor. But anti-Duvalier protests resumed in the poverty-ridden country in the autumn of 1985, and at the end of January 1986 the government in Washington declined to certify the Duvalier regime's compliance with human rights standards, a signal that the United States would reduce its modest assistance grant to Haiti. On that same day, the U.S. ambassador in Port-au-Prince, Clayton McManaway, Jr., met with Duvalier and discussed the possibility that the dictator might quit his office and depart the country. One week later, Duvalier summoned McManaway to the presidential palace and asked that the United States provide him with a getaway plane. The Washington government acceded to Duvalier's request, and at 3:46 A.M., on February 7, 1986, a U.S. Air Force C-141 transport plane dispatched from Fort Bragg, North Carolina, took off from the François Duvalier airport, and whisked Duvalier, his family, and members of his entourage to exile in France.

By the time "Baby Doc" landed near Paris, a few hours later, Haitians by the tens of thousands were celebrating almost without restraint in the streets of Port-au-Prince and other cities and towns of the republic.

The people of the United States took satisfaction in the part taken by the administration of Ronald Reagan in bringing about the demise of the Marcos dictatorship in the Philippines and the Duvalier dictatorship in Haiti. More than a year later, in 1987, they felt satisfaction anew, this time when Reagan's administration nudged the Washington government's longtime ally in Northeast Asia, the Republic of Korea, in the direction of democracy.

The constitution of the ROK, adopted in 1948, provided for a democratic system of government, but Presidents Syngman Rhee (1948–1960) and Park Chung Hee (1961–1979) had ruled the fledgling republic with an iron hand, jailing their more vehement critics and muzzling the press. Rhee and Park, moreover, had looked the other way while underlings harvested the pecuniary rewards of administration. After Park fell to an assassin's bullet in October 1979, Maj. Gen. Chun Doo Huan moved to the leadership of the Seoul government, and in May 1980 dispatched special forces of the ROK army to the provincial capital of Kwangju to put down student-led demonstrations against the arbitrary behavior of the central government. The result was a violent confrontation that claimed the lives of more than 150 protestors. A short time later, in the summer of 1980, Chun secured election to the presidency, then proceeded to move against academics, journalists, and politicians whom he considered hostile. Whatever his impulse to repression, Chun in February 1981 became the first chief of state to meet with Ronald Reagan after the latter's accession to the presidency in Washington. During the meeting, Reagan promised continued U.S. support of South Korea.

The situation in South Korea remained fairly calm over the next several years, in part, no doubt, because the country was achieving industrial growth and experiencing a level of prosperity that would have boggled the minds of Theodore Roosevelt and other Occidentals who at the turn of the twentieth century had viewed Koreans as a hopelessly backward, decadent, and lazy people. Indeed, South Korea by the mid-1980s had established itself as a veritable economic powerhouse, a country that could no longer be defined as a "developing" member of the Third World.

But then, in the spring of 1987, angry students began to storm through the streets of Seoul and other South Korean cities demanding an end to what they denounced as the Chun dictatorship. The students, who were vigorously countered by tough riot policemen, had the undisguised support of a wide spectrum of the South Korean population, including many businesspeople and much of the ROK's large community of Catholic and Protestant Christians.

Behind the scenes, meanwhile, the administration of Ronald Reagan urged the government in Seoul to strike a compromise with its opponents. The actual effect of the urging emanating from Washington remains unclear, but in late June of 1987 the presidential candidate of Chun's Democratic National Justice Party, Roh Tae Woo, announced support of demands by opposition parties for a popularly elected president (instead of one elected, in accord with the existing constitution, by the National Assembly); restoration of the political rights of Kim Dae Jung (a popular leftist who was under a 20-year sentence for sedition); release of political prisoners; and also measures to promote human rights and freedom of the press. The upshot was revision of the ROK constitution and, in December 1987, a presidential election by popular ballot. Because the two principal opposition parties failed to unite behind a single candidate, Roh Tae Woo won the election, although he polled only 36.6 percent of the vote.

Whether South Korea would stay on the path of popular democracy remained to be seen. Still, government by intimidation and repression had suffered several spectacular reverses in various parts of the world in recent years: in the Philippines, Haiti (where, sadly, the overthrow of Jean-Claude Duvalier did not bring an end to violence and arbitrary rule), South Korea, and also in Argentina, where a popularly elected civilian regime replaced a barbarous military junta in 1983, and Brazil, where a civilian regime chosen by an electoral college replaced a junta in 1985.

## THE MIDDLE EAST

As during his first term in the White House, the Middle East was never far from the thoughts of President Reagan during his second term. Of special concern, particularly in the first year or so of the second term, were the depredations of Middle Eastern terrorists.

Less than five months after Reagan repeated the presidential oath for the second time, in June 1985, Shiite militants of Lebanon highjacked Flight 847 of Trans World Airlines (TWA) as it departed Athens, forced the pilot to fly the red-and-white Boeing 727 to Beruit, then to Algiers, then back to Beruit—back to Algiers and back to Beruit again. Aboard the craft were 145 passengers, 39 of them Americans, and during the second stopover in Beruit the terrorists shot Robert D. Stetham, a U.S. Navy diver, and tossed his body out of the plane onto the runway. The principal demand of the terrorists was release by Israel of 766 Lebanese captives, most of them Shiites. At length, after two weeks, the terrorists, apparently responding to pressure applied on Shiite leaders by Pres. Hafiz al-Assad of Syria, released the hostages—after Israel, on request by the United States, had agreed to a gradual release of Shiite captives.

Three months later, in October 1985, Palestinian terrorists, demanding the release of Palestinians being held captive in Israel, seized the Italian cruise liner *Achille Lauro* off the coast of Egypt, shot a wheelchair-bound American tourist, Leon Klinghoffer, and dumped his body into the sea. When Israel declined to meet their demands, the terrorists surrendered to authorities in Egypt. But the drama of the *Achille Lauro* had not played out. When American F-14 jets intercepted the Egyptian airliner that was transporting the terrorists out of Egypt and forced it to land in Italy, the government in Cairo was incensed. And when Italy released the terrorist who had masterminded the hijacking, the government in Washington was incensed. One month later, in

October 1985: Security police guard the gangplank leading to the Italian cruise liner *Achille Lauro*, anchored at Port Said in Egypt, a few days after four Palestinian terrorists had hijacked the vessel and murdered a disabled American passenger.

November 1985, Palestinian terrorists hijacked an Egyptian airliner, forced it to land in Malta, and began shooting passengers one by one until Egyptian commandos stormed the plane. When the smoke had cleared, 59 people were dead, one of them an American woman. At the end of December 1985, Palestinian terrorists, hurling grenades and firing submachine guns, killed 16 people, 4 of them Americans, in coordinated attacks at the check-in counters of El Al Israeli Airlines at airports in Rome and Vienna. Thought to be responsible for the latter outrages was a renegade Palestinian group headed by the shadowy Abu Nidal, who had broken with Yasir Arafat's mainstream group of the PLO in 1974. Aiding and abetting the renegade Palestinians was the Libyan government of Col. Muammar el-Qaddafi. Or so alleged the administration of Pres. Ronald Reagan.

The United States now began to move toward confrontation with Libya. President Reagan in early January 1986 issued executive orders prohibiting virtually all trade between Libya and the United States, ordering the fifteen hundred Americans (many of them oil technicians) who were in Libya to leave the country, and freezing an estimated $2.5 billion of Libyan assets in the United States. He also appealed to the European allies of the United States to join in an economic boycott of Libya. The European allies politely declined. Meanwhile, aircraft of the U.S. Sixth Fleet resumed operations over the Gulf of Sidra, international waters in the view of Americans, territorial waters of Libya in the view of Libyans, and on March 24, 1986, Libyan missile batteries fired on U.S. aircraft as they maneuvered over the gulf. In retaliation, aircraft launched from three U.S. aircraft carriers that were deployed near the gulf destroyed the missile batteries and sank two Libyan patrol boats.

A few days later, on April 2, 1986, a bomb tore a hole in the side of a TWA airliner en route from Rome to Athens. Four passengers who were sucked through the hole, one of them an infant, plunged to their deaths. A group called the Arab Revolutionary Cells issued a statement that the bombing was in retaliation for "American arrogance" and for the recent action by the United States against Libya. Two days later, a bomb exploded in a disco in West Berlin frequented by U.S. servicemen. The blast killed two people, one of them a GI, and injured 155. Unable to establish a link between the Qaddafi government and the explosion aboard the TWA airliner, the government in Washington claimed to have evidence proving Libyan complicity in the attack at the disco in West Berlin.

The climax of the U.S. confrontation with Libya transpired on April 15, 1986, when bombing planes of the U.S. Air Force that were based in the United Kingdom and bombers and fighters of the U.S. Navy, operating from carriers in the Mediterranean, raided targets near the Libyan capital of Tripoli and the town of Benghazi that, according to the Washington government, were parts of Libya's terrorist infrastructure. The raid claimed the lives of perhaps 20 Libyan civilians—also 2 American fliers whose plane went down in the Gulf of Sidra. Intoned President Reagan in an address to his compatriots, "Today we have done what we had to do. If necessary we shall do it again." Although most Americans, taking the president at his word, approved of the raid against Libya, the raid generated angry protest throughout much of the rest of the world, including Western Europe.

Colonel Qaddafi's Libya appeared to fade from the view of Americans in the aftermath of the confrontation of April 1986, at least until the last week of 1988, when President Reagan threatened to unleash American bombing planes against an alleged chemical weapons factory in Libya. Meanwhile, the people of the United States became increasingly aware of what was widely referred to as a shipping war in the Persian Gulf, a consequence of the brutal armed conflict that had convulsed Iraq, an Arab state, and the Ayatollah Khomeini's Islamic republic of Iran, a non-Arab state, since September 1980.

Beginning in 1984, Iraq had sought to strangle Iran by impeding the flow of oil from Iran by attacking Iran's oil-export terminal as well as tankers carrying oil from Iran. Inasmuch as Iraq's oil reached the outer world via pipeline, the Iranians were not able to interrupt the shipment of Iraqi oil. But they undertook reprisals by attacking ships calling at the ports of other Arab states bordering the Persian Gulf. A special object of Iranian attacks were ships moving in and out of Kuwait, an oil-rich Arab emirate that was a principal source of funding of the Iraqi war effort. Then, in the spring of 1987, the government in Washington entered a delicate negotiation that resulted in an agreement whereby 11 Kuwaiti tankers would be "reflagged" with the Stars and Stripes and sail under the protection of the U.S. Navy. The purpose of what amounted to an American armed intervention in the gulf war in 1987? In part (so it appeared) to counter the likelihood of increased Soviet naval activity in the gulf, in part to regain credibility with Arab states of the gulf that had felt betrayed when confronted with the shocking disclosure that, to secure release of Americans being held hostage in Lebanon by Islamic fundamentalists allied with Iran, the United States had sold arms to the Ayatollah Khomeini's government in Teheran. Before completion of the negotiation between Kuwait and the United States, Americans became painfully aware of the risks of military-naval intervention in the Persian Gulf: 37 American seamen died when an Exorcet missile apparently fired accidentally by an Iraqi fighter pilot crashed into the frigate USS *Stark* in the waters off Bahrain.

At length, in July 1987, the first reflagged Kuwaiti tanker entered the Persian Gulf, and two days later struck a mine, apparently planted in the sea by the Iranians. A fortnight later, a U.S.-owned tanker hit a mine in the adjacent Gulf of Oman. During the following month, September 1987, a U.S. Army helicopter disabled and Navy commandos captured an Iranian vessel that was laying mines in the Persian Gulf off the coast of Bahrain. In mid-October, Iranian "Silkworm" missiles of Chinese manufacture struck an American-owned tanker and a reflagged Kuwaiti tanker. In retaliation, U.S. ships a few days later shelled two Iranian offshore oil platforms that, according to Americans, doubled as gunboat bases, and also dispatched commandos who destroyed a third platform that the Iranians had converted into a military command post.

Following a succession of savage attacks on shipping in the Persian Gulf by both Iran and Iraq, in December 1987, the pace of combat in the shipping war appeared to subside. But then, on July 3, 1988, the war produced a monstrous accident: A missile fired by the destroyer USS *Vincennes*, an ultramodern cruiser laden with space-age electronic gear and weapons, sent an Iranian Air Airbus that was making a regularly scheduled flight from Bandar Abbas in Iran to Dubai in the United Arab Emirates crashing into the gulf just west of the Strait of Hormuz. All of the 290 people aboard the twin-jet Airbus perished. What had gone wrong? Misinterpreting radar signals, the crewmen of the *Vincennes*, just minutes after their ship had attacked three Iranian gunboats (and sunk two of them) that were thought to have fired on a U.S. helicopter, concluded that the Airbus was an Iranian F-14 Tomcat fighter—and also that the aircraft was approaching the *Vincennes* in an attack pattern. Chagrined by the tragedy, the Washington government pledged monetary compensation to the families of its 290 victims.

Did the tragedy in the Persian Gulf in July 1988 beget a comparable tragedy, one that came to pass five months later, on December 21, 1988, when a bomb ripped open Pan American Flight 103 as it soared 31,000 feet above Lockerbie, Scotland, en route from Frankfurt to New York via London? All 259 of the passengers aboard Flight 103, a Boeing 747 jetliner named Maid of the Seas, and 11 people on the ground perished in the resultant crash. Anonymous callers claimed that Islamic fundamentalists had perpetrated the outrage in retribution for destruction of the Iranian Air Airbus by the *USS Vincennes* the previous summer. But another anonymous caller claimed that Flight 103 had been destroyed in retaliation for the U.S. aerial attack on Libya in April 1986, while analysts who specialized in terrorist activity suspected that, in view of their history of hijacking and bombing airliners, radical Palestinians were the probable culprits.

Whatever the connection, if any, between the tragedies of the Iranian Air Airbus and Pan Am Flight 103, the murderous Iran-Iraqi war—which over the past year had yielded chilling evidence that the Iraqis were employing chemical weapons (poison gas)—had, mercifully, moved to a termination. A mere fortnight after destruction of the Airbus by the *Vincennes*, Ayatollah Khomeini advised Secretary General Javier Pérez de Cuéllar of the United Nations that Iran now accepted UN Resolution 598 of July 1987 calling for a cease-fire in the long and bloody war. Said Khomeini, who at one point had pledged to continue the fighting against Iraq with "the last blood of my body," "Making this decision was more deadly than drinking poison. I submitted myself to God's will and drank this drink for his satisfaction." Perhaps. But the unvarnished facts were that during the past year Iraq had gained the initiative in the war, and the will of the people of Iran to continue the bloodletting had clearly begun to flag. As for the Iraqis, flushed by recent battlefield successes but weary of the nearly eight-year war (which their strongman, Pres. Saddam Hussein Takriti, had started back in 1980), they were quite ready to consent to a cease-fire.

The breaking out of peace in the Persian Gulf was a glorious happening. Still, the interminable Israeli-Arab conflict betrayed no sign of resolution, and of course remained a source of tension and violence, not to mention a potential source of international crisis, in the Middle East. Inasmuch as only a scattering of Arab diehards continued to believe the destruction of Israel even a remote possibility, it was a conflict that by 1987 centered on the question of the political status and conditions of life of some 1.8 million Palestinians, all of them stateless and virtually bereft of political rights, many them living in squalor, who resided in the Israeli-occupied West Bank and Gaza.

The Arab-Israeli conflict took a new turn in late 1987 when Palestinians in the West Bank and Gaza suddenly accelerated street demonstrations protesting the Israeli occupation of the two territories. Most dramatically, bands of youthful Palestinians, hurling stones and Molotov cocktails (homemade firebombs), began to clash with troops of the Israeli army in almost daily confrontations. The latter displays of bravado by "children of the stones" fired the spirits of ordinary Palestinians, and generated unprecedented sensitivity to the sad plight of the Palestinian people in every corner of the world. Vigorously countered by Israel's armed forces, the Palestinian *intifadeh* (uprising) continued with only intermittent letup through the following year, and by the end of 1988 had resulted in death for more than three hundred Palestinians and perhaps a dozen Israelis.

Meanwhile, the Israeli government headed by Prime Minister Yitzhak Shamir, his intransigence supported by most of his compatriots, refused to consider any settlement of the conflict resting on establishment of an independent Palestinian state in the West Bank and Gaza, and also refused to consider negotiations, direct or indirect, with Yasir Arafat and the PLO. The goal of Israelis? Many Israelis sought outright annexation by Israel of the West Bank and Gaza. Believing that annexation of two territories occupied by 1.8 million Palestinians would prove subversive of the unique character of the Jewish nation-state, other Israelis favored a settlement that would allow local autonomy for the Palestinians in the West Bank and Gaza in confederation with Jordan.

As for the government in Washington when 1987 gave way to 1988, it supported, as it had since Ronald Reagan's accession to the presidency, the Israeli refusal to consider establishment of an independent Palestinian state in the West Bank and Gaza, and like its counterpart in Jerusalem refused to consider negotiations with Arafat and the PLO, on the grounds that the latter were committed to the destruction of Israel and were exponents of terrorism. It shared the view of those Israelis who opposed annexation of the West Bank and Gaza by Israel and favored instead self-determination for Palestinians in confederation with Jordan. Leaders of the Reagan administration, indeed, had become mesmerized by the so-called Jordanian option for resolving the Israeli-Palestinian conflict. But then, in July 1988, the Jordanian option turned to ashes when King Hussein of Jordan (whose kingdom had ruled the West Bank from the time of the Arab-Israeli war of 1948–1949 until that of 1967) disavowed all responsibility for affairs in the West Bank. He thus made it clear that the Israelis and Americans, if they wished to work out a settlement with the Palestinians, would have to deal with Palestinians—in truth, with the PLO, the only organization that commanded the loyalty of a majority of Palestinians.

The foregoing notwithstanding, both the governments in Jerusalem and Washington continued to resist all suggestions, for example, by West Europeans, that they talk with Arafat and the PLO. Then, as 1988 was drawing to a close, Arafat and fellow leaders of the PLO and the Palestine National Council, in a dramatic meeting in Algiers, proclaimed the independence of Palestine, its territory presumably comprising the West Bank and Gaza, which territory of course, the Israelis continued to occupy. The Washington government no less than that in Jerusalem appeared singularly unimpressed. But a short time later, Arafat publicly acknowledged Israel's right to exist, that is, renounced the longtime PLO determination to destroy the Jewish nation-state, and renounced terrorism "in all of its forms." In so doing, he removed the two obstacles which, leaders in Washington had long insisted, prevented a dialogue between the United States and the PLO. Whereupon the Washington government, to the acute consternation of Israelis, began cautious conversations with the PLO in Tunis. Whether the latter conversations might portend a peaceful settlement of one of the most bitter and prolonged of the world's controversies in modern times remained to be seen.

## IRAN-CONTRA SCANDAL

As mentioned, leaders of Arab states in the region of the Persian Gulf that were friendly to the United States, all of them nervous lest their peoples be swept up by the tide of Islamic fundamentalism that Ayatollah Khomeini had unleashed in Iran, felt betrayed when they learned in 1986 that the administration in Washington had sold arms (more than fifteen hundred TOW antitank missiles and a handful of HAWK antiaircraft missiles) to Khomeini's government in Teheran in the hope of securing release of seven Americans being held hostage by Islamic fundamentalists in Lebanon. Not necessarily consumed by feelings of betrayal, Pres. Ronald Reagan's compatriots certainly felt thunderstruck when in November 1986 it was disclosed that his administration had traded arms for hostages. Small wonder. As later remarked in the *Report of the Congressional Committees Investigating the Iran-Contra Affair*, released in the autumn of 1987, "Few principles of U.S. policy were stated more forcefully by the Reagan Administration than refusing to traffic with terrorists or sell arms to the Government of the Ayatollah Khomeini of Iran."

Neither Arab leaders in the region of the Persian Gulf nor ordinary citizens in the United States had any inkling that the Washington government had sold arms to Iran when on November 2, 1986, a Shiite Muslim group in Lebanon that had close ties with Iran released a U.S. citizen, 55-year-old David P. Jacobsen, held hostage by the group for the past 17 months. A statement issued by President Reagan in Washington hailed Jacobsen's release. Then, on the very next day, *Al-Shiraa*, an obscure magazine published in Beruit, disclosed that a U.S. emissary had recently sought to work out a deal with Ayatollah Khomeini's government by which the United States would provide spare parts for Iranian military equipment. *Al-Shiraa*, it turned out, had published only a fraction of the story of recent dealings involving the Washington government and Iran, a sworn enemy of the United States. Subsequent reports pieced together by the news media disclosed that American emissaries had met several times with Iranian officials during the past 16 months and struck a bargain whereby the United States would ship arms to Iran and the Iranians would arrange for the release of Americans being held hostage by Shiite militants in Lebanon.

As noted, the people of the United States were thunderstruck. More than that, they were incredulous. But at length, on November 13, 1986, President Reagan confirmed that the United States had indeed made secret shipments of arms to Iran. Conceding that "to effect the safe return of all hostages" had been an objective of the transaction, he insisted that the shipments had not been part of a deal to gain release of American hostages. Rather, he explained, the purpose had been to bring about improved relations between the governments in Washington and Teheran. Only a comparative handful of die-hard

Reagan partisans accepted the president's disclaimer that the transaction with Iran had not been one of arms for hostages.

A fortnight later, on November 25, 1986, a new bombshell disclosure rocked the United States. Like that of November 13, this one emanated from the White House itself.

After summoning reporters to a special briefing, the president disclosed that, as a consequence of an inquiry conducted by Attorney General Meese, he realized that he had not been "fully informed" about "one of the activities" relative to the arms transactions with Iran. His demeanor somber, the chief executive thereupon turned over the briefing to Meese, who proceeded to explain that the activity in question was the diversion of proceeds from the Iranian arms sales to aid the contras in Nicaragua in their struggle against the ruling Sandinistas. Who was responsible for the diversion of proceeds from the Iranian arms deal to Nicaragua's rebels? According to Meese, responsibility did not rest with Ronald Reagan. The president, he insisted, had known nothing about the diversion until recent days. By the attorney general's account, the culprit had been 43-year-old Lt. Col. Oliver L. North of the Marine Corps, a member of the staff of the National Security Council who operated from an office across the street from the White House. North had allegedly engineered the contra scam without the knowledge of anyone in authority save his immediate superior, the national security adviser, Vice Adm. John M. Poindexter of the Navy. The attorney general reported further that Reagan had accepted Poindexter's resignation and fired North (the latter of whom, a much-decorated combat veteran of the war in Vietnam, Reagan described as "a national hero").

Millions of Americans found Meese's assertion that North had managed the diversion of millions of dollars of federal funds to the contras without the president's knowledge and consent incredible. But Reagan stood by what a few of his cynical compatriots described as "the dunce defense," and on December 2, 1986, announced that he would request appointment of an independent council (or special prosecutor) to investigate charges that his underlings had acted contrary to the law. Appointed later in that same month, the independent counsel was Lawrence E. Walsh, a former federal prosecutor, judge, and deputy attorney general.

The president in December 1986 also appointed a commission composed of former-Senator John G. Tower, Republican of Texas, former-Senator and former-Secretary of State Edmund S. Muskie, Democrat of Maine, and a former national security adviser (in the administration of Gerald Ford), retired-General Brent Scowcroft of the Air Force, to look into the procedures of the National Security Council. Issued in February 1987, the report of the so-called Tower Commission offered scathing criticism of the Reagan administration: "The common ingredients of the Iran and contra policies were secrecy, deception, and disdain for the law. . . . The administration's departure from democratic process created the conditions for policy failure and led to contradictions which undermined the credibility of the United States."

While Reagan was enduring what *Newsweek* described as "the White House Crisis," in early December of 1986, Oliver North and John Poindexter were summoned to testify before committees of the House and Senate. His chest bristling with ribbons and medals, North appeared at the hearing outfitted in an olive drab Marine Corps uniform. Of North's testimony, *Newsweek* reported, "He bit his lip. His boyish face grimaced and his voice quavered. Tears all but welled as he told the hushed hearing room: 'I don't think there's another person in America that wants to tell this story as much as I do.' But instead, on his lawyer's advice, North invoked his right not to testify under the Fifth Amendment." Poindexter, too, invoked the protection provided by the Fifth Amendment to the federal Constitution against self-incrimination.

However stymied in the hearings of December 1986, Congress had no intention of giving up its quest to get to the bottom of the Iran-contra affair, hence in that same month the Senate and House appointed select committees to undertake a joint investigation. The first witness to testify when the congressional select committees at length opened televised hearings in the venerable Senate Caucus Room, on May 5, 1987, was Richard V. Secord, a retired major general of the Air Force whom Oliver North had hired to oversee the sale of arms to Iran and divert profits deriving from the sales to the Nicaraguan contras. To the latter purposes, Secord had set up an elaborate network of bank accounts, companies, and individuals that was code-named the Enterprise. According to Secord, North had described conversations with Reagan in which he and the president had discussed the diversion of funds from the arms sales to the contras—in one of which North claimed to have remarked about the irony of arranging for Ayatollah Khomeini to unwittingly finance the Nicaraguan rebels.

Former National Security Adviser Robert C. McFarlane told the select committees that Reagan had become obsessed with the cause of the Nicaraguan contras, and after Congress in 1984–1985 forbade funding of the contras by the Washington government, the president had directed the NSC staff to keep the contra cause afloat. North's attractive secretary Fawn Hall testified that she had shredded so many documents when the Iran-contra connection became public in November 1986 that the shredding machine in North's office broke down. In defense of what North and she had done, she made perhaps the most memorable utterance of the Iran-contra hearings, "Sometimes you have got to go above the written law." Secretary of State George Shultz told the select committees that he had opposed the sale of arms to Iran from the outset, been lied to by various officials of the administration in the matter of the sales, and come to feel a sense of estrangement from the NSC staff and other White House officials as a result of his opposition to the Iranian initiative. Secretary of Defense Caspar Weinberger also had opposed the sales, and at one point thought his advice to the president to reject arms sales to Iran had succeeded in having "this baby strangled in the cradle."

The star witness in the Iran-contra hearings, of course, was Oliver North, according to the final report of the select committes "the central figure in the scandal," the man who "coordinated all of the activities and was involved in

July 1987: Lt. Col. Oliver North testifies before congressional select committees in Washington during the so-called Iran-contra hearings.

all aspects of the secret operations." His appearance before the select committees (and millions of citizens who were witnessing the interrogation of the uniformed marine officer via television) exuded high drama. Indeed, it will doubtless remain etched in the national memory for many years to come. Wrote Larry Martz in a report that appeared in *Newsweek* in July 1987, "Lt. Col. Oliver L. North charged up Capitol Hill last week as the Rambo of diplomacy, a runaway swashbuckler who had run his own private foreign policy from the White House basement." In a report for *Time*, Lance Morrow wrote that North arrived on Capitol Hill surrounded by an aura of injured virtue. "The force was with him. He played brilliantly upon the collective values of America, upon its nostalgias, its memories of a thousand movies . . . and Norman Rockwell Boy Scout icons. Ironically, he played precisely those American chords of myth and dreaming with which Ronald Reagan orchestrated his triumphal campaigns of 1980 and 1984."

"Ollemania" (as the outpouring of popular support for North came to be referred to) aside, North during his six days of testimony insisted that he had done nothing that his superiors had not approved: "I was authorized to do everything that I did." Although he never "personally discussed" the matter with the president, he assumed that Reagan knew of the diversion of funds from the Iranian arms sales to the Nicaraguan contras. Alas, he had "no recollection" of having seen the president's initials or check of approval on any documents relating to said diversion. He acknowledged that he had shredded documents and misled Congress. "Lying does not come easy to me," North told the committees. "But we all had to weigh in the balance the difference between lives and lies." He often responded to questions by members of the select committees by saying he did not recall. Wrote Ed Magnuson for a report that appeared in *Time*, "In his final morning in the week's testimony, the selective memory of the obviously bright officer failed on no fewer than 30 occasions."

John Poindexter followed North to the witness chair of the select committees. Testified Reagan's former national security adviser, "The buck stops here, with me." By his account, it was he who had authorized the diversion of profits from arms sales to Iran to fund the Nicaraguan contras—and, so he testified, he had not informed the president of the diversion. Poindexter's insistence that he had acted without approval or knowledge of the occupant of the Oval Office clearly ended what had never been more than a remote possibility that Reagan might face impeachment proceedings on the grounds that he had violated the Boland amendment prohibiting funding of the contras by the Washington government. But had Poindexter told the truth? Certainly many observers of politics, perceiving Poindexter as the consummate bureaucrat, found it incredible that he had diverted proceeds from arms sales to the contras without at least a wink or a nod from the president. Remarked Henry Kissinger, "I was a far more assertive security adviser than Poindexter, and I would never have dreamed of making a decision like that."

The final report of the select committees was scathing in its criticism of the administration in its quest to exchange arms for hostages, an activity that resulted in the release of three U.S. hostages but did not prevent pro-Iranian terrorists in Lebanon, in early 1987, from seizing three other Americans and making them hostages. Observing that statutory law required notification of Congress about each covert action, the report scalded the administration for failing to advise Congress of the covert operations of Oliver North and his confederates. Asserted the report, "The common ingredients of the Iran and Contra policies were secrecy, deception, and disdain for the law. A small group of senior officials believed that they alone knew what was right. They viewed knowledge of their actions by others in the Government as a threat to their objectives. They told neither the Secretary of State, the Congress nor the American people of their actions. When exposure was threatened, they destroyed official documents and lied to Cabinet officials, to the public, and to elected representatives in Congress. They testified that they even withheld key facts from the President. . . . The Administration's departure from democratic processes created the conditions for policy failure, and led to contradictions which undermined the credibility of the United States."

Meanwhile, Independent Counsel Walsh continued his inquiry, and in March 1988 a federal grand jury returned a 23-count indictment in the cases of Albert Hakim (a partner in the Enterprise), Oliver North, John Poindexter, and Richard Secord. Sixteen of the 23 counts were drawn against North. Among the 16 counts: in violation of the law prohibiting the expenditure of federal funds to provide military assistance to the contras; conspired to defraud the United States by diverting profits from the Iranian arms sales to provide arms to the contras; stole government property (to wit, the proceeds from the arms sales to Iran); made false statements on four separate occasions, three times to Congress, once to the attorney general; concealed, falsified, or destroyed official documents; received an illegal gratuity (a security fence for his residence valued at $13,000). Trials of the accused men were expected to take place in 1989.

Incredibly, the tawdry Iran-contra affair resulted in no more than a temporary relaxing of President Reagan's grip on the affections of a majority of his compatriots. But it severely crippled his quixotic crusade to rid Central America of the scourge of Marxism by rallying the Nicaraguan contras against the Sandinista regime in Managua.

In truth, Reagan's policies in Central America, such as they were, appeared to be in tatters as his presidency approached its end. Few of the president's compatriots retained any enthusiasm whatever for the enterprise of supporting the contras, who clearly had no chance at all of taking the measure of the Sandinistas in the absence of a sudden determination by the Nicaraguan people to join what had become the moribund contra campaign to rid Nicaragua, its economy a shambles, of its inefficient and repressive Marxist regime. At the dawn of 1989, signs that such a determination by Nicaraguans might come to pass were nonexistent. In a word, the Sandinista regime, to Reagan's dismay and acute disappointment, appeared quite secure, for the time being at any rate. The latter regime, moreover, apparently had no intention of complying with terms of the regional peace treaty signed by Costa Rica, El Salvador, Guatemala, Honduras, and Nicaragua in August 1987 calling for periodic free elections and promotion of "pluralistic democracies." In neighboring El Salvador, meanwhile, President Duarte was suffering the throes of terminal cancer, and tranquility and stability appeared to be no closer at hand in that tormented country than when Reagan, during his first term, made tranquility and stability in El Salvador under a noncommunist regime an object of his policy in Central America. Adding insult to injury in the matter of U.S. policy vis-à-vis Central America during the last year or so of the Reagan presidency, the unsavory dictator of Panama, Gen. Manuel Antonio Noriega, indicted in the United States in 1988 for trafficking in narcotics, continued to preside over the long-suffering Panamanian republic, notwithstanding a concerted and highly publicized effort by the Reagan administration to topple him by the application of diplomatic pressure and economic sanctions.

## FAREWELL TO THE EVIL EMPIRE

Historians of the future are apt to give Ronald Reagan low marks for his approach to Central America during his second term in the White House (and probably the first term as well). But they may very well accord him high marks for his approach to the Soviet Union, at least during the final two years of his presidency. Indeed, it appears not unlikely that future scholars will decide that the course charted by his administration in its dealings with the rival superpower during 1987–1988 constituted the crowning achievement of Reagan's eight-year occupancy of the White House.

Relations between the United States and what President Reagan perceived to be "the evil empire" had sunk to their lowest point since the dark days of the Cuban missile crisis of 1962 when, in November 1982, death claimed the Soviet chieftain of the past 18 years, the strong-willed and stolid president and general secretary, Leonid Brezhnev. Relations between the superpowers underwent no noticeable improvement following accession to leadership in the Kremlin of 68-year-old Yuri V. Andropov, the longtime chief of the KGB (security police). As fate would have it, the tenure of Andropov, a man of surprising sophistication who appeared to be animated by an impulse to reform, would prove brief—only 14 months. Andropov died of kidney failure in February 1984. His successor, 72-year-old Konstantin U. Chernenko, a plodding protégé of Brezhnev, experienced an equally brief tenure as Soviet chieftain. Chernenko died in March 1985, only seven weeks after Ronald Reagan had repeated the presidential oath in Washington for the second time. Chernenko's successor was 54-year-old Mikhail S. Gorbachev.

Observers of Soviet affairs in the West were cautiously optimistic that the new general secretary in the Kremlin might bring a fresh perspective to the task of governing the Soviet empire and managing its relations with the rest of the world. He was, after all, the first of the post–World War II generation of Soviet politicians to reach the top of the Soviet hierarchy, and also the first chieftain of the Soviet empire whose upward movement in that hierarchy owed nothing to the favor of the infamous Josef Stalin. During a visit to Great Britain in 1984, moreover, Gorbachev had made a favorable impression in the West by displaying a pleasant mixture of charm and wit. If no less committed to Marxism-Leninism than his predecessors, he appeared to be more open and pragmatic and less rhetorical and confrontational than previous Soviet leaders.

During his first year at the helm of the Eurasian superpower, Gorbachev consolidated his own position in the Soviet hierarchy and set about to revitalize the Soviet Union's decrepit economic mechanism. But to the annoyance of the leaders in Washington, he sanctioned acceleration of shipments of Soviet arms and supplies to the Sandinista regime in Nicaragua, endorsed Fidel Castro's appeal that the poor countries of the Third World repudiate their debts to the principal lending countries, and tried to lure West Europeans away from their alliance with the United States by ordering a modest reduction in the number of Soviet IRBMs targeted on Western Europe.

Meanwhile, Ronald Reagan had begun to moderate his hostility to the Soviet Union. The new impulse to moderation in his approach to the rival superpower came as a total surprise to many of his compatriots, but not to those who were close observers of Reagan and his presidency.

During his campaign for the White House in 1980, Reagan signaled his disdain for the policy of striving to achieve détente in America's relations with the Soviet Union. He also assailed the SALT II treaty. And after moving into the White House, he turned aside all suggestions that he consider a summit meeting with his counterpart in the Kremlin. As mentioned, he also denounced the Soviet Union as "the focus of evil in the modern world." Still, as his first term in the presidency neared its conclusion, in September 1984, Reagan agreed to meet with the Soviet foreign minister, Andrei Gromyko, a sour-faced diplomatist with whom American leaders had been wrangling for forty years, a veritable symbol of the Cold War. Then, a few days before repeating the presidential oath for the second time, in January 1985, the chief executive sanctioned renewal of arms control negotiations with the Soviet Union after a 13-month suspension. Begun in March 1985, the latter negotiations were intended to achieve agreement regarding weapons in space, strategic weapons systems, and intermediate-range ballistic missiles. At the time of Chernenko's death, Reagan invited Mikhail Gorbachev to meet with him in the United States. Gorbachev declined, but a few months later agreed to meet with Reagan in Geneva the following autumn.

At length, in November 1985, Reagan and Gorbachev made their way to Geneva for the first summit meeting involving U.S. and Soviet leaders since Jimmy Carter's meeting with Brezhnev in 1979. During the three-day meeting, Gorbachev pressed Reagan without success to give up his Strategic Defense ("Star Wars") Initiative. Reagan pressed Gorbachev to terminate Soviet involvement in Afghanistan, Angola, and Ethiopia. Declared the president at one point, "You have no right to be in Afghanistan, Ethiopia, Angola. No right! This is Soviet aggression. It is destabilizing." Responded Gorbachev, "There is no basis for this! None at all! These [Afghans, Angolans, and Ethiopians] are people struggling for national liberation." Arriving at Brussels to brief leaders of NATO on what had taken place at Geneva, Reagan told reporters, "Neither side got everything they wanted." In truth, neither side "got" anything at all of much import. But the president also reported that he and Gorbachev "got very friendly" during the summit meeting in Switzerland. In time, the latter happening would appear to have been a genuine achievement of the Gorbachev-Reagan summit of November 19–21, 1985.

Three months after the summit meeting with Reagan in Geneva, General Secretary Gorbachev, in February 1986, allowed the Jewish dissident Anatoly Scharansky, a brilliant mathematician and computer scientist, to emigrate to Israel. Then, a few days later, in a speech to the twenty-seventh congress of the Communist party of the Soviet Union, he assailed the inertia and apathy of the Soviet bureaucracy, and urged increased flexibility in the management of the stagnant Soviet economy. In a word, he urged *perestroika*, a restructuring of the Soviet political and economic system. He also urged greater openness or *glasnost* in Soviet society. Glasnost was to generate a freer exchange of ideas and increased publicity concerning the shortcomings of life in the Soviet homeland.

Gorbachev's policy of perestroika resulted in important changes in 1986, although resistance to the policy within the Soviet bureaucracy was pervasive. Drawing the most attention in the outer world was adoption of a law that, effective May 1, 1987, would legalize private part-time businesses in such

November 21, 1985: President Reagan and General Secretary Gorbachev prepare to make final remarks at the end of their summit meeting in Geneva.

areas as tailoring, house and car repair, and tutoring. As for glasnost, the new policy appeared to flunk its first test, in May 1986, when the Kremlin was painfully slow to release information concerning the meltdown of Reactor No. 2 at the Chernobyl nuclear generating plant near Kiev in the Ukraine. And Gorbachev sternly refused appeals that the celebrated dissident Andrei Sakharov be allowed to emigrate (on the grounds that Sakharov knew too many secrets that were critical to Soviet security). Still, Sakharov was allowed to return to Moscow after years of exile in the city of Gorky. The system of state censorship was relaxed, and Soviet artists and intellectuals expressed their ideas and ideals with an abandon that they would not have dreamed of only a few years before.

Perestroika and glasnost aside, relations between the Soviet Union and the United States tended to be strained during 1986. When U.S. aircraft attacked "terrorist centers" in Libya in April 1986, the Kremlin accused the North American superpower of "contempt for international law and morality." To the disappointment of the Kremlin, President Reagan in May 1986 announced that the United States would no longer comply with limitations established in the dormant SALT II treaty unless the Soviets stopped violating the treaty. The Soviets denied any violation of the treaty, and in November 1986 the United States openly exceeded limits in strategic weapons prescribed by SALT II, "a major mistake," in the words of Gorbachev. Meanwhile, the government in Washington, contending that the Soviet Union had completed modernization of its nuclear arsenal and the United States had not, turned aside an appeal by Gorbachev for adoption of a treaty prohibiting all testing of nuclear weapons. But the nadir of superpower relations in 1986 came to pass on October 11–12 at Reykjavik in Iceland.

Out of the proverbial blue, in early October 1986, the governments in Moscow and Washington agreed that General Secretary Gorbachev and President Reagan would meet at Reykjavik in a "preliminary" summit, that is, discussions that would be a prelude to a full-dress summit meeting in Washington at a later date. Amid the usual fanfare, the two leaders and their entourages jetted off to Iceland. Then, when discussions got under way, Gorbachev made a bombshell proposal that the superpowers reduce their arsenals of strategic weapons by 50 percent within five years and prohibit deployment of space-based ("Star Wars") weapons for ten years. Taken aback, Reagan countered by proposing total elimination of all ballistic missiles within ten years. The general secretary acceded to Reagan's counterproposal, and also agreed to elimination of all medium-range missiles based in Europe and to reduction of testing of nuclear weapons. But only on one condition, to wit, that the president agree to "strengthen" the SALT I (ABM) treaty of 1972 and confine research on space weapons to the laboratory. When Reagan insisted on the right to test as well as continue research on SDI, the summit meeting collapsed amid charges by each side that the other was to blame. Suspecting that Reagan had missed a golden opportunity to reach an historic agreement that would have turned the tide of the nightmarish competition by the superpowers to achieve supremacy in nuclear weapons, many of the president's compatriots tended to concur with the Soviets.

Brushing aside whatever disappointment he may have felt over the outcome of the Reykjavik summit, Gorbachev in the months that followed pressed ahead with the policies of perestroika and glasnost, and at a plenum of the Central Committee of the Soviet Communist party, in January 1987, delivered a scathing critique of the Soviet system. He charged that "authoritarian appraisals" and opinions had become irrefutable truths during the era of Josef Stalin, and had continued to shackle the Soviet people and the regime in Moscow for three decades after the death of the tyrannical "man of steel." He even spoke of the desirability of bringing a measure of democracy, for example, contested elections and secret ballots, to the Soviet political process. Unfortunately, many of Gorbachev's colleagues in the Soviet hierarchy, while generally supporting the general secretary's initiatives aimed at making the moribund Soviet economy function more efficiently, took a jaundiced view of any reforms that might weaken their hold on the instruments of power.

Meanwhile, the Soviet Union and the United States continued their dialogue in the area of arms control. Few ordinary Americans paid much attention. The superpowers, after all, had been wrestling with minimal success with the tangled question of arms control for years. But then, in December 1987, General Secretary Gorbachev and President Reagan put their hands to a historic treaty by which the superpowers for the first time agreed to a reduction of their nuclear arsenals. In a word, the Soviet Union and the United States would not merely limit further growth of a category (or family) of nuclear weapons. Rather, they would destroy an entire category of nuclear-tipped missiles.

It was in early December of 1987 that Gorbachev traveled to Washington to engage in his third summit meeting with President Reagan. Accompanying him was his fashionable wife Raisa. The trip was a rousing tour de force by the Soviet general secretary. Wrote Michael Mandelbaum in *U.S. News & World Report*, "The direct political descendant of the ascetic revolutionary V. I. Lenin, the murderous tyrant Joseph Stalin, the bumptious son of a coal miner Nikita Khrushchev and the dour apparatchik Leonid Brezhnev swept Washington off its feet last week." At one point, in the heart of downtown Washington, Gorbachev ordered the driver of his limousine to stop, whereupon he bounded out of the vehicle to press flesh with ordinary Americans. Mandelbaum observed that a T-shirt on sale in Washington offered Gorbachev's likeness above the caption "Gorbachev Glasnost Tour, 1987," then remarked that the caption might have read "The Return of Détente." In any event, the two chiefs of state smiled frequently and clinked champagne glasses. Striking a friendly note at the outset of the summit, Reagan told Gorbachev, "My name is Ron." Responded Gorbachev, "Mine is Mikhail."

The climactic moment of the three-day summit meeting took place in the East Room of the White House, on December 10, 1987, when Gorbachev and Reagan signed what was generally referred to as the INF (Intermediate Nuclear Forces) treaty. The treaty provided for the dismantling over the next three years of all 1,752 Soviet and 859 U.S. missiles having ranges of 300 to 3,400 miles, most of them presently deployed in Europe. It also provided for inspectors of both powers to observe the burning, crushing, exploding, smashing, or launching into oblivion of the dismantled missiles. Following the ceremony of signature, the two leaders exchanged pens, which were to be souvenirs of the occasion. Said Reagan, "We can only hope that this history-making agreement will not be an end in itself, but the beginning of a working relationship that will enable us to tackle . . . other issues."

No small number of Americans suspected that the INF treaty would stand as the crowning achievement of the Reagan presidency. And in the perception of partisans of President Reagan, it was an achievement that had resulted from Reagan's grim determination during his first term, in the face of angry protests in both Western Europe and America, that NATO would deploy Pershing 2 and Tomahawk intermediate-range missiles in Europe. That perception is hard to confute. In light of the events that culminated in the INF treaty, the parallel perception that negotiating from a position of strength is more apt to yield arms-control agreements is likewise hard to confute. Still, as a few observers pointed out, the Soviets, who had rejected Reagan's so-called zero-option proposal (whereby the Soviets would dismantle their SS-20 IRBMs in Europe and the Far East and the United States would refrain from deploying Pershing 2s and Tomahawks in Western Europe), set out in late 1981, compelled the United States to accept the huge expense of building and deploying the Pershing 2s and Tomahawks in Western Europe before consenting to dismantle their own IRBMs. In a word, they refused to allow the United States to secure an INF treaty on the cheap.

Although the issue of "Star Wars" prevented the superpowers from completing a START (Strategic Arms Reduction) treaty, relations between the United States and the onetime "evil empire" remained cordial during the remainder of Ronald Reagan's time in the White House. Ignoring suspicions of various of their compatriots, most of them political conservatives, who doubted that provisions for verifying Soviet compliance with its terms would prove effective and feared that removal of American intermediate-range missiles would leave Western Europe vulnerable to a conventional attack by forces of the Warsaw Pact, the U.S. Senate in May 1988 consented to the INF treaty. During that same month, the Soviets announced that they were terminating their bloody and costly nine-year Afghan adventure, and would soon withdraw the first contingent of the 115,000 Soviet troops who were deployed in Afghanistan. Gorbachev indicated that the withdrawal of Soviet troops from Afghanistan would be completed by early 1989. Meanwhile, the general secretary undertook a diplomatic offensive that was breathtaking in scope. He intimated a willingness to discuss termination of Soviet assistance to the Sandinista regime in Nicaragua, permitted the Soviet-backed Marxist government in Angola to begin negotiations aimed at terminating the 13-year civil war that had ravaged the latter country, reduced Soviet military assistance to the Marxist regime in Mozambique. He urged the PLO to recognize Israel's right to national existence, pressed the Soviet Union's Vietnamese allies to remove their troops from Kampuchea (Cambodia), ordered the withdrawal of undisclosed numbers of Soviet troops from the Sino-Soviet frontier, urged the Soviet satellites in Eastern Europe to reform their economies and improve relations with the West.

Then, in June 1988, General Secretary and Mrs. Gorbachev welcomed President and Mrs. Reagan to Moscow. The pilgrimage of Reagan to the citadel of world communism, of course, abounded with irony. Of that pilgrimage, the reporter Hugh Sidey wrote in *Time*, "The most powerful anti-Soviet crusader of the modern era has become its most determined summiteer." And Reagan himself said, "I never expected to be here." Otherwise, the president repeatedly jangled the nerves of his hosts by hectoring them about violations of human rights. But most of the time he exuded warmth and good humor. As for conversations between Gorbachev and Reagan, they tended to be pro forma, and resulted in no agreements of any substance.

The months that followed were difficult for the general secretary. After three years of Gorbachev's reforms, the Soviet economy remained stagnant: Clothing, food, housing, and other essentials remained in short supply; the national living standard had actually declined. Affording intellectuals and ordinary citizens of the Soviet empire an opportunity to voice grievances, glasnost had generated unrest, particularly among national minorities in Estonia, Latvia, and Lithuania in the northwestern reaches of the empire to Armenia in the southwestern reaches. Although it appeared unlikely that any Soviet leader could turn back the national clock to the time of Stalin or even Brezhnev, the survival of glasnost and perestroika appeared less certain than a year or so before.

It was against the foregoing background of frustration and dissension inside the Soviet empire that Gorbachev (who, as a result of constitutional changes engineered by the Kremlin, was now President Gorbachev), in early December of 1988, made his way to New York to address the General Assembly of the UN and say farewell to President Reagan, who would retire from the White House on January 20, 1989. The address to the General Assembly proved the high point of the general secretary's latest visit to the United States. During the address, Gorbachev conceded that "closed societies" did not function as they should and that the Kremlin did not possess "the ultimate truth." He said that "the use or threat of force" was not a legitimate tool of foreign policy, then made a pronouncement that appeared destined to assure the address a place in history: During the next two years the Soviet Union would reduce its conventional armed forces by 500,000 troops and 10,000 tanks—reductions that Gorbachev clearly needed to execute in order to generate funds with which to stimulate his country's stagnant economy. Alas, before completing his itinerary in New York, the general secretary received devastating news: A horrendous earthquake had rocked the Soviet republic of Armenia, claiming the lives of more than fifty thousand Armenian citizens. With heavy heart, Gorbachev rushed back to his homeland to survey the tragedy and oversee relief efforts.

## ELECTION OF 1988

Nineteen hundred and eighty-eight, the year of President Reagan's remarkable trip to Moscow and President Gorbachev's pronouncement that the Soviet Union would reduce its conventional forces, was, of course, an election year in the United States. As usual, popular attention centered on the contest for the most exalted office in the republic, namely, the presidency.

Scarcely had Ronald Reagan repeated the presidential oath for the second time, on January 20, 1985, before the presidential campaign of 1988 got under way. Or so it appeared. Be that as it may, the campaign had begun to move into high gear by the turn of 1987. The odds-on favorite to win the Republican nomination for president in 1988 as the year 1987 unfolded was Vice Pres. George Bush, notwithstanding the much-publicized fact that no incumbent vice president had won election to the presidency since Martin Van Buren in 1836. Still, Bush did not want for challengers, among them Sen. Robert J. Dole of Kansas, former-Governor Pierre S. "Pete" du Pont IV of Delaware, former-Secretary of State Alexander M. Haig, Jr., Rep. Jack F. Kemp of New York, and the televangelist, the Reverend Pat Robertson. Among the Democrats who at the dawn of 1987 were competing for the presidential nomination of their party were former-Governor Bruce E. Babbitt of Arizona, Sen. Joseph R. Biden, Jr., of Delaware, Gov. Michael S. Dukakis of Massachusetts, Rep. Richard A.

Gephardt of Missouri, Sen. Albert Gore, Jr., of Tennessee, former-Senator Gary Hart of Colorado, the Reverend Jesse L. Jackson, and Sen. Paul Simon of Illinois. The front-runner among the Democrats appeared to be Gary Hart—until reports hinting that Hart had dallied with a voluptuous young woman devastated his candidacy. Most Democrats, in truth, expressed little enthusiasm for any of the men who were competing for their party's presidential nomination, and many, frankly, hoped (in vain, as matters turned out) that Gov. Mario Cuomo of New York, Sen. Bill Bradley of New Jersey, or Sen. Sam Nunn of Georgia would enter the contest. At length, in early 1988, the inevitable process of winnowing out of candidates began when Iowa held party caucuses and New Hampshire a primary election. When the process finally ended, in early June of 1988, the survivors were 64-year-old George Bush and 54-year-old Michael Dukakis.

The Democrats held their national convention of 1988 at Atlanta in July. Commanding almost as much attention as Dukakis when delegates assembled was Jesse Jackson, who had finished second in the primary balloting and clearly sought the vice presidential nomination. But Jackson, black and ultraliberal, was anathema to millions of his white compatriots, particularly those of moderate and conservative political orientation. So to the acute disappointment of Jackson and millions of his partisans, Dukakis asked delegates to the convention to nominate the moderately conservative senator of Texas, 67-year-old Lloyd Bentsen, to be his vice presidential running mate. Otherwise, the conclave in Atlanta was a rousing convention, and when delegates, after nominating Dukakis and Bentsen and adopting a brief and moderately liberal platform, departed Atlanta they felt confident that they had launched their party on the road to victory in the balloting in November. Their confidence seemed well founded. Opinion polls disclosed that the country's voters favored Dukakis, widely perceived to be a competent, no-nonsense governor who had presided over revitalization of the economy of Massachusetts, over Bush, widely perceived as a wimpy yes-man who had betrayed no qualities of leadership while serving a succession of GOP presidents in secondary capacities, by a margin of 54 percent to 36 percent.

But for whatever reason—Democrats later accused Dukakis of having rested on his lead—opinion polls disclosed a steady erosion of Dukakis's standing among voters during the weeks that followed the Democratic convention. And by the time delegates to the Republican national convention assembled in New Orleans in mid-August 1988 the two men, Dukakis and Bush, were dead even in the polls. Various pundits suspected that Bush had made a horrendous miscalculation when at the outset of the GOP convention he selected the youthful and handsome and very conservative Sen. J. Danforth "Dan" Quayle of Indiana to be his vice presidential running mate, the more so when it was disclosed that Quayle had opted for service in the National Guard in order to avoid the draft (and possible combat duty) during the war in Vietnam. But Bush delivered a powerful acceptance speech to climax the convention, and within days opinion polls disclosed that a plurality of the country's voters now favored the vice president over Dukakis.

Try as he might, Dukakis during the weeks that followed could not close the gap separating his name and Bush's in the opinion polls. Disappointed Democrats would subsequently allege that the Dukakis campaign organization had been inept and that Dukakis himself lacked the passion required to ignite voters. Meanwhile, the richly endowed Republican campaign performed like a well-oiled engine, and Bush clearly won the competition of the "sound bites," that is, pungent 20- or 30-second pronouncements uttered by the candidates nearly every day in the hope that they would be beamed into tens of millions of households that evening via the news programs of the major television networks. Moreover, Bush found a mark with millions of his compatriots when he repeatedly pledged "no new taxes," then challenged anyone who doubted the pledge to "read my lips." He also found a mark with voters when he portrayed Dukakis as a liberal who, if elected president, would increase federal spending and ask Congress to increase taxes. Meanwhile, to the disgust of millions of voters, he pressed (at the same time that he was promising "a kinder, gentler society") a variety of "hot button" issues, that is, issues that touched the emotions of great numbers of voters. Most notably, he intimated that Dukakis was "soft" on crime and flawed in his patriotism—was the governor who had made possible a weekend leave for the convicted rapist and murderer Willie Horton (who had committed new outrages during his leave) and refused to support legislation requiring teachers in Massachusetts to lead schoolchildren in daily recitation of the pledge of allegiance to the national flag. During two televised "debates," Dukakis failed completely to stay the tide of the Bush campaign.

Mercifully, the tedious and uninspiring campaign ground to a termination on November 8, 1988, and when votes were tabulated the ticket of Bush-Quayle had buried that of Dukakis-Bentsen. Winning 54 percent of the popular votes to 46 percent for their opponents, Bush and Quayle won the electoral votes of 40 of the 50 states. (In addition to 10 states, Dukakis-Bentsen won the electoral votes of the District of Columbia.) But, as had become customary in recent times, the electorate, whatever its preference for Republican candidates for the presidency and vice presidency, displayed an affinity for Democratic candidates for seats in both houses of Congress. Accordingly, the forty-first president would face a national legislature commanded by the opposition party.

## RETROSPECT

Dazed Democrats found it hard to understand why the electorate accorded George Bush victory in the presidential election in the autumn of 1988, by landslide proportions no less. After all, Bush had offered himself to voters as the heir apparent of Ronald Reagan, the candidate who would proceed in accord with perceptions and purposes that had animated the executive branch of the national government during the eight years of "the Gipper" (as Reagan, who, as previously mentioned, had played the legendary football player George

Gipp in one of his Hollywood films, was often referred to). The latter perceptions and purposes had prompted the president and his official family to tolerate monstrous deficits in the federal budget that had resulted in an incredible doubling of the national debt since 1980, to take a casual view of the plight of the country's poor and homeless, to give short shrift to the causes of civil rights, protection of the natural environment, and protection of consumers, to betray scant concern over a steady erosion in recent years in the standards of labor in the United States, the manifest inadequacies of education at all levels in the country, and the inability of millions of Americans to afford adequate health care. Those perceptions and purposes, in the perspective of Democrats, had encouraged a dubious and largely unsuccessful policy in Central America—and, more than that, encouraged a kind of cowboy diplomacy that had culminated in the Iran-contra travesty. They had resulted in toleration by the administration in Washington of the repressive regime of South Africa and other repressive noncommunist regimes as well.

Many Democrats, of course, were not dazed or mystified in the aftermath of Bush's destruction of Dukakis. They understood that in the perspective of a preponderance of Americans the federal budgetary deficits and the national debt were incomprehensible abstractions. They understood, too, that most Americans in 1988 were not poor or homeless and most were not blacks or Indians or Hispanics who nearly every day of their lives endured the consequences of historic discrimination and abuse—also that legions of Americans admired the spirit that had prompted Oliver North to do what he could, whether legal or not, to reinforce Central America's "freedom fighters" and really were not overwrought about white supremacy and apartheid in South Africa. What mattered to a majority of Americans in 1988 as they pondered the years that Ronald Reagan had presided over the national destiny and weighed the candidacies of George Bush and Michael Dukakis was the fact that, notwithstanding seemingly astronomical budgetary deficits and a soaring national debt, not to mention out-of-control deficits in the country's balance of international trade and "the buying of America" by foreign investors, and a burgeoning crisis in the savings and loan (S&L) industry that threatened to cost taxpayers an incredible $100 billion (because accounts in S&Ls were insured by the federal government), the national economy had generated a peacetime record of six consecutive years of prosperity (1983–1988), and that as a consequence most Americans could afford late-model cars, comfortable housing, stereos, VCRs, annual vacations, and uncounted other fruits valued by a consumption-oriented people. Responsible for that prosperity had been the structure of low taxes put in place by the initiative of President Reagan and what most Americans perceived to have been a concerted effort by the Reagan administration to limit federal spending. A majority of the electorate reckoned that a national administration presided over by George Bush was more apt than one presided over by "Mike" Dukakis to urge retention of the structure of low taxes and keep a lid on federal spending—was more apt, in a phrase of recent decades, to keep the good times rolling.

But support of Bush certainly transcended the economic self-interest of a majority of the country's voters. Although born to a measure of wealth and a style of life that only a tiny handful of citizens could ever hope to achieve, Bush more than Dukakis appeared to be animated by personal and social values that tens of millions of Americans cherished. Like those latter Americans, Bush was exuberantly patriotic. He betrayed little compassion for the perpetrators of crime and violence against citizens who abided by the law. He opposed abortion. Unabashedly committed to Protestant Christianity, he favored the right of schools to set aside time for prayer or meditation by their students. More than that, George Bush was a manifestly good and decent man (as was Michael Dukakis). He was not driven by a compulsion to keep his emotions in check. But he was also, in the view of most Americans, a sensible man who could be trusted to exercise good judgment as he guided the North American superpower into the 1990s and toward the twenty-first century.

By choosing Ronald Reagan's vice president to succeed "the Gipper"—indeed choosing the man Reagan had quietly anointed to be his successor—a majority of the voters of the United States had, in fact, registered a dramatic endorsement of the stewardship from 1981 to 1989 of the fortieth chief executive. It remained to be seen whether history would record a similar verdict.

# Chapter
## 14

# Beginning
# of the
# Bush Era

$S$hortly after noon, on January 20, 1989, George Bush placed his left hand on one of two Bibles held by his wife Barbara, raised his right hand, and repeated the presidential oath after Chief Justice William Rehnquist. Flanking the forty-first president were his 87-year-old mother, Vice President and Mrs. Quayle, President and Mrs. Reagan, and a host of relatives, friends, and other dignitaries. Announcing that "a new breeze is blowing," the new chief executive in his inaugural address exhorted his compatriots to "use power to help people." In the view of the editors of *Time*, his speech appeared to signal "a new altruism, a move away from the Reagan era's tacit approval of selfishness, an end to the glorification of greed."

## GEORGE H. W. BUSH

Born on June 12, 1924, in Milton, Massachusetts, George Bush grew up in Greenwich, Connecticut, an affluent suburb of New York City. His father, Prescott Bush, was a successful Wall Street investment banker who in the twilight of his life, from 1962 to 1972, served in the U.S. Senate as a Republican from Connecticut. After graduating in 1942 from Phillips Academy, an exclusive preparatory school, George Bush enlisted in the Navy, underwent flight training, and was assigned to a squadron of torpedo bombers aboard the small aircraft carrier USS *San Jacinto*. During the months that followed, while the "San Jack" was deployed against the Japanese in the Western Pacific, he made 58 combat missions, the most memorable of which took place on September 2, 1944. During the latter mission, a bombing raid against Japanese installations on the island of Chichi Jima in the Bonin Islands, Bush's plane was riddled by antiaircraft fire while attacking an enemy radio station. But, according to the citation that accompanied his award of the Distinguished Flying Cross, "In spite of smoke and flames from the fire in his plane, he continued his dive and scored damaging bomb hits on the radio station, before bailing out of his plane." After spending what he later described as "four terrifying hours in the water," Bush was rescued by the submarine USS *Finback*. In December 1944, the blue-eyed, 6-foot-2-inch airman was rotated back to the United States, and a few weeks later, in January 1945, he married Barbara Pierce, the daughter of the publisher of *McCall's* and *Redbook* magazines.

Released from active duty in the Navy, he enrolled at Yale University in September 1945, majored in economics, and played first base for the Yale baseball team. He was an excellent student, and won election to Phi Beta Kappa. Turning aside offers to join a prestigious investment banking firm in New York, Bush, in 1948, loaded his wife and infant son in a car and made his way to western Texas, where he took a job with an oil-field supply company. At length, in 1954 (the year after his daughter Robin died of leukemia), he became president of Zapata Offshore Company, a developer of drilling equipment for use in offshore oil operations. In 1958, he moved the headquarters of Zapata Offshore to Houston, where he and his wife and their five children had taken up residence.

Long interested in politics, Bush, an unflinching Republican, went down in defeat in 1964 when he ran for a seat in the U.S. Senate. During the campaign, he vigorously supported the Republican candidate for president, Barry Goldwater, and to his discredit assailed the historic civil rights legislation that Lyndon Johnson had recently maneuvered through Congress. Undaunted by defeat, he threw himself into a campaign in 1966 to represent the Seventh Congressional District of Texas in the U.S. House of Representatives. His enterprise yielded victory, and two years later he easily won re-election. Urged on by President Nixon, he made a second run for the Senate in 1970, only to go down in defeat in a contest in which he was pitted against a moderately conservative Democrat, Lloyd M. Bentsen, Jr., notwithstanding heavy support by the oil industry and a secret (and illegal) fund of $100,000 channeled to his campaign by the White House. Having given up his seat in the House to run for the Senate, Bush was now out of a job, whereupon Nixon, in December 1970, appointed him to be the U.S. ambassador at the United Nations. In early 1973, he left the UN when the president appointed him to the chairmanship of the Republican Party. As the Watergate scandal closed in around Nixon, in 1973–1974, Bush remained a stalwart defender of the beleaguered president—until the White House tapes, belatedly surrendered by Nixon on order of the Supreme Court, proved that the president had sought to obstruct the FBI's investigation of the Watergate break-in. At that point, on August 7, 1974, Bush delivered a letter to his mentor of recent years requesting that Nixon resign the presidential office.

A short time later, in the autumn of 1974, Bush accepted a new appointment proffered by President Ford: chief of the U.S. Liaison Office in the People's Republic of China. Fourteen months after that, in late 1975, Ford asked him to return to the United States and assume the directorship of the CIA, its prestige and the morale of its personnel at an all-time low as a result of recent disclosures that the agency had often violated its statutory mandate. Although he headed the CIA for less than a year—he resigned in the aftermath of the Democratic victory in the presidential election of 1976—he received considerate praise for having presided over the drafting of a new charter for the agency and helping to restore the morale of its personnel.

Bush's gaze now turned to the White House, and in May 1979 he announced that he was a candidate for the Republican nomination for president. But, as matters turned out, he proved no match for Ronald Reagan when serious campaigning got under way in early 1988, and he quit the campaign after Reagan rolled over him in Bush's home state of Texas.

Fortunately, Bush had refrained from attacking Reagan during the primary campaign, save for an offhand remark that the tax cuts Reagan was urging amounted to "voodoo economics." So when Reagan and former-President Ford, during the Republican national convention in the summer of 1980, failed to strike a bargain whereby Ford would become Reagan's vice presidential running mate in the impending campaign against the Democrats, Reagan invited Bush to take second place on the national ticket of the GOP. Bush accepted the invitation with unabashed enthusiasm. Reagan and Bush, of course, romped to victory over President Carter and Vice President Mondale on Election Day in November 1980, and on January 20, 1981, Bush became vice president. Reagan and Bush repeated their electoral triumph of 1980 four years later, this time at the expense of Walter Mondale and Geraldine Ferraro.

As vice president from 1981 to 1989, Bush established an easy intimacy with President Reagan, and never wavered in his loyalty to the chief executive. Although many of President Reagan's more dedicated partisans doubted Bush's commitment to Reagan's ultraconservative ideology, the fortieth chief executive, as election year 1988 approached, left no doubt that Bush was his choice to be the next president.

By the time he achieved the presidency, George Bush had failed to stir the passions of any substantial number of his compatriots. He struck many Americans as one who had been an obsequious servant of Presidents Nixon, Ford, and Reagan—as a fawning and servile man who had never established a politi-

January 20, 1989: George Bush repeats the presidential oath after Chief Justice Rehnquist on a platform atop the west steps of the Capitol.

cal identity of his own. Such Americans had been inclined during the Reagan years to view Bush as a wimp (that is, according to *Webster's New World Dictionary*, "a weak, ineffectual, or insipid person"). Legions of his compatriots also ridiculed what they perceived to be his prep school (or "preppy") persona, the more so when Bush, a man who had grown up amid wealth and privilege, sought to convey a down-home image by professing a love of country music, pork rinds, and horseshoe pitching. Still, the new president struck most Americans as a decent and honorable man, one who was bright, knowledgeable, and prudent. His frequent profession of commitment to conservative principles notwithstanding, he seemed to be a pragmatic man rather than an ideologue. After having been led for eight years by an apparent ideologue (who, in truth, was more pragmatic than most Americans realized), the citizenry appeared comfortable with the prospect of falling in behind a president who would not be inclined to allow ideological principles to command high policy.

## BEYOND THE WHITE HOUSE

While George Bush was settling into the Oval Office and meeting the initial challenges of his presidency during the early months of 1989, the people of the United States experienced, often via reports and commentaries by the communications media, a succession of happenings and developments that had little or nothing to do with the new president and the policies and initiatives of his administration. Those happenings and events were nothing if not diverse.

A few days after Bush's inauguration, the San Francisco Forty-Niners overcame the Cincinnati Bengals in professional football's Super Bowl. Caught up in a web of gambling charges, Pete Rose, the manager of the Cincinnati Reds and holder of one of the premier records in sports (the most base hits achieved by a player in the course of a major league baseball career) was the subject of endless speculation regarding his future in baseball. Huge audiences flocked to experience the film *Rain Man,* a bittersweet saga of a youthful hustler (Tom Cruise) and his autistic brother (Dustin Hoffman). Meanwhile, television viewers were tuning in by the millions to the weekly situation comedy "Roseanne" in which the plump and feisty Roseanne Barr played an unfettered and street-smart working wife and mother.

On a more serious note, Americans at the onset of the era of George Bush pondered what most of them reckoned was a new malady: Lyme disease, first identified in Lyme, Connecticut, in 1975. Borne by infected ticks that live in wooded areas and tall grass, Lyme disease can cause arthritis, facial palsy, heart arrhythmias, joint and neurological damage, loss of sensation, and severe headaches. More distressing in the view of many Americans were outbreaks of violence that marked the first months of the presidency of a man who yearned for a kinder and gentler society. Some of the worst violence of those months, ironically perhaps, occurred only a short distance from the gleaming white residence of President Bush himself, in the drug-infested ghettos of Washington, where drug traffickers and their hit men were reinforcing the federal city's claim to the title (gained in 1988, when it displaced Detroit) as the murder capital of the republic. During the months of January through May of 1989, there were 95 homicides in Washington. More upsetting in the view of many Americans was the foray through Central Park in New York City, on a clear evening in April of 1989, by a pack of teenage boys, who according to the boys, were merely looking for something to do. In addition to introducing into the lexicon of urban violence a new word, "wilding" (a term some of them invoked to describe their activity), the boys allegedly assaulted a succession of strollers and at least one male jogger. At length, they encountered a 28-year-old woman jogger whom they chased into a gully, beat senseless with a rock and metal pipe, and left for dead.

## THE ENVIRONMENT AND NUCLEAR FUSION

No less worrisome than urban drug wars and "wilding" in the estimate of many Americans during the pristine months of the Bush presidency were warnings by scientists that the much-discussed "greenhouse" phenomenon, that is, a warming of the earth as a result of destruction of the ozone layer by carbon dioxide and other gases spewed into the atmosphere by humankind's power plants, factories, motor vehicles, landfills, and cattle feedlots, was no chimera, and that an environmental crisis of global dimension was pending if destruction of the ozone layer continued.

Alas, doomsday warnings by scientists regarding the ozone layer appeared to make less of an imprint on the popular consciousness than an environmental disaster that befell the republic two months after George Bush repeated the presidential oath. The foregoing disaster came to pass in the predawn hours of March 24, 1989, when the 987-foot supertanker *Exxon Valdez* plowed into a reef in Prince Edward Sound shortly after leaving the tanker terminal near Valdez, Alaska. The reef tore a hole in the hull of the *Exxon Valdez* from which a quarter-million barrels of Alaskan crude seeped into the sea. The result was an oil slick that covered nearly 1,000 square miles, befouled the shorelines of several large islands, and devastated uncounted marine animals, birds, and fish.

While the cleanup of the enormous oil spill was making uncertain progress, environmentalists reiterated an argument they had made many times over the past two decades, to wit, that the oil industry and Alaska's delicate

April 1989: Troy Anderson and Nicolette Heaphy, at the bird cleaning center in Valdez, Alaska, clean a cormorant that had been covered with crude oil following the wreck of the supertanker *Exxon Valdez*.

ecology were incompatible. Aware that they could not force termination of existing oil operations in Alaska, which fed an average of more than two tankersful of crude each day to refineries on the West Coast of the forty-eight contiguous states of the United States, they hoped at the very least to prevent drilling in the Arctic National Wildlife Refuge on Alaska's northern shore. They found small comfort in words uttered by President Bush, who during his campaign for the White House had proclaimed himself an environmentalist of the Theodore Roosevelt genre. According to Bush, there was no connection between the wreck of the *Exxon Valdez* and drilling in the Arctic National Wildlife Refuge. In a word, he had no intention of preventing companies from exploring for oil in the wildlife preserve. Explained the occupant of the Oval Office, "We are becoming increasingly dependent on foreign oil, and that is not acceptable to any president."

In some measure because electric generating plants powered by "cold" (room temperature) fusion reactors would present almost no danger to the natural environment—that is, they release into the atmosphere no gases that damage the ozone layer or cause acid rain, and (unlike existing atom-splitting nuclear power plants) present no threat of running amok and produce little radioactive waste—millions of Americans responded excitedly to reports that rocketed about the world a few days before the wreck of the *Exxon Valdez* that two chemists, Stanley Pons of the University of Utah and Martin Fleischmann of the University of Southampton in Great Britain, claimed to have produced cold nuclear fusion. (*Webster's New World Dictionary* defines nuclear fusion as "the fusion of lightweight atomic nuclei, as of deuterium or tritium, into a nucleus of heavy mass, as of helium, with a resultant loss in the combined mass, which is converted into energy.") The chemists reported that they had produced fusion in a bottle, using palladium (a metallic chemical element), platinum, "heavy" water (in which deuterium had replaced hydrogen), and electricity. The excitement stirred by the claims of Pons and Fleischmann, to be sure, transcended environmental concerns, for fusion reactors would be fueled by cheap and inexhaustible materials, hence could provide all of the low-cost electricity that the world's populations could ever consume. The economic and social consequences of the perfection of fusion reactors were beyond comprehension.

The scientific community, of course, was agog during the weeks that followed the announcement by Pons and Fleischmann, and millions of nonscientists tried to figure out as best they could the phenomenon of nuclear fusion. Hundreds of laboratories around the world sought to duplicate the experiments of Pons and Fleischmann, and several reported at least a measure of success. Scarcely six weeks after the remarkable announcement by the two chemists, however, it was reported that none of the major laboratories of the United States had achieved positive results when trying to duplicate the Pons-Fleischmann experiments. On the other side of the Atlantic, the editor of the prestigious British journal *Nature* asserted simply that the claim of Pons and Fleischmann "is literally unsupported by the evidence."

## THE TRIAL OF OLIVER NORTH

Touching the emotions, indeed the passions, of millions of Americans in April of 1989, was the long-awaited trial of Oliver North, a central figure in the so-called Iran-contra scandal. The trial took place after the prosecution had dropped its most explosive charges against the onetime colonel of the Marine Corps, notably those pertaining to the diversion of funds from Iranian arms sales to the Nicaraguan contras. Prosecution of North on those charges would require the introduction of top-secret documents that the White House refused to release—because, according to the White House, the national security required that the documents remain secret.

At the onset of the trial, the defense read to the jury an extraordinary "admission of facts" charging that, contrary to his repeated denials, President Reagan had, in fact, been involved in secret efforts to provide aid to the Nicaraguan contras. The admission of facts also charged that Vice President Bush in March 1985 had told the president of Honduras (in apparent violation of the so-called Boland amendment prohibiting aid by the U.S. government to the contras) that the United States would strike a quid pro quo bargain with the Hondurans whereby the Washington government would increase and expedite its military and economic assistance to Honduras if the government in Tegucigalpa, in return, would continue to allow the contras to operate from base camps in Honduran territory and transfer military supplies to the Nicaraguan rebels. (Bush, now the president, looked into TV cameras a short time later and, in reference to his discussions with the Honduran president in 1985, said emphatically, "There was no quid pro quo.") As for North, he insisted that he had been "a pawn in a chess game being played by giants" in the matter of the Iran-contra affair—had been a mere underling who sought to carry out the policies of superiors (after the fashion of German "war criminals" who had sat in the dock at Nuremberg in 1945–1946).

After deliberating for 12 days, the jury found North guilty of aiding and abetting an obstruction of Congress; altering, concealing, and destroying National Security Council documents; and receiving an illegal gratuity (a security fence for his residence). It acquitted him on charges of obstructing and lying to Congress (when he told a congressional committee in 1985 that the NSC was not providing aid to the contras, a lie that North had admitted); obstructing a congressional inquiry (when he told the Congressional Intelligence Committee in 1986 that he was providing no military advice to the contras, another acknowledged lie); and three other charges.

That the jury had found North guilty on any charges at all outraged millions of citizens who continued to view the former marine as a national hero, one who, in what his partisans perceived to be a just and honorable cause, namely, to fight communism in Central America by helping the Nicaraguan contras, had every license to bend or even break the law, the more so when he was merely carrying out the manifest will if not the explicit orders of the president. Other Americans, many of them unsympathetic to the cause of assisting the contras, reckoned that North had been made the scapegoat for the excesses (and perhaps crimes) of his superiors.

At length, on July 5, Judge Gerhard Gesell, asserting that North had willingly and sometimes excessively done the bidding of cynical superiors, announced North's punishment: a three-year suspended prison sentence, a fine of $150,000, and contribution of 1,200 hours of community service in a program aimed at assisting inner-city youths to counter drugs. Still, the drama of Iran-contra had not yet played its final scene. Former-National Security Adviser John M. Poindexter, North's immediate superior at the time the Iran-contra affair unraveled, was scheduled to go on trial in the summer or autumn of 1989—on six counts, including the two main conspiracy and theft charges that the prosecution had dropped in the case against North because the White House would not release relevant classified documents.

## AT THE SUPREME COURT

The pristine months of the Bush presidency were a busy time for the nine justices of the Supreme Court. Indeed, the justices handed down a succession of rulings that touched the emotions and interests of great numbers of Americans: one that the constitutional ban on "cruel and unusual punishments" does not prevent the execution of young people who commit capital crimes at age 16 or 17, or, in certain circumstances, felons who are retarded; four decisions that civil rights activists denounced as constituting a disastrous turning back of the clock in the area of the civil rights of racial minorities and women (most notably, perhaps, a ruling that imposed a barrier against the invocation by minority workers of statistical data to prove that they have been victims of racial discrimination—a heavy blow to affirmative action programs, it was widely surmised); a decision that so-called "dial-a-porn" legislation enacted by Congress in 1988 criminalizing "obscene and indecent" telephone message services (passed largely in response to complaints by parents that "sexy" phone communications were unduly accessible to children) was overly restrictive—that only obscene messages, not those adjudged to be indecent, might be prohibited.

Generating a far more vehement public response than the foregoing decisions was one handed down in June 1989: The high court ruled that the First Amendment guarantee of free speech protects individuals who burn the Stars and Stripes as an act of political protest. Explained Justice William Brennan, "We do not consecrate the flag by punishing its desecration, for in so doing [that is, by punishing desecraters of the national banner] we dilute the freedom that this cherished emblem represents." Few citizens appeared to agree. Declared a veteran of World War II and the Korean War, "Nobody, but nobody, should ever deface the American flag. I don't give a damn whether it's the civil right [of the protester] or not. I fought to protect the American flag, not him." Sharing (or at least reflecting) the popular outrage, the Senate, by a vote of

97 to 3, passed a resolution expressing "profound disappointment" with the Supreme Court's decision in the flag-burning case. The House passed a similar resolution by a vote of 411 to 5. Declaring that the flag was "a unique national symbol," President Bush appealed for a constitutional amendment that would prohibit desecration of the Stars and Stripes.

Still, it seems fair to say, most Americans did not consider the Supreme Court's ruling in the flag-burning case to be nearly so important as that handed down on July 3, 1989, in the case of *William L. Webster* v. *Reproduction Health Services*. The case, in which an abortion clinic in St. Louis challenged a law enacted by the legislature of Missouri in 1986 proclaiming that "life begins with conception" and imposing restrictions on abortion within the state of Missouri, required the Supreme Court to pass judgment anew on its ruling in *Roe* v. *Wade* in 1973, a ruling that had virtually eliminated restrictions on abortion in the United States.

During the spring and early summer of 1989, proponents of choice in the matter of abortion (that is, citizens who demanded that the justices uphold the almost unlimited right of an expectant mother to abort her embryo or fetus as guaranteed by the high court in its earlier ruling in *Roe*) and pro-lifers (citizens who demanded that the justices overturn *Roe* and allow each state to regulate, or outlaw, abortion as it saw fit) made concerted efforts to rally popular support to their respective points of view (and hopefully to influence the justices of the Supreme Court). An estimated 300,000 pro-choice advocates conducted a march through the streets of Washington to draw attention to their views. They pressed the argument that, should *Roe* be overturned, desperate women who could not afford to travel to states in which abortion remained legal would seek illegal abortions. Said Molly Yard of the National Organization of Women (NOW), "Women will have abortions, legal or not. The question is whether they will be legal, medically safe, and available to every woman who needs one." Antiabortion activists, meanwhile, pressed the argument that abortion is tantamount to murder, displayed emotion-rocking pictures of aborted fetuses, many of them having the appearance of perfectly formed babies, some of them bearing burn marks from the saline solution sometimes used in the abortion procedure—also photos of mothers holding healthy infants whom they had considered aborting before birth. Other activists picketed abortion clinics and heckled women who were entering the clinics to secure abortions.

Then, on July 3, 1989, while thousands of impassioned opponents and proponents of abortion chanted and waved placards on the plaza outside the Supreme Court building, the high court handed down its ruling in the Webster case. By a vote of 5 to 4, the justices upheld the abortion statute enacted in Missouri in 1986, and in so doing cleared the way for the states to impose sharp restrictions on abortion within their jurisdictions. Although the high court stopped short of overturning its decision of 1973 in *Roe* v. *Wade*, various commentators predicted that during the next term, when they considered new abortion cases, the justices might, in fact, nullify the *Roe* decision.

Future rulings aside, proponents of the right of a woman to choose to abort an embryo or fetus that was living in her womb appeared to share the view of Molly Yard of NOW that the high court's decision in *Webster* was "a total disaster." Proponents of the right of an embryo or fetus to survive and at length achieve birth as a fully developed baby hailed the decision as a major victory for the right-to-life crusade. Justice Harry Blackmun, the author of the court's decision in *Roe* back in 1973, lamented that the decision "casts into darkness the hopes and vision of every woman in the country who had come to believe that the Constitution guaranteed her the right to exercise some control over her unique ability to bear children." Of the decision, Archbishop John May of St. Louis said, "The biggest winners are the tiniest people of all—children within the womb."

Still, one thing appeared certain: The great controversy over abortion, one that had divided the people of the United States as had few other controversies across the decades of the country's history, was far from over. In the view of one observer in July of 1989, abortion would be "our Vietnam of the 1990s."

## BUSH AT THE HELM

Meanwhile, the six months of the Bush presidency came and went. Dominating the opening weeks of Bush's occupancy of the White House was a wrangle over Bush's nominee to be secretary of defense, former-Senator John Tower of Texas, a onetime chairman of the Armed Services Committee. After a bruising battle in which Tower was accused (among other things) of alcohol abuse, the Senate rejected the Tower nomination. Given his pique over the no-holds-barred handling of his nominee to be secretary of defense, Bush might have been excused if he found satisfaction two months later, in May of 1989, when two prominent Democrats fell from power, one of them Rep. Jim Wright of Texas. The speaker of the House (and thus second, after Vice President Quayle, in the line of presidential succession), Wright had been ensnarled for months in allegations that he had wantonly violated the congressional code of ethics. Not only did Wright feel compelled to resign the speakership; he gave up his seat in Congress as well.

Of greater moment than the political fate of Tower and Wright were an array of questions that commanded the attention of the new president, among them that of what the federal government should do regarding the embattled savings and loan (or "thrift") industry. Largely because of poor management and rampant fraud, several hundred of the country's 3,150 federally insured thrift institutions ("S&Ls") were insolvent or teetering toward insolvency when Bush moved into the White House. Because collapse of the savings and loan industry would strike hard at the general economy, and also at the federal government (which guaranteed deposits in S&Ls), Bush had little choice than to offer a plan for rescuing the industry. His plan, offered in February 1989, called upon the S&Ls and the country's taxpayers to share the cost of a gargantuan rescue program, the estimated cost of which would come to a staggering $126 billion over the next decade.

May 31, 1989: Holding a copy of his autobiography, Representative Jim Wright resigns as speaker of the House of Representatives. Critics had accused Wright of improperly selling bulk copies of the book to groups that he had addressed.

At the same time that he was wrestling with the S&L problem, the new president confronted the task of reducing the federal budgetary deficit from $170 billion to $100 billion by 1990. Otherwise, the previously discussed Gramm-Rudman-Hollings buzz saw would mandate automatic "across-the-board reductions in federal spending.

Bush outlined his budgetary proposals in his first address to Congress a few weeks after moving into the White House. He sketched new or expanded programs in the areas of drug abuse and education, and proposed increased outlays for child care, clean air, the homeless, impoverished mothers, medical research, and space exploration. He urged that Congress reduce taxes on long-term capital gains to 15 percent, a reduction that he contended would result in increased revenues for the federal treasury and at the same time stimulate investment. But, true to the pledge he had made repeatedly during the recent electoral campaign, he proposed no new taxes. How could the federal government finance new programs without raising taxes? Largely, it appeared, as a result of the increased revenues that Bush thought would cascade into the national treasury in the coming year. Why would there be increased revenues? Because, according to the calculus of the White House, of abnormal economic growth. Various economists ridiculed the White House calculus. The economy, they suspected, was more apt to experience a recession than above-normal growth. The result of a recession—or anything less than above-normal growth—would be revenues that would not come close to meeting the bright predictions of the president. Revenues that fell below the presidential predictions would doubtless result in a budgetary deficit well in excess of $100 billion.

Whatever the reservations of various economists, the national economy continued to prosper during the first months of the Bush presidency, and in June 1989 the Dow Jones average of leading industrial stocks passed 2,530—which meant that the Dow had regained approximately 700 of the nearly 1,000 points it had lost at the time of the great stock market crash of 1987. Meanwhile, Bush feared that a new round of inflation might be about to ravage the economy. Lest it contribute to inflation, he therefore took a critical view of increasing the federal minimum wage standard. Still, he proposed that the minimum wage, which had remained unchanged through the 1980s (while living costs inched upward), be raised from $3.35 an hour to $4.25 by 1992—but he wanted to retain the $3.35 rate as a "training wage" for first-time employees. When Congress passed legislation that would have raised the minimum wage to $4.55 and permitted no training wage, the president exercised his veto power.

During his campaign for presidency, George Bush had pledged to do what every informed citizen knew was impossible, at least in the near term, namely, to win the so-called drug war. To coordinate the activities of the various agencies that were responsible for actually waging the war (the FBI, U.S. Customs Service, and Drug Enforcement Administration), the forty-first president appointed William J. Bennett, a rumpled and iconclastic onetime secretary of education (in the Reagan administration). To invoke a popular phrase, Bennett had "his work cut out for him", particularly with regard to cocaine, the drug that had come to dominate the concerns of Americans when their thoughts turned to drugs. As the supply of cocaine available in the United States in recent years had enlarged, prices had plummeted—and consumption of the dangerous substance had skyrocketed, particularly in inner city ghettos. (As reported by the *Wilson Quarterly* in summer of 1989, consumption of cocaine by Americans in middle- and upper-income groups had declined sharply in the past couple of years: "Once considered glamerous and safe, cocaine is now widely viewed [by middle- and upper-income Americans] as a menace.") Selling the cocaine derivative crack on the street for ten times the price paid to South American cocaine barons, a small-time drug entrepreneur in New York City could net hundreds of thousands of dollars annually; various of his assorted "hawkers," "steerers," "stashers," "runners," "lookouts," and "bang bang" (armed males who guarded the operation), some of them young children, could clear several hundred dollars per day. Or so the author Terry Williams was expected to report in a forthcoming book entitled *The Cocaine Kids*.

The frontline troops in the drug war, as well as the never-ending war against crime in general, were the police. The police across much of the republic, or so it appeared during the first months of the Bush presidency, were fighting a losing battle against crime. Why were they fighting a losing battle? In part, because in order to reduce the pressure on overcrowded prisons, prosecutors were increasingly negotiating plea bargains with indicted felons (which often meant that the felons returned to the streets without serving any time at all in prison), and prison officials were relying increasingly on so-called early release programs that returned criminals to the streets before they completed prison terms. Also, many cities that faced budgetary crises had sharply reduced the manpower of their police forces over the past decade. To reinforce the country's beleaguered police, President Bush, in May 1989, announced a $1.2 billion plan to build more federal prisons and strengthen federal penalties for drug-related crimes. The country's cops, clearly outmanned and outgunned in many locales, seemed only mildly impressed.

A few weeks after announcing his plan to relieve the burden of the police, the president, proclaiming that too many Americans "breathe dirty air," announced an ambitious plan that he hoped would liberate most cities of the republic of urban smog by the year 2000 and drastically reduce pollution that causes acid rain. To that purpose, he urged the passage of legislation that would require automobile manufacturers to build and sell methanol-powered cars in nine of the country's cities that were plagued by dirty air, tighten limits on tailpipe emissions of hydrocarbons by existing cars, reduce sulphur dioxide emissions from coal-burning power plants (a major cause of acid rain) by 50 percent, and require industry to install new technology to curb the release of cancer-causing toxic chemicals into the atmosphere.

Meanwhile, President Bush could only cringe when he pondered reports emanating from the subcommittee of the Government Operations Committee of the House of Representatives headed by Tom Santos, Democrat of California, that greedy people had plundered the Department of Housing and Urban Development (HUD) of billions of dollars during the eight years of what Bush, during his campaign for the presidency, had often referred to as the Reagan-Bush administration. (Dubbed "Robin-HUD" by the news media, one employee of HUD admitted to embezzling $5.5 million, most of which, she testified, she had spent on or given to poor people.) Said Secretary of Housing and Urban Development Jack Kemp of the agency he recently had taken charge of, "I knew it was a swamp. I just didn't know it was at the level it is."

## DEFENSE AND ARMS CONTROL

When he became president, George Bush faced an agenda of challenges that, to say the least, was daunting. Among the challenges were the S&L crisis, the federal budgetary deficit, and the war on drugs. Another was that presented by the national defense behemoth.

Most Americans accepted the proposition that their superpowerful republic had no choice than to maintain a fearsome military-naval establishment. Still, great numbers of them fretted over the mind-boggling expense of providing for the defense of the United States and its far-flung strategic and economic (or "vital") interests. (During the eight years of the Reagan presidency, the Washington government had spent more than $2 trillion on the armed forces!) The upset of such Americans increased at the dawn of the era of George Bush when they assessed the B2 "Stealth" bombing plane, unveiled in California the previous November, each copy of which would cost taxpayers in excess of a half billion dollars (more, it was reported, than the cost of constructing six skyscrapers in Manhattan). The Air Force hoped to procure no fewer than 132 of the B2s, although critics contended that during a nuclear showdown with the rival superpower the Stealths would stand very little chance of penetrating Soviet air defenses, buttressed as those defenses were by 100,000 surface-to-air (SAM) missiles. By contrast, the cost of an MX missile, invulnerable to Soviet SAMs, came to a mere(?) $60 million, or about one-ninth the cost of a Stealth.

As for Bush, he recognized the weariness of his compatriots with rampaging defense costs. Moreover, he was under heavy pressure to reduce federal spending in the interest of reducing the deficit in the federal budget. So in his message to Congress on the buget, in February 1989, he proposed a freeze in the defense budget for the coming year—$291 billion plus an adjustment to account for inflation.

The budget was scarcely the only question in the realm of national defense with which Bush had to grapple during his first months in the White House. There was the question of whether to procure additional MX ICBMs (highly accurate and armed with 10 warheads each, 50 of which were already deployed in hardened silos) for deployment aboard railway cars, or single warhead and much more expensive (compared with the MX) Midgetman missiles for deployment on tractor-drawn mobile launchers. The deployment of one or more mobile missile systems presumably would ensure that a sufficient number of weapons would survive a surprise first strike against U.S. ICBMs by the Soviets so that the North American superpower would have the capability of retaliating with a devastating strike of its own. That the United States must always have the capability of so retaliating in the event of a surprise attack by Soviet nuclear-tipped missiles on America's ICBMs had been a fundamental principle of America's deterrence strategy since the dawn of the missile age some three decades before. (Critics argued that 5,300 warheads aboard the country's nuclear submarines and 4,700 nuclear warheads awaiting delivery on enemy tar-

gets by bombing planes provided the United States with the requisite retaliatory capability should the Soviets launch a surprise first strike on its ICBMs.)
The best guess was that Bush would opt for deployment of both weapons systems, that is, MXs on rail cars and Midgetmen on tractor-drawn launchers.

While the president pondered mobile ICBMs, Secretary of State James A.
Baker III traveled to Vienna in March 1989, where, in the glittering Hofburg
Palace, he joined the foreign sinisters of 34 other governments in the opening
session of the Negotiations on Conventional Armed Forces in Europe—the so-
called CFE talks. The goal was a reduction in the manpower and firepower of
the conventional forces that NATO and the Warsaw Pact deployed in Europe
to a point where neither alliance could hope to make a successful conventional
attack on the other. Recalling that the moribund Mutual and Balanced Force
Reduction (MBFR) negotiations had accomplished next to nothing over a period of 15 years, nobody expected achievement of the goal of CFE talks to come
easily. Indeed, a Soviet diplomat remarked, "This is the most complicated diplomatic task since the end of World War II."

Scarcely anyone in Europe or the United States failed to appreciate the
blessings to be derived from a CFE treaty. Still, great number of Americans
believed it far more important that the superpowers negotiate a strategic arms
reduction (START) treaty. A few of them even complained that the Bush administration was so preoccupied with conventional arms reduction that it was
giving short shrift to the task of reducing strategic arms. Administration
spokespeople denied that such was the case. In any event, START negotiations, recessed for several months, resumed in Geneva in the summer of 1989.

Meanwhile, in April of 1989, the question of arms control produced what
newspeople described as the first foreign policy crisis of the Bush presidency.
The would-be crisis took form when Chancellor Helmut Kohl of West Germany, responding to a yearning by most of his compatriots that German soil
be rid of nuclear weapons, demanded immediate East-West negotiations aimed
at securing a treaty to eliminate all short-range nuclear forces (SNF) in Europe.
SNF comprised the short-range (300 miles or less) missiles, nuclear-tipped artillery shells, and nuclear bombs that comprised NATO's on-site deterrent (as
opposed to the deterrent provided by ICBMs, SLBMs, and intercontinental
bombers deployed far from the probable location of any hostilities that might
break out in Middle Europe) to an attack by the vastly superior conventional
forces of the Warsaw Pact. Kohl's proposal infuriated leaders in Washington,
who insisted that NATO must continue to deploy SNF weapons until the Warsaw Pact (translated, the Soviet Union) agreed to give up the Eastern bloc's
overwhelming advantage in tanks and other conventional forces. In truth,
leaders of the United States obviously hoped to use NATO's SNF systems as
a bargaining chip in the aforementioned CFE negotiations, just as it had used
the cruise missiles and IRBMs that it deployed in Western Europe in the early
1980s as chips in the negotiations that resulted in the INF treaty.

A few weeks later, at the end of May of 1989, Bush was on his way to
Brussels to participate in the celebration of the fortieth anniversary of the for-

mation of NATO and confer with leaders of other NATO countries. At the time of his arrival, his standing among his European colleagues was low. The colleagues appeared to share the conviction of many Europeans that Bush was a passive and unimaginative leader who clearly lacked the vision to compete with Mikhail Gorbachev, the dynamic Soviet chieftain who in recent months had mesmerized Europeans by offering a succession of proposals to refashion the military balance in the Old Continent. But then Bush strode to the podium and outlined an imaginative plan, one that appeared more far-ranging than any of the initiatives recently proposed by Gorbachev, to accelerate negotiations aimed at achieving deep reductions in conventional forces deployed by NATO and the Warsaw Pact in Europe.

The response to his NATO speech fired the spirit of the American president, the more so when commentators in Europe as well as the United States credited him with having revived a NATO alliance that many observers thought had become old and creaky. Even the West Germans appeared satisfied, although a fortnight later they accorded Gorbachev a tumultuous reception when the Soviet leader made a state visit to West Germany—and pollsters reported that more than 90 percent of the people of West Germany had a favorable view of Gorbachev, barely 50 percent a favorable view of Bush.

## IN THE OUTER WORLD

How the United States should cope with the world beyond its shores and borders was not an overarching theme of George Bush's campaign for the White House in 1988. Still, the forty-first president understood full well, when he repeated the presidential oath on January 20, 1989, that foreign relations would command a great deal of his attention, just as they had commanded much of the attention of all of his predecessors over the past half century.

A fortnight before Bush became president, two F-14 Tomcat fighters of the U.S. Navy shot down two Libyan MiG fighters over the Mediterranean, 120 miles beyond Libyan territorial waters. According to the American pilots, the Libyan planes had pursued the Tomcats while the latter aircraft were providing protection for the carrier USS *John F. Kennedy*. Although the skill of the crewmen of the Tomcats doubtless stirred the pride of many Americans, the shoot-out over the Mediterranean brought small comfort to the government in Washington. Arab delegates at the UN denounced America's "brutal aggression" against Libya, while the Kremlin described the American action as "state terrorism." The shoot-out also distracted attention from the allegation of the United States that a chemical plant recently built by the government of the strongman Muammar Qaddafi in the Libyan desert was intended primarily to produce mustard gas and chemical nerve agents, sometimes described as the atomic bombs of the poor countries of the Third World (inasmuch as chemical weapons are relatively inexpensive to produce and have fearsome potential as killing instruments in war). As matters turned out, Libya and its chemical plant in the desert near Tripoli ceased to be front page news after Bush took command of the White House. Still, few Americans reckoned that Libya had ceased to be a thorn in the side of the North American superpower.

The new president meanwhile pondered other problems and happenings in the outer world. A problem of incalculable magnitude was the so-called debt crisis that burdened Argentina, Brazil, Mexico, Venezuela, and other Latin American countries. To meet the crisis, the Bush administration, in March 1989, urged commercial banks, in exchange for guarantees that some of the debt would be repaid, to forgive a major part of what the Latin Americans owed them. Then there was the problem that was apt to face the United States in 1992 when the European Community (EC), or Common Market, in accord with an agreement worked out by members of the EC in 1988, would complete implementation of a "unified international market" in which people, goods, services, and capital would move among the 12 member countries unhampered by political boundaries and economic barriers. Businesspeople in the United States feared that when the EC eliminated internal barriers to commerce, it would erect external barriers that would impede the importation of goods and services from the United States and the other non-EC countries of the world.

Of more immediate concern to President Bush and his compatriots was the economic performance and behavior of Japan. Indeed, news commentaries on Bush's trip to Tokyo in February 1989 to attend the funeral of Emperor Hirohito tended to concentrate on what *Newsweek* described as "the Asian challenge"—largely a Japanese challenge—to America's longtime economic supremacy in the world and, more than that, to the latter's ability to control its own economic destiny in the years to come. Statistics indicated to millions of Americans that the United States was failing to meet the challenge. The direct investment by Japanese corporations and entrepreneurs in the United States at the dawn of 1988 had been $33.4 billion, the direct investment of Americans in Japan, $14.3 billion. Japanese exports to the United States in 1987 had totaled $83.6 billion, American exports to Japan, $31.5 billion. Japan imported 108,000 new cars from the United States in 1987, the United States imported 2.4 million new cars from Japan. Japanese foreign exchange holdings at the end of 1987 totaled $75.7 billion, U.S. foreign exchange holdings, $13.1 billion.

According to a Washington Post/ABC News Poll, 44 percent of the people of the United States believed at the onset of the Bush presidency that Japan's economic muscle constituted a greater threat to the security of the United States than the nuclear-tipped ICBMs of the Soviet Union. That belief prompted many Americans to respond angrily in early 1989 when they learned that the Reagan administration had approved a deal whereby the General Dynamics Corporation would sell the top secret "technical data package" of the prized F-16 fighter plane (for a price that amounted to a tenth of what the package had cost U.S. taxpayers) to the Japanese in connection with a joint Japanese-American venture to develop a new fighter plane, the FSX. Such

Americans had visions of the Japanese using American technology that they had obtained on the cheap to produce high-performance jet fighters for sale in the international arms market.

As for the Bush administration, it stood by the FSX deal. But it indicated a willingness to relax enforcement of antitrust laws to allow such companies as AT&T and IBM to jointly develop high-definition television (HDTV), the new technology that produces supersharp TV pictures and is expected to revolutionize household entertainment and telecommunications in the 1990s. The Japanese had already made important strides in the development of HDTV. Then, a short time later, in late May of 1989, the administration, in accord with a provision (known as Super 301) of the trade bill approved by Congress in 1988, singled out Japan—also Brazil and India—as countries that systematically restricted access to their markets by American corporations and entrepreneurs. The United States charged the Japanese with restricting the importation of supercomputers and satellites made in the United States, as well as American lumber. In accord with Super 301, the United States would negotiate with Japan for removal of the barriers. Should no progress result, the Washington government might impose retaliatory tariffs against some Japanese imports in the United States.

Meanwhile, President Bush shared the satisfaction of his compatriots when the last Soviet troops, in early 1989, departed Afghanistan, but doubtless shared their disappointment when, contrary to expectations, the Afghan *mujahidin* failed to drive the Soviet-sponsored communist regime from Kabul in the months that followed. What the president thought about the announcement in April 1989 that Vietnam would end its ten-year occupation of Cambodia (or Kampuchea) and that the last Vietnamese troops would leave the long-suffering Khmer nation by September 30, 1989, is not clear. It appeared probable that many Vietnamese troops, disguised as Cambodians, would remain in Cambodia. Moreover, it appeared that Cambodia was apt to endure a time of intense civil strife involving the Vietnamese-sponsored government in Phnom Penh and various opposition factions—including the infamous Khmer Rouge. A Chinese-supported communist faction headed by the murderous Pol Pot, the Khmer Rouge had made Cambodia the land of "the killing fields" (by savaging to death between a half million and 2 million Cambodian people during the years 1975 to 1979 when it commanded the central government in Phnom Penh).

More comforting to President Bush than goings-on in Cambodia, no doubt, was the arrival of a UN peacekeeping force in newly independent Namibia, wracked by two decades of inconclusive fighting between South African colonial forces and guerrillas of the Soviet-supported South West Africa People's Organization (SWAPO), and the departure from the country of the last military contingents of Namibia's longtime South African occupiers. The arrival of UN troops and departure of the South Africans was the result of an agreement mediated by the United States in December 1988, during the last weeks of the Reagan administration, with the assistance of the Soviet Union. How Bush and his compatriots would react if, as expected, SWAPO, an avowedly Marxist organization, prevailed in the popular elections that were to take place in Namibia was another question.

President Bush no doubt shared the dismay of most of his compatriots when the clashes between stone-throwing Palestinian youths and Israeli troops in the West Bank continued, month after dreary month, and no apparent headway was made toward achievement of a settlement that would secure justice for both the Palestinians and Israelis—also when South Korean students, screaming anti-American slogans and demanding the withdrawal of U.S. forces from South Korea, continued their intermittent antigovernment demonstrations. Like nearly every American, Bush felt outrage when Ayatollah Khomeini of Iran, in early 1989, denounced the novel *The Satanic Verses* as blasphemous (because of its treatment of Islam) and Khomeini's followers put a price on the head of the novel's author, Indian-born Salman Rushdie. Like many other Americans, he may have breathed a sigh of relief in June of 1989 when the 88-year-old Khomeini, a decade-long nemesis of the United States ("the Great Satan," in the ayatollah's lexicon), passed to his reward.

Regarding Nicaragua, a source of protracted querulousness between the Reagan administration and the Democratic-controlled Congress in recent years, the Bush administration worked out a "gentleman's agreement" with Congress in March 1989 whereby the United States would provide the Nicaraguan contras, most of them presently encamped in Honduras, with $4.5 million of nonmilitary aid per month for the next 11 months—provided the 12,000-man contra army stayed in its camps and refrained from new acts of violence. Meanwhile, diplomats would strive to nudge the Marxist Sandinistas, who continued to preside over the government in Managua, in the direction of democracy. How the Washington government was apt to react if the Sandinistas refused to go through with the democratic elections they had promised to arrange in February 1990 was anybody's guess.

Like millions of his compatriots, Bush felt disappointment in March 1989 when a majority of voters in El Salvador elected Alfredo Christiani of the right-wing National Republican Alliance (ARENA) to be president of the long-suffering Central American republic. As for ARENA, it was a paramilitary organization-turned-political-party that had been closely linked with the infamous right-wing death squads which had carried out thousands of political murders in El Salvador over the past decade. Its victory marked the failure of the Washington government's policy (bolstered since 1984 by support to the government in San Salvador in the amount of $1.5 million per day) of building the centrist Christian Democratic Party, headed until recently by José Napoleón Duarte, into a bulwark against both the communist insurgents and ARENA. Following ARENA's victory in the balloting in March 1989, the U.S. State Department reminded El Salvador's new president that the Washington government's relationship with the new regime in San Salvador would depend on the latter regime's respect for human rights.

To the south of El Salvador and Nicaragua lay Panama, still presided over at the time George Bush moved into the White House in Washington by the strongman and alleged kingpin in a network that delivered Latin American cocaine and heroin to the United States, Gen. Manuel Antonio Noriega. The strongman had remained in power in spite of a concerted effort by the government in Washington over the past 11 or so months to arrange his downfall. Still, Bush and his compatriots had reason to hope that the people of Panama themselves might rid the hemisphere of the despicable Noriega, in a general election on May 7, 1989. Unfortunately, the hopes of Bush and other North Americans were dashed when Noriega, his handpicked candidate for president having lost in the popular balloting by a margin of 2 to 1, nullified the fraud- and violence-plagued election (which fraud and violence were largely the work of Noriega partisans), then, three days after the election, turned his goon squads loose on his political opponents. Photographs that were beamed almost instantaneously across the world showed club- and pipe-wielding Noriega thugs chasing and beating the opposition candidate for second vice president of Panama, Guillermo Ford, his white shirt drenched with his own blood.

As for President Bush, he dispatched an additional 1,800 U.S. troops to Panama, ostensibly to assure the safety of the 52,000 American civilians and military personnel who lived and worked in Panama (but in fact to put pressure on Noriega). He also recalled the U.S. ambassador from Panama City, and vowed to continue the economic sanctions imposed against Panama the year before by the Reagan administration. Beyond such feeble gestures, he could do little, for other Latin American governments, while condemning the theft of the Panamanian election by Noriega, made it clear that they would respond angrily to any armed intervention in Panama by the United States—and Bush appeared to be of no mind to stir the anger of friendly governments in Latin America.

## END OF THE COLD WAR? COMMUNISM IN ECLIPSE?

"The cold war of poisonous Soviet-American feelings, of domestic political hysteria, of events enlarged and distorted by East-West confrontation, of almost perpetual diplomatic deadlock is over." So asserted an editorial that appeared in the *New York Times* on April 2, 1989, 73 days into the administration of President George Bush. "The we-they world that emerged after 1945 is giving way to the more traditional struggles of great powers. That contest is more manageable. It permits serious negotiations. It creates new possibilities—for cooperation in combating terrorism, the spread of chemical weapons and common threats to the environment, and for shaping a less violent world." The editors of the *Times* reached their conclusion after pondering the observations and assessments set out in a two-month series of essays by observers and scholars of Soviet-American relations that had appeared on the newspaper's op-ed pages over the previous two months. The essays had addressed the question, "Is the Cold War over?"

For a couple of generations of Americans, many of whom could remember previous occasions when prophets of hope had predicted the demise of the

Cold War, it was hard to believe that what the *Economist* of London defined as the nonlethal struggle for advantage between the superpowers and their respective allies and clients actually belonged to history. The Cold War had gone on for so long, to paraphrase what a historian once wrote about the thoughts of soldiers in the trenches of the Western Front during the Great War of 1914–1918, that they had come to assume it would go on forever. Well, in all candor, undisclosed numbers of Americans doubted that the Cold War had, in fact, ended—or even was coming to an end. Their views were given sometimes eloquent expression on June 19, 1989, by the columnist William F. Buckley, Jr., and others during a debate on the question, "Resolved, the Cold War Is Not Coming to an End," that was televised across the republic from the campus of Northwestern University by PBS.

Why did a fair number of people in the United States and around the world surmise at the dawn of George Bush's presidency that the Cold War was a phenomenon (or nightmare) of the past? In no small measure, because of initiatives taken over the past three or so years by the Soviet chieftain Mikhail Gorbachev, described by the distinguished scholar-diplomat George F. Kennan (in an interview by Robert MacNeil of the "MacNeil/Lehrer News Hour" in December 1988) as "a most remarkable man."

As Jeremy Stone of the Federation of American Scientists observed in his op-ed essay in the *New York Times*, Gorbachev had agreed to vastly disproportionate reductions in the Soviet Union's medium-range missiles and pledged substantial unilateral reductions in Soviet forces deployed in Middle Europe. He had withdrawn Soviet forces from Afghanistan, urged political settlements in strife-torn Angola and Cambodia, and pressed the PLO leader Yasir Arafat to renounce terrorism and accept the existence of Israel. He also had cooperated with the United States to bring an end to the bloodletting in Namibia, and was reported to have told Fidel Castro of Cuba and Daniel Ortega of Nicaragua that their Marxists governments would have to manage with reduced support by the Soviet Union.

Inside the Soviet empire, meanwhile, Gorbachev, via his *perestroika* (restructuring) initiative, had set about to reform and revitalize (largely be decentralizing) the stagnant Soviet economy, and, via the *glasnost* (openness) initiative, was encouraging Soviet citizens to express themselves with a measure of freedom that few of them had ever experienced. Then, at the end of March of 1989, as a consequence of a *demokratizatsiia* (democratization) initiative, he arranged for the first contested elections (albeit single-party elections) across the width and breadth of the Eurasian behemoth since 1917. And on election day, citizens from Siberia to Lithuania voted overwhelmingly against hacks of the Communist party establishment.

In a word, after 70 years of socioeconomic regimentation, rampant denial of what people in the Western democracies understood to be essential human rights, and government by a dictatorial and often brutal party, Gorbachev appeared to be moving the Soviet Union, however gingerly, toward a more open and humane, less regimented and democratic society. Gorbachev's Soviet Union, morever, apparently would be less preoccupied than the Soviet Union of Stalin, Khrushchev, and Brezhnev had been with building ever more powerful weapons systems and spreading the gospel of Marxism-Leninism to every corner of the earth. As Graham Allison of Harvard's Kennedy School had written in his op-ed essay, such a reshaping of Soviet society and alteration of the outlook and behavior of the leaders in the Kremlin had been objects of U.S. policy since World War II. If that reshaping and alteration actually came to pass and became permanent, the raison d'être of the Cold War would disappear, or so reasoned fair numbers of Americans.

Most observers and analysts in the West reckoned that Gorbachev was not acting to move the Soviet Union away from the rigid dogmas of Marx and Lenin out of the goodness of his spirit. Rather, they thought, he understood that the application of those dogmas had produced a nation-state whose economic life was hopelessly stagnant. As Gorbachev doubtless remembered, the Soviet Communist party in 1961 had proclaimed that by the 1970s the Soviet Union would surpass the United States in per capita production, and Soviet communism would reach full flower. That bright prediction had come to nothing. Indeed, by the mid-1970s, while the stolid Leonid Brezhnev commanded the Kremlin, the Soviet economy, measured in GNP, fell further behind that of the United States—and, more than that, was passed by the economy of Japan. Wrote the Soviet historian Leonid Batkin in 1988, "While the Brezhnev system was reducing our country to a state of mediocrity, the world was developing lasers and personal computers and witnessing the explosion of the postindustrial revolution." As an exporter of manufactured merchandise, the Soviet Union slipped from a ranking among the world's exporting nation-states and colonies from eleventh in 1973 to fifteenth in 1985, having been passed by Taiwan, South Korea, Hong Kong, and Switzerland. Observed Zbigniew Brzezinski in his book *The Grand Failure: The Birth and Death of Communism in the Twentieth Century* (1989), ". . . in the seventy years of Soviet rule not a single [consumer] item capable of competing on the world market has yet been produced [in the Marxist-Leninist-Stalinist empire]."

Brzezinski's book, in truth, dealt with what the author described as the terminal crisis of communism across the world. Of his volume, the respected academic and onetime national security adviser (in the White House of Jimmy Carter) wrote, "It describes and analyzes the progressive decay and the deepening agony both of its system and of its dogma. It concludes that in the next century communism's irreversible historical decline will have made its practice and dogma largely irrelevant to the human condition. Prospering only where it abandons its internal substance even if still retaining some of its external labels, communism will be remembered as the twentieth century's most extraordinary political and intellectual aberration."

The proposition that communism, a socioeconomic system that had fired the imaginations of many Americans idealists during the 1920s and 1930s (even at a time when, on the order of, or as a consequence of, the policies and programs of the butcher Stalin, literally tens of millions of Soviet citizens perished), was in the decline and perhaps inching toward oblivion was hard to confute as the era of George Bush got under way. Dramatically reinforcing the proposition that communism was in decline were goings-on in Eastern Europe and China.

## EASTERN EUROPE AND CHINA

Poland had been rumbling off and on since the summer of 1980, when millions of Poles, sick and tired of the domination of their country by the Soviet Union as well as the stifling rigidities imposed by the Marxist-Leninist-Stalinist regime in Warsaw, rallied around the newly organized Solidarity trade union, led by the shipyard worker Lech Walesa. The inept Warsaw government had tried without success to suppress Solidarity. Meanwhile, the condition of the Polish economy, burdened by a huge external debt and bureaucratic inefficiency, had gone from awful to absolutely awful. Complicating matters for the communists, the Polish citizenry, inspired in some measure by the currents of reform that Mikhail Gorbachev had unleashed in the Soviet empire, became increasingly restless.

Then, in the spring of 1989, the communist chieftains in Warsaw, almost in desperation, agreed to recognize the legality of Solidarity and sanction the first contested elections in Poland in more than 40 years. Held on June 4, 1989, the elections resulted in a crushing defeat for the communists, although communists would continue to dominate the Sejm, or lower house of the national parliament, inasmuch as their opponents had been allowed to contest only a third of the seats. All save a handful of Solidarity's candidates emerged victorious, and only 2 of 35 top incumbent (communist) members of the Sejm who ran unopposed on a "National List" secured the 50 percent vote that was required for re-election. Solidarity candidates won 92 of 100 seats in a newly constituted Senate, or upper chamber, of the national legislature.

Poland was not the only East European nation-state that was struggling to break loose from the bondage of Sovietism and forge a more democratic and productive political and social order. Another was Hungary. Indeed, Hungary recently had carried out reforms that moved the Hungarian economy in the direction of free enterprise. By 1989, Hungarian reformers prevailed on the current Communist party chieftain, Karoly Groez, to consent to a multiparty political system for Hungary—also to independent trade unions and a new constitution that no longer reserves a commanding role for the Communist party. Then, in the spring of 1989, while reformers talked of loosening Hungary's ties with the Warsaw Pact and eventually turning Hungary into a neutral nation-state after the fashion of Austria and Sweden, Hungarian soldiers set about to cut the barbed wire fences, that is, a segment of the infamous Iron Curtain, separating Hungary from neighboring Austria.

At the same time that Poland and Hungary appeared to be edging their way out of the Soviet empire, the manifestly anti-Soviet populations of the onetime independent Baltic republics of the Soviet Union, Estonia, Latvia, and Lithuania, were becoming increasingly restive under Soviet rule. As reported in *Time* in April of 1989, secessionist winds were blowing in the Baltic states.

And in the Soviet republic of Uzbek, a predominantly Muslim area to the north of Afghanistan, anti-Soviet rioting prompted Mikhail Gorbachev to dispatch troops of the Red Army to put down the disturbances. But the most dramatic display of opposition to communist authority during the first months of the presidency of George Bush came to pass in China, the homeland of well over a billion people.

During the years following the establishment of formal diplomatic relations between the Washington and Beijing governments, in 1979, tens of thousands of Chinese students made their way to colleges and universities in the United States, and many American youths went off to study in China. Substantial numbers of American scholars, businesspeople, and tourists likewise traveled to the ancient Middle Kingdom, and most of them appeared to be charmed by the Chinese people and their ancient culture. Meanwhile, China's communist leader, Deng Xiaoping, who had suffered dreadfully as a result of Mao Zedong's "cultural revolution" during the 1960s, set about to modernize and stimulate China's hopelessly backward and unproductive economy by relaxing Marxist-Leninist strictures against free enterprise and Maoist strictures against what Mao had contended were the decadent behavior and social practices of the West. But Deng, however perceived by Americans to be a benign and pragmatic communist of a new genre, made no move to relax the iron grip of the Communist party on the instruments of political power in China. And in early 1989, authorities in Beijing dispatched army troops to the legendary city of Lhasa to put down demonstrations in which Tibetans were demanding greater autonomy for Tibet, ruled by China since 1950. The troops may have killed more than a hundred Tibetans in the resulting melee.

Several weeks after the Beijing government suppressed the demonstrators in Tibet, in April of 1989, Chinese students by the tens of thousands began to gather in Tiananmen Square in Beijing to demand an increase in "democracy" in China. In the main, the students, some of whom had studied in America and Europe, and most of whom probably had heard the democratic message on their transistor radios, that is, had listened to broadcasts of the Voice of America, as well as broadcasts emanating from Hong Kong and elsewhere, appeared to want a curtailment of restrictions on freedom of expression, fewer restrictions on the communications media, and an end to alleged corruption in high places. Triggering the demonstrations was the funeral of Hu Yaobang, the onetime secretary-general of the Chinese Communist party whom hardliners in the party hierarchy had ousted in 1987 after accusing him of failing to combat "bourgeois liberalism," translated, democratic ideas of the West, in China. Before long, the demonstrations had spread to other major cities, including Nanjing, Shanghai, and Tianjin.

The people of the United States responded warmly to the goings-on in China, which were closely monitored by the American news services, both print and electronic, the more so when students in Tiananmen Square quoted the writings of Thomas Jefferson and fashioned a plaster statue that resembled the Statue of Liberty (although the Chinese explained that the statue was intended to resemble an ancient Chinese goddess).

June 3, 1989: On the day before the infamous massacre in Tiananmen Square in Beijing, a young woman is caught between fellow pro-democracy demonstrators and helmeted soldiers as thousands of demonstrators attempt to prevent the troops from entering the square.

Meanwhile, the demonstrations continued, week after week. As for the communist authorities, they appeared confused—for a time, perhaps, because of their determination to do nothing that might interfere with a state visit to Beijing by Mikhail Gorbachev. But then, a fortnight after the Gorbachev visit, in late May of 1989, those authorities summoned units of the Chinese army to deploy in the vicinity of Tiananmen Square, and Americans thrilled to the dramatic pictures of a lone white-shirted civilian, exuding courage and quiet dignity, causing a column of tanks to come to a halt by placing himself in their path. Then, in the early hours of Sunday morning, June 4, 1989, the army set about to crush the demonstrations. The outcome was a massacre that shocked people across the world (the communist leaders of East Germany constituting a vocal exception). Estimates of the death toll among the demonstrators ranged from 500 to 2,000. In the aftermath of the massacre, which the communist authorities blatantly denied had taken place, the regime set about to seek out and execute the leaders of the demonstrations. One of those who was reportedly executed was the brave man who had stopped the column of tanks.

As for President Bush, he deplored the massacre of its own people by the Chinese government, ordered the Immigration and Naturalization Service to extend the visas of Chinese students in the United States (many of whom had demonstrated in support of the students in Tiananmen Square) who might be afraid to return to China, and suspended sales of U.S. military hardware to the Beijing government. Some of his compatriots thought his "measured" response unduly tepid. The president, of course, determined to take no action that might shatter the relationship which the governments in Washington and Beijing had carefully nurtured since President Nixon's momentous journey to China in 1972.

Meanwhile, Americans hoped that Zbigniew Brzezinski and other commentators might be correct in their conviction that communism, at least as it has existed since the time of the Bolshevik Revolution in 1917, was passing into eclipse. True, the winds of change that recently had blown across the Soviet Union, Poland, Hungary, and China had scarcely been felt (or so it seemed) in such hard-line citadels of Marxism-Leninism-Stalinism as Bulgaria, Cuba, East Germany, North Korea, Romania, and Vietnam. And the authorities in Beijing, for the time being at any rate, had apparently succeeded in their effort to subdue those winds in the ancient Middle Kingdom. Still, the winds had not died—and the communist tyrants were not about to rid their domains of the omnipresent transistor radios, cassette recorders, and other wonders of modern communication by which people, even in closed societies, were now able to keep abreast of goings-on across the world and gain access to subversive ideas regarding freedom and democracy. That tyrants and would-be tyrants could no longer stem the flow of information and ideas, indeed, was perhaps the greatest blow to tyranny in its long and tortured history.

## RETROSPECT

To paraphrase the words of Gen. Douglas MacArthur, given in his "Old Soldiers Never Die" speech of April 1951, the world, by 1989, had turned over many times since that day in 1944 when the submarine *Finback* rescued the boyish George Bush from the rolling waters of the western Pacific. The national population had enlarged from approximately 140 million to 247 million, and its balance had shifted steadily to the west and south of the sprawling republic. The United States had propelled the world into the nuclear era, one in which the threat of doomsday was never far from the consciousness of national leaders and ordinary earthlings alike. It had endured a bone-chilling "cold war" and two agonizing "limited" wars. Contrary to an opinion advanced by various scholars and pundits, the United States, if it often behaved imperiously, had never made a large part of the world its empire, that is (applying the definition of empire provided in *Webster's New World Dictionary*), had never exercised supreme rule, absolute power or authority, or dominion over any substantial area of the world beyond its own national domain (save, of course, for Japan, southern Korea, and the parts of the former German Reich that it occupied in the immediate aftermath of World War II). But it had cast aside what the historian Selig Adler once identified as an isolationist impulse that animated its political relations with the outer world during its first 164 years by accepting the responsibility of global leadership. And while its power to determine global events had declined over the past two decades, it remained, in 1989, the premier power of the world.

Since that day when George Bush was fished out of the Pacific, the United States (and the rest of the world) had experienced scientific and technological developments that few people in 1944 even remotely suspected might be in the offing—scientific and technological developments that had revolutionized communications, information (or data) processing, and transportation, not to mention the processes of agriculture and manufacturing; opened grand new vistas in the prevention and treatment of disease and disability; wrought dramatic and, arguably, revolutionary change in the way ordinary and nonordinary citizens alike passed their daily lives; enabled Americans and others to explore the reaches of outer space and the depths of the world's oceans. The decades since World War II had been, by and large, a time of steady economic growth and, for the most part, rampant prosperity for the United States, but also a time when the country's economic life became enmeshed with the economic life of the rest of the world to an extent that was without precedent (as the world increasingly became a global market)—a time when the North American colossus lost a good deal of its longtime ability to control its economic destiny.

The years since World War II had been a time when traditional American values were under frequent attack, a time when the manners, mores, and morals (regarding sex and marriage, for example) of a substantial percentage of the citizenry underwent far-ranging (and, for many citizens, wrenching) change. The decades since 1944–1945 had been a time when millions of Americans experimented with new and what many of them thought were exotic lifestyles—a time when the use of mind-affecting drugs literally exploded.

The decades since World War II had been a time of change in the political map of the United States. Most notably perhaps, the southern region of the republic, in 1944–1945 a citadel of the Democratic party (what American beyond the age of 50 does not remember the "solid South" of yesteryear?), had by the 1980s become a citadel of the party of Abraham Lincoln and Ronald Reagan. Of greater moment, the decades since the global war had been a time of important change in relations between the races in the United States, a time when the self-proclaimed citadel of democracy made halting and unsatisfactory headway—but headway nonetheless—toward the goal of eliminating its infamous racial caste system. Those decades had been a time of impressive growth of the country's Hispanic population, not to mention its Asian population, a time when American Indians (or, as they preferred to be called, Native Americans) asserted their civil rights with renewed determination and became increasingly conscious of their rich heritage.

The years since 1944–1945 had witnessed a rebirth of the feminist movement, as well as a dramatic change in the place of women in the national society, in the dynamics of the nuclear family, in attitudes regarding abortion. They had witnessed the emergence of homosexuals by the millions from the proverbial closet, as well as a revival and then steady decline in the influence of religion in the lives of the people of the United States. They had been years in which Americans, as never before, became conscious of the imperative that humankind must act boldly and decisively if it is to preserve the fragile natural environment.

The years since 1944–1945 had been a time when Americans became conscious as never before of the transparent imperfections and shortcomings of their national society. Still, a preponderance of them had never wavered in their commitment to the essentials of representative democracy and free enterprise. And during the first months of George Bush's presidency, as they pondered what was happening in nation-states ruled by dictators and dictatorial parties and ordered by the rigidities of Marxism-Leninism, that commitment took on renewed strength.

As for the first six or so months of 1989, they were, of course, the time when George Bush settled into the White House. Opinion polls taken during those months disclosed that most of his compatriots took a warm view of the new chief executive. Still, many observers of American politics complained during those same months that the Bush presidency was getting off to an agonizingly slow start, and that the forty-first chief executive was squandering the so-called honeymoon period of his occupancy of the White House, that is, a time when, according to conventional wisdom, the people and their representatives in Congress are most apt to respond favorably to presidential initiatives. And at the end of April, on completion of the first 100 days of the Bush administration, assorted pundits concluded that Bush had to that point been a mediocre president.

Happily, Bush's standing with the more critical of his compatriots appeared to improve in the late spring of 1989, notably when he made his dramatic speech in Brussels proposing an acceleration of the arms-control process. Still, historians in years to come are not apt to concentrate on the performance of George Bush (or rulings by the Supreme Court, the performance of the U.S. economy, or the trial of Oliver North) when considering the beginning of the so-called Bush era. Rather, they are apt to concentrate on the apparent passing of the Cold War and the almost cosmic events that transpired in the Soviet empire from Eastern Europe to Siberia and in China. Indeed, should history eventually record that during the first half of 1989 the Cold War was finally and properly consigned to the scrap heap of history and the crisis of communism entered a terminal stage—if it turns out that, as President Bush said at the Karl Marx Institute in Budapest during a trip to Poland and Hungary in July 1989, "We are on the threshold of a new era"—scholars of the future might very well look upon the beginning months of the presidency of George Herbert Walker Bush as an epochal time, that is (as noted in Chapter 1), a time that marks the start of a new period or era in the unfolding of nature or in the affairs of humans.

# Additional
# Reading

An array of books of various lengths offer general treatments of the experience of the United States and its people during the decades after World War II. Perhaps the best of the shorter volumes is Allan M. Winkler, *Modern America: The United States from World War II to the Present* (1985). Other sharply written and cogently argued surveys of under three hundred pages are Melvyn Dubofsky and Athan G. Theoharis, *Imperial Democracy: The United States Since 1945* (1988); Norman L. Rosenberg et al., *In Our Times: America Since World War II* (1976); and William E. Leuchtenburg, *A Troubled Feast: American Society Since 1945* (1973). Two brightly illustrated volumes in the 300-

page range are Douglas T. Miller, *Visions of America: Second World War to the Present* (1988), and David A. Horowitz et al., *On the Edge: A History of America Since World World War II* (1989). See also James Gilbert, *Another Chance: Postwar America, 1945–1985* (1986), and Carl N. Degler, *Affluence and Anxiety, 1945–Present* (1968). Finally, one must take note of the sixth edition of *American Epoch: The United States Since 1900* (1987), the first edition of which, authored by Arthur S. Link, one of the country's most renowned historians, appeared in the 1950s and quickly established itself as a standard survey of the United States in the 20th century. Volume II of the sixth edition of *American Epoch*, by Arthur S. Link, William A. Link, and William B. Catton, covers the years 1936–1985.

Another excellent survey by a premier historian is Norman A. Graebner, *The Age of Global Power: The United States Since 1939* (1979). James T. Patterson, like Graebner one of the finest scholars of recent U.S. history, provides a comparatively brief and lucid coverage of the national experience after 1945 in *America in the Twentieth Century* (1976). Howard Zinn, *The Twentieth Century: A People's History* (1983), views the American experience in recent times from the perspective of citizens who have endured political and economic exploitation. See also Lawrence S. Wittner, *Cold War America: From Hiroshima to Watergate* (1974); Alonzo L. Hamby, *The Imperial Years: The United States Since 1939* (1976); and George Moss, *America in the Twentieth Century* (1989). For the years 1960–1980, one might examine Charles R. Morris, *A Time of Passion* (1984), a volume described by its author as a personal exploration of what he perceives to have been a time of momentous change.

Other volumes cover the period (or much of it) in greater detail. Arguably, the best of the longer books is James MacGregor Burns, *The Crosswinds of Freedom* (1989), the third and final volume in Burns's trilogy, *The American Experiment. Crosswinds of Freedom* chronicles and interprets the American experience from 1932 to 1988. A first-rate volume of about four hundred pages is Dewey W. Grantham, *Recent America: The United States Since 1945* (1987), and still another is Robert D. Marcus and David Burner, *America Since 1945* (1985). A much-acclaimed book that is especially strong in the area of the social and cultural experience of the United States and its people during the decades following the global war is William H. Chafe, *America Since World War II* (1986). See also Richard S. Kirkendall, *A Global Power: America Since the Age of Roosevelt* (1980); Albert C. Ganley et al., *After Hiroshima: America Since 1945* (1985); Frederick F. Siegel, *Troubled Journey: From Pearl Harbor to Ronald Reagan* (1984); and George E. Mowry and Blaine A. Brownell, *The Urban Nation, 1920–1981* (1981). Paul Johnson, *Modern Times: The World from the '20s to the '80s* (1982), offers an incisive survey of the history of the entire world over a period of more than six decades. The reader might also wish to examine Clifton Daniel (ed.), *Chronicle of the 20th Century* (1987), a weighty volume that offers newspaperlike accounts and pictures of important events in America and the rest of the world for each month of every year from 1900 through 1987.

## CHAPTERS 1 AND 2

For the closing stages of World War II, the reader might consult Volume 2 of A. Russell Buchanan, *The United States in World War II* (1964). A stirring account of the final months of the war in Europe is John Toland, *The Last 100 Days* (1966). For the last months of the Roosevelt presidency and the death of FDR, see James MacGregor Burns, *Roosevelt: The Soldier of Freedom* (1970), and Jim Bishop, *FDR's Last Year: April 1944–April 1945* (1975). A plethora of books take up the fabrication and detonation of the first atomic bomb, the most recent of which is Richard Rhodes, *The Making of the Atomic Bomb* (1986). See also McGeorge Bundy, *Danger and Survival: Choices About the Bomb in the First Fifty Years* (1988), Paul Boyer, *By the Bomb's Early Light: American Thought and Culture at the Dawn of the Atomic Age* (1985), and Carl B. Feldbaum and Ronald J. Bee, *Looking the Tiger in the Eye: Confronting the Nuclear Threat* (1988). A fascinating account of the atomic raids on Hiroshima and Nagasaki appears in Fletcher Knebel and Charles W. Bailey II, *No High Ground* (1960). For a view of the first atomic raid from the perspective of the raid's victims, see John Hersey, *Hiroshima* (1946). For the diplomatic events that led to Japan's surrender, see Herbert Feis, *Japan Subdued: The Atomic Bomb and the End of the War in the Pacific* (1961), and Robert J. C. Butow, *Japan's Decision to Surrender* (1962). For the trials of German war criminals, see Bradley F. Smith, *Reaching Judgment at Nuremberg* (1977). For the early years of the United Nations, see Evan Luard, *A History of the United Nations*, I, *The Years of Western Domination, 1945–1955* (1982).

Assorted biographies of Harry Truman and surveys of the Truman presidency consider most of the happenings and developments treated in both Chapters 1 and 2. A short and readable biography of Truman is Robert H. Ferrell, *Harry S. Truman and the Modern Presidency* (1983). A first-rate study of the Truman presidency is Donald R. McCoy, *The Presidency of Harry S. Truman* (1984). See also William E. Leuchtenburg's consideration of Truman's presidency in his book *In the Shadow of FDR: From Harry Truman to Ronald Reagan* (1983). A two-volume account of Truman's presidency is Robert J. Donovan, *Conflict and Crisis: The Presidency of Harry S. Truman, 1945–1948* (1979), and *Tumultuous Years: The Presidency of Harry S. Truman, 1949–1953* (1982).

George T. Mazuzan and J. Samuel Walker, *Controlling the Atom: The Beginnings of Nuclear Regulation, 1946–1962* (1984), provides an excellent account of the attempt to regulate the awesome power unleashed at Alamogordo in the summer of 1945. For the formulation of deterrence strategy and nuclear weapons during the postwar years, see Richard G. Hewlett and Francis Duncan, *A History of the United States Atomic Energy Commission*, II, *Atomic Shield, 1947–1952* (1969), and Henry R. Borowski, *A Hollow Threat: Strategic Air Power and Containment Before Korea* (1982).

A basic book for the reader who wishes to understand Truman's approach to policy in the realm of home affairs is Alonzo L. Hamby, *Beyond the New*

*Deal: Harry S. Truman and American Liberalism* (1973). A variety of other books take up developments and problems in the area of domestic politics during the Truman presidency, among them R. Alton Lee, *Truman and Taft-Hartley: A Question of Mandate* (1966); Monte M. Poen, *Harry S. Truman Versus the Medical Lobby: The Genesis of Medicare* (1979); William Howard Moore, *The Kefauver Committee and the Politics of Crime, 1950–1952* (1974); and Maeva Marcus, *Truman and the Steel Seizure Case: The Limits of Presidential Power* (1977). An excellent analysis of the controversy over civil rights from 1945 to 1953 is Donald R. McCoy and Richard T. Reutten, *Quest and Response: Minority Rights and the Truman Administration* (1973). See also Morris J. MacGregor, Jr., *Integration of the Armed Forces, 1940–65* (1981). For Truman's battles with Republicans in Congress, see Susan M. Hartman, *Truman and the 80th Congress* (1971).

Perhaps the most respected analysis of the coming of the Cold War is John Lewis Gaddis, *The United States and the Origins of the Cold War, 1941–1947* (1972). Less analytical but no less powerful is Herbert Feis, *From Trust to Terror: The Onset of the Cold War, 1945–1950* (1970). A more recent study is Hugh Thomas, *Armed Truce: The Beginnings of the Cold War* (1987). Robert J. Maddox, *From War to Cold War: The Education of Harry S. Truman* (1988), provides a splendid and brief analysis of the breakdown of the Grand Alliance and the opening stages of the Cold War. See also Thomas G. Paterson, *On Every Front: The Making of the Cold War* (1979); Greg Herkin, *The Winning Weapon: The Atomic Bomb in the Cold War, 1945–1950* (1980); and Fraser J. Harbutt, *The Iron Curtain: Churchill, America, and the Origins of the Cold War* (1986). For the interpretation of the origins of the Cold War by the New Left or Cold War revisionist school, see Joyce and Gabriel Kolko, *The Limits of Power: The World and United States Foreign Policy, 1945–1954* (1972), and Lloyd C. Gardner, *Architects of Illusion: Men and Ideas in American Foreign Policy, 1941–1949* (1970). Robert J. Maddox, *The New Left and the Origins of the Cold War* (1973), offers a biting critique of New Left scholarship. A provocative look at more recent trends in Cold War scholarship may be found in John Lewis Gaddis et al., "The Emerging Post-Revisionist Synthesis on the Origins of the Cold War," *Diplomatic History*, VII, 3, Summer 1983.

Several volumes of memoirs can add to one's understanding of the early years of the Cold War, among them, James F. Byrnes, *Speaking Frankly* (1947); Dean G. Acheson, *Present at the Creation: My Years at the State Department* (1969); and George F. Kennan, *Memoirs, 1925–1950* (1967). An indispensable biographical study is Forrest C. Pogue, *George C. Marshall: Statesman, 1945–1959* (1987). Michael J. Hogan, *The Marshall Plan: America, Britain, and the Reconstruction of Western Europe, 1947–1952* (1987), provides a brilliant treatment of the historic program to regenerate noncommunist Europe in the aftermath of the global war. For the Berlin blockade and airlift, see Ann Tusa and John Tusa, *The Berlin Airlift* (1988), and Richard Collier, *Bridge Across the Sky: The Berlin Blockade and Airlift, 1948–1949* (1978).

Michael Schaller, *The American Occupation in Japan: The Origins of the Cold War in Asia* (1985), and Theodore Cohen, *Remaking Japan: The Ameri-*

*can Occupation as New Deal* (1987), are valuable studies of what the United States did and tried to do in postwar Japan. D. Clayton James, *The Years of MacArthur, III, Triumph & Disaster, 1945–1964* (1985), offers a careful and insightful account of General MacArthur's management of the occupation of Japan from 1945 to 1951.

A fair number of books and essays have appeared over the past decade or so that consider the part taken by the United States in the birth of Israel; the best of them, arguably, is Kenneth Ray Bain, *The March to Zion: United States Policy and the Founding of Israel* (1979). Evan Wilson, *Decision on Palestine* (1979), offers a sharp critique of the Washington government's policy vis-à-vis the Palestinian question in 1945–1948. For other aspects of the Washington government's Middle Eastern policy during the Truman years, see Aaron David Miller, *The Search for Security: Saudi Arabian Oil and American Foreign Policy, 1939–1949* (1980), and Barry Rubin, *Paved with Good Intentions: American Experience in Iran* (1980).

A useful study of the presidential election of 1948 in the United States is Irwin Ross, *The Loneliest Campaign: The Truman Victory of 1948* (1968). A first-rate study of the scandals that tarnished the Truman administration is Andrew J. Dunar, *The Truman Scandals and the Politics of Morality* (1984).

Harold A. Bierck, *The United States and Latin America, 1933–1968: From the Good Neighbor to the Alliance for Progress* (1969) considers the Latin American policy of the Truman administration. For the origins and early years of the North Atlantic alliance, see Lord Ismay Hastings, *NATO: The First Five Years, 1948–1954* (1955), and Lawrence S. Kaplan, *The United States and NATO: The Formative Years* (1984). John C. Campbell, *Tito's Separate Road: America and Yugoslavia in World Politics* (1967), offers a concise and sharply written account of U.S. relations with Marshal Tito's communist regime in Yugoslavia during the administrations of Truman and Eisenhower. An array of books and essays have examined U.S. relations with China during the years of Truman, 1945–1953, among them Michael Schaller, *The United States Crusade in China, 1938–1948* (1979); Dorothy Borg and Waldo Heinrichs (eds.), *Uncertain Years: Chinese-American Relations, 1947–1950* (1980); and Robert M. Blum, *Drawing the Line: The Origins of the American Containment Policy in East Asia* (1982).

Shortly after completion of the Maoist conquest of China—also soon after explosion of a nuclear device by the Soviet Union—the Washington government decided to build a thermonuclear or hydrogen bomb. David Alan Rosenberg has offered an incisive account of that decision in "American Atomic Strategy and the Hydrogen Bomb Decision," *Journal of American History*, LXVI, June 1979. See also Herbert F. York, *The Advisors: Oppenheimer, Teller, and the Superbomb* (1975).

The anticommunist crusade in America in the postwar years and the enterprise of Sen. Joseph R. McCarthy have generated many books and essays. Athan G. Theoharis, *Seeds of Repression: Harry S. Truman and the Origins of McCarthyism* (1971), is sharply critical of the performance of the Truman administration during what has sometimes been identified as the country's

"Second Red Scare" (the First Red Scare having taken place in 1919–1920). See also Athan G. Theoharis and Stuart John Cox, *The Boss: J. Edgar Hoover and the Great American Inquisition* (1988). Like Theoharis, Richard M. Freeland in *The Truman Doctrine and the Origins of McCarthyism: Foreign Policy, Domestic Politics, and Internal Security, 1946–1948* (1969), assigns considerable blame to the Truman administration for the anticommunist hysteria that seemed to grip the country in the latter 1940s and early 1950s. See also Peter L. Steinberg, *The Great 'Red' Menace: United States Prosecution of American Communists, 1947–1952* (1984), and Larry Ceplair and Steven England, *The Inquisition in Hollywood: Politics in the Film Community, 1930–1960* (1980). Near the center of any account of the controversy over domestic communism during the postwar years is the affair of Alger Hiss. The definitive study of the affair is Allen Weinstein, *Perjury: The Hiss-Chambers Case* (1978). Starting his research with the conviction that Hiss was innocent, Weinstein concluded that he was, after all, guilty. In *Alger Hiss: The True Story* (1977), John Chabot Smith insists that Hiss was, in fact, innocent.

Another cause célèbre that stirred the embers of the Second Red Scare was the case of the atomic spies Julius and Ethel Rosenberg. A fascinating argument for the guilt of the Rosenbergs appears in Ronald Radosh and Joyce Milton, *The Rosenberg File: A Search for the Truth* (1983). Whereas Radosh and Milton affirm the guilt of the Rosenbergs, Walter and Miriam Schneir assert their innocence in *Invitation to an Inquest* (1983). The reader who wishes to learn more about the state of the Communist party in the United States during the years immediately following the global war might examine Joseph R. Starobin, *American Communism in Crisis, 1943–1957* (1972). For the division between political liberals and radicals in the United States that resulted from the communist controversy during the postwar years, see William O'Neill, *A Better World: The Great Schism: Stalinism and the American Intellectuals* (1983).

A sprightly critique of Senator McCarthy is Richard H. Rovere, *Senator Joe McCarthy* (1959). First-rate analyses of McCarthy and the McCarthy phenomenon appear in Robert Griffith, *The Politics of Fear: Joseph R. McCarthy and the Senate* (1970), and Richard M. Fried, *Men Against McCarthy* (1976). More detailed and more recent is David M. Oshinsky, *A Conspiracy So Immense: The World of Joe McCarthy* (1983). See also Mark Landis, *Joseph McCarthy: The Politics of Chaos* (1987); Donald F. Crosby, *God, Church, and Flag: Senator Joseph R. McCarthy and the Catholic Church, 1950–57* (1978); and Ellen W. Schrecker, *No Ivory Tower: McCarthyism and the Universities* (1986).

Transpiring against the background of the Second Red Scare and McCarthyism was the Korean War. One might do well to begin a study of the Korean War with Robert M. Slusser, "Stalin's Far Eastern Policy, 1945–50: Stalin's Goals in Korea," in Yonosuke Nagai and Akira Irye (eds.), *The Origins of the Cold War in Asia* (1977). Exploring America's road to the Korean War are Charles M. Dobbs, *The Unwanted Symbol: American Foreign Policy, the Cold*

*War, and Korea, 1947–1950* (1981); William W. Stueck, Jr., *The Road to Confrontation: American Policy Toward China and Korea, 1947–1950* (1981); and James I. Matray, *The Reluctant Crusade: American Foreign Policy Toward China and Korea, 1947–1950* (1985).

Joseph C. Goulden has offered a hefty and readable volume relating the military and political dimensions of the Korean War, *Korea: The Untold Story of the War* (1982). A sharply written and comparatively brief history of the Korean War that focuses on the military events is Max Hastings, *The Korean War* (1987). No less sharply written and considerably more detailed is Clay Blair, *The Forgotten War: America in Korea, 1950–1953* (1987), a stirring piece of military history. A vivid report of the nitty-gritty of combat during the Korean War is S. L. A. Marshall, *Pork Chop Hill: The American Fighting Man in Action* (1953). A careful study of what was, arguably, the most grisly combat involving Americans during the Korean War is Roy E. Appleman, *East of Chosin: Entrapment and Breakout in Korea, 1950* (1987). Of continuing fascination to students of history is the controversy between MacArthur and Truman that, at length, resulted in MacArthur's dismissal. In addition to the aforementioned volume by D. Clayton James, the reader wishing to learn more about the controversy might examine John Spanier, *The MacArthur Controversy and the Korean War* (1959).

Unlike the two world wars and the war in Vietnam, the Korean War has brought forth no coherent study of the American home front during the time of the war. All that has appeared in print to date is John E. Wilz, "The Korean War and American Society," in Francis H. Heller (ed.), *The Korean War: A 25-Year Perspective* (1977). John Robert Greene, *The Crusade: The Presidential Election of 1952* (1985), considers the first Eisenhower-Stevenson contest for the presidency. See also John Bartlow Martin, *Adlai Stevenson of Illinois: The Life of Adlai E. Stevenson* (1976).

## CHAPTER 3

The reader who wishes to learn more about Dwight D. Eisenhower before he became president ought to examine Stephen E. Ambrose, *Eisenhower, I, Soldier, General of the Army, President-Elect, 1890–1952* (1983). The best account of Eisenhower the president is Stephen E. Ambrose, *Eisenhower, II, The President* (1984). See also Herbert S. Parmet, *Eisenhower and the American Crusades* (1972); Robert F. Burk, *Dwight D. Eisenhower: Hero and Politician* (1986); and Piers Brendon, *Ike: His Life and Times* (1986). Two memoirs by members of the Eisenhower administration offer insight into the thirty-fourth president's leadership style: Emmet John Hughes, *The Ordeal of Power: A Political Memoir of the Eisenhower Years* (1963), and Arthur Larson, *Eisenhower: The President Nobody Knew* (1968). Fred I. Greenstein, *The Hidden Hand Presidency: Eisenhower as Leader* (1982), provides a scholarly and much-acclaimed analysis of Eisenhower's style of leadership. See also Blanche

Wiesen Cook, *The Declassified Eisenhower: A Divided Legacy* (1981), and Robert Griffith, "Dwight D. Eisenhower and the Corporate Commonwealth," *American Historical Review*, LXXXVII, 1, February 1982.

Various of the books mentioned in the preceding section consider the Eisenhower administration's response to the phenomenon of McCarthyism. See also Allen Yarnell, "Eisenhower and McCarthy: An Appraisal of Presidential Strategy," *Presidential Studies Quarterly*, X, 1, Winter 1980. Several books consider the ultraconservative John Birch Society that came to touch the consciousness of Americans during the 1950s, among them Gene Grove, *Inside the John Birch Society* (1961).

An array of books describe and analyze the civil rights crusade during the 1950s and the Eisenhower administration's response to that crusade, one of the most widely acclaimed of which is Juan Williams, *Eyes on the Prize: America's Civil Rights Years, 1954–1965* (1987). Other important titles are Harvard Sitkoff, *The Struggle for Black Equality, 1954–1980* (1981); Manning Marable, *Race, Reform, and Rebellion: The Second Reconstruction in Black America, 1945–1982* (1984); Louise Meriwether, *Don't Ride the Bus on Monday: The Rosa Parks Story* (1973); Robert F. Burk, *The Eisenhower Administration and Black Civil Rights* (1984); and Tony Freyer, *The Little Rock Crisis: A Constitutional Interpretation* (1984).

It was during the Eisenhower years of course that Martin Luther King, Jr., emerged as a leader of the civil rights crusade. For the life and career of King, see Steven B. Oates, *Let the Trumpet Sound: The Life of Martin Luther King, Jr.* (1982); David J. Garrow, *Bearing the Cross: Martin Luther King, Jr., and the Southern Christian Leadership Conference* (1986); and Adam Fairclough, *To Redress the Soul of America: The Southern Christian Leadership Conference and Martin Luther King, Jr.* (1987). See also Taylor Branch, *Parting the Waters: America in the King Years, 1954–63* (1988). Also an important player in the civil rights crusade was the Supreme Court. Paul Murphy, *The Constitution in Crisis Times, 1918–1969* (1972), and J. Harvie Wilkinson III, *From Brown to Bakke: The Supreme Court and School Integration, 1954–1978* (1979), consider initiatives by the high court in the matter of civil rights during the years of Eisenhower. Richard Kluger, *Simple Justice: The History of Brown v. Board of Education and Black America's Struggle for Equality* (1976), analyzes the historic school desegregation decision by the Supreme Court. See also two first-rate biographies of the man who presided over the Supreme Court in those years, G. Edward White, *Earl Warren: A Public Life* (1982), and Bernard Schwartz, *Super Chief: Earl Warren and His Supreme Court* (1983). Clifton E. Marsh, *From Black Muslims to Muslims: The Transition from Separation to Islam, 1930–1980* (1984), provides insight regarding Elijah Muhammad and the Black Muslims who stirred the fears of many white Americans during the time of Eisenhower.

Walter A. MacDougall, *The Heavens and the Earth: A Political History of the Space Age* (1985), and Richard S. Lewis, *Appointment on the Moon* (1969), consider the beginning of space exploration by the United States during the years of Eisenhower. Barbara Barksdale Clowse, *Brainpower for the Cold War:*

*The Sputnik Crisis and the National Defense Education Act of 1958* (1981), takes up the psychic and political consequences of the launching by the Soviets of the first Sputnik spacecraft. The defense policies of the Eisenhower administration are considered in E. Bruce Geelhoed, *Charles E. Wilson and Controversy at the Pentagon, 1953 to 1957* (1979). Richard G. Hewlett and Jack M. Holl, *Atoms for Peace and War, 1953–1961* (1989), considers nuclear policy-making at the highest level of the Eisenhower administration.

The Cold War was the overbearing reality in American foreign relations during the Eisenhower years, and Robert A. Divine, *Eisenhower and the Cold War* (1981) offers an insightful summary of the diplomacy of the Eisenhower administration in the matter of the Cold War. See also Richard Melanson and David Mayers (eds.), *Reevaluating Eisenhower: American Foreign Policy in the 1950s* (1987). Burton I. Kaufman, *Trade and Aid: Eisenhower's Foreign Economic Policy, 1953–1961* (1982), considers a central aspect of the Washington government's diplomacy during the years of Eisenhower. An excellent study of the North Atlantic alliance during the presidency of Eisenhower is Lawrence S. Kaplan, *The United States and NATO: The Formative Years* (1984). Adam B. Ulam, *The Rivals: America and Russia Since World War II* (1971), considers the Cold War policies of the superpowers during the years of Eisenhower.

Kermit Roosevelt, *Countercoup: The Struggle for the Control of Iran* (1979), offers an eyewitness account of U.S. intervention in Iran in 1953 by the man who orchestrated it. Donald Neff, *Warriors at Suez* (1981), considers the Suez crisis of 1956. Roger J. Spiller, *"Not War But Like War": The American Intervention in Lebanon* (1981), addresses the U.S. intervention in Lebanon in 1958.

Foster Rhea Dulles, *American Policy Toward Communist China*, offers a lucid analysis of the Eisenhower administration's policies regarding the People's Republic of China. It was during the years of Eisenhower, of course, that the United States first escalated its involvement in the conflict in Indochina. A fair number of books consider that escalation—and also its antecedents, among them Bernard B. Fall, *The Two Viet-Nams: A Political and Military Analysis* (1964); Stanley Karnow, *Vietnam: A History* (1983); George C. Herring, *America's Longest War: The United States and Vietnam, 1950–1975* (1979); and George McT. Kahin, *Intervention: How America Became Involved in Vietnam* (1986). For Eisenhower's response to the siege at Dien Bien Phu in 1954, see Melanie Billings-Yun, *Decision Against War: Eisenhower and Dien Bien Phu* (1988).

The best book on the Eisenhower administration's policies vis-à-vis Latin America is Stephen G. Rabe, *Eisenhower and Latin America: The Foreign Policy of Anticommunism* (1988). For U.S. intervention in Guatemala in 1954, see R. H. Immerman, *The CIA in Guatemala: The Foreign Policy of Intervention* (1982), and Stephen C. Schlesinger and Stephen Kinzer, *Bitter Fruit: The Untold Story of the American Coup in Guatemala* (1982). An excellent book taking up the Eisenhower administration's response to the Castro revolution in Cuba is Richard E. Welch, Jr., *Response to Revolution: The United States* and the Cuban Revolution, 1959–1961 (1985). See also Morris H. Morley, *Imperial State and Revolution: The United States and Cuba, 1952–1986* (1987), and Wayne S. Smith, *The Closest of Enemies: A Personal and Diplomatic Account of U.S.-Cuban Relations Since 1957* (1987).

## CHAPTER 4

Several authors have written useful surveys of all or part of the social history of the United States during the fifteen or so years after World War II, the best of which, arguably, is Geoffrey Perrett, *A Dream of Greatness: The American People, 1945–1963* (1979). See also William L. O'Neill, *American High: The Years of Confidence, 1945–1960* (1989); Marty Jezer, *The Dark Ages: Life in the United States, 1945–1960* (1982); Joseph C. Goulden, *The Best Years, 1945–1950* (1976); Jeffrey P. Hart, *When the Going Was Good! American Life in the Fifties* (1982); and Douglas T. Miller and Marion Nowak, *The Fifties: The Way We Really Were* (1977).

Kenneth Fox, *Metropolitan America: Urban Life and Urban Policy in the United States, 1940–1980* (1980), considers the continuing growth of cities in America during the years after the global war and the consequences of that growth. See also Blake McKelvey, *The Emergence of Metropolitan America, 1915–1966* (1969), and John C. Teaford, *The Twentieth-Century American City: Problems, Promise, and Reality* (1986). Kenneth T. Jackson, *The Crabgrass Frontier: The Suburbanization of the United States* (1985), takes up the growth of suburbia in America in the years after 1945.

Harold G. Vatter, *The U.S. Economy in the 1950's: An Economic History* (1963), provides an incisive treatment of the economic life of the United States during the 1950s. See also the appropriate chapters of Robert Sobel, *The Age of Giant Corporations: A Microeconomic History of American Business, 1914–1984* (1984). Herbert Stein, *The Fiscal Revolution in America* (1969), considers the changing fiscal policies of the United States in the aftermath of the global war. Robert H. Zeiger, *American Workers, American Unions, 1920–1985* (1986), addresses the condition of working people in the United States in the decades after World War II. For American agriculture during those same decades, see John T. Schlebecker, *Whereby We Thrive: A History of American Farming, 1607–1972* (1975).

Donald M. Itzkoff, *Off the Track: The Decline of the Intercity Passenger Train in the United States* (1985), analyzes the American passenger train from "the glory years" of rail passenger travel through the 1970s. See also John F. Stover, *The Life and Decline of the American Railroad* (1970). Lawrence J. White, *The Automobile Industry Since 1945* (1971), has written a useful study of the automobile industry during the first quarter century after the global war. C. Gayle Warnock, *The Edsel Affair: . . . What Went Wrong?* (1980), considers the automobile industry's most celebrated fiasco of the years 1945–1960. The title of John B. Rae, *Climb to Greatness: The American Aircraft Industry, 1920–1960* (1968), is self-explanatory.

J. Harry DuBois, *Plastics History U.S.A.* (1972), traces the growth of the plastics industry. Several books consider the evolution and development of the computer, among them Herman H. Goldstine, *The Computer: From Pascal to Von Neumann* (1972). But the premier studies of the history of the computer are the volumes of the *MIT Press Series in the History of Computing* edited by J. Bernard Cohen and William Aspray. Three admirable volumes in the series have appeared to date: Emerson W. Pugh, *Memories That Shaped an Industry* (1984); Maurice V. Wilkes, *Memoirs of a Computer Pioneer* (1985); and Charles J. Bashe et al., *IBM's Early Computers* (1986). John Swift, *Adventure in Vision: The First Twenty-Five Years of Television* (1950), traces the origins and pristine years of television transmission. More useful is Erik Barnouw, *The Tube of Plenty: The Evolution of American Television* (1975).

The relevant chapters of James Bordley III, and A. McGehee Harvey, *Two Centuries of American Medicine, 1776–1976* (1976), provide excellent sketches of medical developments during the first three decades following World War II. Richard Carter, *Breakthrough: The Saga of Jonas Salk* (1966), essays the most publicized achievement of medical science during the years 1945–1950, namely, the discovery of the vaccine to prevent poliomyelitis. Daniel J. Kevles, *The Physicists: The History of a Scientific Community in Modern America* (1978), considers an important group of scientists in the United States in the twentieth century. A plethora of books consider the discovery of penicillin and other antibiotic drugs, among them Gladys L. Hobby, *Penicillin: Meeting the Challenge* (1985), and Selman Abraham Waksman, *The Antibiotic Era: A History of the Antibiotics and of Their Role in the Conquest of Infectious Diseases and in Other Fields of Human Endeavor* (1975).

David A. Spaeth, *Mies van der Rohe* (1985), considers the foremost architect of the years immediately following the global war. See also Dora P. Crouch, *History of Architecture: Stonehenge to Skyscrapers* (1985).

James Gilbert, *A Cycle of Outrage: America's Reaction to the Juvenile Delinquent in the 1950s* (1986), considers an aspect of crime that touched the consciousness of millions of Americans during the 1950s. As for organized crime, an array of first-rate books consider that unfortunate phenomenon in American society, among them Frederic Sonder, *Brotherhood of Evil: The Mafia* (1959), and Humbert S. Nelli, *Business of Crime: Italians and Syndicate Crime in the United States* (1976).

Mary J. Bane, *Here to Stay: American Families in the Twentieth Century* (1976), illuminates the condition of the American family during the early postwar years. Birth control became a subject of increased public discussion during the decade and a half after World War II. For enlightenment on the subject, one might consult Linda Gordon, *Woman's Body, Woman's Right: A Social History of Birth Control* (1977), and James Reed, *From Private Vice to Public Virtue: The Birth Control Movement and American Society Since 1830* (1978). Leila J. Rupp and Verta Taylor, *Survival in the Doldrums: The America Women's Rights Movement, 1945 to 1960* (1987), considers feminism in the United States in the early postwar years.

For the work of the sex researcher Alfred Kinsey, see Wardell B. Pomery,

*Dr. Kinsey and the Institute for Sex Research* (1982). Diane Ravitch, *The Troubled Crusade: American Education, 1945–1980* (1983), is, arguably, the best study of education in the United States during the postwar decades. Two contemporary works that generated widespread debate regarding the schools during the 1950s are Arthur E. Bestor, *Educational Wastelands: The Retreat from Learning in Our Public Schools* (1953), and Hyman G. Rickover, *Education and Freedom* (1959).

Two important studies of religion in the United States in the years since the global war are Robert Wuthnow, *The Restructuring of American Religion: Society and Faith Since World War II* (1988), and Mark Silk, *Spiritual Politics: Religion and America Since World War II* (1988). An excellent survey of popular culture in America by the country's premier historian of popular culture is Russel B. Nye, *The Unembarrassed Muse: The Popular Arts in America* (1970). Leonard Quart and Albert Auster, *American Film and Society Since 1945* (1984), considers American films during the first two decades after the global war. Matthew Baigell, *A Concise History of American Painting and Sculpture* (1984), offers an excellent survey of painting and sculpture in the United States. Alan Howard Levy, *Musical Nationalism: American Composers' Search for Identity* (1983), offers insight into classical music in the United States during the years after the global war.

Robert E. Kiernan, *American Writing Since 1945: A Critical Survey* (1983), and Warner Berthoff, *A Literature Without Qualities: American Writing Since 1945* (1979), treat literature in the United States during the decades after World War II. Martin Gottfried, *A Theater Divided: The Postwar American Stage* (1967), offers a useful account of the American theater. Rock 'n' roll took form in the United States during the decade and a half following the global war. Charlie Gillett, *The Sound of the City: The Rise of Rock and Roll* (1984), offers a useful account of the birth and early development of rock 'n' roll. The undeniable king of rock 'n' roll, of course, was Elvis Presley. Marge Crumbaker, *Up and Down with Elvis Presley* (1981), may be the best book on the incomparable Elvis. John Rockwell, *Sinatra: An American Classic* (1984), considers the premier performer in the field of pop music in American during the decades after World War II. Bill C. Malone, *Country Music, U.S.A.: A Fifty-Year History* (1985), surveys an enduring phenomenon in popular culture in the United States.

Several books have considered the beatnik and hippie phenomena, among them Bruce Cook, *The Beat Generation* (1971). The reader who is interested in the social critics of the early postwar years ought to read the writings of various of the critics themselves, for example, Jack Kerouac, *On the Road* (1955); William H. Whyte, *The Organization Man* (1956); Vance O. Packard, *The Status Seekers* (1959); and John Kenneth Galbraith, *The Affluent Society* (1959).

Library bookshelves abound with books on the numerous dimensions of sports during the decades since World War II. But, arguably, the most important happening in the realm of sports in the United States during that time was the integration of major league baseball in 1947 when Jackie Robinson became the first baseman of the Brooklyn Dodgers. For that historic happening and its import, see Jules Tygiel, *Baseball's Greatest Experiment: Jackie Robinson and His Legacy* (1983).

## CHAPTER 5

The best study of the U-2 affair of the spring of 1960 is Michael R. Beschloss, *MAYDAY: Eisenhower, Khrushchev, and the U-2 Affair* (1986). In the first and, arguably, the best of his widely acclaimed "making of the president" series of studies of American presidential elections, Theodore H. White, *The Making of the President, 1960* (1961), offers a stirring and incisive firsthand account of the contest for the White House between John F. Kennedy and Richard Nixon.

A fascinating and critical study of John Kennedy's life and career before his election to the presidency is Herbert S. Parmet, *Jack: The Struggles of John F. Kennedy* (1980). See also James MacGregor Burns, *John Kennedy: A Political Profile* (1960), and Joan Blair and Clay Blair, *The Search for J.F.K.* (1976). Various members of Kennedy's New Frontier administration have written their own recollections and impressions of the youthful chief executive, among them Arthur M. Schlesinger, Jr., *A Thousand Days: John F. Kennedy in the White House* (1965); Theodore Sorenson, *Kennedy* (1965); and Pierre Salinger, *With Kennedy* (1966). A recent, sharply written, and brief study of Kennedy and his presidency is David Burner, *John F. Kennedy and a New Generation* (1988). Herbert S. Parmet, *JFK: The Presidency of John F. Kennedy* (1983), provides a useful survey of Kennedy's performance in the White House. See also Jim F. Heath, *Decade of Disillusionment: The Kennedy-Johnson Years* (1975), and J. Richard Snyder (ed.), *John F. Kennedy: Person, Policy, Presidency* (1988). Allen J. Matusow, *The Unraveling of America: A History of Liberalism in the 1960s* (1984), takes a critical view of the liberal consensus that commanded American politics for a time during the years of Kennedy and Johnson. See also David Burner and Thomas R. West, *The Torch Is Passed: The Kennedy Brothers and American Liberalism* (1984), Garry Wills, *The Kennedy Imprisonment* (1982), and Nancy Gager Clinch, *The Kennedy Neurosis* (1973), offer critical analyses of the influence of the Kennedy personality on the politics of the 1960s, David Halberstam, *The Best and the Brightest* (1972), a biting critique of American political leaders during the 1960s and their assumptions.

An array of topics, among them "John F. Kennedy and the Economy" and "Kennedy, Defense and Arms Control," are treated in Kenneth W. Thompson (ed.), *The Kennedy Presidency: Seventeen Intimate Perspectives of John F. Kennedy* [*Portraits of American Presidents*, IV] (1985). Grant McConnell, *Steel and the Presidency—1962* (1963), takes up Kennedy's confrontation with the steel industry. Richard Harris, *The Real Voice* (1964), considers Kennedy's part in passage of drug-control legislation in 1962. Other useful books on Kennedy and his presidency include Donald C. Lord, John F. Kennedy, *The Politics of Confrontation and Conciliation* (1977); Jim F. Heath, *John F. Kennedy and the*

*Business Community* (1969); and Lawrence H. Fuchs, *John F. Kennedy and American Catholicism* (1967). Carl M. Brauer, *John F. Kennedy and the Second Reconstruction* (1977), takes a favorable view of the performance of the Kennedy administration in the area of civil rights, Victor S. Navasky, *Kennedy Justice* (1971), a more critical view.

Desmond Ball, *Politics and Force Levels: The Strategic Missile Program of the Kennedy Administration* (1980), offers an excellent analysis of Kennedy's strategic nuclear policy. The centerpiece of the space program during the years of Kennedy, of course, was Project Mercury. Lloyd S. Swenson, Jr., et al., *This New Ocean: A History of Project Mercury* (1966), and M. Scott Carpenter, *We Seven: By the Astronauts Themselves* (1962), provide information and insight regarding the Mercury project. See also William R. Shelton, *Man's Conquest of Space* (1968), and Evgeny Riabchikov, *Russians in Space* (1971).

Richard J. Walton, *Cold War and Counterrevolution: The Foreign Policy of John F. Kennedy* (1972), provides a critical analysis of the foreign policies of the Kennedy administration. See also Louise FitzSimons, *The Kennedy Doctrine* (1972). A sharply written analysis by a member of the Kennedy administration is Roger Hilsman, *To Move a Nation: The Politics of Foreign Policy in the Administration of John F. Kennedy* (1967). Montague Kern et al., explore Kennedy's relations with the communications media by examining several crises in foreign relations in *The Kennedy Crises: The Press, the Presidency, and Foreign Policy* (1983). Warren I. Cohen, *Dean Rusk* (1980), provides an admirable portrait of the secretary of state during the presidencies of Kennedy and Johnson. The Peace Corps is the subject of Gerald T. Rice, *The Bold Experiment: JFK's Peace Corps* (1985). William D. Rogers, *The Twilight Struggle: The Alliance for Progress and the Politics of Development in Latin America* (1967), and Jerome Levinson and Juan de Onís, *The Alliance That Lost Its Way: A Critical Report on the Alliance for Progress* (1970), consider Kennedy's bold initiative aimed at the regeneration of Latin America. Trumbull Higgins, *The Perfect Failure: Kennedy, Eisenhower, and the CIA at the Bay of Pigs* (1988), and Peter Wyden, *Bay of Pigs: The Untold Story* (1979), offer authoritative studies of the most glaring debacle of the years of Kennedy's presidency.

The previously noted volumes by George McT. Kahin, Stanley Karnow, and George Herring survey the enlargement of America's commitment in Vietnam during the years of the Kennedy presidency. See also Ralph B. Smith, *An International History of the Vietnam War: The Kennedy Strategy* (1985), and Ellen J. Hammer, *A Death in November: America in Vietnam, 1963* (1988). P. J. Honey (ed.), *North Vietnam Today: Profile of a Communist Satellite* (1962), affords a critical view of North Vietnam at the time Kennedy undertook to enlarge U.S. involvement in the conflict in Southeast Asia. Chester L. Cooper, *The Lost Crusade: America in Vietnam* (1970), provides an eloquent account by a foreign service officer who participated extensively in the United States effort in Vietnam. A vigorous—and, as matters turned out, prescient—contemporary critique of America's involvement in Vietnam during the early 1960s is David Halberstam, *The Making of a Quagmire* (1965). Neil Sheehan, *A Bright and Shining Lie: John Paul Vann and America in Vietnam* (1988), a searing volume that should command the attention of any reader seeking enlightenment about America's part in the war in Vietnam, reiterates Halberstam's essential arguments.

Richard D. Mahoney, *JFK: Ordeal in Africa* (1983), consider's Kennedy approach to Africa, particularly his response to the crisis in the Congo. Curtis Cate, *The Ides of August: The Berlin Wall Crisis, 1961* (1978), analyzes America's confrontation with the Soviet Union in the matter of Berlin in 1961. See also Robert M. Slusser, *The Berlin Crisis of 1961: Soviet-American Relations and the Struggle for Power in the Kremlin, June–November 1961* (1973). Several useful books provide insight regarding the Cuban missile crisis of 1962, among them Herbert S. Dinerstein, *The Making of a Missile Crisis: October 1962* (1976), and David Detzer, *The Brink* (1979). See also Robert F. Kennedy's remembrance of the crisis, *Thirteen Days: A Memoir of the Cuban Missile Crisis* (1969). Glenn T. Seaborg, *Kennedy, Khrushchev, and the Test Ban* (1981), considers negotiation of the nuclear test-ban treaty of 1963. A. Paul Kubricht, "Politics and Foreign Policy: A Brief Look at the Kennedy Administration's Eastern European Diplomacy," *Diplomatic History*, XI, 1, Winter 1987, offers a brief assessment of Kennedy's policy vis-à-vis Eastern Europe.

Jim Bishop, *The Day Kennedy Was Shot* (1968), narrates the last day in the life of John F. Kennedy. William R. Manchester, *The Death of a President: November 20–November 25, 1963* (1967), offers a detailed and emotion-rocking account of the death of the thirty-fifth president and the ceremonies and observances that followed until his burial. A succession of books have debated the Kennedy assassination and offered scenarios and theories, most of them highly imaginative. The best source on the assassination remains the report of the Warren Commission, *Report of the President's Commission on the Assassination of President John F. Kennedy* (1964).

## CHAPTER 6

A fair number of books have considered the life and presidency of Lyndon Johnson. Robert Caro, *The Years of Lyndon Johnson: The Path to Power* (1982), is a scathing attack on the character and purposes of the prepresidential Johnson. More sympathetic is Ronnie Dugger, *The Life and Times of Lyndon Johnson: The Drive to Power, from the Frontier to Master of the Senate* (1982). Resting heavily on interviews with Johnson after he left the presidency, Doris Kearns, *Lyndon Johnson and the American Dream* (1976), offers a psychobiography of the thirty-sixth president. But the most satisfactory biography of Johnson is Paul K. Conkin, *Big Daddy from the Pedernales: Lyndon Baines Johnson* (1986). See also Robert A. Divine, *The Johnson Years*, I, *Exploring the Johnson Years* (1981), and II, *Vietnam, the Environment, and Science* (1987). Eric F. Goldman, *The Tragedy of Lyndon Johnson: A Historian's Personal Interpretation* (1969), is an insightful memoir by a brilliant historian who for a time served as resident intellectual in the Johnson White House. Jack Valenti, *A Very Human President* (1975), is a sympathetic memoir by one of Johnson's closest political confidants.

For Johnson's first months in the White House, see Michael Amrine, *This*

*Awesome Challenge: The Hundred Days of Lyndon Johnson* (1964). See also Jack Bell, *The Johnson Treatment: How Lyndon B. Johnson Took Over the Presidency and Made It His Own* (1965). Theodore H. White, *The Making of the President, 1964* (1965), considers the presidential election in which Johnson, in a hackneyed political phrase, won election in his own right. See also Richard Rovere, *The Goldwater Caper* (1965). Emmette S. Redford and Richard T. McCulley, *White House Operations: The Johnson Presidency* (1986), considers the inner workings of the Johnson White House. James E. Anderson, *Managing Macroeconomic Policy: The Johnson Presidency* (1986), analyzes the Johnson administration's approach to the economy.

Sheri I. David, *With Dignity: The Search for Medicare and Medicaid* (1985), offers a first-rate account of the legislative struggle that resulted in passage of the King-Anderson Act of 1965, Hugh Davis Graham, *The Uncertain Triumph: Federal Education Policy in the Kennedy and Johnson Years* (1984), an equally first-rate study of educational initiatives that resulted in the federal education legislation of 1965. David Zarefsky, *President Johnson's War on Poverty: Rhetoric and History* (1986), is a useful study of the antipoverty initiatives of the thirty-sixth president. Anyone striving for enlightenment on the antipoverty initiatives of the Kennedy-Johnson years should examine Michael Harrington, *The Other America: Poverty in the United States* (1962), a best-selling book that nudged the consciences of uncounted Americans during the early 1960s and kindled the concern of the Kennedy and Johnson administrations. Another indispensable book for anyone undertaking to study the antipoverty crusade in America is James T. Patterson, *America's Struggle Against Poverty, 1900–1980* (1981).

Biographical studies of Martin Luther King, Jr., which are noted under Chapter 3, are essential to any serious study of the civil rights crusade during the 1960s. See also David Thelen et al., "A Round Table: Martin Luther King, Jr., and the Spirit of Leadership." *Journal of American History*, LXXIV, 2, September 1987, and Martin Luther King, Jr., *Why We Can't Wait* (1964). David J. Garrow, *Protest at Selma: Martin Luther King, Jr., and the Voting Rights Act of 1965* (1978), considers what, arguably, was the premier triumph of King's career. David J. Garrow, *The FBI and Martin Luther King, Jr.: From 'Solo' to Memphis* (1981), offers a critical study of the surveillance of King by the FBI. A general study of the civil rights crusade during the era of Kennedy and Johnson is Rhoda Lois Blumberg, *Civil Rights: The 1960s Freedom Struggle* (1984). James Silver, a professor of history at the University of Mississippi who had the courage to speak out in support of integration of the university, wrote two important books: *Mississippi: The Closed Society* (1964), and a memoir of his own experiences, *Running Scared: Silver in Mississippi* (1984). Seth Cagan and Philip Dray. *We Are Not Afraid: The Story of Goodman, Schwerner, and Chaney and the Civil Rights Campaign for Mississippi* (1988), discusses the infamous murder of three civil rights workers in Mississippi in 1964. See also Sally Belfrage, *Freedom Summer* (1965).

No coherent survey of the foreign policies of the Johnson administration has appeared to date, but perhaps the best book on the subject is Warren I.

Cohen's *Dean Rusk*, noted previously. Abraham Lowenthal, *The Dominican Intervention* (1972) offers a useful account of U.S. intervention in the civil conflict in the Dominican Republic in 1965. At the center of Johnson's concern in foreign affairs, of course, was the war in Vietnam. The volumes by Herring, Karnow, Sheehan, and Cooper mentioned in the preceding section are basic to any consideration of Johnson's escalation of U.S. involvement in the war and his efforts to prevail on the communists to accept a negotiated settlement of the conflict. Herbert Y. Schandler, *The Unmaking of a President: Lyndon Johnson and Vietnam* (1977), considers the devastating consequences that the war had on Johnson and his presidency. Kathleen J. Turner, *Lyndon Johnson's Dual War: Vietnam and the Press* (1985), offers an insightful account of the effect of the war on Johnson's relations with the communications media. Daniel C. Hallin, *The "Uncensored War": The Media and Vietnam* (1989), offers a careful account of what Americans read and watched in the matter of Vietnam. Thomas Powers, *Vietnam: The War at Home: Vietnam and the American People, 1964–1968* (1984), and Nancy Zaroulis and Gerlad Sullivan, *Who Spoke Up? American Protest Against the War in Vietnam, 1963–1975* (1984), offer incisive accounts of the antiwar movement in the United States during the war in Vietnam. Gabriel Kolko, *Anatomy of a War: Vietnam, the United States, and the Modern Historical Experience* (1985), is a searing indictment of America's involvement in Vietnam by a prominent scholar of the New Left persuasion. For a defense of American involvement in Vietnam by a political conservative, see Norman Podhertz, *Why We Were in Vietnam* (1982). See also Michael P. Sullivan, *The Vietnam War: A Study in the Making of American Policy* (1985). George C. Herring, "America and Vietnam: The Debate Continues," *American Historical Review*, XCII, 2, April 1987, analyzes the scholarly debate relating to U.S. involvement in the war in Vietnam.

Bruce Palmer, Jr., *The 25-Year War: America's Military Role in Vietnam* (1984), offers a useful survey of the military involvement of the United States during the war in Vietnam. Harry G. Summers, *On Strategy: A Critical Analysis of the Vietnam War* (1982), is a provocative study that blames a flawed military strategy for America's frustration in Vietnam. Norman B. Hannah, *The Key to Failure: Laos and the Vietnam War* (1987), offers an argument similar to that advanced by Summers. S. L. A. Marshall, *Battles in the Monsoon: Campaigning in the Central Highlands* (1967), provides a moving account that catches the terror and tedium endured by U.S. infantrymen in Vietnam. See also Mark Baker, *Nam: The Vietnam War in the Words of the Men and Women Who Fought There* (1981), and Charles R. Anderson, *The Grunts* (1976). Seymour M. Hersh, *My Lai 4: A Report on the Massacre and Its Aftermath* (1970), narrates what, probably, was the most shameful episode involving Americans during the war in Vietnam. Jonathan Schell, *The Military Half: An Account of Destruction in Quang Ngai and Quang Tin* (1968), captures the brutality and devastation of American operations in Vietnam. Robert Pisor, *The End of the Line: The Siege of Khe Sanh* (1982), considers one of the most publicized military actions of the war. Paul Frederick Cecil, *Herbicidal Warfare: The Ranch Hand Project in Vietnam* (1986), provides a careful account of what the United States did and did not do in its defoliation activities in Vietnam. Tom Mangold and John Penycate, *The Tunnels of Cu Chi* (1985), offers fascinating insight into the ingenuity and determination of America's enemies in the Vietnamese conflict.

## CHAPTER 7

The best survey of the social and cultural experience of the United States during the 1960s is William L. O'Neill, *Coming Apart: An Informal History of America in the 1960's* (1971). More impassioned perhaps is Milton Viorst, *Fire in the Street: America in the 1960s* (1979). Two more recent studies of the seventh decade of the twentieth century in the United States are Todd Gitlin, *The Sixties: Years of Hope, Days of Rage* (1987), and Gary H. Koerselman, *The Lost Decade: A Story of America in the 1960s* (1987). See also Gerald Howard (ed.), *The Sixties* (1982).

The reader seeking insight on the environmental movement of the 1960s ought to examine Rachel Carson, *Silent Spring* (1962), the book widely credited with giving birth to the environmental movement. See also Samuel P. Hays, *Beauty, Health, and Permanence: Environmental Politics in the United States 1955–1985* (1987). For the consumer protection movement, one might examine Ralph Nader, *Unsafe at Any Speed* (1965), a book that did not touch off the consumer protection movement but certainly provided it with a great deal of impetus.

The revived feminist movement has been the object of a plethora of books. Again, the reader is advised to examine a book that has been credited with inciting a movement, in this instance Betty Friedan's *The Feminine Mystique* (1963). Rochelle Gatlin, *American Women Since 1945* (1987) is a recently published general study of the experience of women in America that considers the revived feminist movement of the 1960s. See also Cynthia Ellen Harrison, *On Account of Sex: The Politics of Women's Issues, 1945–1968* (1988); William Chafe, *Women and Equality: Changing Patterns in American Culture* (1977); and Gerda Lerner, *The Majority Finds Its Past: Placing Women in History* (1979).

Volumes noted under Chapters 5 and 6 are essential to any serious consideration of the experience of black Americans during the 1960s. Several contemporary volumes illuminate the problems confronting blacks in the United States in the 1960s and before, among them Kenneth Clark, *Dark Ghetto* (1965); Claude Brown, *Manchild in a Promised Land* (1965); Eldridge Cleaver, *Soul on Ice* (1969); and James Baldwin's searing and brilliant *The Fire Next Time* (1963). For the ghetto uprising of 1965 in the Los Angeles suburb of Watts, see Jerry Cohen and William S. Murphy, *Burn, Baby, Burn: The Los Angeles Race Riot, August 1965* (1966). For an insightful study of the causes of violence in Watts and other urban ghettos during the 1960s, see *Report of the National Advisory Commission on Civil Disorders* (1968), that is, the report of the celebrated Kerner Commission. James Haskins provides insights regarding the proponents of black power in *Profiles in Black Power* (1972).

A recently published study by Rodolfo Acuna entitled *Occupied America: A History of Chicanos* (1988), provides an excellent survey of the experience of Mexican Americans. Manuel P. Servin (compiler), *Mexican Americans: An Awakened Minority* (1972), considers the new impulse to activism among Mexican Americans during the 1960s and early 1970s. For the enterprise of César Chavez, see Ronald B. Taylor, *César Chavez and the Farm Workers* (1975).

John D'Emilio and Estelle Freedman, *Intimate Matters: A History of Sexuality in America* (1988), discusses the so-called sexual revolution of the 1960s. Martin A. Lee and Bruce Shlain, *Acid Dreams: The CIA, LSD, and the Sixties Rebellion* (1985), considers happenings relating to the exploding drug culture of the latter decade. The youth rebellion and counterculture of the 1960s have generated an array of books. Peter Clecak, *America's Quest for the Ideal Self: Dissent and Fulfillment in the 60s and 70s* (1983), assesses the youth rebellion. For the counterculture, see Theodore Roszak, *The Making of the Counter Culture: Reflections on the Technocratic Society and Its Youthful Opposition* (1969). Communes are discussed in Ron E. Roberts, *The New Communes: Coming Together in America* (1971), and Laurence R. Veysey, *The Communal Experience: Anarchist and Mystical Counter Cultures in America* (1973). The most infamous name identified with the counterculture of the 1960s was that of Charles Manson. For Manson and the horrors he and his "family" perpetrated, see Vincent Bugliosi, *Helter Skelter: The True Story of the Manson Murders* (1976). Robert S. Spitz, *Barefoot in Babylon: The Creation of the Woodstock Music Festival, 1969* (1979), describes the climactic moment of the youth rebellion in the 1960s.

Two excellent accounts of the so-called New Left that took form during the 1960s are Irwin Unger, *The Movement: A History of the American New Left* (1974), and Maurice Isserman, *If I Had a Hammer: The Death of the Old Left and the Birth of the New Left* (1987). The best known of the New Left organizations during the 1960s was the Students for a Democratic Society. The most recent study of the SDS appears in James Miller, *"Democracy in the Streets": From Port Huron to the Siege of Chicago* (1987). See also Kirkpatrick Sale, *SDS* (1971). Abbie Hoffman, *Revolution for the Hell of It* (1968), and Jerry Rubin, *Do It: Scenarios of the Revolution* (1970), are polemics in support of the enterprise of the Youth International Party (or Yippies) by its best-known leaders. Harold Jacobs (compiler), *Weatherman* (1970), discusses the purposes and methods of the radical Weatherman organization.

C. Wright Mills, *The Power Elite* (1956), scores America's so-called military-industrial complex. Less impassioned analyses are offered in Sidney Lens, *The Military-Industrial Complex* (1970), and Paul A. C. Koistinen, *The Military-Industrial Complex: A Historical Perspective* (1980). For development of electrostatic photocopying machines, see John H. Dessaner and Harold E. Clark (eds.), *Xerography and Related Processes* (1965), and John H. Dessaner,

*My Years with Xerox: The Billions Nobody Wanted* (1971). No happening in the field of medicine stirred the interest of Americans so much as the transplantation of human hearts. A pioneer in the field was the South African surgeon Christiaan Barnard. For Barnard and his enterprise, see Peter Hawthorne, *The Transplanted Heart: The Incredible Story of the Epic Heart Transplant Operations by Professor Christiaan Barnard and His Team* (1968). The premier scientific accomplishment of the time was, arguably, the perfection of hybrid grains that resulted in the Green Revolution. For a study of that accomplishment, see Stanley Johnson, *The Green Revolution* (1972).

Essays in Gerald Howard (ed.), *The Sixties: Art, Attitudes, Politics, and Media of Our Most Explosive Decade* (1982), provide insight regarding various aspects of American culture during the 1960s. Morris Dickstein, *Gates of Eden: American Culture in the Sixties* (1977), discusses literature, rock music, and social protest during the 1960s. It was during the 1960s that the Beatles first imprinted the cultural scene in America. For the Beatles and their enterprise, see Philip Norman, *Shout: The Beatles and Their Generation* (1981), and Terence J. O'Grady, *The Beatles: A Musical Evolution* (1983). More durable than the Beatles have been the Rolling Stones. David Dalton, *The Rolling Stones: The First Twenty Years* (1981), offers a first-rate account of the Stones and their music. Michael O'Brien, *Vince: A Personal Biography of Vince Lombardi* (1987), considers one of the premier figures in professional sports in America during the 1960s. Ray Kroc, *Grinding It Out: The Making of McDonald's* (1977), and Harland Sanders, *Life as I Have Known It Has Been Finger Lickin' Good* (1974), are autobiographical accounts by the two most renowned fast-food impresarios of the 1960s. Another premier personality in the world of pop culture during the 1960s was Hugh Hefner, the founder of *Playboy* magazine and related ventures. For Hefner and his enterprise, see Frank Brady, *Hefner* (1974), and Russell Miller, *Bunny: The Real Story of Playboy* (1985).

## CHAPTERS 8 AND 9

The opening sections of Chapter 8 consider the tumultuous year 1968, viewed by assorted observers of the recent past as a watershed year in the American experience. Charles Kaiser, *1968 in America: Music, Politics, Chaos, Counterculture, and the Shaping of a Generation* (1988), provides a readable survey of that year, one that is particularly strong in the matter of social and cultural happenings. More impressive is David Caute, *The Year of the Barricades: A Journey Through 1968* (1987), a provocative account of what has been described as the most destabilizing year experienced by the United States during the twentieth century. See also Irwin Unger and Debi Unger, *Turning Point: 1968* (1988), Hans Koning, *Nineteen Sixty-Eight: A Personal Report* (1987), and George Katisiaficas, *The Imagination of the New Left: A Global Analysis of 1968* (1987). Early in the year 1968, the capture of the USS *Pueblo* by North Korean gunboats stirred the people of the United States. Several books offer accounts and analyses of the affair of the *Pueblo*, among them Daniel V. Gallery, *The Pueblo Incident* (1970); Lloyd M. Bucher, *Bucher: My Story* (1970); and Eleanor V. B. Harris, *The Ship That Never Returned* (1974). While weighing the seizure of the *Pueblo,* Americans confronted the *Tet* offensive unleashed by the communists in South Vietnam. Don Oberdorfer, *Tet!* (1971), provides a readable account of that offensive. Peter Baestrup, *The Big Story: How the American Press and Television Reported and Interpreted the Crisis of Tet 1968 in Vietnam and Washington* (1979), offers a critique of the way the communications media reported the *Tet* offensive.

For the murder of Martin Luther King, Jr., see the various King biographies previously noted. Eugene McCarthy's campaign for the Democratic nomination for president is described and analyzed in Jeremy Larner, *Nobody Knows: Reflections on the McCarthy Campaign of 1968* (1970), and Richard T. Stout, *People* (1970). See also Eugene J. McCarthy, *The Year of the People* (1969), and Albert Eisele, *Almost to the Presidency* (1972). Jules Witcover, *85 Days: The Last Campaign of Robert Kennedy* (1969), considers Kennedy's campaign for the Democratic presidential nomination of 1968. See also David Halberstam, *The Unfinished Odyssey of Robert Kennedy* (1968), and Arthur M. Schlesinger, Jr., *Robert Kennedy and His Times* (1978). Jody Carlson, *George C. Wallace and the Politics of Powerlessness: The Wallace Campaigns for the Presidency, 1964–1976* (1981), discusses the presidential campaign of the governor of Alabama in 1968. James Miller, *Democracy in the Streets* (1987), and David R. Farber, *Chicago '68* (1988), assess the so-called Battle of Chicago during the Democratic national convention of 1968. Jules Witcover, *The Resurrection of Richard Nixon* (1970), explains the remarkable political comeback of Nixon during the middle 1960s. Theodore H. White, *The Making of the President, 1968* (1969), and Lewis Chester et al., *An American Melodrama: The Presidential Campaign of 1968* (1969), offer general accounts of the presidential election of 1968. See also Joe McGinniss, *The Selling of the President, 1968* (1969).

An array of books consider the life and presidency of Richard Nixon. Stephen Ambrose, *Nixon: The Education of a Politician, 1913–1962* (1987), traces Nixon's life and career through the year of his defeat when he ran for governor of California. See also Roger Morris, *Iron Destinies, Lost,* I, *To the Threshold of Power* (1989). Nixon's memoirs, *RN: The Memoirs of Richard Nixon* (1978), set out Nixon's view of his life and presidency. Garry Wills, *Nixon Agonistes: The Crisis of the Self-Made Man* (1972), and Rowland Evans and Robert Novak, *Nixon in the White House: The Frustration of Power* (1972), offer contemporary (and pre-Watergate) appraisals of Nixon the president. William Safire, *Before the Fall: An Inside View of the Pre-Watergate White House* (1975), is a massive book that is at once insightful and splendidly written. Other useful volumes by members of the Nixon White House are John Ehrlichman, *Witness to Power: The Nixon Years* (1982); H. R. Haldeman, *The Ends of Power* (1978); and Raymond Price, *With Nixon* (1977). Henry A. Kissinger, *The White House Years* (1979), and *Years of Upheaval* (1982), in addition to offering insights regarding the character and personality of Nixon, are indispensable sources for any study of foreign policy during the years of the Nixon and Ford presidencies.

William E. Leuchtenburg, *In the Shadow of FDR*, previously noted, considers the Nixon presidency, as does Otis L. Graham, Jr., *Toward a Planned Society: From Roosevelt to Nixon* (1976). Arthur M. Schlesinger, Jr., discusses the imperiousness of Nixon and other presidents in his widely acclaimed book *The Imperial Presidency* (1973). Jonathan Schell, *The Time of Illusion: An Historical and Reflective Account of the Nixon Era* (1975), provides a sharp critique of the national stewardship of Nixon. A variety of authors have sought to analyze the personality and character of Richard Nixon: James David Barber, *The Presidential Character: Predicting Performance in the White House* (1972); Bruce Mazlish, *In Search of Nixon: A Psychohistorical Inquiry* (1972); Eli S. Chesen, *President Nixon's Psychiatric Profile: A Psychodynamic-Genetic Interpretation* (1973); David Abrahamsen, *Nixon vs. Nixon: An Emotional Tragedy* (1976); and Fawn M. Brodie, *Richard Nixon: The Shaping of His Character* (1981).

The aforementioned volumes by Henry Kissinger detail the policies and initiatives of the Nixon administration in the realm of foreign affairs. Seymour M. Hersh, *The Price of Power: Kissinger in the Nixon White House* (1983), offers a scathing portrait of Kissinger and his performance as national security adviser and eventually secretary of state in the Nixon administration. Tad Szulc, *The Illusion of Peace: Foreign Policy in the Nixon Years* (1978), is equally unflattering in its assessment of American foreign relations during the Nixon years. Raymond L. Garthoff, *Détente and Confrontation: American-Soviet Relations from Nixon to Reagan* (1985), provides a judicious analysis of Nixon's management of relations between the United States and the rival superpower. See also Robert S. Litwak, *Détente and the Nixon Doctrine: Foreign Policy and the Pursuit of Stability* (1984). Boris Meissner, *The Brezhnev Doctrine* (1970), discusses a pronouncement by the Soviet chieftain that nettled the Washington government during the years of Nixon. John Newhouse, *Cold Dawn: The Story of SALT* (1973); Samuel B. Payne, *The Soviet Union and SALT* (1980); and Gerard C. Smith, *Doubletalk: The Story of the First Strategic Arms Limitation Talks* (1980), consider negotiations that resulted in a treaty that has been widely viewed as a premier achievement of the Nixon presidency. Melvin Gurtov and Ray Maghoori, *The Roots of Failure: United States Policy in the Third World* (1984), and John Stockwell, *In Search of Enemies: A CIA Story* (1978), analyze the approach of the Nixon administration to the developing countries.

For the Nixon administration's policy regarding the war in Vietnam, see the previously noted volumes by Stanley Karnow and George Herring. Guenter Lewy, *America in Vietnam* (1978), is generally supportive of Nixon's approach to the intractible problem of Vietnam. Allan E. Goodman, *The Lost Peace: America's Search for a Negotiated Settlement of the Vietnam War* (1978), discusses the Nixon administration's attempt to work out a settlement with the Vietnamese communists. Leslie H. Gelb and Richard K. Betts, *The Irony of Vietnam: The System Worked* (1979), defends the role of the national security adviser in the search for a negotiated settlement. Nguyen Tien Hung and Jerrold L. Schecter, *The Palace File* (1986), sets out the remarkable story of secret letters dispatched by Presidents Nixon and Ford to Pres. Nguyen Van Thieu of

South Vietnam pledging continued U.S. support to the Saigon government in the latter's struggle for survival against the Vietnamese communists in the aftermath of the armistice of January 1973. William Shawcross, *Sideshow: Kissinger, Nixon and the Destruction of Cambodia* (1979), blames Nixon and Kissinger for the tragedy that engulfed Cambodia during the 1970s. For the Nixon-Kissinger approach to problems in the Middle East, see Edward R. F. Sheehan, *The Arabs, Israelis, and Kissinger: A Secret History of American Diplomacy in the Middle East* (1976).

The space program of the United States registered some of its most spectacular achievements during the time of the Nixon presidency. Most outstanding were the flights to the moon by the astronauts of Project Apollo. John Noble Wilford, *We Reach the Moon: The New York Times Story of Man's Greatest Adventure* (1969), and Davis Thomas, *Moon: Man's Greatest Adventure* (1970), describe the flight of Apollo 11, the first voyage to the lunar surface. See also Edwin E. Aldrin, *Return to Earth* (1973); Henry S. F. Cooper, *Thirteen: The Flight That Failed* (1973); and Bernie Lay, *Earthbound Astronauts: The Builders of Apollo-Saturn* (1971). For unmanned flights into space, see William K. Hartmann and Odell Raper, *The New Mars: The Discoveries of Mariner 9* (1974), and Henry S. F. Cooper, *Imaging Saturn: The Voyager Flights to Saturn* (1982).

Theodore H. White, *The Making of the President, 1972* (1973), provides an assessment of the presidential campaign that White later revised in the aftermath of the expanding scandal of Watergate. See also Gary W. Hart, *Right from the Start: A Chronicle of the McGovern Campaign* (1973), and George S. McGovern, *Grassroots: The Autobiography of George McGovern* (1977). Athan G. Theoharis, *Spying on Americans: Political Surveillance from Hoover to the Huston Plan* (1978), and Fred J. Donner, *The Age of Surveillance: The Aims and Methods of America's Political Intelligence System* (1980), discuss the political surveillance of American citizens during the years of Nixon.

The impulse to surveillance led to the Watergate affair and the downfall of the Nixon presidency. Perhaps the best source for Watergate is Congressional Quarterly, *Watergate: Chronology of a Crisis* (1974), two volumes. J. Anthony Lukas, *Nightmare: The Underside of the Nixon Years* (1976), offers a detailed and readable account of the dubious activities, including the break-in at the Watergate, undertaken by members of the Nixon administration and the Committee to Re-elect the President. Carl Bernstein and Bob Woodward, *All the President's Men* (1974), describes the efforts of the reporters Bernstein and Woodward to discern the truth of the Watergate affair. See also Theodore H. White, *Breach of Faith: The Fall of Richard Nixon* (1975). An array of participants in the Watergate drama have written books that shed light on the scandal: E. Howard Hunt, *Undercover: Memoirs of an American Secret Agent* (1974); James W. McCord, *Pieces of Tape: The Watergate Story, Fact and Fiction* (1974); G. Gordon Liddy, *Will: The Autobiography of G. Gordon Liddy* (1980); John W. Dean III, *The White House Years: Blind Ambition* (1976); Maurice H. Stans, *The Terror of Justice: The Untold Story of Watergate* (1978); Sam J. Ervin, Jr., *The Whole Truth: The Watergate Conspiracy* (1980); Samuel Dash, *Chief Counsel: Inside the Ervin Committee—The Untold Story of Wa-*

*tergate* (1976); and Leon Jaworski, *The Right and the Power: The Prosecution of Watergate* (1976). Philip Kurland, *Watergate and the Constitution* (1978), assesses the constitutional implications of the Watergate scandal; John E. Labovitz, *Presidential Impeachment* (1978), addresses the move in Congress to impeach President Nixon. New York Times, *The White House Transcripts* (1973), provides transcripts of the tapes of conversations in the Nixon White House that related to Watergate. See also Bruce Oudes, *From the President: Nixon's Withheld Memoranda* (1988). David Frost, *"I Gave Them A Sword": Behind the Scenes of the Nixon Interviews* (1978), treats television interviews of Nixon by David Frost. Carl Bernstein and Bob Woodward, *The Final Days* (1976), chronicles the concluding days of the Nixon presidency. Richard M. Cohen and Jules Witcover, *A Heartbeat Away: The Investigation and Resignation of Vice President Spiro T. Agnew* (1974), considers the disgrace of Nixon's vice president.

Gerald R. Ford, *A Time to Heal: The Autobiography of Gerald R. Ford* (1979), summarizes Ford's view of his life and his presidency. Hugh Sidey, *Portrait of a President* (1975), provides a sympathetic view of Gerald Ford. See also Congressional Quarterly, *President Ford: The Man and His Record* (1974); Clark R. Mollenhoff, *The Man Who Pardoned President Nixon* (1976); Richard Reeves, *A Ford, Not a Lincoln* (1975); and John R. Hersey, *The President* (1975). Various men who served Ford during his brief presidency have written recollections of their service and observations: John J. Casserly, *The Ford White House: The Diary of a Speechwriter* (1977); Robert T. Hartmann, *Palace Politics: An Insider's Account of the Ford Years* (1980); and Ron Nessen, *It Sure Looks Different from the Inside* (1978). See also the volume prepared by the press secretary in the Ford White House who resigned as a result of the pardon of Nixon, Jerald F. terHorst, *Gerald Ford and the Future of the Presidency* (1974). James Reichley discusses Ford in *Conservatives in an Age of Change: The Nixon and Ford Administrations* (1981), as does James L. Sundquist in *The Decline and Resurgence of Congress* (1981). John J. Sirica, *To Set the Record Straight: The Break-In, the Tapes, the Conspirators, the Pardon* (1979).

Alan Dawson, *55 Days: The Fall of South Vietnam* (1977), describes the most traumatic happening of the years of the Ford presidency. See also Arnold R. Isaacs, *Without Honor: Defeat in Vietnam and Cambodia* (1983). Nguyen Van Toai and David Chanoff, *The Vietnamese Gulag* (1986), and Nguyen Van Canh (with Peter Cooper), *Vietnam Under Communism, 1975–1982* (1983), consider conditions in Vietnam after the communist conquest of South Vietnam.

# CHAPTER 10

Roy Rowan, *The Four Days of Mayaguez* (1975), and Richard G. Head, *Crisis Resolution: Presidential Decision Making in the Mayaguez and Korean Confrontations* (1978), describe and analyze the *Mayaguez* affair of the spring of

1975. For the affair of the *Mayaguez* and other aspects of the foreign policy of the Ford administration in the months following the fall of South Vietnam to the communists, see Henry A. Kissinger, *Years of Upheaval*, previously noted. American Revolution Bicentennial Administration, *The Bicentennial of the United States of America: A Final Report to the People* (1977), five volumes, is the best source for the observance of the two hundredth anniversary of the birth of the republic. Jules Witcover, *Marathon: The Pursuit of the Presidency, 1972–1976* (1977), offers detailed coverage of the presidential election of 1976. Sidney Kraus (ed.), *The Great Debates: Carter vs. Ford, 1976* (1979), assesses the televised "debates" between the challenger Jimmy Carter and the incumbent, President Ford, during the presidential campaign of 1976.

Jimmy Carter, *A Government as Good as Its People* (1977), sets out the political views and perceptions of Jimmy Carter. Richard Hyatt, *The Carters of Plains* (1977), offers a portrait of the family of Jimmy Carter. William L. Miller, *Yankee from Georgia* (1978), and Bruce Mazlish, *Jimmy Carter: A Character Portrait* (1979), provide insight regarding the character and personality, intellect and temperament of the thirty-ninth president. Jimmy Carter, *Keeping Faith: Memoirs of a President* (1982), sets out Carter's own recollections of his years in the White House. Carter's press secretary Jody Powell has recalled the Carter presidency in *The Other Side of the Story* (1984). Another member of Carter's inner circle during the White House years, Hamilton Jordan, has recalled the final tumultuous year of the Carter presidency in *Crisis: The Last Year of the Carter Presidency* (1982).

Edwin C. Hargrove, *Jimmy Carter as President: Leadership and the Politics of the Public Good* (1988), a volume in the *Miller Center Series on the American Presidency*, offers an incisive and balanced appraisal of the thirty-ninth president. See also William E. Leuchtenburg, *In the Shadow of FDR*, previously noted. Robert Shogan, *Promises to Keep: Carter's First Hundred Days* (1977), offers a sympathetic analysis of Carter's pristine months in the White House. Clark R. Mollenhoff, *The President Who Failed: Carter Out of Control* (1980), provides a scathing portrait of the Carter presidency. Charles O. Jones, *Trusteeship Presidency: Jimmy Carter and the United States Congress* (1988), assesses Carter's troubled relations with the national legislature. See also Laurence E. Lynn, *The President as Policymaker: Jimmy Carter and Welfare Reform* (1981).

Bruce W. Jentleson, *The Complex Political Economy of East-West Energy Trade* (1986), and Richard H. K. Vietor, *Energy Policy in America Since 1945: A Study in Business-Government Relations* (1984), consider a problem that caused President Carter a great deal of anguish. Nathan Glazer (ed.), *Clamor at the Gates: The New American Immigration* (1985), and David Reimers, *Still the Golden Door: The Third World Comes to America* (1985), provide insight regarding the large-scale migration of people from economically and politically distressed areas of the world to the United States during the years of President Carter. See also Bruce Grant, *The Boat People: An "Age" Investigation* (1979).

A center of public controversy during the years of the Ford and Carter presidencies was the CIA. President Carter's director of the CIA, Stanfield Turner, offers an insightful view of the business of espionage in the modern world in *Secrecy and Democracy: The CIA in Transition* (1985). John Ranelagh, *The Agency: The Rise and Decline of the CIA* (1986), considers the agency's tribulations in recent times. See also Rhodri Jeffrey Jones, *The CIA and American Democracy* (1988). Gaddis Smith, *Morality, Reason, and Power: American Diplomacy in the Carter Years* (1986), offers a balanced and incisive examination of American foreign relations during the presidency of Jimmy Carter. Indispensable sources for the study of the diplomacy of the Carter presidency are the memoirs by the secretary of state during most of that presidency and by Carter's national security adviser: Cyrus Vance, *Hard Choices: Critical Years in America's Foreign Policy* (1983), and Zbigniew K. Brzezinski, *Power and Principle: Memoirs of the National Security Adviser, 1977–1981* (1985). Walter La Feber, "From Confusion to Cold War: The Memoirs of the Carter Administration," *Diplomatic History*, VIII, 1, Winter 1984, offers a critique of the memoirs by Carter, Vance, and Brzezinski. See also Davis S. McLellan, *Cyrus Vance* (1985), a volume in the distinguished series, *The American Secretaries of State and Their Diplomacy.*

Jerel A. Rosati, *The Carter Administration's Quest for Global Community: Beliefs and Their Impact on Behavior* (1987), assesses the perceptions and convictions of the Carter administration in the realm of foreign policy. Joshua Maravchik, *The Uncertain Crusade: Jimmy Carter and the Dilemmas of Human Rights* (1986), provides a less than satisfactory discussion of the human rights initiatives of the Carter administration. Raymond L. Garthoff, *Détente and Confrontation: American-Soviet Relations from Nixon to Reagan*, previously noted, considers relations between the superpowers during the years of the Carter presidency. Strobe Talbott, *Endgame: The Inside Story of SALT II* (1979), discusses the negotiation of the SALT II treaty during the Carter presidency. David D. Newsom, *The Soviet Brigade in Cuba: A Study in Personal Diplomacy* (1987), considers Carter's response to the disclosure that a Soviet army brigade was deployed in Cuba. Anthony Arnold, *Afghanistan: The Soviet Invasion in Perspective* (1985), comments on the U.S. response to the Soviet adventure in Afghanistan.

Tom Gervasi, *The Myth of Soviet Military Supremacy* (1985), discusses what the author thinks have been the intellectual and statistical inconsistencies that have plagued discussions regarding the strategic nuclear balance between the superpowers. A more controversial question for the Carter presidency was whether to build and deploy the MX missile. For the MX debate, see Colin S. Gray, *The MX ICBM and National Security* (1981), and Herbert Scoville, Jr., *MX: Prescription for Disaster* (1981).

George D. Moffett III, *The Ratification of the Panama Canal Treaties* (1985), James Michael Hogan, *The Panama Canal in American Politics: Domestic Advocacy and the Evolution of Policy* (1986), and J. P. Morray (ed.), *The View from Panama* (1978), assess the negotiation and ratification of the Panama Canal treaties during the Carter presidency. For the so-called Camp David accords, one ought to examine Melvin A. Friedlander, *Sadat and Begin: The Domestic Politics of Peacemaking* (1983). A variety of books examine U.S.

relations with Iran and the crisis resulting from the seizure of American citizens by Iranian militants in 1979. James A. Bill, *The Eagle and the Lion: The Tragedy of American-Iranian Relations* (1987), provides an excellent analysis of relations between the United States and Iran. Robert Huyser, *Mission to Tehran* (1985), describes the mission to Iran in 1979 by an American general, ordered by President Carter, to determine whether the regime of the shah might be saved. Pierre Salinger, *America Held Hostage: The Secret Negotiations* (1981), weigh the secret negotiations aimed at securing release of the American hostages. Paul B. Ryan, *The Iranian Rescue Mission: Why It Failed* (1985), discusses the attempt to rescue the American hostages in the spring of 1980.

## CHAPTER 11

The society of the United States during the 1970s and 1980s, of course, was a vast and complicated phenomenon. A useful source with which to begin a study of that phenomenon is Andrew Hacker (ed.), *U/S: A Statistical Portrait of the American People* (1983).

Sex and pornography remained near the center of the national consciousness during the 1970s and 1980s. Daniel Yankelovich, *The New Morality: A Profile of American Youth in the 1970s* (1974), provides a statistical analysis of the sexual mores of youthful Americans. Laura Lederer (ed.), *Take Back the Night: Women on Pornography* (1980), views pornography from a feminist perspective. See also Murray S. Davis, *Smut: Erotic Reality/Obscene Ideology* (1983), and David Alexander Scott, *Pornography—Its Effects on Family, Community, and Culture* (1985). Seth Cagin, *Hollywood Films of the Seventies: Sex, Drugs, Violence, Rock 'n' Roll & Politics* (1984), addresses the many dimensions of American movies during the eighth decade of the twentieth century. Women who deplore the addiction of men to televised football games might wish to examine Phil Patton, *Razzle Dazzle: The Curious Marriage of Television and Professional Football* (1984).

Peter N. Carroll, *It Seemed Like Nothing Happened: The Tragedy and Promise of America in the 1970s* (1982), laments the decline of youthful activism during the 1970s. Christopher Lasch, *The Culture of Narcissism: American Life in an Age of Diminishing Expectations* (1979), offers an incisive and often biting critique of the values that had come to animate Americans by the latter 1970s. Affluent consumerism is discussed in Deborah Silverman, *Selling Culture: Bloomingdale's Diana Vreeland and the New Aristocracy of Taste in Reagan's America* (1986).

Barbaralee Diamonstein, *American Architecture Now* (1980), considers architecture in the United States at the end of the 1970s. Eric Salmon, *Is the Theatre Still Dying?* (1985), assesses the state of the theater in America in the 1980s. Peter S. Prescott, *Never in Doubt: Critical Essays on American Books, 1972–1985* (1986), analyzes American writing during the 1970s and early 1980s.

David Halberstam, *The Reckoning* (1986), compares Japanese and American automobile manufacturers—to the detriment of the Americans. Lee Ia-cocca, *Iacocca: An Autobiography* (1984), celebrates the life and career of America's best-known businessperson of the contemporary period. Theodore Roszak offers a critique of the computer culture in *The Cult of Information: The Folklore of Computers and the True Art of Thinking* (1986).

Those black holes that generated so much popular interest during the 1970s are discussed in Walter Sullivan, *Black Holes: The End of Space, The Edge of Time* (1979). A variety of books have examined the technique of cloning, a phenomenon which also caught the attention of millions of Americans in the 1970s, among them Margery Facklam and Howard Facklam, *From Cell to Clone: The Story of Genetic Engineering* (1979). Nan Tilton and Todd Tilton and Gaylen Moore, *Making Miracles: In Vitro Fertilization* (1985), considers so-called test-tube babies. Peter Singer and Deane Wells, *Making Babies: The New Science and Ethics of Conception* (1985), addresses the ethical and moral issues raised by IVF. Noel P. Keane, *The Surrogate Mother* (1981), considers the controversial topic of surrogate motherhood. Ann Giudici and William A. Check, *The Truth About AIDS: Evolution of an Epidemic* (1984), and Frederick P. Siegal, *AIDS: The Medical Mystery* (1983), discuss the almost sudden appearance of AIDS and its early consequences.

Bookshelves fairly abound with titles dealing with religion in the very recent past. Ronald B. Flowers, *Religion in Strange Times: The 1960s and 1970s* (1984), considers the changing religious environment in America over the past generation or so. Wade Clark Roof and William McKinney, *American Mainline Religion: Its Changing Shape and Future* (1987), evaluates the declining religious commitment of a majority of Americans from the middle 1960s through the 1980s. Andrew M. Greeley, *American Catholicism Since the Council: An Unauthorized Report* (1985), weighs what has widely been perceived to be a crisis within American Catholicism resulting largely from the declining commitment of Catholic Americans to traditional values. Stephen M. Cohen, *American Assimilation or Jewish Revival?* (1988), and Charles E. Silberman, *A Certain People: American Jews and Their Lives Today* (1985), consider the Jewish revival of the past generation and the thorny question of assimilation of Jews in the wider culture. Robert S. Ellwood, *Alternative Altars: Unconventional and Eastern Spirituality in America* (1979), addresses the enlarging interest among Americans in Eastern mysticism. Margaret M. Poloma, *The Charismatic Movement: Is There a New Pentecost?* (1982), discusses a movement that has captivated substantial numbers of Protestants and Catholics in America. David Bromley, *Strange Gods: The Great American Cult Scare* (1981), addresses the growth of religious cults in the United States during recent decades. The most notorious of the religious cult leaders, of course, was Jim Jones. George Klineman, *The Cult That Died: The Tragedy of Jim Jones and the Peoples Temple* (1980), describes Jones and the demise of his followers. See also David Chidester, *Salvation and Suicide: An Interpretation of Jim Jones, The Peoples Temple, and Jonestown* (1988).

Ben Armstrong, *The Electric Church* (1979), and Razelle Frankl, *Televangelism: The Marketing of Popular Religion* (1987), critique the phenomenon of televangelism and the individuals responsible for it. Arguably, the best known of the televangelists has been the fundamentalist minister the Reverend Jerry Falwell. Falwell himself has considered fundamentalism in Jerry Falwell, (ed.), *The Fundamentalist Phenomenon: The Resurgence of Conservative Christianity* (1981). For the Reverend Jim Bakker and his scandal-ridden ministry, see Joe E. Barnhart, *Jim and Tammy: Charismatic Intrigue Inside the PTL* (1988). Steve Bruce, *The Rise and Fall of the Christian Right: Conservative Protestant Parties in America, 1978–1988* (1988), discusses the role of religion in politics in the United States during recent years.

Peter Gluck, *Cities in Transition: Social Changes and Institutional Responses in Urban Development* (1979), considers the city in contemporary America. Robert L. Weinstein and Robert E. Firestine, *Regional Growth and Decline in the United States: The Rise of the Sunbelt and the Decline of the Northeast* (1978), addresses the so-called Sunbelt phenomenon. Jeanne Dosch, *Family: Changing Faces of American Families* (1985), considers the challenge to the nuclear family in modern America. Edgar W. Butler, *Traditional Marriage and Emerging Alternatives* (1979), and Andrew J. Cherlin, *Marriage, Divorce, Remarriage* (1981), assess the state of marriage in contemporary times. Vance O. Packard, *Our Endangered Children, Growing Up in a Changing World* (1983), weigh the problems confronting America's children in the 1980s. A variety of books address the plight of elderly citizens in a youth-oriented society, among them Charles H. Percy, *Growing Old in the Country of the Young* (1974). E. Fuller Torrey, *Nowhere to Go: The Tragic Odyssey of the Homeless Mentally Ill* (1988), is one of a variety of books dealing with the saddening phenomenon of homelessness in contemporary America.

Crime in the 1970s and 1980s has generated a fair number of books. Jonathan Kwitny, *Vicious Circles: The Mafia's Control of the American Marketplace, Food, Clothing, Transportation, Finance* (1979), discusses the enterprise of organized criminals, Peter Reuter, *Disorganized Crime, The Economics of the Visible Hand* (1983), crime of the less organized genre. The most publicized criminal escapade of recent times was that involving Patricia Hearst. For Hearst and her activities, see Vin McLellan and Paul Avery, *The Voices of Guns: The Definitive and Dramatic Story of the Twenty-two-month Career of the Symbionese Liberation Army—One of the Most Bizarre Chapters in the History of the American Left* (1976).

Immigrants have cascaded into the United States in increasing numbers over the past two decades. And, of course, race and ethnicity have continued to make an imprint on American life. Nathan Glazer (ed.), *Clamor at the Gates: The New American Immigration* (1985), considers immigration in the United States in recent times. Reynolds Farley and Walter R. Allen, *The Color Line and the Quality of Life in America* (1987), uses the federal census as a basis for determining the importance of race in fixing the place of Americans in the national life. Joel Dreyfuss, *The Bakke Case: The Politics of Inequality* (1979), discusses a court case that touched the emotions of millions of America's blacks and whites. Relland Dewing, *The Wounded Knee: The Meaning and Significance of the Second Incident* (1985), assesses the affair involving

Indian Americans at Wounded Knee, South Dakota, in 1973. Philip Reno, *Mother Earth, Father Sky, and Economic Development* (1981), considers economic aspects of the lives of Indian Americans in contemporary times.

Peter Schrag, *The Decline of the WASP* (1976), considers what the author perceives to be the waning influence in American life of white Anglo-Saxon Protestants. Richard Krickus, *Pursuing the American Dream: White Ethnics and the New Populism* (1976), weighs the attempt by white ethnics to press their interests via the political process. See also Nathan Glazer, *Ethnic Dilemmas, 1964–1982* (1983). Cuban Americans have become increasingly visible and assertive in the United States over the past three decades. Several books illuminate the experience of Cuban Americans, among them José Llanes, *Cuban Americans: Masters of Survival* (1982). Norris Hundley, Jr. (ed.), *The Asian American: The Historical Experience* (1976), discusses a genre of Americans who, like the Cuban Americans, have become increasingly visible and assertive in the United States. See also Howard Brett Melendy, *Asians in America: Filipinos, Koreans, and East Indians* (1977).

Barbara Ehrenreich, *The Hearts of Men: The Flight from Commitment* (1983), laments what the author perceived to be a decline in the influence of the feminist movement by the early 1980s. More upbeat is the view of the feminist movement offered by Ethel Klein in *Gender Politics: From Consciousness to Mass Politics* (1984). Pamela Johnston Conover and Virginia Gray consider the feminist movement's enduring confrontation with political conservatives in *Feminism and the New Right: Conflict over the American Family* (1983). The failure of the Equal Rights Amendment is analyzed in Joan Hoff-Wilson (ed.), *Rights of Passage: The Past and Future of the ERA* (1986), and Mary Frances Berry, *Why ERA Failed: Politics, Women's Rights, and the Amending Process of the Constitution* (1986).

Another cause close to the hearts of many feminists has been the right to a choice about abortion. A fair number of books consider the abortion and "right-to-life" question. Lawrence Lader, *Abortion II: Making the Revolution* (1973), is a veritable celebration of abortion. Nanett J. Davis, *From Crime to Choice: The Transformation of Abortion in America* (1985), likewise takes a positive view of abortion, whereas Bernard N. Nathanson, *Aborting America* (1979), and Jerry Falwell, *If I Should Die Before I Wake* (1986), take a negative view. Lauren R. Sass (ed.), *Abortion: Freedom of Choice and the Right to Life* (1978), and Bonnie Szumski (ed.), *Abortion: Opposing Viewpoints* (1986), offer essays arguing both sides of the abortion question.

Homosexuality became a subject of public discussion during the 1970s. Two recent books on homosexuality are Stephen Stewart, *Positive Image: A Portrait of Gay America* (1985), and Barry D. Adams, *The Rise of a Gay and Lesbian Movement* (1987). For an attack on gay liberation, see Anita Bryant, *The Anita Bryant Story: The Survival of Our Nation's Families and the Threat of Militant Homosexuality* (1977).

Victor Ferkiss, *The Future of Technological Civilization* (1974), considers the ecological threat presented by modern civilization. Jonathan Schell, *The Fate of the Earth* (1982), weighs the threat to the natural environment presented by nuclear energy. Philip L. Cantelon and Robert C. Williams, *Crisis Contained: The Department of Energy at Three Miles Island* (1982), and Daniel F. Ford, *Three Mile Island: Thirty Minutes to Meltdown* (1982), consider America's most frightening nuclear accident. Adeline Gordon Levine, *Love Canal: Science, Politics, and People* (1982), and Lois Marie Gibbs, *Love Canal: My Story* (1982), describe America's most publicized toxic waste scandal. See also Michael H. Brown, *The Toxic Cloud, A Cross-Country Report on the Poisoning of America's Air* (1987).

## CHAPTERS 12 AND 13

The overbearing political phenomenon of the 1970s and 1980s in the United States was the renaissance of conservatism. David W. Reinhard, *The Republican Right Since 1945* (1983), surveys the ups and downs of Republican conservatives since World War II. F. Clifton White, *Why Reagan Won: A Narrative History of the Conservative Movement, 1964–1981* (1981), considers the condition of conservatism in the United States from the Goldwater debacle of 1964 to the Reagan triumph of 1980. Alan Crawford, *Thunder on the Right: The "New Right" and the Politics of Resentment* (1980), discusses the conservative revival on the eve of Ronald Reagan's election to the presidency. See also Gilliam Peele, *Revival and Reaction: The Right in Contemporary America* (1984). Thomas Ferguson and Joel Rogers, *Right Turn: The Decline of the Democrats and the Future of American Politics* (1987), offers a more critical analysis of the conservative revival. Randall Rothenberg, *The Neoliberals: Creating the New American Politics* (1984), considers the condition of the liberal movement in America during the Reagan era.

An array of biographies of Ronald Reagan and analyses of the Reagan presidency illuminate many of the points in Chapters 12 and 13. Anne Edwards, *Early Reagan* (1987), considers the pristine years of the life and career of Ronald Reagan. Lou Cannon, *Reagan* (1982), offers a sharply written and critical account of Reagan's life and career through his election to the presidency in 1980. See also Rowland Evans and Robert Novak, *The Reagan Revolution* (1981), and Peter Hannaford, *The Reagans: A Political Portrait* (1983). Laurence Leamer, *Make-Believe: The Story of Nancy & Ronald Reagan* (1983); Paul D. Erickson, *Reagan Speaks: The Making of an American Myth* (1985); and Michael J. Rogin, *Ronald Reagan the Movie, and Other Episodes of Political Demonology* (1987), offer caustic critiques of Reagan. Equally biting and more sharply written is Garry Wills, *Reagan's America: Innocents at Home* (1987).

Ronnie Dugger, *On Reagan: The Man and His Presidency* (1983), considers Reagan and his first year or so in the White House. The newsman Laurence I. Barrett's *Gambling with History: Reagan in the White House* (1983), provides an account of the pristine period of Reagan's presidency that is at once balanced, insightful, and detailed. John L. Palmer and Isabel V. Sawhill (eds.), *The Reagan Record: An Assessment of America's Changing Domestic Priorities*

(1984), provides a dispassionate consideration of policies and initiatives by the Reagan administration in the area of home affairs during the administration's first three years. See also Fred I. Greenstein (ed.), *The Reagan Presidency: An Early Assessment* (1983). Robert Dallek, *Ronald Reagan: The Politics of Symbolism* (1984), is sharply critical of Reagan and his presidency. See also Theodore J. Lowi, *The Personal President: Power Invested, Promises Unfulfilled* (1985), and Richard Reeves, *The Reagan Detour: Conservative Revolutionary* (1985). David Boaz (ed.), *Assessing the Reagan Years* (1988), and Martin Anderson, *Revolution* (1988), provide rousing defenses of the Reagan presidency. Michael K. Deaver, *Behind the Scenes: In Which the Author Talks About Ronald and Nancy Reagan . . . and Himself* (1987); Larry Speakes, *Speaking Out: The Reagan Presidency from Inside the White House* (1988); and Donald T. Regan, *For the Record: From Wall Street to Washington* (1988), are memoirs by members of the Reagan administration.

David Stockman, *The Triumph of Politics: Why the Reagan Revolution Failed* (1986), offers a biting analysis of the formulation of economic policy during the early years of the Reagan presidency by Reagan's first director of the Office of Management and Budget. Less critical is *Reagonomics: An Insider's Account of the Policies and the People* (1988), by William A. Niskanen, a member of the Council of Economic Advisers during Reagan's first term in the White House. See also Robert Lekachman, *Greed Is Not Enough: Reaganomics* (1982); Paul Craig Roberts, *The Supply-Side Revolution: An Insider's Account of Policymaking in Washington* (1984); and Michael J. Boskin, *Reagan and the Economy: Successes, Failures, Unfinished Agenda* (1987). Daniel Bell, *The Deficits: How Big? How Dangerous?* (1985), addresses the thorny question of federal budgetary deficits during the Reagan years.

Greg J. Duncan, *Years of Poverty, Years of Plenty: The Changing Economic Fortunes of American Workers and Families* (1984), weighs the effect of Reagan's economic policies on "ordinary" Americans. Clyde V. Prestowitz, Jr., *Trading Places: How We Allowed Japan to Take the Lead* (1988), and Martin Tolchin and Susan Tolchin, *Buying into America: How Foreign Money Is Changing the Face of Our Nation* (1988), consider developments that came to cause Americans no little concern during the Reagan years. Paul Kennedy, *The Rise and Fall of the Great Powers: Economic Change and Military Conflict from 1500 to 2000* (1987), a book that likewise generated concern among the people of the United States, suggests that the power of the United States, like that of Great Britain a half century or so before, may be moving into eclipse. Also addressing economic problems that became increasingly apparent during the Reagan years are Paul M. Kamer, *The U.S. Economy in Crisis: Adjusting to the New Realities* (1988), and John E. Ullman, *The Anatomy of Decline: Productivity, Investment, and Location in U.S. Manufacturing* (1988).

Paul Light, *Artful Work: The Politics of Social Security Reform* (1985), and Michael J. Boskin, *Too Many Promises: The Uncertain Future of Social Security, A twentieth Century Fund Report* (1986), consider a problem that came to a head during the Reagan years. Ruben J. Dunn, *The Crash Put Simply: October 1987* (1988), explains the stock market collapse of the autumn of

1987. Detrick Bell, *And We Are Not Saved: The Elusive Quest for Racial Justice* (1987), assesses the legacy of the civil rights crusade in the latter years of the Reagan presidency. Lincoln Caplan, *The Tenth Justice: The Solicitor General and the Rule of Law* (1987), considers the politicization of the role of the solicitor general during the Reagan era.

A volume that is packed with tightly argued essays on virtually every aspect of foreign policy during much of the Reagan era—relations with the Third World, energy policy, and relations with the Soviet Union, China, the NATO allies, Japan, Latin America, and the Middle East—is Kenneth A. Oye et al., (eds.), *Eagle Resurgent? The Reagan Era in American Foreign Policy* (1987). Alexander M. Haig, Jr., Reagan's first secretary of state, weighs foreign policy during the pristine years of the Reagan presidency in *Caveat: Realism, Reagan, and Foreign Policy* (1984). Walter Russell Mead, *Mortal Splendor: The American Empire in Transition* (1987), explains the changing face of what the author perceives to be the "empire" of the United States (that is, the United States and all of its allies and friends across the world) during the years of Reagan. Joseph Churba, *The Reagan Retreat: The Reagan Foreign and Defense Policy* (1984); Jay Peterzell, *Reagan's Secret Wars* (1984); James T. Hackett (ed.), *The State Department vs. Ronald Reagan: Four Ambassadors Speak Out* (1985); and Joel Krieger, *Reagan, Thatcher, and the Politics of Decline* (1986), provide critiques of the foreign policies of President Reagan.

Raymond L. Garthoff, *Détente and Confrontation*, and Richard W. Stevenson, *The Rise and Fall of Détente: Reflections of Tensions in U.S.-Soviet Relations, 1953–84*, previously noted, consider relations between the United States and the Soviet Union during Reagan's first years in the White House. Strobe Talbott, *The Russians and Reagan* (1984), offers an assessment of Reagan's approach to the Soviets during the early years of his presidency. Michael Mandelbaum and Strobe Talbott, *Reagan and Gorbachev* (1987), assesses Reagan's relations with the dynamic leader who took over the Kremlin in 1984. See also Mikail Gorbachev, *Perestroika: New Thinking for Our Country and the World* (1987).

Strobe Talbott, *Deadly Gambits: The Reagan Administration and the Stalemate in Nuclear Arms Control* (1984), assesses the Strategic Arms Reduction Talks and the approach of the Reagan administration to the question of controlling nuclear weapons systems. Stephen J. Cimbala (ed.), *Strategic Arms Control After SALT* (1989), offers essays that analyze the various dimensions of arms control during the years of Reagan, among them the problems of evolving technology, the philosophical implications of active defense, and the question of strategic surprise. An array of books consider the threat posed to humanity by nuclear arms and the resultant antinuclear movement that captivated millions of Americans during Reagan's first term in the White House, the most formidable of which, arguably, is Jonathan Schell, *The Fate of the Earth* (1982). See also Judith Bentley, *The Nuclear Freeze Movement* (1984); Carla P. Johnston, *Reversing the Nuclear Arms Race* (1986); and Paul Rogat Loeb, *Hope in Hard Times: America's Peace Movement and the Reagan Era* (1987). John Tirman (ed.), *The Fallacy of Star Wars: Based on Studies by the Union of Concerned Scientists* (1984), and Robert Bowman, *Star Wars: A Defense Insider's Case Against the Strategic Defense Initiative* (1986), set out arguments in opposition to Reagan's Strategic Defense Initiative. More balanced considerations appear in Arthur G. J. Chalfont, *Stars Wars: Suicide or Survival?* (1985), and P. Edward Haley and Jack Merritt (ed.), *Strategic Defense Initiative: Folly or Future?* (1986).

Steven L. Spiegel, *Making America's Middle East Policy: From Truman to Reagan*, previously noted, discusses the Washington government's policy in the Middle East during Reagan's first term in the White House. George W. Ball, a highly respected former assistant secretary of state, weighs relations between the United States and Israel during the early years of the Reagan presidency in *Error and Betrayal in Lebanon: An Analysis of Israel's Invasion of Lebanon and the Implications for U.S.-Israeli Relations* (1984). Cheryl Rubenberg questions the long-standing premises of the American-Israeli relationship in *Israel and the American National Interest: A Critical Examination* (1986). See also Noam Chomsky, *The Fateful Triangle: The United States, Israel, and the Palestinians* (1983).

Bob Woodward, *Veil: The Secret Wars of the CIA, 1981–1987* (1987), narrates and analyzes the enterprise of the CIA in Nicaragua, El Salvador, and other troubled areas that commanded the attention of President Reagan and his CIA director, William Casey. Otherwise, a variety of books are available to the reader seeking insight on initiatives by the Reagan administration in Central America, among them E. Bradford Burns, *At War in Nicaragua: The Reagan Doctrine and the Politics of Nostalgia* (1986). Leslie Cockburn, *Out of Control: The Story of the Reagan Administration's Secret War in Nicaragua, the Illegal Arms Pipeline, and the Contra Drug Connection* (1987), and Roy Gutman, *Banana Diplomacy: The Making of American Policy in Nicaragua, 1981–1987* (1988), offer scathing indictments of the Reagan administration's policy vis-à-vis Nicaragua. For the U.S. invasion of Grenada, see Anthony Payne et al., *Grenada: Revolution and Invasion* (1984), and Peter Dunn and Bruce W. Watson (ed.), *American Intervention in Grenada: The Implications of Operation "Urgent Fury"* (1985).

Jack Germond and Jules Witcover, *Wake Us When It's Over: Presidential Politics of 1984* (1985); Michael Nelson, *The Election of 1984* (1985); and Gerald M. Pomper et al., *The Election of 1984: Interpretations* (1985), consider the political canvass that resulted in Ronald Reagan's re-election to a second term in the White House. Imprinting the campaign of 1984, particularly in its pre-convention stage, was the black activist Jesse Jackson. For Jackson and his politics, see Sheila D. Collins, *The Rainbow Challenge: The Jackson Campaign and the Future of U.S. Politics* (1986), and Bob Faw, *Thunder in America* (1986). Kathleen Hall Jamieson, *Packaging the Presidency: A History and Criticism of Presidential Campaign Advertising* (1988), is a prizewinning study of campaign advertising in recent presidential elections.

Jane Mayer and Doyle McManus, *Landslide: The Unmaking of the President, 1944–1988* (1988), offers a caustic portrait of Ronald Reagan during his second term in the White House. Howard Blum, *I Pledge Allegiance: The True*

*Story of the Walkers: An American Spy Family* (1987), considers one of the espionage cases that haunted the United States during the Reagan years. Jonathan Kwitny, *The Crimes of Patriots: A True Tale of Dope, Dirty Money, and the CIA* (1987), describes alleged misdeeds involving America's intelligence community during the Reagan era.

Reagan's pilgrimage to the cemetery at Bitburg is considered in Ilya Levkov (ed.), *Bitburg and Beyond: Encounters in American, German, and Jewish History* (1987). Vigorous criticism of U.S. policy vis-à-vis the Republic of South Africa during the years of Reagan appears in David Mermelstein (ed.), *The Anti-Apartheid Reader: The Struggle Against White Racist Rule in South Africa* (1987). See also Christopher Coker, *The United States and South Africa, 1968–1985* (1986). For America's confrontation with Col. Muammar el-Qaddafi's Libya during the years of Reagan, see Aftab Kamal Pasha, *Libya and the United States: Qaddafi's Response to Reagan's Challenge* (1984), and Ronald B. St. John, *Qaddafi's World Design: Libyan Foreign Policy, 1969–1987* (1987).

Jonathan Marshall et al., *The Iran-Contra Connection: Secret Teams and Covert Operations in the Reagan Era* (1987), and Ben Bradlee, Jr., *Guts and Glory: The Rise and Fall of Oliver North* (1988), consider the so-called Iran-contra affair, the premier political scandal in the United States during the Reagan years. But the best source for the Iran-contra affair is the report entitled "Iran-Contra Investigation: Joint Hearing Before the Select Committee to Investigate Covert Arms Transactions with Iran" and the *Senate Select Committee on Secret Military Assistance to Iran and the Nicaraguan Opposition, 100th Congress, 1st Session* (1988). The editors of *Time* Magazine, *The Winning of the White House 1988* (1989), describes and analyzes the presidential election of 1988. See also Nicholas King, *George Bush: A Biography* (1986); Doug Wead and George Bush, *Man of Integrity* (1988); Richard Gaines, *Dukakis and the Reform Impulse* (1987); and Charles Kennedy and Robert L. Turner, *Dukakis: An American Odyssey* (1988). A problem that nettled President Reagan—and would nettle his successor—was drugs. Library shelves, of course, groan under the weight of books that describe and analyze the drug problem. Among the more recent of those books are: Cheryl Carpenter et al., *Kids, Drugs, and Crime* (1988); Paul Eddy et al., *The Cocaine Wars* (1988); Patricia G. Erickson et al., *The Steel Drug: Cocaine in Perspective* (1987); Seymour Fisher et al. (eds.), *Cocaine, Clinical and Behavioral Aspects* (1987); Lester Grinspoon and James B. Bakalar, *Cocaine: A Drug and Its Social Evolution* (1985); Herbert Hendin et al., *Living High: Daily Marijuana Use Among Adults* (1987); Chris-Ellyn Johanson, *Cocaine: A New Epidemic* (1986); Ibe Kachikwu, *Cocaine Connection* (1987); Joseph Kennedy, *Coca Exotica: The Illustrated History of Cocaine* (1985); Scott B. MacDonald, *Dancing on a Volcano: The Latin American Drug Trade* (1988); James Mills, *The Underground Empire: Where Crime and Governments Embrace* (1986); Michael D. Newcomb and Peter M. Bentler, *Consequences of Adolescent Drug Use* (1988); Peter Reuter et al., *Sealing the Borders: The Effects of Increased Military Participation in Drug Interdiction* (1988); William O. Walker III, *Drug Control in the Americas* (1989).

# Index